Contents

APPENDICES

Introduction

STEFAN COLLINI

ANY VOLUME OF OCCASIONAL WRITINGS, especially those of an author who, according to his own unapologetic testimony, had, and never hesitated to express, strong views on "most of the subjects interesting to mankind,"[1] is bound to appear diverse in character, and no attempt will here be made to hide or apologize for this diversity. Indeed, part of the value of a collected edition lies precisely in the reminder it provides to later and more specialized ages of the range and interconnectedness of a major writer's concerns. But in the present case the appearance of the contents-page may actually exaggerate the heterogeneity of the material in this volume. One way to counteract this judgment is to observe the thematic overlapping of the subject-matter. Even with an author whose intellectual ambitions were less systematic than Mill's, writings on the topics of equality and law could hardly be remote from each other, and in Mill's case, furthermore, his whole theory of social and moral improvement was in one obvious sense educational, so that his views on particular educational ideals and institutions can, without strain, be seen as further corollaries of those same basic principles which underlie his other writings, including those on equality and law. But even if one considers the categories in isolation for a moment, the list of contents may still convey a misleading impression of how the items are distributed among them: considered purely quantitatively, more than half the volume falls primarily under the heading of "equality"; "law" accounts for just over one quarter, and "education" for a little under a fifth. The most important concentration of all, however, is chronological, despite the fact that the earliest piece reproduced here was published forty-six years before the last. For in fact, about three-quarters of the volume is occupied by material published in the thirteen years between 1859 and 1871. This period, of course, marked the very peak of Mill's reputation and influence as a public figure, and he very deliberately set about exploiting his recently established authority to promote his particular social and political views

---

[1]*The Later Letters of John Stuart Mill [LL]*, ed. Francis E. Mineka and Dwight N. Lindley, *Collected Works of John Stuart Mill [CW]*, XIV-XVII (Toronto: University of Toronto Press, 1972), XIV, 205.

as they related to the leading public issues of the day, utilizing all those means of addressing the relevant audiences which become available to an established public figure—pamphlets and manifestos as well as books, formal lectures as well as testimony to Royal Commissions, and, above all, articles, reviews, and letters in the periodical press. The essays in this volume are largely the fruit of this activity.

Readers of this edition need hardly be told that some phases of Mill's career and aspects of his writing have been subjected to intensive, or at least repeated, study and are now comparatively familiar. Works expounding and criticizing his major theoretical writings in philosophy, politics, and economics exist in industrial quantities, and of course the earlier stages of his intellectual development have come to constitute one of the best-known identity crises in history. But neither his less extended mature writings nor the final, and in some ways quite distinct, phase of his career have received anything like such close attention; therefore, as a preliminary to a more detailed discussion of the individual pieces reprinted in this volume, it may be helpful to consider in a fairly general way Mill's performance in the role of public moralist, and to try to place him in that world of High-Victorian polemical and periodical writing to which he was such a notable contributor. This is not simply a question of the set of doctrines which could be extracted from these essays. As a practitioner of the higher moralizing, Mill established a particular tone and level of discussion and employed certain characteristic modes of argument and other means of persuasion that together account for many of the features, often the most interesting features, common to the following pieces.

MILL AS PUBLIC MORALIST

WITH HIS REPUTATION will stand or fall the intellectual repute of a whole generation of his countrymen. . . . If they did not accept his method of thinking, at least he determined the questions they should think about. . . . The better sort of journalists educated themselves on his books, and even the baser sort acquired a habit of quoting from them. He is the only writer in the world whose treatises on highly abstract subjects have been printed during his lifetime in editions for the people, and sold at the price of railway novels. Foreigners from all countries read his books as attentively as his most eager English disciples, and sought his opinions as to their own questions with as much reverence as if he had been a native oracle.[2]

It is, no doubt, difficult to write the obituary of an oracle, and John Morley's prose here betrays the strain. Yet his studied hyperbole, or at least his apparent need to resort to it even when writing for a sympathetic audience, suitably indicates the quite extraordinary public standing that Mill achieved in the last decade or so of his life. We must be careful not to let the development of his reputation during the earlier stages of his career be obscured by or assimilated to its final remarkable apotheosis: in the 1830s he was best known as a leading representative of an

[2]John Morley, "The Death of Mr. Mill," *Fortnightly Review*, n.s. XIII (June, 1873), 670.

extreme and unpopular sect; in the 1840s and into the 1850s his double-decker treatises on logic and political economy won him a reputation that was formidable but restricted in scope and limited in extent. After all, up until 1859 these were the only books he had published (apart from the rather technical and commercially never very successful *Essays on Some Unsettled Questions of Political Economy*), and although his articles and reviews continued to appear during these decades, he did not, before his retirement from the East India Company and his wife's death in 1858, deliberately and consistently seek the limelight by publication or any other means. It is interesting to reflect how different the obituaries would have been had Mill died in the mid-1850s, as seemed to him very likely at the time. Not only would his place in the history of political thought, for example, be comparatively negligible, but he would be seen as one of those distinguished figures in the history of thought who never achieved full recognition in their lifetimes, and whose subsequent reputation partly derived from incomplete or posthumous works, with the result that they stood in a quite different relation to their contemporary audiences. Nor, of course, would he have served his term in Parliament, the extraordinary manner of his election to which was both a symptom of his peculiar standing and a cause of its further growth.

Mill himself was well aware of the influence this lately acquired reputation gave him. Of his spate of publications after 1859, he says to an American correspondent in 1863, "They have been much more widely read than ever [my longer treatises] were, & have given me what I had not before, popular influence. I was regarded till then as a writer on special scientific subjects & had been little heard of by the miscellaneous public," and, he adds with evident satisfaction, "I am in a very different position now."[3] The triumphant note of realized ambition is even clearer in his reflection recorded during his Westminster candidacy of 1865: "I am getting the ear of England."[4] He did not hesitate to bend that ear, and although he did not exactly pour honey into it, he was well aware of the persuasive arts needed to hold its attention. There may well be figures who conform to the stereotype of the theorist, working out ideas on abstract subjects heedless of the world's response, but Mill cannot be numbered among them. Nor should his justly celebrated defence of the ideals of toleration and many-sidedness obscure the fact that on nearly all the issues of his time, intellectual as well as practical, he was rabidly partisan; as "a private in the army of Truth"[5] he frequently engaged in hand-to-hand combat, offering little quarter to the unhesitatingly identified forces of Error.

---

[3]Letter to Charles A. Cummings, *LL*, *CW*, XV, 843 (23 Feb., 1862). Cf., for further "proof of the influence of my writings," Mill's letter to Helen Taylor, *ibid.*, 673 (7 Feb., 1860).

[4]Letter to Max Kyllmann, *LL*, *CW*, XVI, 1063n (30 May, 1865). Mill may have felt uneasy with the tone of this passage since he cancelled it from his draft.

[5]The phrase is John Sterling's, recorded by Caroline Fox in her *Memories of Old Friends*, ed. Horace N. Pym, 2 vols. (London: Smith, Elder, 1882), II, 8.

A revealing statement of Mill's own conception of his role as a public moralist is seen in his reply in 1854 to the secretary of the charmingly named Neophyte Writers' Society, which had invited him to become a member of its council:

So far as I am able to collect the objects of the Society from the somewhat vague description given of them in the Prospectus, I am led to believe that it is not established to promote any opinions in particular; that its members are bound together only by the fact of being writers, not by the purposes for which they write; that their publications will admit conflicting opinions with equal readiness; & that the mutual criticism which is invited will have for its object the improvement of the writers merely as writers, & not the promotion, by means of writing, of any valuable object.

Now I set no value whatever on writing for its own sake & have much less respect for the literary craftsman than for the manual labourer except so far as he uses his powers in promoting what I consider true & just. I have on most of the subjects interesting to mankind, opinions to which I attach importance & which I earnestly desire to diffuse; but I am not desirous of aiding the diffusion of opinions contrary to my own; & with respect to the mere faculty of expression independently of what is to be expressed, it does not appear to me to require any encouragement. There is already an abundance, not to say superabundance, of writers who are able to express in an effective manner the mischievous commonplaces which they have got to say. I would gladly give any aid in my power towards improving their opinions; but I have no fear that any opinions they have will not be sufficiently well expressed; not in any way would I be disposed to give any assistance in sharpening weapons when I know not in what cause they will be used.

For these reasons I cannot consent that my name should be added to the list of writers you send me.[6]

It could be argued that almost his entire mature career is a gloss on this letter; with an eye to the contents of the present volume, let us concentrate on just three aspects of it.

First of all, Mill was no tyro as far as the means for diffusing his opinions were concerned. Morley called him the best-informed man of his day: certainly he was one of the most attentive readers of the great reviews, then in their heyday. His correspondence is studded with references to the latest issue of this or that journal, the political and intellectual character of each being duly noted; a more than casual interest in the medium is revealed when a man spends several weeks systematically catching up on back issues of a periodical, as Mill did in 1860 with the *Saturday Review*, despite the fact that it was largely a journal of comment on the ephemeral topics of the day.[7] He was always alive to the nature of the different audiences he could reach through these journals. He cultivated his connection with the *Edinburgh Review*, for example, despite the defects of its increasingly hide-bound Whiggism, because appearing in its pages conferred greater authority and respectability than any of its lesser rivals could offer; on the other hand,

---

[6]Letter to the Secretary of the Neophyte Writers' Society, *LL*, *CW*, XIV, 205 (23 Apr., 1854).

[7]See his letters to Helen Taylor for January and February, 1860, *LL*, *CW*, XV, 660-87. The exercise was no labour of love: he observed at the end, after grudgingly conceding the quality of much of its writing, that the review "is among the greatest enemies to our *principles* that there now are" (687).

particularly contentious or merely slight pieces were seen as needing more congenial company. Thus, to do justice to Austin's reputation nothing less than the *Edinburgh* would do (and the subject was anyway a "safe" one), but the *Westminster* was a better platform from which to issue a timely puff in favour of Cairnes' controversial *The Slave Power*. As Bain tersely put it: "He chose the *Westminster* when he wanted free room for his elbow."[8] The importance Mill attached to the maintenance of "an organ of really free opinions," shows clearly his belief, whether justified or not, that it would otherwise be difficult to get a hearing for "advanced" opinions.[9] When coaching the young Lord Amberley on how best to put a shoulder behind the wheel of Progress, he remarks: "The greatest utility of the Westminster Review is that it is willing to print bolder opinions on all subjects than the other periodicals: and when you feel moved to write anything that is too strong for other Reviews, you will generally be able to get it into the Westminster."[10] For this reason Mill remained willing, long after he had relinquished ownership of the paper, to sink money in its never very promising battle against low circulation figures, and in this he was only one among several contemporary public men to whom the prestige or accessibility of a review of a congenial temper justified often quite substantial subsidies.[11] When in the last decade of his life the *Fortnightly Review* got under way, it fulfilled this role more successfully, especially while edited by his self-proclaimed disciple, John Morley, and several of Mill's later pieces, including the last article reprinted here, were written for it. Testimony of a different kind about the importance Mill attached to such a review is provided by the fact that he should have offered, at the age of sixty-four and with numerous other claims on his time, to occupy the editor's chair during Morley's threatened absence rather than have the *Fortnightly* fall into the wrong hands or suffer a break in publication.[12]

Although he was predictably censorious of "professional excitement-

---

[8]Alexander Bain, *John Stuart Mill, a Criticism: With Personal Recollections* (London: Longmans, 1882), 118. For an interesting example of Mill's wishing to use the *Edinburgh* in this way and agreeing to "put what I have to say in a form somewhat different from that in which I should write for another publication," see his correspondence in 1869 with its editor, Henry Reeve, about a proposed review of his friend W.T. Thornton's *On Labour*; eventually, Mill was unwilling to meet Reeve's stipulations, and his review of Thornton, which contained his famous recantation of the wages-fund doctrine, appeared in the *Fortnightly* instead. See *LL*, *CW*, XVII, 1574-82.

[9]See, for examples, *ibid.*, XIV, 62, 72.

[10]Letter to Lord Amberley, *ibid.*, XVI, 1007 (8 Mar., 1865).

[11]See the essays in *The Victorian Periodical Press: Samplings and Soundings*, ed. Joanne Shattock and Michael Wolff (Leicester: Leicester University Press; Toronto: University of Toronto Press, 1982), especially the essay by Sheila Rosenberg on John Chapman's proprietorship of the *Westminster*.

[12]Letter to John Morley, *LL*, *CW*, XVII, 1785 (28 Nov., 1870). Cf. his letter to Morley of 11 May, 1872, hoping that the latter will not stand for the Chair of Political Economy at University College London "lest the undertaking of additional work might possibly affect either your health or the time you can give to the Fortnightly. I am very desirous that the F. sh^d continue, & increase rather than diminish in importance & I think you exercise a wider influence through it than you could do through the Professorship" (*ibid.*, 1892).

makers,"[13] Mill's mastery of his role also extended to that other important requirement, a sense of timing. In writing to the editor of the *Westminster* about a proposed article by another contributor, Mill reported: "he does not like the idea of its not appearing till April, and I should certainly think January would be a better time, as giving it a chance of helping to shape the speeches in Parliament or at public meetings, and the newspaper articles, by which alone any impression can be made upon unwilling Finance Ministers."[14] In issuing his own work, Mill calculated the moment for making the maximum "impression": he delayed full expression of his unpopular views on the American Civil War until there was a "chance of getting a hearing for the Northern side of the question," and later congratulated himself that "The Contest in America" had appeared at just the right moment to influence opinion.[15] Similarly, he delayed publication of *The Subjection of Women* (which was written in 1861) until the campaign for the suffrage, which he helped to orchestrate, had created a more receptive audience.[16] Judicious distribution of off-prints of his articles was intended to increase this impact, just as the pamphlet form of both his "Remarks on Mr. Fitzroy's Bill" and his evidence to the Royal Commission on the Contagious Diseases Acts gave his views on these subjects a wider currency. And of course he was no less careful in judging the occasion for publishing further Library editions of his earlier works, as well as the cheap People's Editions that, beginning in 1865, gave wide circulation to his major works.[17] Having got "the ear of England," Mill did not intend to let it go.

The second aspect of Mill's performance in the role of public moralist that concerns us here is the fact that his views were always likely to be unpopular with the majority of the educated classes, or at least—what may be rather more interesting—Mill always thought of himself as the holder of unpopular views, despite the success of his writings. In very general terms it is true that Mill's beliefs on "most of the subjects interesting to mankind" were those of an advanced Radical—secular, democratic, egalitarian, actively sympathetic to Socialism and the emancipation of women, yet more actively hostile to privilege and injustice and to the moral callousness he took to underlie these evils—and these views

[13]Letter to John Elliot Cairnes, *ibid.*, XVI, 1003 (5 May, 1865).

[14]Letter to John Chapman, *ibid.*, XV, 733 (12 July, 1861).

[15]Letter to Cairnes, *ibid.*, 767 (20 Jan., 1862); *Autobiography and Literary Essays*, ed. John M. Robson and Jack Stillinger, *CW*, I (Toronto: University of Toronto Press, 1981), 268.

[16]*Autobiography*, *CW*, I, 265. Cf. letter to Alexander Bain, *LL*, *CW*, XVII, 1623 (14 July, 1869), on how the strategy of *The Subjection of Women* was now appropriate in a way it would not have been "ten years ago."

[17]In fact, 1865 marked an extraordinary peak of simultaneity in the publication of Mill's work: "In addition to the two editions of *Representative Government*, the fifth editions of both the *Logic* and the *Principles*, the People's Editions of *On Liberty* and the *Principles*, the periodical and first book editions of *Auguste Comte and Positivism*, and the first and second editions of the *Examination of Sir William Hamilton's Philosophy*" all appeared in that year (Textual Introduction, *Essays on Politics and Society*, *CW*, XVIII-XIX [Toronto: University of Toronto Press, 1977], XVIII, lxxxix).

hardly commanded immediate assent in the smoking-rooms of mid-Victorian England. But it may have become important to Mill to exaggerate the extent to which he was a lonely crusader, lacking a supporting army (a few white knights aside), sustained only by the righteousness of the cause and the kinship of a scattering of rare spirits in other countries. Certainly, it is an identity which a self-described "radical" thinker is always likely to find comforting, since it simultaneously flatters the intellect, provides a sense of purpose, and explains away failure. Occasionally there is an almost paranoid note in Mill's writing—it is part of what gives *On Liberty* its somewhat shrill tone—and although it is true that Mill was frequently reminded of the unpopularity of many of his causes, it is also true that magnifying the strength of the Forces of Darkness in his typically Manichaean vision of the world was essential to his polemical strategy. There are numerous instances of this in the present volume: to take but one, consider how often in the opening paragraphs of *The Subjection of Women* he depicts his task as "arduous," emphasizing the great "difficulty" of "contend[ing] against . . . a mass of feeling," and leading up to the subtly self-flattering self-excusing statement: "In every respect the burthen is hard on those who attack an almost universal opinion. They must be very fortunate as well as unusually capable if they obtain a hearing at all." (261.) The first two editions of the book, it should be noted, sold out within a few months.

As the metaphor of "advanced" or "progressive" opinion suggests, Mill projected his differences with the majority of his contemporaries into a reassuring historical dimension. Mankind were strung out in an enormous caravan, slowly and often unwillingly trudging across the sands of time, with the English governing classes, in particular, reluctant to move on from their uniquely favoured oasis. Mill, some way in advance of the main party, could see distant vistas hidden from their view: the task was to convince the more susceptible among them to move in the right direction, and crucial to this task was showing that the recommended route was but an extension of the path successfully followed so far. Mill, unlike several of the most prominent nineteenth-century social thinkers, did not elaborate a fully teleological account of history, but he frequently resorted to the claim that there had been a discernible line of moral improvement, not dissimilar to what T.H. Green was to call "the extension of the area of the common good,"[18] whereby the circle of full moral recognition was gradually being extended to all those hitherto neglected or excluded, whether they were English labourers or negro slaves or—the argument is used to particularly good effect here—women. It is always an advantage to portray one's opponents as committed to defending a quite arbitrary stopping-place along the route of progress, and the argument had a particular resonance when addressed to an audience of mid-

---

[18]See Thomas Hill Green, *Prolegomena to Ethics*, ed. Andrew Cecil Bradley (Oxford: Clarendon Press, 1883), 217.

nineteenth-century English liberals who regarded such moral improvement as the chief among the glories of their age.

As this account reveals, Mill did not in fact stand in such a purely adversary relation to his culture as he sometimes liked to suggest, since he was constantly appealing to certain shared values when berating his contemporaries for failing either to draw the right inferences from their professed moral principles in theory or to live up to their agreed standards in practice. Mill—it is one of the few things about him one can assert with reasonable security against contradiction—was not Nietzsche. He was not, that is, attempting fundamentally to subvert or reverse his society's moral sensibilities, but rather to refine them and call them more effectively into play on public issues (examples will be noted below). In these circumstances, the moralist runs the risk of priggishness, as he contrasts the consistency of his own position and the purity of his own motives with the logical confusions and self-interested prejudices that he must impute to those who, sharing the same premises, fail to draw the same conclusions.

This consideration brings us to the third aspect of Mill's performance as public moralist to be discussed here, his characteristic style and manner of argument. Coleridge's dictum, "*Analogies* are used in aid of *Conviction*: *Metaphors* as means of *Illustration*,"[19] catches and at the same time explains one of the most characteristic features of Mill's style. His prose, typically, is didactic and forensic, conducting the reader through the logical deficiencies of arguments like a severe, slightly sarcastic, and not altogether patient tutor dissecting a pupil's essay. He wrote to convince, and where he could not convince, to convict. No one has ever doubted the power of sustained analysis that he could command, but the pieces in this volume also display his mastery of the blunter weapons of controversy. One would be wise to respect an opponent who could begin a paragraph with a bland enquiry into the nature of Confederate society and then move smoothly to the conclusion: "The South are in rebellion not for simple slavery; they are in rebellion for the right of burning human creatures alive" (136). The invention of imaginary opponents underlined the gladiatorial nature of Mill's dialectic, and he could be as unfair to them as Plato often is to Socrates' stooges (who provide Mill's model), as when in *The Subjection of Women* we are told what a "pertinacious adversary, pushed to extremities, may say," only to discover a few lines later that this "will be said by no one now who is worth replying to" (292; cf. 310-11). But perhaps his most common rhetorical strategy is the *reductio ad absurdum*—and this observation underlines the earlier point about Mill's reliance on a certain community of values between himself and his readers, without which the reductions would seem either not absurd or else simply irrelevant. Similarly, the use of analogy requires that the characterization of one term of the analogy be

[19]Quoted in John Holloway, *The Victorian Sage: Studies in Argument* (London: Macmillan, 1953), 13-14, from Coleridge's *Aids to Reflection* (London: Taylor and Hessey, 1825), 198 (Aph. 104 in other eds.).

beyond dispute: if it is not, the alleged extension will have no persuasive force. Arguments about equality are particularly likely to involve appeals to analogy; indeed, the whole of *The Subjection of Women* could be regarded as one long elaboration of the basic analogy between the historical position of slaves and the present position of women. And finally, the gap between profession and practice, to which Mill was constantly calling attention, invites the use of irony, though it must be said that his efforts at irony often sailed close to mere sarcasm and ridicule; his own highly developed sense of being, and having to be seen to be, "a man of principle" did not, perhaps, leave much room for that more generous and tolerant perception of human limitation which sustains the best forms of irony.

As a medium for addressing the reader of the periodicals of general culture, Mill's prose was certainly not without its drawbacks. Carlyle's ungenerous description of Mill's conversation as "sawdustish"[20] could also be applied to some of his writing. He was aware, Bain tells us, that he lacked that facility of illustration which would have mitigated the overly abstract texture which characterizes almost all his work, and a compendium of Mill's wit would be a slim volume indeed. His scorn for the mere "literary craftsman" quoted above was of a piece with his own avoidance of those arts common among the more winning essayists and reviewers in the nineteenth century. He never quite hits off the ideal tone for such writing in the way in which, say, Bagehot or Leslie Stephen did: he never manages to create that sense of intimacy between reader and author, that warming feeling of sharing a sensible view of a mad world. But in some ways the achievement of this effect would have been foreign to Mill's purpose, for the sense of complicity it nurtured was to him only a subtler form of that complacency which he saw as the chief danger of modern society, the *fons malorum* that, above all else, required constant criticism: and here we come to the heart of his role as a public moralist.

Behind the particular issues to which the topical pieces in this volume were addressed there runs a common theme: the moral health of society is the highest good, calling, as the metaphor suggests, for constant care and sustenance if decay is not to set in.[21] Mill is here acting as moral coach, keeping the national conscience in trim, shaming it out of flabbiness, urging it on to yet more strenuous efforts. In some ways this is an ancient role, and he sometimes hits a surprisingly traditional note: when, in defending the military action of the Northern states, he declared that "war, in a good cause, is not the greatest evil which a nation can suffer. . . . [T]he decayed and degraded state of moral and patriotic feeling which thinks nothing *worth* a war, is worse" (141), we are reminded more of the language of Machiavelli and civic *virtù* than that of Cobden and Bright and the age of pacific commercialism. But for the most part the conception of morality to which Mill

---

[20]Quoted in Bain, *John Stuart Mill*, 190.
[21]Cf. his reply of 6 Dec., 1871, to a correspondent who had asked him if he thought France was "en décadence": "A mon sens, la décadence morale est toujours la seule réelle" (*LL, CW*, XVIII, 1864).

appeals appears unambiguously Victorian, both in its emphasis upon the active shaping of "character," that constantly self-renewing disposition to form virtuous habits of conduct, and in its focus on the welfare of others as the object of moral action, and even, indeed, on the duty of altruism. What Mill is trying to do, beyond keeping this conception in good repair, is to mobilize its power in areas outside those over which it was conventionally granted sovereignty. In assessing England's foreign policy he makes questions of moral example paramount; in discussing attitudes towards the American Civil War the moral tone of opinion in England is his chief concern; in opposing the Contagious Diseases Acts it is their public endorsement of vice he most objects to.

As prompter of the national conscience, Mill derived certain advantages from his deliberately nurtured position as an outsider among the English governing classes. Where the aim is to make one's readers morally uncomfortable, too great an intimacy can be an obstacle; Mill seems to have felt that his avoidance of Society helped to provide the requisite distance as well as to preserve a kind of uncorrupted purity of feeling (he, though not he alone, attributed the allegedly superior moral insight of the labouring classes to the same cause). More obviously, he claimed a special authority on account of his familiarity (his unique familiarity, he sometimes seems to imply) with the main currents of Continental, and especially French, thought. Reproaches to his countrymen for their insular prejudice and ignorance are a staple ingredient in Mill's writing, whether he is castigating them for their aversion to theories of history or upbraiding them for their unresponsiveness to the beauties of art. This is a further aspect of the didactic voice: tutor and pupil are not equals. An interesting complication emerges, however, where the comparative moral achievements of the English are concerned, for he repeatedly asserts that England is the superior of other nations in its "greater tenderness of conscience" (though characteristically he cannot resist the censorious warning, "I am not sure that we are not losing" the advantage [253]). As far as individual conduct was concerned, he could still maintain that its tendency to harden into a narrow "Hebraizing" called for correction from larger views of life that needed, on the whole, to be imported. But where national policy was at issue, Mill conceded England's superior reputation, only to treat it as the source of an enlarged duty: as "incomparably the most conscientious of all nations" in its "national acts" (115), England had a special responsibility for maintaining and improving standards of international morality. In either case there was no rest for the virtuous. Since the English, according to Mill, were perpetually liable to complacency, a critic who could keep a more strenuous ideal before their minds would never want for employment.

It may help us to place that role as Mill's practice defined it if we contrast it with two others, which were certainly no less available in mid-Victorian England, and which may, for convenience, simply be labelled those of the Sage and the Man of

Letters.[22] Claims to both these titles could be made on Mill's behalf, yet their ultimate inappropriateness as descriptions of the author of the pieces in this volume (and, I think, of most of Mill's mature *oeuvre*) is revealing of his position in the intellectual life of his time. The Sage (to construct a highly simplified ideal-type) trades in wisdom and new visions of experience as a whole. Typically, he is not so much attempting to *argue* his readers out of false beliefs as to reveal to them—or, better still, to put them in the way of discovering for themselves—the limitations of that perception of the world upon which they purport to base all their beliefs. The ineffable constantly looms, and he frequently employs a highly idiosyncratic vocabulary in an effort to disclose those dimensions of experience which the conventional categories are said to distort or obscure. Coleridge, Carlyle, and Newman might be taken as obvious nineteenth-century examples of this type, their very heterogeneity ensuring that it will not be understood to imply a set of common doctrines. Now, for all his Coleridgean and Carlylean flirtations in the late 1820s and early 1830s, I think it is clear that Mill does not belong in this *galère*. The *Logic* is hardly attempting to awaken in us a sense of the mysteries of the universe, and none of the essays in the volumes of *Dissertations and Discussions* leaves us feeling that we now possess our experience in a quite new way. Nothing in Mill's philosophy strains at the limits of the plainly expressible, and if this restriction gives his prose a rather pedestrian quality by comparison with that of the Sages, we should remember that it is part of the definition of the pedestrian that he has his feet on the ground. After all, when Mill clashes directly with Carlyle over "the Negro Question" (85-95), it is not obvious that the latter's esoteric vision yields the more appealing view, still less that it provides the more persuasive basis for action.

As one who wrote so extensively for the great Victorian reviews and on such a diverse range of subjects, Mill might seem to have a better claim to be included in the more capacious category of Man of Letters. His literary essays of the 1830s could be cited as one qualification for membership, his later reviews on historical and classical subjects, more dubiously, as another, and in any inclusive survey of the type Mill ought arguably to find a place. But even then he seems to be at most a kind of honorary member, too important to be left out, too individual to be conscripted, and his reply to the Neophyte Writers' Society again provides the clue which helps us to pin down his distinctiveness. It is not only that Mill aimed to instruct rather than to delight, though it is worth recalling the disdain he entertained for what he dismissively termed "the mere faculty of expression"; he could never have subscribed to the view expressed in Francis Jeffrey's defence of the lively style of the early *Edinburgh Review*: "To be learned and right is no doubt the first requisite, but to be ingenious and original and discursive is perhaps more

---

[22]For suggestive uses of these terms, which I have drawn upon but not strictly followed, see Holloway, *Victorian Sage*, and John Gross, *The Rise and Fall of the Man of Letters: Aspects of English Literary Life since 1800* (London: Weidenfeld and Nicolson, 1969).

than the second in a publication which can only do good by remaining popular."[23] But Mill is not divided from the best practitioners of literary journalism in his day only by a difference of tactics: there is the far deeper difference that he was not sufficiently interested in the variousness of literary achievement, not drawn to those exercises in appreciation, discrimination, and evocation that bulked so large in the reviews of the day. Where others collected their essays under such titles as "Hours in a Library," "Literary Studies," or simply "Miscellanies," Mill quite accurately called his "Dissertations and Discussions." Interestingly, he never wrote that kind of extended meditation on and appreciation of the work of a single figure which is among the chief essayistic glories of, say, Macaulay or Bagehot or Stephen, or even, more revealingly, of Morley, more revealingly because Morley was close to Mill in both doctrine and temperament. It is hard to imagine Mill, had he lived another ten years, contributing to Morley's English Men of Letters series. Of the two books which Mill did devote to individual figures, that on Hamilton is a massive display of destructive criticism and dialectical overkill, while even the briefer and more general assessment of Comte remains firmly tied to an analytical discussion of the strengths and weaknesses of Comte's *theory*. The nearest Mill had earlier come to this genre was in his famous essays on Bentham and Coleridge, yet even these were thinly disguised instalments in Mill's own philosophical progress, less essays in appreciation than occasions for further synthesis. Similarly, his pieces on the French historians were intended to be contributions towards the development of a general historical theory, just as his reviews of Grote's history were in effect manifestos for democracy, and so on. "I have on most of the subjects interesting to mankind, opinions to which I attach importance & which I earnestly desire to diffuse." In pursuing this goal, the mature Mill husbanded his energies with principled care; perhaps he could not afford to explore other voices. At all events, as a moralist he never missed a chance to instruct, reproach, and exhort.

Such a figure is bound to excite strong feelings of one kind or another. In the pieces collected here, Mill, as a contemporary comment on his writings on the American Civil War put it, "ceases to be a philosopher and becomes the partisan,"[24] and they are for that reason an excellent corrective to caricatures of Mill as the irenic spokesman for some factitious "Victorian orthodoxy." It was because of such writings, above all, that he was regarded in many respectable circles as incorrigibly "extreme," a zealous root-and-branch man; even many of those who had been enthusiastic admirers of his earlier works in philosophy and political economy found these later writings too "doctrinaire."[25] Others regarded

[23]Quoted in William Thomas, *The Philosophic Radicals: Nine Studies in Theory and Practice, 1817-1841* (Oxford: Clarendon Press, 1979), 160.

[24]"J.S. Mill on the American Contest," *The Economist*, XX (8 Feb., 1862), 144.

[25]For examples of this response see Christopher Harvie, *The Lights of Liberalism: University Liberals and the Challenge of Democracy, 1860-86* (London: Lane, 1976), 152-3; cf. John Vincent,

them as among his best works.[26] It may be appropriate, therefore, to conclude this general discussion with two contemporary judgments which are both, it will be seen, essentially responses to those features of Mill the moralist we have been dealing with. A reviewer of *The Subjection of Women*, irked by Mill's "assumption of especial enlightenment—of a philosophic vantage-ground from which he is justified in despising the wisdom of mankind from the beginning of things," saw in this the source of his considerable unpopularity: "His intense arrogance, his incapacity to do justice to the feelings or motives of all from whom he differs, his intolerance of all but his own disciples, and lastly, in natural consequence of these qualities, his want of playfulness in himself and repugnance to it in others, all combine to create something like antipathy."[27] On the other hand, John Morley, commending Mill's "moral thoroughness," concluded: "The too common tendency in us all to moral slovenliness, and a lazy contentment with a little flaccid protest against evil, finds a constant rebuke in his career. . . . The value of this wise and virtuous mixture of boldness with tolerance, of courageous speech with courageous reserve, has been enormous."[28]

EQUALITY

MILL'S WRITINGS ON EQUALITY included in this volume fall into two main groups, which it will be convenient to discuss separately: they are those that deal with what might be loosely termed "the negro question," including, in addition to the piece of that name, his essays on the American Civil War and the papers of the Jamaica Committee; and those that deal with women, including, as well as the obvious items, his evidence on the Contagious Diseases Acts. (The two complementary pieces on foreign affairs—"A Few Words on Non-Intervention" and "Treaty Obligations"—will be discussed with the first group since they directly bear on the related question of the moral considerations that ought to govern England's international conduct.) But, as the earlier remarks about analogy suggest, the arguments deployed in the two groups were very closely connected in Mill's mind, and so it may be helpful to make a preliminary point about the chief feature they have in common.

Alexander Bain, increasingly sceptical of Mill's later political enthusiasms,

---

The Formation of the British Liberal Party, 1857-1868 (London: Constable, 1966), 190. It is a view which pervades Bain's account: see, for example, *John Stuart Mill*, 91.

[26]For John Morley, for example, they represented "the notable result of this ripest, loftiest, and most inspiring part of his life," and he regarded *The Subjection of Women*, in particular, as "probably the best illustration of all the best and richest qualities of its author's mind" ("Mr. Mill's Autobiography," *Fortnightly Review*, n.s. XV [Jan., 1874], 15, 12).

[27]Anne Mozley, "Mr. Mill *On the Subjection of Women*," *Blackwood's Magazine*, CVI (Sept., 1869), 320-1.

[28]Morley, "Death of Mr. Mill," 673, 672.

considered the "doctrine of the natural equality of men" to be his master's greatest error as a "scientific thinker."[29] Mill certainly presented the issue as essentially a matter of scientific method, making his opponents' belief in natural inequalities seem a corollary of their defective grasp of the nature of induction. He constantly maintained that no reliable inference about what men and, more particularly, women would be like under a quite different set of circumstances could be made on the basis of our knowledge of their behaviour under the circumstances of systematic inequality which, he alleged in a rather brisk characterization of human history, had shaped that behaviour up to the present. His belief in the indefinite malleability of human nature provided one crucial ingredient of this claim, though here as elsewhere he was hampered (as he at times acknowledged) by his failure with his pet project of an "Ethology," the scientific demonstration of the ways in which character is formed by circumstances.[30] But in a way his view reflects the larger problem of negative evidence, a recurring motif in radical arguments against the existing order of things. That is to say, to the premise that individuals should be treated equally unless good cause can be shown to do otherwise, Mill wants to attach the rider that history could not *in principle* furnish the evidence needed to show such cause in the case of traditionally subordinate groups such as "the lower races," the lower classes, or women. Actually, of course, Mill does wish to appeal to history in one way, namely (as suggested in general terms above), to present it as exhibiting a broad movement towards equality, but he is not, strictly speaking, attempting to have it both ways: the historical and epistemological claims are logically independent of each other. After all, it would be possible to uphold a belief in equality as in some sense "natural" whilst acknowledging that the march of history seemed to be in the direction of ever greater inequality, though unless buttressed by some ingenious supporting arguments this position might make the initial claim less plausible as well as, and perhaps more consequentially, less inspiriting. In practice, needless to say, Mill combined the two claims to good polemical effect: "the course of history, and the tendencies of progressive human society, afford not only no presumption in favour of this system of inequality of rights, but a strong one against it; and . . . so far as the whole course of human improvement up to this time, the whole stream of modern tendencies, warrants any inference on the subject, it is, that this relic of the past is discordant with the future, and must necessarily disappear" (272). He did not, in fact, always press the second, quasi-historicist, claim quite so hard; but he squeezed the first, negative,

[29]Bain, *John Stuart Mill*, 146.

[30]For his conception of Ethology, see *A System of Logic, Ratiocinative and Inductive*, CW, VII-VIII (Toronto: University of Toronto Press, 1973), VIII, 861-74 (Bk. VI, Chap. v). For his "failure" with it, see Bain, *John Stuart Mill*, 78-9. His correspondence reveals that he continued to entertain hopes of returning to the project: e.g., letter to Alexander Bain of 14 Nov., 1859, where he referred to it as "a subject I have long wished to take up, at least in the form of Essays, but have never yet felt myself sufficiently prepared" (*LL, CW*, XV, 645). For an example of his acknowledgment that "there is hardly any subject which, in proportion to its importance, has been so little studied," see 277 below.

point very hard indeed, and it is this, above all, that imparts such a strongly destructive flavour to some of these pieces.

"The Negro Question" (1850), the earliest of the first group, was published in the form of a letter to the editor of *Fraser's* replying to Carlyle's "Occasional Discourse on the Negro Question" published in the preceding number.[31] Mill's friendship with Carlyle had cooled—indeed, all but lapsed—since the days of Mill's heady, discipular enthusiasm in the early 1830s,[32] and Carlyle's ever more vehement denunciations of the sentimental cant of humanitarian reformers placed a very large obstacle in the way of any genuine intellectual rapprochement. This and other uncongenial themes, including the Divine sanction to the rule of the strongest, and the heroic, Promethean conception of work, were all rehearsed in this latest intemperate satire on the misguided world of Exeter Hall and "The Universal Abolition of Pain Association," so that Mill's reply involved a repudiation of the whole Carlylean vision. The exchange also prefigured the far more significant confrontations over the Governor Eyre controversy sixteen years later, when Mill and Carlyle were to emerge as leaders of the rival public committees, and when the lines of division were very much those canvassed in the earlier exchange.

The bare structure of Mill's argument follows the basic pattern referred to above: what Carlyle takes as the distinctive and self-evidently inferior "nature" of the negro is in fact the result of the historical circumstances of subjection under which that character has been formed, and it is the distinctive mark of the modern age to be bent on mitigating or abolishing such subjection. Both science and history, therefore, tell against the view that the negro—"Quashee," to use Carlyle's mischievously provocative term—must perpetually work under the lash of a white master. But though Mill's reply is, as ever, analytically sharp, it may seem to leave untouched the deeper sources of Carlyle's rhetorical power. For example, in replying that the abolition of slavery "triumphed because it was the cause of justice," not because the age itself was enslaved to a "rose-pink sentimentalism" (88), Mill does not really engage with that transvaluation of all values that lay at the root of Carlyle's particular gibes (the appropriateness of the Nietzschean phrase is itself an indication of the systematically subversive nature of Carlyle's assault on the moral truisms of his day). Mill's criticisms are decisive in their own terms, but they bounce like small-arms fire off Carlyle's armour-plated vision of the enthusiasm for human justice as itself part of that weak-kneed, self-deluded evasion of the facts of a power-governed universe. Carlyle, hardly surprisingly, thought Mill's reply "most shrill, thin, poor, and insignificant."[33]

[31]For more detailed comments on the publishing history of each of the items reprinted here, see the Textual Introduction below.

[32]See especially Mill's letters to Carlyle for the years 1832-35, in *The Earlier Letters of John Stuart Mill* [*EL*], ed. Francis E. Mineka, *CW*, XII-XIII (Toronto: University of Toronto Press, 1963).

[33]See Carlyle's journal for 7 Feb., 1850, quoted in Emery Neff, *Carlyle and Mill: An Introduction to Victorian Thought*, 2nd ed. (New York: Columbia University Press, 1926), 43.

One significant feature of Mill's attack was his prescient concentration on the prospects for slavery in the United States, and on the support given to "the owners of human flesh" by Carlyle's flinging "this missile, loaded with the weight of his reputation, into the abolitionist camp" (95). Mill always followed American developments very closely, convinced that they would eventually prove decisive for several of the causes he cared most about:[34] the fate of popular government, in particular, seemed to Mill and many others in England to be bound up with the successes and failures of "the great democratic experiment" of the United States.[35] Although Mill shared many of Tocqueville's misgivings about the pressures making for mediocrity and conformity in American society, he did not let these misgivings override his principled optimism about the future of democracy, and he was always alert to the ways in which anti-democratic opinion in England, with *The Times* in the van, tried to exploit the acknowledged weaknesses of American political life and constitutional arrangements to discredit all popular causes at home. The Civil War, therefore, touched several nerves in Mill's moral physiology; not only did it involve the most blatant case of institutionalized inequality in the civilized world and the whole question of popular government's ability to combine freedom with stability, but, always powerfully active in determining Mill's interest in public issues, it provided a thermometer with which to take the moral temperature of English society as a whole.

The question of British attitudes towards the American Civil War is a notoriously complex and disputed one,[36] but it is uncontentious to say that in the early stages of the war a very large majority among the articulate was hostile to the North, and that within that majority there was an influential body actively sympathetic to the Confederate cause. It was not simply that the upper classes largely sided with what was perceived as the aristocratic or gentlemanly character of plantation society, nor even that for many in all classes commercial self-interest seemed to dictate a prudent regard for the prosperity and independence of the cotton-exporting states. It was also that the Confederate cause was widely represented as the cause of freedom, that in defending their "right to secede" in the face of the superior force of an essentially alien power, the Southern states were

---

[34]It is even possible that in this respect America was coming to replace France in Mill's thinking, especially once France was saddled with the despotism of Napoleon III, which he so abhorred. In 1849 he could still write: "The whole problem of modern society however will be worked out, as I have long thought it would, in France & nowhere else" (letter to Henry Samuel Chapman, *LL, CW,* XIV, 32 [28 May, 1849]); but for later remarks which seem to assign at least equal importance to the United States see *ibid.,* 1307 and 1880; see also *Autobiography, CW,* I, 266-8.

[35]There is a useful survey in D.P. Crook, *American Democracy in English Politics, 1815-1850* (Oxford: Clarendon Press, 1965).

[36]The standard account was for long Ephraim Douglass Adams, *Great Britain and the American Civil War,* 2 vols. (London: Longmans, 1925); a strongly revisionist attack on the view that the cotton workers of Lancashire had, against their economic interest, supported the North is provided in the controversial study by Mary Ellison, *Support for Secession: Lancashire and the American Civil War* (Chicago: University of Chicago Press, 1972); there is a judicious synthesis in D.P. Crook, *The North, the South and the Powers, 1861-1865* (New York: Wiley, 1974).

acting analogously to those peoples "rightly struggling to be free" who had aroused such enthusiasm in Britain in the preceding decade: Jefferson Davis was elevated to stand alongside Kossuth and Garibaldi. The issue was thus not one on which opinion divided (in so far as it very unequally did divide) along party lines: Gladstone and Russell were among those who considered the Federal attempt to "coerce the South" to be unwarranted, while Radicals were told by some of their spokesmen that "the first doctrine of Radicalism . . . was the right of a people to self-government."[37]

Mill, to whom the real issue at stake in the war had from the outset been the continued existence of slavery, considered that much of this sympathy for the South rested on ignorance or, even more culpably, moral insensibility, and "The Contest in America" (1862) was his attempt to educate English opinion on both counts. He expected it, Bain recorded, "to give great offence, and to be the most hazardous thing for his influence that he had yet done."[38] He made this judgment not simply because he found himself on the side of the minority, and a pretty small one at that; this he had taken to be the more or less constant character of his intellectual life from his earliest Benthamite propaganda onwards. Bain's phrase suggests, rather, that Mill was now the self-conscious possessor of a "reputation" which he was about to deploy in an outspoken condemnation of the moral myopia of the reputation-making classes. For, "the tone of the press & of English opinion," as he confided to Thornton, "has caused me more disgust than anything has done for a long time";[39] he regarded the "moral attitude" displayed by "some of our leading journals" (*The Times* and the *Saturday Review* particularly galled him) as betraying an unavowed partiality for slavery. In some cases, he sneered, this arose from "the influence, more or less direct, of West Indian opinions and interests," but in others—and here he warms to a favourite theme—it arose

from inbred Toryism, which, even when compelled by reason to hold opinions favourable to liberty, is always adverse to it in feeling; which likes the spectacle of irresponsible power exercised by one person over others; which has no moral repugnance to the thought of human beings born to the penal servitude for life, to which for the term of a few years we sentence our most hardened criminals, but keeps its indignation to be expended on "rabid and fanatical abolitionists" across the Atlantic, and on those writers in England who attach a sufficiently serious meaning to their Christian professions, to consider a fight against slavery as a fight for God (129).

Slavery is thus treated by Mill as the extreme form of undemocracy, a kind of Toryism of race to match the "Toryism of sex" that he saw in women's exclusion from the franchise.[40] The "warmth of his feelings" on the issue was remarked by

---

[37]Quoted in Ellison, *Support for Secession*, 9.

[38]Bain, *John Stuart Mill*, 119.

[39]Letter to William Thomas Thornton of 28 Jan., 1862, where he also places his characteristic two-way bet that his article "if noticed at all is likely to be much attacked" (*LL, CW*, XV, 774).

[40]He used this phrase in a reference to the exclusion of women from the suffrage in the otherwise unusually democratic Australian colonies (letter to Henry Samuel Chapman, *LL, CW*, XV, 557 [8 July, 1858]).

friends and opponents alike: he was, Grote recorded, "violent against the South . . . ; embracing heartily the extreme Abolitionist views, and thinking about little else in regard to the general question."[41] It was the outspoken public expression of this passion which, more than anything else, gave Mill that identity as a "partisan" controversialist which was such a marked feature of his reputation in the last decade of his life.

Mill was adamant that even if secession were the main issue at stake, this would still not automatically entitle the South to the support of those who thought of themselves as ranged on the side of freedom. Brandishing his own radical credentials, he announced, "I have sympathized more or less ardently with most of the rebellions, successful and unsuccessful, which have taken place in my time," but emphasized that it was not simply their being rebellions that had determined their moral status: "those who rebel for the power of oppressing others" were not to be seen as exercising "as sacred a right as those who do the same thing to resist oppression practised upon themselves" (137). The nature and aims of Southern society were the decisive test, and in educating English opinion on this matter Mill found his chief ally in the Irish economist John Elliot Cairnes. The younger man had already won his senior's approval with his very Millian statement of the method of classical political economy,[42] and when in the summer of 1861 he sent Mill the manuscript of a course of lectures that he had just delivered on the nature of American slavery, Mill immediately recognized their polemical value and urged their publication.[43] The resulting book, accurately entitled *The Slave Power: Its Character, Career, and Probable Designs: Being an Attempt to Explain the Real Issues Involved in the American Contest*,[44] fully satisfied Mill's expectations, and led to the growth between the two men of what Mill, in a revealing phrase, referred to as "the agreeable feeling of a brotherhood in arms."[45]

The chief contentions of Cairnes' book were that the nature of Southern society was determined by its basis in the economy of slavery, that such a system of production needed, under American conditions, continually to expand the territory cultivated by slave labour, and that this inherent dynamic accounted for the expansionist activities of the Southern states which, when the action of the Federal government threatened to curb them, naturally led to war. Secession was not,

[41]Harriet Grote, *The Personal Life of George Grote* (London: Murray, 1873), 264. Recommending Mill's article to Gladstone, the Duke of Argyle particularly emphasized how "the cold-blooded philosopher comes out with much warmth" (quoted in Adelaide Weinberg, *John Elliot Cairnes and the American Civil War: A Study in Anglo-American Relations* [London: Kingswood Press, 1969], 22). See also *The Economist*'s suggestion that on this issue Mill was carried away "by the very warmth of his own feelings" ("Mill on the American Contest," 171).

[42]*The Character and Logical Method of Political Economy* (London: Longman, *et al.*, 1857). For Mill's favourable view, see letter to Cairnes, *LL, CW*, XV, 554 (22 Apr., 1858).

[43]Letter to Cairnes, *ibid.*, 738 (18 Aug., 1861); cf. 750.

[44]London: Parker, 1862; 2nd ed., London: Macmillan, 1863. For details, see Weinberg, *Cairnes and the American Civil War*, esp. Chap. ii.

[45]Letter to Cairnes, *LL, CW*, XV, 785 (24 June, 1862).

therefore, a demand of an oppressed people to be left alone: it was the inevitable outcome of an insatiably aggressive policy, which could only be halted by the destruction of slavery itself.

Mill was obviously right about the topical resonance of the work, which received considerable critical attention and was republished in a second, enlarged edition in 1863. But it is worth noting that Cairnes himself recorded that his purpose had initially been of "a purely speculative kind—my object being to show that the course of history is largely determined by the action of economic causes."[46] Now, in one sense, Cairnes' procedure was naturally likely to be to Mill's methodological taste: the argument of the book relies, to a quite surprising degree, on deduction from its small set of basic premises.[47] Cairnes remarks at one point how the "political economist, by reasoning on the economic character of slavery and its peculiar connection with the soil, [may] deduce its leading social and political attributes, and almost construct, by way of a priori argument, the entire system of the society of which it forms the foundation," and later he says that he has been examining "the direction in which, under ordinary circumstances, and in the absence of intervention from without, the development of such a system proceeds";[48] or, in other words, that he was employing the kind of hypothetical reasoning, setting aside "disturbing causes," which Mill had long ago insisted was the proper procedure for political economy, and which Cairnes had elaborated, with Mill's enthusiastic endorsement, in his first book. That Mill should here welcome the use of this method in treating a type of subject that, in his canonical statement of the method of the moral sciences in Book VI of his *Logic*, he had assigned to the province of sociology may simply be one among many indications of the extent to which in practice he ignored the grand design for a science of society that he had laid out in 1843 and fell back upon more traditional enterprises like political economy.[49] But it is perhaps more surprising that he should let Cairnes' historical materialism pass without comment, since Mill was in general so concerned to insist that moral and intellectual rather than economic causes are the motor of history. He presumably felt that this was no time to be parading differences over the finer points of method; brothers-in-arms have more important things to do than criticizing the cut of each other's armour.

The review of Cairnes, the first half of which is a faithful paraphrase of the original in both tone and content, provided Mill with another opportunity to read a lesson on the debased state of "public morality" in England, "this sad aberration of

---

[46]*Slave Power*, vii.

[47]For Mill's classic statement, see his "On the Definition of Political Economy; and on the Method of Investigation Proper to It," in *Essays on Economics and Society*, CW, IV-V (Toronto: University of Toronto Press, 1965), IV, 309-39, as well as his treatment in Book VI of the *Logic*.

[48]*Slave Power*, 69, 171.

[49]This is argued more fully in Stefan Collini, Donald Winch, and John Burrow, *That Noble Science of Politics: A Study in Nineteenth-Century Intellectual History* (Cambridge: Cambridge University Press, 1983), 127-59.

English feeling at this momentous crisis," which he contrasted unfavourably with the right-mindedness of liberal feeling in France.[50] As he recognized, opinion in England was at first very much affected by estimates of the likely outcome of the military struggle—in 1861 and early 1862 many people were not convinced that the North would win—and throughout the war there was hostility to the North on the grounds that even if it did win it could not permanently govern the South in a state of subjection. Indeed, the one point on which Mill and Cairnes initially differed was that the latter thought that the best outcome would be an independent South confined, fatally for its slave economy, to the existing slave states, whereas the former looked for nothing short of complete surrender and re-incorporation in the Union on the North's terms, a view with which Cairnes seems to have come to agree by 1865.[51] It is indicative of Mill's passion on the subject that he immediately fastened on a potentially valuable aspect of Lincoln's assassination: "I do not believe the cause will suffer," he wrote to one correspondent. "It may even gain, by the indignation excited."[52] Keeping the indignation-level well topped-up in such cases Mill seems to have regarded as one of the routine tasks of the public moralist, and he hoped that one consequence of the feelings aroused by the assassination would be to "prevent a great deal of weak indulgence to the slaveholding class, whose power it is necessary should be completely and permanently broken at all costs."[53]

This disposition to fight *à l'outrance* manifested itself even more strikingly in Mill's contribution to the Governor Eyre controversy, which flared up later in 1865. This was one of those great moral earthquakes of Victorian public life whose fault lines are so revealing of the subterranean affinities and antipathies of the educated classes which the historian's normal aerial survey of the surface cannot detect. Faced with a native insurrection of uncertain proportions in October, 1865, the English Governor of Jamaica had declared martial law, under which justification he apparently condoned several brutal acts of suppression carried out by his subordinates, some of them after the danger was, arguably, past, and including the summary execution of the leader of the native opposition party in the local assembly.[54] Considerable uncertainty at first surrounded many of the facts of the case, but opinion in England immediately divided: on the one side were those who thought that, though the reported brutality was no doubt regrettable, Eyre's unorthodox and vigorous action in a situation of great danger had saved the population, especially the white population, from far worse evils (the Indian Mutiny, after all, was still fresh in the memory); on the other side were those,

---

[50]Letter to Cairnes, *LL*, *CW*, XV, 750 (25 Nov., 1861); cf. Cairnes, *Slave Power*, 16.

[51]See below (162-4) for the point of difference, and Weinberg, *Cairnes and the American Civil War*, 42, 42n, for Cairnes' later agreement.

[52]Letter to John Plummer, *LL*, *CW*, XVI, 1042 (1 May, 1865).

[53]Letter to William E. Hickson, *ibid.*, 1044 (3 May, 1865).

[54]For an account of this episode which pays considerable attention to Mill's role, see Bernard Semmel, *The Governor Eyre Controversy* (London: MacGibbon and Kee, 1962).

including Mill, who regarded Eyre's actions as both morally unpardonable and flagrantly illegal, and who thought it their duty to see that he was brought to justice, and the moral stain on the character of English rule thereby removed. The intensity of Mill's commitment to this view is strikingly illustrated by his comment in December, 1865, on the next session's business in Parliament: "There is no part of it all, not even the Reform Bill, more important than the duty of dealing justly with the abominations committed in Jamaica."[55] He immediately joined the Jamaica Committee, which was founded in the same month to ensure that Eyre and his subordinates were brought to justice, and when its first Chairman, Charles Buxton, thinking it sufficient simply to secure Eyre's dismissal and disgrace without also having him prosecuted for murder, resigned in June, 1866, Mill, then in Parliament and sternly resisting further calls on his time even for causes to which he was sympathetic, took over the chairmanship and retained it until the Committee was wound up in May, 1869.[56]

The three aims of the Committee were summarized in the progress report which Mill, together with the Treasurer and the Secretary, issued to members in July, 1868 (and which is reproduced as part of Appendix E below): "to obtain a judicial inquiry into the conduct of Mr. Eyre and his subordinates; to settle the law in the interest of justice, liberty and humanity; and to arouse public morality against oppression generally, and particularly against the oppression of subject and dependent races" (433). On the first point they had to acknowledge defeat: despite repeated efforts, which had earned for Mill, in particular, a reputation as the vindictive persecutor of the unfortunate Eyre, no court had proved willing to put him on trial. The second aim had met with some success as far as the status of martial law within the English legal system was concerned, though whether the inconclusive outcome of the whole affair vindicated the principle of "government by law," which Mill had always insisted was at stake in the matter, is open to question.[57] Quite what counted as success on the third point was obviously harder to say. "A great amount of sound public opinion has been called forth" (434), the statement reported, and for Mill this effect was something of an end in itself, though it is not obvious that the campaign exercised that morally educative influence which he always looked for in such cases. T.H. Huxley, predictably a member of the Jamaica Committee, may have been nearer the mark when he wrote to Charles Kingsley that "men take sides on this question, not so much by looking

[55]Letter to William Fraser Rae, *LL*, *CW*, XVI, 1126 (14 Dec., 1865).

[56]He considered his contribution to the debate on this issue in July, 1866, as the best of his speeches in Parliament (*Autobiography*, *CW*, I, 281-2). For an indication of the importance Mill attached to making a stand on this issue whether or not the prosecution proceedings were successful, see letter to Lindsey Middleton Aspland, *LL*, *CW*, XVI, 1365 (23 Feb., 1868).

[57]In his speech in Parliament Mill had insisted that if Eyre were not brought to justice "we are giving up altogether the principle of government by law, and resigning ourselves to arbitrary power"; and he defended his speech as "not on this occasion standing up for negroes, or for liberty, deeply as both are interested in the subject—but for the first necessity of human society, law" (speech of 31 July, 1866, *PD*, 3rd ser., Vol. 184, col. 1800; and letter to David Urquhart, *LL*, *CW*, XVI, 1205 [4 Oct., 1866]).

at the mere facts of the case, but rather as their deepest political convictions lead them."[58] Certainly, attitudes towards the working class and democracy at home played a large part in the controversy; Eyre's supporters were not slow to suggest, for example, that the Hyde Park riots of 1866 called for a similarly vigorous use of force by the authorities. Conversely, as far as Mill was concerned, right feeling on the matter transcended more pragmatic party loyalties: when in 1871 the Liberal government decided to honour a previous Tory promise to pay Eyre's legal expenses, Mill, deeply disgusted, announced: "After this, I shall henceforth wish for a Tory Government."[59] Such issues of public righteousness provide surer touchstones by which to understand Mill's later career than do any of the conventional political labels; it will always be difficult to say with certainty which of those liberal and reforming measures enacted in the decades after his death he would have approved of, but there can surely be no doubt that had he lived he would have been among the leaders of the agitation against the Bulgarian atrocities in 1876.[60]

The question of the proper conduct of nations towards each other, particularly the appropriate English role in international affairs, was one which exercised Mill throughout the latter part of his life. Although observations on it can be found in several of his other writings, most notably in *Considerations on Representative Government*, only two essays, both reprinted here, were devoted exclusively to it. The first, "A Few Words on Non-Intervention" (1859), was occasioned by Palmerston's reported attempt to defeat an international project to build a Suez canal, on the grounds of the harm it might do to England's commercial and strategic position in the East. Mill's particular concern here was with England's moral reputation, and with the harm done to that reputation by statements which seemed to confine English policy to the pursuit of purely selfish aims.[61] But, as he says in the *Autobiography*: ". . . I took the opportunity of expressing ideas which had long been in my mind (some of them generated by my Indian experience and others by the international questions which then greatly occupied the European public) respecting the true principles of international morality and the legitimate modifications made in it by difference of times and circumstances. . . ."[62] His premise was that nations, like individuals, "have duties . . . towards the weal of the human race," and that the whole issue must accordingly be considered "as a really moral question" (116, 118), a phrase that always signals a change of key in Mill's compositions. Viewing the question from this higher ground, he showed himself to have little sympathy with a policy of strict and complete "non-intervention," a

---

[58]Quoted in Semmel, *Governor Eyre*, 122.

[59]Letter to Cairnes, *LL, CW*, XVII, 1828-9 (21 Aug., 1871).

[60]Cf., in what is still the best study of one of the issues, R.T. Shannon, *Gladstone and the Bulgarian Agitation, 1876* (London: Nelson, 1963), 208.

[61]See letter to Bain, *LL, CW*, XV, 646 (14 Nov., 1859), for the view that the "affair is damaging the character of England on the Continent more than most people are aware of" (a remark in which his sense of his special intimacy with Continental opinion is again evident).

[62]*Autobiography, CW*, I, 263-4.

policy much canvassed in England in the 1850s and often popularly, if not altogether justifiably, associated with the names of Cobden and Bright. Mill disavowed slavish adherence to this (or any other) maxim in foreign affairs, just as he did to that of laissez-faire in domestic policy: the decisive test was rather whether intervention might promote the good of enabling a people with legitimate aspirations to independence to render themselves fit to exercise genuine self-government, a view with special resonance in the period of liberal nationalist uprisings in Europe. The stage of civilization reached by the society in question was a crucial consideration here; as he demonstrated in his better-known works on liberty and representative government, Mill thought a civilized power might have a duty *not* to leave a backward people stagnating in a freedom they could make no profitable use of. Where, on the other hand, a foreign despotism had been enlisted to suppress a genuine popular movement in another country, a liberal power had a duty to intervene, and it is an illustration of the seriousness with which Mill regarded this duty that he even maintained that England should have acted to prevent the Austrian suppression, with Russian aid, of the Hungarian uprising of 1849 (124). One of the things that drew Mill to Gladstone in the 1860s, however much they differed on specific policies, was the latter's professed commitment to determining England's international role by such moral principles.[63]

That this idealism was at the same time tempered by a kind of realism is suggested by the second piece reprinted here, the brief article on "Treaty Obligations" (1870), which was written in response to a different kind of crisis. On 31 October, 1870, Russia declared its intention of repudiating the clause in the Treaty of Paris—the peace forced on Russia by the victorious Anglo-French alliance at the conclusion of the Crimean War in 1856—whereby the Black Sea was to remain neutral waters. This declaration produced an ill-considered cry in England for war against Russia to force her to honour the agreement, during which agitation the principle of the indefinite inviolability of treaty obligations was frequently invoked. Mill regarded the whole agitation as resting on this mistaken notion that treaties forced upon defeated powers ought to be regarded as binding in perpetuity: "Were they terminable, as they ought to be, those who object to them would have a rational hope of escape in some more moral way than an appeal to the same brute force which imposed them."[64] But as ever, he was also addressing himself to the state of mind—or, more accurately, the state of character—of which such misguided public responses were symptomatic. In both cases, it was "that laxity of principle which has almost always prevailed in public matters" which he denounced with especial warmth, moved yet again by the conviction that the unrebuked expression of such views was "injurious to public morality" (343, 345).

In turning to Mill's writings on women, one approaches an area where the

---

[63]For Mill's enthusiasm for Gladstone at this point, see Vincent, *Formation of the Liberal Party*, 160-1.

[64]Letter to Morley, *LL*, *CW*, XVII, 1778 (18 Nov., 1870). See also Mill's letters to *The Times*, 19 Nov., 1870, 5; and 24 Nov., 1870, 3.

interplay between his private convictions and his public statements as well as between his biography and his reputation is particularly complex and controversial. It is deeply ironical that the interpretation of so much of the work of a man who reckoned the sexual urge to be a grossly overrated and ultimately insignificant part of human life should have come to be so completely entangled with, even determined by, competing assessments of the influence exercised over him by the woman he loved. Needless to say, this irony applies with especial force to his writings on women, so much so that we could reverse his dictum that "one can, to an almost laughable degree, infer what a man's wife is like, from his opinions about women in general" (278). Even at the time, critics, especially once primed by the revelations of the *Autobiography*, were not slow to turn this remark against Mill, while even his admirers deplored the turn which Harriet was taken to have given to his thought on this and other questions. Any complete account of Mill's thinking on the subject of women would have to come to terms with the role of this very clever, imaginative, passionate, intense, imperious, paranoid, unpleasant woman. Here, fortunately, it is appropriate to offer only a few prolegomena to *The Subjection of Women*, the last book published by Mill in his lifetime and the most substantial of the works included in the present volume.

It is at least clear, where so much is unclear, that Mill's belief in the equality of the sexes was well established before he met Harriet. When at the opening of *The Subjection of Women* he refers to it as "an opinion I have held from the very earliest period when I had formed any opinions at all on social and political matters" (261), he seems, as far as the evidence allows us to judge, to be stating a literal truth. It occasioned, for example, his one point of dissent from his father's *Essay on Government* at the time when he was in all other ways the most faithful and zealous expounder of the latter's views, and even as a matter of tactics in the unpromising political climate of England in the 1820s he considered his father's acceptance of women's temporary exclusion from the suffrage to be "as great an error as any of those against which the Essay was directed."[65] Indeed, this ardent and uncompromising advocacy may have been one of the things that first attracted Harriet's favourable attention. Their oddly formal exchange of statements, some two years after they met in 1830, about the position of women in relation to marriage was by then the rehearsal of shared views, and may be seen in Mill's case as the bizarre courting behaviour of an over-intellectualized man. Not that this was not the way to Harriet's heart: Mill could bask in the implied praise of her complaint that "it seems now that all men, with the exception of a few lofty-minded, are sensualists more or less," to which she firmly added, "Women on the contrary are quite exempt from this trait, however it may appear otherwise in the cases of some" (375).

[65]*Autobiography*, *CW*, I, 107 (it should not be inferred, nor does Mill's account strictly imply, that his father was in principle opposed to the enfranchisement of women). For an early example of his public criticism of prevailing attitudes towards women, see his "Periodical Literature: Edinburgh Review" (1824), in *CW*, I, 311-12.

Understandably, this exchange between an unhappily married woman and her yearning admirer revolves around the question of the dissolubility of the marriage tie. Harriet's soaring idealism is evident in her greater readiness to do "away with all laws whatever relating to marriage" (376). Mill, characteristically, subjects the arguments to careful analysis before concluding in favour of "leaving this like the other relations voluntarily contracted by human beings, to depend for its continuance upon the wishes of the contracting parties" (49). Clearly, though he may have sighed like a lover, he could still write like the son of James Mill. This expression of his view in a purely private form has a particular interest in that his avoidance of a clear recommendation about divorce in *The Subjection of Women* was to be a major point of criticism.[66]

It is worth remarking that even in this unconstrained expression of belief in the natural equality of the sexes, he still adhered to some rather more traditional notions about their distinctive roles. "In a healthy state of things," he maintained, "the husband would be able by his single exertions to earn all that is necessary for both; and there would be no need that the wife should take part in the mere providing of what is required to *support* life: it will be for the happiness of both that her occupation should rather be to adorn and beautify it" (43). In a phrase which should remind us, if we need reminding, that Mill is not an unproblematic recruit to the ranks of late-twentieth-century feminism, he blandly laid down that a woman's task in life is "accomplished rather by *being* than by *doing*" (43). While he always strenuously disputed, on essentially epistemological grounds, all assertions about "natural" differences between the sexes, this is an early indication—there are several later ones—that he was in practice willing to endorse certain conventional assumptions about the most "appropriate" sphere for women's activity.

Despite the importance he attached to the subject—he later remarked that the "emancipation of women, & cooperative production, are . . . the two great changes that will regenerate society"[67]—Mill published nothing substantial on it until 1869. In part this was a matter of waiting for a less hostile phase of public opinion. (Mill, surely influenced here by Harriet's paranoid attitude to society in general, was particularly pessimistic about the state of opinion in England in the 1850s.) As he explained to the editor of the *Westminster* in 1850: "My opinions on the whole subject are so totally opposed to the reigning notions that it would probably be inexpedient to express all of them."[68] In 1854 he and Harriet included it among the subjects on which they hoped to leave some record of their thoughts, but it was not

---

[66]Note also his statement in a letter to an unidentified correspondent in 1855: "My opinion on Divorce is that though any relaxation of the irrevocability of marriage would be an improvement, nothing ought to be ultimately rested in, short of entire freedom on both sides to dissolve this like any other partnership" (*LL, CW*, XIV, 500). Compare this with the view referred to at xxxvi below.

[67]Letter to Parke Godwin, *LL, CW*, XVII, 1535 (1 Jan., 1869).

[68]Letter to William Hickson, *ibid.*, XIV, 48 (19 Mar., 1850).

until some two years after Harriet's death that Mill wrote *The Subjection of Women*, and only nine years later still that he considered the world ready to receive it. It may also have been the case that Mill's failure to make any progress with the Ethology deterred him from attempting a systematic exploration of an issue which, as suggested above, was so closely dependent on that project as he conceived it. The extent to which his dispute with Comte over the alleged differences between the sexes turned on what Mill regarded as the questions to be settled by Ethology is very suggestive here.[69] In complaining to Harriet in 1849 about the prevalence of false assumptions about woman's "nature" ("on which the whole of the present bad constitution of the relation rests"), he declared: "I am convinced however that there are only two things which tend at all to shake this nonsensical prejudice: a better psychology & theory of human nature, for the few; & for the many, more & greater proofs by example of what women can do."[70]

Most of all, he may have considered that his views on sexual equality had been given adequate public expression for the present—by Harriet. "I do not think that anything that could be written would do nearly so much good on that subject the most important of all, as the finishing your pamphlet. . . ."[71] Quite how much Mill contributed to the writing of "The Enfranchisement of Women," published in the *Westminster* in 1851, remains unclear, but there seems little doubt that it is substantially Harriet's work, though Mill seems to have thought it prudent to let the editor assume it was by him (see the Textual Introduction, lxxv-lxxvii below). Mill certainly held a correspondingly inflated view of it: when asked by later correspondents to recommend reading on this subject he always put his wife's article at the head of the list, and there is no doubt that he whole-heartedly subscribed to its contents, though his own expression of essentially the same views in *The Subjection of Women* is occasionally somewhat more circumspect. A list of the more obvious similarities between the two works could begin with the analogy with "the kindred cause of negro emancipation," and go on to include the identification of custom as the great enemy, the interpretation of history as the prolonged repeal of the law of the strongest, the assertion that free competition will assign each to his or her appropriate role, and the appeal to the demonstrated practical ability of famous queens (401-2). After Harriet's death, Mill included the article in his *Dissertations and Discussions* in 1859, with an embarrassing eulogy of its author (see 393-4), though he emphasized that it was far from being a complete statement of the case.

When Mill did decide that the time was ripe to issue a systematic statement of his views it was a ripeness he had played an important role in bringing on by his activities in Parliament. In particular, his presentation in June, 1866, of a petition for the extension of the suffrage to women, and his proposal during the debates of May, 1867, to amend the Reform Bill then before the House by omitting reference

[69]See *EL*, *CW*, XIII, 604-11, 616-17, 696-8.
[70]*LL*, *CW*, XIV, 12-13.
[71]*Ibid.*, 13.

to the gender of householders entitled to the vote, had aroused a great deal of attention, not all of it hostile.[72] That his amendment received the support of over seventy M.P.s, including John Bright, Mill found "most encouraging," and in the wake of this triumph the National Society for Women's Suffrage was formed, actively prompted by Mill and Helen Taylor.[73] When *The Subjection of Women* was published, therefore, Mill was unusually optimistic about the progress the cause was likely to make in the immediate future.[74]

This short book, little more than an extended pamphlet as the nineteenth century knew that genre, offers the whole world of Mill's characteristic political and moral arguments in microcosm: themes whose best known *loci* are in the *Principles*, *On Liberty*, or *Representative Government* are here drawn together and focussed on a single issue. This is true of such questions as the role of an élite who have the feelings of the future, the indispensability of liberty to individual happiness, the educative as well as defensive importance of participation in public affairs, and much more. At the same time, the work is a deliberately provocative and splendidly sustained polemic, one of the peaks of Mill's rhetorical achievement as a public moralist. Considered in this light, two features of the book call for comment.

First there is the general question of argumentative strategy mentioned above. Mill attempts systematically to undermine the standing of *any* evidence about the "natural subordination" of women drawn from past experience, just as in his claims about Socialism elsewhere he sometimes rules out of court all objections based on the selfishness of human nature as manifested in the past under non-socialist arrangements.[75] In both cases, the move is one of considerable high-handedness, and not all readers have been disposed to go along with this dismissal of mankind's accumulated experience. In fact, as we saw, Mill's ban on evidence drawn from history is only partial: where that evidence may seem to suggest a positive conclusion about women's capacities, as in the case of notable female monarchs,[76] its doubtful epistemological credentials are treated more leniently, just as he considered examples of successful cooperative production to

---

[72]Mill considered his proposal of this amendment as "by far the most important, perhaps the only really important public service [he] performed in the capacity of a Member of Parliament" (*Autobiography*, *CW*, I, 285).

[73]Letter to Cairnes, *LL*, *CW*, XVI, 1272 (26 May, 1867). See Ann P. Robson, "The Founding of the National Society for Women's Suffrage," *Canadian Journal of History*, VIII (Mar., 1973), 1-22; and, for women's suffrage organizations in general, see Constance Rover, *Women's Suffrage and Party Politics in Britain, 1866-1914* (London: Routledge and Kegan Paul, 1967).

[74]For an example of this optimism, see Mill's letter to Charles Eliot Norton, *LL*, *CW*, XVII, 1618 (23 June, 1869). The optimism was, of course, misplaced in that no women received the vote in national elections until 1918. Consider here Bain's judgment: "His most sanguine hopes were of a very slow progress in all things; with the sole exception, perhaps, of the equality-of-women question, on which his feelings went farther than on any other" (*John Stuart Mill*, 132).

[75]E.g., in his "Chapters on Socialism," in *Essays on Economics and Society*, *CW*, V, 736.

[76]For an indication of the weight Mill attached to these cases, see how eagerly he seizes upon the "new evidence" of the practical capacities of Elizabeth I provided by Froude (letter to John Nichol, *LL*, *CW*, XVII, 1632-4 [18 Aug., 1869]).

be admissible evidence in the parallel case. But, further, as in his early essay on marriage, Mill does not in fact exclude all current assumptions about distinctively feminine qualities or spheres of activity; for example, he holds that "the common arrangement, by which the man earns the income and the wife superintends the domestic expenditure, seems to me in general the most suitable division of labour between the two persons," and "in an otherwise just state of things, it is not, therefore, I think, a desirable custom, that the wife should contribute by her labour to the income of the family" (297-8). Complaints about his "failure to question the social institutions of his time" (and about his "taking the bourgeois family as his model")[77] will recommend themselves to those who are irritated by the "failure" of historical figures to express approved modern views, but they miss the main point. It is not that Mill should be expected to have transcended the categories embodied in the common experience of his time—that is always a surprising achievement—it is rather that he takes some of these categories for granted when it suits his argument, after having had the methodological hubris to claim that all such experience was necessarily beside the point.

The other feature of the book calling for comment here is its concern with moral education. The forensic centrepiece of the work is its condemnation of existing marriage arrangements: as he pungently put it, "There remain no legal slaves except the mistress of every house" (323). He was, of course, arguing for far more than the removal of the legal disabilities of married women, important though he always considered the law as a means of wider improvement. He was also proposing a different conception of marriage, in which the couple, meeting as equals, are held together by the bonds of affection and mutual respect. But his concern in doing so goes beyond that of improving woman's lot: he constantly treats marriage as "a school of genuine moral sentiment" (293), demonstrating once again his intense preoccupation with the consequences institutions have on the character and moral habits of those whose lives they structure. "Any society [in the sense of social contact] which is not improving, is deteriorating, and the more so, the closer and more familiar it is" (335). This, Mill argued (it was another point that had been made in Harriet's article of 1851), was why "young men of the greatest promise generally cease to improve as soon as they marry, and, not improving, inevitably degenerate" (335). Marriage for a man whose closest daily contact is with someone whom he regards as his inferior, and who herself acts as his inferior, becomes "a school of wilfulness, over-bearingness, unbounded self-indulgence, and a double-dyed and idealized selfishness" (289). Mill's argument here can be represented as a localized variant of Hegel's famous parable of the need to recognize another's autonomy and worth before that person's response could provide any worthwhile confirmation of one's own identity and

---

[77]See, for example, Susan Moller Okin, *Women in Western Political Thought* (Princeton: Princeton University Press, 1979), 229, 226.

value. "The relation of superiors to dependents is the nursery of these vices of character" (288).

Mill's critics found his ideal of marriage a little too much like a two-member Mutual Improvement Society. "To him marriage was a union of two philosophers in the pursuit of truth," was how Goldwin Smith unkindly but not altogether unfairly put it, adding "not only does he scarcely think of children, but sex and its influences seem hardly to be present to his mind."[78] Certainly his prim dismissal of the role of the "animal instinct" might well be seen as something of a handicap for anyone wishing to alter the relations between the sexes. Bain, who thought Mill deficient in "sensuality" ("he made light of the difficulty of controlling the sexual appetite"), presented this criticism in the cautious form of reported speech: "It was the opinion of many, that while his estimate of pure sentimental affection was more than enough, his estimate of the sexual passion was too low."[79] Mill's own professed view was that "the force of the natural passions" has been "exaggerated": "I think it most probable that this particular passion will become with men, as it already is with a large number of women, completely under the control of the reason," which surprising proposition he sought to buttress with a somewhat feeble appeal to authority—"I have known eminent medical men, and lawyers of logical mind, of the same opinion."[80]

Faced with Mill's call for a radical alteration in the nature of marriage as commonly understood, an alteration which women did not by and large seem to be demanding for themselves, contemporary critics were inclined to ask *Cui bono?*[81] But for Mill this was not a matter of sectional interests. It was not just that wives were denied opportunities for self-fulfilment: he saw the existing pattern of marriage as systematically warping the moral sensibilities of men as well, and thus inhibiting the moral growth of society as a whole. "The moral regeneration of mankind will only really commence, when the most fundamental of the social relations is placed under the rule of equal justice, and when human beings learn to cultivate their strongest sympathy with an equal in rights and in cultivation" (336). The emphatic, insistent note here—"only," "really," "most fundamental," "strongest," and so on—is a sign of Mill's anxiety that in these matters those who listen do not hear, while "moral regeneration" (the implication of the peculiarly debased state of the present is the cultural critic's occupational failing) shows what high stakes are being played for.

In more immediate terms, the three legal issues with which the whole question

[78]Goldwin Smith, "Female Suffrage," *Macmillan's Magazine*, XXX (June, 1874), 140; see also Brian Harrison, *Separate Spheres: The Opposition to Women's Suffrage in Britain* (London: Croom Helm, 1978), 62.

[79]Bain, *John Stuart Mill*, 149, 89-90.

[80]Letter to Lord Amberley, *LL, CW*, XVII, 1693 (2 Feb., 1870).

[81]The most persistent criticism of the feminist position was to be found in the *Saturday Review*, for Mill's hostility to which see x and xxiii; Harrison, *Separate Spheres*, 104; and Merle Mowbray Bevington, *The Saturday Review, 1855-1868* (New York: Columbia University Press, 1941), 114-18.

was inseparably connected were property rights, divorce, and the suffrage. The first issue is fully and vigorously explored in *The Subjection of Women*,[82] but the second, which had been central to the early essays, is deliberately avoided. As Mill explained to a correspondent in the following year:

The purpose of that book was to maintain the claim of women, whether in marriage or out of it, to perfect equality in all rights with the male sex. The relaxation or alteration of the marriage laws . . . is a question quite distinct from the object to which the book is devoted, and one which, in my own opinion, cannot be properly decided until that object has been attained. It is impossible, in my opinion, that a right marriage law can be made by men alone, or until women have an equal voice in making it.[83]

But this conviction only made the third issue, the suffrage, all the more crucial, and here the book was unequivocal: "Under whatever conditions, and within whatever limits, men are admitted to the suffrage, there is not a shadow of justification for not admitting women under the same" (301). Bain's comment that *The Subjection of Women* constituted "the most sustained exposition of Mill's life-long theme—the abuses of power"[84] is apposite here, for in writing on the one subject on which he had from the outset criticized his father's essay "Government," he echoed that work's arguments throughout. Though his mind brooded on the prospects for moral progress in the long term, he never doubted that the key to the immediate relief of woman's estate was her possession of the vote. In a letter to Florence Nightingale two years before, he had expressed this belief in a way that made its Philosophical Radical pedigree particularly clear. Nightingale had affirmed her preference for concentrating on other improvements in women's position, expressing the hope that enlightened governments could be persuaded to bring about such improvements without women themselves having the vote. In reply, Mill gave her a brisk tutorial on the fundamentals of democratic political theory. He granted that "a ruling power" *might* be moved to alleviate the disabilities of the ruled: "The question is, has it ever seemed to them urgent to sweep away these disabilities, until there was a prospect of the ruled getting political power?" Even under an enlightened government, the interests of the ruled were constantly at risk, "for no earthly power can ever prevent the constant unceasing unsleeping elastic pressure of human egotism from weighing down and thrusting aside those who have not the power to resist it." Ultimately, it was the primacy of the political that Mill was trying, unsuccessfully, to bring Nightingale to recognize: "political power is the only security against every form of oppression."[85] So much did this issue dominate the last years of Mill's life—Helen

---

[82]For an account, with ample reference to Mill, see Lee Holcombe, *Wives and Property: Reform of the Married Women's Property Law in Nineteenth-Century England* (Toronto: University of Toronto Press, 1983).

[83]Letter to Henry Keylock Rusden, *LL*, *CW*, XVII, 1751 (22 July, 1870).

[84]Bain, *John Stuart Mill*, 130.

[85]Letter to Florence Nightingale, *LL*, *CW*, XVI, 1343-4 (31 Dec., 1867). In drawing up his condemnation of the frustrations of the life of the typical woman of the prosperous classes, Mill had

Taylor showed some of her mother's skill here—that Mill could announce in 1872: "The time, moreover, is, I think now come when, at parliamentary elections, a Conservative who will vote for women's suffrage should be, in general, preferred to a professed Liberal who will not. . . . [T]he bare fact of supporting Mr Gladstone in office, certainly does not now give a man a claim to preference over one who will vote for the most important of all political improvements now under discussion."[86]

Mill's concern not just with the rights of women but with the moral sensibility exhibited in publicly condoned attitudes towards them came strongly to the fore in the agitation against the Contagious Diseases Acts from which the last of the items here reprinted takes its origin. These Acts, passed between 1864 and 1869, provided for the compulsory medical inspection and, if necessary, treatment of women suspected of being prostitutes in certain specified garrison towns, in an attempt to control the incidence of venereal disease among the troops stationed there. The Acts raised several questions of principle in relation to police powers and the treatment of women, as well as provoking a variety of less rational responses, and in 1869 a public campaign for the repeal of the Acts was launched with Josephine Butler at its head.[87] Mill supported the campaign—"Of course one need scarcely say that to any man who looks upon political institutions & legislation from the point of view of principle the idea of keeping a large army in idleness & vice & then keeping a large army of prostitutes to pander to their vices is too monstrous to admit of a moment's consideration"—though he was anxious lest the peculiarly emotional controversy that it aroused should injure the campaign for the suffrage.[88] The agitation led to the setting up of a Royal Commission on the Acts in 1870; by Easter, 1871, it had heard forty-eight witnesses in favour of the maintenance or extension of the Acts and only twelve in favour of their repeal. The National Association for the Repeal of the Contagious Diseases Acts argued that it should hear more witnesses known to favour repeal, and Mill was among those

---

already made use of Nightingale's *Suggestions for Thought*, 3 vols. (London: privately published, 1860) (see Francis Barrymore Smith, *Florence Nightingale: Reputation and Power* [London: Croom Helm, 1982], 187).

[86]Letter to George Croom Robertson, *LL*, *CW*, XVII, 1917 (5 Nov., 1872); it should be remembered that Mill was already disillusioned with the Gladstone ministry by this point—see above, xxviii. For a sharp assessment of Helen Taylor's influence over Mill on this subject, see the editor's introduction in *LL*, *CW*, XIV, xxxvi-xxxvii.

[87]For details of the campaign and the issues it raised see Francis Barrymore Smith, "Ethics and Disease in the Later-Nineteenth Century: The Contagious Diseases Acts," *Historical Studies* (Melbourne), XV (1971), 118-35; and Paul McHugh, *Prostitution and Victorian Social Reform* (London: Croom Helm, 1980).

[88]Letter to William T. Malleson, *LL*, *CW*, XVII, 1688 (18 Jan., 1870). For the anxiety that to "the mass of the English people, as well as to large numbers already well disposed towards some little improvement in women's condition, the union of the C.D.A. agitation with that for the suffrage, condemns the latter utterly, because they look upon it as indelicate and unfeminine," see Mill's letter to Robertson, *LL*, *CW*, XVII, 1854 (15 Nov., 1871).

called as a result.[89] It is worth observing in passing that Mill was called as a witness despite having no official standing in any of the organizations or professions involved, having no expert knowledge of the subjects at issue, and having, on his own admission, made no special study of the working of the Acts; as with the Westminster candidacy in 1865, his being John Stuart Mill was sufficient recommendation. In fact he proved to be a model witness as, under hostile and unfair questioning from some members of the Commission, he maintained a calm and lucid hold on the essential questions of principle.[90]

What is striking about Mill's evidence, particularly when read in conjunction with his discussion of related issues in *On Liberty*, is the extent to which he makes the question of the Acts' official endorsement of vice the chief ground of his objection to them. This is not to say that he scouts objections based on the Acts' potential invasion of individual liberty or the inequity of their effectively penalizing women but not men, for he puts both very forcibly. But when the hypothetical case is put to him of women voluntarily submitting to the examination and treatment, he replies: "I still think it objectionable because I do not think it is part of the business of the Government to provide securities beforehand against the consequences of immoralities of any kind" (353). Similarly, his primary objection to any system of licensing prostitutes is that licences "have still more the character of toleration of that kind of vicious indulgence" (356). And although he would not be opposed in principle to state provision of hospitals for the treatment of all contagious diseases, he insists that it would be improper to provide treatment for this class of disease alone, as again condoning publicly the sexual activity that led to it. As things stand, he fears that the troops themselves infer from the very existence of the Acts "that Parliament does not entertain any serious disapprobation of immoral conduct of that kind" (360), and he concludes his testimony by reiterating that the tendency of such Acts is "to do moral injury" (371). Furthermore, he places great weight on the distinction between the provision of assistance for those whose conduct has left them unable to provide it for themselves (essentially the principle of the Poor Law), and the provision, before the event, of securities against the natural consequences of immoral or imprudent conduct (the principle, as Mill sees it, of the Contagious Diseases Acts). Not only may the latter provision be taken as encouraging or endorsing the behaviour in question, but the crucial unstated premise of Mill's objection to such provisions is that they interfere with the proper operation of the calculation of consequences upon the formation of the will. Ultimately, this moral psychology lies at the heart of all Mill's reflections on the shaping of character by institutions, whether the character in question is that of a selfish voter at the polls, or of a feckless peasant on his smallholding, or of a randy young trooper in Aldershot.

---

[89]McHugh, *Prostitution and Social Reform*, 61.
[90]Cf. *ibid.*, 63: "The most impressive witness of all was John Stuart Mill."

LAW

HAD THE YOUNG JOHN STUART MILL not entered the service of the East India Company in 1823, he might have had a very distinguished legal career. His father at first intended him for the Bar,[91] that great avenue of advancement for ambitious but impecunious young men, and although his extreme radical views would have made him an unlikely candidate for the Bench, it is not hard to imagine the brilliant, analytical, outspoken young barrister commanding the intricacies of the English law as well as cutting a considerable figure in public life. But this reflection only reminds us how surprisingly slight was Mill's actual involvement with the law in his mature years. He had, after all, been brought up in a milieu suffused with legal categories and with a sense of the importance of the law; the whole fabric of Bentham's theory, to take the central intellectual component in that milieu, had grown out of a concern with legal reform and was primarily constituted by the project of a science of legislation, imparting an emphasis that endured into early Philosophic Radical thought. Moreover, the young Mill's most extensive literary work was the editing of the five volumes of Bentham's *Rationale of Judicial Evidence*, and not only did this work contain "the most elaborate exposure of the vices and defects of English law, as it then was," but in preparation for its editing Mill read "the most authoritative treatises on the English Law of Evidence, and commented on a few of the objectionable points of English rules, which had escaped Bentham's notice."[92]

Certainly, several of Mill's later writings on politics, both at the topical and systematic levels, were concerned in a general sense with questions of legislation, and even at the height of his preoccupation with the power of sociological and moral forces he retained the conviction that the law was the most important instrument a government could exercise directly for influencing both the actions and the character of its citizens. But this is obviously still some distance either from a sustained concentration on jurisprudential issues, or even from the working-out of a political and social theory pervaded by legal categories. There is no need to exaggerate this perception into a paradox: the trajectory of Mill's actual intellectual development sufficiently accounts for his not having followed either of these courses. Still, even if we merely remark the fact that jurisprudence found no place in his map of the moral sciences in Book VI of the *Logic*, or that, in striking contrast to his wide-ranging work in several branches of philosophy, logic, politics, and political economy, he made no original contribution to legal thought, we thereby register how comparatively slight was the residue from his early exposure to the law.

[91]*Autobiography, CW*, I, 67.
[92]*Ibid.*, 119, 117. See also Mill's Preface to Jeremy Bentham, *Rationale of Judicial Evidence Specially Applied to English Practice*, 5 vols. (London: Hunt and Clarke, 1827), I, v-xvi.

At a less elevated level, a large part of the political activity of the circle of young Radicals that formed around Bentham and James Mill in the 1820s was addressed to legal issues.[93] Naturally, any proposals for change grounded in Benthamite political theory were likely to treat the law as the chief means by which self-interested individuals could be prompted to contribute to the general happiness. But such Radical critics went further, identifying the existing state of English law as an elaborate protective screen to disguise the oppressive reality of aristocratic privilege. Laws restricting freedom of expression, in particular, were regarded as the chief obstacle to any fundamental political improvement, since in the years immediately following the Napoleonic wars an anxious and twitchy government readily resorted to them as a way of suppressing any expression of views that could be construed as seditious. The close connection in this period between certain kinds of political radicalism and blasphemous or obscene literature facilitated the use of the very wide-ranging laws of libel to silence all kinds of critics of the established order, and some of the young Mill's earliest publications were outspoken denunciations of such religious and political censorship.[94]

The first of the pieces included in this volume is a good example of this vein of criticism. Ostensibly a review-article on two works on the law of libel, it is essentially a rehearsal of some of the central tenets of the radical political theory developed by James Mill out of Bentham's Utilitarianism. Written when the younger Mill was eighteen, it is a product of that phase of his life when, on his own later admission, he was little more than the mouthpiece of his father's views on politics as on so much else.[95] These views had attained their greatest circulation in the series of articles James Mill contributed to the *Supplement to the Fourth, Fifth, and Sixth Editions of the Encyclopaedia Britannica*, where the basic tenets of Philosophic Radical thought were insinuated through respectable encyclopaedia entries. On the subject of liberty of expression, his celebrated article on "Liberty of the Press," written in 1821, provided the classic statement of the Radical case, and it is the immediate source for several of the arguments in his son's article.[96] Partly for this reason, the younger Mill's article is itself of no great theoretical or literary interest; like several of his other early contributions to the *Westminster*, it is repetitive, somewhat crude, and at times simply boring. Its simplistic deductive logic is the hallmark of this early propagandistic phase; in fact the first and more general part of the article is an attempt to deduce the necessity for complete freedom of the press from "the great principles of human nature" (19). The

[93]See *Autobiography*, *CW*, I, 91, for some remarks on their criticism of "that most peccant part of English institutions and of their administration."

[94]See the pieces collected in *Prefaces to Liberty*, ed. Bernard Wishy (Boston: Beacon Press, 1959).

[95]*Autobiography*, *CW*, I, Chap. iv, 89-135.

[96]James Mill, "Liberty of the Press" (1821) in the *Supplement to the Fourth, Fifth, and Sixth Editions of the Encyclopaedia Britannica*, 6 vols. (Edinburgh: Constable, 1824), V, 2, 258-72; rpt. *Essays* (London: Innes, [1825]).

premise, most famously expressed in his father's essay "Government," is that rulers will, unless checked, necessarily abuse their power to further their own self interest.[97] Criticism by their subjects is the essential check, but since the rulers cannot be allowed to determine *which* criticism may be expressed, there is no logical stopping-place short of complete freedom of expression. In practice, it could not be denied, a more limited form of freedom did exist, but this, too, was testimony to the power of opinion that, even in post-Waterloo England, would not tolerate complete suppression.[98] It was characteristic of Philosophic Radical political criticism to reduce to such elemental forces the traditional claims about the ways in which the glorious constitution protected the historic rights of Englishmen. From the first page of this article, where he seeks to show that "the Law of England is as unfavourable to the liberty of the press, as that of the most despotic government which ever existed," Mill indulges this iconoclastic hostility to invocations of the virtues of the constitution, all of which he treats as mystifications designed to protect the privileges of the established classes.

To this political antagonism towards the law-making class was added an intellectual impatience with the sheer muddle of English law at the beginning of the nineteenth century. This had been the spur which, half a century earlier, had stirred Bentham to pursue what became his lifelong project, and the hope of bringing some order to the ancient intricacies of English legal practice continued to animate the analytical jurisprudence of his successors. Radical critics complained that in many cases there existed no definitive statement of the law, that the latitude allowed judicial interpretation was practically limitless. Mill here traces the extraordinary variations in the existing libel laws to this source: "it is an evil inseparable from a system of common law" (20). His later support for measures for the limited codification of English law had its roots in this distrust, at once political and intellectual, of a legal system that was, in the dismissively pejorative sense of the term, merely "empirical." Any move towards a more rational treatment of legal problems met with Mill's approval, as witnessed by the two short pieces reprinted here, "On Punishment" and "Smith on Law Reform," the first recommending a Utilitarian justification of punishment, the second displaying his hostility to the antiquarian character of so much English legal discussion.

Preceding those just mentioned is another short piece, his 1832 review of Austin's *Province of Jurisprudence Determined*, discussion of which naturally leads on to the most substantial of his jurisprudential writings, his well-known essay of 1863 on Austin's *Lectures on Jurisprudence*, consideration of which

[97]James Mill, "Government" (1820), in *Essays*, 5.

[98]Mill's argument here—"Even a Turkish Sultan is restrained by the fear of exciting insurrection" (7)—echoes David Hume's famous dictum, "It is . . . on opinion only that government is founded," and so even "the soldan of Egypt" must cultivate the opinion of his mamalukes ("Of the First Principles of Government," *Essays Moral, Political, and Literary*, in *Philosophical Works* [1882], ed. Thomas Hill Green and Thomas Hodge Grose, 4 vols. [Aalen: Scientia, 1964], III, 110).

introduces a relationship requiring somewhat fuller discussion. That the signifi-cance of Mill's connection with Austin should be tantalisingly elusive is appropriate, for Austin is one of the great shadowy figures of English nineteenth-century intellectual history. After his death he came to occupy a commanding place in the legal thought of the second half of the century, and no small proportion of the political theory of that period was devoted to discussion, usually critical, of his classic analyses of the central concepts of law and morality.[99] The attention paid to his rather slight legacy of published work chiefly resulted, by an obvious paradox, from the very swing in intellectual fashion away from the kind of deductive method he was taken to have employed and towards more historical and evolutionary approaches. Austin was treated, especially and most influentially by Sir Henry Maine, as the chief exemplar of this outmoded method, and he, together with Ricardo, became a largely symbolic representative of the alleged methodological weaknesses of the moral sciences in the first half of the century.[100] Changes in legal education, also, particularly following the recommendations of the Committee on Legal Education of 1846, meant that the second half of the century saw a new demand for a systematic textbook of jurisprudence, and Austin's work thus had classic status thrust upon it.[101] The fact that this celebrity was almost entirely posthumous only adds to the elusiveness of the man himself, who, however, we know played an important part in Mill's early development.

Called to the bar in 1818, at the age of twenty-eight, after having abandoned a military career, Austin conducted a somewhat desultory practice in Lincoln's Inn for seven years, in the first of several unsatisfactory attempts to find a suitable setting for his talents.[102] He became a close associate of Bentham during this period, but, though a convinced Utilitarian, he maintained a characteristic distance from the extreme political radicalism of the circle gathered around the sage of

[99]See Frederick Pollock, *An Introduction to the History of the Science of Politics* (1890), new ed. (London: Macmillan, 1911), 109-11.

[100]Maine's criticisms of Austin were most explicitly set out in his *Lectures on the Early History of Institutions* (London: Murray, 1875), Chaps. xii and xiii, where the parallel with political economy is also developed. Austin and Ricardo were bracketed together in this way in Fitzjames Stephen's article of 1861 cited by Mill at 169 below.

[101]For the Committee on Legal Education see the references given in Peter Stein, *Legal Evolution: The Story of an Idea* (Cambridge: Cambridge University Press, 1980), 78-9. For Austin's position in the syllabus (his work "is the staple of jurisprudence in all our system of legal education"), see Edwin Charles Clark, *Practical Jurisprudence: A Comment on Austin* (Cambridge: Cambridge University Press, 1883). See also Sarah Austin's letter to Guizot of 2 Mar., 1863, quoted in Janet Ross, *Three Generations of Englishwomen*, 2 vols. (London: Murray, 1888), II, 138: ". . . I must tell you that his book is daily rising into fame and authority to a degree which I never hoped to live to witness, and which he would never have believed. It is become an examination book at both Oxford and Cambridge, and I am assured by barristers that there is a perfect enthusiasm about it among *young* lawyers—men among whom it was unknown till since [*sic*] I published the second edition."

[102]For information about Austin's life, see Sarah Austin's "Preface" to the 2nd ed. of the *Lectures*, 3 vols. (London: Murray, 1861-63), I, iii-xxxvi, and Ross, *Three Generations, passim.*

Queen Square. He was nonetheless held in high esteem by those few who knew him well, and when James Mill thought of preparing his eldest son for the Bar, it was natural to send him to be coached by Austin, under whose supervision the young Mill read Roman Law and the works of Blackstone and Bentham in 1821 and 1822.[103] Mill's most sustained exposure to Austin's own legal thought came after the latter was appointed to the Chair of Jurisprudence at the newly founded University College, London. Having first spent two years in Germany to prepare himself, Austin began lecturing in the autumn of 1828, and continued, with some intermissions, until the spring of 1833. After a promising start, the lectures quickly dwindled in popularity, but Mill remained one of the faithful to the end: in his correspondence in 1832 and 1833 he recorded that Austin was lecturing to "a very small but really select class," only six or seven students "but those of a *kind* he likes" (his audience included several others who were to attain distinction, including G.C. Lewis, John Romilly, and Charles Buller).[104] Austin clearly had all the qualities that make for a really unsuccessful lecturer—he was painstakingly thorough, unrelievedly dry, remorselessly analytical. "He never had the slightest idea of rendering his subject popular or easy," his formidable wife, Sarah, later recalled with loyal respect, but also, perhaps, with a hint of exasperation (her own energies were of a more practical and direct kind).[105] As Leslie Stephen coolly observed: ". . . Austin thought it a duty to be as dry as Bentham, and discharged that duty scrupulously."[106] When his introductory lectures were published in 1832 these same qualities were much in evidence. "It must be admitted that the reception given to his book at first was not encouraging," his wife reported, and the major reviews ignored it.[107] But "some eulogistic articles appeared in journals of less general currency," the chief of these being the brief notice by Mill in the short-lived *Tait's Edinburgh Magazine*, which, its author confided to Carlyle, "was chiefly intended as a recommendation of that work."[108] Most of the points made in this review, and even some of the phrasing, recur in the larger essay thirty years later, though it is noticeable how Mill, in his high Carlylean phase, recruits Austin to his own campaign against the debased tastes of an increasingly democratic culture (54).

Austin, as we have already remarked, never shared the ardent democratic enthusiasms of James Mill and his immediate circle,[109] and there is some reason to

[103]*Autobiography*, *CW*, I, 67; *EL*, *CW*, XII, 13.

[104]*EL*, *CW*, XII, 51, 107, 134, 141.

[105]Austin, "Preface," xxxii.

[106]Leslie Stephen, *The English Utilitarians*, 3 vols. (London: Duckworth, 1900), III, 318.

[107]Austin, "Preface," xv.

[108]*EL*, *CW*, XII, 117.

[109]Cf. Sarah Austin's recollection of her husband's relations with Bentham on this score: "My husband used vainly to represent to him that the ignorance and wrong-headedness of the people were fully as dangerous to good government as the 'sinister interests' of the governing classes. Upon this point they were always at issue." (Letter to Guizot of 18 Dec., 1861, in Ross, *Three Generations*, II, 114.)

think that his reservations about such matters, especially his ideas about the proper authority of the more enlightened elements in society, played an important part in fostering the young Mill's reaction against this inherited creed.[110] In the later 1830s and 1840s, however, Austin's apprehensive political sensibilities led him to develop an increasingly conservative line of thought, opposing all further reform, in which Mill was unwilling to follow him. This difference of view reached its peak in a strong disagreement over the French Revolution of 1848 (Mill was a warm advocate of the popular cause), and some real or imagined slights by Sarah Austin to Harriet over her relations with Mill brought about a complete estrangement between the two couples, marked by that unyielding bitterness which characterized all Harriet's social antagonisms.[111] On John Austin's death Mill could at first bring himself to write only a stiff, brief note to the Austins' granddaughter, later checking with Helen Taylor to ensure that any further communication with Sarah Austin was consistent with what her mother would have wished.[112] Despite these differences, Mill always retained his regard for Austin's intellect and character, and when in 1863 Sarah Austin published her edition of her husband's full lecture notes under the title of *Lectures on Jurisprudence*, Mill took the opportunity publicly to pay his respects to his former tutor and, in passing, to display his own command of the subject.

Bain, always relieved when the later Mill followed his analytical rather than his polemical inclinations, ranked the essay on Austin as "among the best of his minor compositions," adding, "It does not seem to contain much originality, but it is a logical treat."[113] Mill would no doubt have acknowledged the justice of both parts of this judgment. He had himself described Austin's project as an enquiry into "the logic of law," and his review made clear that he extended full and sympathetic approval to this project, dissenting from Austin's analysis only on one point of substance (see his discussion of Austin's definition of a "right," 178-81). Later commentators have not always found it so easy to characterize the nature of the project of analytical jurisprudence practised by Austin and endorsed by Mill. The chief difficulty seems to lie in determining what relation the apparently *a priori* analysis of the essence of law has to the variety of actual historical legal systems, especially when Austin's subject-matter is defined, as it is by Mill at one point below, as "positive law—the legal institutions which exist, or have existed, among mankind, considered as actual facts" (169). The way both Austin and Mill seem to contrast the philosophy of law with the history of law only makes the difficulty

---

[110]See especially the excellent discussion by Richard B. Friedman, "An Introduction to Mill's Theory of Authority," in *Mill: A Collection of Critical Essays*, ed. J.B. Schneewind (Garden City, N.Y.: Doubleday, 1968), 379-425.

[111]*EL, CW*, XIII, 734. Under Harriet's influence, Mill penned a very harsh portrait of Sarah Austin in the early draft of the *Autobiography*, which he later omitted from the published version (see *Autobiography, CW*, I, 186).

[112]*LL, CW*, XV, 658, 671. Cf. the Textual Introduction, lxv below.

[113]Bain, *John Stuart Mill*, 124.

more acute: as Mill puts it in a revealing phrase, existing bodies of law "having grown by mere aggregation," they are subject to "no authoritative arrangement but the chronological one," and therefore do not furnish the student with any general principles of classification. The task of the philosopher of law is thus that of "stripping off what belongs to the accidental or historical peculiarities" of any given system in order to identify the "universal" elements (171, 173).

In this last phrase the suggestion of the ancient ambition to distinguish essences from accidents points in the right direction, and one may recall one of Austin's few self-revealing remarks here: "I was born out of time and place. I ought to have been a schoolman of the twelfth century—or a German professor."[114] The primary task of jurisprudence as Austin conceived it was essentially classificatory. It involved "clearing up and defining the notions which the human mind is compelled to form, and the distinctions which it is necessitated to make, by the mere existence of a body of law of any kind. . . ." It is true that to this statement Mill appended the potentially relativizing rider, "or of a body of law taking cognizance of the concerns of a civilized and complicated state of society" (168-9); but in practice neither he nor Austin allowed this consideration to limit the effectively universalist ambitions of analytical jurisprudence. These ambitions rested on the confidence that all legal systems in fact have certain features in common, since they are "designed . . . for the same world, and for the same human nature" (170). These similarities are not merely contingent: "There are certain combinations of facts and of ideas which every system of law *must* recognise . . ." (170), and the analyst must "free from confusion and set in a clear light those *necessary* resemblances and differences, which, if not brought into distinct apprehension by all systems of law, are latent in all, and do not depend on the accidental history of any" (172; my emphases). But in Mill's view, developed in general terms in his *System of Logic*, establishing such connections was not a purely *a priori* procedure. As one commentator has aptly summarized the procedure in the present case: "Through factual investigations of the objects which possess the combination of attributes specified in the definition, one can discover (by various methods which Mill outlines) that these attributes cause other attributes to be present along with themselves; in other words, a necessary connection exists between the attributes specified in the definition and those discovered by an investigation of the objects possessing them."[115] Hence Mill's confidence that the resulting system of classification would have a general purchase on all legal systems: "The same terminology, nomenclature, and principle of arrangement, which would render one system of law definite, clear, and (in Bentham's language) cognoscible, would serve, with additions and variations in minor details, to render the same office for another" (171). Indeed, rather than creating a system of classification of

---

[114]Quoted in Austin, "Preface," xviii.
[115]W.L. Morison, "Some Myth about Positivism," *Yale Law Journal*, LXVIII (Dec., 1958), 226-7.

his own, Austin took that displayed in Roman law (albeit Roman law as systematized and abstracted by the Pandectists) as his basis, a decision that Mill warmly defended: "the legal system which has been moulded into the shape it possesses by the greatest number of exact and logical minds, will necessarily be the best adapted for the purpose; for, though the elements sought exist in all systems, this is the one in which the greatest number of them are likely to have been brought out into distinct expression, and the fewest to remain latent" (173). Though the goal is recognizably Benthamite, the route may seem curiously roundabout: English lawyers (but not lawyers alone) of the 1860s are being urged to think about the nature of law in terms of a set of principles developed in the 1820s out of Austin's encounter with the German Pandectist rationalization of the legal system of the Roman Empire. Of course, the hostility to the common law which Austin and Mill shared came into play here: "Turning from the study of the English, to the study of the Roman Law," Austin declared, "you escape from the empire of chaos and darkness, to a world which seems by comparison, the region of order and light."[116] It is noticeable how by far the longest extract from Austin's work Mill permits himself to reproduce is that wherein Austin demolishes the common arguments against codification. The argument is conducted in general terms, but there is no doubting the moral Mill intended his contemporaries to draw from it.

This underlying preoccupation with reform also explains why Mill can so unequivocally commend the work of Henry Maine, who drew very different conclusions from the study, in his case the historical and comparative study, of Roman law. Some explanation is called for, since Maine's *Ancient Law*, published in 1861, posed a fundamental methodological challenge to Austin's work (and hence to Mill's endorsement of it), and called into doubt some of its most central elements, such as the definitions of law and sovereignty.[117] Nonetheless, Mill had been among the earliest admirers of the book, and his reference to it in the 1862 edition of his *Principles* as a "profound work" set the tone for all his future citations, of which there were several in the next decade, culminating in a glowing review in 1871 of Maine's second book, *Village-Communities in the East and West*.[118] In the present essay he treats Maine's work as complementary to Austin's without really drawing attention to the differences of approach and sensibility that informed them. But the terms of the commendation reveal that the focus of Mill's attention is elsewhere: "the historical value" of such studies as Maine's, he announces, "is the smallest part of their utility. They teach us the highly practical

---

[116]Austin, *Lectures*, I, xciv.

[117]For a discussion of Maine's work in these terms, see J.W. Burrow, *Evolution and Society: A Study in Victorian Social Theory* (Cambridge: Cambridge University Press, 1966), Chap. v; and Stein, *Legal Evolution*, Chaps. iv and v.

[118]*Principles of Political Economy*, *CW*, II-III (Toronto: University of Toronto Press, 1965), II, 219; "Maine on Village-Communities," *Fortnightly Review*, n.s. IX (May, 1871), 543-56.

lesson, that institutions which, with more or less of modification, still exist, originated in ideas now universally exploded; and conversely, that ideas and modes of thought which have not lost their hold even on our own time, are often the artificial, and in some sort accidental product of laws and institutions which exist no longer, and of which no one would now approve the revival." (170.) Similarly, his use of *Ancient Law* in his *Principles* is to buttress his claim that existing property arrangements cannot be taken as natural or unalterable; Maine's book is cited to demonstrate that no "presumption in favour of existing ideas on this subject is to be derived from their antiquity."[119] As so often, the heat of Mill's enthusiasms is sufficient to melt the awkwardly hard edges of the authors whom he discusses: in his account, Maine and Austin stand side by side as contributors to "the improvement of law" (170).

"Austin on Jurisprudence" offers one of the best examples of Mill's use of an extended essay in one of the great reviews to instruct the relevant section of the reading public on abstract subjects. The value of Austin's rigorous analysis, he asserts, transcended its contribution to the special science of jurisprudence: it functioned "as a training school for the higher class of intellects" (167), and Mill's own essay was intended as a small instalment of this training. It proceeds on the assumption that the readers of the *Edinburgh Review*—a class which even the critics of that journal could not by this date suggest was confined to Scotch lawyers—would be willing as part of their general self-culture to apply themselves to such subjects as the classification of public and private wrongs in the *corpus juris*. Mill's prose betrays none of that defensiveness of the teacher who needs to justify his subject; on the contrary, the voice expresses confidence in an advanced community of interest: "We would particularly direct attention to the treatment of *Dominium* or Property, in its various senses, with the contrasted conception of *servitus* or easement" (198). How far his audience in fact met these expectations it is impossible to say; certainly Mill's later correspondence suggests there were always some readers who received, and sometimes challenged, instruction at the appropriate level. But it is Mill's own untroubled self-assurance as he moves across the details of yet another field of knowledge which is most remarkable. To have been able to give such a clear and forceful précis of the agonizingly involuted contents of Austin's three volumes, and to have been able to take him on as an equal on disputed points, is some indication that Mill's early immersion in the law was not, after all, without its effect, and a reminder that once he had mastered a subject he could always thereafter lay out its structure with impressive authority. For several generations of jurisprudence students Mill's essay was required reading, and it is striking testimony to the qualities of his mind displayed in what is, after all, in the corpus of his work as a whole, a relatively minor, occasional

---

[119]*Principles, CW*, II, 218-19. This passage dated from the first edition; the reference to *Ancient Law* was simply appended to it in 1862.

composition, that almost a century later the leading scholarly authority on Austin should still rank Mill's essay as one of "the best comprehensive accounts" of its subject.[120]

EDUCATION

WITH A WRITER WHO SAYS that by education he means "whatever helps to shape the human being; to make the individual what he is or hinder him from being what he is not" (217), it hardly seems appropriate to group so few of his writings together as representing his views on the subject. While he endorsed Helvétius' dictum, "l'éducation peut tout,"[121] we might, conversely, say that for Mill everything can be education. In one sense, no doubt, something similar could be said of any major social theorist: all is *Bildung*. But even by these standards, Mill's conception of society is an exceptionally and pervasively educative one. We have already seen some instances of how he makes their effect on the shaping of character the ultimate test of all institutions and policies, and one could without strain regard his whole notion of political activity itself as an extended and strenuous adult-education course. Thus, the whole of this collected edition of his works, and not just part of one volume within it, might not improperly be subtitled "Essays on Education." Even if we confine ourselves to education in the narrower sense of the business carried on in schools and universities, still the one major and two minor pieces included here could be augmented by essays in other volumes. For example, the general basis of the views on educational endowments expounded below (209-14) receives fuller treatment in his later article on "Endowments" in *Essays on Economics and Society* (Vol. V of the *Collected Works*), just as his account of the ideal university syllabus in his *Inaugural Address* (217-57) can be compared with his discussion of the same subject in his "Sedgwick's Discourse" and "Civilization" (in Vol. X, *Essays on Ethics, Religion, and Society*, and Vol. XVIII, *Essays on Politics and Society*, respectively); the appearance of these three pieces in three *different* volumes of this edition is itself an indication of the artificiality, albeit inescapable, of appearing to imply that the pieces included here are an exhaustive representation of Mill on education.[122]

Mill was, of course, in no position to minimize the influence of education. His own extraordinary upbringing, while it might leave him with a dismissive scorn for what mere schooling usually accomplished, was hardly calculated to make him

[120]H.L.A. Hart, "Introduction" to Austin, *The Province of Jurisprudence Determined* (London: Weidenfeld and Nicolson, 1954), xx.

[121]Claude Adrien Helvétius, *De l'homme, de ses facultés intellectuelles, et de son éducation* (1772), in *Oeuvres complètes d'Helvétius*, 10 vols. in 5 (Paris: Garnéry, and Dugour, 1793-97), IX, 191.

[122]"Endowments" (1869), in *Essays on Economics and Society*, V, 613-29; "Sedgwick's Discourse" (1835), in *Essays on Ethics, Religion, and Society*, CW, X (Toronto: University of Toronto Press, 1969), 31-74; "Civilization" (1836), CW, XVIII, 117-47.

sceptical of the formative power of a properly conceived and rigorously administered education. Indeed, one of his professed reasons for writing the *Autobiography* was precisely to demonstrate "how much more than is commonly supposed"[123] might be achieved if schoolmasters generally approximated more closely to the model of James Mill, which is one reason why that work reads more like Rousseau's *Emile* than like his *Confessions*. For the younger Mill was, as he acknowledged only half regretfully, a guinea-pig upon whom his father tried out his educational theories, and so it was by both precept and experience that he absorbed the latter's "fundamental doctrine . . . the formation of all human character by circumstances, through the universal Principle of Association, and the consequent unlimited possibility of improving the moral and intellectual condition of mankind by education."[124] Whatever other aspects of his intellectual inheritance Mill may have rejected or modified, on this count he was James Mill's eldest boy to the last.

This optimistic doctrine formed one of the cornerstones of Philosophic Radical political theory in the 1820s and 1830s, and there were few existing practices dealt with more severely by those critics of all things established than what they regarded as the feeble provision for education in England, especially as contrasted with what was increasingly being provided under the auspices of the state in France and Prussia. The latter, in particular, was frequently cited as an example of what enlightened and efficient administration could achieve, and the architect of the Prussian education system, Wilhelm von Humboldt (from whom Mill was later to take the epigraph for *On Liberty*), ranked only below "the god-like Turgot" as a recent example of a statesman with genuinely philosophic vision.[125] A report on Prussian education by another eminent philosopher and educational reformer, Victor Cousin, was, therefore, a naturally congenial document to the Philosophic Radical circle, one that could serve as a useful weapon with which to beat a government then showing some disposition to take up the question of national education, which had been pressed upon it very forcibly in the debates of 1833 by Molesworth and, above all, Roebuck. It seemed, as Mill says below, "an auspicious moment for inviting the attention of the English public to that highest and most important of all the objects which a government can place before itself" (63), and he took the opportunity to press the case in a favourable notice of Sarah Austin's translation of Cousin's book.

Although Mill had reported to Carlyle that Mrs. Austin's preface was "the truest & best piece of printed writing I have read for many months,"[126] his review was,

---

[123]*Autobiography*, *CW*, I, 5.

[124]*Ibid.*, 111.

[125]For von Humboldt and Mill's relation to him, see the editor's introduction to Wilhelm von Humboldt, *The Limits of State Action*, ed. J.W. Burrow (London: Cambridge University Press, 1969). "The godlike Turgot" is a phrase of John Austin's quoted not only by Mill (204), but by (among others) Morley in his "Death of Mr. Mill," 671.

[126]Letter to Carlyle, *EL*, *CW*, XII, 225 (28 Apr., 1834).

even by early-nineteenth-century standards in these matters, a mere pretext for a bit of propagandizing about the deplorable state of English schools. There is practically no reference to Cousin's work itself, and only one substantial quotation from the translator's preface; instead the article is fleshed out with several lengthy extracts from an unflattering contemporary account of Church of England elementary schools, references to congenial speeches in Parliament, and, under the cover of anonymity, a long quotation from his own article on the abuses of church and corporation property published in the previous year. The article makes no constructive proposals, Mill contenting himself with exhorting the House of Commons committee on education to pursue "the reform of such abominations" (73). It is noticeable how slight and mechanical such early polemical pieces seem when juxtaposed to some of Mill's later performances as a public moralist.

If the elementary education of the many had been culpably neglected, the ancient public schools and universities, on which the privileged classes were wont to congratulate themselves, Mill always regarded as grossly overvalued. The inefficient cramming of the rudiments of Latin and Greek carried on at many of the former was invariably referred to sarcastically, and even the better of them were berated for concentrating on what always seemed to Mill the least valuable part of such an education, the imitation of classical verse models. These sentiments can be found in works published in the 1860s as well as the 1830s, and his correspondence abounds with remarks about the "miserable pretence of education, which those classes now receive," and especially about the "disgraceful" failure even to teach the ancient languages properly.[127] In the 1830s Oxford and Cambridge, too, came in for some very sharp criticism, the great flaw and foundation of all other vices in these institutions being their position as virtual seminaries for the Established Church: "While their sectarian character, while the exclusion of all who will not sign away their freedom of thought, is contended for as if life depended on it, there is hardly a trace in the system of the Universities that any other object whatever is seriously cared for."[128] Education was naturally one of Mill's favoured examples of the cramping effect of religion on English life, whether in the form of the conformity-exacting complacency of Anglicanism or the bigoted sectarianism of the Dissenters, and his repeated pleas for freedom of thought in education have to be seen in this context. His having neither received a religious education nor attended a school or university of any kind constituted an important element in his identity as an outsider, and meant that he never displayed that indulgent, forgiving piety towards the ancient educational foundations which marked the attitudes of the vast majority of the governing class who had passed through them.

If in the earlier part of the century the schoolmaster was abroad in the land, by the 1860s it was the school inspector, backed by the power of several Royal

[127]Letter to Henry William Carr, *LL*, *CW*, XIV, 80 (7 Jan., 1852); letter to T.H. Huxley, *ibid.*, XVI, 1092 (18 Aug., 1865). Cf. "Civilization," *CW*, XVIII, 138-9; and 221-2 below.
[128]"Civilization," *CW*, XVIII, 142.

Commissions, who represented the essence of recent developments. The spirit of administrative reform was now breathing down the necks of lowly ushers in dames' schools and of great pashas in public schools alike. Royal Commissions on the two extremities of the system, the leading public schools and "popular education," were succeeded at the end of 1864 by a long-lived Commission with the self-consciously miscellaneous title of an enquiry into those schools "not comprised within Her Majesty's two recent Commissions," soon casually identified as "middle-class schools." The Commission, usually referred to as the Taunton Commission after its Chairman Henry Labouchere, Baron Taunton, sent sets of questions to various possible witnesses, including Mill, who was at the time in Parliament and in fairly close contact with some members of the Commission.[129] On matters of this type Mill often sought, and even more often received, coaching from Edwin Chadwick, whose tactlessness was always liable to obstruct the proper deployment of his expertise. In this case, Mill asked Chadwick to "cram" him on the subject, and submitted a draft of his replies for the latter's approval.[130] These comparatively slight replies (Chadwick had favoured the earlier Commission on popular education with 160 pages of information and advice) constitute a typically Chadwickian plea for administrative efficiency based on the recognizably Benthamite "conjunction of duty-and-interest" principle alluded to at their opening as the "fundamental" maxim governing "the conduct of business of any kind by a delegated agent" (209).

If one is not to exaggerate considerations of this sort in Mill's thinking about education, however, these replies need to be read in conjunction with his article on "Endowments" published three years later (which includes several commendations of the Commission's eventual report), wherein he considers the value of educational endowments from the wider perspective of his general social thought. In the later piece he makes clear, for example, that however much he might have been in favour of "payment by results" (the slogan made popular a few years earlier by Robert Lowe) as the foundation of efficient teaching in state schools, he did not regard education generally as a commodity that the operation of market forces could be expected to provide satisfactorily. Thus, endowments are assigned a crucial role in making available secondary education for those who would profit from it but would not otherwise be able to afford it (a meritocracy in which women are emphatically included), and the larger principle which this satisfies is that of preserving, and where necessary providing, variety. "It is desirable that every particular enterprise for education or other public objects should be organized; that is, its conductors should act together for a known object, on a definite plan,

---

[129]For the Taunton Commission see H.C. Barnard, *A History of English Education from 1760*, 2nd ed. (London: University of London Press, 1961), 128-34; see also Mill's letter to Edwin Chadwick, *LL*, *CW*, XVI, 1168 (21 May, 1866).

[130]Letters to Edwin Chadwick, *LL*, *CW*, XVI, 1168, 1172, and 1190 (21 May, 31 May, and 9 Aug., 1866).

without waste of strength or resources." This is the typically Benthamite-Chadwickian note. "But it is far from desirable that all such enterprises should be organized exactly alike. . . . [W]hat the improvement of mankind and of all their works most imperatively demands is variety, not uniformity."[131] This is the distinctively Millian voice. Although he came to regard it as part of the duty of the state to see that all children received a certain level of education, he always thought it positively dangerous for the state to provide all the schools to which those children were to be sent.

By the 1860s Mill also recognized that the English universities, goaded by yet more Royal Commissions, fed by rejuvenated public schools, and prompted by reformers from within, were responding to the spirit of improvement.[132] The beginnings of an expansion of the traditional classics- and mathematics-based curriculum formed part of a larger national debate on the proper role of the universities, which revived once again the challenge, endlessly offered and almost as endlessly refused in English educational history, of science to the dominant position held by the humanities. Mill's own influence at Oxford and Cambridge was at its peak in this decade, an influence which was seen to tell on the side of "modern" studies. In accepting the invitation of the St. Andrews students to deliver a Rectorial address, Mill clearly saw an opportunity to deploy his influence in this debate, as well, perhaps, as to do a little homage to the Scottish university tradition, respect for which had been bred into him by his Edinburgh-educated father.

Mill's Address, which took three hours to deliver ("a very lengthened performance," Bain grumbled), does not rank with the speeches of Gladstone or Macaulay among the masterpieces of Victorian oratory, but it has some of the same monumental quality. Having taken as his theme "every essential department of general culture . . . considered in its relation to human cultivation at large . . . [and] the nature of the claims which each has to a place in liberal education" (220), Mill was in no position to be brief, though it must be said that the Address concludes with those headmasterly platitudes whose natural home is the school prize-giving: "what we achieve depends less on the amount of time we possess, than on the use we make of our time. You and your like are the hope and resource

---

[131]"Endowments," *CW*, V, 617. See also Mill's article of 1833 on "Corporation and Church Property," *CW*, IV, 193-222, where he had had to insist more strenuously on the right of the state to interfere with such endowments at all; by 1869 he felt that the contrary case most needed to be stated.

[132]In reprinting "Civilization" in 1859, for example, Mill added a footnote conceding that "much of what is here said of the Universities has, in a great measure, ceased to be true" (*CW*, XVIII, 143n). Cf. Mill's letter to Mrs. Henry Huth of 7 Jan., 1863: "Twenty years ago [Oxford and Cambridge] were about the last places which I should have recommended in any parallel case; but they are now very much changed, and free enquiry and speculation on the deepest and highest questions, instead of being crushed or deadened, are now more rife there than almost anywhere else in England" (*LL*, *CW*, XV, 819). For the whole question of the revival of the universities, see Sheldon Rothblatt, *The Revolution of the Dons: Cambridge and Society in Victorian England* (London: Faber and Faber, 1968); Rothblatt, *Tradition and Change in English Liberal Education: An Essay in History and Culture* (London: Faber and Faber, 1976); and Harvie, *Lights of Liberalism*.

of your country in the coming generation" (257), and so on. Bain, a Professor at a Scottish university, thought the Address a "mistake" in its setting because Mill "had no conception of the limits of a University curriculum."[133] Certainly Mill was describing a course of study for which a couple of decades would not have been too generous a provision of time. He professed himself "amazed at the limited conception which many educational reformers have formed to themselves of a human being's power of acquisition" (221), but if his Address was intended as a practical proposal then it was one of those occasions when Mill was afflicted with a kind of solipsism in his judgment of human capacities (we have already seen something similar at work in his view of sex). And past experience is again denied authority as a guide: with all the optimism of one who had never taught in a university, Mill insists, "let us try what conscientious and intelligent teaching can do, before we presume to decide what cannot be done" (221). In fact the Address is not best read as a constructive proposal for reform of the syllabus, but rather as a statement of the values Mill wished to see fostered in higher education, and of his own distinctive conception of the contributions the various branches of knowledge could make to this goal. It thus serves as a good sketch-map of the geography of Mill's mature thought on abstract subjects, embracing in its way a wider territory even than that mapped out in the *Logic*.

Although Mill affected to regard the dispute between the claims of classics and the claims of science as needless, in that any worthwhile education should include both, the stand he actually took on this issue was bound to appear a conservative one. For he pressed the case for the classics in the strongest possible terms: "The only languages . . . and the only literature, to which I would allow a place in the ordinary curriculum, are those of the Greeks and Romans; and to these I would preserve the position in it which they at present occupy" (225). It may be said that Mill slightly mis-states the import of his argument here, since the position these studies then occupied was confined by the traditional philological and textual preoccupations of English classical scholarship, whereas Mill was pressing for a much broader study of the ancient world (his tastes and loyalties were in fact always far more Greek than Roman) in which history and, above all, philosophy would predominate. He certainly did not see himself as endorsing the empty versifying of the English classical schools. But he was bound to appear to be upholding the traditional primacy of the classics: Huxley, for example, on a celebrated parallel occasion, responded in this way in contrasting his own call for the teaching of science at universities with Mill's eulogy of the classics.[134] Moreover, at a time when there was something of a crisis of confidence about just

---

[133]Bain, *John Stuart Mill*, 127; cf. Bain's remark on Mill's strictures on universities in his "Sedgwick" article: "Such a view of the functions of a University would not be put forth by any man that had ever resided in a University; and this is not the only occasion when Mill dogmatized on Universities in total ignorance of their working" (46).

[134]In his Rectorial Address at Aberdeen in 1874, Huxley explicitly challenged the pre-eminence which he took Mill to be assigning to the classics; see "Universities: Actual and Ideal," in Thomas Henry Huxley, *Science and Education* (New York: Collier, 1902), 183-4.

what constituted the distinctive merits of a classical education, and when the discrepancies and contradictions between the various justifications were occasioning some embarrassment,[135] Mill's brisk amalgamation of the various arguments hit a particularly confident and unyielding note: the classics display the most polished examples of literary form, *and* they contain unrivalled wisdom and truth in their content; the grammatical structures of the ancient languages uniquely fit them to provide mental training, *and* exposure to the operation of minds so unlike our own is itself a most valuable discipline, and so on.

Mill had presented a brief defence of a classical education in slightly different and rather more revealing terms twenty-seven years earlier when he endorsed Tocqueville's view of the importance to be attached to the ancient literatures "not as being without faults, but as having the contrary faults to those of our own day." There, in more sociological vein, he suggested that these literatures, produced in "the military and agricultural commonwealths of Antiquity," exhibit "precisely that order of virtues in which a commercial society is apt to be deficient." The justification is unequivocally a moral one. And on these grounds he was, in 1840, already worried about the future of the classics: "If, as everyone may see, the want of affinity of these studies to the modern mind is gradually lowering them in popular estimation, this is but a confirmation of the need of them, and renders it more incumbent upon those who have the power, to do their utmost towards preventing their decline."[136] Here surely is the key to his decision to devote almost half his Address to a defence of that feature of university education which the existing system already fostered beyond all others. (For once, Bain failed to see that Mill was talking about a tendency, not a realized fact, commenting with some exasperation: "Mill had taken it into his head that the Greek and Roman classics had been too hardly pressed by the votaries of science, and were in some danger of being excluded from the higher teaching. . . .")[137] A glance at the development of the university syllabus in the last third of the nineteenth century hardly vindicates Mill's anxiety that the study of the classics was on the point of extinction. But just as his ideal of what such a study should consist in and produce was far removed from the actual practice of the day which he seemed to be defending, so his anxiety about the fate of that study was not a realistic assessment of purely educational

---

[135]For a good example of contemporary soul-searching on this topic, see the collection of essays edited by Frederic William Farrar, *Essays on a Liberal Education* (London: Macmillan, 1867). For discussion, see Rothblatt, *Liberal Education*, Chap. v; Harvie, *Lights of Liberalism*, Chap. vii; and, for the corresponding but distinctive Scottish debate, George Davie, *The Democratic Intellect: Scotland and Her Universities in the Nineteenth Century* (Edinburgh: Edinburgh University Press, 1961).

[136]"De Tocqueville on Democracy in America [II]," *CW*, XVIII, 195. Cf. Mill's letter to Herbert Spencer of 9 Feb., 1867, replying to Spencer's comment on the *Address*: "In regard to classical instruction, I do not altogether agree with you that the side favourable to it is too strong; for I think there is a growing reaction to the opposite extreme, producing a danger on that side which being the side most in harmony with modern tendencies has the best chance of being ultimately the stronger" (*LL*, *CW*, XVI, 1237).

[137]Bain, *John Stuart Mill*, 126.

changes, but an example of his familiar and more personal anxiety about the need for countervailing forces to the increasingly conformist pressure of modern society.

Another way of indicating how far removed Mill was from those pressing the claims of scientific and technological education is to point to the fact that his case for science is almost entirely couched in terms of its value as a training in method. Science provides, above all, "models of the art of estimating evidence" (235), and the term "models" naturally suggests that the particular content is of secondary importance. What Mill chiefly offers his audience here is a brisk summary of the *Logic*, taking the opportunity to press the *correct* method in circles all too prone to various forms of Intuitionism. Comte's classification of the sciences is followed from mathematics up to physiology, but at that point Mill reverts to the older British tradition of "the science of mind," referred to indifferently as psychology or philosophy (Comte had moved directly from physiology, the study of man's physical constitution, including phrenology, to sociology, the study of the laws governing man's action in society). Thus, that part of Mill's Address which lays down "the outline of a complete scientific education" concludes, revealingly, by prescribing the works of Hobbes, Locke, Reid, Stewart, Hume, Hartley, and Brown. To this he appends a brief section on those sciences that deal with "the great interests of mankind as moral and social beings" (243-4), brief because so few of the attempts at systematic study of these topics are considered to have attained the rank of sciences. Political economy and jurisprudence are treated as the only secure possessors of that status, and the account of jurisprudence is only one of several ways in which this section differs interestingly from the parallel discussion in Book VI of the *Logic*.

Only after having devoted three-quarters of his Address to what he called "intellectual education" did Mill move onto moral and aesthetic education; but these proportions are misleading if they suggest that his audience had not been kept constantly aware of the moral purposes all education was meant to serve. For example, in introducing the student to the philosophic view of history as the development of stages of civilization (a view with appropriately strong Scottish connections), the university would thereby—Mill seems to regard the connection as too obvious to need spelling out—be cultivating a conception of life as "an unremitting conflict between good and evil powers, of which every act done by any of us, insignificant as we are, forms one of the incidents; a conflict in which even the smallest of us cannot escape from taking part, in which whoever does not help the right side is helping the wrong, and for our share in which, whether it be greater or smaller, and let its actual consequences be visible or in the main invisible, no one of us can escape the responsibility" (244). The Headmaster has clearly moved over from the lectern to the pulpit; whatever a university teaches, "it should teach as penetrated by a sense of duty; it should present all knowledge as chiefly a means to worthiness of life, given for the double purpose of making each of us practically useful to his fellow-creatures, and of elevating the character of the species itself" (248).

The voice of the moralist sounds out equally clearly in Mill's discussion of the value of art. Considered at this level of abstraction, this is one of those quicksand-like questions whose chief role seems to be to reveal the blind spots in any philosopher's sensibilities. For Mill, step-child of English Romanticism, the cultivation of the feelings is the core of the aesthetic experience, but only a certain, rather narrow, selection of feelings seems to be involved. His residual Words-worthianism surfaces here: natural beauty, for example, is said to make us "feel the puerility of the petty objects which set men's interests at variance, contrasted with the nobler pleasures which all might share" (255). Mill's aesthetic does not easily accommodate the tragic; where values appear to clash, there is a presumption that selfishness is at work somewhere. Indeed, not only does art not create a potential rival realm of value for Mill: beauty is not even allowed to be morally indifferent. "There is . . . a natural affinity between goodness and the cultivation of the Beautiful, when it is real cultivation, and not a mere unguided instinct. He who has learnt what beauty is, if he be of virtuous character, will desire to realize it in his own life—will keep before himself a type of perfect beauty in human character, to light his attempts at self-culture." (255.) The rider "if he be of virtuous character" threatens to reduce the proposition to a tautology, a process which is assisted by his sliding from "beauty" in general to "beauty in human character." It is a tension which, in other forms, appears elsewhere in Mill's thought, most notably in *On Liberty*: the goal of self-development rests on a restricted notion of the self, a self whose development not only does not impede, but positively fosters, the moral interests of others. Once again, the dim outline of the idea of a common good is discernible in Mill's thinking here. It is, in fact, the obverse of his Manichaeanism, which is itself another strategy for simplifying the disorderly actualities of moral experience. Launched into his peroration, Mill quite naturally makes "the ultimate end" from which his prescribed course of studies takes its "chief value" that of "making you more effective combatants in the great fight which never ceases to rage between Good and Evil" (256). Inaugural Addresses form an inescapably programmatic genre, and for that reason Mill's displays several of his chief intellectual virtues to good effect: the magisterial survey is his natural medium, all of human knowledge his familiar bailiwick. His occasional tendency to a narrow and hectoring moralism finds only a subdued expression here, while the awesome range and dazzling lucidity of his mind are exhibited at their formidable, impressive best.

Textual Introduction

JOHN M. ROBSON

EQUALITY, as Stefan Collini asserts in the Introduction above, is the dominant theme in this volume. Perhaps because the word does not appear in the title of any of Mill's great essays, its importance in his thought and life is not often emphasized. The materials now gathered, which demonstrate its significance in his thought on education and law as well as on sexual, racial, and domestic issues, derive from each of the decades of his writing career, that is, from the 1820s to the 1870s.[1] They also cover a wide range in provenance.[2] The majority, eleven of the eighteen in the text proper, originated as reviews or essays in periodicals: three in each of the *Westminster Review* and *Fraser's Magazine*, two in the *Monthly Repository*, and one in each of *Tait's Edinburgh Magazine*, the *Edinburgh Review*, and the *Fortnightly Review*. Of these eleven, three were reprinted during Mill's lifetime in the British edition of *Dissertations and Discussions*, one ("Treaty Obligations") was republished in the posthumous fourth volume, and one ("The Slave Power") in the U.S. editions of that collection. Two of the items, the *Inaugural Address at St. Andrews* (originally a speech) and *The Subjection of Women*, appeared as books; and one, *Remarks on Mr. Fitzroy's Bill*, as a pamphlet. Parliamentary evidence, in written form and as a transcription of oral answers (republished in pamphlet form), supplies two further items. And two more not published by Mill are presented from manuscript. The appendices given to ancillary textual matter include essays and fragments by Harriet Taylor Mill, only one of which was published in her lifetime (in the *Westminster*), a manuscript

---

[1]Of course, full appreciation of his thought on these matters requires reference to other volumes of the *Collected Works*: to cite only the most obvious cases, the parallels between *The Subjection of Women* and *On Liberty* will lead readers of this volume to *Essays on Politics and Society*, Vols. XVIII and XIX of the *Collected Works*, and the educational writings will suggest consultation of the *Autobiography* in Vol. I.

[2]Bibliographic details are given in the Editor's Note to each item. These include information about provenance ("not republished" means not republished by Mill), evidence for attribution and dating, listing of copies in Mill's library, Somerville College, Oxford, and the entry in Mill's bibliography of his published writings, which has been edited by Ney MacMinn, J.M. McCrimmon, and J.R. Hainds, *Bibliography of the Published Writings of J.S. Mill* (Evanston: Northwestern University Press, 1945), this edition being identified as "MacMinn."

fragment of the *Inaugural Address*, and three publications of the Jamaica Committee under Mill's chairmanship.

These disparities make it convenient to discuss textual matters not according to dominant focus[3] or provenance, but chronologically, beginning with "Law of Libel and Liberty of the Press" (April, 1825). Nothing specific is known of Mill's relevant activities at this time, though he was in 1825 immersed in the massive task of editing Jeremy Bentham's *Rationale of Judicial Evidence* (published in 1827). The essay, remarkable as the work of a youth still in his eighteenth year, reveals some Benthamic echoes (for example, the reference to judge-made law on 20), as well as much material from Francis Place, whose pamphlet on libel Mill is reviewing along with Richard Mence's *The Law of Libel*. It will be noted that Place's pamphlet was published in 1823 (in fact its separate essays first appeared at the end of 1822); and Mill had already reviewed it favourably in the *Morning Chronicle* on 1 January, 1824, 2, more than a year before the article here reprinted. Quite apparent is Mill's heavy dependence on his father, James Mill, whose arguments in "Liberty of the Press" and whose habits of thought and phrasing reverberate throughout the essay. "We have no higher ambition," anonymously and collectively says the young Mill, "than that of treading in [James Mill's] steps [in "Liberty of the Press"]; and, taking his principles as our guide, we shall endeavour to unravel the sophistry, and expose the mischievous designs of the enemies to free discussion."[4] This article, Mill's fifth for the *Westminster* since its founding at the beginning of 1824, was the first of his to be given pride of place in the Radical review.

The wide gap in approach and style between that essay and the manuscript we have entitled "On Marriage" is explained by Mill's internal declaration of independence after his "mental crisis" and his meeting Harriet Hardy Taylor who, twenty years later, was to marry him. This essay, with her companion piece (printed here as Appendix A), examines in a highly personal tone questions that had the greatest practical import for their relations.[5] It is therefore very annoying not to be able precisely to date the manuscripts. The evidence is slight: the watermarks, some of Mill's letters, although none mentions the essays, and the reference in Mill's essay to Robert Owen's definitions of chastity and prostitution.

[3]Eight of the items are directly related to equality of various kinds, seven to legal issues, and three to education; they of course differ greatly in length, so that, as is argued in the Introduction above, more than one-half of the volume concerns equality, with the remainder divided almost equally between law and education.

[4]See 4. Other familiar phrases include "It thus appears, by the closest ratiocination" (6); "a proposition which rests upon the broadest principles of human nature" (8); "that universal law of human nature" (11); "all history bears testimony" (13); "security for good government" and "see-saw" (18).

[5]Friedrich A. Hayek, whose researches during the 1940s did much to bring Mill back into scholarly and public repute, published these essays in his valuable and readable *John Stuart Mill and Harriet Taylor: Their Friendship and Subsequent Marriage* (London: Routledge and Kegan Paul, 1951), from which their frequent reprinting and quotation unfortunately perpetuated the errors in transcription.

The watermarks, 1831 and 1832,[6] led Professor Hayek to postulate a date of 1832, which presents no obvious difficulty when placed in the context of our general knowledge of their developing relations. Helen, the last of the Taylors' three children, was born in July, 1831; Harriet Taylor's attitudes towards marriage were consistently—and sensibly—coloured by her sense of responsibility to her children, and the views expressed in her and in Mill's essays suggest a prior and protracted discussion of the effect of frequent births on a young and inexperienced mother. By 1832 they clearly had reached emotional intimacy, if the earliest of Mill's surviving letters to her is correctly dated to August of that year.[7] Another likely occasional cause for the essays appears in the marital disruption in the household of W.J. Fox, their friend, whose wife began to live separately from him though in the same house, her place being taken by his ward, Eliza Flower, Harriet Taylor's closest and most admired companion. Again, the essays may well have preceded the six-month trial separation between Harriet and John Taylor beginning in September, 1833, when she went to Paris, to be joined there by Mill in October.[8] The citation of Robert Owen's definitions of chastity and prostitution proves less helpful in dating the essay than one would hope. The Owenite attitude to marriage had been known in the 1820s, particularly in the United States, where an account of one of Owen's speeches in 1827 concludes with mention of his promptly complying with a request for his opinions on marriage which, having "before been promulgated in various ways, it is not thought necessary here to recapitulate."[9] But where and when would Mill have heard or read the definitions? He had, of course, debated with Owen's adherents in 1825, and his father had known Owen for many years, but it is not known whether or not marriage was a moot issue in the debates and conversations. The closest wording to that appearing in Mill's footnote is in the published account of an unbelievably long debate between Owen and Alexander Campbell in Cincinnati from 13 to 21 April, 1829, in which Owen is reported as saying: "For real chastity consists, in connexion

[6]Mill's essay (British Library of Political and Economic Science, Mill-Taylor Collection, Vol. XLI, No. 1) is on seven sheets of paper watermarked "E. Wise 1831" (probably East India Co. paper), folded once to make fourteen folios, c. 34.0 cm. x 21.1 cm., written recto and verso on the right-hand side of each folio, leaving the left side free for notes and revisions (as Mill commonly did in these years, for example in his "Notes on Some of the More Popular Dialogues of Plato," reprinted in *Essays on Philosophy and the Classics, CW*, XI). Harriet Taylor's companion essay (Mill-Taylor Collection, Box III, No. 79) is on two sheets of paper watermarked "J. Morbey & Co 1832", folded once to make four folios, c. 19.8 cm. x 25.0 cm., written recto and verso on all sides.

[7]*EL, CW*, XII, 114. Hayek's inferred date of July, 1832, which is followed by Michael St.J. Packe in his *Life of John Stuart Mill* (London: Secker and Warburg, 1954), is rejected by Professor Mineka because of the reference to flowers gathered in the New Forest, where Mill had been on a walking tour from 19 July to 6 Aug.

[8]See Mill to W.J. Fox, *EL, CW*, XII, 185-9 (5 or 6 Nov., 1833).

[9]*Address Delivered by Robert Owen, at a Public Meeting, Held at the Franklin Institute, in the City of Philadelphia, on Monday Morning, June 25, 1827* (Philadelphia: Gould, and Mortimer, 1827), 39.

with affection, and prostitution, in connexion without affection."[10] It is hard to believe that Mill (or anyone) read the two thick volumes of that account, which cannot have had much of a sale in Britain. The first of Owen's statements in Britain that approximates Mill's wording was not made until 1 May, 1833, in London:[11] Mill is likely to have heard of it—and could even have heard it—and if this was his first acquaintance with Owen's precise views, the manuscript must be dated as late at least as May, 1833, not by any means an impossible date, but one that would slightly revise the received view of the rate at which his intimacy with Harriet Taylor had developed. The exchange of statements between them at that time would, in fact, help explain the crisis in their affairs that led to the flight to Paris in September, 1833. It could even be argued that Mill's reference (39) to Thomas Carlyle simply by his last name implies a closeness of acquaintance on his part not reached until 1833. But this evidence is very tenuous, and it seems wise, unless and until further evidence emerges, to assign only a tentative "1832-33?" to the essays.

About the date of the next item, "Austin's Lectures on Jurisprudence," there is no such mystery: Mill had finished and sent off the review by 13 September, 1832,[12] and it appeared in *Tait's Edinburgh Magazine* for December of that year. A devoted friend of John and Sarah Austin at this time, Mill had read law while staying with them at Norwich a decade earlier, attended in 1829 the lectures he is here reviewing, advised John Austin (through Sarah) about the lectures in 1830, was now addressing Mrs. Austin as "My Dear Mütterlein," and toured part of Cornwall with them in the interval between the writing and publishing of the review. It is not, however, mere puffery or "doctrinal matter";[13] nor was it composed because Mill was unoccupied. Indeed in five or six weeks he also wrote two other important—and very different—essays, "Corporation and Church Property" and "On Genius."[14]

The same personal connection lies behind Mill's "Reform in Education," a review of Sarah Austin's translation of Victor Cousin's *Report on the State of Public Instruction in Prussia*. The personal note is muted, sounding only innocently in the recommendation that her preface to the translation "well deserves to be separately printed and widely circulated," because it shows "force and conclusiveness," and a "happy union . . . of an earnest spirit and a conciliatory and engaging tone" (64). Probably Mill got from Sarah Austin other information used

---

[10]*Debate on the Evidences of Christianity*, 2 vols. (Bethany, Va.: Campbell, 1829), I, 120 (15 Apr., forenoon).

[11]See "The Address of Robert Owen, at the Great Public Meeting, . . . on the 1st of May, 1833, Denouncing the Old System of the World, and Announcing the Commencement of the New," *The Crisis*, II (11 May, 1833), 141. The passage is quoted in App. G, 472-3 below.

[12]See Mill's letters to Sarah Austin and to Thomas Carlyle, *EL, CW*, XII, 116 (13 Sept., 1832) and 117 (17 Sept., 1832).

[13]*Ibid.*, 117.

[14]Printed respectively in *CW*, IV, 193-222, and *CW*, I, 327-39.

in the review; in any case the first generation of Philosophic Radicals had engaged both theoretically and practically in the controversies over Lancasterian and National Schools that occupy much space in Mill's review, especially in the long quotations from Biber. Mill also quotes from his own "Corporation and Church Property," modifying the wording slightly as indicated in the variant notes:[15] one merits mention here. Everywhere and always, Mill says in the original essay, and in its reprint in *Dissertations and Discussions*, "enlightened individuals and enlightened governments should . . . bestir themselves to provide (though by no means forcibly to impose) that good and wholesome food for the wants of the mind" that "the mere trading market" does not supply (65-6). As quoted in his review of Sarah Austin, the passage lacks the parenthesis, and it may be that at this particular time (though only a year had passed since the first version in "Corporation and Church Property") Mill had entered one of his fiercer moods, and was less reluctant to restrain benevolent leaders.

The next two items, short reviews separated in time by seven years, reflect Mill's continued interest in legal questions, especially those having to do with reform. "On Punishment" (1834) gives some hints of attitudes seen in newspaper articles of the 1850s by Harriet and John Mill, in *Remarks on Mr. Fitzroy's Bill*, and in his later comments on justifications for corporal and capital punishment. It is the earliest of the pieces in this volume to have textual corrections based on Mill's emendations in his own copy in the Somerville College Library; all such corrections are described in the headnotes.

The second of these short reviews, "Smith on Law Reform" (1841), was written when Mill, though busy finishing his *System of Logic* for the press, felt obliged to help work off a debt to William Hickson, who had taken over the *Westminster Review* from him in the preceding year. It presents no textual problems.

While there is another gap of nine years between that review and the next essay, "The Negro Question" (1850), one should not infer that Mill lacked interest in issues of equality, law, or education during the 1840s, which was one of his greatest decades as an author.[16] Indeed, "The Negro Question," occasioned by Carlyle's "Occasional Discourse on the Negro Question,"[17] was Mill's second public disagreement on questions of justice and equality with his earlier intimate, for he had responded, in "England and Ireland" (*Examiner*, 13 May, 1848), to an article by Carlyle advocating forceful subjugation of the Irish anarchy. From this time, justice between blacks and whites became a leading theme in Mill's writings, as the later essays in this volume clearly indicate. The attack on Carlyle was

[15]Most of the variants record changes made when "Corporation and Church Property" was revised for *Dissertations and Discussions*.

[16]Of special relevance are his "Claims of Labour" (1845), his extended series of newspaper leading articles on Ireland (1846-47), and the 1st (1848) and 2nd (1849) eds. of his *Principles of Political Economy*.

[17]Carlyle, totally contemptuous of Mill's response, lengthened his diatribe and republished it with the title altered to "The Nigger Question."

reprinted in the *Daily News*, with three substantive and several accidental variants; the substantive changes are given here in notes although there is no reason to think the reprinted text was supervised by Mill.[18]

The next item is Mill's formal moral renunciation of the legal powers that would result from his impending marriage to Harriet Taylor, written on 6 March, prior to their wedding on 21 April, 1851.[19] The text is taken from the facsimile reproduced in Hugh S.R. Elliot's edition of Mill's letters;[20] the present location of the manuscript is unknown. It is not surprising that chronologically the preceding items in the present volume are Harriet Taylor's fragments (here printed in Appendix B), and the succeeding ones are her "Enfranchisement of Women" (Appendix C) and the pamphlet *Remarks on Mr. Fitzroy's Bill*, in all of which the abuse of power in sexual and familial relations is central. The last of these, the pamphlet, prompted by the introduction in Parliament on 10 March, 1853, of a bill to improve the protection of women and children from assaults, was jointly written by the two Mills.[21] At this time Mill was publishing little, though he was beginning, with his wife, to draft what was finally published as his *Autobiography*, and to sketch out other important essays, including *On Liberty* and *Utilitarianism*.[22]

In the year after his wife's death in 1858 came a great burst of books and articles, many of the latter on political issues, such as "A Few Words on Non-Intervention" (*Fraser's Magazine*, December, 1859), the first of the items in this volume to have been reprinted in full by Mill himself. It is also the first to be explicitly mentioned in the *Autobiography*, where Mill explains his being prompted to write it by a desire to defend England against imputations of habitual selfishness in foreign affairs, and to account for the colour given to such imputations by the "low tone" of governmental pronouncements and behaviour (especially Palmerston's).[23] This

---

[18]The change at 92[b-b] shows someone correcting a first-person singular non-emphatic "will" to "shall," a solecism that my mentor A.S.P. Woodhouse, with quite unnecessary exaggeration, said no Englishman was ignorant enough to commit, and no Scot learned enough to avoid (he was implicating me, like Mill a second-generation Scot).

[19]That Mill did not view the marriage with insouciance is shown even more in the letter he wrote to his wife *fifteen months* after their union in the Registry Office at Melcombe Regis, suggesting that because his signature in the register was irregular, they should be married again—in a church (*LL*, XIV, 96-7).

[20]*The Letters of John Stuart Mill*, 2 vols. (London: Longmans, Green, 1910); the printed text in Elliot (I, 158-9), has in the concluding sentence one manifest error, "pretence" for "pretension".

[21]This echo of the title of Gertrude Himmelfarb's book on Mill is somewhat ironical, but unavoidable. Mill, in his bibliography of his published writings, says of this pamphlet: "In this I acted chiefly as amanuensis to my wife." As we cannot apportion responsibility for parts of this work, we have included it, like other "joint productions" (to use Mill's usual term)—which include the *Principles* and *On Liberty*—in the text proper rather than in an appendix.

[22]He also made, with her help, very extensive revisions of the 3rd eds. of both *A System of Logic, Ratiocinative and Inductive* (1851) and the *Principles* (1852). For comment on the former, see John M. Robson, "'Joint Authorship' Again: The Evidence in the Third Edition of Mill's *Logic*," *Mill News Letter*, VI (Spring, 1971), 15-20.

[23]*Autobiography*, *CW*, I, 263-4.

retrospective account is borne out by a letter of 14 November, 1859, to Alexander Bain, in which he also says he has just sent the article from Avignon to J.W. Parker for December publication in *Fraser's*.[24] He had the article offprinted (without revision), hoping it would have quick public effect, and was pleased with the response.[25] The reprint in *Dissertations and Discussions* reveals very few changes;[26] in this respect it is typical of Mill's essays revised between 1859 and 1867 for Volume III of *Dissertations and Discussions* (which then first appeared, along with the 2nd edition of Volumes I and II).

"The Contest in America" (*Fraser's*, February, 1862) was also reprinted in Volume III of *Dissertations and Discussions*. That reprinting suggests the importance Mill attached to this (and of course the preceding) essay, though a glance at the contents of Volume III shows that one criterion he had established in his Preface to the first two volumes in 1859 was somewhat loosely interpreted; he had excluded papers dominated by comments "on passing events."[27] Because his more enduring attitudes are also expressed, no question would be raised were it not that the companion essay (also 1862), "The Slave Power," which moreover was a review of a work by his great friend John Elliot Cairnes, was not reprinted in the British version of *Dissertations and Discussions*. In any case, Mill thought "The Contest in America" had been timely and influential. He had withheld public comment on the American war because of the *Trent* incident; feelings over it having abated, he wrote the essay quickly in mid-January while in Avignon.[28] Writing to William T. Thornton before the essay appeared in the February number of *Fraser's*, Mill said his views, if noticed at all, would probably be much attacked, as opposed to the "tone of the press & of English opinion, a tone which," he remarks, "has caused me more disgust than anything has done for a long time."[29] Reports of the article's reception cheered him,[30] and his retrospective view in the *Autobiography* is self-congratulatory or—more accurately—congratulatory of Helen Taylor:

. . . I shall always feel grateful to my daughter that her urgency prevailed on me to write it when I did: for we were then on the point of setting out for a journey of some months in Greece and Turkey, and but for her, I should have deferred writing till our return. Written

[24]*LL, CW*, XV, 646. Mill, still in Avignon, received the number through the post on 8 Dec. (*ibid.*, 652).

[25]*Ibid.*, to Edwin Chadwick, 655 (20 Dec., 1859).

[26]Normally spelling changes are not recorded in our variant notes, but here the change from "rivality" to "rivalry" is given, as calling attention to a different form, also used in a manuscript by Mill (114).

[27]The Preface is reprinted as App. A, *Essays on Ethics, Religion, and Society, CW*, X; see 493.

[28]See letters to George Grote and Cairnes, *LL, CW*, XV, 764 (10 Jan., 1862) and 767 (20 Jan., 1862).

[29]*Ibid.*, 774 (28 Jan., 1862). Cf. the discussion in the Introduction, xxiii above.

[30]In letters to Henry Fawcett, Cairnes, and Theodor Gomperz, *ibid.*, 776 (6 Mar., 1862), 783 (15 June, 1862), and 809 (14 Dec., 1862). In the second of these he qualifies his apparently favourable judgment on Seward's despatch "as a whole" in response to Cairnes' dissatisfaction.

and published when it was, the paper helped to encourage those Liberals who had felt overborne by the tide of illiberal opinion, and to form in favour of the good cause a nucleus of opinion which increased gradually, and after the success of the North began to seem probable, rapidly. When we returned from our journey I wrote a second article, a review of Professor Cairnes' book published in the *Westminster Review*. England is paying the penalty, in many uncomfortable ways, of the durable resentment which her ruling classes stirred up in the United States by their ostentatious wishes for the ruin of America as a nation; they have reason to be thankful that a few, if only a few known writers and speakers, standing firmly by the Americans in the time of their greatest difficulty, effected a partial diversion of these bitter feelings, and made Great Britain not altogether odious to the Americans.[31]

The essay was offprinted in a textually unchanged version,[32] and published as a pamphlet in Boston (Little, Brown, 1862) that went through two printings within a year. Of the changes between the versions in *Fraser's* and in *Dissertations and Discussions* only one is important, the addition of a long footnote at 133, consisting mostly of quotation from a letter from Wendell Phillips correcting Mill's statements about the Abolitionists. Of the minor alterations, perhaps the most interesting (as typical of Mill's search for the accurate word) is his describing Henry Carey as a "high authority" in 1862 and an "unimpeachable" one in 1867 (132^{e-e}).

The review of Cairnes' *The Slave Power*, as suggested above, is closely related to "The Contest in America" in time as well as theme; it appeared, however, in the *Westminster* rather than *Fraser's*, was not offprinted by Mill, and was excluded from the British *Dissertations and Discussions*. Like "The Contest in America" it was published as a pamphlet in the United States, and was included in American editions of *Dissertations and Discussions*. There is no indication that these versions were supervised by Mill, so our copy-text is the original and only British version; but substantive variants in the American versions, all minor, are given in notes.[33] The epistolary record will make twentieth-century authors again sorrowful that technological progress has made haste rather less than slowly. While travelling with his stepdaughter after completing "The Contest in America," Mill offered to review Cairnes for the *Westminster*. John Chapman, its editor, having accepted, Mill—now back in Avignon—promised on 31 August, 1862, to have it to Chapman by 20 September at the latest, as it was important to call attention to Cairnes' book as soon as possible.[34] He actually sent the review from Avignon on 11 September, asking for proof or, if there was not time, to have

[31]*CW*, I, 268.

[32]One typographical error was introduced, another was not corrected, and the page numbers were changed.

[33]One change in the pamphlet, from "round" to "around", is not so recorded. The accidentals show undoubted intervention on the western side of the ocean: for example, where Mill uses a quotation of Cairnes from Clay, both have "neighbours" for Clay's "neighbors"—but the American versions delete the non-U.S. "u."

[34]*LL, CW*, XV, 788, 789.

"some careful person . . . collate the proof with the manuscript." But there was time, and thirteen days later, after two postal journeys between Avignon and London, setting, and proof-correction, the last page of proof was returned to Chapman.[35]

The intimacy that obtained between Mill and the Austins in the 1820s and '30s did not survive political and personal differences in the late '40s; indeed, when John Austin died late in 1859, Mill acknowledged his debt to him in a note to their granddaughter, Janet Duff-Gordon, without even mentioning Sarah.[36] He brought himself, however, shortly thereafter, to recommend to her that all of her husband's lectures be published, revised only to remove the repetitions; when the 2nd edition of the *Province* appeared in 1861, Mill actually defended those repetitions as necessary in lectures to students, against the criticism of James Fitzjames Stephen in the *Edinburgh*.[37] In assembling her husband's manuscripts, Sarah Austin found some gaps in the lectures; Mill, hearing of the problem, wrote to Henry Reeve, her nephew, offering his notes taken thirty years earlier, "to supply, in however imperfect a manner, the hiatus."[38] This typical meticulousness led to the restoration of important parts of the text, particularly much of Lecture 39 and all of Lecture 40, when, six years later, Robert Campbell prepared a so-called 3rd edition of the *Lectures on Jurisprudence*.[39]

To avoid confusion about the status of the edition Mill reviewed in October, 1863, a few words about the publishing history of Austin's lectures are needed. The edition he reviewed is known as the 2nd, and Campbell's is known as the 3rd, but those identifications are not exactly right: the 2nd edition of the *Province*, published in 1861, was also designated as Volume I of the three-volume edition of the *Lectures* in 1863 (the version Mill reviewed, though the original heading of his article refers to them as separate works, and in his notes he cites Volumes II and III as Volumes I and II). That is, Volumes II and III of the *Lectures on Jurisprudence* first appeared, and that title was first used, in 1863, so the edition of 1869 was really the 2nd, not the 3rd, edition of the *Lectures*, though (counting the 1861 and 1863 issues as one edition) it was the 3rd of the *Province* (though that title was not separately used in 1869). The matter is even further complicated by the issuance in 1863 as a separate publication of *On the Uses of Jurisprudence* "from the Third Volume of 'Lectures on Jurisprudence'"; in the heading of Mill's article it is so identified, although, as mentioned above, the *Lectures* are said in that heading to consist of only two volumes.

[35]*Ibid.*, 792, 798.
[36]*Ibid.*, 658.
[37]*Ibid.*, 674 (10 Feb., 1860), and 757-8 (20 Dec., 1861).
[38]*Ibid.*, 822 (15 Jan., 1863); see also 823 (17 Jan., 1863), XVI, 1142-3 (30 Jan., 1866), and XVII, 1625 (26 July, 1869).
[39]London: Murray, 1869. There, in the "Advertisement to this Edition," I, v-vi, and again in a note at II, 705, Campbell explains the part Mill's notes played in his reconstruction of the text. (Apart from Lectures 39 and 40, Lectures 3, 4, 5, 22, 28, and 29 were improved and/or expanded.)

Mill's interest having been both stimulated and revealed to Austin and Reeve, it is not surprising that he reviewed the volumes, thus giving himself, as he says in the *Autobiography*, "an opportunity of paying a deserved tribute" to Austin's memory, and also of "expressing some thoughts on a subject on which, in my old days of Benthamism, I had bestowed much study."[40] Correspondence concerning the review itself has not survived, except in a letter to Henry Samuel Chapman of 5 October, 1863, which mentions that it is about to appear in the *Edinburgh*.[41] By that time Mill was occupied with the first draft of his *Examination of Sir William Hamilton's Philosophy* (completed by November), and was thinking of the form his judgments of Auguste Comte should take, and so, given the detail and length of the article, it is likely that he worked on it early in the year.[42] The close attention to the subject matter did not preclude the kind of personal touch that heightens the sense of mastery, as in the indications that he heard the lectures (179, 204), and had knowledge of the manuscripts (192). There is also an echo (though the terms of the metaphor have altered) of his earlier assessments of Bentham, who is here portrayed as employing a "battering ram" rather than a "builder's trowel" (168). And there is another reflection that Mill himself may not have been conscious of, and that his contemporaries certainly could not have seen: in saying that Austin "has been in nothing more useful than in forming the minds by which he is, and will hereafter be, judged" (167), Mill comes very close to the views expressed by his wife and himself about their role as guides for the future.[43]

Like other articles of this period, the review of Austin was little revised for republication. It was offprinted without alterations, and only five minor changes (including two reflecting the difference in provenance and two corrections of misprints) were made for *Dissertations and Discussions*. There are rather more accidental changes than usual, probably because the *Edinburgh*'s preferred spellings ("s" rather than "z" in participles and hyphens inserted in some compound words) and punctuation (especially lighter use of commas) differed more from Longman's (and Mill's) style than did that of the other journals printing his essays at the time.

The next few years brought Mill to the height of his public acclaim as new books and editions poured forth and his election as M.P. for Westminster highlighted his ideas and public character. One inevitable result was a great increase in requests for opinions and appearances, his occasional compliance with which is witnessed in the next two items in this volume, his evidence to the Taunton Schools Inquiry Commission and his *Inaugural Address* at St. Andrews. Anticipating a request for

[40]*Autobiography, CW*, I, 268.

[41]*LL, CW*, XV, 889.

[42]He spent the first part of the year in London, going to Avignon for April and May, returning to London in June, and then again to Avignon from September until January, 1864. From April to June he was troubled by Theodore Gomperz's unrequited infatuation with Helen Taylor.

[43]See, for one of the less attractive statements, his letter to her of 29 Jan., 1854 (*LL, CW*, XIV, 141-2).

his opinion on educational endowments, he wrote on 21 May, 1866, to his lifelong friend Edwin Chadwick for information and advice; Chadwick, ever willing, complied, and some time in the next two months, busy as Mill was with political affairs (the great Hyde Park Reform agitation occurred in July, when he also assumed the Chair of the Jamaica Committee), he sent a draft of his paper to Chadwick for comment. He requested its return on 5 August, and, having made "various alterations and insertions" to comply with those comments, sent his answers to the Commission on 9 August, at the same time conveying his thanks to Chadwick.[44] The text, taken from *Parliamentary Papers*, has been altered slightly to conform to that used in this edition for all of Mill's interrogations and evidence for parliamentary committees and royal commissions; the most significant typographical feature is the placing of the questions in italic type to contrast with the roman of Mill's answers.

The other item directly related to Mill's public stature is his *Inaugural Address* delivered to the University of St. Andrews on 1 February, 1867, and quickly published in an edition of 1000 copies, a 2nd edition of 500 being called for in the same month, and a cheap People's Edition of 2000 copies in March, with another issue of 1000 in June. The students, in electing Mill Rector, were obviously partaking in a widespread expectation of sagacity from him, and seeking to honour him, rather than to have him serve them in very material ways.[45] The general rather than local aims—though the praise of Scottish universities and the concluding references to theological studies show his attention to *pathos* and *ethos*[46]—are clear in the few sentences he gives to the *Address* in his *Autobiography*:

In this Discourse I gave expression to many thoughts and opinions which had been accumulating in me through life respecting the various studies which belong to a liberal education, their uses and influences, and the mode in which they should be pursued to render those influences most beneficial. The position I took up, vindicating the high educational value alike of the old classic and the new scientific studies, on even stronger grounds than are urged by most of their advocates, and insisting that it is only the stupid inefficiency of the usual teaching which makes those studies be regarded as competitors instead of allies, was, I think, calculated, not only to aid and stimulate the improvement which has happily commenced in the national institutions for higher education, but to diffuse juster ideas than we often find even in highly educated men on the conditions of the highest mental cultivation.[47]

This account suggests both the time and the care he spent in preparing the *Address* (probably in Avignon, where he spent much of the inter-parliamentary recess);

[44]*Ibid.*, XVI, 1168, 1172, 1187-8, 1190.

[45]For details of his election and his performance of Rectorial duties, see Anna J. Mill, "The First Ornamental Rector at St. Andrews University," *Scottish Historical Review*, XLIII (1964), 131-44.

[46]Cf. Bain, *John Stuart Mill*, 128.

[47]*CW*, I, 287. Of the specific notions in the *Address*, several permit of fuller elucidation than they have received; in one place, for instance, he makes the point later fully elucidated by R. H. Tawney, saying that British character has been shaped since the Stuarts by two influences: "commercial money-getting business, and religious Puritanism" (253).

however, he gave little time to St. Andrews, arriving only on 31 January, and leaving again on 2 February for two speaking engagements in Manchester before returning to London on the 5th. (This flurry of activity outside London was quite untypical; Mill delivered public speeches rarely, even during his parliamentary career, and almost always in London.) He undoubtedly had a printed version in mind from the beginning, though perhaps he thought a three-hour speech was fitting to the occasion. The full transcription of his speech in those capacious repositories, the contemporary newspapers, as well as the quick publication in book form, gave publicity to his ideas, and the response to them was generally favourable, though, as Stefan Collini points out (liii-liv above), there was criticism of his support for classical studies. The *Address* was widely read in the United States (it appeared in *Littell's Living Age*, in book form, and in the U.S. editions of *Dissertations and Discussions*); it was, like almost all his works, quickly translated into German, and, unusually, into Hungarian.

The printed text is uncomplicated, with but one variant, probably from the compositor's misreading of "lines" for "times." A portion of what would appear to be a first draft exists, which differs in a multitude of details from the printed version; the differences are so numerous that attention to them might divert the reader from the main argument, and so they are given in Appendix D, as variant notes to the fragment in its draft version.

The *Inaugural Address* provides a broad and relatively objective survey of many of Mill's concerns, public and private; the second book in this volume, *The Subjection of Women*, gives his fullest argument for the most passionately felt of these, sexual equality. The book's antecedents may be inferred in part from other items here included: the companion essays on marriage, the fragments printed in Appendix B, and Harriet Mill's "Enfranchisement of Women" (Appendix C). Mill so determinedly and correctly asserted that his attitude to sexual equality preceded her teaching of him that his main statement deserves quotation in full:

The steps in my mental growth for which I was indebted to her were far from being those which a person wholly uninformed on the subject would probably suspect. It might be supposed, for instance, that my strong convictions on the complete equality in all legal, political, social and domestic relations, which ought to exist between men and women, may have been adopted or learnt from her. This was so far from being the fact, that those convictions were among the earliest results of the application of my mind to political subjects, and the strength with which I held them was, as I believe, more than anything else, the originating cause of the interest she felt in me. What is true is, that until I knew her, the opinion was, in my mind, little more than an abstract principle. I saw no more reason why women should be held in legal subjection to other people, than why men should. I was certain that their interests required fully as much protection as those of men, and were quite as little likely to obtain it without an equal voice in making the laws by which they are to be bound. But that perception of the vast practical bearings of women's disabilities which found expression in the book on *The Subjection of Women*, was acquired mainly through her teaching. But for her rare knowledge of human nature and comprehension of moral and social influences, though I should doubtless have held my present opinions I should have had a very insufficient perception of the mode in which the consequences of the inferior position of women intertwine themselves with all the evils of existing society and with all the difficulties of human improvement. I am indeed painfully conscious how much of her best thoughts on the subject I have failed to reproduce, and how greatly that little treatise falls short of what would have been given to the world if she had put on paper her entire mind on this question, or had lived to revise and improve, as she certainly would have done, my imperfect statement of the case.[48]

It seems likely, though not provable, that the priority of publication of her "Enfranchisement of Women" in 1851 inhibited the preparation of a fuller work by them together or by him alone. When, three years later, they were planning their life's work, their list of subjects only hints at aspects of the question.[49] "Differences of character," including those arising from sex, "Love," "Education of tastes," "Family & Conventional," all bear some relation to the themes of *The Subjection of Women*, but none is specially close except the first (which clearly suggests the "Ethology" that Mill never wrote) and the last two (which, especially the final one, are touched on in Harriet Taylor's manuscript fragments). A month later, in March, 1854, however, when they agreed not to accept John Chapman's request to reprint the "Enfranchisement," a work more specifically like *The Subjection of Women* is implied. "I think that to refuse was best, on the whole," Mill writes to his wife, "for I should not like any more than you that that paper should be supposed to be the best we could do, or the real expression of our mind on the subject. . . . I only wish the better thing we have promised to write were already written instead of being in prospect."[50] It remained in prospect, however, until 1860, when Mill felt ready to put down his own thoughts at length. Writing to Henry Fawcett on 24 December, he remarked that he had finished two works (*Considerations on Representative Government* and *Utilitarianism*), and had "made good progress with a third," that is, *The Subjection of Women*.[51] It was, like most of his other works, including the other two just mentioned, not occasional, and his explanation in the *Autobiography* of its genesis and delayed publication is plausible if not fully conclusive:

It was written at my daughter's suggestion that there might, in any event, be in existence a written exposition of my opinions on that great question, as full and conclusive as I could make it. The intention was to keep this among other unpublished papers, improving it from time to time if I was able, and to publish it at the time when it should seem likely to be most useful. As ultimately published it was enriched with some important ideas of my daughter's, and passages of her writing. But in what was of my own composition, all that is

---

[48]*Autobiography*, *CW*, I, 253n.

[49]The full list reads (in "confused order," as Mill said): "Differences of character (nation, race, age, sex, temperament). Love. Education of tastes. Religion de l'Avenir. Plato. Slander. Foundation of morals. Utility of religion. Socialism. Liberty. Doctrine that causation is will. To these," already agreed on, he continues, "I have now added from your letter: Family, & Conventional" (*LL*, *CW*, XIV, 152 [7 Feb., 1854]). For comment on most of these see *CW*, X, cxxii-cxxiv.

[50]*LL*, *CW*, XIV, 189-90 (20 Mar., 1854).

[51]*Ibid.*, XV, 716.

most striking and profound belongs to my wife; coming from the fund of thought which had been made common to us both, by our innumerable conversations and discussions on a topic which filled so large a place in our minds.[52]

At any rate, when he decided to publish the book in 1869, after his help in founding and promoting the Women's Suffrage Society and his advocacy of the cause in the House of Commons, he seems to have chosen his time well. Three British editions, each of 1500 copies, appeared in May, June, and October, 1869, and two in the United States in that year; and it was translated almost immediately into French, Danish, German, Italian, Polish, and Russian.[53] Even a casual glance through Mill's correspondence for 1869 and 1870 will show just how much interest and admiration *The Subjection of Women* earned; indeed, on the surviving evidence, no other of his works drew so much immediate correspondence. (The comparison is of course skewed because both his public position and his circle of acquaintance were greater in 1869 than when his earlier works appeared.)

As well as enthusiastic supporters, and such vituperative opponents as J.F. Stephen, there were some allies who thought Mill's message was untimely if not excessive; Bain was one, and Mill's reply to him strongly asserts the ripeness of the time. Mill's impassioned plea, too long for full quotation here, deserves to be read, but Bain's subdued summary gives the sense:

> Without entering into an argument with him on his equality view, I expressed my doubts as to the expediency of putting this more strongly than people generally would be willing to accept; inasmuch as the equality of rights did not presuppose absolute equality of faculties. He replied with much warmth, contending that the day of a temporizing policy was past; that it was necessary to show, not simply that the removal of restrictions would leave things as they are, but that many women are really capable of taking advantage of the higher openings. And further, he urged, it was necessary to stimulate the aspirations of women themselves, so as to obtain proofs from experience as to what they could do.[54]

The rapid exhaustion of the first two editions meant that Mill had little time to reconsider, and so it is not surprising that the only textual change is the correction in the 2nd edition of a misprint ("progressive" for "progessive" at 276.16), or that one evident error remained in all editions ("she" at 324.20, corrected in this edition

---

[52]*CW*, I, 265; he habitually referred to his stepdaughter, Helen Taylor, as his daughter. Later in the *Autobiography*, in his one-paragraph concluding summary of his post-parliamentary career, he says: "I . . . have published *The Subjection of Women*, written some years before, with some additions by my daughter and myself . . ." (*ibid.*, 290). It cannot be superfluous, in the light of these disclaimers, to point to some isolated passages that show his personal touch: for example, the echo of Bentham's tone and terminology in the reference to "the power of the scold, or the shrewish sanction" (289); the claim to personal knowledge of Indian government (303n); the comment, going back to discussions with his father, that "sensibility to the present, is the main quality on which the capacity for practice, as distinguished from theory, depends" (305); the typical notion that echoes the passage here being footnoted, that men verify and work out women's original thoughts (316); and, perhaps strongest of all, the account of feelings on emerging from boyhood (337).

[53]It is surprising that *The Subjection of Women* is not listed in Mill's bibliography of his published writings, but perhaps the amanuensis simply failed to copy the entry.

[54]Bain, *John Stuart Mill*, 131; for Mill's statement see *LL, CW*, XVII, 1623-4 (letter to Bain, 14 July, 1869).

to "he"). Like *On Liberty* and *Utilitarianism*, *The Subjection of Women* has few even implicit references; unlike them, and in this respect unique among Mill's books, for no evident reason it lacks chapter titles.

The campaign for women's rights occupied much of Mill's time and energy for the remainder of his life, sharing primacy with the movement for reform of land tenure, but he, deeply concerned like many others over the European situation, did not ignore international relations. "Treaty Obligations," published over his name in the *Fortnightly Review* in December, 1870, shows his concern, as do the associated letters he wrote to *The Times*. They were, indeed, written at the same time, for the letters appeared on 19 and 24 November, and Mill returned the proofs of "Treaty Obligations" on the 28th.[55] In her continuation of Mill's *Autobiography*, Helen Taylor refers to the publication of the article, and says:

he also wrote two letters to the *Times* in the month of November 1870 on the same topic. They were called forth by a cry, that arose at that time in a portion of the English press, for plunging England into a war with Russia. They were the first protest that appeared in any well known name against such a war; they called forth others and helped to calm down the warlike excitement that was being aroused.[56]

Again the text provides no problems: the article was not republished in Mill's lifetime, and the posthumous version in Volume IV of *Dissertations and Discussions* (1875), edited by Helen Taylor, shows a corrected typographical error (a comma was removed), one minor substantive ("which" changed to "that", a change purists wish had been more often made in Mill's works), and one altered spelling ("s" to "z" in "demoralizing").

The final item in the main text is Mill's evidence, given on 13 May, 1871, before the Royal Commission on the Contagious Diseases Acts of 1866 and 1869. Busy as ever, he was engaged—aided, abetted, and led by Helen Taylor—in controversy over leadership of the women's suffrage movement,[57] and active in the Land Tenure Reform Association, having written its *Explanatory Statement* in March, and making a speech for it on 15 May. He also published "Maine on Village Communities" in that month, and was understandably fussed over getting rid of his Blackheath house, where he had lived since his marriage, preparatory to moving to his last London home in apartments in Victoria Street. He must have had little time to consider the details of the administration and operation of the Contagious Diseases Acts, of which he certainly had no personal knowledge, and so his answers, firm and persistent, draw, as Stefan Collini argues, on principle and reason, not facts and induction.

The text presents problems that are disguised in other cases where Mill's oral

---

[55]With the proofs went his offer (cf. xi above) to act as editor of the *Fortnightly* while Morley regained his strength.

[56]*CW*, I, 626.

[57]One reason for the split was the desire of Mill's group, the London National Society for Women's Suffrage, to dissociate itself officially from the campaign to repeal the Contagious Diseases Acts, despite their admitted noxiousness. See *LL*, *CW*, XVII, 1818n.

evidence is included in this edition, because here there are two versions, one in *Parliamentary Papers* and one in a pamphlet issued by the National Association for the Repeal of the Contagious Diseases Acts that says on its title page, quite wrongly, "Reprinted Verbatim from the Blue Book." Under normal circumstances, which there is no reason to believe did not obtain, the evidence in the Blue Books gives what the recorder took down, amended—not by the witness—merely to ensure sense. Nothing is known that would indicate Mill's control over the pamphlet text, and neither version is in Mill's library, and so one is left with two differing versions with competing authority. It appears, however, that the pamphlet was printed, if not verbatim, at least on the basis of the Blue Book, and not from some version amended by Mill or another.[58] The later version has some evident corrections ("fail" for "fall" at 365.40, and "care" for "cure" at 366.47), and in general the pamphlet reflects some attention to clarity. We therefore have adopted it as copy-text, but have given the variant readings from *Parliamentary Papers* in notes,[59] and accepted, where sense and consistency demanded, some accidentals from the earlier version. (The resisted urge to do more emendation was very strong, as will be realized by anyone who has seen supposedly verbatim reports of her or his lectures or conversation.) The format, as with all such verbal evidence, has been slightly modified to ease reading: questions are italicized; the "*Q.*" and "*A.*" that precede questions and answers in the pamphlet version are omitted, as are the numbers of the questions in the Blue Book version; and the full names of the commission members are given before the first question each asks.

APPENDICES

THE APPENDED MATERIALS are of four kinds: (a) essays and fragments by Harriet Taylor, before and after her marriage to Mill, that are cognate to his writings on sexual equality, and in the writing of which he had an indirect or even a direct hand, (b) a draft fragment in his hand, (c) material that is not certainly of Mill's own composition, though issued over his name with his authority, and (d) editorial materials.

In the first group fall Appendices A, B, and C. The first of these is Harriet Taylor's early essay,[60] which we have entitled, like Mill's companion piece, "On Marriage" (see above, lviii-lx).[61] The evidence for dating, as indicated above, is

---

[58]For instance, errors in the Blue Book are repeated in the pamphlet; and one word in the pamphlet is hyphenated to reproduce an end-of-line hyphen in the Blue Book, while elsewhere in both versions it appears as one word.

[59]It should be noted that more than half the variants occur in the questions put to Mill, rather than in his answers.

[60]For a description of the manuscript, see n. 6 above.

[61]The manuscript is accompanied by two drafts, which are reprinted, with commentary, in John M. Robson, "Harriet Taylor on Marriage: Two Fragments," *Mill News Letter*, XVIII (Summer, 1983), 2-6.

slight. One related fragment is on paper watermarked 1831; the other, closer to our text, is like it on paper watermarked 1832.[62] So we have contented ourselves with the rather hollow certainty that her essay is of the same unascertained but probable date as his, i.e., 1832-33. The essay is of interest biographically, and also as tending to support, if not confirm, his assertion about her role in giving him ideas that he developed. The most obvious one here is in the concluding sentence, "It is for you . . . to teach, such as may be taught, that the higher the *kind* of enjoyment, the greater the *degree* . . ."; this hint, coupled as it is with the notion of the lofty "poetic nature," adumbrates a central issue in Mill's ethics.

Appendix B is made up of five items that we attribute jointly to Harriet Taylor and J.S. Mill. They are all in Mill's hand, except the title of the first and some corrections on the first and fourth, which are in hers, but that title, "Rights of Women—and Especially with Regard to the Elective Franchise—By a Woman—Dedicated to Queen Victoria," the character, tone, and syntax of the pieces, and our slight knowledge of their working habits, all suggest that Mill wrote them at her dictation and/or copied them from now lost drafts in her hand. They all, in subject and in argument, can be interpreted as preliminary to her "Enfranchisement of Women" (discussed below), especially as the paper that is watermarked is of 1847, but there is no reference to them in extant correspondence or memoirs.

The first and most extensive is on paper of 1847.[63] The editorial notes indicate where Taylor's changes can be made out (she made alterations in pencil that Mill traced over in ink), and where the length of text on a side suggests piece-meal composition.

The text of the second manuscript, entitled in Mill's hand "Women—(Rights of)," is reconstructed from two now separate items in the Mill-Taylor Collection.[64] No explanation has been found for the curious condition of this manuscript: the first two sheets having been cut in half, Taylor pencilled a circled "A" at the end of the text on f. 1r and a circled "B" at the end of f. 2r of No. 2; she then, in the blank space at the bottom of 3v, wrote (all in faded pencil, except for the first

---

[62]Harriet Taylor's hand has provided no good clues: the most promising feature, an occasional long "s," appears on other fragments in the collection on paper of 1831 and of 1832, but not in these manuscripts and not later; one might therefore infer that these are later than other fragments written on paper of the same date, but the evidence is too slight for confident assertion. Indeed almost all of her extant papers are in Box III of the collection, mostly on paper of 1832 and (less commonly) of 1831, but this chance survival does not justify a conclusion that she was specially stimulated to begin much, but finish nothing, in the early 1830s.

[63]Mill-Taylor Collection, Vol. XLI, No. 2, numbered 22 to 31, watermarked "J Whatman 1847." It consists of five sheets, c. 37.0 cm. x 22.7 cm., folded to make twenty sides, c. 18.4 cm. x 22.7 cm. (the last two sheets interfolded, so that the fourth sheet makes ff. 13-14, 19-20), written recto and verso, numbered by Mill on every fourth folio in the top right corner. There are current cancellations and interlinings in Mill's hand, occasionally confirming in ink changes made in pencil by Taylor.

[64]*Ibid.*, ff. 15-17, and 6, ff. 50-1. No. 2 consists of three separate slips written recto and verso, the first two cut across between lines of text; all are c. 18.4 cm. broad, the height being, respectively, c. 12.7 cm., 15.2 cm., and 22.8 cm. The third is in fact full size, for the two scraps making up No. 6, ff. 50-1, are the missing bits of No. 2; measuring respectively c. 10.1 cm. x 18.5 cm.and 7.6 cm. x 18.5 cm., they fit exactly (by text and watermark as well as measurement) the first two scraps of No. 2. The watermark is again "[J Wh]atman [1]847."

twenty words of "B," where the pencil has been inked over), following a circled "A" and "B," the same words that Mill wrote in ink on 1r and 2r of No. 6—i.e., the parts of 1r and 2r of No. 2 that were cut off. Also, after the first word on No. 6, f. 1v ("extinction."), which ends a paragraph, she has pencilled "Rights of women." Whatever the explanation, there can be no doubt that the sequence of scraps is (as here published) No. 2, f. 1r; No. 6, f. 1r; No. 2, f. 1v; No. 6, f. 1v; No. 2, f. 2r; No. 6, f. 2v (because the slip is bound in backwards); No. 2, f. 2v; No. 6, f. 2r; No. 2, f. 3r; No. 2, f. 3v (top half).

The third manuscript, headed rather ungrammatically in Mill's hand "The Rights of Women to the Elective Franchise and Its Advantages," is clearly an outline rather than a finished document or even a draft.[65] The fourth manuscript, headed in Mill's hand "Why Women Are Entitled to the Suffrage,"[66] and the fifth unheaded manuscript[67] are even more patently outlines.

Although only preliminary workings, these are all informative, not least in their expressing radical feminist principles rather more openly than do "The Enfranchisement of Women" and *The Subjection of Women*. It may be noted incidentally that the title of the latter is adumbrated at the opening of the second paragraph of "Women—(Rights of)." Certainly the manuscripts indicate singly and collectively the extent to which questions of sexual equality were in the minds of Taylor and Mill in the late 1840s when, it seems fair to say, their effective authorial collaboration was really beginning, as Mill's account in the *Autobiography* of her part in *Principles of Political Economy* and his dedication of that work to her assert so strongly.[68]

Appendix C, "The Enfranchisement of Women," was the only published expression of their views on sexual equality during Harriet Taylor Mill's lifetime. That the items included in Appendix B are related to its composition is suggested by Mill's letter to her of 21 February, 1849, wherein he says that the best contribution to improved relations between women and men would be for her to finish her "pamphlet—or little book rather, for it should be that." He adds: "I do hope you are going on with it—gone on with & finished & published it *must be*, & next season too."[69] That urgency was not complied with, but just over a year later, on 19 March, 1850, when writing to Hickson about the possibility of articles for the *Westminster*, Mill says that he may be moved to write on the whole question of the effect of laws and customs on the status of women.[70] The occasion for completing

---

[65]*Ibid.*, ff. 33-4. The identifying part of the watermark is not on this sheet, which is folded once to make two folios, c. 19.0 cm. x 22.8 cm., written 1r, 1v, 2r (top only).

[66]*Ibid.*, ff. 20-1. Again the identifying part of the watermark is not on this sheet, which is folded once to make two folios, c. 18.7 cm. x 22.5 cm., written 1r (1/4 left blank), 1v (2/5 left blank), 2r (1/4 left blank).

[67]*Ibid.*, f. 32. Once more the identifying part of the watermark is not on this single folio, c. 18.2 cm. x 22.1 cm., written recto only.

[68]See *CW*, I, 255-7, and III, 1026.

[69]*LL, CW*, XIV, 13.

[70]*Ibid.*, 47-8.

the essay came in October, when the *New York Tribune* reported on the Women's Rights Convention in Worcester, Massachusetts; here obviously was a chance to show advanced British opinion that the United States was leading the way. But the essay was not finished before 3 March, 1851, when Mill offered to send it to Hickson within a week for the April number of the *Westminster*.[71] Indeed, it was not quite ready even then, for, learning that the April number was full, Mill delayed a little further, but finally sent it for the July number (expressing relief that it escaped association with the "despicable trash" printed in the April number).[72] Hickson was at this time trying vainly to get Mill to reassume editorship of the review, but Mill, who had—after over twenty years of love—finally married Harriet Taylor on 21 April, seems not to have been seriously tempted.[73] In an undated letter, probably of late May, Mill wrote again to Hickson, to say that he wished to keep the proof, which had just arrived, as long as was convenient, it being "necessary on such a subject to be as far as possible invulnerable." "I have not," he continues, "quite fixed on a heading. The best I have thought of is 'Enfranchisement of Women.' The one you propose with the word 'sex' in it would never do. That word is enough to vulgarize a whole review. It is almost as bad as 'female.'"[74] The touchiness here evident is much more pronounced in the next letter to Hickson on 9 June:

I am surprised to see by the revise of my article that you have made two verbal alterations. I gave you the article on an understood consideration, the only one on which I ever write, that no alterations should be made by anyone but myself, & from this condition I cannot depart. I have returned the corrected revise to the printer. I should be obliged by your letting me have (if possible before the review is out) twenty-five separate copies, at my expense. I wish for no title page, but in place of it a page with only the words "Reprinted from the Westminster Review for July 1851." I should like to see a proof of the reprint.[75]

It will have been noted that in the correspondence with Hickson Mill consistently refers to the article as his own; because Hickson was familiar with Mill's handwriting, one may infer that the manuscript was in his hand (as are those in Appendix B). There is, therefore, on this evidence some uncertainty about authorship, and the essay has been attributed to Mill by some. As will be seen, however, most of the evidence lies in the other scale. Mill, it will be recalled, had urged Harriet Taylor to finish *her* "pamphlet" or "little book." After its publication (and their marriage), he wrote to Anna Blackwell, on 16 August, 1851, noting that the article was anonymous, and declining her attribution of it to him.[76] This is a quiet hint, but the next is more vehement: in a letter to his wife on 6 March, 1854, when reporting a letter from John Chapman proposing to reprint the article, which

[71]*Ibid.*, 55-6.
[72]*Ibid.*, 56 (10 Mar.), 56-7 (19 Mar.), and 61-2 (14 Apr.).
[73]*Ibid.*, 62 and 63 ([28?] and 29 Apr.).
[74]*Ibid.*, 66.
[75]*Ibid.*, 69.
[76]*Ibid.*, 75.

Chapman "vulgarly calls . . . the article on Woman," Mill says, "How *very* vulgar all his notes are. I am glad however that it is your permission he asks." He goes on to ask her what to do.[77] She, as always, complied, and he reported to her on 20 March:

I sent to Chapman the letter you drafted, exactly as it was, only choosing the phrases I preferred where you gave the choice of two. I think that to refuse was best, on the whole, for I should not like any more than you that that paper should be supposed to be the best we could do, or the real expression of our mind on the subject. This is not supposed of a mere review article written on a special occasion as that was, but would perhaps be so if the same thing were put out, years after, under our own auspices as a pamphlet. I only wish the better thing we have promised to write were already written instead of being in prospect. In any case the article will of course be in any collection or rather *se*lection of articles which we may either publish in our life, or leave for publication afterwards, & whichever we do it shall be preceded by a preface which will shew that much of all my later articles, & all the best of that one, were, as they were, my Darling's.[78]

On any assumption about authorship it is difficult to interpret the remark, "I should not like any more than you that that paper should be supposed to be the best we could do," and the comment that "the best" of the "Enfranchisement" was hers leaves open the interpretation that the rest, the "worst," was his. In the preface to the article when republished, he says more clearly that the essay is different from the "joint productions," in that his share in it was "little more than that of an editor and amanuensis" (393). He also elaborates the excuse for the essay's failure to do her mind justice, and says, in my view conclusively, that her authorship was known at the time. Indeed, in an angry letter to George Jacob Holyoake of 21 September, 1856, he is explicit on the subject:

On returning a few days ago from the Continent I found your note inclosing the reprint of my wife's article in the W.R. on the enfranchisement of women. I think you are not justified in reprinting it without asking the permission of the author which you could easily have done through me, still less with many errors in the reprint. I have marked the principal of them in the margin of the copy you sent. One particularly offensive is the excessive vulgarity of substituting "woman" for "Women"; this occurs in several places and in the first paragraph. One of the purposes of writing the article was to warn the American women to disunite their cause from the feeble sentimentality which exposes it to contempt & of which the stuff continually talked & written about "woman" may be taken as a symbol & test,—& it is therefore very disagreeable to the writer to see this piece of vulgarity prominent on the face of the article itself.[79]

And later, in 1865, in agreeing to the publication of his articles by his election

---

[77]*Ibid.*, 177.

[78]*Ibid.*, 189-90; part of this letter is quoted above (lxix) with reference to "the better thing," i.e., *The Subjection of Women.*

[79]*LL, CW*, XV, 509-10. In quoting from J.G. Forman's "Women's Rights Convention" in the "Enfranchisement," Harriet Mill was careful to alter the vulgar "Woman" to "women"; see the collation in App. G, 458-9 below.

committee, he says that if the "Enfranchisement" is reprinted, "it must be as my wife's, not as mine"; and in thanking Moncure Conway for his report of the article's value in the U.S.A., he comments on how much pleasure its author would have taken from the movement's progress, "had she lived to see it."[80] Finally, in preparing for the reprinting of the essay as a pamphlet, with "by Mrs. Stuart Mill" on the cover, he describes it to Herbert Spencer as "Mrs Mill's paper," and after the publication refers to it in correspondence as hers.[81] It is not fanciful, further, to see the delay in completing the article and the spiteful annoyance over details as not being characteristic of Mill in reference to writings unmistakably his own. One may safely conclude that the article is, on the common understanding of authorship, Harriet Taylor Mill's; on her and her husband's understanding, it is a "joint production"; but to accept that description here is surely to weaken the claim that she played a major role in those joint productions that appeared under his name. Attributing it to her, of course, again strengthens the case for her influence on Mill's thought (see the Introduction, xxxii above, for resemblances).

The transmission of text among the different versions seems clear: the original article (or its textually identical offprint) served as base text for the 1st edition of *Dissertations and Discussions*, in which nine substantive changes were introduced. The 2nd edition of *Dissertations and Discussions* was based on the first, four substantive changes being made. None of these appears in the pamphlet of 1868, and only one of the nine introduced in 1859 is seen there, while the pamphlet differs from all other versions in twenty-two substantives. The inference that the version of 1868 was based on that of 1851 is borne out by a study of the accidental variants, where in punctuation those two agree as against *Dissertations and Discussions* in sixteen cases compared with one agreement between 1868 and *Dissertations and Discussions* as against 1851.[82] No elaborate conclusions seem necessary or justified: it appears probable that Mill, having made the changes for the 1st edition of *Dissertations and Discussions* himself, thought little about the (typically) minor changes for the 2nd edition, but called on Helen Taylor's collaboration in preparing the pamphlet, for which they used the most convenient base text, a copy of the offprint.

The second kind of material in the appendices is found in Appendix D, the draft of part of the *Inaugural Address*, which has a quite different, and much slighter, interest, as giving one of the rare glimpses of Mill, late in life, revising a work

---

[80]*Ibid.*, XVI, 1059 (letter to Chadwick, 28 May, 1865), and 1106-7 (23 Oct., 1865). With the latter, cf. *ibid.*, 1289 (letter to Parker Pillsbury, 4 July, 1867).

[81]*Ibid.*, 1270 (letter to Spencer, 24 May, 1867), XVII, 1610 (letter to Emile Cazelles, 30 May, 1869), and 1670 and 1747-8 (letters to Paulina Wright Davis, 11 Dec., 1869 and 22 July, 1870). Twice, in recommending it, he does not give an author (*ibid.*, XVI, 1451 [27 Sept., 1868], and 1476 [3 Nov., 1868]).

[82]The varied spellings (including hyphenation and initial capitalization) are less conclusive but also less significant: in five cases 1868 is consonant with 1851; in ten with the 2nd ed. of *Dissertations and Discussions* (in eight of these the 1st ed. also agrees); and in nine its reading is unique.

thoroughly as to wording, but not finding it necessary to make structural or argumentative changes. Both economy and precision were well served in what must have been a rapid rewriting. This fragment was probably preserved merely by accident when many of the Mill-Taylor papers were destroyed in Avignon after Helen Taylor's return to England in 1905; it found a place in a miscellaneous collection bought from the Avignon bookseller J. Roumanille by George Herbert Palmer, and eventually was deposited in the Houghton Library, Harvard University.

Appendix E is of the third kind; it consists of three documents issued by the Jamaica Committee under Mill's chairmanship, one dating from 1866, and two from 1868. Mill's name appears first among the signatories of each, and he must have approved, even if he did not draft, the contents of each. His passionate involvement in the attempt of the Committee to bring Governor Eyre to trial, discussed in the Introduction (xxvi-xxviii), is fully illustrated in his parliamentary career, both in his speeches and actions and in attacks on and defences of him in Parliament and the press. The texts for the documents are based on different sources. The first, the extensive "Statement of the Jamaica Committee," 27 July, 1866, is taken from Volume III of the series of *Jamaica Papers* issued from time to time by the Committee. It also appeared in the press. No official copy has been found of the second document, an address to friends of the Committee, dated October, 1866. Our text is taken from the *Examiner* of 13 October, where the format appears less altered by newspaper practice than that in the *Daily News* of 12 October. The third, the concluding statement by the Committee, dated 15 July, 1868, and indicating the winding up of its business, comes from a printed letter, two copies of which are in the Mill-Taylor Collection; no full version has been found in the press, which by then reflected the general public indifference or hostility to the Committee's cause, though a summary of the statement is in the *Daily Telegraph* of 24 July.

The final two appendices contain editorial materials. Appendix F lists the textual emendations, most of which are corrections of typographical errors. Appendix G, the Bibliographic Appendix, provides a guide to Mill's references and quotations, with notes concerning the separate entries, and a list of substantive variants between his quotations and their sources. The items in this volume contain references to more than 150 publications (excluding Statutes and Parliamentary Papers and unidentified anonymous quotations, but including classical tags and references that occur in quotations from others). Mill quotes from over seventy of these, including the eight works he reviews. The most extensive quotation is, as one would expect, from the reviewed works; a large number of the shorter quotations (some of which are indirect) are undoubtedly taken from memory, with no explicit references being given, and the identification of some of these is inescapably inferential.

Because Appendix G serves as an index to persons, writings, and statutes, references to them do not appear in the Index proper, which has been prepared by Dr. Jean O'Grady.

TEXTUAL PRINCIPLES AND METHODS

AS THROUGHOUT THIS EDITION, the copy-text for each item is that of the final version supervised by Mill.[83] Details concerning revisions are given in the headnotes to each item and in the discussion above.

Method of indicating variants. All the substantive variants are governed by the principles enunciated below; "substantive" here means all changes of text except spelling, hyphenation, punctuation, demonstrable typographical errors, and such printing-house concerns as type size, etc. The substantive variants are of three kinds: addition of a word or words, substitution of a word or words, deletion of a word or words. The following illustrative examples are drawn, except as indicated, from "The Contest in America."

Addition of a word or words: see 128 $^{a-a}$. In the text, the last word of the passage "A nation which has made the professions that England has made" appears as "^{a}made^a"; the variant note reads "$^{a-a}$+67". The plus sign indicates an addition in the edition signalled by the following numbers. The editions are always indicated by the last two numbers of the year of publication: here 67 indicates 1867 (the 2nd edition of Volumes I and II of *Dissertations and Discussions*). Information explaining the use of these abbreviations is given in each headnote, as required. Any added editorial comment is enclosed in square brackets and italicized.

Placing this example in context, the interpretation is that when first published (1862) the reading was "A nation which has made the professions that England has"; this reading was retained in the offprint (also 1862); but in 1867 the reading of the concluding clause became "that England has made".

Substitution of a word or words: see 129 $^{d-d}$. In the text the passage "Now that the mind of England" appears as "Now ^{d}that^d the mind of England"; the variant note reads "$^{d-d}$62^{1,2} , when". Here the word following the edition indicator is that for which "that" was substituted; applying the same rules and putting the variant in context, the interpretation is that when first published in 1862 (indicated by 62^1) the reading was "Now, when the mind of England"; this reading was retained in the offprint (indicated by 62^2); in 1867 it was altered to "Now that the mind of England".

Deletion of a word or words: see 141 ^{j} and 65 $^{c-c}$. The first of these is typical, representing the most convenient way of indicating deletions in a later edition. In the text on 141 a *single* superscript ^{j} appears *centred* between "repudiation." and

---

[83]The argument for this practice is given in my "Principles and Methods in the Collected Edition of John Stuart Mill," in *Editing Nineteenth-Century Texts*, ed. John M. Robson (Toronto: University of Toronto Press, 1967), 96-122.

"Unless"; the variant note reads "^{j}62^{1,2} Mississippi was the first state which repudiated, Mr. Jefferson Davis was Governor of Mississippi, and the Legislature of Mississippi had passed a Bill recognizing and providing for the debt, which Bill Mr. Jefferson Davis repudiated." Here the sentence following the edition indicator was deleted. Applying the same rules and putting the variant in context, the interpretation is that when first published (1862) and offprinted (also 1862) the sentence appeared between "repudiation." and "Unless"; in 1867 it was deleted.

The second example (65$^{c\text{-}c}$) illustrates the method used to cover more conveniently deletions when portions of the copy-text were later reprinted, as in the case of "Reform in Education," in which Mill quotes from his own "Corporation and Church Property," which was republished in *Dissertations and Discussions*, Volume I. (That is, there is here, exceptionally, a later version of part of the copy-text, whereas normally the copy-text is the latest version.) In the text the words "a particle worse than" appear as "^{c}a particle^{c} worse than"; the variant note reads "$^{c\text{-}c}$−59,67". The minus sign indicates that in the editions signified the words enclosed were deleted. Putting the example in context, the interpretation is that when first published (1834) the reading was (as is clear in the text) "a particle worse than"; this reading was altered in 1859 (the 1st edition of *Dissertation and Discussions*) to "worse than"; and the altered reading was retained in 1867.

Dates of footnotes: see 133n. In this edition the practice is to place immediately after the footnote indicator, in square brackets, the figures indicating the edition in which Mill's footnote first appeared. In the example cited, "[67]" signifies that the note was added in 1867. In the only other instance in this volume (at 420n) "[−67]" signifies that the footnote in the draft manuscript was removed for the printed version. Elsewhere, where no such indication appears, the note is in all versions.

Punctuation and spelling. In general, changes between versions in punctuation and spelling are ignored. Those changes that occur as part of a substantive variant are included in that variant, and the superscript letters in the text are placed exactly with reference to punctuation. Changes between italic and roman type are treated as substantive variants except in titles of works, abbreviations, and in one case ("prima facie" at 275.33) a foreign phrase. One unusual old form ("began" rather than "begun" at 315.15) has been retained, as it persists through three editions.

Other textual liberties. Some of the titles have been modified or supplied, but most are those found in the copy-texts. "Law of Libel and Liberty of the Press" and "Austin's Lectures on Jurisprudence" are taken from the running titles. The manuscripts, if not entitled, are given titles reflecting their contents, as are the short review "Smith on Law Reform" and the two extracts from *Parliamentary Papers*. The headnotes give information about original headings and titles (the running titles, when cited, are standardized in capitalization and font). The dates added to the titles are those of first publication or, for manuscripts, composition.

When footnotes to the original titles of articles gave bibliographic information, these have been deleted, and the information given in the headnotes. The original headnote to "The Negro Question," which was supplied by the editor of *Fraser's Magazine*, is given as a footnote.

Typographical errors have been silently corrected in the text; they are listed in Appendix F. Some of these, as well as some variants, are indicated by Mill in copies now in Somerville College, Oxford (signified by "SC" in our notes). In the headnotes, errors in the quotations from Mill's bibliography, the manuscript of which is a scribal copy, are also silently corrected; the note below lists them.[84] While the punctuation and spelling of each item are retained, the style has been made uniform: for example, periods are deleted after references to monarchs (for example, "Charles I."), dashes are deleted when combined with other punctuation before a quotation or reference, and italic punctuation after italic passages has been made roman. For consistency, in a few places titles are given an initial capital, and at 270.10 an initial capital has been placed on "parliament". In monarchs' titles the sequential designations have been regularized to roman numerals (for example, "Francis the First" is given as "Francis I"). Indications of ellipsis have been normalized to three dots plus, when necessary, terminal punctuation. The positioning of footnote indicators has been normalized so that they always appear after adjacent punctuation marks; in some cases references have been moved from the beginning to the end of quotations for consistency. Where the copy-text is manuscript, the ampersand is given as "and"; in those in Appendix B contractions such as "w^{d}" are expanded and superscripts lowered.

Also, in accordance with modern practice, all long quotations have been reduced in type size and the quotation marks removed. In consequence, it has occasionally been necessary to add square brackets around Mill's words in quotations; there is little opportunity for confusion, as there are no editorial insertions except page references. Double quotation marks replace single, and titles of works originally published separately are given in italics. At 198.3 and 245.26-7 quotation marks have been placed around "Vision" (i.e., Addison's "Vision of Mirzah") and "Hymn to Intellectual Beauty" by Shelley. Mill's references to sources, and additional editorial references (in square brackets), have been normalized. When necessary his references have been corrected; a list of the corrections and alterations is given in the note below.[85]

---

[84]The corrected scribal errors (the erroneous reading first, with the corrected one following in square brackets) are:

62.5   Miss [Mrs.]
86.5   negroes" [negroes,']
216.4   in [on]

[85]Following the page and line notation, the first reference is to Mill's identification; the corrected identification (that which appears in the present text) follows in square brackets. There is no indication of the places where a dash has been substituted for a comma to indicate adjacent pages, where "P." or

As indicated above, the format of "The Contagious Diseases Acts" has been made compatible with that used elsewhere in this edition for Mill's parliamentary evidence: the numbers of the questions have been deleted; the questioners' names are given in full; and the questions are given in italic (this practice is also followed in "Educational Endowments," where Mill's evidence was given in writing rather than *viva voce*).

ACKNOWLEDGMENTS

FOR PERMISSION TO PUBLISH manuscript material, we are indebted to the British Library of Political and Economic Science, the Houghton Library, Harvard University, and the National Provincial Bank (literary executors and residual legatees of Mary Taylor, Mill's step-granddaughter). Stefan Collini and I have also received gracious help from the staffs of the Aberdeen University Library, the British Library (with the regrettable exception of one librarian at Colindale), the Central Library of the City of Manchester, Dr. Williams's Library, the History of Ideas Unit, Australian National University (particularly Sam Goldberg and Barry Smith), the Instituto Internacional de Estudios Avanzados, Caracas (especially Luis Castro), the Jamaica Archives, the Lindsay Institute (Lanark), the London Library, the Longmans Archive, Reading University, the National Library of Jamaica, the National Library of Scotland, Somerville College Library, the University of London Library, the University of Toronto Library, Victoria University Library, and Yale University Library. The unflagging personal and technical help of the staff of the University of Toronto Press, and especially of our copy-editors, Rosemary Shipton and Margaret Parker, deserve only our richest

---

"Pp." replaces "p." or "pp." (or the reverse), or where the volume number has been added to the reference.
18.33   45 [45-6]
24n.3   75 [75-6]
29n.2   V.527 [Vol. XIV, col. 1128] [*JSM was using a different version*]
29n.4   ix [XVII]
29n.5   *Ibid.* [XVII . . . 112] [*for the vol. no. of* State Trials *and the page no. of* Holt, *which is* 111 *in the previous note*]
78.21   22, 23 [73]
174n.3   xciv [xciv n]
177.13   116 [116n]
185n.10   273 [273-4]
194.15   278 [278-9]
197n.1   134 [134-5]
201n.1   439 [439-40]
204n.2   24 [24-5]
204n.4   150 [150n]

thanks. Individuals whose aid we are delighted to acknowledge include the members of the Editorial Committee, and Robin Alston, John Burrow, D.G. Clarke, Peter Clarke, G.M. Craig, John Dinwiddy, Claire Gobbi, Joseph Hamburger, Geoffrey Hawthorn, Bruce L. Kinzer, David Lieberman, J. McGarrity, W.E. McLeod, Kenneth McNaught, Francis E. Mineka, Ruth Morse, Stephen B. Oates, William, John, and Ann Christine Robson, C.A. Silber, John Thompson, Donald Winch, and Elizabeth Zyman.

Our greatest benefactor is the Social Sciences and Humanities Research Council of Canada, whose generous Major Editorial Project Grant supports both publication and the work of our talented and dedicated editorial team. For this volume, much of the credit belongs to Jean O'Grady, Marion Filipiuk, Maureen Clarke, Rea Wilmshurst, Allison Taylor, and Jonathan Cutmore. My wife, Professor Ann P. Robson, to whom my greatest debt is owed, will not object to my linking her and our favourite publishing house in saying, with Horace, "Domus et placens uxor."

LAW OF LIBEL AND LIBERTY OF THE PRESS

1825

EDITOR'S NOTE

Westminster Review, III (Apr., 1825), 285-321. Headed: "Art. I. *On the Law of Libel; with Strictures on the self-styled Constitutional Association.* [By Francis Place.] 8vo. pp. 73. London. John Hunt. 1823. / *The Law of Libel.* By Richard Mence, Esq. of the Middle Temple, Barrister. 8vo. 2 Vols. in one, pp. 595. London [: Pople], 1824." Running titles: "Law of Libel and Liberty of the Press." Unsigned; not republished. Identified in Mill's bibliography as "An article on the Liberty of the Press, in the sixth number of the Westminster Review" (MacMinn, 6). Vol. III of the *Westminster* in the Somerville College Library has no corrections or alterations. For comment on the review, see xl-xli and lviii above.

Law of Libel and Liberty of the Press

THE TWO PUBLICATIONS which we have chosen to head this article, possess considerable merit, and we do not hesitate to recommend them to our readers, as worthy of an attentive perusal.

The first, though no name appears in the title-page, is the acknowledged production of a known and tried friend of the people.[*] It consists of a series of essays, all of which, except the last, appeared nearly two years since in a weekly newspaper. It comprises a summary exposure of many of the abominations contained in what is called the Law of Libel, as well as in the administration of that Law; and a brief review of the acts of a body of men, now sunk into obscurity, who were at one time notorious under the name of the Constitutional Association. We will not say that the author has completely exhausted the subject; but we consider no small praise to be his due, for having said so much, and so much to the purpose, in the narrow compass within which, by the original design, he was unavoidably confined.

Mr. Mence's work attracted our attention, from being advertised as dedicated to the Constitutional Association. What might be expected from a work, appearing under such auspices, our readers have no occasion to be informed. We, however, had not proceeded far in the perusal, before we found Mr. Mence to be, not a humble aspirant after ministerial patronage, content to lend himself to the purposes of those who would keep the human mind in perpetual bondage; but one who does not shrink from exposing, even at the risk of his professional success, the vices of existing institutions; one who dares give utterance to great and important truths, however little acceptable, to the rich and powerful; and who would be, for that reason alone, deserving of high praise, had he executed his task with far less ability than he has displayed.

Without entering into a critical examination of the merits and defects of these two works, we embrace this opportunity of delivering our sentiments upon the highly important subject to which they refer: availing ourselves of the language of either or both of them, as often as it appears peculiarly adapted to our purpose.

We shall divide our remarks into two parts; in one of which we shall discuss the

[*Francis Place. The essays (except the last) first appeared in weekly front-page instalments in the *British Luminary and Weekly Intelligencer* from 3 Nov. to 22 Dec., 1822.]

general question, to what extent restraints upon the freedom of the press can be considered as warranted by sound principles of political philosophy; and in the other, we shall take a brief review of the English Law, and of the doctrines of English Lawyers, on this subject: and we pledge ourselves to prove, that the Law of England is as unfavourable to the liberty of the press, as that of the most despotic government which ever existed; and, consequently, that whatever degree of that liberty is enjoyed in this country, exists, not in consequence of the law, but in spite of it.

The general question has usually been disposed of in a very summary way. It has, in fact, been regularly assumed, first, that to employ the press in any other than a certain manner, is inconceivably wicked; and secondly, that, for this reason, it is the duty of the magistrate to prevent it, by fine and imprisonment, if not by means still more certainly and more promptly effectual.

The author of the article "Liberty of the Press," in the Supplement to the *Encyclopaedia Britannica*, has, however, set the example of rather a different sort of reasoning; and (what was never completely or consistently done before) he has pointed out the considerations on which this question really turns. We have no higher ambition than that of treading in his steps; and, taking his principles as our guide, we shall endeavour to unravel the sophistry, and expose the mischievous designs of the enemies to free discussion.

That the press may be so employed as to require punishment, we are very far from denying: it may be made the instrument of almost every imaginable crime.

There is scarcely a right,* for the violation of which, scarcely an operation of government, for the disturbance of which, the press may not be employed as an instrument. The offences capable of being committed by the press are indeed nearly coextensive with the whole field of delinquency.

It is not, however, necessary to give a separate definition of every such violation or disturbance, when committed by the press, for that would be to write the penal code a second time; first describing each offence as it appears in ordinary cases; and then describing it anew for the case in which the press is the particular instrument.

If, for the prevention of the violation of rights, it were necessary to give a separate definition, on account of every instrument which might be employed as a means of producing the several violations, the penal code would be endless. In general the instrument or means is an immaterial circumstance. The violation itself, and the degree of alarm which may attend it, are the principal objects of consideration. If a man is put in fear of his life, and robbed of his purse, it is of no consequence whether he is threatened with a pistol, or with a sword. In the deposition of a theft, of a fraud, or a murder, it is not necessary to include an account of all the sorts of means by which these injuries may be perpetrated. It is sufficient if

---

*Article "Liberty of the Press" [1821] (in the *Supplement to the* [*Fourth, Fifth, and Sixth Editions of the*] *Encyclopaedia Britannica* near the beginning). [James Mill, *Essays* (London: Innes, [1825]), pp. 3-4; J.S. Mill is using this text rather than that in the *Supplement*.] This invaluable essay is from the pen of Mr. Mill, the historian of British India. [The concluding reference is to *The History of British India*, 3 vols. (London: Baldwin, *et al.*, 1817 [1818]).]

the injury itself is accurately described. The object is, to prevent the injury, not merely when produced by one sort of means or another sort of means, but by any means.

As far as persons and property are concerned, the general definition of the acts by which rights are liable to be violated, has always been held sufficient; and has been regarded as including not less the cases in which the instrumentality of the press has been employed, than those in which any other means have been employed to the same end. Nobody ever thought of a particular law for restraining the press on account of the cases in which it may have been rendered subservient to the perpetration of a murder or theft. It is enough that a law is made to punish him who has been guilty of the murder or theft, whether he has employed the press or any thing else as the means for accomplishing his end.*

There are some species of acts, however, of which the press if not the sole, may, at any rate, be regarded as the most potent instrument: these are, the publication of facts, and the expression of opinions; and to one or other of these heads belong those uses of the press, against which the Law of Libel is principally directed.

It is not pretended that, in the language of English Law, the word Libel is strictly confined to one meaning. It includes, on the contrary, a number of acts, of a very heterogeneous nature, resembling one another scarcely at all, except in having penalties attached to them by the authorized interpreters of the law. A threatening letter, demanding money, is a libel. An indecent picture is a libel. For the present, however, we may confine our remarks to the question regarding the publication of facts and the expression of opinions.

To begin with the latter. If the magistrate is to be intrusted with power to suppress all opinions which he, in his wisdom, may pronounce to be mischievous—to what control can this power be subjected? What security is it possible to take against its abuse? For without some security all power, and of course this power, is sure to be abused, just as often as its abuse can serve any purpose of the holder.

It is the boast of English lawyers that the offence of treason is defined; so strictly defined, that nothing is ambiguous, nothing arbitrary, nothing left to the discretion of the judge. This, they tell us, is one of the chief bulwarks of our liberty: implying, that if it *were* left to the judge to say what should, and what should not be

---

*Montesquieu saw pretty clearly the only case in which the expression of opinions and sentiments could be a fit object of punishment: although he did not venture to extend the doctrine further than to the case of *words*, and even among words, only to these which are called treasonable.

"Les paroles qui sont jointes à une action, prennent la nature de cette action. Ainsi un homme qui va dans la place publique exhorter les sujets à la révolte, devient coupable de lèse-majesté, parce que les paroles sont jointes à l'action, et y participent. Ce ne sont point les paroles que l'on punit; mais une action commise dans laquelle on emploie les paroles. Elles ne deviennent des crimes, que lorsqu'elles préparent, qu'elles accompagnent, ou qu'elles suivent une action criminelle. On renverse tout, si l'on fait des paroles un crime capital, au lieu de les regarder comme le signe d'un crime capital." [Charles Louis de Secondat, baron de la Brède et de Montesquieu, *De l'] Esprit des Lois* [2 vols. (Geneva: Barrillot, 1748), Vol. I, pp. 313-14], Liv. XII, Chap. 12.

treason, every thing would be treason which the government did not like. Yet why should definition be required in the case of treason, not required in the case of libel? Is the government less interested in misdecision? Is the judge less dependent on the government? Is a packed special jury less subservient? Or are the judge and jury angels when they judge of libel, men only when they judge of treason?

It would be hardy to assert, that to give the right of pronouncing upon libels to the judge, is any thing more than another name for giving it to the government. But there are many subjects, and these the most important of all, on which it is the interest of the government, not that the people should think right, but, on the contrary, that they should think wrong: on these subjects, therefore, the government is quite sure, if it has the power, to suppress, not the false and mischievous opinions, but the great and important truths. It is the interest of rulers that the people should hold slavish opinions in politics: it is equally so, that they should hold slavish opinions in religion: all opinions, therefore, whether in politics or religion, which are not slavish, the government, if it dares, will be sure to suppress. It is the interest of rulers that the people should believe all their proceedings to be the best possible: every thing, therefore, which has a tendency to make them think otherwise, and among the rest, all strictures, however well deserved, government will use its most strenuous exertions to prevent. If these endeavours could succeed, if it could suppress all censure, its dominion, to whatever degree it might pillage and oppress the people, would be for ever secured.

This is so palpable, that a man must be either insincere or imbecile to deny it: and no one, we suppose, will openly affirm that rulers should have the power to suppress all opinions which they may call mischievous—all opinions which they may dislike. Where, then, is the line to be drawn? At what point is the magistrate's discretionary power of suppressing opinions to end? Can it be limited in such a manner as to leave him the power of suppressing really mischievous opinions, without giving him that of silencing every opinion hostile to the indefinite extension of his power?

It is manifest, even at first sight, that no such limit can be set. If the publication of opinions is to be restrained, merely because they are mischievous, there must be somebody to judge, what opinions are mischievous, and what the reverse. It is obvious, that there is no certain and universal rule for determining whether an opinion is useful or pernicious; and that if any person be authorized to decide, unfettered by such a rule, that person is a despot. To decide what opinions shall be permitted, and what prohibited, is to choose opinions for the people: since they cannot adopt opinions which are not suffered to be presented to their minds. Whoever chooses opinions for the people, possesses absolute control over their actions, and may wield them for his own purposes with perfect security.

It thus appears, by the closest ratiocination, that there is no medium between perfect freedom of expressing opinions, and absolute despotism. Whenever you invest the rulers of the country with any power to suppress opinions, you invest them with *all* power; and absolute power of suppressing opinions would amount, if it *could* be exercised, to a despotism far more perfect than any which has yet existed, because there is no country in which the power of suppressing opinions has ever, in practice, been altogether unrestrained.

How, then, it may be asked, if to have any power of silencing opinions is to have all power—since the government of Great Britain certainly has that power in a degree—how do we account for the practical freedom of discussion, which to a considerable extent undoubtedly prevails in this country? The government having the power to destroy it, why is it suffered to exist?

Why? For the same reason for which we have a habeas corpus act,[*] with a government possessing the power to suspend or repeal it: for the same reason for which a jury is sometimes allowed to acquit a prisoner, whom the aristocracy wish to destroy: for the same reason for which we are not taxed up to the highest amount which could be extorted from us, without impairing our power of being useful slaves. The aristocracy do not submit to these restraints because they like them, but because they do not venture to throw them off. This is conformable to the theory of the British constitution itself.

Even a Turkish Sultan is restrained by the fear of exciting insurrection. The power of shackling the press may, like all other power, be controlled in its exercise by public opinion, and to a very great, though far from a sufficient, extent, it has been and is so controlled in Great Britain. By law, however—notwithstanding the assertions of lawyers, which assertions, when it suits them, they never scruple to contradict—liberty of discussion, on any topic by which the interests of the aristocracy can be affected, does not exist at all in this country, as we have already shewn, upon general principles, and shall prove in the sequel from the actual words of the highest legal authorities.

The preliminary inquiry, however, would not be complete, unless, having discussed the consequences of restraining the press, we were also to inquire what would be the consequences of leaving it free.

It is evident, at first sight, that, whatever might be the evils of freedom, they could not be worse than the evils of restraint. The worst that could happen, if the people chose opinions for themselves, would be, that they would choose wrong opinions. But this evil, as we have seen, is not contingent, but unavoidable, if they allow any other person to choose opinions for them. Nor would it be possible that the opinions, however extravagant, which might become prevalent in a state of freedom, could exceed in mischievousness those which it would be the interest, and therefore the will, of rulers, to dictate: since there cannot be more mischievous opinions, than those which tend to perpetuate arbitrary power. There would, however, be one great difference. Under a free system, if error would be

[*31 Charles II, c. 2 (1679).]

promulgated, so would truth: and truth never fails, in the long run, to prevail over error. Under a system of restraint, the errors which would be promulgated from authority would be the most mischievous possible, and would not be suffered to be refuted.

That truth, if it has fair play, always in the end triumphs over error, and becomes the opinion of the world, is a proposition which rests upon the broadest principles of human nature, and to which it would be easy to accumulate testimonials from almost every author, whatever may be his political leanings, who has distinguished himself in any branch of politics, morals, or theology. It is a proposition which the restrictors themselves do not venture to dispute. They continually protest, that their opinions have nothing to fear from discussion; the sole effect of which, according to them, is, to exhibit their irrefragable certainty in a still stronger light than before. And yet they do not scruple to punish men for doing that which, if their own assertions be correct, merits not punishment, but reward.

Although, however, the worst enemies of discussion, do not deny, as a general proposition, its tendency to unveil the truth, there is a certain number of subjects on which, if they are to be believed, discussion tends, not to enlighten, but to mislead. Among these are all the subjects on which it is the interest of rulers that the people *should* be misled; the political religion of the country, its political institutions, and the conduct and character of its rulers.

On the first of these topics, we have delivered our opinions so fully in our third number,[*] that we shall in the present confine ourselves principally to the three latter: all of which substantially resolve themselves into one.

That there is no subject of greater importance, no one needs to be told: and to say this, is to say that there is no subject on which it is of greater importance that the people should be rightly informed. As the stability of a good government wholly depends upon its being acknowledged by the people to be good, so, on the other hand, the reform of a bad one wholly depends upon its being believed by the people to be bad. In the correctness of the estimate which the people form of the goodness of their government, their whole happiness is involved; since misgovernment includes every misery which is capable of afflicting mankind: and misgovernment is alike the consequence, whether the people believe a good government to be a bad one, or a bad government to be a good one.

We have been thus particular in laying down first principles, because the language held on this subject by rulers implies, that it is indeed the greatest of calamities, for the people to believe a good government to be bad, but that their considering a bad government to be good, is no evil at all, or at most a very trifling one. The evil, however, as we have already observed, is in both cases the same; or rather, the one is an evil, chiefly because it leads to the other: that the people should

[*William Johnson Fox, "Religious Prosecutions," *Westminster Review*, II (July, 1824), 1-26.]

think ill of a good government is principally to be lamented, because it may occasion their acquiescence in a worse.

If, therefore, there be any subject on which the people cannot, without the greatest danger, trust the power of choosing opinions for them out of their own hands, it is this. And if such power cannot safely be given to any one, least of all can it be given to the rulers of the country.

If the people were compelled to take their opinions implicitly from some one who might have an interest in persuading them that their government is worse than it is, the greatest evils, it is admitted, would be the consequence. To think ill of a good government, and well of a bad one, are evils of equal magnitude. If, therefore, the privilege of dictating opinions to the people, on the subject of their government, be intrusted to persons interested in persuading them that their government is better than it is, the mischief cannot consistently be affirmed to be less. That rulers are so interested, will not be denied. What inference, then, are we to draw? or rather, how can the inference be evaded, that, if rulers are suffered to choose what opinions the people shall hold concerning their government, all the evils of misrule are rendered perpetual?

Such a choice, however, is made by rulers, as often as they inflict punishment upon any person for criticizing institutions, or censuring the conduct of government: unless they are willing to prohibit, under equal penalties, the expression of praise.

To forbid the expression of one opinion, and give encouragement to that of another, is surely to make a choice. To punish censure of rulers, while praise is permitted, is to say, 'tis fit that the people should think well of their government, whether good or bad; and to take the most effectual mode of compelling them to do so.

Against this reasoning it is impossible that any rational objection can be urged. Cavils, indeed, may be brought against it: but there are few conclusions of equal importance, the proof of which affords so little hold even for cavil.

When it is asserted, that to restrain discussion is to choose opinions for the people, and that rulers, if permitted to dictate opinions to their subjects, having an interest in choosing the most mischievous of all opinions, will act as that interest directs; there is only one objection which can by possibility be raised. It cannot be said, that to fetter discussion is not to choose opinions, nor that rulers are not interested in making a bad choice. But, it may be said, that our rulers are men in whom the confidence of the people may be reposed; and that, although it be confessedly their interest to make a bad choice, they will disregard that interest, and make a good one.

To such a pinnacle of absurdity men may always be driven, when they attempt to argue in defence of mischievous power. They begin by boldly denying the possibility of abuse: when this can no longer be maintained, they fly for refuge to the characters of the individuals, and insist with equal pertinacity, that in their hands power may be trusted without fear of being abused. This is a compliment of which the rulers for the time being, be they who they may, always receive as much as they can pay for: dead rulers are not so fortunate. That all rulers in time past abused their power when they could, is allowed: but an exception is made in favor of the present. This is a species of reasoning, however, which will pass current with nobody in the present day: we cannot be forced back to the times when rulers were thought not to be made like human beings, but to be free from all the passions and appetites by which other men are misled. If uncontrolled power can exist, and not be abused, then away with the British, and all other constitutions, and let us return to the despotism of our wise and venerable ancestors. But if men will abuse all other powers, when unrestrained, so they will that of controlling the press: if rulers will avail themselves of all other means to render themselves despotic, they will not pass over an expedient so simple and effectual as that of suppressing, in as far as they dare, all opinions hostile to the extension of their authority. And perfect freedom of discussion is, as we have already proved, the only alternative.

The objections which have been urged against the principle of free discussion, though infinitely diversified in shape, are at bottom only one assertion: the incapacity of the people to form correct opinions. This assumption is indeed the stronghold of all the disguised or undisguised partisans of despotism. It has been the unremitting, and hitherto, unhappily, the successful endeavour of rulers, to make it be believed that the most dreadful calamities would be the effect of any attempt to obtain securities that their power should be employed for the benefit, not of themselves, but of the community. With this view, it has been their uniform practice to vilify those whom they are striving to enslave. If the people were permitted to choose opinions for themselves, they would be sure, it is alleged, to choose the most mischievous and dangerous opinions. Being utterly incapable either of thinking or of acting for themselves, they are quite sure, unless kept in awe by priests and aristocracies, to become blind instruments in the hands of factious demagogues, who would employ them to subvert all establishments, and to throw every thing into the wildest anarchy and confusion. This language, by the way, is a practical illustration of the impartiality of the Law of Libel. It restrains all declaration, even of unfavourable truth with regard to the aristocracy: it gives full indulgence, and there is plenty of encouragement, to the propagation of all manner of unfavourable lies against the people. The conspiracy have thus all that is necessary for their purpose. Give a dog a bad name, and hang him: so they try with the people. Whether the object be to coerce them by standing armies, or to muzzle them by libel law, the motive always is pure loving-kindness, to save the unoffending, that is, the aristocratic part of mankind, from the jaws of those ravenous wolves and tigers, the people.

Such a language is calculated to act upon men by their fears, not by their reason: otherwise a little reflection would show, that the incapacity of the people, were it admitted, proves nothing, or, at least, nothing to the purpose. The practical conclusion would be the same, even if the people were so destitute of reasoning power, as to be utterly incapable of distinguishing truth from falsehood: since there is no alternative, but to let them choose their own opinions, or to give the choice to persons interested in misleading them.

An ignorant man, even if he decide at hap-hazard, has at least a chance of being sometimes in the right. But he who adopts every opinion which rulers choose to dictate, is always in the wrong, when it is their interest that he should be so, that is, on the most momentous of all topics.

Another question, which it does not suit those who make the ignorance of the people a plea for enslaving them to put, is, why are they ignorant? because to this question there can be only one answer, namely, that if they are ignorant, it is precisely because that discussion, which alone can remove ignorance, has been withheld from them. And although their masters may find it convenient to speak of their ignorance as incurable, we take the liberty of demurring to this conclusion, until the proper remedy shall have been tried. This remedy is, instruction: and of instruction, discussion is the most potent instrument. Discussion, therefore, has a necessary tendency to remedy its own evils. For the evils which spring from an undue veneration for authority, there is no such cure: and the longer the disease continues, without the remedying influence of discussion, the more inveterate it becomes.

But, the assertion itself, by which so many terrors have been conjured up—the incapacity of the people to choose correct opinions—upon what evidence does it rest? Upon history? No: for history proves, that just in proportion as the people have been permitted to choose opinions for themselves, in that proportion have they been moral, intelligent, and happy: and it is precisely in those countries in which the greatest pains has been taken to shut out discussion, that the people, when once roused from their habitual apathy, have proved themselves to be most ignorant and ferocious. No people which had ever enjoyed a free press, could have been guilty of the excesses of the French Revolution. By what artifices, then, have governments contrived to spread a vague apprehension of danger from discussion so widely among the unthinking part of mankind? By availing themselves of that universal law of human nature, by which men are prone to dread whatever they do not understand, and they who foresee the least, uniformly fear the most. The evils which they endure, habit has rendered tolerable: but change, because they cannot foresee its consequences, is the object of their terror and aversion. And though history does not prove that discussion produces evil, but the contrary, there is abundant proof from history, that it produces change: change, not indeed in any thing good, but in every thing that is bad, bad laws, bad judicature, and bad government. That it leads to such changes is the very reason for which it is most to be desired, but it is also the reason why short-sighted persons hold it in terror.

Nor is there any difficulty in convincing the understanding of any one who will coolly apply his attention to the subject. The real difficulty is, to quiet fears. We cannot confide in persons whose fears appear to us to fall always in the wrong place. Nothing is more to be feared than a habit of fearing, whenever any thing is proposed for the good of mankind. The man who is always fearing evil to the many from the many, never from the few, appears to us an object of very rational fear.

The ignorance of the people is a mere pretext for a line of conduct which would have been equally pursued without any such pretext. This appears from the little regard paid to it in the practice of rulers themselves. The proper course in regard to ignorant persons, they say truly, is to guard them against deception: now, as rulers dare not openly lay claim to impeccability, they cannot deny that there may be deception on both sides: on the side of praise, as well as on the side of blame. To praise, however, both of rulers and of institutions, the most unlimited latitude has been given: censure alone has been restricted. Every one is free to represent the government and its functionaries as better than they are; and that to any extent: but woe to him who presumes, with whatever truth, to cast any blame upon either! Does this look as if it were believed that the people are ignorant? No! it looks as if it were feared that they would be too clear-sighted.

It seems not very consistent, in those whose case rests wholly upon the people's incapacity of judging, to propose as a remedy for that incapacity, that nothing but an ex-parte statement should be presented to them. Is incapacity to judge cured by hearing only one side? Is ignorance remedied by placing it in a situation where the most perfect wisdom could scarcely escape being misled? To make the ignorance of the people a pretext for refusing them the means of judging, when it is precisely on account of their ignorance that they stand most in need of those means, would excite laughter, if it did not excite indignation. In other countries, it is maintained that the people ought not to judge of public affairs. To prevent them from hearing evidence, therefore, is, at any rate, consistent. In this country it is admitted that the people should judge; and it is, nevertheless, asserted, that they should hear only one side!

To support this monstrous absurdity, there is, in addition to the grand assumption of the incapacity of the people, another question which it has been customary to beg. This is, that the people hate their rulers, and are strongly disposed to judge unfavorably, both of them and of their actions. So utterly false is this assumption, that, on the contrary, there is no fact to which the testimony of experience is more unvarying, than to the strong disposition of the people, to think much better of their rulers and of their institutions than they deserve. The love of ease, perhaps the strongest principle of human nature, and beyond all comparison stronger, in the majority of mankind, than the hope of any remote and contingent advantage, is constantly urging them to avoid innovation, and rest satisfied with things as they are:[*] with what success, every one has it in his power to observe. Who

[*The concluding phrase, often used ironically by the Philosophic Radicals, probably is taken from the title of William Godwin's *Things As They Are; or, The Adventures of Caleb Williams*, 3 vols. (London: Crosby, 1794).]

is there that has not seen a hundred instances of evil needlessly endured, for one of good wantonly abandoned and evil adopted? Is there, then, no inconsistency in supposing that in public matters the case is directly reversed? Nor is the love of ease the only principle which is constantly in operation, to warp the judgments of the people in favour of their rulers. He must have looked at mankind with a resolution not to see the truth, who can be blind to the excessive veneration of the poor for title, rank, and riches, a veneration arising from the habitual propensity of mankind to over-estimate advantages which they do not possess; and which was enumerated by Adam Smith among the most fertile sources of false judgments in morality which could be named.[*] With these two principles strongly on one side, and nothing but reason on the other, knowledge must be far advanced among the people before they learn to venerate rulers only as far as they deserve veneration. Accordingly, all history bears testimony to the constancy with which the most dreadful mis-government has been suffered to prevail in almost every country of the globe: but the advocates of restriction may safely be challenged to produce one instance from history, in which the people have risen against a good government and overthrown it.

So strong, and so durable, is the veneration of the people for their rulers: nor has it ever yet been eradicated by anything short of the most grinding oppression. What epithet, then, can be too severe for the conduct of those who would prevent this feeling from giving way, like all other mischievous feelings, with the progress of civilization; who would deny a hearing to opinions and arguments which tend to weaken the inordinate reverence of the people for every ruler, good or bad, and give free scope to those which tend to render that blind reverence, and all its consequent miseries, everlasting!

Although our sentiments on the subject of free discussion in religion have already been fully stated, we will quote one passage from an essay to which we have before referred: merely to show that the same arguments apply to religion, which we have already stated with a more immediate reference to politics:

Religion, in some of its shapes, has in most countries been placed on the footing of an institution of the state. Ought the freedom of the press to be as complete with regard to this, as we have seen that it ought to be in regard to all other institutions of the state? If any one says that it ought not, it is incumbent upon him to shew, wherein the principles which are applicable to the other institutions, fail in their application to this.

We have seen, that, in regard to all other institutions, it is unsafe for the people to permit any but themselves to choose opinions for them. Nothing can be more certain, than that it is unsafe for them to permit any but themselves to choose for them in religion.

If they part with the power of choosing their own religious opinions, they part with every power. It is well known with what ease religious opinions can be made to embrace every thing upon which the unlimited power of rulers and the utmost degradation of the people

[*The Theory of Moral Sentiments (1759), 6th ed., 2 vols. (London: Strahan and Cadell; Edinburgh: Creech and Bell, 1790), Vol. I, p. 146 (Pt. 1, Sect. III, Chap. iii); the passage alluded to first appeared in this ed.]

depend. The doctrine of *passive obedience* and non-resistance was a *religious doctrine*. Permit any man, or any set of men, to say what shall and what shall not be religious opinions, you make them despotic immediately.

This is so obvious, that it requires neither illustration nor proof.

But if the people here, too, must choose opinions for themselves, discussion must have its course; the same propositions which we have proved to be true in regard to other institutions, are true in regard to this; and no opinion ought to be impeded more than another, by any thing but the adduction of evidence on the opposite side.*

The argument drawn from the unsafeness of permitting governments to choose a religion for their subjects, cogent as it is, ranks only as one among a host of arguments, for leaving the people to follow their own reason, in matters of religion, as in every thing else.

In an age when the slightest difference of opinion on such a subject was deemed a perfectly sufficient reason for bringing the unhappy minority to the stake, it was not wonderful that Infidelity also should be considered a crime. But now, when a Churchman no more thinks of persecuting a Calvinist, or a Calvinist of persecuting a Churchman, than we think of punishing a man because he happens to be taller, or shorter, than ourselves; it is truly strange that there should be any one who can so blind himself as not to see, that the same reasons which make him a friend to toleration in other cases, bind him also to tolerate Infidelity.

The expression of opinions having been disposed of, it remains to be considered, whether in any case there is sufficient reason for placing restrictions upon the statement of facts. It must be admitted that the case of facts, and that of opinions, are not precisely similar. False opinions must be tolerated for the sake of the true: since it is impossible to draw any line by which true and false opinions can be separated from one another. There is no corresponding reason for permitting the publication of false statements of fact. The truth or falsehood of an alleged fact, is matter, not of opinion, but of evidence; and may be safely left to be decided by those, on whom the business of deciding upon evidence in other cases devolves.

It is maintained, however, by lawyers, that there ought to be other restrictions upon the statement of facts, besides the punishment of falsehood: there being some facts, as they allege, which, even if true, ought not to be made public. On this it is to be observed, that the same reasoning which proves that there should be perfect freedom of expressing opinions, proves also that there should be perfect freedom of expressing true facts. It is obviously upon facts, that all true opinions must be founded; if rulers, therefore, have, on any subject, on their own conduct, for example, the power of keeping from the knowledge of the people all facts which it does not suit them to disclose, they do, in fact, choose opinions for the people on that subject, just as completely as if they assumed the power of doing so, by a positive enactment.

There is one case, and only one, in which there might appear to be some doubt of

*The Article "Liberty of the Press," near the end [in *Essays*, p. 34].

the propriety of permitting the truth to be told without reserve. This is, when the truth, without being of any advantage to the public, is calculated to give annoyance to private individuals. That there are such cases must be allowed; and also that it would be desirable, in such cases, that the truth should be suppressed, if it could be done by any other means than law, or arbitrary power. It must, however, be borne in mind, that, if there are cases in which a truth unpleasant to individuals is of no advantage to the public, there are others in which it is of the greatest; and that the truths which it most imports to the public to know, are precisely those which give most annoyance to individuals, whose vices and follies they expose. Tory lawyers, indeed, for whom no doctrine is too extravagant which tends to uphold their power, or that of their employers, have asserted that one man has no right whatever to censure another: that to do so is an act of judicial authority which no individual is entitled to exercise: and that to expose vices and follies, instead of being one of the most important of all services to mankind, is a gross and unwarrantable usurpation of superiority.* We hope that none but Tory lawyers are hardy enough to profess concurrence in doctrines like these. Since, then, there is no one who can be trusted to decide which are useful, which the unimportant truths; and the consequences of suppressing both would, beyond comparison, exceed in mischievousness the consequences of allowing both to be heard; the practical conclusion needs not to be stated.

We have yet to notice a shift, to which recourse has frequently been had, since the spread of liberal opinions has rendered it scarcely safe to acknowledge the same degree of enmity to discussion, which was formerly avowed. We allude to the doctrine, that *calm* and *fair* discussion should be permitted, but that ridicule and invective ought to be chastised.

This is so much the doctrine which has been fashionable of late, that most of our readers probably believe it to be the law: and so, according to the *dicta* of judges, it is: but according to other *dicta* of the same judges, it is also the law, that any discussion, unless it be all on one side, and even a bare statement of acknowledged facts, is a libel.

The doctrine, however, being as we have said, a fashionable one, it is necessary to say something on it; and we observe, in the first place, that if argument may be permitted with safety, there can be little hazard in tolerating ridicule and invective; since, on all questions of importance, it is, in the long run, the balance of argument which always determines the decision of the majority. First, from the very nature of the weapons themselves: the operation of invective and ridicule being in a great measure limited to those whose minds are already made up. They may stimulate partizans, but they are not calculated to make converts. If a man does not renounce his opinion from conviction, it is scarcely by hearing himself laughed at, or reviled

*See Holt on the Law of Libel, *passim*. [Francis Ludlow Holt, *The Law of Libel* (London: Reed; Dublin: Phelan, 1812).]

for holding it, that he will be prevailed upon to give it up. Such means usually have no effect but to make him adhere to his opinion still more pertinaciously than before. And secondly, because ridicule and invective, if they may be used on one side, may be used also on the other; and against falsehood, for obvious reasons, with greater effect than against truth.

In the next place, if exclusion is to be put upon ridicule and invective, why is it not impartial? If any advantage can be derived from the employment of such weapons, why is it permitted to one set of opinions, withheld from another? Or is it that ridicule and invective then only tend to mislead, when they are employed on the side adverse to rulers? To deny any advantage to censure, which is extended to praise, is the same thing, though in a less aggravated degree, with the total prohibition of censure. Its effect, in as far as it has any, is to give an undue preponderance to praise: its tendency is, to make the people think better of their rulers than they deserve; and, to that extent rulers are enabled to oppress with impunity.

Suppose, for instance, that a writer is permitted to say, in as many words, that ministers or parliament have acted improperly, have engaged, for instance, in an unjust war; but, if he says this, and moreover expresses indignation that it should be so, he is punished. By expressing indignation, he gives it to be understood, that the evil, in his opinion, is great, and its authors deserving of punishment. If he refrains from expressing indignation, he virtually says, that the evil is not great, and its authors not deserving of punishment. Is it of no consequence, then, that the public should be informed, whether an evil is great or small? whether its authors are criminal, or the reverse? We fully subscribe to the manly and liberal sentiments of Mr. Mence on this subject. "It is not only no crime, but a positive duty, never to state crimes drily and coldly, and without the language of just and honest indignation. And our law, or supposed law of libel, by repressing the exercise of this duty, ministers to and encourages every kind of vice; and corrupts and undermines the manners and morals of the people." (Vol. I, p. 162.)

Great as are these evils, they are not the greatest which the prohibition of ridicule and invective carries along with it: nor is it for the mere purpose of securing exclusively to themselves any advantage which such weapons can bestow, that rulers cling so closely to the privilege of putting them down. It is because they know well that, if they are permitted to suppress ridicule and invective, they have it in their power to suppress all unfavourable representation. Who is to judge, what is invective, and what is fair and temperate discussion? None but rulers themselves: for no line can be drawn. All censure is invective. To censure is to ascribe misconduct. Even error is misconduct, in those to whose management the great affairs of a community are intrusted. When to err is to put to hazard the welfare of a nation, it is a crime for those who cannot avoid error to remain at the helm. To impute even error, therefore, is equivalent to invective, and might be construed as employing it. The mere statement of a great crime is itself invective. It implies, and is meant to imply, moral guilt: if it fails of doing so, the statement is so far imperfect. It is impossible, therefore, to prohibit invective, without prohibiting all discussion, or leaving it to rulers to decide what sort of discussion shall be punished, and what left free.

The question is, whether *indecent* discussion should be prohibited? To answer this question, we must, of course, inquire what is meant by indecent.

In English libel law, where this term holds so distinguished a place, is it not defined?

English legislators have not hitherto been good at defining; and English lawyers have always vehemently condemned, and grossly abused it. The word "indecent," therefore, has always been a term under which it was not difficult, on each occasion, for the judge to include whatever he did not like. "Decent" and "what the judge likes," have been pretty nearly synonymous.*

And while *indecent* discussion is prohibited by law, they always will be synonymous.

The doctrine which we have now exposed, is merely one of the shifts to which English rulers, from their peculiar situation, have been compelled to have recourse.

In other countries, where the system to be upheld is one of undisguised despotism, the utter incapacity of the people to judge rightly, and the unspeakable wickedness of their presuming to judge at all, on the subject of government, are the avowed doctrines of rulers. The people, it is there contended, have no business to form any opinion on the acts of government. They have nothing to do with their rulers except to obey them.[*] The magistrate, as he ought to have absolute control over the actions of all under his dominion, ought likewise to have power equally unlimited over their opinions. And this doctrine, if it has no other merit, has at least the recommendation of consistency.

The language of English rulers, down to the Revolution in 1688, was precisely similar. At that period, however, a new government was established; and this government, having come in upon the popular ground of resistance to kings, could not avoid admitting, that the people ought to be permitted to judge both of rulers and of institutions; since to deny this, would have been to give up the principle upon which its own dominion was founded. At the same time, having the same interests as any other government, it was desirous of suppressing, as far as possible, all censure upon its proceedings. Accordingly, the course which, since that time, it has pursued, has been one of perpetual compromise. It has admitted, in the fullest and most unequivocal terms, that discussion on all subjects of government and legislation ought to be free. It has even maintained, that the privilege of canvassing the acts of their government, is the birthright of Englishmen: that we owe to it all that we hold dear: that, without it, there can be no

*Article "Liberty of the Press," as before referred to [in *Essays*, p. 30].

[*Cf. Samuel Horsley, Speech of 6 Nov., 1795, in *The Speeches in Parliament of Samuel Horsley*, ed. H. Horsley (Dundee: Chalmers, 1813), pp. 167-8.]

security for good government. At the same time, in the teeth of these large professions, it has maintained, that censure of established governments ought not to be permitted; and it has assumed to itself, in practice, the privilege of visiting such censure, as often as it has thought fit, with some of the severest penalties of the law.

In this see-saw, English rulers have been followed by English lawyers. We shall select our first instances from Mr. Holt's celebrated treatise on the Law of Libel: a work which, having been declared by the late Lord Ellenborough from the bench to contain an accurate expression of his own sentiments, and being now generally received among lawyers as one of their standard works, may be considered unexceptionable authority, both for the law itself, and for the sentiments of rulers upon it. Observe what he says of the unspeakable importance of free discussion:

> Our constitution, in fact, as it at present exists, in a church reformed from the errors of superstition, and in a system of liberty equally remote from feudal anarchy, and monarchical despotism, is almost entirely, under Providence, the fruit of a free press. It was this which awakened the minds of men from that apathy in which ignorance of their rights, and of the duties of their rulers, left them. It was by these means that moral and religious knowledge, the foundations of all liberty, was refracted, multiplied, and circulated; and instead of existing in masses, and in the single points of schools and universities, was rendered the common atmosphere in which we all live and breathe. It was from the press that originated, what is, in fact, the main distinction of the ancient and modern world, public opinion. A single question will be sufficient to put the importance of this subject in the strongest point of view. In the present state of knowledge and manners, is it possible that a Nero or Tiberius would be suffered to live or reign? (1st ed., pp. 39, 40.)

Judging from this passage, who would not conceive it to be the doctrine of English lawyers, that mankind are indebted for all that is of greatest value, to censure of existing institutions: such censure as tends to produce the most radical changes, both in church and state, and even the dethronement and destruction of a bad sovereign?

Now mark the language of the same writer, only a few pages afterwards.

"In *every society*, therefore, the liberty of the press may justly be restricted within those limits which are necessary to maintain the establishment, and are necessary to maintain its exercise." (Pp. 45-6.)

"Every society" admits of no exception. It includes the worst governed, as well as the best. According to Mr. Holt, therefore, in this passage, all governments, no matter how bad, should be maintained. They are establishments, and that alone is a sufficient recommendation. It is to a free press, indeed, that we owe "a church reformed from the errors of superstition, and a system of liberty equally remote from feudal anarchy and monarchical despotism;" but as these were obtained by overthrowing a former system, and as "the limits necessary to maintain the establishment" are by no means to be passed, the writings which led to the Revolution ought to have been suppressed, and that great event, with all its glorious consequences, ought never to have been suffered to take place.

The difference, therefore, between the doctrine of rulers in England, and that of rulers elsewhere, exists only in name; and is not indicative of any difference in their real sentiments, but only in their power of giving expression to them without danger.

If there be any truth in the great principles of human nature, or any validity in the reasoning, upon which the British constitution is founded, there is no ruler who would not, if he could, suppress all censure of himself, of his measures, or of any of the arrangements which contribute to this authority. The British constitution supposes, that rulers always wish to abuse their power, and, of course, wish to remove every check which has a tendency to prevent them from abusing their power. But the great check to abuses of all sorts, is a free press. It is of the utmost importance, therefore, to observe, that all rulers have the strongest possible interest in destroying the freedom of the press: that they are under an absolute necessity of hating it; and that although they may not, at any one moment, have a fixed and regular plan for effecting its destruction, they are obstinately averse to any, even the most trifling, extension of it; and are eager to seize every opportunity for restraining it within the narrowest practicable limits.

The necessity for veiling this disposition by the tricks of language, has taught our rulers to devise a number of artful phrases, by the help of which they contrive, in the same breath, to give and take away the right of free discussion, and which, as often as they have occasion for the punishment of an obnoxious writer, serve them to beg the question in favour of their object. A trick of this kind, which has done them much good service, is the well-known profession, that they are friends to the *liberty* of the press, but enemies to its *licentiousness*.

Let us examine what this means. The liberty of the press, we are told, is good; that is, as we suppose, discussion, if not in all cases, at any rate in some cases, ought to be free. But the licentiousness of the press, it seems, is an evil; which we must presume to mean, that there are certain other cases in which discussion ought not to be free: but what cases? Of this we are not informed; for the word licentiousness, far from marking the distinction, is merely a vague epithet of blame. Their meaning, therefore, must be, that they are to judge what is the liberty of the press, and what is licentiousness. But this is to have the whole power of choosing opinions for the people. Allow them to decide what is, or is not licentiousness, and every thing will be licentiousness which implies censure of themselves, which involves any doctrine hostile to the indefinite increase and perpetual duration of their power. With them, indeed, to use the language of Mr. Mence, "the liberty of the press is a liberty of flattering, fawning, trifling, prosing, but not of writing freely, or fairly, or usefully, or in a way to engage attention, or have a chance of exciting interest, upon men or manners, or upon political, or legal, or religious, or moral subjects." (Vol. I, p. 206.)

It now remains to exhibit the actual state of the law of this country, with respect to the liberty of the press.

It is proper here to take notice of a very elaborate attempt made by Mr. Mence, to prove that the law really is not so unfavourable to free discussion as is commonly supposed.

The whole of the law by which the offence of libel is created, exists only in the state of common or unwritten law, of precedent, or custom. But this circumstance is so far from being peculiar to libel, that more than one half of the law of England exists in no other shape.

Mr. Mence alleges, and endeavours to prove—perhaps (for we shall not enter into so unimportant an inquiry) he has succeeded in proving, that the precedents on which the law of libel is founded, are not older than the star-chamber (printing itself, indeed, was not older); and from this he infers, that they are not, to use a legal phrase, *good law*; that there is, therefore, no law of libel, and that the punishments which have been inflicted upon alleged libellers are illegal.[*] Mr. Mence, however, is not the interpreter of the law. It belongs to the judges, and to them alone, to say what is, and what is not law. It is true, that the instances of omission are far more numerous than the instances of execution, and in the eye of reason, are equally entitled to be considered as precedents. It is true, that the judge hears a case, or refuses to hear it, as he pleases, and, therefore, makes the law, *toties quoties*, under the guise of declaring it. Nothing, indeed, can be more shocking, more grossly inconsistent with all ideas of good law, or good judicature, than this; but it is an evil inseparable from a system of common law, and if the law of libel be not, technically speaking, good law, we can scarcely be said to have any law at all, since even statutes are for the most part built upon the common law, and taking the offence for granted, confine themselves to regulating the punishment.

It is of little importance in itself, what the law is, if the practice be bad: but it is of the greatest importance that the public should not be made to believe that the law, if it were executed, would afford a security, when in reality it would afford no security at all; and it is because Mr. Mence has taken, as we conceive, so erroneous a view of this question, that we think it necessary to caution our readers against being misled by an author, from whom, in other respects, they may derive so much information.

Our own view of the state of the law will be collected, partly from Mr. Holt's work, which is a digest of the cases, and which, as we have already observed, carries with it all the weight of Lord Ellenborough's authority,[†] partly from the *dicta* of judges themselves.

The object being to asertain, what meaning the English law attaches to the term libel, it is natural to begin by asking, what definition of libel it affords? To which we answer, none: nothing which deserves the name of a definition ever having been adduced.

[*See Mence, Vol. I, pp. 287-386.]
[†Holt's work is dedicated (pp. iii-iv) to Edward Law, Lord Ellenborough.]

Mr. Holt says, "A libel is a malicious defamation, expressed either in printing or writing, or by signs, pictures, &c., tending either to blacken the memory of one who is dead, with an intent to provoke the living, or the reputation of one who is alive, and thereby exposing him to public hatred, contempt and ridicule." (P. 50.)

What can be more absurd than to put forth such a definition as this, with great parade too of exactness, and fortified by references to no less than six legal authorities;[*] and in the very next sentence, enumerating the species of libel, to talk of libels against *religion*, against *morality*, against *the constitution*.[†] Mr. Holt's definition, by whomsoever devised, was obviously intended only for private libel; and if applied to any thing else, is unintelligible. It necessarily supposes a person libelled. Religion, morality, &c. are not persons, either dead or alive, but abstract terms. Considered only as a definition of private libel, it is abundantly mischievous, since it informs us, that to give publicity to vice, in other words, to take the only effectual security against its overspreading the earth, is, according to English law, a crime. And this doctrine, Mr. Holt, in another place, does not scruple openly to avow.[‡]

This is, at any rate, an attempt to define. In most law books, if we look for a definition of libel, we find nothing but a fiction. Libel is punishable, we are there told, because it tends to provoke a breach of the peace. The person libelled, may, out of resentment, commit the crime of assault against his accuser: it is fit, therefore, that the law should extend its protecting shield over the libeller, and save him from the chance of a broken head, by inflicting upon him a year's imprisonment. A tweak by the nose, according to this doctrine, should be more criminal than any libel, for it is certainly far more likely to provoke the species of retaliation alluded to. Miserable as this fiction is, it has served as a foundation to lawyers for building up the excellent law maxim, "the greater the truth, the greater the libel." A bad man, it is alleged, is more easily provoked than a good man! and a true accusation being usually more cutting than a false one, exposes the accuser to a greater hazard of being knocked down!

One might almost as reasonably contend, [says Mr. Mence,] that it ought to be criminal in point of law for any person to carry money about him, lest it should tempt some scoundrel to pick his pocket or knock his brains out. The punishment in such a case, as the law now stands, would fall upon the thief, instead of the tempter. And the peace would be at least as well secured, and the interests of morality much better consulted, in cases of alleged libel, by punishing not the man who exposes vice and holds it up to deserved infamy; but the man whose vicious conduct is exposed, and who to his crimes has added the farther crime of braving the disgrace, and committing violence upon the person who may justly and meritoriously have exposed him. (Vol. I, p. 136.)

[*William Blackstone, Edward Coke, William Hawkins, John Holt, Lloyd Kenyon, and Thomas Wood; for the specific citations, see under their names in App. G below.]
[†Holt, p. 51.]
[‡*Ibid.*, Chap. x, pp. 160-220.]

The reader may be curious to learn for what purpose this ludicrous fiction was invented. The purpose was, to render libel a penal offence, instead of being merely a civil injury. Had it been classed among private offences, under the head of injuries to reputation, it would have been necessary to prove, in the first place, that an injury had really been sustained; and then the damages awarded would not have exceeded a fair compensation for the actual injury which had been proved. To make it a public offence, it was erected into a sort of virtual breach of the peace, which, again, by another equally contemptible fiction, is the king's peace; and thus, a libel against an individual became an offence against the king. Englishmen, who have been accustomed to hear, and to believe, that the law is the perfection of human reason,[*] will be astonished to learn, that there is scarcely one, even of its good principles, which has any thing better than such fictions as the above for its basis. *In fictione juris semper aequitas*, say the lawyers. It is an assertion which they would not venture to put forth, were not the apathy of the public a sufficient security for its being believed without inquiry. Yet here is, at any rate, one instance, (and every one who has examined the law without a resolution to find every thing as it should be,[†] can supply many more), in which such fictions have been devised for the most mischievous of all purposes.

This technical definition answered to admiration, so long as there were no libels but against individuals, all the rest being heresy or treason; but when times altered, and it was no longer practicable to hang, draw, and quarter men for libel, judges were put to their shifts for a definition which should give them power really unlimited, without the appearance. The late Lord Ellenborough, who, from his greater boldness of character, was in the habit of giving utterance to the pernicious doctrine with less of restraint and disguise than is usual, once said from the bench, that a libel was *any thing which hurts the feelings of any body*.[‡] This was acknowledging more than was quite safe. It was admitting, that, according to English law, as administered by English judges, it is a crime to impute either error or criminality to public functionaries or to individuals; since to impute even error to any one, if it does not in all cases actually hurt his feelings, has, at least, always a tendency to do so.

The words of an indictment for public libel, which, in the absence of a definition, are, it must be presumed, intended to give some indication of the meaning and import of the charge, are "tending to bring our Lord the King and his

---

[*See Edward Coke, *The First Part of the Institutes of the Lawes of England* (London: Society of Stationers, 1628), p. 97 (Lib. II, Cap. vi, Sect. 138).]

[†See Jeremy Bentham, *A Fragment on Government* (1776), in *Works*, ed. John Bowring, 11 vols. (Edinburgh: Tait; London: Simpkin, Marshall; Dublin: Cumming, 1843), Vol. I, p. 230.]

[‡See Edward Law, Charge to the Jury in the Trial of William Cobbett, 1804, in *A Complete Collection of State Trials*, ed. Thomas Bayly Howell, 34 vols. (London: Longman, *et al.*, 1809-28), Vol. XXIX, col. 49.]

administration," or "the constitution and government of these realms," or "the two Houses of Parliament," or "the administration of justice, the trial by jury," &c. "into *great and public hatred and contempt.*"[*]

Lord Ellenborough's *dictum* itself is not better adapted to bear out the judge in the most mischievous exertion of power, than this. It is criminal to bring rulers into "hatred and contempt." But hatred is the legitimate consequence of guilt; contempt the legitimate consequence of folly. To impute either guilt or folly, either intentional or unintentional error, to rulers, is, therefore, by English law, a crime.

The attempts at definition, bad as they are, have only been exceptions: the general rule has been, to maintain, that libel, though it ought to be punished, cannot, and ought not to be defined. The conspiracy, in truth, have a good reason for leaving the offence of libel undefined: for they would not dare to include in a definition all that the support of the conspiracy requires to be included. They would not dare to assume, by a specific law, all the power which they hope to enjoy by usurpation. Were they to make a definition which included all that they wish to be included, common feeling would be shocked; neither they nor other men would bear to look at it. Nothing, however, can be more gross than the inconsistency into which this necessarily drives them. They insist that libel cannot be defined, yet they say that twelve unlettered men are to judge what is libel and what is not. How can any man know what is included in a general rule, if he knows not what that rule is?

On the subject of libels against the constitution, the following is the language of Mr. Holt:

If the law protects the subject in his rights, and punishes every invasion of them, much more does it protect that system from which all these rights proceed, and by which alone they can be maintained. The government and constitution being the common inheritance, every attack made upon them, which affects their permanence and security, is in a degree an attack upon every individual in the state, and concerns the rights of all. If it be the highest crime known to our laws, to subvert by force that constitution and polity which the wisdom and valour of our ancestors have erected and confirmed, it is certainly a crime, though of inferior magnitude, yet of great enormity, to endeavour to despoil it of its best support, the veneration, esteem, and affection of the people. It is, therefore, a maxim of the law of England, flowing by natural consequence and easy deduction from the great principle of self-defence, to consider as libels and misdemeanours every species of attack by speaking or writing, the object of which is *wantonly to defame*, or *indecorously to calumniate*, that economy, order, and constitution of things, which make up the general system of the law and government of the country. (P. 74.)

Considering the parade of logic, which characterizes Mr. Holt's book, it is not a little remarkable that, on the most important point of all, he should be detected in using language so utterly destitute of any definite or precise meaning. Such

[*For similar wording, see the indictment in the "Trial of John Lambert and James Perry, for a Libel upon His Majesty George the Third," *ibid.*, Vol. XXXI, cols. 335-6; cf. 60 George III and 1 George IV, c. 8 (1819).]

vagueness can have but one object; namely, to hide the absolute power which the words that he uses are intended to confer upon the judge.

In the first place, he is pleased to represent the constitution as a person, and talks of *defaming* the constitution, *calumniating* the constitution, as if an abstract term could be defamed or calumniated. Then it is *wantonly* to defame, and *indecorously* to calumniate. Whether any thing be added to, or taken from the sense by these epithets, we profess ourselves unable to understand.

What is the constitution? merely the aggregate of the securities for good government, which are provided by the existing law, whatever those securities may be, more or less complete.[*] This must be the meaning of the word, constitution, if it has any: and if by a sort of metaphor we speak of the constitution as being calumniated, we can only mean, that these securitites are represented as insufficient for the prevention of mis-government; that the constitution is represented as not attaining its end.

Consider what is implied, when it is said, that the securities for good government which, being taken collectively, we call the constitution, are inadequate to their end. It is implied, that, to a certain extent at least, if not altogether, we are as if we had no constitution; and that rulers have the power to tyrannize over us with impunity. If this be true, it will not be openly asserted that, to make it known would not be highly meritorious. The supposition, therefore, must be, that it is not true. This cannot be proved, without suffering those who deny it to be heard. It is, therefore, taken for granted without proof.

It being, therefore, according to this doctrine, allowable for English rulers to take for granted, without proof, that their own form of government is the best possible, it must be equally allowable for all other rulers to make the same assumption in favour of theirs. It will not, however, be contended, that all forms of government are the best. The doctrine, therefore, of the law of England, as expounded by Mr. Holt, is, that any rulers, in any country, may justly assume that the most detestable of all governments is the best, and upon that assumption may with perfect propriety inflict punishment to any extent upon all who presume to call in question its excellence.

Higher authorities than Mr. Holt have propounded the same doctrine. Lord Camden says,

"All governments must set their faces against libels, and whenever they come before a court and a jury, they will set their faces against them. And if juries do not prevent them, they may prove fatal to liberty, destroy government, and introduce anarchy; but tyranny is better than anarchy, and the worst government better than none at all."*

[*Cf. James Mill, "Government" (1820), in *Essays*, pp. 16-19; Jeremy Bentham, *Constitutional Code*, in *Works*, Vol. IX, p. 9.]

*Entick *v.* Carrington, 2 *Wils.* *K.B.* 275, apud Holt, pp. 75-6 [95 *English Reports* 818].

It is here pretty distinctly intimated, that the worst government is justified in punishing all who hold it up to that detestation which it deserves; and the premises are equally edifying with the conclusion: if a tyrannical government be subverted, it is possible that anarchy may ensue; and anarchy, in the opinion of Lord Camden and of Mr. Holt, is a greater evil than the worst possible government. Adam Smith, indeed, thought differently; in the opinion of that great philosopher and practical judge of human nature, despotism is "more destructive of leisure and security, than anarchy itself."* His lordship is welcome, however, as far as we are concerned, to whatever advantage he can derive from this assumption. But we submit that, if the worst possible government may be succeeded by anarchy, it may also be succeeded by a good government; and how must his mind be constituted who, if it were necessary, would fear to risk a few years, even of anarchy, for such a possibility!

In this investigation we have purposely avoided making the supposition, that the British constitution really is not the best possible. It is obvious, however, how much, if it be not, the strength of the argument is increased.

If we were as firmly convinced that the British constitution is, as we are convinced that it is not, the best possible government, we should be willing to expose even such a government to a very considerable degree of risk, rather than support it by means, which if they may be used for the preservation of the best government, may be equally used to perpetuate all the atrocities of the worst. But if the constitution be really imperfect—and who shall say that it is otherwise, if gainsayers are not suffered to be heard? then how greatly is the atrocity aggravated! and what are we to think of those who wickedly endeavour to prop up a bad cause, by means which even the best ought to reject with horror!

Mr. Holt seems to have been in some degree aware, that the mischievous purpose of the law would shew itself even through the vague and evasive language in which he has clothed it. After telling us that the judges have the power to punish every thing which they may pronounce intended to "despoil the constitution of its best support, the veneration, esteem, and affection of the people," he has thought it expedient to say something with a view to make it appear that they *have not* this power.

The constitution of this country, which is nothing but perfect reason, acknowledges in every man a right to set forth a general or individual hardship, and to suggest error, even in the highest branch of the magistracy. The constitution, indeed, is too wise not to acknowledge that the best interest of the state, as of human society at large, is truth. It opens, therefore, a ready ear to honest and useful truth of all kinds; and as it receives this truth from human beings, and therefore can only expect it as mingled up and adulterated with human passions, it will often pardon and overlook a natural warmth, for the sake of the truth which it produces. This is the character of the constitution with respect to public libels

*Essay on the History of Astronomy, [in *Essays on Philosophical Subjects*, ed. Joseph Black and James Hutton (London: Cadell and Davies, 1795),] p. 27.

in good times. But every right has its limits. The right is given by the constitution, in so far as it is necessary and salutary, for the purposes of reminding kings of their duty, and parliaments of their trusts; the right stops at that point where its exercise would endanger the permanence and due weight of government; that is, where it serves no other purpose than to revive the original anarchy and to spread disaffection and tumult through the state. (P. 76.)

It is not easy to enumerate all the gratuitous assumptions, all the shifts and evasions, which this one passage contains.

In the first place, it is assumed, that to "endanger the permanence of government" (such are the words of Mr. Holt) can have no object but to "revive the original anarchy:" which is precisely the assumption by which all bad rulers, from time immemorial, have begged the question in favour of themselves.

In the next place, we are informed that the right of unfavourable representation is allowed, so far as is necessary to "remind kings of their duty, and parliaments of their trusts;" but not to such a degree as to "spread disaffection through the state." So said the Mogul emperor: his subjects might state their grievances for his information, and if he thought fit, he would redress them; with this reservation, however, that if he should happen to take offence at their representations, he might cut off their heads upon the spot.[*]

But, thirdly, it seems, even this limited right of unfavourable representation is allowed only in good times; the question, what are and are not good times, being of course left to be decided by the government itself. It is not difficult to see what, by such a judge, would be pronounced to be good times. So long as the people were perfectly quiet, and any breath of censure which might be heard boded no danger to profitable abuses, that censure might be tolerated, simply because there would be no motive for its suppression. But as soon as a feeling began to be excited, that there was something wrong, something calling for reformation; as soon as there began to be a chance, that unfavourable representations, if they continued, might at length have the effect of forcing upon rulers some degree of amendment; then would be the time for declaring that the "permanence and due weight of government" were endangered: then would be the time for suspending the habeas corpus act, and extending, like Mr. Pitt, the strong arm of power, to crush every writer who presumed to insinuate, that all was not for the best.[†]

One admission, however (we shall see how far it is sincere), is made in the above passage; that the constitution does permit censure, if not at all times, and on

[*See the reference to the Emperor Jehangir in William Finch, "Observations of William Finch, Merchant, Taken out of His Large Journall," in Samuel Purchas, *Purchas His Pilgrimes*, 4 vols. (London: Fetherstone, 1625), Vol. I, p. 439.]

[†For Pitt's actions, see "The King's Proclamation against Seditious Writings" (21 May, 1792), in *Parliamentary History of England*, ed. William Cobbett and John Wright, 36 vols. (London: Bagshaw, Longmans, 1806-20), Vol. XXIX, cols. 1476-7; see also 34 George III, c. 54 (1794).]

all subjects, yet at some times, and on some subjects. Now mark the language of Mr. Holt, a few pages afterwards:

"If" a writer, "forgetting the wholesome respect which is due to authority and to the maintenance of *every system*, proposes to reform the evils of the state by *lessening the reverence of the laws*; the law, under such circumstances, considers him as abusing to the purposes of anarchy, what it has given him for the purposes of defence." (P. 103.)

It is not to the doctrine, that not only a good system, but every system ought to be maintained, that we would at present direct the attention of our readers. It is to the declaration, that nothing must be done tending to lessen the reverence for the laws: that to whatever degree a law may be bad, its badness shall not be suffered to be exposed, nor any representation to be made which shall convince the people of the necessity for its repeal. What, then, is to be said of the assertions that "the constitution acknowledges the best interest of the state to be truth"; that it "opens a ready ear to honest and useful truth of all kinds?" What, but that they are cant, disgusting from its hypocrisy, as mischievous as false, and put forth solely to deceive the people into a belief that the constitution and the law are much better than they really are?

From libels on the constitution, Mr. Holt passes to libels on the king and his government, and to this subject we shall follow him, promising to the reader, that, after all that we have already said, we shall not detain him long.

From Mr. Holt's general view of the law on this subject, one passage has been already extracted. We now give it entire.

Every Englishman has a clear right to discuss public affairs freely, inasmuch as, from the renewable nature of the popular part of our constitution, and the privilege of choosing his representatives, he has a particular, as well as a general interest in them. He has a right to point out error and abuse in the conduct of the affairs of state, and freely and temperately to canvass every question connected with the public policy of the country. But, if instead of the sober and honest discussion of a man prudent and attentive to his own interests, his purpose is, to misrepresent, and find a handle for faction; if, instead of the respectful language of complaint and decorous remonstrance, he assumes a tone and a deportment which can belong to no individual in civil society; if, forgetting the wholesome respect which is due to authority, and to the maintenance of every system, he proposes to reform the evils of the state by lessening the reverence of the laws; if he indiscriminately assigns bad motives to imagined errors and abuses; if, in short, he uses the liberty of the press to cloak a malicious intention, to the end of injuring private feeling, and disturbing the peace, economy, and order of the state; the law, under such circumstances, considers him as abusing to the purposes of anarchy what it has given him for the purposes of defence. (Pp. 102-3.)

For the exposure of this doctrine, a few words are sufficient.

In the first place, the distinction between the censure which is permitted, and the censure which is prohibited, turns out to be, not any thing in the censure itself, but something in the intention. By what evidence is the intention to be ascertained? By the greater severity of the censure? No: for it surely does not follow, that a man must necessarily intend to misrepresent because he censures severely; unless it is contended that governments can never act in such a manner as to merit severe censure.

To obtain reform, you must point out defects. By pointing out defects, you bring discredit on the government. By pointing out defects and seeking remedies, you shew your malice. Yes; the same sort of malice which a man shews towards himself by going to a physician to know the defects of his constitution, and how to remedy them.

Some parts of Mr. Holt's language, however, seem to insinuate, what he himself in other places denies, that censure may be freely applied, provided it be without assigning bad motives. "The law," says he, "in this respect, follows in the line of our duty. Invective, and the assignment of bad motives, can evidently answer no good purpose. No man assuredly can justify such contumely, even towards a private individual, and society at least should have dignity enough to commmunicate something of its sacredness to its officers." (P. 103.)

What is meant by the dignity of society, and communicating sacredness to its officers, we do not pretend to understand. What Mr. Holt, or the judges, would consider as bad motives, we do not know. Perhaps, by bad motives he means criminality, as distinguished from innocent error; and, in that case, we utterly deny the assertion, that no good purpose is to be answered by exposing it. Is it of no importance that the public should know the character of those in whose hands the disposal of their whole happiness is placed? Apply this doctrine to the crimes of individuals: would Mr. Holt assert that it can answer no good purpose to distinguish between wilful murder and accidental homicide?

This part of the law of libel, as expounded by the judges, and by Mr. Holt, is, like all other parts of it, purposely left in such a state of vagueness, as to place every public writer absolutely at the mercy of the judge.

"Every thing," says Mr. Holt, "is a libel, the purpose of which is, to misrepresent and find a handle for faction." But what is faction? Every man opposing ministers. What is misrepresentation? Falsehood. Who is to judge what is falsehood? The government: and the government, therefore, is to judge in its own cause; the government is to decide upon the truth or falsehood of a charge of error or crime against itself, and if it pronounces the charge to be false, it is to have the power of inflicting punishment, to any extent, upon the accuser!

It may be thought, perhaps, that Mr. Holt has distorted the law. To prove that he has not, we shall next quote some of the *dicta* of judges; than which nothing can be more explicit, as to the illegality of all censure upon the government.

LORD HOLT. They say that nothing is a libel but what reflects on some particular person. But this is a very strange doctrine, to say that it is not a libel reflecting on the government; endeavouring to possess the people that the government is mal-administered by corrupt persons that are employed in such stations, either in the navy or army. To say that corrupt officers are appointed to administer affairs is certainly a reflection on the government. If men should not be called to account for possessing the people with an ill opinion of the government, no government can subsist.*

According to this judge, nothing is to be permitted which tends to possess the people with an ill opinion of the government; that all censure has this for its object, it is unnecessary to remark. All censure, therefore, is prohibited.

LORD CHIEF JUSTICE RAYMOND. Even a private man's character is not to be scandalized, either directly or indirectly; because there are remedies appointed by law, in case he has injured any person, without maliciously scandalizing him in his character. And much less is a magistrate, minister of state, or other public person's character to be stained, either directly or indirectly. And the law reckons it a greater offence when the libel is pointed at persons in a public capacity, as it is a reproach to the government to have corrupt magistrates, &c. substituted by his majesty, and tends to sow sedition, and disturb the peace of the kingdom.[†]

From this we learn two things: first, that nothing is permitted to be said which can be construed as either directly or by implication a reproach upon the government. And secondly, that all persons whatever, public or private, are guaranteed by the law against all exposure of any misconduct, however glaring, and however hurtful to the community.

SIR PHILIP YORKE (afterwards Lord Chancellor Hardwicke). He (the printer) is not to publish any thing reflecting on the character, and reputation, and *administration* of his majesty, or his ministers.[‡]

This doctrine, which is honoured with the peculiar approbation of Mr. Holt (p. 111), is in substance the same with that which we last quoted; with this addition, that it contains a prohibition of strictures, even upon particular measures. The "*administration* of his majesty, or his ministers," is not to be reflected upon.

On the trial of Woolston for a deistical work,[*] the Court said, "that the Christian religion is established in this kingdom; and therefore they would not allow any books to be written which should tend to alter that establishment."[§] Christianity is to be made an instrument of persecution because it is an *establishment*; no books are to be written which tend to alter *establishments*. What sort of a doctrine is this?

*[John Holt, Charge to the Jury in the Trial of John Tutchin, 1704, in] *Holt K.B.* 424 [90 *English Reports* 1133], and [Howell,] *State Trials*, Vol. XIV, col. 1128, apud Holt, p. 108.

[†][Robert Raymond, Speech in the Trial of Richard Francklin, 1731, in Howell,] *State Trials*, Vol. XVII [cols. 658-9], apud Holt, p. 111.

[‡]*Ibid.* [Speech for the Plaintiff in the Trial of Richard Francklin, 1731, in Howell, *State Trials*, Vol. XVII, col. 670; quoted in Francis Holt, p. 112.]

[*Thomas Woolston was tried in 1729 for his *A Discourse on the Miracles of Our Saviour, in View of the Present Controversy between Infidels and Apostates*, 6 pts. (London: the Author, 1727-29).]

[§][Robert Raymond, Speech in the Trial of Thomas Woolston, 1729, in 94 *English Reports* 113,] Holt, p. 55.

LORD ELLENBOROUGH. It is no new doctrine, that if a publication be calculated to alienate the affections of the people, by *bringing the government into disesteem*, whether the expedient be by ridicule or obloquy, the person so conducting himself is exposed to the inflictions of the law. It is a crime, it has ever been considered as a crime, whether wrapt in one form or another.*

Having commented at so much length upon similar doctrines, we are under no inducement to spend time upon this.

The two trials of Mr. Wooler, in the year 1817, for seditious libels, teem with similar *dicta*, both of the attorney-general who prosecuted, and the judge who presided. We quote a report which was printed *verbatim* from the manuscript of an eminent short-hand writer. On that occasion, the then attorney-general, the present Master of the Rolls, and, if report say true, the future Lord Chancellor, delivered himself in the following terms:

To impute to the ministers under any form of government, whether monarchy or any other established form of government, wicked and corrupt motives of a pecuniary nature, or of another and a worse sort, viz. that corruption arising from a desire to destroy the liberties and the constitution of their country, and to take away from the subjects of the state all the happiness intended to be given by the laws and constitution, is, I take leave boldly to state, without hazard of contradiction from any lawyer in the country, a libel against the administration of the government: against the ministers employed in that administration.[†]

It would appear at first sight, to an incautious reader, that the improved spirit of the times had produced some effect, even upon his majesty's attorney-general. The doctrine, that all censure of ministers is a libel, was no longer dared to be openly avowed. What was avowed, however, is, that when ministers aim at subverting the constitution, at subverting that, which, according to the attorney-general, is our only security against every horror which mankind have, at any period of history, endured from bad rulers; that when ministers aim at taking away this security, and plunging us into these evils, no one shall be allowed to say so. That this is an unfair interpretation we deny. Is it, or is it not, possible, that ministers should wish to be absolute? If it be answered, that such a design is possible, but that in this instance it was unjustly ascribed to them, we answer, that if despotism has been the aim of some ministers, it may be the aim of the present, and we are not to believe that to be impossible which all experience proves to be certain, merely because the attorney-general thinks proper to deny it. This modest claim, however, he did not scruple to prefer. "They (the ministers) would not make

*Case of the King *v.* Cobbett, apud Holt, p. 119.

[†]*Trials of Mr. Wooler* [i.e., Thomas Jonathan Wooler, *A Verbatim Report of the Two Trials of Mr. T. J. Wooler, Editor of the Black Dwarf* (London: Wooler, 1817)], pp. 5-6. [The Attorney-General at the time was Samuel Shepherd; Mill is confusing him with the Solicitor-General, Robert Gifford, who was Master of the Rolls in 1825, and was expected to be the next Lord Chancellor.]

their will the general law, but it is not that they dare not, but, I take leave to state, because they cannot and will not."*

Here we are asked to believe that ministers are not men of ordinary virtue, nor even men of extraordinary virtue, but something infinitely superior to all men who ever did, or can exist. Not so says the law of England. That law always presumes that men act according to their interest. So far is this principle carried, that, if a man has a single shilling to gain by perjury, the law presumes that he will perjure himself for that shilling, and refuses to hear his evidence. And here we are called upon to take it for granted, not only that the strongest conceivable temptations are weaker than the virtue of ministers, but that a man ought to be severely punished for insinuating the contrary. And why? Because such is the *ipse dixit* of his majesty's attorney-general.

The present Chief Justice Abbott, on the same occasion, was pleased to deliver, as has been recently the usual practice, two contrary doctrines; both of which, of course, by his pronouncing them, became equally the law of the land.

It is open to every subject of the country to discuss the measures of government, provided he do it reasonably, fairly, and impartially; but if, instead of reasoning and discussing upon measures general or particular, a person chooses to issue forth to the world slander and calumny against the government, or against the authors of those measures, he then becomes amenable to the law; if I may so say, where reasoning ends and slander and calumny begin, there is the line by which a judgment is to be formed.[†]

This is one doctrine. Shortly afterwards he, in a passage too long to quote, propounds, and praises Lord Holt for propounding, the other.[*] This is, that it is libellous in any way to reflect upon, that is, to censure, the government, and to bring into discredit, that is again to censure, the two Houses of Parliament.

We will take the least bad doctrine of the two: that which asserts that reasoning is permitted, but slander and calumny prohibited.

What is the use of reasoning? To draw conclusions, we suppose. All reasoning is, we apprehend, for the sake of the conclusion. Reasoning, it seems, is fit and proper: is it proper to draw conclusions? If they are favourable, yes; if unfavourable, no; because in that case, they are slander and calumny.

We might quote many cases posterior to this, but we shall stop here, partly because we have already exhibited enough, partly because the more recent trials have not been published in an equally authoritative form. It is not because there is nothing to say on the trial of Mr. Harvey for a libel on a living king, or on that of Mr. John Hunt, for a libel on a dead one,[†] that we refrain from particularly

Ibid., p. 14.
†*Ibid.*, p. 80.
[*Ibid.*, p. 82.]
[†Daniel Whittle Harvey was tried in 1823 for libelling George IV; John Hunt, in 1824, for libelling George III.]

alluding to what was said by lawyers and judges on those memorable occasions. It is because it was not in our power to quote any better authority than newspaper reports; and it is not enough for us that our assertions are true; we would have them exempt even from the possibility of suspicion.

We notice the head "Libels against the two Houses of Parliament,"[*] only to say that, according to Mr. Holt, the one thing to which all the influence of public opinion over those assemblies is owing, the publication of their proceedings—is illegal.

Under the head, "Libels against Courts of Justice,"[†] Mr. Holt says,

It is, undoubtedly, within the natural compass of the liberty of the press, to discuss, in a peaceable and temperate manner, the decisions and judgments of a court of justice; to suggest even error, and, provided it be done in the language, and with the views, of fair criticism, to censure what is apparently wrong, but with this limitation, that no false or dishonest motives be assigned to any party.*

"Any public reflection," he continues, "on the ministration of justice, is unquestionably libellous."[‡]

Here are two assertions: the one, that the law permits censure; the other that it does not. We shall now see which of them is borne out by the *dicta* of judges. And we shall content ourselves with quoting the first case, related under this branch of his subject, by Mr. Holt himself.

JUSTICE BULLER. Nothing can be of greater importance to the welfare of the public, than to put a stop to the animadversions and censures which are so frequently made upon courts of justice in this country. They can be of no service, and may be attended with the most mischievous consequences. Cases may happen, in which the judge and jury may be mistaken; when they are, the *law has afforded a remedy*, and the party injured is entitled to pursue every method which the law allows to correct the mistake. But, when a person has recourse either by writing like the present, by publications in print, or by any other means, to calumniate the proceedings of a court of justice, the obvious tendency of it is, to weaken the administration of justice, and, in consequence, to sap the very foundation of the constitution itself.[†]

The law has afforded a remedy! Yes; the injured party, if he can afford it, may move the very judge by whom he was condemned, for a new trial; and if by miracle he should obtain it, he may go again to be tried before the same, or a brother judge, subject to the same sinister interest,[§] and a jury under the same influence. We

[*Francis Holt, Chap. vi, pp. 121-36.]
[†*Ibid.*, Chap. vii, pp. 137-49.]
Ibid., p. 144.
[‡*Ibid.*]
†[Francis Buller, Judgment in the Case of R. *v.* Archer, 1788, in 100 *English Reports* 113,] Holt, p. 145.
[§For the term, see, e.g., Bentham, *Plan of Parliamentary Reform* (1817), in *Works*, Vol. III, pp. 440, 446.]

may be permitted to doubt, however, whether his chance of obtaining redress in this way be so considerable, as to render all other means superfluous; or whether he would have any chance whatever of obtaining it, if he had not the means of influencing public opinion in his favour.

The doctrine inculcated in the above *dictum*, that it is criminal to censure the proceedings of a court of judicature, and that whoever presumes to do so, is an enemy to the administration of justice, became unhappily, by the artifices of judges and the influence of rulers, deeply rooted in the minds of Englishmen. It was long the prevailing cry, that the administration of justice must be preserved free from suspicion, that no reflections must be permitted on the administration of justice: as if any mischief could be done to good judges, and good judicature, by the exposure of bad; as if it were not the greatest possible injury to a good judge, to render it impossible for the public to distinguish him from a bad one.

So far is the conduct of judges from requiring no *surveillance*, that there is scarcely any set of public functionaries, whose conduct requires it so much. Receiving their appointments from government; having, of necessity, from the course they must have adopted to obtain those appointments, all their leanings on the side of power; having, most of them, sons and nephews at the bar, for whom they are in the habit of looking to advancement and patronage at the hands of government; vested with power, which, if thrown into the scale of government, goes so far to render it despotic, that no sacrifice, on the part of rulers, can be too great, by which their co-operation can be obtained; it is not easy for any set of persons to be exposed to stronger temptations: and that those temptations have invariably proved too strong for the virtue even of the best judges, we have only to look at the records of libel cases, to be convinced.

We are perpetually boasting, [says the writer of the pamphlet which stands, together with Mr. Mence's work, at the head of this article,] We are perpetually boasting of the integrity of the judges. The judges on the bench are always, for the time being, the best of judges, the wisest and most upright of men, men who will neither do nor suffer injustice, men who will drive from their presence all who seek to pervert the law, or who take advantage of its defects to do injury to any one. Woe to him who shall dare to impeach the conduct of a living judge!

Yet how few are the dead judges whose conduct has not been impeached, and that, too, on good grounds. Were the judges really and truly independent of the executive power, and were the people at liberty, as they ought to be, but as, with the consent of the judges, they never will be, were they at liberty to canvass the conduct of a living judge to the necessary extent, so that no judge could commit acts of folly or of injustice with impunity, very few such acts would be committed. Had this security been taken, and this freedom been enjoyed in time past, the evils which have been accumulating for ages would have had no existence, the law would have been precise, clear, and sufficient, and its administration very different indeed from that which we are compelled to witness.*

*[Place, *On the Law of Libel*,] pp. 5-6.

We regard it, then, as one of the most favourable signs of the times, that this indiscriminating reverence for all the instruments of judicature is giving way; that the proceedings of judges begin to obtain their due share of examination, and their misconduct of reprobation. And we take this opportunity of declaring our conviction, that this great and salutary change has been in a great degree owing to the indefatigable exertions of the *Morning Chronicle*; a journal, in which we have now been long accustomed to look for excellence of all sorts, but which has displayed, more particularly, in its strictures on the language and conduct of judicial functionaries, a degree of true courage, of ability, and of morality in its highest and least common shape, which it has been but too rarely our lot to witness in the periodical press of this country.

The two following conclusions may now, we think, be regarded as fully established:

That the law of England, as delivered by its authorized interpreters, the judges, however earnestly the same judges may occasionally disavow this doctrine, prohibits all unfavourable representation with respect to institutions, and with respect to the government and its acts:

And, consequently, that if any freedom of discussion is permitted to exist, it is only because it cannot be repressed; the reason why it cannot be repressed, being, the dread of public opinion.

And now, having established these two propositions, we have only further to recommend them to the most serious consideration of our readers.

The importance of free discussion, though frequently dwelt upon by public writers, is seldom fully appreciated by those who, not being themselves exposed to the danger of becoming its martyrs, erroneously consider themselves little affected by its violations. It concerns in fact equally every member of the community. It is equal in value to good government, because without it good government cannot exist. Once remove it, and not only are all existing abuses perpetuated, but all which, in the course of successive ages, it has overthrown, revive in a moment, along with that ignorance and imbecility, against which it is the only safeguard. Conceive the horrors of an oriental despotism—from this and worse we are protected only by the press. Carry next the imagination, not to any living example of prosperity and good government, but to the furthest limit of happiness which is compatible with human nature; and behold that which may in time be attained, if the restrictions under which the press still groans, merely for the security of the holders of mischievous power, be removed. Such are the blessings of a free press: and again and again be it repeated, there cannot be a free press without freedom of censure.

ON MARRIAGE

1832-33?

EDITOR'S NOTE

Holograph MS, Mill-Taylor Collection, British Library of Political and Economic Science, London School of Economics. Untitled and unsigned, but in Mill's hand. Dated on physical evidence. Not published (and therefore not in Mill's bibliography). For a description of the MS, and comment on it, see xxx-xxxi and lviii-lx above.

On Marriage

SHE TO WHOM MY LIFE IS DEVOTED has wished for a written exposition of my opinions on the subject which, of all connected with human Institutions, is nearest to her happiness. Such as that exposition can be made without *her* to suggest and to decide, it is given in these pages: she, herself, has not refused to put into writing for *me*, what she has thought and felt on the same subject, and *there* I shall be taught all perhaps which I have, and certainly all which I have not, found out for myself. In the investigation of truth as in all else, "it is not good for man to be alone."[*] And more than all, in what concerns the relations of Man with Woman, the law which is to be observed by both should surely be made by both; not, as hitherto, by the stronger only.

How easy would it be for either me or you, to resolve this question for ourselves alone! Its difficulties, for difficulties it has, are such as obstruct the avenues of all great questions which are to be decided for mankind at large, and therefore not for natures resembling each other, but for natures or at least characters tending to all the points of the moral compass. All popular morality is as I once said to you a compromise among conflicting natures; each renouncing a certain portion of what its own desires call for, in order to avoid the evils of a perpetual warfare with all the rest. That is the best popular morality, which attains this general pacification with the least sacrifice of the happiness of the higher natures; who are the greatest, indeed the only real, sufferers by the compromise: for *they* are called upon to give up what would really make them happy; while others are commonly required only to restrain desires the gratification of which would bring no real happiness. In the adjustment, moreover, of the compromise, the higher natures count only in proportion to their number, how small! or to the number of those whom they can influence: while the conditions of the compromise weigh heavily upon them in the ratio of their greater capacity of happiness, and its natural consequence, their keener sense of *want* and disappointment when the degree of happiness which they know would fall to their lot but for untoward external circumstances, is denied them.

By the higher natures I mean those characters who from the combination of natural and acquired advantages, have the greatest capacity of feeling happiness,

[*Genesis, 2:18.]

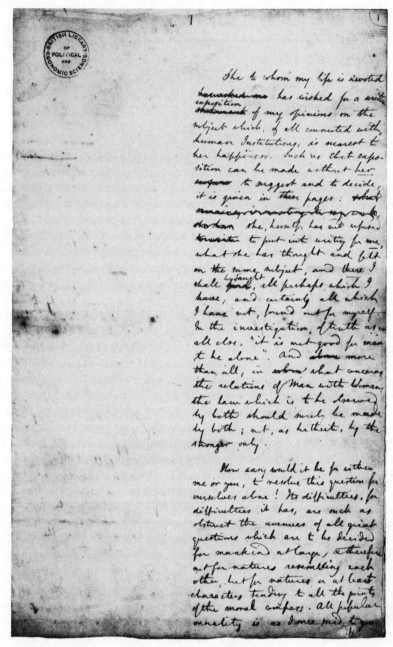

Folio 1r of "On Marriage"
British Library of Political and Economic Science

and of bestowing it. Of bestowing it in two ways: as being beautiful to contemplate, and therefore the natural objects of admiration and love; and also as being fitted, and induced, by their qualities of mind and heart, to promote by their actions, and by all that depends upon their will, the greatest possible happiness of all who are within the sphere of their influence.

If all persons were like these, or even would be guided by these, morality might be very different from what it must now be; or rather it would not exist at all as morality, since morality and inclination would coincide. If all resembled you, my lovely friend, it would be idle to prescribe rules for them. By following their own impulses under the guidance of their own judgment, they would find more happiness, and would confer more, than by obeying any moral principles or maxims whatever; since these cannot possibly be adapted beforehand to every peculiarity of circumstance which can be taken into account by a sound and vigorous intellect *worked* by a strong *will*, and guided by what Carlyle calls "an open loving heart."[*] Where there exists a genuine and strong desire to do that which is most for the happiness of all, general rules are merely aids to prudence, in the choice of means; not peremptory obligations. Let but the desires be right, and the "imagination lofty and refined":[†] and provided there be disdain of all false seeming, "to the pure all things are pure."[‡]

It is easy enough to settle the moral bearings of our question upon such characters. The highest natures are of course impassioned natures; to such, marriage is but one continued act of self-sacrifice where strong affection is not; every tie therefore which restrains them from seeking out and uniting themselves with some one whom they can perfectly love, is a yoke to which they cannot be subjected without oppression: and to such a person when found, they would naturally, superstition apart, scorn to be united by any other tie than free and voluntary choice. If such natures have been healthily developed in other respects, they will have all other good and worthy feelings strong enough to prevent them from pursuing this happiness at the expense of greater suffering to others: and that is the limit of the forbearance which morality ought in such a case to enjoin.

But will the morality which suits the highest natures, in this matter, be also best for all inferior natures? My conviction is, that it will: but this can be only a happy accident. All the difficulties of morality in any of its branches, grow out of the conflict which continually arises between the highest morality and even the best popular morality which the degree of developement yet attained by average human nature, will allow to exist.

[*Thomas Carlyle, "Biography," *Fraser's Magazine*, V (Apr., 1832), 259.]
[†William Wordsworth, "Weak is the will of Man, his judgment blind," Miscellaneous Sonnets, Pt. I, xxxi, in *The Poetical Works*, 5 vols. (London: Longman, *et al.*, 1827), Vol. II, p. 285 (l. 10).]
[‡Titus, 1:15.]

If all, or even most persons, in the choice of a companion of the other sex, were led by any real aspiration towards, or sense of, the happiness which such companionship in its best shape is capable of giving to the best natures, there would never have been any reason why law or opinion should have set any limits to the most unbounded freedom of uniting and separating: nor is it probable that popular morality would ever, in a civilized or refined people, have imposed any restraint upon that freedom. But, as I once said to you, the law of marriage as it now exists, has been made *by* sensualists, and *for* sensualists, and *to bind* sensualists. The aim and purpose of that law is either to tie up the sense, in the hope by so doing, of tying up the soul also, or else to tie up the sense because the soul is not cared about at all. Such purposes never could have entered into the minds of any to whom nature had given souls capable of the higher degrees of happiness: nor could such a law ever have existed but among persons to whose natures it was in some degree congenial, and therefore more suitable than at first sight may be supposed by those whose natures are widely different.

There can, I think, be no doubt that for a long time the indissolubility of marriage acted powerfully to elevate the social position of women. The state of things to which in almost all countries it succeeded, was one in which the power of repudiation existed on one side but not on both: in which the stronger might cast away the weaker, but the weaker could not fly from the yoke of the stronger. To a woman of an impassioned character, the difference between this and what now exists, is not worth much; for she would wish to be repudiated, rather than to remain united only because she could not be got rid of. But the aspirations of most women are less high. They would wish to retain any bond of union they have ever had with a man to whom they do not prefer any other, and for whom they have that inferior kind of affection which habits of intimacy frequently produce. Now, assuming what may be assumed of the greater number of men, that they are attracted to women solely by sensuality or at best by a transitory *taste*; it is not deniable, that the irrevocable vow gave to women when the passing gust had blown over, a permanent hold upon the men who would otherwise have cast them off. Something, indeed *much*, of a community of interest, arose from the mere fact of being indissolubly united: the husband took an interest in the wife as being *his* wife, if he did not from any better feeling: it became essential to his respectability that his wife also should be respected; and commonly when the first revulsion of feeling produced by satiety, went off, the mere fact of continuing together, if the woman had anything loveable in her and the man was not wholly brutish, could hardly fail to raise up some feeling of regard and attachment. She obtained also, what is often far more precious to her, the certainty of not being separated from her children.

Now if this be all that human life *has* for women, it is little enough: and any woman who feels herself capable of great happiness, and whose aspirations have not been artificially checked, will claim to be set free from *only* this, to seek for more. But women in general, as I have already remarked, are more easily contented. And this I believe to be the cause of the general aversion of women to the idea of facilitating divorce. They have a habitual belief that their power over men is chiefly derived from men's sensuality; and that the same sensuality would go elsewhere in search of gratification, unless restrained by law and opinion. They, on their part, mostly seek in marriage, a home, and the state or condition of a married woman, with the addition or not as it may happen, of a splendid establishment &c. &c. These things once obtained, the indissolubility of marriage renders them sure of keeping. And most women, either because these things really give them all the happiness they are capable of, or from the artificial barriers which curb all spontaneous movements to seek their greatest felicity, are generally more anxious not to peril the good they have than to go in search of a greater. If marriage were dissoluble, they think they could not retain the position once acquired; or not without practising upon the affections of men by those arts, disgusting in the extreme to any woman of simplicity, by which a cunning mistress sometimes establishes and retains her ascendancy.

These considerations are nothing to an impassioned character; but there is something in them, for the characters from which they emanate—is not that so? The only conclusion, however, which can be drawn from them, is one for which there would exist ample grounds even if the law of marriage as it now exists were perfection. This conclusion is, the absurdity and immorality of a state of society and opinion in which a woman is at all dependent for her social position upon the fact of her being or not being married. Surely it is wrong, wrong in every way, and on every view of morality, even the vulgar view,—that there should exist any motives to marriage except the happiness which two persons who love one another feel in associating their existence.

The means by which the condition of a married woman is rendered artificially desirable, are not any superiority of legal rights, for in that respect single women, especially if possessed of property, have the advantage: the civil disabilities are greatest in the case of the married woman. It is not law, but education and custom which make the difference. Women are so brought up, as not to be able to subsist in the mere physical sense, without a man to keep them: they are so brought up as not to be able to protect themselves against injury or insult, without some man on whom they have a special claim, to protect them: they are so brought up, as to have no vocation or useful office to fulfil in the world, remaining single; for all women who are educated for anything except to *get* married, are educated to *be* married, and what little they are taught deserving the name useful, is chiefly what in the ordinary course of things will not come into actual use, unless nor until they are married. A single woman therefore is felt both by herself and others as a kind of excrescence on the surface of society, having no use or function or office there. She is not indeed precluded from useful and honorable exertion of various kinds: but a married woman is *presumed* to be a useful member of society unless there is evidence to the contrary; a single woman must establish, what very few either women or men ever do establish, an *individual* claim.

All this, though not the less really absurd and immoral even under the law of marriage which now exists, evidently grows out of that law, and fits into the general state of society of which that law forms a part; nor could continue to exist if the law were changed, and marriage were not a contract at all, or were an easily dissoluble one. The indissolubility of marriage is the keystone of woman's present lot, and the whole comes down and must be reconstructed if that is removed.

And the truth is, that this question of marriage cannot properly be considered by itself alone. The question is not what marriage ought to be, but a far wider question, what woman ought to be. Settle that first, and the other will settle itself. Determine whether marriage is to be a relation between two equal beings, or between a superior and an inferior, between a protector and a dependent; and all other doubts will easily be resolved.

But in this question there is surely no difficulty. There is no natural inequality between the sexes; except perhaps in bodily strength; even *that* admits of doubt: and if bodily strength is to be the measure of superiority, mankind are no better than savages. Every step in the progress of civilization has tended to diminish the deference paid to bodily strength, until now when that quality confers scarcely any advantages except its natural ones: the strong man has little or no power to employ his strength as a means of acquiring any other advantage over the weaker in body. Every step in the progress of civilization has similarly been marked by a nearer approach to equality in the condition of the sexes; and if they are still far from being equal, the hindrance is not now in the difference of physical strength, but in artificial feelings and prejudices.

If nature has not made men and women unequal, still less ought the law to make them so. It may be assumed, as one of those propositions which would almost be made weaker by anything so ridiculous as attempting to prove them, that men and women ought to be perfectly coequal: that a woman ought not to be dependent on a man, more than a man on a woman, except so far as their affections make them so, by a voluntary surrender, renewed and renewing at each instant by free and spontaneous choice.

But this perfect independence of each other for all save affection, cannot be, if there be dependence in pecuniary circumstances: a dependence which in the immense majority of cases must exist, if the woman be not capable, as well as the man, of gaining her own subsistence.

The first and indispensable step, therefore, towards the enfranchisement of woman, is that she be so educated, as not to be dependent either on her father or her husband for subsistence: a position which in nine cases out of ten, makes her either the plaything or the slave of the man who feeds her; and in the tenth case, only his humble friend. Let it not be said that she has an equivalent and compensating advantage in the exemption from toil: men think it base and servile in men to accept food as the price of dependence, and why do they not deem it so in women? solely because they do not desire that women should be their equals. Where there is strong affection, dependence is its own reward: but it must be voluntary dependence; and the more perfectly voluntary it is,—the more exclusively each owes every thing to the other's affection and to nothing else,—the greater is the happiness. And where affection is not, the woman who will be dependent for the sake of a maintenance, proves herself as low-minded as a man in the like case—or *would* prove herself so, if that resource were not too often the only one her education has given her, and if her education had not also taught her not to consider as a degradation, that which is the essence of all prostitution, the act of delivering up her person for bread.

It does not follow that a woman should *actually* support herself because she should be *capable* of doing so: in the natural course of events she will *not*. It is not desirable to burthen the labour market with a double number of competitors. In a healthy state of things, the husband would be able by his single exertions to earn all that is necessary for both; and there would be no need that the wife should take part in the mere providing of what is required to *support* life: it will be for the happiness of both that her occupation should rather be to adorn and beautify it. Except in the class of actual day-labourers, that will be her natural task, if task it can be called which will in so great a measure, be accomplished rather by *being* than by *doing*.

We have all heard the vulgar talk that the proper employments of a wife are household superintendance, and the education of her children. As for household superintendance, if nothing be meant but merely seeing that servants do their duty, that is not an occupation; every woman who is capable of doing it at all can do it without devoting anything like half an hour every day to that purpose peculiarly. It is not like the duty of a head of an office, to whom his subordinates bring their work to be inspected when finished: the defects in the performance of household duties present *themselves* to inspection: skill in superintendance consists in knowing the right way of noticing a fault when it occurs, and giving reasonable advice and instruction how to avoid it; and more depends upon establishing a good *system* at first, than upon a perpetual and studious watchfulness. But if it be meant that the mistress of a family shall herself do the work of servants, *that* is good and will naturally take place in the rank in which there do not exist the means of hiring servants; but nowhere else.

Then as to the education of children; if by that term be meant, instructing them in particular arts or particular branches of knowledge, it is absurd to impose that upon mothers: absurd in two ways: absurd to set one-half of the adult human race to perform each on a small scale, what a much smaller number of teachers could accomplish for all, by devoting themselves exclusively to it; and absurd to set all mothers doing that for which some persons must be fitter than others, and for which average mothers cannot possibly be *so* fit as persons trained to the profession. Here again, when the means do not exist of hiring teachers, the mother is the natural teacher: but no special provision needs to be made for that case. Whether she is to teach or not, it is desirable that she should *know*; because knowledge is desirable for its own sake; for its uses, for its pleasures, and for its beautifying influence when not cultivated to the neglect of other gifts. What she knows, she will be able to teach to her children if necessary: but to erect such teaching into her occupation whether she can better employ herself or not, is absurd.

The education which it *does* belong to mothers to give, and which if not imbibed from them is seldom obtained in any perfection at all, is the training of the affections; and through the affections, of the conscience, and the whole moral being. But *this* most precious, and most indispensable part of education, does not take up *time*; it is not a business, an occupation; a mother does not accomplish it by sitting down with her child for one or two or three hours to a task. She effects it by *being* with the child; by making it happy, and therefore at peace with all things; by checking bad habits in the commencement; by loving the child, and by making the child love her. It is not by particular efforts, but imperceptibly and unconsciously that she makes her own character pass into the child; that she makes the child love what she loves, venerate what she venerates, and imitate as far as a child can, her example. These things cannot be done by a hired teacher; and they are better and greater, than all the rest. But to impose upon mothers what hired teachers *can* do, is mere squandering of the glorious existence of a woman fit for woman's highest destiny. With regard to such things, her part is to see that they are rightly done, not to do them.

The great occupation of woman should be to *beautify* life: to cultivate, for her own sake and that of those who surround her, all her faculties of mind, soul, and body; all her powers of enjoyment, and powers of giving enjoyment; and to diffuse beauty, and elegance, and grace, everywhere. If in addition to this the activity of her nature demands more energetic and definite employment, there is never any lack of it in the world. If she loves, her natural impulse will be to associate her existence with him she loves, and to share *his* occupations; in which if he loves her (with that affection of *equality* which alone deserves to be called love) she will naturally take as strong an interest, and be as thoroughly conversant, as the most perfect confidence on his side can make her.

Such will naturally be the occupations of a woman who has fulfilled what seems to be considered as the end of her existence, and attained what is really its happiest state, by uniting herself to a man whom she loves. But whether so united or not, women will never be what they should be, nor their social position what it should be, until women, as universally as men, have the power of gaining their own livelihood: until, therefore, every girl's parents have either provided her with independent means of subsistence, or given her an education qualifying her to provide those means for herself. The only difference between the employments of women and those of men will be, that those which partake most of the beautiful, or which require delicacy and taste rather than muscular exertion, will naturally fall to the share of women: all branches of the fine arts in particular.

In considering, then, what is the best law of marriage, we are to suppose that women already are, what they would be in the best state of society; no less capable of existing independently and respectably without men, than men without women. Marriage, on whatever footing it might be placed, would be wholly a matter of choice, not, as for a woman it now is, something approaching to a matter of necessity; something, at least, which every woman is under strong artificial motives to desire, and which if she attain not, her life is considered to be a failure.

These suppositions being made; and it being no longer any advantage to a woman to be married; merely for the sake of being married; why should any woman cling to the indissolubility of marriage, as if it could be for the good of one party that it should continue when the other party desires that it should be dissolved?

It is not denied by anyone, that there are numerous cases in which the happiness of both parties would be greatly promoted by a dissolution of marriage. We will add, that when the social position of the two sexes shall be perfectly equal, a divorce if it be for the happiness of either party, will be for the happiness of both. No one but a sensualist would desire to retain a merely animal connexion with a person of the other sex, unless perfectly assured of being preferred by that person, above all other persons in the world. This certainty never can be quite perfect under the law of marriage as it now exists: it would be nearly absolute, if the tie were merely voluntary.

Not only there are, but it is in vain to hope that there will not always be, innumerable cases, in which the first connexion formed will be one the dissolution of which if it *could* be, certainly would be, and ought to be, effected. It has long ago been remarked that of all the more serious acts of the life of a human being, there is not one which is commonly performed with so little of forethought or consideration, as that which is irrevocable, and which is fuller of evil than any other act of the being's whole life if it turn out ill. And this is not so astonishing as it seems: The imprudence, while the contract remains indissoluble, consists in marrying at all: If you *do* marry, there is little wisdom shewn by a very anxious and careful deliberation beforehand. Marriage is really, what it has been sometimes called, a lottery; and whoever is in a state of mind to calculate the chances calmly and value them correctly, is not at all likely to purchase a ticket. Those who marry after taking great pains about the matter, generally do but buy their disappointment dearer. For the failures in marriage are such as are naturally incident to a first trial: the parties are inexperienced, and cannot judge. Nor does this evil seem to be remediable. A woman is allowed to give herself away for life, at an age at which she is not allowed to dispose of the most inconsiderable landed estate: what then? if people are not to marry until they have learnt prudence, they will seldom marry before thirty: can this be expected, or is it to be desired? To direct the immature judgment, there is the advice of parents and guardians: a precious security! The only thing which a young girl can do, worse than marrying to please herself, is marrying to please any other person. However paradoxical it may sound to the ears of those who are reputed to have grown wise as wine grows good, by *keeping*, it is yet true, that A, an average person, can better know what is for his own happiness, than B, an average person, can know what is for A's happiness. Fathers and mothers as the world is constituted, do not judge more wisely than sons and daughters; they only judge differently: and the judgments of both being of the ordinary strength, or rather of the ordinary weakness, a person's own self has the advantage of a considerably greater number of *data* to judge from, and the further one of a stronger interest in the subject. Foolish people will say, that being interested in the subject is a disqualification; strange that they should not distinguish between being interested in a cause as a party before a judge, i.e., interested in deciding one way, right or wrong,—and being interested as a person is in the management of his own property, interested in deciding right. The parties themselves are only interested in doing what is most for their happiness; but their relatives may have all sorts of selfish interests to promote by inducing them to marry or not to marry.

The first choice, therefore, is made under very complicated disadvantages. By the fact of its being the *first*, the parties are necessarily inexperienced in the particular matter; they are commonly young (especially the party who is in greatest peril from a mistake) and therefore inexperienced in the knowledge and judgment of mankind and of themselves generally: and finally, they have seldom had so much as an opportunity afforded them, of gaining any real knowledge of each other, since in nine cases out of ten they have never been once in each other's society completely unconstrained, or without consciously or unconsciously acting a part.

The chances therefore are many to one against the supposition that a person who requires, or is capable of, great happiness, will find that happiness in a first choice: and in a very large proportion of cases the first choice is such that if it cannot be recalled, it only embitters existence. The reasons, then, are most potent for allowing a subsequent change.

What there is to be said in favor of the indissolubility, superstition apart, resolves itself into this: that it is highly desirable that changes should not be frequent; and desirable that the first choice should be, even if not compulsorily, yet very generally, persevered in: That consequently we ought to beware lest in giving facilities for retracting a bad choice, we hold out greater encouragement than at present for making such a choice as there will probably be occasion to retract.

It is proper to state as strongly as possible the arguments which may be advanced in support of this view of the question.

Repeated trials for happiness, and repeated failures, have the most mischievous effect on all minds. The finer spirits are broken down, and disgusted with all things: their susceptibilities are deadened, or converted into sources of bitterness, and they lose the power of being ever *contented*. On the commoner natures the effects produced are not less deplorable. Not only is their capacity of happiness worn out, but their morality is depraved: all refinement and delicacy of character is extinguished; all sense of any peculiar duties or of any peculiar sacredness attaching to the relation between the sexes, is worn away; and such alliances come to be looked upon with the very same kind of feelings which are now connected with a passing intrigue.

Thus much as to the parties themselves: but besides the parties, there are also to be considered their children; beings who are wholly dependent both for happiness and for excellence upon their parents; and who in all but the extreme cases of actual profligacy, or perpetual bickering and disunion, *must* be better cared for in both points if their parents remain together.

So much importance is due to this last consideration, that I am convinced, if marriage were easily dissoluble, two persons of opposite sexes who unite their destinies would generally, if they were wise, think it their duty to avoid having children until they had lived together for a considerable length of time, and found in each other a happiness adequate to their aspirations. If this principle of morality were observed, how many of the difficulties of the subject we are considering would be smoothed down! To be jointly the parents of a human being, should be the very last pledge of the deepest, holiest, and most durable affection: for *that* is a tie which independently of convention, is indeed indissoluble: an additional and external tie, most precious where the souls are already indissolubly united, but simply burthensome while it appears possible to either that they should ever desire to separate.

It can hardly be anticipated, however, that such a course will be followed by any but by those who to the greatest loftiness and delicacy of feeling, unite the power of the most deliberate reflexion. If the feelings be obtuse, the force of these considerations will not be felt; and if the judgment be weak or hasty, whether from inherent defect or from inexperience, people will fancy themselves in love for their whole lives with a perfect being, when the case is far otherwise, and will suppose they risk nothing by creating a new relationship with that being, which can no longer be got rid of. It will therefore most commonly happen that when circumstances arise which induce the parents to separate, there will be children to suffer by the separation: nor do I see how this difficulty can be entirely got over, until the habits of society allow of a regulated community of living, among persons intimately acquainted, which would prevent the necessity of a total separation between the parents even when they had ceased to be connected by any nearer tie than mutual good will, and a common interest in their children.

There is yet another argument which may be urged against facility of divorce. It is this. Most persons have but a very moderate capacity of happiness; but no person ever finds this out without experience, very few even with experience: and most persons are constantly wreaking that discontent which has its source internally, upon outward things. Expecting therefore in marriage, a far greater degree of happiness than they commonly find; and knowing not that the fault is in their own scanty capabilities of happiness—they fancy they should have been happier with some one else: or at all events the disappointment becomes associated in their minds with the being in whom they had placed their hopes—and so they dislike one another for a time—and during that time they would feel inclined to separate: but if they remain united, the feeling of disappointment after a time goes off, and they pass their lives together with fully as much of happiness as they could find either singly or in any other union, without having undergone the wearing of repeated and unsuccessful experiments.

Such are the arguments for adhering to the indissolubility of the contract: and for such characters as compose the great majority of the human race, it is not deniable that these arguments have considerable weight.

That weight however is not so great as it appears. In all the above arguments it is tacitly assumed, that the choice lies between the absolute interdiction of divorce, and a state of things in which the parties would separate on the most passing feeling of dissatisfaction. Now this is not really the alternative. Were divorce ever so free, it would be resorted to under the same sense of moral responsibility and under the same restraints from opinion, as any other of the acts of our lives. In no state of society but one in which opinion sanctions almost promiscuous intercourse, (and in which therefore even the indissoluble bond is not practically regarded,) would it be otherwise than disreputable to either party, the woman especially, to change frequently, or on light grounds. My belief is, that in a tolerably moral state of society, the first choice would almost always, especially where it had produced children, be adhered to, unless in case of such uncongeniality of disposition as rendered it positively uncomfortable to one or both of the parties to live together, or in case of a strong passion conceived by one of them for a third person. Now in either of these cases I can conceive no argument strong enough to convince me, that the first connexion ought to be forcibly preserved.

I see not why opinion should not act with as great efficacy, to enforce the true rules of morality in this matter, as the false. Robert Owen's definitions* of chastity

---

Chastity, sexual intercourse *with* affection. *Prostitution*, sexual intercourse *without* affection. [Owen's views on marriage were promulgated, especially in the United States, in the 1820s. Mill's wording is closest to that found in Robert Owen and Alexander Campbell, *Debate on the Evidences of Christianity*, 2 vols. (Bethany, Virginia: Campbell, 1829), Vol. I, p. 120; however, he may be echoing a later version, delivered in London, contained in "The Address of Robert Owen, at the Great Public Meeting, Held at the National Labour Exchange, Charlotte-street, Fitzroy-square, on the 1st of May, 1833, Denouncing the Old System of the World, and Announcing the Commencement of the New," *The Crisis*, II (11 May, 1833), 141.]

and prostitution, are quite as simple and take as firm a hold of the mind as the vulgar ones which connect the ideas of virtue and vice with the performance or non-performance of an arbitrary ceremonial.

The arguments, therefore, in favour of the indissolubility of marriage, are as nothing in comparison with the far more potent arguments for leaving this like the other relations voluntarily contracted by human beings, to depend for its continuance upon the wishes of the contracting parties. The strongest of all these arguments is that by no other means can the condition and character of women become what it ought to be.

When women were merely slaves, to give them a permanent hold upon their masters was a first step towards their elevation. That step is now complete: and in the progress of civilization, the time has come when women may aspire to something more than merely to find a protector. The condition of a single woman has ceased to be dangerous and precarious: the law, and general opinion, suffice without any more special guardianship, to shield her in ordinary circumstances from insult or injury: woman in short is no longer a mere property, but a person, who is counted not solely on her husband's or father's account but on her own. She is now ripe for equality. But it is absurd to talk of equality while marriage is an indissoluble tie. It was a change greatly for the better, from a state in which all the obligation was on the side of the weaker, all the rights on the side of the physically stronger, to even the present condition of an obligation nominally equal on both. But this nominal equality is not real equality. The stronger is always able to relieve himself wholly or in a great measure, from as much of the obligation as he finds burthensome: the weaker cannot. The husband can ill-use his wife, neglect her, and seek other women, not perhaps altogether with impunity, but what are the penalties which opinion imposes on him, compared with those which fall upon the wife who even with that provocation, retaliates upon her husband? It is true perhaps that if divorce were permitted, opinion would with like injustice, try the wife who resorted to that remedy, by a harder measure than the husband. But this would be of less consequence. Once separated she would be comparatively independent of opinion: but so long as she is forcibly united to one of those who *make* the opinion, she must to a great extent be its slave.

AUSTIN'S LECTURES ON JURISPRUDENCE

1832

EDITOR'S NOTE

Tait's Edinburgh Magazine, II (Dec., 1832), 343-8. Title footnoted: *"The Province of Jurisprudence Determined.* By John Austin, Esq., Barrister at Law. [London: Murray, 1832.]" Running titles as title. Unsigned; not republished. Identified in Mill's bibliography as "A review of Austin's Lectures on Jurisprudence in the 9th number of Tait's Edinburgh Magazine (December 1832.)" (MacMinn, 23.) The Somerville College copy (tear-sheets) has three inked corrections by Mill that are adopted in the present text: at 53.1 "early a brilliant" is altered to "early or brilliant"; at 54.19 "people. Our" is altered to "people; Our" (we complete the correction by printing "our"); and at 56.10 "as an author" is changed to "as our author". For comment on the review, see xli-xliii and lx above.

Austin's Lectures on Jurisprudence

IF WE COULD ANTICIPATE early or brilliant success for this work, we should think more highly of the wisdom of the book-buying public than we fear there are grounds for. This is a reading age; and precisely because it is so reading an age, any book which is the result of profound meditation, is perhaps less likely to be duly and profitably read than at a former period. The world reads too much, and too quickly, to read well. When books were few, to get through one was a work of time and labour: what was written with thought was read with thought, and with a desire to extract from it as much of the materials of knowledge as possible. But when almost every person who can spell, can and will write, what is to be done? It is difficult to know what to read, except by reading every thing; and so much of the world's business is now transacted through the press, that it is necessary to know what is printed if we desire to know what is going on. Opinion weighs with so vast a weight in the balance of events, that ideas of no value in themselves, are of importance from the mere circumstance that they *are* ideas, and have a *bona fide* existence as such anywhere out of Bedlam. The world, in consequence, gorges itself with intellectual food of all qualities, and in order to swallow the more, *bolts* it. Nothing is now read slowly, or twice over. Books are run through with no less rapidity, and scarcely leave a more durable impression than a newspaper article. It is for this, among other causes, that so few books are produced of any value. The lioness in the fable boasted that though she produced only one at a birth, that one was a lion.[*] But if each lion only counted for one, and each leveret for one, the advantage would all be on the side of the hare. When every unit is individually weak, it is only multitude that tells. Who wonders that the newspapers should carry all before them? A book produces no greater effect than an article, and there can be three hundred and sixty-five of these in one year. He, therefore, who should and would write a book, and write it in the proper manner of writing a book, now dashes down his first hasty thoughts, or what he mistakes for thoughts, in a periodical. And the public is in the predicament of an indolent man, who cannot bring himself to apply his mind vigorously to his own affairs; and over whom,

[*"The Lioness and the Vixen," *Aesop's Fables*, trans. Vernon Stanley Vernon Jones (London: Heinemann; New York: Doubleday, Page, 1912), p. 91.]

therefore, not he who speaks most wisely, but he who speaks most frequently, obtains the influence.

At such a period, any person who once more gives to mankind a philosophical work, which he has conscientiously endeavoured to make as good as he could, by unsparing labour and meditation, make it, performs an act the more meritorious, as it is the less likely to meet with any reward; and if, like Mr. Austin, he is qualified for the more successful and profitable kinds of literary composition, yet deliberately prefers the more instructive, the greater is his deserving. There are passages in the volume before us, which shew that if the author chose, he could excel as a popular writer; and the mere clippings and parings of a work like this, would be material enough to be wrought up into more than one popular book. But Mr. Austin knows, that in order to make an impression upon careless, rapid, and impatient readers, it is necessary to avoid calling upon them for a vigorous effort of attention, and that without such an effort, no ideas can be imbibed but such as are loose and vague. And knowing that there are many persons who are competent to explain popularly, all that can be popularly explained; for one who can follow out a long train of thought, and conceive and express it at once with clearness and with precision; that the former may teach the people, but it belongs to the latter only to teach the teachers of the people; our author has chosen for himself the higher, and more difficult, though less conspicuous and less honoured part.

He has accordingly produced a work which requires to be read, in the antique sense of that term, not as we read a novel, but rather as men read for honours at the University. But the work will repay those who shall so read it. As all know who have ever really *learnt* any thing, real knowledge never comes by easy reading. Nobody ever set about learning Latin by *running* through the Latin Grammar. Mr. Austin's work is part of the grammar of a science. As such, it is not a book for any but persons who are really anxious to learn; but to them, it is such a book as they delight in. The author's style is a model of perspicuity: the concatenation of his propositions is free from all obscurity; and the reader will find no difficulty but that which is inseparable from the attempt to communicate precise ideas.

The volume consists of the preliminary lectures of a course delivered by Mr. Austin at the University of London, and which we had the good fortune of hearing. An outline of the entire course is annexed to the present publication.

We shall endeavour to give as sufficient a conception as can be given in a few words, of what our author understands by Jurisprudence, as distinguished from the philosophy of Legislation.

Both these sciences are conversant with laws; namely, laws in the strict sense, laws set to man by man, in the character of a political superior. But though the subject-matter of both sciences be the same, both do not look at it under the same aspect.

The philosophy of legislation is conversant with laws, as a contrivance for accomplishing certain *ends*. It considers what are the purposes of law; and judges of the means, according as they are well or ill adapted to the accomplishment of those purposes. It teaches the requisites of a *good* law; and what particular laws would be good or bad, either universally, or under any supposable set of circumstances.

Jurisprudence, on the other hand, does not take any direct cognizance of the goodness or badness of laws, nor undertake to weigh the motives which lead to their establishment: it assumes their existence as a fact, and treats of their nature and properties, as a naturalist treats of any natural phenomenon. It furnishes an analytical exposition, not indeed of any particular system of existing laws, but of what is common to all or most systems of law.

In the first place, the very notion of a *law* is an extremely complex idea: that of a *body* of laws, still more so. These ideas have to be analyzed. The component elements of a law, and of a body of laws, and the suppositions which they involve, must be precisely determined and cleared up. For instance, a *law* supposes a *political superior* from whom the law emanates: what is a political superior? All laws create *obligations*, and are clothed with *sanctions*; all laws (certain peculiar cases excepted) create *rights*: but what is meant by an obligation, a sanction, a right? Every body of laws recognises a distinction between *civil* law and *criminal* law, between *private* law and *constitutional* law: is there any rational foundation for these distinctions, and what is it?

Further, laws operate only by creating *rights*, and *duties*, or *obligations*. The rights and duties which the law of any country creates, are the *law* itself. Now these rights and duties fall so naturally into certain classes, form themselves so naturally into certain groups, that in all or almost all bodies of law, which men have tried to reduce into any thing like a systematic order, an effort has been made to grasp these very groups, and bind them together by appropriate technical terms. But the attempt has generally been a most lame and impotent one,[*] partly for want of what may be called the *coup d'oeil* of a practised logician, which enables him, like an experienced general, to survey an entire field at once, and either comprehend an actual arrangement, or frame an imaginary one, without being bewildered by the multitude of details; and still more for want of mastery over the casual associations connected with familiar terms, and of the capacity to wield every word as a mere instrument to convey a thought; an instrument which may be taken up and laid down at pleasure. The classes which have been formed are not properly classes at all, for they are not separated by plain well-marked boundaries, but cross one another in all directions. It is impossible to define them, because no property can be found common to an entire class; or none but what may also be found in something that is absurdly left out of the class. Yet, as before observed, the authors of these unskilful classifications have always had indistinctly before their eyes

[*Cf. William Shakespeare, *Othello*, II, i, 161; in *The Riverside Shakespeare*, ed. G. Blakemore Evans (Boston: Houghton Mifflin, 1974), p. 1213.]

certain natural groups, which they have been ineffectually attempting to hit, and to find some means of circumscribing within the bounds of a general expression. Hence, if we were to strip off from the arrangement and technical language of each system of law, whatever is purely accidental, and (as it may be termed) historical, having a reference solely to the peculiar history of the institutions of the particular people; if we were to take the remainder, and regularize and correct it according to its own general conception and spirit; we should bring the nomenclature and arrangement of all systems of law existing in any civilized society, to something very nearly identical.

Now the science of jurisprudence, as our author conceives it, endeavours to disentangle these natural groups (with which all classifications coincide in the gross, and none accurately) from the environment which surrounds them, of terms without any precise meaning, except perhaps a historical one; and distinctions answering to no difference, except, perhaps, one which has ceased to exist. The natural groups are thus brought into strong relief; a distinct conception is gained of their boundaries; and compact and precise names may be obtained to designate them by. When this is done, a commanding view may be taken of the detailed provisions of any existing body of law, the rights and duties which it establishes: they may be rendered *cognoscible*, as Mr. Bentham would say;[*] a common framework is obtained, into the compartments of which all bodies of law may be distributed; and a systematic exposition might be given with comparative ease, either of one or of any number of legal systems, in parallel columns.

Thus prepared, the student of any existing system of law would no longer find it a mass of inextricable confusion; he would be enabled, in a comparatively short time, to obtain a far more perfect mastery of the system than was ever possessed by those who made it. An expository law book would then be so constructed as to be a lesson of clear ideas, instead of being almost enough to incapacitate the mind from ever forming one. And the legislator who would either reduce any existing body of laws into a code, or draw up an improved system, would reap two benefits. The whole of the rights and duties which past legislators have thought it desirable to create, would be brought compendiously under his view; and he would have an arrangement, and a technical language ready made, which would be an excellent basis for him to start from in framing his own. For though classification is not made by nature, but is wholly an affair of convenience, one most important part of the convenience of any classification is, that it shall coincide, as far as possible, with the mode in which the ideas have a natural tendency to arrange themselves.

Unfortunately, the science of jurisprudence as thus conceived, mostly remains still to be created. No person, however, is qualified to do more towards creating it

[*Jeremy Bentham, *Papers Relative to Codification and Public Instruction* (1817), in *Works*, ed. John Bowring, 11 vols. (Edinburgh: Tait; London: Simpkin, Marshall; Dublin: Cumming, 1843), Vol. IV, p. 454.]

than the author whose work is now before us. Whatever assistance is to be derived on the one hand from the Roman lawyers and their German successors; on the other, from our own immortal Bentham, he has thoroughly possessed himself of. And his course of lectures, if it were completed as it has been begun, would, we think, leave little for any successor in the same field. The present work, however, is merely an introduction; and even in his oral lectures, the Professor had not space to complete more than a small part of his intended scheme. There are portions, however, of what he has actually delivered (and which we hope may one day be published) still more instructive and interesting than what is here given.

The volume now published is occupied in "determining the province of jurisprudence," by analyzing the notion of a law, in the strict sense of the term; namely, a law set by a political superior;—and discriminating it from whatever else has received the name of law; whereof our author distinguishes three kinds, namely, laws set to man by God; laws (analogically so called) which may be said to be prescribed by *opinion*; and laws so called only by metaphor, as when we speak of the *law* of gravitation.[*]

These various notions are defined and discriminated from one another with rare logical power, and superiority over the trammels of language. In addition to this main object of the work, it abounds in valuable discussions on incidental topics. To mention only one of these discussions, (the largest, and most important,) that great question which has occupied so many of the most gifted minds, the foundation of moral obligation, and the nature of the standard or test of right and wrong, whether it be utility or an instinctive principle, forms the principal subject of no less than three lectures; being introduced under the head of the Divine Law, in the form of an inquiry, in what way the unrevealed portion of that law is made known to us.[†] This investigation will be the most interesting part of the present volume to the general reader. Mr. Austin is a strong partisan of the doctrine which considers utility as the test or index to moral duty. Though he has stated some, he has omitted others of the essential explanations with which we think that this doctrine should be received; but he has treated the question in a most enlarged and comprehensive spirit, and in the loftiest tone of moral feeling; and has discussed certain branches of it in a manner which we have never seen equalled.

Valuable as this work is in the intrinsic merits of its contents, its greatest value, after all, is, we think, as a logical discipline to the mind. We hardly ever read a book which appears to us, if duly studied, to have so great a tendency to accustom the mind to habits of close and precise thinking; of using every word with a meaning, or meanings accurately settled, rigidly adhered to, and always present to the mind; of never leaving off with a half-solution of a doubt or difficulty, but sticking to it till nothing remains unexplained.

[**Province*, p. vii, e.g.]
[†*Ibid.*, Lectures II-IV, pp. 31-125.]

Mr. Austin's style is more remarkable for clearness and precision than ease; but it is perfectly unaffected; and his language is the rich, expressive, homely English, of his favourite writers, Hobbes and Locke.

It would be injustice to our author to conclude this notice without affording him an opportunity of speaking for himself; but it would be still greater injustice to exhibit a mere fragment of a philosophic investigation, the merit of which must of course be mainly dependent upon its connected and systematic character. Our specimens must necessarily be selected from the merely parenthetical passages. The following may perhaps serve, as well as any others, to give a conception of our author's general turn of thought and expression.

The first passage that we shall quote is a Pisgah view[*] of the future improvement of the moral sciences:

If there were a reading public, numerous, discerning, and *impartial*, the science of ethics, and all the various sciences which are nearly related to ethics, would advance with unexampled rapidity.

By the hope of obtaining the approbation which it would bestow upon genuine merit, writers would be incited to the patient research and reflection, which are not less requisite to the improvement of ethical, than to the advancement of mathematical science.

Slight and incoherent thinking would be received with general contempt, though it were cased in polished periods, studded with brilliant metaphors. Ethics would be considered by readers, and, therefore, treated by writers, as the matter or subject of a *science*; as a subject for persevering and accurate investigation, and not as a theme for childish and babbling rhetoric.

This general demand for truth, (though it were clothed in homely guise,) and this general contempt of falsehood and nonsense, (though they were decked with rhetorical graces,) would improve the method and the style of inquiries into ethics, and into the various sciences which are nearly related to ethics. The writers would attend to the suggestions of Hobbes and of Locke, and would imitate the method so successfully pursued by geometers: though such is the variety of the premises which some of their inquiries involve, and such are the complexity and ambiguity of some of the terms, that they would often fall short of the perfect exactness and coherency which the fewness of his premises, and the simplicity and definiteness of his expressions, enable the geometer to reach. But, though they would often fall short of geometrical exactness and coherency, they might always approach, and would often attain to them. They would acquire the art and the habit of defining their leading terms; of steadily adhering to the meanings announced by the definitions; of carefully examining and distinctly stating their premises; and of deducing the consequences of their premises with logical vigour. Without rejecting embellishments which might happen to fall in their way, the only excellencies of style for which they would seek are precision, clearness, and conciseness; the first being absolutely requisite to the successful prosecution of inquiry, whilst the others enable the reader to seize the meaning with certainty, and spare him unnecessary fatigue.

And, what is equally important, the protection afforded by this public to diligent and honest writers would inspire into writers upon ethics, and upon the nearly related sciences, the spirit of dispassionate inquiry: the "indifferency" or impartiality in the pursuit of truth, which is just as requisite to the detection of truth as continued and close attention, or

[*See Deuteronomy, 3:27.]

sincerity and simplicity of purpose. Relying on the discernment and the justice of a numerous and powerful public, shielded by its countenance from the shafts of the hypocrite and the bigot, indifferent to the idle whistling of that harmless storm, they would scrutinize established institutions, and current or received opinions, fearlessly but coolly, with the freedom which is imperiously demanded by general utility, but without the antipathy which is begotten by the dread of persecution, and which is scarcely less adverse than "the love of things ancient" to the rapid advancement of science.

This patience in investigation, this distinctness and accuracy of method, this freedom and indifferency in the pursuit of the useful and the true, would thoroughly dispel the obscurity by which the science is clouded, and would clear it from most of its uncertainties. The wish, the hope, the prediction of Mr. Locke, would, in time, be accomplished; and "ethics would rank with the sciences which *are capable of demonstration*."[*] The adepts in ethical, as well as in mathematical science, would commonly agree in their results; and, as the jar of *their* conclusions gradually subsided, a body of doctrine and authority, to which the *multitude* might trust, would emerge from the existing chaos. The direct examination of the multitude would only extend to the elements, and to the easier, though more momentous of the derivative practical truths. But none of their opinions would be adopted blindly, nor would any of their opinions be obnoxious to groundless and capricious charge. Though most or many of their opinions would still be taken from *authority*, the authority to which they would trust might satisfy the most scrupulous reason. *In the unanimous or general consent of numerous and impartial inquirers*, they would find that mark of trustworthiness which justifies reliance on authority, wherever we are debarred from the opportunity of examining the evidence for ourselves. (Pp. 81-4.)

We had marked several passages for quotation: but space presses, and we must conclude with the following estimate of Dr. Paley:

The treatise by Dr. Paley on Moral and Political Philosophy[†] exemplifies the natural tendency of narrow and domineering interests to pervert the course of inquiry from its legitimate purpose.

As men go, this celebrated and influential writer was a wise and a virtuous man. By the qualities of his head and heart, by the cast of his talents and affections, he was fitted, in a high degree, to seek for ethical truth, and to expound it successfully to others. He had a clear and a just understanding; a hearty contempt of paradox, and of ingenious but useless refinements; no fastidious disdain of the working people, but a warm sympathy with their homely enjoyments and sufferings. He knew that they are more numerous than all the rest of the community, and he felt that they are more important than all the rest of the community to the eye of unclouded reason and impartial benevolence.

But the sinister influence[‡] of the position, which he unluckily occupied, cramped his generous affections, and warped the rectitude of his understanding.

A steady pursuit of the consequences indicated by *general* utility, was not the most obvious way to professional advancement, nor even the short cut to extensive reputation. For there was no impartial public, formed from the community at large, to reward and encourage with its approbation an inflexible adherence to truth.

[*John Locke, *An Essay Concerning Human Understanding* (1690), in *Works*, new ed., 10 vols. (London: Tegg, *et al.*, 1823), Vol. II, pp. 368-9 (Bk. IV, Chap. iii, Sect. 18).]

[†William Paley, *The Principles of Moral and Political Philosophy* (1785), 15th ed., 2 vols. (London: Faulder, 1804).]

[‡For the term, see, e.g., Bentham, *Plan of Parliamentary Reform* (1817), in *Works*, Vol. III, pp. 440, 446.]

If the bulk of the community had been instructed, so far as their position will permit, he might have looked for a host of readers from the middle classes. He might have looked for a host of readers from those classes of the working people, whose wages are commonly high, whose leisure is not inconsiderable, and whose mental powers are called into frequent exercise by the natures of their occupations or callings. To readers of the middle classes, and of all the higher classes of the working people, a well-made and honest Treatise on Moral and Political Philosophy, in his clear, vivid, downright, *English* style, would have been the most easy and attractive, as well as instructive and useful, of abstract or scientific books.

But those numerous classes of the community were commonly too coarse and ignorant to care for books of the sort. The great majority of the readers who were likely to look into his book, belonged to the classes which are elevated by rank or opulence, and to the peculiar professions or callings which are distinguished by the name of "liberal." And the character of the book which he wrote, betrays the position of the writer. In almost every chapter, and in almost every page, his fear of offending the prejudices, commonly entertained by such readers, palpably suppresses the suggestions of his clear and vigorous reason, and masters the better affections which inclined him to the *general* good.

He was one of the greatest and best of the great and excellent writers, who by the strength of their philosophical genius, or by their large and tolerant spirit, have given imperishable lustre to the Church of England, and extinguished or softened the hostility of many who reject her creed. He may rank with the Berkeleys and Butlers, with the Burnets, Tillotsons, and Hoadleys.

But in spite of the esteem with which I regard his memory, truth compels me to add, that the book is unworthy of the man. For there is much ignoble truckling to the dominant and influential few. There is a deal of shabby sophistry in defence or extenuation of abuses which the few are interested in upholding. (Pp. 79-81.)

REFORM IN EDUCATION

1834

EDITOR'S NOTE

Monthly Repository, n.s. VIII (July, 1834), 502-13. Headed: "Mrs. Austin's Translation of M. Cousin's Report on the State of Public Instruction in Prussia." Title footnoted: "[London:] Effingham Wilson [, 1834]." Running titles: "Reform in Education." Unsigned; not republished. Identified in Mill's bibliography as "A review of Mrs. Austin's Translation of Cousin's Report on the State of Public Instruction in Prussia, in the Monthly Repository for July 1834" (MacMinn, 40). There are no corrections or emendations in the Somerville College copy (tear-sheets). For comment on the review, see xlix-l and lx-lxi above.

The long quotation at 65-6 from Mill's "Corporation and Church Property" has been collated with its successive versions; in the variant notes "33" indicates *Jurist* (and the offprint, which does not differ), "59" indicates *D&D*, 1st ed. (1859), and "67" indicates *D&D*, 2nd ed. (1867).

Reform in Education

IN A RECENT NUMBER we briefly announced the appearance of this important document in an English form.[*] We now return to it, because the reception of Mr. Roebuck's motion by the House of Commons,[†] and the appointment of a committee to consider the subject of national education,[‡] are tokens, among many others, that the present is an auspicious moment for inviting the attention of the English public to that highest and most important of all the objects which a government can place before itself, and to the great things which have been accomplished by another nation in the prosecution of that object.

The value of M. Cousin's Report does not consist in the details, though without the details it would be comparatively of little interest. It throws no new or unexpected light upon the means of educating a people; it simply enables us to realize the fact that a government exists virtuous enough to will the end. The machinery is no other than that which common sense suggests, and would suggest to any government animated by the same spirit. Schools for *all*,[§] without distinction of sect, and without imposing upon any sect the creed or observances of another; the superintendence shared between a Minister of Public Instruction, and local committees of a most democratic constitution, (a fact perfectly accordant with the spirit of the Prussian government, whose municipal institutions are among the freest in Europe;) and finally, that without which the remainder of the system would be of little value, schools for teachers.[¶] In all this there is nothing intricate or recondite; what is memorable is not the conception, but that it has found hands to execute it: that the thing is actually done; done within two days' journey of our own shores, done throughout a great country, and by a government unrivalled in the art of doing well whatever it does at all, because surpassing all other

[*See "New Publications," *Monthly Repository*, n.s. VIII (May, 1834), 383.]

[†John Arthur Roebuck, Speech in Introducing a Motion on National Education (3 June, 1834; Commons), *Parliamentary Debates* (hereafter cited as *PD*), 3rd ser., Vol. 24, cols. 127-30.]

[‡See "Report from the Select Committee on the State of Education," *Parliamentary Papers* (hereafter cited as *PP*), 1834, IX, 1-261.]

[§Cf. James Mill, *Schools for All, in Preference to Schools for Churchmen Only* (London: Longman, *et al.*, 1812).]

[¶See Cousin, pp. 23-33, 4-21, and 62-7, respectively.]

governments in the systematic choice, for whatever it wishes done, of the persons fittest for doing it.

The spirit which has accomplished this, with us is still to be created; and in the hope of contributing to the creation of such a spirit, Mrs. Austin has employed herself in rendering M. Cousin's Report accessible to the English reader.

> Constituted, [says she,] as the government of this country is, and accustomed as it is to receive its impulses from without, (a state of things approved and consecrated by the national ways of thinking,) it would be contrary to reason and to experience to expect it to originate any great changes. This is not recognised, either by governors or governed, as any part of its duty. It is to the public mind, therefore, that those who desire any change must address themselves. (P. viii.)

The preface, from which the above is an extract, well deserves to be separately printed and widely circulated; by the force and conclusiveness with which it combats the shallow opinions and groundless feelings which oppose themselves in this country to a national education, and by the happy union which it exhibits of an earnest spirit and a conciliatory and engaging tone.

If, as from a speech of the Lord Chancellor a year ago[*] we might suppose to be his opinion, it were enough that schools exist, and it mattered not what they teach, or in what method they teach it, we might in this country expect to see all the ends of a national education speedily attained with little assistance from government.

> In a country containing thirteen millions of people, the whole expense of the schools to the state, not only for the lower but for the middling classes, did not amount, in the year 1831, to 35,000*l*. When we remember that, as it is asserted on the highest authority, 1,200,000*l*. are voluntarily raised for the support of our extremely defective popular schools, we have surely no reason to despair that if our management were equal to our means, ample provision would be found for the suitable education of the whole people.*

The £20,000 granted by Parliament last year for building schoolhouses called forth private contributions of nearly treble the amount. Independently of all this, we have the immense endowments which the charity commissioners have brought to light, and proved to have been for generations embezzled and wasted. As far, therefore, as *quantity* of teaching is concerned, the education of our people is, or will speedily be, amply provided for. It is the *quality* which so grievously demands the amending hand of government. And this is the demand which is principally in danger of being obstructed by popular apathy and ignorance. The very first condition of improvement is not yet realized; the public are not sufficiently

---

[*Henry Peter Brougham, Speech on National Education (14 Mar., 1833; Lords), *PD*, 3rd ser., Vol. 16, cols. 632-8.]

*Sir W. Molesworth's speech [on National Education (3 June, 1834; Commons), reported in *The Cornish Guardian and Western Chronicle* (Truro), 13 June, 1843, pp. 2-3]. [The report of the speech in *PD*, 3rd ser., Vol. 24, cols. 130-1, does not contain the passages quoted here and at pp. 66 and 67 below.].

discontented. They are not yet alive to the bad quality of the existing tuition. The very people who furnish so vast an annual sum for the maintenance of schools, often oppose themselves to the wish of their own schoolmasters to give valuable instruction. With many of these patrons of education, whose support Lord Brougham fears will be withdrawn if a state provision be made for education,[*] the constant alarm is, not lest too little, but lest too much, should be taught. And even where the state of their inclinations is unexceptionable, can we expect any judgment or intelligence in providing education for their inferiors in the scale of society, from people who allow the places of education for their own children to be in the wretched state in which we find almost all the schools for the higher and middle classes of England? Are not those schools, and the influence which parents exercise over them, correctly described in the following passage:

a Let us *b* look at home, and examine whether with all the grievous abuses of the endowed seminaries of Great Britain, they are, after all, *c*a particle*c* worse than, or even so bad as, almost all our other places of *d*education. *d* We may ask, whether the desire to gain as much money with as little labour as is consistent with saving appearances, be peculiar to the endowed teachers? Whether the plan of nineteen-twentieths of our unendowed schools be not an organized system of charlatanerie for imposing upon the ignorance of *e*the*e* parents? Whether parents do, in point of fact, prove themselves as solicitous, and as well qualified, to judge rightly of the merits of places of education, as the theory of Adam Smith supposes?[†] Whether the truth be not, that, for the most part, they bestow very little thought upon the matter; or, if they do, show themselves in general the ready dupes of the very shallowest artifices? Whether the necessity of keeping parents in good humour does not too often, instead of rendering the education better, render it worse; the real ends of instruction being sacrificed, not solely (as would *f*be the case under other circumstances*f*) to the ease of the teacher, but to that, and *g*also*g* to the additional positive vices of clap-trap and lip-proficiency? We may ask, whether it is not matter of experience, that a schoolmaster who endeavours really to educate, instead of endeavouring only to seem to educate, and laying himself out for the suffrages of those who never look below the surface, and only for an instant at that, is almost sure, unless he have the genius and the ardour of a Pestalozzi, to make a losing speculation? Let us do what we may, it will be the study of the *h*mere*h* trading schoolmaster to teach down to the level of the parents, be that level high or low; as it is of the trading author to write down to the level of his readers. And in the one shape as in the other, it is *i*at*i* all times and in all places indispensable, that enlightened individuals and

[*Brougham, speech of 14 Mar., 1833, col. 634.]
[†See Adam Smith, *An Inquiry into the Nature and Causes of the Wealth of Nations*, 2 vols. (London: Strahan and Cadell, 1776), Vol. II, pp. 185, 206.]

*a*33,59,67   [*no paragraph*]
*b*33,59,67   even
c-c−59,67
*d-d*59,67   education?
e-e−59,67
*f-f*59,67   otherwise be the case
*g-g*59,67   also
*h-h*59,67   merely
*i-i*59,67   in

enlightened governments should, from other motives than that of pecuniary gain, bestir themselves to provide ^{j} that good and wholesome food for the wants of the mind, for which the competition of the mere trading market affords in general so indifferent a substitute.*

To quote another author:

As regards the common run of day and boarding schools, it is well known that they are, as much as any shopkeepers, obliged to gratify the tastes, and satisfy the wishes of their customers; and that, even if some establishments have risen into such popularity, as to render it truly difficult to insure places in them, this enables them no more to resist and combat the prevailing prejudices, than the most fashionable shop in the metropolis has it in its power to abolish all fanciful fashions, and to introduce a plain and simple dress. Their high popularity is founded upon the opinion, that by them the public taste will be gratified more than anywhere else; but let it for a moment be suspected, that there is a design radically to reform that taste, or merely to correct and purify it, and all the popularity will be gone in an instant. Nowhere is there a more extensive application made of the maxim, *Mundus vult decipi, ergo decipiatur*;[*] that is to say, in education,—the vanity and folly of the parents will be flattered, therefore let us flatter them. And although the weakness of the parents, and the servility of schoolmasters, has been fully explored, and although they heartily despise one another, yet the practical language of a father, when putting his child to school, is still, "I want to be deceived,—I want to be flattered;" and the schoolmaster's answer is no less, "You may rely upon it, it shall be done, in general matters, on the usual terms, and in special matters, at so much extra."[†]

What wonder, then, if they who so ill provide for what most nearly concerns themselves, should be the wretchedest purveyors for the wants of others? What wonder that, as Sir William Molesworth affirmed in his speech on seconding Mr. Roebuck's motion,

The so-called education, provided for the working classes of England, deficient as it is admitted to be in quantity, is immeasurably more deficient in quality; as *instruction*, it is lamentably meagre, incomplete, and inappropriate; as *education*, as nearly as possible, absolutely null. All instruction consists in the mere repetition by rote of certain words, to which the children affix either no idea at all, or ideas too indistinct to have any hold on their minds, or influence on their conduct.[†]

"The schoolmaster," (says the Cornish paper from which we take our report of

---

*From a pamphlet, entitled, "Corporation and Church Property resumable by the State. From the *Jurist* of February, 1833." [An offprint of the article by Mill, "Corporation and Church Property," *Jurist*, IV (Feb., 1833), 1-26; in *Essays on Economics and Society*, Vols. IV-V of *Collected Works* (hereafter cited as *CW*) (Toronto: University of Toronto Press, 1967), Vol. IV, pp. 214-15.]

[*The maxim combines elements found in Sebastian Franck, *Paradoxa ducenta octogenta* ([Ulm: Varnier, 1535]), p. 141 (no. 237), and Auguste De Thou, *Historia sui temporis*, 5 vols. (Paris: Drouart, 1604-08), Vol. II, p. 299.]

†[George Edward] Biber's Lectures on Christian Education [*Christian Education, in a Course of Lectures* (London: Wilson, 1830)], p. 181.

[†Molesworth, speech of 3 June, 1834, p. 2.]

^{j}33,59,67   (though by no means forcibly to impose)

this excellent speech,) "the schoolmaster may be abroad,* but it is in quest of his daily bread, which he earns hardly and ungratefully," and with as little thought and as little labour to himself as possible.

Well was it said by Sir W. Molesworth, that,

In order to obviate all doubts upon this subject, and at the same time to provide us with the data required for legislation on it, some means should immediately be adopted to ascertain distinctly what is actually taught in the popular schools throughout the country.[*]

Such should be the main object of the committee recently appointed by the House of Commons: and a committee being essentially an unfit instrument for conducting inquiries which must be protracted far beyond the duration of the session, and for collecting from all parts of the country evidence much of which can be obtained only on the spot; the best proof which the committee could afford of wisdom and zeal in the cause, would be to follow the example of the committee on municipal corporations, and recommend an address to the king for the appointment of a commission, to inquire into the quality of the existing popular education in all its branches.[†]

The sort of facts which such an inquiry would elicit, may be judged by the passages we are about to quote from a series of Lectures on Christian Education, delivered in 1829 and published in 1830, by Dr. Biber; a man of remarkable powers and attainments, and a most unexceptionable witness to the narrowing and perverting tendency of the religious instruction pretended to be given at our schools; as his own religious sentiments are most fervent, and his hostility to latitudinarianism in religion touches the verge of intolerance.

Of the Church-of-England, or self-styled National, schools:

What affords the most convincing evidence on this subject, and what I wish, therefore, all those that are interested in it to witness themselves, if they have the opportunity, is the yearly public examination of the central school at Baldwin's Gardens. I have been present on one of those occasions, and what I then witnessed, far exceeded all my conceptions of manufacture-teaching. What struck my mind most forcibly in the whole display, was a sort of co-operative plan in the solution of an arithmetical question. This was done, like all the rest, in rotation, the first boy beginning, for instance, 6 times 3 are 18; *second boy*: put 8 and carry 1; *third boy*: 6 times 2 are 12; *fourth boy*: 12 and 1 are 13; *fifth boy*: put 3 and carry 1; *sixth boy*: 6 times 7 are 42; *seventh boy*: 42 and 1 are 43; *eighth boy*: put 3 and carry 4: and so all round and round, again and again, till the whole of it was gone through. Now, although unquestionably all the children could, with a moderate degree of attention, get the ciphers correctly on their slates, it is evident that, with all this, there might, perhaps, not have been more than two in the whole number, who could have solved the same problem for

The Cornish Guardian and Western Chronicle, published at Truro (June 13, 1834). [An anonymous leading article, on Henry Peter Brougham, Speech on the Address on the King's Speech (29 Jan., 1828; Commons), *PD*, n.s., Vol. 18, col. 58.]

[*Molesworth, speech of 3 June, 1834, p. 2.]

[†"First Report of the Commissioners Appointed to Inquire into the Municipal Corporations in England and Wales," *PP*, 1835, XXIII, 48.]

themselves. But what is far more important is, that such a plan of instruction is the direct way of preventing them from ever thinking about what they are doing, and thus cutting off every chance of their understanding it. With their memory-knowledge of the multiplication, addition, and other tables, they are put into this machinery, which, like the wheel of a treadmill, although put in motion by the joint exertions of those in it, overpowers the individual, and forces him to go on at any rate, whether he be disposed to do so or not. Not to mention the absolute ignorance in which the children in those schools always remain concerning *number*, their attention being only directed to *ciphers*, I question whether the above plan is calculated to make even good cipherers. For if there be no knowledge of numbers, there should be some understanding, at least as far as it can be had without the other, of the ciphering system, that the pupil may not be the blind instrument of rules, blindly learned by rote. Nevertheless the solution of the question, as I have described it to you, gave general satisfaction to a number of the bishops, and a large public, assembled on the occasion; and so did the reading of a long list of alms—or reward—givings, at the end of the examination, decreeing to one girl an apron, to another girl a pair of shoes, to such a boy half a crown, to such another boy a pair of trowsers, &c.; that both the givers and receivers might be seen and known of men! The observations I made at that examination, I found confirmed by private visits to the schools; and, among the rest, to one which I may, with the more propriety, instance in support of the charges I have brought against the system, as I can, from personal acquaintance, bear the highest testimony to the zeal, as well as the generally enlightened views, of the clergyman who presides over it, and in whose company I visited it. I asked the children to read the parable of the Prodigal Son,[*] and among other questions which I put to them was this: "What is meant by riotous living?" "Dissipated living." "And what does dissipated living mean?" "Wasteful living." "And what is the meaning of wasteful living?" To this question, as their collection of synonymes was exhausted, I received no answer, and therefore, to get upon intelligible ground I asked then what things were necessary for subsistence, and what not; when some of the girls contended that beer, and cheese, and cakes, and patties, were indispensably necessary for life. And as in this case, so I found it invariably, whenever and wherever I travelled out of the road of those questions, which have for their object to direct the children's attention to mere words; on the most common subjects I found their ideas unclear and confused, and the same children, who would use the most correct language as long as they remained in the track of what they were just then reading, or what they had learned by rote, were unable to express themselves even with tolerable correctness on other matters; a clear proof that their apparent knowledge was a mere word-knowledge, in the acquisition or advantages of which the mind had no share. Thus, on another visit, the boys were exhibiting their slates, on which they had written various words. I stopped one among the rest, who had the word "*disadvantageous.*" "What does that word mean, my boy?" "I don't know." "You know, perhaps, what *disadvantage* means?" "No." "Do you know what *advantageous* means?" "No." "Or, have you ever heard the word *advantage*, what does that mean?" "I don't know." "Well, but suppose you lost your jacket, would that be an advantage or a disadvantage to you?" "An advantage!" was his answer.

It would be unfair, however, to let it be supposed that facts, such as these, are only to be met with in National schools. On this head the British system is quite as defective. Its method of ciphering, though different in some of the details, is, on the whole, no less objectionable, as it is, like the other, a mere mechanical application of the mechanical rules of ciphering, mechanically inculcated into the memory. And, as regards the preposterous exercise of learning to read and to write words, selected merely from a regard to the number

[*Luke, 15:11-32.]

of their syllables, by which the children are so stupified, that they lose the habit of thinking altogether, and do not care about the meaning even of that which they might understand, I recollect a fact which far outdoes the boy, who thought it an advantage for him to lose his jacket. It was at a Lancasterian school, and one which has the name of being among the best conducted; so at least I was told by my friend who went with me, and who is one of the managers. When we entered the room, we found the boys engaged in writing words of different lengths, according to the order of their seats; I passed by those in which such words as "approximation, superintendency," and the like, caught my eye, and, looking over the sentences which some of the more advanced boys were writing, I found one who had copied, about half a dozen times, the words "Live in love." "What are you writing here?" I asked. "Live in love." "And what does that mean?" "I don't know!" "You don't know! But don't you know what 'love' means?" "No!" "Or do you know what 'live' means?" "No!" "What must you do to live in love?" "I don't know!" "Do you know what you must not do, to live in love!" "No, I don't." "Well, but you should know something about what 'Live in love' means. Does it mean that you are to fight with the other boys?" "I can't tell!" "Well," said I, turning to my friend, "what do you say to this?" Upon which the school-master, observing somewhat of the scope of our conversation, came up to us and said, "I dare say you might ask such questions all over the school, without getting a better answer; they none of them know what they are writing."[*]

Of the Lancasterian schools:

It is worth while to examine, in detail, the operations of this system. "Tickets of nominal value are given to deserving boys each school time, which are called in at the end of every three months, and rewards are paid to the holders in exchange. These tickets are valued at the rate of eight for one penny." It is not a mere prospect of reward, by which the pupils are encouraged; a prize stuck up at the end of a long career, which they must run through to attain it:—no, a reward is immediately bestowed upon every performance of duty, the very same morning or afternoon. A distant prospect, it is apprehended, might not act powerfully enough; thus the children are accustomed to "love a reward upon every cornfloor,"[†] and in whatsoever they do, instead of doing it, according to the apostle's injunction, for the glory of God,[‡] to "love gifts, and follow after rewards."[§] So effectual is the operation of this admirable principle, that the fact has actually occurred in a Lancasterian school that, upon the mistress proposing a task of rather a novel description, the girls asked her, whether they should have tickets for doing it, openly declaring, that if there was no reward attached to it, they would not do it. "*Point d'argent, point de Suisse.*"[¶] The daily getting of a reward for every thing that is called "deserving," by the British system, is, however, not sufficient, properly to cultivate an hireling spirit. To complete this part of its education, the system gives proper encouragement to a calculating spirit; first of all by the conversion of the reward tickets into substantial rewards every three months, and, secondly, by a popish sort of indulgence-trade, which the children are permitted to carry on with them before their conversion into real property, and by which those reward tickets come fully under the denomination of the "Mammon of unrighteousness."[‖] Under the head "Punishments," we

[*Biber, pp. 162-5.]
[†Hosea, 9:1.]
[‡I Corinthians, 10:31.]
[§Isaiah, 1:23.]
[¶Jean Baptiste Racine, *Les plaideurs* (1668), in *Oeuvres*, 7 vols. (Paris: Le Normant, 1808), Vol. II, p. 277 (I, i, 15).]
[‖Luke, 16:9.]

are informed that at the close of each school-time, "the bad boys are classed into divisions, corresponding with the number of their offences, and are required to pay one ticket for each offence; those who do so are dismissed, and those who have no tickets are confined a quarter of an hour for every offence reported against them." And lest any doubt should remain on the subject, it is further stated that "in all cases, the parties may be excused from confinement, if they are in possession of reward tickets, by forfeiting them, at the rate of one ticket for every quarter of an hour's detention." Not enough that the child is taught to do his duty, not from conscientious feeling of obligation, but for reward's sake; he is also taught, and that in the most effectual manner, viz., by practice, that past good conduct amounts to a license for the commission of sin. This may not be the intention of the framers of those ill-contrived regulations, but it is the necessary effect of them. How easy is it, for instance, for a clever boy to gain reward tickets, to a considerable amount, by attention to reading, spelling, and arithmetic, all of which he may, if he prefer present indulgence to future gratification, convert into as many tickets of license for the perpetration of such offences as are particularly to his taste. I call upon those that are candid, among the advocates of the British system, to deny, if they can, on the score of principle, that from such causes such effects must follow, or, on the ground of practical experience, that such effects are actually taking place. And if they have not been observed as frequently as might be anticipated, is there not reason to suppose, that this may partly be owing to the want of close contact, on the part of the master, with every individual child, an evil which is the necessary consequence of the much-extolled machinery of the British system, and which, on more than one ground, calls loudly for a remedy? Be that as it may, the effect of the remission of punishment, for the forfeiture of rewards, is obvious enough, and the fact has been admitted to me by some who have had opportunities, more than myself, of watching the practical effects of the system. But even without such an admission it would be evident, from the combination of all the influences enumerated, that the British system must beget a set of hirelings, who, for hire's sake, do the good, and, for hire's sake, abstain from evil. But, as if there had been an anxiety to collect, on the score of motives, all that is unscriptural, and to put it into practice in those schools, the conversion of the reward tickets into actual rewards, at the expiration of each three months, is celebrated in the following manner: "When all the boys have received the prizes, they are conducted round the school-room by the general monitors, who proclaim that they have obtained their prizes for good behaviour, regular attendance, and improvement in learning; after walking two or three times round the school, they are permitted to go home." Is not this, in plain language, sounding a trumpet before the boys?

Now, I would ask my Christian friends—for so, I know, some of the managers and supporters of the British system will permit me to call them, in spite of what I have said against that system—I would ask them, as Christians, whether they can justify any of these practices individually: the setting aside of genuine moral feeling; the stimulus of appearing greater and better, one than the other; the seeking a reward for every performance of duty; the exemption from punishment through rewards before gained; the calculation of the total amount of these rewards within a given period; and lastly, the going round "the corners" of the school, with the monitors as trumpeters before them?[*]

Lastly, of the infant schools: and this is the most frightful perversion of all. That any kind of technical instruction should, in vulgar and unintelligent hands, degenerate into mechanical routine, is less wonderful: but that an institution designed for *moral* culture only—a place where the child learned nothing, in the

[*Biber, pp. 167-70.]

vulgar sense of learning, but only learned to live; that places designed exclusively for the cultivation of the kindly affections, should by dulness, hardness, and miserable vanity, be converted into places for parroting gibberish; this is a more wretched example than any other, of the state of mind of the people who subscribe the 1,200,000*l.* which Lord Brougham is afraid they should prefer to keep in their pockets if more rational views of education were substituted for their own.[*]

The original design of the infant system has been entirely perverted; and, as a natural consequence of this, the system itself has undergone considerable alterations. The first idea, if I am correctly informed, was to collect those children who were below the grasp of the other systems, and to endeavour, at the very tenderest age, to awaken them to a life of love and intelligence.[†] Positive instruction was not made an object of, but merely considered as a means for the attainment of that higher object, the developement of the soul in the true life. With this view, the first infant schools were founded, and it seemed as if, from the mouths of babes, the public would receive evidence, to convince them of the errors of long cherished prejudices. But, as it is written, "Though thou shouldest bray a fool in a mortar among wheat, with a pestle, yet will not his foolishness depart from him,"[‡] so did it prove to be the case with the prejudices of the public. Infant schools, indeed, became the fashion; for there was a something in them to win the feelings, which has since very much worn off, but which, then, was in all its freshness, and made converts by hundreds. But the consequence of this was, not that the public adopted the principles of the new system, but that they grafted upon it their old prejudices, their sectarian sympathies and antipathies, and all their paltry party feelings and interests. Originally, the infant schools were calculated to show, what could be done by appealing to a principle of love in the child, which would subdue the wrath of its nature, and to a principle of truth, which would enlighten its darkness; and thereby eventually to subvert those systems in which, as we have seen, the evil tendencies of our nature are made the levers of education. This was no sooner discovered, than a stir was made, for the purpose of suppressing the rising opposition in its very germ. A society was formed, which, under the pretence of advocating the infant system, succeeded in gradually commuting it into the very reverse of what it was originally meant to be, and which, after having accomplished so praiseworthy an object, has at length absconded, by a sort of mystification, in a stationer's shop. But although the agents have vanished, the baneful effects of their labours have remained. The infant schools are now no more than preparatory for the Lancasterian and National schools, especially the latter, which had most to dread from the rising system, and whose influence, therefore, was most powerfully exerted in defeating its success. The machinery of those two systems has found its way into the infant schools, and has made them, with rare exceptions, mere miniature pictures of the others. You see the little monitors spelling, with their classes, over the A, B, C, and a variety of lesson tables without sense and meaning; you hear them say, by rote, the multiplication table, the pence table, and so on. The same things are repeated over and over again, so that a parrot hung up for some time in one of those schools, would unquestionably make as good an infant school mistress as any. There is hardly one of the means introduced at the beginning, which has not been turned to a bad purpose. Thus, for instance, among other things, sets of geometrical figures and bodies, cut out of wood, were used, for the

[*Cf. p. 65 above.]
[†See Robert Owen, *A New View of Society* (London: Cadell and Davies, 1813), Essay III, pp. 2-4.]
[‡Proverbs, 27:22.]

purpose of questioning the children respecting the number and proportion of their angles, sides, &c.; but, instead of making them the means of intellectual exercises, in which the children would be led every day to make new discoveries, and to think for themselves, those figures are now pulled out, chiefly in the presence of visitors, and then the whole school bawls out together, "This is a pentagon—this is a hexagon—this is an octagon, and so on." One of the most pleasing features of the infant system, in its origin, was the social feeling, the cordiality, and cheerfulness of the little company, which was greatly promoted by some short and easy tunes, to which occasionally some infantine words were sung. The effect which this had, in soothing the irritation of some, moderating the violence of others, and arousing the dull ones into life, was truly wonderful; but no sooner was the discovery made, that there was, so early in life, a way to man's heart and mind by singing, than the machinists of education availed themselves of this fact, for the purpose of conveying to the memory some of their dead stock, which would not otherwise have found its way there so easily; and, presently, the multiplication, and other ciphering tables, the pence table, avoirdupois weight, and more of the like kind, were set to music, and occasionally better fitted for the infantine taste, at least so it was supposed, by the addition of the most silly rhymes. What intellectual or moral effect, I should like to know, can be anticipated from a child learning such a verse as this:

> Forty pence are three and four pence,
>   A pretty sum, or I'm mistaken;
> Fifty pence are four and two pence,
>   Which will buy five pounds of bacon;

Or, still more vulgar, in the song about the cow:

> And when she's dead, her flesh is good,
> For beef is our true English food;
> But though 'twill make us brave and strong,
> To eat too much, we know, is wrong.[*]

In one infant school, I have known the children to be made to laugh, or to cry, or to look happy, or unhappy, or kind, or angry, at the master's command; in another school, in which the picture of a farm yard was hung up on the wall, the master assured me that he was expressly enjoined by his committee, to ask the children for scripture references to every object represented in that picture. Thus, when he pointed to a cow, the children were to quote him chapter and verse of those passages in scripture in which a cow was mentioned; the same with the sheaves, the clouds, and whatever else the picture contained; this was considered, by the committee, as an excellent method of connecting religious instruction with all other subjects. To enumerate all the nonsense that has been practised, and is still practised, in this manner, would be an endless task; but what has most effectually contributed to the ruin of the infant system, is the manner of propagating it. The renown of the system penetrates into some country place, or into some district of a large town, and some persons take it into their heads, upon hearing what excellent things the infant schools are, that they too will have an infant school. They then go in search of a place, and find out

[*Cf. Samuel Wilderspin, *The Infant System, for Developing the Intellectual and Moral Powers of All Children from One to Seven Years of Age* (1823), 6th ed. (London: Simpkin and Marshall, 1834), pp. 265, 277.]

some old barn, or coach-house, which, with a few alterations, can be turned into a school-room. So far all is right; for it is better that a good school should be in a wretched place, than, as we so often see it before our eyes in the metropolis, that a wretched school should be in a splendid place. But the great difficulty arises in the choice of the future master or mistress. Each of the originators and patrons of the proposed institution, has some client in view, whom he has nominated in his heart. A poor fellow, a tailor, a shoe-maker, or a fiddler by trade, who is not prosperous in the exercise of his calling, has the suffrage of the most active member of the committee; or an old dame, whose school would suffer by the opposition of the new system, is patronized by some charitable ladies; or the richest contributor has an old servant, whom she wants to put into a snug place; a struggle arises between these contending interests, the result of which is, that the client of the most influential party is selected for the situation, although, perhaps, the most unfit of all the candidates. The next question then is, how the new master or mistress is to learn the system, of which they must be presumed to be entirely ignorant. Some friend, perhaps, advises the committee to send the teacher to London, or some other place, for three months, and have him regularly trained under a good infant school master. In vain! they cannot wait so long, it will protract the business, and the zeal of the good people in the town might get cool in the mean time. The infant school must be opened in a fortnight or three weeks at the latest, and this is consequently all the time that can be permitted to the newly chosen master for his preparation. The question of time being settled, another arises: to what place is he to be sent? The expense of sending him up to London, or to some other place of note, is found too great, particularly for so short a time, and it seems, therefore, better that he should be sent the least distance possible, to the nearest infant school, to "catch" the system. But suppose even he come to London, or to Exeter, or Bristol, to one of the best schools that are, what can he learn in so short a time? What strikes him chiefly, is the singing of the tables, the distribution in classes, the marching round the room, the clapping of hands, and all the other machinery. This he catches, as well as he can, and back he goes, and opens his school, and his chief endeavour is to follow the system which he has caught, as closely as he can. And what can be expected after this? What else, but that the infant school should become a treadmill for the minds of the poor children!

Such has been the history of the infant system; it has been misapprehended by prejudice and narrow-mindedness, and perverted by bigotry and false zeal, so much so, that those who were its warmest advocates, are tempted to wish that never so much as one infant school had been established in the country.[*]

We can add nothing to this. Surely every member of the committee of the House of Commons who reads it, will be eager to make the labours of that committee instrumental to the reform of such abominations.

We conclude in the words of the same author, with the following general summary, every word of which accords with all our own information.

I have had a sad picture to lay before you, when speaking of the neglect of education, and of the numbers of children who are left without any instruction at all; but no less sad is the picture of the present state of our charity schools. All the evils under which society at large labours are, as it were, concentrated upon this point, as if to destroy the very vitals of the nation. The universal motive is money-getting; the means are all devised upon the analogy

[*Biber, pp. 172-7.]

of large manufactures, carried on by mechanical power; and, to make the measure of evil full, the cloak of it all is a dead profession of the gospel. The principle of mammon is recognized as the life of education, the existence of mental and moral powers is set aside, and the spirit of religion is supplanted by the letter. Such is the general character of the education which is imparted to the poorer classes of this country, whatever may be the name of the system under which it is done. I leave you to judge, what must become of the nation![*]

[*Ibid., pp. 177-8.]

ON PUNISHMENT

1834

EDITOR'S NOTE

Monthly Repository, n.s. VIII (Oct., 1834), 734-6. Title footnoted: "Remarks on Criminal Law; with a Plan for an Improved System, and Observations on the Prevention of Crime. [By Thomas Jevons. London: Hamilton, Adams; Edinburgh: Waugh and Innes; Dublin: Curry; Liverpool: Marples, 1834.]" Running titles as title. Unsigned; not republished. Identified in Mill's bibliography as "An article headed 'On Punishment' being a review of an anonymous work by Mr. Jevons of Liverpool; in the Monthly Repository of October 1834" (MacMinn, 42). In the Somerville College copy (tear-sheets) there are two corrections by Mill that are adopted in the present text: at 78.6 the question mark after "another" is deleted (we substitute a period); and at 79.17 "merely" is altered to "surely". For comment on the review, see xli and lxi above.

On Punishment

THE FREE AND BOLD SPIRIT OF INQUIRY, and the benevolence of heart, which breathe through this little tract, and which are characteristic of the supposed writer, render his speculations on the now hacknied subject of penal law, deserving of an attention, which the degree of truth or of practical applicability which they possess, would not of itself have entitled them to. The author, in fact, deals with punishment as Mr. Owen deals with the institution of private property. He makes out a case of manifest hardship and cruelty against the one, as Mr. Owen does against the other, and with as little difficulty, for the materials are ample; and like Mr. Owen, he helps out his case by including in his enumeration not only the evils inseparable from the institution itself, but all those which are actually attendant on it in its present form, however easily remediable. He then gravely proposes that punishment should be abolished, and the prevention of crime attempted by other means; as one might conceive a philanthropist enlarging upon the nauseousness of medicine, its injurious effects upon the constitution, the hardship of administering it to persons who are ill and helpless and not their own masters, and concluding that medicine be abolished, and that mankind should endeavour to preserve their health in some other manner.

The author's substitute for punishment is itself a punishment, though one of the mildest kind. He proposes that those who are convicted of offences, whether of the slightest or of the gravest description, should be no otherwise ill-treated than by being compelled to live as a community apart, in a portion of the country specially allotted to them, in which they should have the same opportunities of gaining their livelihood as the rest of the the community, and from which they should be liberated on proof of continued good conduct. Within this district there should be a smaller enclosure, to which those should be again banished who have violated the laws of the criminal community to which they were first relegated; and within this second a third, in which again, as the last resort, there should be a prison. But no one is to be incarcerated in this prison without having the alternative offered to him of going into perpetual exile.

In the subordinate arrangements there is some good sense and much ingenuity: and as one among many systems of reformatory discipline, the plan of our author seems worthy to be tried by way of experiment upon the less corrupted of the persons convicted of minor offences. But as a plan of systematic treatment for all offenders, to be adopted in lieu of every other punishment, it would be a more utter failure than the worst of the penal systems, for it would fail to deter from crime. On whom would the penalty of temporary banishment from the society of the honest, operate as a sufficient motive to restrain from the violation of the laws? Upon the honest; upon those who are already sufficiently restrained by their own disposition, or by the opinion of one another. All who required restraint, would find this restraint inefficacious; and if all who, in any manner violated the laws, were removed into such a place of reformation, the inhabitants of the reformatory would speedily outnumber the remainder of the community, and would become themselves the rulers of the country.

Even this consequence were it admitted by the author, would not, perhaps, decide the question in his mind; for he considers the infliction of punishment for the purpose of prevention, as in itself an immorality and an injustice.

"To punish one man," says he, "in order that some other unknown person may be deterred from the commission of crime, is an iniquitous practice, and cannot be justified even if its consequences, so far as the public is affected by the exhibition, were beneficial in ever so great a degree, and could be calculated upon with certainty." [P. 72.]

He calls the infliction of punishment "for example's sake," a debasing practice: and expresses his "earnest wishes that so wicked a principle may never again be adopted as the motive and guide by which the high and mighty may rule their low and erring brethren." (P. 73.)

Here is much good indignation thrown away on an occasion, when there is nothing to call for it but a form of words. You do not punish one person in order that another may be deterred. The other is deterred, not by the punishment of the first, but by the expectation of being punished himself: and as the punishment you threaten him with, would have no effect upon his conduct, unless he believed that it would really be inflicted, you are obliged to prove the reality of your intention, by keeping your word whenever either he, or any other person, disregards your prohibition. This is no injustice to the sufferer, because he, too, has been warned beforehand; unless indeed, not the punishment merely, but the law itself, be unjust, and an improper restriction upon his freedom. If the acts which the law prohibits, were such as he had no right to do, and if he had full warning of all the consequences to which he would subject himself by violating it, he has no ground of complaint that its full penalties are inflicted, not to deter others, but in order that what really deters others, the threat of punishment to themselves, may not be an idle mockery.

Our author's objection is only valid against either *ex post facto* laws, or laws which are in themselves unjust, independently of the means by which they are enforced. In all other cases the offender himself, and not the legislator, is responsible for the evil which falls upon him by his voluntary breach of a just law.

We may add, that if the principles laid down by our author constitute a valid objection to the existing notions of punishment, they apply with exactly the same force to his own system of banishment to a particular place. If what he acknowledges to be "the fundamental principle that should govern the criminal code of every enlightened state, viz. protection of person and property," (p. 23,) will justify the infliction of the smallest atom of pain upon offenders, it will justify the infliction of any amount necessary for the end; unless such as would outweigh all the benefits of which the security of person or property is the cause. The only right by which society is warranted in inflicting any pain upon any human creature, is the right of self-defence; and if this will justify it in interfering with the natural liberty of its offending members, by the degree of coercion implied in removing them to the reformatory and keeping them there, it will warrant any greater degree of coercion which may be found necessary to protect the innocent part of the community against their encroachments. On any other principle, instead of relegating offenders to a particular part of the country, or tendering to them the alternative of voluntary exile, the utmost rights of honest people would extend no further than to remove out of harm's way, by going into exile themselves. But this is surely being scrupulous in the wrong place. If we were attacked by robbers or savages, and in danger of our lives, no one ever questioned our right to defend ourselves even to the death of the assailant; and we cannot conceive a greater piece of inconsistency than, admitting this, to deny us the liberty of declaring before-hand to all robbers, that if they attack us we will put them to death. No doubt if we can protect ourselves as effectually with less evil to them, it is our duty to do so; and we ought to try the experiment in all ways which afford a chance of success, before we give it up as hopeless. But our right to punish, is a branch of the universal right of self-defence; and it is a mere subtlety to set up any distinction between them.

Some of the author's minor suggestions are well deserving of the attention of an enlightened legislature. We would notice in particular [p. 95] his idea of restraining juvenile delinquency by holding the parents legally responsible instead of the children.

SMITH ON LAW REFORM

1841

EDITOR'S NOTE

Westminster Review, XXXV (Jan., 1841), 239-40. In the Miscellaneous Notices section, under "Law," headed: "Remarks on Law Reform; addressed more particularly to the general reader. By William Smith, Esq., of the Middle Temple, barrister at law. [London:] Maxwell: 1840." Running title to section, not to article. Signed "A." Not republished. Identified in Mill's bibliography as "A short notice of a pamphlet on Law Reform by William Smith, in the Miscellaneous Notices of the Westminster Review for January 1841. (No. 68.)" (MacMinn, 53.) There is no copy in the Somerville College Library. For comment, see xli and lxi above.

Smith on Law Reform

THIS IS SUCH A PAMPHLET as we have long wished to see. The question of Law Reform has usually either been treated bit by bit, on the principle of suggesting no more at once than could be carried at once, or it has been kept so completely *in generalibus* that although the existing system might be shown to be bad, it seemed as if nothing could be done to amend it except by beginning from the foundations and reconstructing the whole fabric. There was wanted a writer who, with the requisite knowledge of the existing law, but with the capacity also of distinguishing principles of universal legislation from the technicalities of a conventional system, should review the whole of our jurisprudence, and examine how much of the absurdity which disfigures, and the complication which embarrasses it, is capable of being removed in that piecemeal mode in which parliament legislates, and in a country like ours, or, at least, in the present state of general opinion, must legislate.

Mr. Smith has attempted a portion of this task, and has executed it with a high degree of merit. He thoroughly understands his subject, he has the art of popular and lively exposition, and on the whole we know not any work where in so small a compass so great a number of important law reforms, practicable at the present moment, are pointed out, and the expediency of them so briefly and forcibly, and at the same time popularly demonstrated. The defects upon which he chiefly animadverts are some of the peculiarities of the system of pleading; some of the exclusionary rules of evidence; the doctrine of feudal tenures, which, although now a mere mass of fiction, still continues to encumber, by the technical consequences which it involves, the whole of our law of real property; and the fact that three different and conflicting systems of law, administered by three sets of courts, (common law, equity, and ecclesiastical,) co-exist, insomuch that the very same property would often be assigned by these different systems to different persons; and the unseemly spectacle is exhibited of one court giving relief, as it is called, from the disposition of property which would be lawfully and regularly made by another. The practical mischiefs of a most serious kind, arising from these defects in our legal system, are pointed out in a masterly manner by Mr. Smith. The following passage may convey an idea of his style:

If any one expects, by a revision of our laws, to prepare a system so simple that every man may acquire sufficient knowledge of it, that he who runs may read,[*] that no body of professed lawyers will be requisite to conduct litigation or frame legal instruments, he is merely manifesting his total ignorance upon the subject. Jurisprudence, when it advances beyond those simple rules which are dictated by the general sense of what is just or unjust, becomes in some measure arbitrary, and inevitably complicate. Rules are then to be laid down, which must be the result of a nice balance of opposite expediencies; and when these, or, indeed, any other rules, are determined, innumerable cases arise, of which again it is difficult to decide whether they are included in the rules. But because jurisprudence must of necessity present to our view a vast and complex system, because it must admit many distinctions, the value and importance of which cannot without much previous study be appreciated, is it therefore to be loaded with any foreign matter whatsoever? Is this a reason for admitting and perpetuating a mass of erudition quite alien to the science itself of jurisprudence? Is it not rather a reason, since law must be difficult, for avoiding every needless cause of difficulty? Again and again I protest against the admixture, still too frequent, of feudalism and antiquarian lore with English jurisprudence. Why am I to be incessantly presented with an historical account of its origin as a sufficient reason for the actual existence of the law which governs me? Doubtless, the antiquarian will be shocked, and denounce me as a man of rude, uncultured taste, if I dispute the necessity of recording by existing laws the ancient feudalism of Europe. What! no trace left of past times? no pride of ancestry increased by the very framework of our jurisprudence? all to be new and scientific? Our laws, he exclaims, will no longer be English, they might as well be French, or Russian, or Chinese; they will not belong to us and to our history. Let him go and study history, and providentially endowed as he is with the love of what is dark and little, connect with it what antiquities he thinks fit; I will listen and will learn of him with pleasure. But why must I meet, to my confusion and dismay, in the real business of life, and at the hazard of my property, these relics, these spectral remains of the maxims and manners of my forefathers? I can read with interest of the struggle maintained by our courts of law against the subtle contrivances of land-loving monks. Must I, therefore, desire that this struggle be recorded in the deed which conveys my property? Think you that law, which is the most ancient matter in this world, and has dealt with the nearest interests of living men through the remotest generations of the earth, needs to be set off with this antique and Gothic tracery? Or is it true that jurisprudence has ends of its own so idle and unimportant to mankind, that it must stand indebted to such sources of interest as an antiquarian society can supply?[†]

[*William Cowper, "Tirocinium," in *The Task, a Poem, in Six Books, to Which Are Added by the Same Author, an Epistle to Joseph Hill, Esq., Tirocinium, or a Review of Schools, and the History of John Gilpin* (London: Johnson, 1785), p. 297 (l. 80).]
  [†Smith, pp. 8-9.]

THE NEGRO QUESTION

1850

EDITOR'S NOTE

Fraser's Magazine, XLI (Jan., 1850), 25-31. Headed and running titles as title. Introduced by an editorial note by John William Parker, Jr., here given in a footnote to the title. Signed "D." Not republished. Identified in Mill's bibliography as "A letter to the Editor of Fraser's Magazine, in answer to an attack by Carlyle on the 'rights of negroes,' published under the signature D in Fraser's Magazine for January 1850. (Copied into the D[aily] News of 2d Jany.)" (MacMinn, 72.) In response to Thomas Carlyle, "Occasional Discourse on the Negro Question," *Fraser's Magazine*, XL (Dec., 1849), 670-9. The Somerville College copy has one pencilled emendation by Mill that is adopted in the present text: at 93.39 "highest" is altered to "briefest". For comment on the essay, see xxi-xxii and lxi-lxii above.

The copy-text is the *Fraser's* version, but collation with the version in the *Daily News* of 2 Jan., 1850, 3, reveals three variants that, as they may be considered improvements, are given in notes; in these notes "50^2" indicates *Daily News*.

The Negro Question*

SIR,

Your last month's Number contains a speech against the "rights of Negroes,"[*] the doctrines and spirit of which ought not to pass without remonstrance. The author issues his opinions, or rather ordinances, under imposing auspices; no less than those of the "immortal gods." [P. 675.] "The Powers," "the Destinies," announce through him, not only what *will* be, but what *shall* be done; what they "have decided upon, passed their eternal act of parliament for." [*Ibid.*] This is speaking "as one having authority;"[†] but authority from whom? If by the quality of the message we may judge of those who sent it, *not* from any powers to whom just or good men acknowledge allegiance. This so-called "eternal Act of Parliament" is no new law, but the old law of the strongest,—a law against which the great teachers of mankind have in all ages protested:—it is the law of force and cunning; the law that whoever is more powerful than another, is "born lord" of that other, the other being born his "servant," [pp. 676-7,] who must be "compelled to work" for him by "beneficent whip," if "other methods avail not." [P. 675.] I see nothing divine in this injunction. If "the gods" [*ibid.*] will this, it is the first duty of human beings to resist such gods. Omnipotent these "gods" are *not*, for powers which demand *human* tyranny and injustice cannot accomplish their purpose unless human beings co-operate. The history of human improvement is the record of a struggle by which inch after inch of ground has been wrung from these maleficent powers, and more and more of human life rescued from the iniquitous dominion of the law of might. Much, very much of this work still remains to do; but the progress made in it is the best and greatest achievement yet performed by mankind, and it was hardly to be expected at this period of the world that we should be enjoined, by way of a great reform in human affairs, to begin *un*doing it.

The age, it appears, is ill with a most pernicious disease, which infects all its proceedings, and of which the conduct of this country in regard to the Negroes is a

---

*If all the meetings at Exeter Hall be not presided over by strictly impartial chairmen, they ought to be. We shall set an example to our pious brethren in this respect, by giving publicity to the following letter. Our readers have now both sides of the question before them, and can form their own opinions upon it.—EDITOR. [John William Parker, Jr.]

[*Carlyle, "Occasional Discourse," p. 670; subsequent references are given in the text.]
[†Matthew, 7:29.]

prominent symptom—the Disease of Philanthropy. "Sunk in deep froth-oceans of Benevolence, Fraternity, Emancipation-principle, Christian Philanthropy, and other most amiable-looking, but most baseless, and, in the end, baleful and all-bewildering jargon," the product of "hearts left destitute of any earnest guidance, and disbelieving that there ever was any, Christian or heathen," the "human species" is "reduced to believe in rose-pink sentimentalism alone." [P. 671.] On this alleged condition of the human species I shall have something to say presently. But I must first set my anti-philanthropic opponent right on a matter of fact. He entirely misunderstands the great national revolt of the conscience of this country against slavery and the slave-trade, if he supposes it to have been an affair of sentiment. It depended no more on humane feelings than any cause which so irresistibly appealed to them must necessarily do. Its first victories were gained while the lash yet ruled uncontested in the barrack-yard and the rod in schools, and while men were still hanged by dozens for stealing to the value of forty shillings. It triumphed because it was the cause of justice; and, in the estimation of the great majority of its supporters, of religion. Its originators and leaders were persons of a stern sense of moral obligation, who, in the spirit of the religion of their time, seldom spoke much of benevolence and philanthropy, but often of duty, crime, and sin. For nearly two centuries had negroes, many thousands annually, been seized by force or treachery and carried off to the West Indies to be worked to death, literally to death; for it was the received maxim, the acknowledged dictate of good economy, to wear them out quickly and import more. In this fact every other possible cruelty, tyranny, and wanton oppression was by implication included. And the motive on the part of the slave-owners was the love of gold; or, to speak more truly, of vulgar and puerile ostentation. I have yet to learn that anything more detestable than this has been done by human beings towards human beings in any part of the earth. It is a mockery to talk of comparing it with Ireland. [P. 672.] And this went on, not, like Irish beggary, because England had not the skill to prevent it,—not merely by the sufferance, but by the laws of the English nation. At last, however, there were found men, in growing number, who determined not to rest until the iniquity was extirpated; who made the destruction of it as much the business and end of their lives, as ordinary men make their private interests; who would not be content with softening its hideous features, and making it less intolerable to the sight, but would stop at nothing short of its utter and irrevocable extinction. I am so far from seeing anything contemptible in this resolution, that, in my sober opinion, the persons who formed and executed it deserve to be numbered among those, not numerous in any age, who have led noble lives according to their lights, and laid on mankind a debt of permanent gratitude.

After fifty years of toil and sacrifice, the object was accomplished, and the negroes, freed from the despotism of their fellow-beings, were left to themselves, and to the chances which the arrangements of existing society provide for those who have no resource but their labour. These chances proved favourable to them, and, for the last ten years, they afford the unusual spectacle of a labouring class whose labour bears so high a price that they can exist in comfort on the wages of a comparatively small quantity of work. This, to the ex-slave-owners, is an inconvenience; but I have not yet heard that any of them has been reduced to beg his bread, or even to dig for it, as the negro, however scandalously he enjoys himself, still must: a carriage or some other luxury the less, is in most cases, I believe, the limit of their privations—no very hard measure of retributive justice; those who have had tyrannical power taken away from them, may think themselves fortunate if they come so well off; at all events, it is an embarrassment out of which the nation is not called on to help them: if they cannot continue to realize their large incomes without more labourers, let them find them, and bring them from where they can best be procured, only not by force. Not so thinks your anti-philanthropic contributor. That negroes should exist, and enjoy existence, on so little work, is a scandal in his eyes, worse than their former slavery. It must be put a stop to at any price. He does not "wish to see" them slaves again "if it can be avoided;" but "decidedly" they "will have to be servants," "servants to the whites," [p. 667,] "compelled to labour," and "not to go idle another minute." [P. 674.] "Black Quashee," [p. 674,] "up to the ears in pumpkins," [p. 671,] and "working about half an hour a day," [p. 672,] is to him the abomination of abominations. I have so serious a quarrel with him about principles, that I have no time to spare for his facts; but let me remark, how easily he takes for granted those which fit his case. Because he reads in some blue-book of a strike for wages in Demerara,[*] such as he may read of any day in Manchester, he draws a picture of negro inactivity, copied from the wildest prophecies of the slavery party before emancipation. If the negroes worked no more than "half an hour a day," would the sugar crops, in all except notoriously bad seasons, be so considerable, so little diminished from what they were in the time of slavery, as is proved by the Customhouse returns?[†] But it is not the facts of the question, so much as the moralities of it, that I care to dispute with your contributor.

A black man working no more than your contributor affirms that they work, is, he says, "an eye-sorrow," a "blister on the skin of the state," [p. 676,] and many other things equally disagreeable; to *work* being the grand duty of man. "To do competent work, to labour honestly according to the ability given them; for that, and for no other purpose, was each one of us sent into this world." Whoever prevents him from this his "sacred appointment to labour while he lives on earth" is "his deadliest enemy." If it be "his own indolence" that prevents him, "the first

[*Carlyle, p. 672; see "First Report from the Select Committee on Ceylon and British Guiana," *PP*, 1849, XI, 114, 129-30.]

[†See, e.g., "An Account Showing the Imports into the United Kingdom of Sugar, Molasses, Rum, Coffee, and Cocoa, from the West Indies and British Guiana, for the Years 1831 to 1847," *PP*, 1847-48, LVIII, 547-9.]

right he has" is that all wiser and more industrious persons shall, "by some wise means, compel him to do the work he is fit for." [P. 673.] Why not at once say that, by "some wise means," every thing should be made right in the world? While we are about it, wisdom may as well be suggested as the remedy for all evils, as for one only. Your contributor incessantly prays Heaven that all persons, black and white, may be put in possession of this "divine right of being compelled, if permitted will not serve, to do what work they are appointed for." [P. 674.] But as this cannot be conveniently managed just yet, he will begin with the blacks, and *"will"* make them work *for* certain whites, those whites *not* working at all; that so "the eternal purpose and supreme will" [*ibid.*] may be fulfilled, and "injustice," which is "for ever accursed," may cease. [P. 676.]

This pet theory of your contributor about work, we all know well enough, though some persons might not be prepared for so bold an application of it. Let me say a few words on this "gospel of work"[*]—which, to my mind, as justly deserves the name of a cant as any of those which he has opposed, while the truth it contains is immeasurably farther from being the whole truth than that contained in the words Benevolence, Fraternity, or any other of his catalogue of contemptibilities. To give it a rational meaning, it must first be known what he means by work. Does work mean every thing which people *do*? No; or he would not reproach people with doing no work. Does it mean laborious exertion? No; for many a day spent in killing game, includes more muscular fatigue than a day's ploughing. Does it mean *useful* exertion? But your contributor always scoffs at the idea of utility.[†] Does he mean that all persons ought to earn their living? But some earn their living by doing nothing, and some by doing mischief; and the negroes, whom he despises, still do earn by labour the "pumpkins" they consume and the finery they wear.

Work, I imagine, is not a good in itself. There is nothing laudable in work for work's sake. To work voluntarily for a worthy object is laudable; but what constitutes a worthy object? On this matter, the oracle of which your contributor is the prophet has never yet been prevailed on to declare itself. He revolves in an eternal circle round the idea of work, as if turning up the earth, or driving a shuttle or a quill, were ends in themselves, and the ends of human existence. Yet, even in the case of the most sublime service to humanity, it is not because it is work that it is worthy; the worth lies in the service itself, and in the will to render it—the noble feelings of which it is the fruit; and if the nobleness of will is proved by other evidence than work, as for instance by danger or sacrifice, there is the same

[*See Carlyle, *Past and Present* (London: Chapman and Hall, 1843), Bk. II, Chaps. xi and xii.]

[†See, e.g., Carlyle, "Signs of the Times," *Edinburgh Review*, XLIX (June, 1829), 453, and *Sartor Resartus* (1833-34), 2nd ed. (Boston: Munroe, 1837), Bk. III, Chap. v.]

a-a–50²

worthiness. While we talk only of work, and not of its object, we are far from the root of the matter; or if it may be called the root, it is a root without flower or fruit.

In the present case, it seems, a noble object means "spices." "The gods wish, besides pumpkins, that spices and valuable products be grown in their West Indies"—the "noble elements of cinnamon, sugar, coffee, pepper black and grey," "things far nobler than pumpkins." [Pp. 674-5.] Why so? Is what supports life, inferior in dignity to what merely gratifies the sense of taste? Is it the verdict of the "immortal gods" that pepper is noble, freedom (even freedom from the lash) contemptible? But spices lead "towards commerces, arts, polities, and social developements." [P. 674.] Perhaps so; but of what sort? When they must be produced by slaves, the "polities and social developements" they lead to are such as the world, I hope, will not choose to be cursed with much longer.

The worth of work does not surely consist in its leading to other work, and so on to work upon work without end. On the contrary, the multiplication of work, for purposes not worth caring about, is one of the evils of our present condition. When justice and reason shall be the rule of human affairs, one of the first things to which we may expect them to be applied is the question, How many of the so-called luxuries, conveniences, refinements, and ornaments of life, are *worth* the labour which must be undergone as the condition of producing them? The beautifying of existence is as worthy and useful an object as the sustaining of it; but only a vitiated taste can see any such result in those fopperies of so-called civilization, which myriads of hands are now occupied and lives wasted in providing. In opposition to the "gospel of work," I would assert the gospel of leisure, and maintain that human beings *cannot* rise to the finer attributes of their nature compatibly with a life filled with labour. I do not include under the name labour such work, if work it be called, as is done by writers and afforders of "guidance," an occupation which, let alone the vanity of the thing, cannot be called by the same name with the real labour, the exhausting, stiffening, stupefying toil of many kinds of agricultural and manufacturing labourers. To reduce very greatly the quantity of work required to carry on existence, is as needful as to distribute it more equally; and the progress of science, and the increasing ascendancy of justice and good sense, tend to this result.

There is a portion of work rendered necessary by the fact of each person's existence: no one could exist unless work, to a certain amount, were done either by or for him. Of this each person is bound, in justice, to perform his share; and society has an incontestable right to declare to every one, that if he work not, at this work of necessity, neither shall he eat. Society has not enforced this right, having in so far postponed the rule of justice to other considerations. But there is an ever-growing demand that it be enforced, so soon as any endurable plan can be devised for the purpose. If this experiment is to be tried in the West Indies, let it be tried impartially; and let the whole produce belong to those who do the work which produces it. We would not have black labourers compelled to grow spices which they do not want, and white proprietors who do not work at all exchanging the spices for houses in Belgrave Square. We would not withhold from the whites, any more than from the blacks, the "divine right" of being compelled to labour. [P. 674.] Let them have exactly the same share in the produce that they have in the work. If they do not like this, let them remain as they are, so long as they are permitted, and make the best of supply and demand.

Your contributor's notions of justice and proprietary right are of another kind than these. Acording to him, the whole West Indies belong to the whites: the negroes have no claim there, to either land or food, but by their sufferance. "It was not Black Quashee, or those he represents, that made those West India islands what they are." [*Ibid.*] I submit, that those who furnished the thews and sinews[*] really had something to do with the matter. "Under the soil of Jamaica the bones of many thousand British men"—"brave Colonel Fortescue, brave Colonel Sedgwick, brave Colonel Brayne," and divers others, "had to be laid." [P. 676.] How many hundred thousand African men laid their bones there, after having had their lives pressed out by slow or fierce torture? They could have better done without Colonel Fortescue, than Colonel Fortescue could have done without them. But he was the stronger, and could "compel;" what they did [p. 674] and suffered therefore goes for nothing. Not only they did not, but it seems they *could* not have cultivated those islands. "Never by art of his" (the negro) "could one pumpkin have grown there to solace any human throat." [P. 675.] They grow pumpkins, however, and more than pumpkins, in a very similar country, their native Africa. We are told to look at Haiti: what does your contributor know of Haiti? "Little or no sugar growing, black Peter exterminating black Paul, and where a garden of the Hesperides might be, nothing but a tropical dog-kennel and pestiferous jungle." [*Ibid.*] Are we to listen to arguments grounded on hearsays like these? In what is black Haiti worse than white Mexico? If the truth were known, how much worse is it than white Spain?

But the great ethical doctrine of the Discourse, than which a doctrine more damnable, I should think, never was propounded by a professed moral reformer, is, that one kind of human beings are born servants to another kind. "You will have to be servants," he tells the negroes, "to those that are born *wiser* than you, that are born lords of you—servants to the whites, if they are (as what mortal can doubt that they are?) born wiser than you." [Pp. 676-7.] I do not hold him to the absurd letter of his dictum; it belongs to the mannerism in which he is enthralled like a child in swaddling clothes. By "born wiser," I *b*will*b* suppose him to mean, born more capable of wisdom: a proposition which, he says, no mortal can doubt, but which I will make bold to say, that a full moiety of all thinking persons, who have attended

[*For the phrase, see Walter Scott, *Rob Roy*, 3 vols. (Edinburgh: Constable, 1818), Vol. I, p. 60 (Chap. iii).]

*b-b*50^2 shall

to the subject, either doubt or positively deny. Among the things for which your contributor professes entire disrespect, is the analytical examination of human nature. It is by analytical examination that we have learned whatever we know of the laws of external nature; and if he had not disdained to apply the same mode of investigation to the laws of the formation of character, he would have escaped the vulgar error of imputing every difference which he finds among human beings to an original difference of nature. As well might it be said, that of two trees, sprung from the same stock, one cannot be taller than another but from greater vigour in the original seedling. Is nothing to be attributed to soil, nothing to climate, nothing to difference of exposure—has no storm swept over the one and not the other, no lightning scathed it, no beast browsed on it, no insects preyed on it, no passing stranger stript off its leaves or its bark? If the trees grew near together, may not the one which, by whatever accident, grew up first, have retarded the other's developement by its shade? Human beings are subject to an infinitely greater variety of accidents and external influences than trees, and have infinitely more operation in impairing the growth of one another; since those who begin by being strongest, have almost always hitherto used their strength to keep the others weak. What the original differences are among human beings, I know no more than your contributor, and no less; it is one of the questions not yet satisfactorily answered in the natural history of the species. This, however, is well known—that spontaneous improvement, beyond a very low grade,—improvement by internal developement, without aid from other individuals or peoples—is one of the rarest phenomena in history; and whenever known to have occurred, was the result of an extraordinary combination of advantages; in addition doubtless to many accidents of which all trace is now lost. No argument against the capacity of negroes for improvement, could be drawn from their not being one of these rare exceptions. It is curious withal, that the earliest known civilization was, we have the strongest reason to believe, a negro civilization. The original Egyptians are inferred, from the evidence of their sculptures, to have been a negro race: it was from negroes, therefore, that the Greeks learnt their first lessons in civilization; and to the records and traditions of these negroes did the Greek philosophers to the very end of their career resort (I do not say with much fruit) as a treasury of mysterious wisdom. But I again renounce all advantage from facts: were the whites born ever so superior in intelligence to the blacks, and competent by nature to instruct and advise them, it would not be the less monstrous to assert that they had therefore a right either to subdue them by force, or circumvent them by superior skill; to throw upon them the toils and hardships of life, reserving for themselves, under the misapplied name of work, its agreeable excitements.

Were I to point out, even in the briefest terms, every vulnerable point in your contributor's Discourse, I should produce a longer dissertation than his. One instance more must suffice. If labour is wanted, it is a very obvious idea to import labourers; and if negroes are best suited to the climate, to import negroes. This is a mode of adjusting the balance between work and labourers, quite in accordance with received principles: it is neither before nor behind the existing moralities of the world: and since it would accomplish the object of making the negroes work more, your contributor at least, it might have been supposed, would have approved of it. On the contrary, this prospect is to him the most dismal of all; for either "the new Africans, after labouring a little," will "take to pumpkins like the others," or if so many of them come that they will be obliged to work for their living, there will be "a black Ireland." [P. 672.] The labour market admits of three possibile conditions, and not, as this would imply, of only two. Either, first, the labourers can live almost without working, which is said to be the case in Demerara; or, secondly, which is the common case, they can live by working, but must work in order to live; or, thirdly, they cannot by working get a sufficient living, which is the case in Ireland. Your contributor sees only the extreme cases, but no possibility of the medium. If Africans are imported, he thinks there must either be so few of them, that they will not need to work, or so many, that although they work, they will not be able to live.

Let me say a few words on the general quarrel of your contributor with the present age. Every age has its faults, and is indebted to those who point them out. Our own age needs this service as much as others; but it is not to be concluded that it has degenerated from former ages, because its faults are different. We must beware, too, of mistaking its virtues for faults, merely because, as is inevitable, its faults mingle with its virtues and colour them. Your contributor thinks that the age has too much humanity, is too anxious to abolish pain. I affirm, on the contrary, that it has too little humanity—is most culpably indifferent to the subject: and I point to any day's police reports as the proof. I am not now accusing the brutal portion of the population, but the humane portion; if they were humane *enough*, they would have contrived long ago to prevent ᶜthese ᶜ daily atrocities. It is not by excess of a good quality that the age is in fault, but by deficiency—deficiency even of philanthropy, and still more of other qualities wherewith to balance and direct what philanthropy it has. An "Universal Abolition of Pain Association" [p. 670] may serve to point a sarcasm, but can any worthier object of endeavour be pointed out than that of diminishing pain? Is the labour which ends in growing spices noble, and not that which lessens the mass of suffering? We are told [p. 675], with a triumphant air, as if it were a thing to be glad of, that "the Destinies" proceed in a "terrible manner;" and this manner will not cease "for soft sawder or philanthropic stump-oratory;" but whatever the means may be, it *has* ceased in no inconsiderable degree, and is ceasing more and more: every year the "terrible manner," in some department or other, is made a little less terrible. Is our cholera comparable to the old pestilence—our hospitals to the old lazar-houses—our workhouses to the hanging of vagrants—our prisons to those visited by Howard? It is precisely

ᶜ⁻ᶜ50² those

because we have succeeded in abolishing so much pain, because pain and its infliction are no longer familiar as our daily bread, that we are so much more shocked by what remains of it than our ancestors were, or than in your contributor's opinion we ought to be.

But (however it be with pain in general) the abolition of the infliction of pain by the mere will of a human being, the abolition, in short, of despotism, seems to be, in a peculiar degree, the occupation of this age; and it would be difficult to shew that any age had undertaken a worthier. Though we cannot extirpate all pain, we can, if we are sufficiently determined upon it, abolish all tyranny: one of the greatest victories yet gained over that enemy is slave-emancipation, and all Europe is struggling, with various success, towards further conquests over it. If, in the pursuit of this, we lose sight of any object equally important; if we forget that freedom is not the only thing necessary for human beings, let us be thankful to any one who points out what is wanting; but let us not consent to turn back.

That this country should turn back, in the matter of negro slavery, I have not the smallest apprehension. There is, however, another place where that tyranny still flourishes, but now for the first time finds itself seriously in danger. At this crisis of American slavery, when the decisive conflict between right and iniquity seems about to commence, your contributor steps in, and flings this missile, loaded with the weight of his reputation, into the abolitionist camp. The words of English writers of celebrity are words of power on the other side of the ocean; and the owners of human flesh, who probably thought they had not an honest man on their side between the Atlantic and the Vistula, will welcome such an auxiliary. Circulated as his dissertation will probably be, by those whose interests profit by it, from one end of the American Union to the other, I hardly know of an act by which one person could have done so much mischief as this may possibly do; and I hold that by thus acting, he has made himself an instrument of what an able writer in the *Inquirer* justly calls "a true work of the devil."[*]

[*Anon., "Mr. Carlyle on the Negroes," *The Inquirer*, VIII (8 Dec., 1849), 770.]

STATEMENT ON MARRIAGE

1851

EDITOR'S NOTE

MS facsimile reproduced in Hugh S.R. Elliot, *The Letters of John Stuart Mill*, 2 vols. (London: Longmans, Green, 1910), I, facing 159 and 160. Unheaded. Signed "J.S. Mill" and dated 6 March, 1851. Not published (and therefore not in Mill's bibliography). In Elliot's transcription, "pretension" (l.17) is mistakenly given as "pretence". For comment, see lxii above.

Statement on Marriage

BEING ABOUT, if I am so happy as to obtain her consent, to enter into the marriage relation with the only woman I have ever known, with whom I would have entered into that state; and the whole character of the marriage relation as constituted by law being such as both she and I entirely and conscientiously disapprove, for this among other reasons, that it confers upon one of the parties to the contract, legal power and control over the person, property, and freedom of action of the other party, independent of her own wishes and will; I, having no means of legally divesting myself of these odious powers (as I most assuredly would do if an engagement to that effect could be made legally binding on me), feel it my duty to put on record a formal protest against the existing law of marriage, in so far as conferring such powers; and a solemn promise never in any case or under any circumstances to use them. And in the event of marriage between Mrs. Taylor and me I declare it to be my will and intention, and the condition of the engagement between us, that she retains in all respects whatever the same absolute freedom of action, and freedom of disposal of herself and of all that does or may at any time belong to her, as if no such marriage had taken place; and I absolutely disclaim and repudiate all pretension to have acquired any *rights* whatever by virtue of such marriage.

REMARKS ON MR. FITZROY'S BILL
FOR THE MORE EFFECTUAL PREVENTION
OF ASSAULTS ON WOMEN AND CHILDREN

1853

EDITOR'S NOTE

London: printed "for private distribution," 1853. Anonymous; not republished. Identified in Mill's bibliography as "A pamphlet (a few copies only printed for distribution)—entitled 'Remarks on Mr. Fitzroy's Bill for the more effectual prevention of assaults on women and children.' (In this I acted chiefly as amanuensis to my wife.)" (MacMinn, 79.) Occasioned by Henry Fitzroy's "A Bill for the Better Prevention and Punishment of Assaults on Women and Children," 16 Victoria (10 Mar., 1853), *PP*, 1852-53, I, 9-12, enacted as 16 & 17 Victoria, c.30 (1853). The Somerville College copies have no corrections or emendations. For comment, see lxii above.

Remarks on Mr. Fitzroy's Bill
for the More Effectual Prevention
of Assaults on Women and Children

THE BILL BROUGHT INTO PARLIAMENT BY MR. FITZROY, as the organ of the Home Office, enlarging the powers of magistrates to inflict summary penalties for brutal assaults on women and children, is excellent in design; and if in execution it falls short of what is required to deal adequately with the enormity of the evil, the speech of the Mover indicated that he felt its imperfection, and had done as much as he thought it prudent to attempt without assurance of support.[*] There have since been signs, both in and out of Parliament, that the Minister formed a lower estimate than necessary of what the public would receive at his hands, and that a measure far more likely to be efficacious would have been well received. The following remarks, on what the writer deems the shortcomings of the present Bill, are offered for the consideration of those who interest themselves in its success.

The speech of the Mover showed him to be strongly impressed with the horrible amount of domestic brutality which the law at present existing leaves unrepressed; and he made a selection of recent cases, exhibiting the disgraceful contrast which every reader of police reports is accustomed to see, between the flagrancy of the offence and the insignificance of the penalty.[†] If any deficiency could be remarked in the statement, it is, that all the instances cited were cases of outrage against women, to the exclusion of the brutalities inflicted both by men and women on the still more helpless children. Without reckoning the frightful cases of flogging and starving which so often come to light, there have been two cases within the last few weeks in each of which a woman, entrusted with the care of an infant three or four years old, caused its death by burning with fire.[‡] In one of these cases the woman had forced the infant to grasp a red hot coal in its hand, and

[*Henry Fitzroy, Speech (10 Mar., 1853; Commons), *PD*, 3rd ser., Vol. 124, col. 1417.]
[†*Ibid.*, cols. 1414-16.]
[‡See *The Times*, 3 Jan., 1853, p. 7 (a report of Mary Ann Oldham's cruelty to John Gaywood; his death is reported *ibid.*, 1 Feb., 1853, p. 8), and 19 Jan., 1853, p. 4 (Elizabeth Baker's cruelty to Albert Monks). The Oldham case is the one referred to in the next sentence.]

hold it there for some minutes; and being put on trial before the child had died, but when it was already certain that he would be a cripple for life, was sentenced, not by a police magistrate, but by the Central Criminal Court at the Old Bailey, to—a fortnight's imprisonment! Such cases prove that there is more amiss than an extension of the powers of the subordinate Courts will remedy; that there is not merely a want of power in the administrators of criminal justice to treat such culprits with a severity sufficient for example, but, in some cases at least, a want of will. Merely to authorize a greater amount of punishment for these offences, at the discretion of a judicial officer, is no guarantee against their continuing to be perpetrated with almost as near an approach to impunity as at present. To increase the penalty is an indication of intention on the part of the Legislature. To see that the intention be fulfilled ought to be the care of those with whom rests the choice of judges and of magistrates.

By the existing law, the utmost punishment which can be inflicted by summary sentence is five pounds fine, or two months' imprisonment.[*] The Bill raises this limit to a fine of twenty pounds, or imprisonment for six months, *with or without hard labour*.[†] With regard to the fine, when the prisoner cannot pay it, the power of fining is nugatory. When he can, it is revolting to the commonest sense of justice that any one should be able to buy the privilege of inflicting atrocious cruelty by paying twenty pounds. From the newspaper reports it appears to be the practice of police magistrates, not to pass sentence of imprisonment unless they have first ascertained that the prisoner cannot pay the fine. It is only because these criminals are usually of the most reckless and therefore the most needy portion of the labouring classes, that this power of compounding by payment of blood-money does not operate as an actual licence to the offences intended to be repressed.

Remains the penalty of imprisonment, "with or without" the addition of labour. The remark is applicable to the question of secondary punishment in general, and peculiarly to these offences, that the alternative of imprisonment with or without labour is equivalent to that of conviction with or without punishment. Can it be supposed that any amount of imprisonment without labour (unless in the few jails in which the salutary rule of separation of prisoners has been made universal) has a deterring effect upon criminals of the class who come under the proposed enactment? What is a prison to them? A place where, probably, they are better fed, better clothed, better lodged, than in their own dwellings, with an abundance of society of their own description, while they are exempted from the hard work by which they earned their living until the justice of their country undertook to punish them. In return for this release from all the most disagreeable circumstances of their ordinary condition, they suffer the inconvenience of not being able to get gin

[*9 George IV, c. 31 (1828), Sect. 27.]
[†"A Bill for the Better Prevention and Punishment of Assaults on Women and Children," p. 10.]

and tobacco; that is, they are treated exactly as if they were in the union workhouse, except the hard labour. Even alms are not given to the able-bodied at the expense of the parish, though but for a day, without a day's work in exchange for it;[*] and surely, now that attention has been awakened to these subjects, it must soon be recognized that when imprisonment is imposed as a punishment, even if only for a day, either solitude or hard labour (for those who are capable of it) ought invariably to be a part of the sentence. In the case of the poor, the addition of labour is not even a punishment. Their life when at large must be one of labour, and generally of a restraint even upon their power of locomotion, almost equal to that of imprisonment. With the addition of labour, imprisonment to the ordinary labourer scarcely amounts to a punishment; without labour it is a holiday.

But neither with labour nor without it, is imprisonment in any form a suitable or a sufficient penalty for crimes of brutality. For these nothing will be effectual but to retaliate upon the culprit some portion of the physical suffering which he has inflicted. The beneficial efficacy of the enactment now in contemplation will, it is safe to prophesy, depend on the adoption or not of Mr. Phinn's amendment, making corporal punishment a part of the penalty.[†] The Mover himself did not disguise his conviction that nothing less than this would be adequate to the exigency;[‡] and it is earnestly to be hoped that the many adhesions which the suggestion has since received, including that of one of the most intelligent of the London police magistrates,* will induce Mr. Fitzroy to incorporate it in the Bill.

Overwhelming as are the objections to corporal punishment except in cases of personal outrage, it is peculiarly fitted for such cases. The repulsiveness to standers by, and the degradation to the culprit, which make corporal maltreatment so justly odious as a punishment, would cease to adhere to it, if it were exclusively reserved as a retribution to those guilty of personal violence. It is probably the only punishment which they would feel. Those who presume on their consciousness of animal strength to brutally illtreat those who are physically weaker, should be made to know what it is to be in the hands of a physical strength as much greater than their own, as theirs than that of the subjects of their tyranny. It is the moral medicine needed for the domineering arrogance of brute power. After one or two

[*See "Report from His Majesty's Commissioners for Inquiring into the Administration and Practical Operation of the Poor Laws," *PP*, 1834, XXVII, 146-7, which refers to the desired continuation of the "intent" and "spirit" of 43 Elizabeth, c. 2 (1601) in the new poor law (enacted as 4 & 5 William IV, c. 76 [1834]).]

[†Thomas Phinn, Speech in Amendment to Mr. Fitzroy's Bill (10 Mar., 1853; Commons), *PD*, 3rd ser., Vol. 124, col. 1419.]

[‡Fitzroy, speech of 10 Mar., 1853, col. 1414.]

*Mr. [John] Hammill. "Though he was much gratified at finding that a bill was now under the consideration of the Legislature for more adequately punishing such atrocious offences, he felt satisfied, from the result of his experience, that nothing short of the infliction of corporal punishment would afford an efficient protection to the helpless objects of such brutality." (*The Times*, March 25, [1853, p. 7].)

cases of flogging for this description of crime, we should hear no more of outrages upon women or children for a long time to come. Probably such outrages would cease altogether, as soon as it became well known that the punishment of flogging would be inflicted for them.

With this penalty in the Act, and a clear understanding on the part of magistrates that it was not intended as a *brutum fulmen*, nor to be reserved for those horrible cases for which, as a matter of moral retribution, hanging would scarcely be punishment enough; if the administration of the law were such that the ruffianly part of the population would know that they could not give loose to their brutal rage without imminent risk of incurring in fact, and not nominally, the only punishment which they would dread; the enactment would do more for the improvement of morality, and the relief of suffering, than any Act of Parliament passed in this century, not excepting, perhaps, the Act for the abolition of slavery.[*] But this salutary impression can only be made by rendering punishment prompt and certain in infliction, as well as efficacious in kind; by avoiding, therefore, to let in, by the terms of the Act itself, certainty of delay, and probable chances of escape. This would, however, be an inevitable effect of adopting another amendment, of which notice has been given, allowing an appeal to the quarter sessions.[†] An appeal is often a necessary evil, but in such a case as this, a palpably unnecessary one. These are not cases in which a magistrate, or two magistrates, are likely to err on the side of inflicting too severe a sentence; there is abundant experience that the danger of error is all on the contrary side.

A government which should pass an act embodying these provisions, would confer a more immediate and a more certain benefit on the community, than it is often in the power of legislators to ensure by any enactment. The beneficial fruits of such a law are not to be measured by the crime and suffering which it would directly prevent, though these would be sufficient to stamp it as one of the most beneficent acts yet done by Government for the improvement of our institutions. A measure such as this, is of wider scope, and still more extensive beneficence. It is a measure of moral education. All parties now acknowledge that it is the urgent duty of Government to provide that the people be educated, could they but discover how it is to be done; and the present Ministry made it one of their pledges, on coming into office, that they would do something effectual for education.[‡] But even if the measure they contemplate were far more considerable than they probably have it in their power to make it, what chance is there for education, if the schools teach one lesson, and the laws another contradictory to it? The administration of criminal

[*3 & 4 William IV, c. 73 (1833).]
[†See Phinn, speech of 10 Mar., 1853, col. 1420.]
[‡See John Russell, Speech on Public Business (10 Feb., 1853; Commons), *PD*, 3rd ser., Vol. 124, cols. 18-19.]

justice is one of the chief instruments of moral education of the people. Its lessons of morality are of the utmost importance for good or for ill; for they take effect upon that part of the population which is unreached by any other moralizing influences, or on which others have been tried, and have failed of their effect. The lessons which the law teaches, it cannot fail of teaching impressively. The man who is brought, or who knows himself liable to be brought, to answer for his conduct at the bar of justice, cannot slight or despise the notions of right and wrong, the opinions and feelings respecting conduct and character, which he there finds prevailing. It is the one channel through which the sentiments of the well-conducted part of the community are made operative perforce on the vilest and worst. Yet, in this day of ragged schools, and model prisons, and plans for the reformation of criminals, the most important instrument which society has for teaching the elements of morality to those who are most in need of such teaching, is scarcely used at all. So potent an engine must necessarily act in one way or another, and when it does not act for good, it acts for evil. Is there any system of moral instruction capable of being devised for the populace, which could stand against the lessons of a diametrically opposite tendency, daily given by the criminal courts? The law and the tribunals are terribly in earnest when they set about the protection of property. But violence to the person is treated as hardly deserving serious notice, unless it endangers life; and even then, unless pre-meditated intention is proved by such superfluity of evidence that neither in-genuity nor stupidity can escape from admitting it, the criminal generally gets off almost scot free.* It is of little avail to talk of inculcating justice, or kindness, or self-control, while the judicial and police courts teach by actions, so much more efficacious than words, that the most atrocious excesses of ungovernable violence are, in the eyes of the authorities, something quite venial. The law has the forming of the character of the lowest classes in its own hands. A tithe of the exertion and money now spent in attempting to reform criminals, if spent in reforming the minor criminal laws and their administration, would produce a real diminution of crime, instead of an imaginary reformation of criminals. But then, it must be allowed, it would not serve to fill so much of philanthropic gentlemen's time.

Not only is education by the course of justice the most efficacious, in its own

*Contrast the sentence of *eighteen months' imprisonment*, passed a few days ago, at the Norfolk Assizes, on a man [Samuel Horth] who had attempted to murder a woman [Ann Proudfoot] with a pitch plaster, under about as revolting a combination of circumstances as imagination can conceive, with fourteen years' transportation, awarded on the same day, by the same judge [Jonathan Frederick Pollock], for stealing to the value of a few pence. [See *The Times*, article on the Norfolk Circuit, 21 Mar., 1853, p. 7. The *Morning Chronicle*, 21 Mar., 1853, p. 8, agrees with *The Times* in saying that on the same day, 18 Mar., Pollock sentenced William Jarvis to ten years' transportation for defrauding an insurance company by burning his own house; neither gives the information Mill cites.]

province, of all kinds of popular education, but it is also one on which there needs be no difference of opinion. Churches and political parties may quarrel about the teaching of doctrines, but not about the punishment of crimes. There is diversity of opinion about what is morally good, but there ought to be none about what is atrociously wicked. Whatever else may be included in the education of the people, the very first essential of it is to unbrutalise them; and to this end, all kinds of personal brutality should be seen and felt to be things which the law is determined to put down. The Bill of Mr. Fitzroy is a step in the right direction; but, unless its provisions are strengthened, it will be rather an indication of the wish, than a substantial exercise of the power, to repress one of the most odious forms of human wickedness.

A FEW WORDS ON NON-INTERVENTION

1859

EDITOR'S NOTE

Dissertations and Discussions, III (1867), 153-78, where the title is footnoted, *"Fraser's Magazine*, December 1859." Reprinted from *Fraser's Magazine*, LX (Dec., 1859), 766-76, signed "John Stuart Mill": left running titles as title; right running titles: "Ideas of English Foreign Policy on the Continent" (767; equivalent of 111.20-113.1); "Misrepresentation of the National Feeling" (769; equivalent of 114.14-115.28); "The Isthmus of Suez Question" (771; equivalent of 117.3-118.17); "British Relations with Native Indian States" (773; equivalent of 119.30-121.8); and "How One Free Government May Assist Another" (775; equivalent of 122.21-123.36). Identified in Mill's bibliography as "An article headed 'A few words on Non-Intervention' in Fraser's Magazine for December 1859" (MacMinn, 93). In Somerville College there are no corrections or emendations in the copy of the original (tear-sheets) or in an offprint, which is headed, "[Reprinted from 'Fraser's Magazine' for December, 1859.]" but is otherwise identical. For comment on the article, see xxviii-xxix and lxii-lxiii above.

The text below is that of *D&D*, III (1867), the only edition of that volume in Mill's lifetime. In the four footnoted variants, "59[1]" indicates *Fraser's Magazine*; "59[2]", the offprint.

A Few Words on Non-Intervention

THERE IS A COUNTRY IN EUROPE, equal to the greatest in extent of dominion, far exceeding any other in wealth, and in the power that wealth bestows, the declared principle of whose foreign policy is, to let other nations alone. No country apprehends or affects to apprehend from it any aggressive designs. Power, from of old, is wont to encroach upon the weak, and to quarrel for ascendancy with those who are as strong as itself. Not so this nation. It will hold its own, it will not submit to encroachment, but if other nations do not meddle with it, it will not meddle with them. Any attempt it makes to exert influence over them, even by persuasion, is rather in the service of others, than of itself: to mediate in the quarrels which break out between foreign States, to arrest obstinate civil wars, to reconcile belligerents, to intercede for mild treatment of the vanquished, or finally, to procure the abandonment of some national crime and scandal to humanity, such as the slave-trade. Not only does this nation desire no benefit to itself at the expense of others, it desires none in which all others do not as freely participate. It makes no treaties stipulating for separate commercial advantages. If the aggressions of barbarians force it to a successful war, and its victorious arms put it in a position to command liberty of trade, whatever it demands for itself it demands for all mankind. The cost of the war is its own; the fruits it shares in fraternal equality with the whole human race. Its own ports and commerce are free as the air and the sky: all its neighbours have full liberty to resort to it, paying either no duties, or, if any, generally a mere equivalent for what is paid by its own citizens; nor does it concern itself though they, on their part, keep all to themselves, and persist in the most jealous and narrow-minded exclusion of its merchants and goods.

A nation adopting this policy is a novelty in the world; so much so, it would appear, that many are unable to believe it when they see it. By one of the practical paradoxes which often meet us in human affairs, it is this nation which finds itself, in respect of its foreign policy, held up to obloquy as the type of egoism and selfishness; as a nation which thinks of nothing but of out-witting and out-generalling its neighbours. An enemy, or a self-fancied rival who had been distanced in the race, might be conceived to give vent to such an accusation in a moment of ill-temper. But that it should be accepted by lookers-on, and should pass into a popular doctrine, is enough to surprise even those who have best sounded the depths of human prejudice. Such, however, is the estimate of the foreign policy of England most widely current on the Continent. Let us not flatter ourselves that it is merely the dishonest pretence of enemies, or of those who have their own purposes to serve by exciting odium against us, a class including all the Protectionist writers, and the mouthpieces of all the despots and of the Papacy. The more blameless and laudable our policy might be, the more certainly we might count on its being misrepresented and railed at by these worthies. Unfortunately the belief is not confined to those whom they can influence, but is held with all the tenacity of a prejudice, by innumerable persons free from interested bias. So strong a hold has it on their minds, that when an Englishman attempts to remove it, all their habitual politeness does not enable them to disguise their utter unbelief in his disclaimer. They are firmly persuaded that no word is said, nor act done, by English statesmen in reference to foreign affairs, which has not for its motive principle some peculiarly English interest. Any profession of the contrary appears to them too ludicrously transparent an attempt to impose upon them. Those most friendly to us think they make a great concession in admitting that the fault may possibly be less with the English people, than with the English Government and aristocracy. We do not even receive credit from them for following our own interest with a straightforward recognition of honesty as the best policy. They believe that we have always other objects than those we avow; and the most far-fetched and unplausible suggestion of a selfish purpose appears to them better entitled to credence than anything so utterly incredible as our disinterestedness. Thus, to give one instance among many, when we taxed ourselves twenty millions (a prodigious sum in their estimation) to get rid of negro slavery,[*] and, for the same object, perilled, as everybody thought, destroyed as many thought, the very existence of our West Indian colonies, it was, and still is, believed, that our fine professions were but to delude the world, and that by this self-sacrificing behaviour we were endeavouring to gain some hidden object, which could neither be conceived nor described, in the way of pulling down other nations. The fox who had lost his tail had an intelligible interest in persuading his neighbours to rid themselves of theirs:[†] but we, it is thought by *our* neighbours, cut off our own magnificent brush, the largest and finest of all, in hopes of reaping some inexplicable advantage from inducing others to do the same.

It is foolish attempting to despise all this—persuading ourselves that it is not our fault, and that those who disbelieve *us* would not believe though one should rise from the dead. Nations, like individuals, ought to suspect some fault in themselves when they find they are generally worse thought of than they think they deserve; and they may well know that they are somehow in fault when almost everybody but themselves thinks them crafty and hypocritical. It is not solely because England

[*By 3 & 4 William IV, c. 73 (1833).]

[†Aesop, "The Fox Without a Tail," *Aesop's Fables*, trans. Vernon Stanley Vernon Jones (London: Heinemann; New York: Doubleday, Page, 1912), p. 68.]

has been more successful than other nations in gaining what they are all aiming at, that they think she must be following after it with a more ceaseless and a more undivided chase. This indeed is a powerful predisposing cause, inclining and preparing them for the belief. It is a natural supposition that those who win the prize have striven for it; that superior success must be the fruit of more unremitting endeavour; and where there is an obvious abstinence from the ordinary arts employed for distancing competitors, and they are distanced nevertheless, people are fond of believing that the means employed must have been arts still more subtle and profound. This preconception makes them look out in all quarters for indications to prop up the selfish explanation of our conduct. If our ordinary course of action does not favour this interpretation, they watch for exceptions to our ordinary course, and regard these as the real index to the purposes within. They moreover accept literally all the habitual expressions by which we represent ourselves as worse than we are; expressions often heard from English statesmen, next to never from those of any other country—partly because Englishmen, beyond all the rest of the human race, are so shy of professing virtues that they will even profess vices instead; and partly because almost all English statesmen, while careless to a degree which no foreigner can credit, respecting the impression they produce on foreigners, commit the obtuse blunder of supposing that low objects are the only ones to which the minds of their non-aristocratic fellow-countrymen are amenable, and that it is always expedient, if not necessary, to place those objects in the foremost rank.

All, therefore, who either speak or act in the name of England, are bound by the strongest obligations, both of prudence and of duty, to avoid giving either of these handles for misconstruction: to put a severe restraint upon the mania of professing to act from meaner motives than those by which we are really actuated, and to beware of perversely or capriciously singling out some particular instance in which to act on a worse principle than that by which we are ordinarily guided. Both these salutary cautions our practical statesmen are, at the present time, flagrantly disregarding.

We are now in one of those critical moments, which do not occur once in a generation, when the whole turn of European events, and the course of European history for a long time to come, may depend on the conduct and on the estimation of England. At such a moment, it is difficult to say whether by their sins of speech or of action our statesmen are most effectually playing into the hands of our enemies, and giving most colour of justice to injurious misconception of our character and policy as a people.

To take the sins of speech first: What is the sort of language held in every oration which, during the present European crisis, any English minister, or almost any considerable public man, addresses to parliament or to his constituents? The eternal repetition of this shabby *refrain*—"We did not interfere, because no English interest was involved;" "We ought not to interfere where no English interest is concerned." England is thus exhibited as a country whose most distinguished men are not ashamed to profess, as politicians, a rule of action which no one, not utterly base, could endure to be accused of as the maxim by which he guides his private life; not to move a finger for others unless he sees his private advantage in it. There is much to be said for the doctrine that a nation should be willing to assist its neighbours in throwing off oppression and gaining free institutions. Much also may be said by those who maintain that one nation is incompetent to judge and act for another, and that each should be left to help itself, and seek advantage or submit to disadvantage as it can and will. But of all attitudes which a nation can take up on the subject of intervention, the meanest and worst is to profess that it interferes only when it can serve its own objects by it. Every other nation is entitled to say, "It seems, then, that non-interference is not a matter of principle with you. When you abstain from interference, it is not because you think it wrong. You have no objection to interfere, only it must not be for the sake of those you interfere with; they must not suppose that you have any regard for their good. The good of others is not one of the things you care for; but you are willing to meddle, if by meddling you can gain anything for yourselves." Such is the obvious interpretation of the language used.

There is scarcely any necessity to say, writing to Englishmen, that this is not what our rulers and politicians really mean. Their language is not a correct exponent of their thoughts. They mean a part only of what they seem to say. They do mean to disclaim interference for the sake of doing good to foreign nations. They are quite sincere and in earnest in repudiating this. But the other half of what their words express, a willingness to meddle if by doing so they can promote any interest of England, they do not mean. The thought they have in their minds, is not the interest of England, but her security. What they would say, is, that they are ready to act when England's safety is threatened, or any of her interests hostilely or unfairly endangered. This is no more than what all nations, sufficiently powerful for their own protection, do, and no one questions their right to do. It is the common right of self-defence. But if we mean this, why, in Heaven's name, do we take every possible opportunity of saying, instead of this, something exceedingly different? Not self-defence, but aggrandizement, is the sense which foreign listeners put upon our words. Not simply to protect what we have, and that merely against unfair arts, not against fair ^{a}rivalry^a; but to add to it more and more without limit, is the purpose for which foreigners think we claim the liberty of intermeddling with them and their affairs. If our actions make it impossible for the most prejudiced observer to believe that we aim at or would accept any sort of mercantile monopolies, this has no effect on their minds but to make them think that we have chosen a more cunning way to the same end. It is a generally

$^{a\text{-}a}59^{1,2}$ rivality

accredited opinion among Continental politicians, especially those who think themselves particularly knowing, that the very existence of England depends upon the incessant acquisition of new markets for our manufactures; that the chase after these is an affair of life and death to us; and that we are at all times ready to trample on every obligation of public or international morality, when the alternative would be, pausing for a moment in that race. It would be superfluous to point out what profound ignorance and misconception of all the laws of national wealth, and all the facts of England's commercial condition, this opinion presupposes: but such ignorance and misconception are unhappily very general on the Continent; they are but slowly, if perceptibly, giving way before the advance of reason; and for generations, perhaps, to come, we shall be judged under their influence. Is it requiring too much from our practical politicians to wish that they would sometimes bear these things in mind? Does it answer any good purpose to express ourselves as if we did not scruple to profess that which we not merely scruple to do, but the bare idea of doing which never crosses our minds? Why should we abnegate the character we might with truth lay claim to, of being incomparably the most conscientious of all nations in our national acts? Of all countries which are sufficiently powerful to be capable of being dangerous to their neighbours, we are perhaps the only one whom mere scruples of conscience would suffice to deter from it. We are the only people among whom, by no class whatever of society, is the interest or glory of the nation considered to be any sufficient excuse for an unjust act; the only one which regards with jealousy and suspicion, and a proneness to hostile criticism, precisely those acts of its Government which in other countries are sure to be hailed with applause, those by which territory has been acquired, or political influence extended. Being in reality better than other nations, in at least the negative part of international morality, let us cease, by the language we use, to give ourselves out as worse.

But if we ought to be careful of our language, a thousand times more obligatory is it upon us to be careful of our deeds, and not suffer ourselves to be betrayed by any of our leading men into a line of conduct on some isolated point, utterly opposed to our habitual principles of action—conduct such that if it were a fair specimen of us, it would verify the calumnies of our worst enemies, and justify them in representing not only that we have no regard for the good of other nations, but that we actually think their good and our own incompatible, and will go all lengths to prevent others from realizing even an advantage in which we ourselves are to share. This pernicious, and, one can scarcely help calling it, almost insane blunder, we seem to be committing on the subject of the Suez Canal.

It is the universal belief in France that English influence at Constantinople, strenuously exerted to defeat this project, is the real and only invincible obstacle to its being carried into effect. And unhappily the public declarations of our present Prime Minister not only bear out this persuasion, but warrant the assertion that we oppose the work because, in the opinion of our Government, it would be injurious to the interest of England.[*] If such be the course we are pursuing, and such the motive of it, and if nations have duties, even negative ones, towards the weal of the human race, it is hard to say whether the folly or the immorality of our conduct is the most painfully conspicuous.

Here is a project, the practicability of which is indeed a matter in dispute, but of which no one has attempted to deny that, supposing it realized, it would give a facility to commerce, and consequently a stimulus to production, an encouragement to intercourse, and therefore to civilization, which would entitle it to a high rank among the great industrial improvements of modern times. The contriving of new means of abridging labour and economizing outlay in the operations of industry, is the object to which the larger half of all the inventive ingenuity of mankind is at present given up; and this scheme, if realized, will save, on one of the great highways of the world's traffic, the circumnavigation of a continent. An easy access of commerce is the main source of that material civilization, which, in the more backward regions of the earth, is the necessary condition and indispensable machinery of the moral; and this scheme reduces practically by one half, the distance, commercially speaking, between the self-improving nations of the world and the most important and valuable of the unimproving. The Atlantic Telegraph is esteemed an enterprise of world-wide importance because it abridges the transit of mercantile intelligence merely. What the Suez Canal would shorten is the transport of the goods themselves, and this to such an extent as probably to augment it manifold.

Let us suppose, then—for in the present day the hypothesis is too un-English to be spoken of as anything more than a supposition—let us suppose that the English nation saw in this great benefit to the civilized and uncivilized world a danger or damage to some peculiar interest of England. Suppose, for example, that it feared, by shortening the road, to facilitate the access of foreign navies to its Oriental possessions. The supposition imputes no ordinary degree of cowardice and imbecility to the national mind; otherwise it could not but reflect that the same thing which would facilitate the arrival of an enemy, would facilitate also that of succour; that we have had French fleets in the Eastern seas before now, and have fought naval battles with them there, nearly a century ago; that if we ever became unable to defend India against them, we [b]should[b] assuredly have them there without the aid of any canal; and that our power of resisting an enemy does not depend upon putting a little more or less of obstacle in the way of his coming, but upon the amount of force which we are able to oppose to him when come. Let us assume, however, that the success of the project would do more harm to England

[*See, e.g., Henry John Temple, Speech on the Isthmus of Suez Canal—Resolution (1 June, 1858; Commons), *PD*, 3rd ser., Vol. 150, cols. 1379-84.]

[b-b]59[1,2]   shall

in some separate capacity, than the good which, as the chief commercial nation, she would reap from the great increase of commercial intercourse. Let us grant this: and I now ask, what then? Is there any morality, Christian or secular, which bears out a nation in keeping all the rest of mankind out of some great advantage, because the consequences of their obtaining it may be to itself, in some imaginable contingency, a cause of inconvenience? Is a nation at liberty to adopt as a practical maxim, that what is good for the human race is bad for itself, and to withstand it accordingly? What is this but to declare that its interest and that of mankind are incompatible—that, thus far at least, it is the enemy of the human race? And what ground has it of complaint if, in return, the human race determine to be *its* enemies? So wicked a principle, avowed and acted on by a nation, would entitle the rest of the world to unite in a league against it, and never to make peace until they had, if not reduced it to insignificance, at least sufficiently broken its power to disable it from ever again placing its own self-interest before the general prosperity of mankind.

There is no such base feeling in the British people. They are accustomed to see their advantage in forwarding, not in keeping back, the growth in wealth and civilization of the world. The opposition to the Suez Canal has never been a national opposition. With their usual indifference to foreign affairs, the public in general have not thought about it, but have left it, as (unless when particularly excited) they leave all the management of their foreign policy, to those who, from causes and reasons connected only with internal politics, happen for the time to be in office. Whatever has been done in the name of England in the Suez affair has been the act of individuals; mainly, it is probable, of one individual;[*] scarcely any of his countrymen either prompting or sharing his purpose, and most of those who have paid any attention to the subject (unfortunately a very small number) being, to all appearance, opposed to him.

But (it is said) the scheme cannot be executed. If so, why concern ourselves about it? If the project can come to nothing, why profess gratuitous immorality and incur gratuitous odium to prevent it from being tried? Whether it will succeed or fail is a consideration totally irrelevant; except thus far, that if it is sure to fail, there is in our resistance to it the same immorality, and an additional amount of folly; since, on that supposition, we are parading to the world a belief that our interest is inconsistent with its good, while if the failure of the project would really be any benefit to us, we are certain of obtaining that benefit by merely holding our peace.

As a matter of private opinion, the present writer, so far as he has looked into the evidence, inclines to agree with those who think that the scheme cannot be executed, at least by the means and with the funds proposed. But this is a consideration for the shareholders. The British Government does not deem it any part of its business to prevent individuals, even British citizens, from wasting their

[*Henry John Temple, Lord Palmerston.]

own money in unsuccessful speculations, though holding out no prospect of great public usefulness in the event of success. And if, though at the cost of their own property, they acted as pioneers to others, and the scheme, though a losing one to those who first undertook it, should, in the same or in other hands, realize the full expected amount of ultimate benefit to the world at large, it would not be the first nor the hundredth time that an unprofitable enterprise has had this for its final result.

There seems to be no little need that the whole doctrine of non-interference with foreign nations should be reconsidered, if it can be said to have as yet been considered as a really moral question at all. We have heard something lately about being willing to go to war for an idea. To go to war for an idea, if the war is aggressive, not defensive, is as criminal as to go to war for territory or revenue; for it is as little justifiable to force our ideas on other people, as to compel them to submit to our will in any other respect. But there assuredly are cases in which it is allowable to go to war, without having been ourselves attacked, or threatened with attack; and it is very important that nations should make up their minds in time, as to what these cases are. There are few questions which more require to be taken in hand by ethical and political philosophers, with a view to establish some rule or criterion whereby the justifiableness of intervening in the affairs of other countries, and (what is sometimes fully as questionable) the justifiableness of refraining from intervention, may be brought to a definite and rational test. Whoever attempts this, will be led to recognise more than one fundamental distinction, not yet by any means familiar to the public mind, and in general quite lost sight of by those who write in strains of indignant morality on the subject. There is a great difference (for example) between the case in which the nations concerned are of the same, or something like the same, degree of civilization, and that in which one of the parties to the situation is of a high, and the other of a very low, grade of social improvement. To suppose that the same international customs, and the same rules of international morality, can obtain between one civilized nation and another, and between civilized nations and barbarians, is a grave error, and one which no statesman can fall into, however it may be with those who, from a safe and unresponsible position, criticise statesmen. Among many reasons why the same rules cannot be applicable to situations so different, the two following are among the most important. In the first place, the rules of ordinary international morality imply reciprocity. But barbarians will not reciprocate. They cannot be depended on for observing any rules. Their minds are not capable of so great an effort, nor their will sufficiently under the influence of distant motives. In the next place, nations which are still barbarous have not got beyond the period during which it is likely to be for their benefit that they should be conquered and held in subjection by foreigners. Independence and nationality, so essential to the due growth and development of a people further advanced in

war; the annexation of any civilized people to the dominion of another, unless by their own spontaneous election. Up to this point, there is no difference of opinion among honest people; nor on the wickedness of commencing an aggressive war for any interest of our own, except when necessary to avert from ourselves an obviously impending wrong. The disputed question is that of interfering in the regulation of another country's internal concerns; the question whether a nation is justified in taking part, on either side, in the civil wars or party contests of another; and chiefly, whether it may justifiably aid the people of another country in struggling for liberty; or may impose on a country any particular government or institutions, either as being best for the country itself, or as necessary for the security of its neighbours.

Of these cases, that of a people in arms for liberty is the only one of any nicety, or which, theoretically at least, is likely to present conflicting moral considerations. The other cases which have been mentioned hardly admit of discussion. Assistance to the government of a country in keeping down the people, unhappily by far the most frequent case of foreign intervention, no one writing in a free country needs take the trouble of stigmatizing. A government which needs foreign support to enforce obedience from its own citizens, is one which ought not to exist; and the assistance given to it by foreigners is hardly ever anything but the sympathy of one despotism with another. A case requiring consideration is that of a protracted civil war, in which the contending parties are so equally balanced that there is no probability of a speedy issue; or if there is, the victorious side cannot hope to keep down the vanquished but by severities repugnant to humanity, and injurious to the permanent welfare of the country. In this exceptional case it seems now to be an admitted doctrine, that the neighbouring nations, or one powerful neighbour with the acquiescence of the rest, are warranted in demanding that the contest shall cease, and a reconciliation take place on equitable terms of compromise. Intervention of this description has been repeatedly practised during the present generation, with such general approval, that its legitimacy may be considered to have passed into a maxim of what is called international law. The interference of the European Powers between Greece and Turkey, and between Turkey and Egypt, were cases in point. That between Holland and Belgium was still more so. The intervention of England in Portugal, a few years ago, which is probably less remembered than the others, because it took effect without the employment of actual force, belongs to the same category. At the time, this interposition had the appearance of a bad and dishonest backing of the government against the people, being so timed as to hit the exact moment when the popular party had obtained a marked advantage, and seemed on the eve of overthrowing the government, or reducing it to terms. But if ever a political act which looked ill in the commencement could be justified by the event, this was; for, as the fact turned out, instead of giving ascendancy to a party, it proved a really healing measure; and the chiefs of the so-called rebellion were, within a few years, the honoured and successful ministers of the throne against which they had so lately fought.[*]

With respect to the question, whether one country is justified in helping the people of another in a struggle against their government for free institutions, the answer will be different, according as the yoke which the people are attempting to throw off is that of a purely native government, or of foreigners; considering as one of foreigners, every government which maintains itself by foreign support. When the contest is only with native rulers, and with such native strength as those rulers can enlist in their defence, the answer I should give to the question of the legitimacy of intervention is, as a general rule, No. The reason is, that there can seldom be anything approaching to assurance that intervention, even if success-ful, would be for the good of the people themselves. The only test possessing any real value, of a people's having become fit for popular institutions, is that they, or a sufficient portion of them to prevail in the contest, are willing to brave labour and danger for their liberation. I know all that may be said. I know it may be urged that the virtues of freemen cannot be learnt in the school of slavery, and that if a people are not fit for freedom, to have any chance of becoming so they must first be free. And this would be conclusive, if the intervention recommended would really give them freedom. But the evil is, that if they have not sufficient love of liberty to be able to wrest it from merely domestic oppressors, the liberty which is bestowed on them by other hands than their own, will have nothing real, nothing permanent. No people ever was and remained free, but because it was determined to be so; because neither its rulers nor any other party in the nation could compel it to be otherwise. If a people—especially one whose freedom has not yet become prescriptive—does not value it sufficiently to fight for it, and maintain it against any force which can be mustered *within* the country, even by those who have the command of the public revenue, it is only a question in how few years or months that people will be enslaved. Either the government which it has given to itself, or some military leader or knot of conspirators who contrive to subvert the government, will speedily put an end to all popular institutions: unless indeed it suits their convenience better to leave them standing, and be content with reducing them to mere forms; for, unless the spirit of liberty is strong in a people, those who have the executive in their hands easily work *d*any*d* institutions to the purposes of despotism. There is no sure guarantee against this deplorable issue, even in a country which has achieved its own freedom; as may be seen in the present day by striking examples both in the Old and New Worlds: but when freedom has been achieved *for* them, they have little prospect indeed of escaping this fate. When a

[*Nuño José de Mendonça Rolim de Moura Barreto, Duke of Loulé, and Bernardo Sá de Bandeira.]

*d-d*59[1,2]   *any*

people has had the misfortune to be ruled by a government under which the feelings and the virtues needful for maintaining freedom could not develope themselves, it is during an arduous struggle to become free by their own efforts that these feelings and virtues have the best chance of springing up. Men become attached to that which they have long fought for and made sacrifices for; they learn to appreciate that on which their thoughts have been much engaged; and a contest in which many have been called on to devote themselves for their country, is a school in which they learn to value their country's interest above their own.

It can seldom, therefore—I will not go so far as to say never—be either judicious or right, in a country which has a free government, to assist, otherwise than by the moral support of its opinion, the endeavours of another to extort the same blessing from its native rulers. We must except, of course, any case in which such assistance is a measure of legitimate self-defence. If (a contingency by no means unlikely to occur) this country, on account of its freedom, which is a standing reproach to despotism everywhere, and an encouragement to throw it off, should find itself menaced with attack by a coalition of Continental despots, it ought to consider the popular party in every nation of the Continent as its natural ally: the Liberals should be to it, what the Protestants of Europe were to the Government of Queen Elizabeth. So, again, when a nation, in her own defence, has gone to war with a despot, and has had the rare good fortune not only to succeed in her resistance, but to hold the conditions of peace in her own hands, she is entitled to say that she will make no treaty, unless with some other ruler than the one whose existence as such may be a perpetual menace to her safety and freedom. These exceptions do but set in a clearer light the reasons of the rule; because they do not depend on any failure of those reasons, but on considerations paramount to them, and coming under a different principle.

But the case of a people struggling against a foreign yoke, or against a native tyranny upheld by foreign arms, illustrates the reasons for non-intervention in an opposite way; for in this case the reasons themselves do not exist. A people the most attached to freedom, the most capable of defending and of making a good use of free institutions, may be unable to contend successfully for them against the military strength of another nation much more powerful. To assist a people thus kept down, is not to disturb the balance of forces on which the permanent maintenance of freedom in a country depends, but to redress that balance when it is already unfairly and violently disturbed. The doctrine of non-intervention, to be a legitimate principle of morality, must be accepted by all governments. The despots must consent to be bound by it as well as the free States. Unless they do, the profession of it by free countries comes but to this miserable issue, that the wrong side may help the wrong, but the right must not help the right. Intervention to enforce non-intervention is always rightful, always moral, if not always prudent. Though it be a mistake to *give* freedom to a people who do not value the boon, it cannot but be right to insist that if they do value it, they shall not be hindered from the pursuit of it by foreign coercion. It might not have been right for England (even apart from the question of prudence) to have taken part with Hungary in its noble struggle against Austria; although the Austrian Government in Hungary was in some sense a foreign yoke. But when, the Hungarians having shown themselves likely to prevail in this struggle, the Russian despot interposed, and joining his force to that of Austria, delivered back the Hungarians, bound hand and foot, to their exasperated oppressors, it would have been an honourable and virtuous act on the part of England to have declared that this should not be, and that if Russia gave assistance to the wrong side, England would aid the right. It might not have been consistent with the regard which every nation is bound to pay to its own safety, for England to have taken up this position single-handed. But England and France together could have done it; and if they had, the Russian armed intervention would never have taken place, or would have been disastrous to Russia alone: while all that those Powers gained by not doing it, was that they had to fight Russia five years afterwards, under more difficult circumstances, and without Hungary for an ally. The first nation which, being powerful enough to make its voice effectual, has the spirit and courage to say that not a gun shall be fired in Europe by the soldiers of one Power against the revolted subjects of another, will be the idol of the friends of freedom throughout Europe. That declaration alone will ensure the almost immediate emancipation of every people which desires liberty sufficiently to be capable of maintaining it: and the nation which gives the word will soon find itself at the head of an alliance of free peoples, so strong as to defy the efforts of any number of confederated despots to bring it down. The prize is too glorious not to be snatched sooner or later by some free country; and the time may not be distant when England, if she does not take this heroic part because of its heroism, will be compelled to take it from consideration for her own safety.

THE CONTEST IN AMERICA

1862

EDITOR'S NOTE

Dissertations and Discussions, III (1867), 179-205, where the title is footnoted, *"Fraser's Magazine*, February 1862." Reprinted from *Fraser's Magazine*, LXV (Feb., 1862), 258-68, "By John Stuart Mill" appearing under title: left running titles as title; right running titles: "Attitude of England towards the Northern States" (259; equivalent of 128.22-129.35); "Slavery the One Cause of the War" (261; equivalent of 131.8-132.18); "Tendency of the Struggle towards Abolition" (263; equivalent of 134.29-136.1); "The South Not United" (265; equivalent of 137.17-138.27); and "The Alternatives and Their Consequences" (267; equivalent of 139.38-141.10). Identified in Mill's bibliography as "An article entitled 'The Contest in America' in Fraser's Magazine for February 1862" (MacMinn, 94). In Somerville College there are no corrections or emendations in the offprint, which is headed, "[Reprinted from 'Fraser's Magazine' for February, 1862.]," and is repaged 1-11, but is otherwise identical. For comment on the article, see xxii-xxiv and lxiii-lxiv above.

The text below is that of *D&D*, III (1867), the only edition of that volume in Mill's lifetime. In the footnoted variants, "62[1]" indicates *Fraser's Magazine*; "62[2]", the offprint; and "67", *D&D*.

The Contest in America

THE CLOUD WHICH FOR THE SPACE OF A MONTH hung gloomily over the civilized world, black with far worse evils than those of simple war, has passed from over our heads without bursting. The fear has not been realized, that the only two first-rate Powers who are also free nations would take to tearing each other in pieces, both the one and the other in a bad and odious cause. For while, on the American side, the war would have been one of reckless persistency in wrong, on ours it would have been a war in alliance with, and, to practical purposes, in defence and propagation of, slavery. We had, indeed, been wronged. We had suffered an indignity, and something more than an indignity, which not to have resented, would have been to invite a constant succession of insults and injuries from the same and from every other quarter. We could have acted no otherwise than we have done: yet it is impossible to think, without something like a shudder, from what we have escaped. We, the emancipators of the slave—who have wearied every Court and Government in Europe and America with our protests and remonstrances, until we goaded them into at least ostensibly co-operating with us to prevent the enslaving of the negro—we, who for the last half-century have spent annual sums equal to the revenue of a small kingdom in blockading the African coast, for a cause in which we not only had no interest, but which was contrary to our pecuniary interest, and which many believed would ruin, as many among us still, though erroneously, believe that it has ruined, our colonies,—we should have lent a hand to setting up, in one of the most commanding positions of the world, a powerful republic, devoted not only to slavery, but to pro-slavery propagandism —should have helped to give a place in the community of nations to a conspiracy of slave-owners, who have broken their connexion with the American Federation on the sole ground, ostentatiously proclaimed, that they thought an attempt would be made to restrain, not slavery itself, but their purpose of spreading slavery wherever migration or force could carry it.[*]

[*Constitution, Adopted Unanimously by the Congress of the Confederate States of America, March 11, 1861, Art. VI, Sect. 2 (1, 3) and Sect. 6 (3), in The Federal and the Confederate Constitutions for the Use of Government Officers and for the People (Cincinnati: Watkin, 1862), pp. 17-18.]

A nation which has made the professions that England has *made*, does not with impunity, under however great provocation, betake itself to frustrating the objects for which it has been calling on the rest of the world to make sacrifices of what they think their interest. At present all the nations of Europe have sympathized with us; have acknowledged that we were injured, and declared, with rare unanimity, that we had no choice but to resist, if necessary by arms. But the consequences of such a war would soon have buried its causes in oblivion. When the new Confederate States, made an independent Power by English help, had begun their crusade to carry negro slavery from the Potomac to Cape Horn, who would then have remembered that England raised up this scourge to humanity not for the evil's sake, but because somebody had offered an insult to her flag? Or, even if unforgotten, who would then have felt that such a grievance was a sufficient palliation of the crime? Every reader of a newspaper to the furthest ends of the earth, would have believed and remembered one thing only: that at the critical juncture which was to decide whether slavery should blaze up afresh with increased vigour, or be trodden out—at the moment of conflict between the good and the evil spirit—at the dawn of a hope that the demon might now at last be chained and flung into the pit, England stepped in, and, for the sake of cotton, made Satan victorious.

The world has been saved from this calamity, and England from this disgrace. The accusation would indeed have been a calumny. But to be able to defy calumny, a nation, like an individual, must stand very clear of just reproach in its previous conduct. Unfortunately, we ourselves have given too much plausibility to the *charge: not* by anything said or done by us as a Government or as a nation, but by the tone of our press, and in some degree, it must be owned, the general opinion of English society. It is too true, that the feelings which have been manifested since the beginning of the American contest—the judgments which have been put forth, and the wishes which have been expressed, concerning the incidents and probable eventualities of the struggle—the bitter and irritating criticism which has been kept up, not even against both parties equally, but almost solely against the party in the right, and the ungenerous refusal of all those just allowances, which no country needs more than our own, whenever its circumstances are as near to those of America *at the present moment* as a cut finger is to an almost mortal wound,—these facts, with minds not favourably disposed to us, would have gone far to make the most odious interpretation of the war in which we have been so nearly engaged with the United States, appear by many degrees the most probable. There is no denying that our attitude towards the contending parties (I mean our moral attitude, for politically there was no other course open to us than neutrality)

[a-a]+67
[b-b]62[1,2]   charge. Not
[c-c]+67

has not been that which becomes a people who are as sincere enemies of slavery as the English really are, and have made as great sacrifices to put an end to it where they could. And it has been an additional misfortune, that some of our most powerful journals have been, for many years past, very unfavourable exponents of English feeling on all subjects connected with slavery: some, probably, from the influences, more or less direct, of West Indian opinions and interests: others from inbred Toryism, which, even when compelled by reason to hold opinions favourable to liberty, is always adverse to it in feeling; which likes the spectacle of irresponsible power exercised by one person over others; which has no moral repugnance to the thought of human beings born to the penal servitude for life, to which for the term of a few years we sentence our most hardened criminals, but keeps its indignation to be expended on "rabid and fanatical abolitionists" across the Atlantic, and on those writers in England who attach a sufficiently serious meaning to their Christian professions, to consider a fight against slavery as a fight for God.

Now ^{d}that^d the mind of England, and it may almost be said, of the civilized part of mankind, has been relieved from the incubus which had weighed on it ever since the *Trent* outrage, and when we are no longer feeling towards the Northern Americans as men feel towards those with whom they may be on the point of struggling for life or death; now, if ever, is the time to review our position, and consider whether we have been feeling what ought to have been felt, and wishing what ought to have been wished, regarding the contest in which the Northern States are engaged with the South.

In considering this matter, we ought to dismiss from our minds as far as possible those feelings against the North, which have been engendered not merely by the *Trent* aggression, but by the previous anti-British effusions of newspaper writers and stump orators. It is hardly worth while to ask how far these explosions of ill-humour are anything more than might have been anticipated from ill-disciplined minds, disappointed of the sympathy which they justly thought they had a right to expect from the great anti-slavery people, in their really noble enterprise. It is almost superfluous to remark that a democratic government always shows worst, where other governments generally show best, on its outside; that unreasonable people are much more noisy than the reasonable; that the froth and scum are the part of a violently fermenting liquid that meets the eyes, but are not its body and substance. Without insisting on these things, I contend, that all previous cause of offence should be considered as cancelled, by the reparation which the American Government has so amply made; not so much the reparation itself, which might have been so made as to leave still greater cause of permanent resentment behind it; but the manner and spirit in which they have made it. These have been such as most of us, I venture to say, did not by any means expect. If

$^{d-d}62^{1,2}$, when

reparation were made at all, of which few of us felt more than a hope, we thought that it would have been made obviously as a concession to prudence, not to principle. We thought that there would have been truckling to the newspaper editors and supposed fire-eaters who were crying out for retaining the prisoners[*] at all hazards. We expected that the atonement, if atonement there were, would have been made with reservations, perhaps under protest. We expected that the correspondence would have been spun out, and a trial made to induce England to be satisfied with less; or that there would have been a proposal of arbitration; or that England would have been asked to make concessions in return for justice; or that if submission was made, it would have been made, ostensibly, to the opinions and wishes of Continental Europe. We expected anything, in short, which would have been weak, and timid, and paltry. The only thing which no one seemed to expect, is what has actually happened. Mr. Lincoln's Government have done none of these things. Like honest men, they have said in direct terms, that our demand was right; that they yielded to it because it was just; that if they themselves had received the same treatment, they would have demanded the same reparation; and that if what seemed to be the American side of a question was not the just side, they would be on the side of justice; happy as they were to find, after their resolution had been taken, that it was also the side which America had formerly defended.[†] Is there any one, capable of a moral judgment or feeling, who will say that his opinion of America and American statesmen is not raised by such an act, done on such grounds? The act itself may have been imposed by the necessity of the circumstances; but the reasons given, the principles of action professed, were their own choice. Putting the worst hypothesis possible, which it would be the height of injustice to entertain seriously, that the concession was really made solely to convenience, and that the profession of regard for justice was hypocrisy: even so, the ground taken, even if insincerely, is the most hopeful sign of the moral state of the American mind which has appeared for many years. That a sense of justice should be the motive which the rulers of a country rely on, to reconcile the public to an unpopular, and what might seem a humiliating act; that the journalists, the orators, many lawyers, the Lower House of Congress, and Mr. Lincoln's own naval secretary,[‡] should be told in the face of the world, by their own Government, that they have been giving public thanks, presents of swords, freedom of cities, all manner of heroic honours to the author[§] of an act which, though not so intended, was lawless and wrong, and for which the proper remedy is confession and atonement; that this should be the accepted policy (supposing it to be nothing higher) of a Democratic Republic, shows even unlimited democracy to be a better thing than many Englishmen have lately been in the habit of

[*George Eustis, James E. McFarland, James Murray Mason, and John Slidell.]
[†See William Henry Seward, Letter to Lord Lyons, quoted in "The Trent Affair," *The Times*, 13 Jan., 1862, p. 9.]
[‡Gideon Welles.]
[§Charles Wilkes.]

The present Government of the United States is not an abolitionist government. Abolitionists, in America, mean those who do not keep within the Constitution; who demand the destruction (as far as slavery is concerned) of as much of it as protects the internal legislation of each State from the control of Congress; who aim at abolishing slavery wherever it exists, by force if need be, but certainly by some other power than the constituted authorities of the Slave States.* The

*[67] Since the first publication of this paper, I have been honoured with a communication from Mr. Wendell Phillips, supplying some necessary corrections to the view taken above of the principles and purposes of the Abolitionists. My readers will be glad to see those principles and purposes stated in the very words of that eminent man:

"1. Though repudiating the obligation of any law upon the citizen who deems it immoral, the Abolitionists have put into that category only the *fugitive slave clause* of the Constitution [Art. IV, Sect. 2, p. 11], and refused to obey that only; a refusal in which very many of the Republicans, and all the highest toned men, in political life and out of it, have joined them. This refusal therefore is no distinction between them and their fellow citizens. The Abolitionists, in many instances, not meaning to obey that clause, refused to take office because in that case obliged to swear to *support* the whole Constitution. Others swore, and still, in this particular point, disobeyed the law.

"Though seeking to break the Union and end the Constitution, the Abolitionists have always '*kept within it,*' and been Constitution-and-law-abiding citizens, seeking their ends only by moral and lawful means; what Englishmen call *agitation.*

"2. During the whole thirty years of their action before the war, the Abolitionists never asked to have State legislation overridden by Congress. Since the war, in common with the whole loyal party, they ask Congress to exercise the *war power* [Art. I, Sect. 8, p. 5] which authorizes interference with the *rebel* States and with the whole subject of slavery everywhere. But that claim constitutes no distinction between them and their loyal fellow citizens.

"3. The Abolitionists have never 'aimed at abolishing slavery by force;' on the contrary they have constantly, by word and deed, repudiated that method. They have addressed themselves always to '*the constituted authorities of the Slave States,*' urging them to act on the subject, and allowing that *they only* had the right to act upon it. The exceptions to this, in their ranks, have been too few to require notice, or to characterize the party. John Brown (who himself repudiated the charge of abolishing slavery by *force*), though held in the highest respect by Abolitionists, did not represent them. [See John Brown, Last Speech (2 Nov., 1859), reported in "Brown's Trial," *New York Daily Tribune*, 3 Nov., 1859, p. 5.]

"The Abolitionists were distinguished by these principles:

"They considered slave-holding to be *sin*—any voluntary participation in, or upholding of it, to be sin—any law which authorized or supported it to be *immoral*, and therefore not binding, and not to be obeyed. Thinking the Constitution to contain such a law, many of them refused to take office under it, or swear to support it. They demanded *immediate* and *unconditional* emancipation: thereby differing from gradualists—from those who advocated an apprenticeship system; and from colonizationists, who wished the whole black race exported to Africa, as a condition precedent to emancipation.

"The Abolitionists have from the beginning sought abolition only by lawful and moral means—submitting to every law except that ordering the return of slaves to their masters, and using only the press, the rostrum, politics, and the pulpit, as their means to change that public opinion which is sure to change the law. [See 2nd Congress, Sess. II, c. 7 (1793), and 31st Congress, Sess. I, c. 60 (1850).] This has always been their whole and sole reliance."

Republican party neither aim nor profess to aim at this object. And when we consider the flood of wrath which would have been poured out against them if they did, by the very writers who now taunt them with not doing it, we shall be apt to think the taunt a little misplaced. But though not an Abolitionist party, they are a Free-soil party. If they have not taken arms against slavery, they have against its extension. And they know, as we may know if we please, that this amounts to the same thing. The day when slavery can no longer extend itself, is the day of its doom. The slave-owners know this, and it is the cause of their fury. They know, as all know who have attended to the subject, that confinement within existing limits is its death-warrant. Slavery, under the conditions in which it exists in the States, exhausts even the beneficent powers of nature. So incompatible is it with any kind whatever of skilled labour, that it causes the whole productive resources of the country to be concentrated on one or two products, cotton being the chief, which require, to raise and prepare them for the market, little besides brute animal force. The cotton cultivation, in the opinion of all competent judges, alone saves North American slavery; but cotton cultivation, exclusively adhered to, exhausts in a moderate number of years all the soils which are fit for it, and can only be kept up by travelling farther and farther westward. Mr. Olmsted had given a vivid description of the desolate state of parts of Georgia and the Carolinas, once among the richest specimens of soil and cultivation in the world; and even the more recently colonized Alabama, as he shows, is rapidly following in the same downhill track.[*] To slavery, therefore, it is a matter of life and death to find fresh fields for the employment of slave labour. Confine it to the present States, and the owners of slave property will either be speedily ruined, or will have to find means of reforming and renovating their agricultural system; which cannot be done without treating the slaves like human beings, nor without so large an employment of skilled, that is, of free labour, as will widely displace the unskilled, and so depreciate the pecuniary value of the slave, that the immediate mitigation and ultimate extinction of slavery would be a nearly inevitable and probably rapid consequence.

The Republican leaders do not talk to the public of these almost certain results of success in the present conflict. They talk but little, in the existing emergency, even of the original cause of quarrel. The most ordinary policy teaches them to inscribe on their banner that part only of their known principles in which their supporters are unanimous. The preservation of the Union is an object about which the North are agreed; and it has many adherents, as they believe, in the South generally. That nearly half the population of the Border Slave States are in favour of it is a patent fact, since they are now fighting in its defence. It is not probable that they would be willing to fight directly against slavery. The Republicans well know that if they can re-establish the Union, they gain everything for which they originally

[*Frederick Law Olmsted, *The Cotton Kingdom*, 2 vols. (New York: Mason; London: Low, 1861), Vol. II, pp. 296-9.]

contended; and it would be a plain breach of faith with the Southern friends of the Government, if, after rallying them round its standard for a purpose of which they approve, it were suddenly to alter its terms of communion without their consent.

But the parties in a protracted civil war almost invariably end by taking more extreme, not to say higher grounds of principle than they began with. Middle parties and friends of compromise are soon left behind; and if the writers who so severely criticise the present moderation of the Free-soilers are desirous to see the war become an abolition war, it is probable that, if the war lasts long enough, they will be gratified. Without the smallest pretension to see further into futurity than other people, I at least have foreseen and foretold from the first, that if the South were not promptly put down, the contest would become distinctly an anti-slavery one; nor do I believe that any person, accustomed to reflect on the course of human affairs in troubled times, can expect anything else. Those who have read, even cursorily, the most valuable testimony to which the English public have access, concerning the real state of affairs in America—the letters of the *Times* correspondent, Mr. Russell—must have observed how early and rapidly he arrived at the same conclusion, and with what increasing emphasis he now continually reiterates it. In one of his recent letters he names the end of next summer as the period by which, if the war has not sooner terminated, it will have assumed a complete anti-slavery character.[*] So early a term exceeds, I confess, my most sanguine hopes; but if Mr. Russell be right, Heaven forbid that the war should cease sooner, for if it lasts till then it is quite possible that it will regenerate the American people.

If, however, the purposes of the North may be doubted or misunderstood, there is at least no question as to those of the South. They make no concealment of *their* principles. As long as they were allowed to direct all the policy of the Union; to break through compromise after compromise, encroach step after step, until they reached the pitch of claiming a right to carry slave property into the Free States, and, in opposition to the laws of those States, hold it as property there; so long, they were willing to remain in the Union. The moment a President was elected of whom it was inferred from his opinions, not that he would take any measures against slavery where it exists, but that he would oppose its establishment where it exists not,—that moment they broke loose from what was, at least, a very solemn contract, and formed themselves into a Confederation professing as its fundamental principle not merely the perpetuation, but the indefinite extension of slavery. And the doctrine is loudly preached through the new Republic, that slavery, whether black or white, is a good in itself, and *is* the proper condition of the working classes everywhere.

Let me, in a few words, remind the reader what sort of a thing this is, which the

[*William Howard Russell, "The Civil War in America," *The Times*, 13 Sept., 1861, p. 9.]

ff+67

white oligarchy of the South have banded themselves together to propagate, and establish, if they could, universally. When it is wished to describe any portion of the human race as in the lowest state of debasement, and under the most cruel oppression, in which it is possible for human beings to live, they are compared to slaves. When words are sought by which to stigmatize the most odious despotism, exercised in the most odious manner, and all other comparisons are found inadequate, the despots are said to be like slave-masters, or slave-drivers. What, by a rhetorical licence, the worst oppressors of the human race, by way of stamping on them the most hateful character possible, are said to be, these men, in very truth, are. I do not mean that all of them are hateful personally, any more than all the inquisitors, or all the buccaneers. But the position which they occupy, and *of which they are in arms to vindicate the abstract excellence*, is that which the united voice of mankind habitually selects as the type of all hateful qualities. I will not bandy chicanery about the more or less of stripes or other torments which are daily requisite to keep the machine in working order, nor discuss whether the Legrees or the St. Clairs[*] are more numerous among the slave-owners of the Southern States. The broad facts of the case suffice. One fact is enough. There are, Heaven knows, vicious and tyrannical institutions in ample abundance on the earth. But this institution is the only one of them all which requires, to keep it going, that human beings should be burnt alive. The calm and dispassionate Mr. Olmsted affirms that there has not been a single year, for many years past, in which this horror is not known to have been perpetrated in some part or other of the South.[†] And not upon negroes only; the *Edinburgh Review*, in a recent number, gave the hideous details of the burning alive of an unfortunate Northern huckster by Lynch law, on mere suspicion of having aided in the escape of a slave.[‡] What must American slavery be, if deeds like these are necessary under it? and if they are not necessary, and are yet done, is not the evidence against slavery still more damning? The South are in rebellion not for simple slavery; they are in rebellion for the right of burning human creatures alive.

But we are told, by a strange misapplication of a true principle, that the South had a *right* to separate; that their separation ought to have been consented to, the moment they showed themselves ready to fight for it; and that the North, in resisting it, are committing the same error and wrong which England committed in opposing the original separation of the thirteen colonies. This is carrying the doctrine of the sacred right of insurrection rather far. It is wonderful how easy, and

[*Characters in Harriet Beecher Stowe, *Uncle Tom's Cabin; or, Life among the Lowly*, 2 vols. (Boston: Jewett, 1852).]

[†Olmsted, *The Cotton Kingdom*, Vol. II, p. 354.]

[‡Harriet Martineau, "The United States under the Presidentship of Mr. Buchanan," *Edinburgh Review*, CXII (Oct., 1860), 575.]

*-*62[1,2]   the abstract excellence of which they are in arms to vindicate

liberal, and complying, people can be in other people's concerns. Because they are willing to surrender their own past, and have no objection to join in reprobation of their great-grandfathers, they never put ^{h}to^h themselves the question what they themselves would do in circumstances far less trying, under far less pressure of real national calamity. Would those who profess these ardent revolutionary principles consent to their being applied to Ireland, or India, or the Ionian Islands? How have they treated those who did attempt so to apply them? But the case can dispense with any mere *argumentum ad hominem*. I am not frightened at the word rebellion. I do not scruple to say that I have sympathized more or less ardently with most of the rebellions, successful and unsuccessful, which have taken place in my time. But I certainly never conceived that there was a sufficient title to my sympathy in the mere fact of being a rebel; that the act of taking arms against one's fellow citizens was so meritorious in itself, was so completely its own justification, that no question need be asked concerning the motive. It seems to me a strange doctrine that the most serious and responsible of all human acts imposes no obligation on those who do it, of showing that they have a real grievance; that those who rebel for the power of oppressing others, exercise as sacred a right as those who do the same thing to resist oppression practised upon themselves. Neither rebellion, nor any other act which affects the interests of others, is sufficiently legitimated by the mere will to do it. Secession may be laudable, and so may any other kind of insurrection; but it may also be an enormous crime. It is the one or the other, according to the object and the provocation. And if there ever was an object which, by its bare announcement, stamped rebels against a particular community as enemies of mankind, it is the one professed by the South. Their right to separate is the right which Cartouche or Turpin would have had to secede from their respective countries, because the laws of those countries would not suffer them to rob and murder on the highway. The only real difference is, that the present rebels are more powerful than Cartouche or Turpin, and may possibly be able to effect their iniquitous purpose.

Suppose, however, for the sake of argument, that the mere will to separate were in this case, or in any case, a sufficient ground for separation, I beg to be informed *whose* will? The will of any knot of men who, by fair means or foul, by usurpation, terrorism, or fraud, have got the reins of government into their hands? If the inmates of Parkhurst Prison were to get possession of the Isle of Wight, occupy its military positions, enlist one part of its inhabitants in their own ranks, set the remainder of them to work in chain gangs, and declare themselves independent, ought their recognition by the British Government to be an immediate consequence? Before admitting the authority of any persons, as organs of the will of the people, to dispose of the whole political existence of a country, I ask to see whether their credentials are from the whole, or only from a part. And first, it is necessary

$^{h\text{-}h}$+67

to ask, Have the slaves been consulted? Has *their* will been counted as any part in the estimate of collective volition? They are a part of the population. However natural in the country itself, it is rather cool in English writers who talk so glibly of the ten millions (I believe there are only eight), to pass over the very existence of four millions who must abhor the idea of separation. Remember, *we* consider them to be human beings, entitled to human rights. Nor can it be doubted that the mere fact of belonging to a Union in some parts of which slavery is reprobated, is some alleviation of their condition, if only as regards future probabilities. But even of the white population, it is questionable if there was in the beginning a majority for secession anywhere but in South Carolina. Though the thing was pre-determined, and most of the States committed by their public authorities before the people were called on to vote; though in taking the votes terrorism in many places reigned triumphant; yet even so, in several of the States, secession was carried only by narrow majorities. In some the authorities have not dared to publish the numbers; in some it is asserted that no vote has ever been taken. Further (as was pointed out in an admirable letter by Mr. Carey),[*] the Slave States are intersected in the middle, from their northern frontier almost to the Gulf of Mexico, by a country of free labour—the mountain region of the Alleghanies and their dependencies, forming parts of Virginia, North Carolina, Tennessee, Georgia, and Alabama, in which, from the nature of the climate and of the agricultural and mining industry, slavery to any material extent never did, and never will, exist. This mountain zone is peopled by ardent friends of the Union. Could the Union abandon them, without even an effort, to be dealt with at the pleasure of an exasperated slave-owning oligarchy? Could it abandon the Germans who, in Western Texas, have made so meritorious a commencement of growing cotton on the borders of the Mexican Gulf by free labour? Were the right of the slave-owners to secede ever so clear, they have no right to carry these with them; unless allegiance is a mere question of local proximity, and my next neighbour, if I am a stronger man, can be compelled to follow me in any lawless vagaries I choose to indulge.

But (it is said) the North will never succeed in conquering the South; and since the separation must in the end be recognised, it is better to do at first what must be done at last; moreover, if it did conquer them, it could not govern them when conquered, consistently with free institutions. With no one of these propositions can I agree.

Whether or not the Northern Americans *will* succeed in reconquering the South, I do not affect to foresee. That they *can* conquer it, if their present determination holds, I have never entertained a doubt; for they are twice as numerous, and ten or twelve times as rich. Not by taking military possession of their country, or marching an army through it, but by wearing them out, exhausting their resources, depriving them of the comforts of life, encouraging their slaves to desert, and

[*The French and American Tariffs Compared, pp. 19-20 (Letter 3).]

excluding them from communication with foreign countries. All this, of course, depends on the supposition that the North does not give in first. Whether they will persevere to this point, or whether their spirit, their patience, and the sacrifices they are willing to make, will be exhausted before reaching it, I cannot tell. They may, in the end, be wearied into recognising the separation. But to those who say that because this may have to be done at last, it ought to have been done at first, I put the very serious question—On what terms? Have they ever considered what would have been the meaning of separation if it had been assented to by the Northern States when first demanded? People talk as if separation meant nothing more than the independence of the seceding States. To have accepted it under that limitation would have been, on the part of the South, to give up that which they have seceded expressly to preserve. Separation, with them, means at least half the Territories; including the Mexican border, and the consequent power of invading and overrunning Spanish America for the purpose of planting there the "peculiar institution"[*] which even Mexican civilization has found too bad to be endured. There is no knowing to what point of degradation a country may be driven in a desperate state of its affairs; but if the North *ever*, unless on the brink of actual ruin, makes peace with the South, giving up the original cause of quarrel, the freedom of the Territories; if it resigns to them when out of the Union that power of evil which it would not grant to retain them in the Union—it will incur the pity and disdain of posterity. And no one can suppose that the South would have consented, or in their present temper ever will consent, to an accommodation on any other terms. It will require a succession of humiliations to bring them to that. The necessity of reconciling themselves to the confinement of slavery within its existing boundaries, with the natural consequence, immediate mitigation of slavery, and ultimate emancipation, is a lesson which they are in no mood to learn from anything but disaster. Two or three defeats in the field, breaking their military strength, though not followed by an invasion of their territory, may possibly teach it to them. If so, there is no breach of charity in hoping that this severe schooling may promptly come. When men set themselves up, in defiance of the rest of the world, to do the devil's work, no good can come of them until the world has made them feel that this work cannot be suffered to be done any longer. If this knowledge does not come to them for several years, the abolition question will by that time have settled itself. For assuredly Congress will very soon make up its mind to declare all slaves free who belong to persons in arms against the Union.[†] When that is done, slavery, confined to a minority, will soon cure itself; and the pecuniary value of the negroes belonging to loyal masters will probably not exceed the amount of compensation which the United States will be willing and able to give.

[*For the term, see Article on emigration to Kansas, *New York Tribune*, 19 Oct., 1854, p. 4.]

[†See 37th Congress, Sess. II, c. 195 (1862), Sects. 9, 10; and Abraham Lincoln, *Emancipation Proclamation* (Washington: n.p., 1863).]

The assumed difficulty of governing the Southern States as free and equal commonwealths, in case of their return to the Union, is purely imaginary. If brought back by force, and not by voluntary compact, they will return without the Territories, and without a Fugitive Slave Law. It may be assumed that in that event the victorious party would make the alterations in the Federal Constitution which are necessary to adapt it to the new circumstances, and which would not infringe, but strengthen, its democratic principles. An article would have to be inserted prohibiting the extension of slavery to the Territories, or the admission into the Union of any new Slave State. Without any other guarantee, the rapid formation of new Free States would ensure to freedom a decisive and constantly increasing majority in Congress. It would also be right to abrogate that bad provision of the Constitution (a necessary compromise at the time of its first establishment) whereby the slaves, though reckoned as citizens in no other respect, are counted, to the extent of three-fifths of their number, in the estimate of the population for fixing the number of representatives of each State in the Lower House of Congress.[*] Why should the masters have members in right of their human chattels, any more than of their oxen and pigs? The President, in his Message, has already proposed that this salutary reform should be effected in the case of Maryland, additional territory, detached from Virginia, being given to that State as an equivalent: thus clearly indicating the policy which he approves, and which he is probably willing to make universal.[†]

As it is necessary to be prepared for all possibilities, let us now contemplate another. Let us suppose the worst possible issue of this war—the one apparently desired by those English writers whose moral feeling is so philosophically indifferent between the apostles of slavery and its enemies. Suppose that the North should stoop to recognise the new Confederation on its own terms, leaving it half the Territories, and that it is acknowledged by Europe, and takes its place as an admitted member of the community of nations. It will be desirable to take thought beforehand what are to be our own future relations with a new Power professing the principles of Attila and Genghis Khan as the foundation of its Constitution. Are we to see with indifference its victorious army let loose to propagate their national faith at the rifle's mouth through Mexico and Central America? Shall we submit to see fire and sword carried over Cuba and Porto Rico, and Hayti and Liberia conquered and brought back to slavery? We shall soon have causes enough of quarrel on our own account. When we are in the act of sending an expedition against Mexico to redress the wrongs of private British subjects,[‡] we should do well to reflect in time that the President of the new Republic, Mr. Jefferson Davis,

[*Constitution, Art. I, Sect. 2, p. 2.]
[†Mill's source for this mistaken attribution to Lincoln has not been located.]
[‡See The Times, 1 Oct., 1861, p. 10, and 26 Oct., 1861, p. 12.]

was [i]one of the original apostles[i] of repudiation. [j] Unless we abandon the principles we have for two generations consistently professed and acted on, we should be at war with the new Confederacy within five years about the African slave-trade. An English Government will hardly be base enough to recognise them, unless they accept all the treaties by which America is at present bound; nor, it may be hoped, even if *de facto* independent, would they be admitted to the courtesies of diplomatic intercourse, unless they granted in the most explicit manner the right of search. To allow the slave-ships of a Confederation formed for the extension of slavery to come and go, free and unexamined, between America and the African coast, would be to renounce even the pretence of attempting to protect Africa against the man-stealer, and abandon that Continent to the horrors, on a far larger scale, which were practised before Granville Sharp and Clarkson were in existence. But even if the right of intercepting their slavers were acknowledged by treaty, which it never would be, the arrogance of the Southern slaveholders would not long submit to its exercise. Their pride and self-conceit, swelled to an inordinate height by their successful struggle, would defy the power of England as they had already successfully defied that of their Northern countrymen. After our people by their cold disapprobation, and our press by its invective, had combined with their own difficulties to damp the spirit of the Free States, and drive them to submit and make peace, we should have to fight the Slave States ourselves at far greater disadvantages, when we should no longer have the wearied and exhausted North for an ally. The time might come when the barbarous and barbarizing Power, which we by our moral support had helped into existence, would require a general crusade of civilized Europe, to extinguish the mischief which it had allowed, and we had aided, to rise up in the midst of our civilization.

For these reasons I cannot join with those who cry Peace, peace. I cannot wish that this war should not have been engaged in by the North, or that being engaged in, it should be terminated on any conditions but such as would retain the whole of the Territories as free soil. I am not blind to the possibility that it may require a long war to lower the arrogance and tame the aggressive ambition of the slave-owners, to the point of either returning to the Union, or consenting to remain out of it with their present limits. But war, in a good cause, is not the greatest evil which a nation can suffer. War is an ugly thing, but not the ugliest of things: the decayed and degraded state of moral and patriotic feeling which thinks nothing *worth* a war, is worse. When a people are used as mere human instruments for firing cannon or

---

[i-i]62[1,2] the original inventor

[j]62[1,2] Mississippi was the first state which repudiated, Mr. Jefferson Davis was Governor of Mississippi, and the Legislature of Mississippi had passed a Bill recognizing and providing for the debt, which Bill Mr. Jefferson Davis vetoed. [In this erroneous statement of 1862 (revised in 1867), Mill is accepting the assertions of a Northern agent, Robert James Walker, made most prominently in his *Jefferson Davis and Repudiation* (London: Ridgway, 1863).]

thrusting bayonets, in the service and for the selfish purposes of a master, such war degrades a people. A war to protect other human beings against tyrannical injustice; a war to give victory to their own ideas of right and good, and which is their own war, carried on for an honest purpose by their free choice—is often the means of their regeneration. A man who has nothing which he is willing to fight for, nothing which he cares more about than he does about his personal safety, is a miserable creature who has no chance of being free, unless made and kept so by the exertions of better men than himself. As long as justice and injustice have not terminated *their* ever renewing fight for ascendancy in the affairs of mankind, human beings must be willing, when need is, to do battle for the one against the other. I am far from saying that the present struggle, on the part of the Northern Americans, is wholly of this exalted character; that it has arrived at the stage of being altogether a war for justice, a war of principle. But there was from the beginning, and now is, a large infusion of that element in it; and this is increasing, will increase, and if the war lasts, will in the end predominate. Should that time come, not only will the greatest enormity which still exists among mankind as an institution, receive far earlier its *coup de grâce* than there has ever, until now, appeared any probability of; but in effecting this the Free States will have raised themselves to that elevated position in the scale of morality and dignity, which is derived from great sacrifices consciously made in a virtuous cause, and the sense of an inestimable benefit to all future ages, brought about by their own voluntary efforts.

THE SLAVE POWER

1862

EDITOR'S NOTE

Westminster Review, LXXVIII (Oct., 1862), 489-510. Headed: "Art. VIII.—The Slave Power. / *The Slave Power; its Character, Career, and Probable Designs: being an Attempt to explain the real Issues involved in the American Contest*. By J.E. Cairnes, M.A., Professor of Jurisprudence and Political Economy in Queen's College, Galway; and late Whately Professor of Political Economy in the University of Dublin. London. [Parker, Son, and Bourne,] 1862." Running title as title. Unsigned; not republished in British *Dissertations and Discussions*, but appeared in U.S. editions. Also reprinted in U.S. as a pamphlet (New York: Crowen, 1862). Identified in Mill's bibliography as "A review of Prof. Cairnes's work 'The Slave Power' in the Westminster Review for Oct. 1862" (MacMinn, 94). In the Somerville College Library the two copies (tear-sheets) of the *Westminster* version have no corrections or emendations; Vol. III of the Boston ed. of *D&D*, in which the article appears, is no longer in Somerville. For comment on the review, see xxiv-xxvi and lxiv-lxv above.

The *Westminster* version is used as copy-text; it has been collated with the New York reprint and the 1st American ed. of *D&D* (Boston: Spencer, 1864). In the footnoted variants, "62¹" indicates *WR*; "62²", the pamphlet; "64", the U.S. *D&D*.

The Slave Power

THIS VOLUME HAS A TWOFOLD CLAIM TO ATTENTION; on the author's account, and on its own. Mr. Cairnes, one of the ablest of the distinguished men who have given lustre to the much-calumniated Irish colleges, as well as to the chair of Political Economy, which Ireland owes to the enlightened public spirit of Archbishop Whately, is known to the thinking part of the public as the contributor to English periodicals of the clearest and most conclusive discussions which have yet appeared on some of the most disputed and difficult economical questions of the time. He has now, in a work of larger dimensions, given the result of the study which, both as a first-rate political economist, and in the higher character of a moral and political philosopher, he has devoted to the American contest. A work more needed, or one better adapted to the need, could scarcely have been produced at the present time. It contains more than enough to give a new turn to English feeling on the subject, if those who guide and sway public opinion were ever likely to reconsider a question on which they have so deeply committed themselves. To all who are still open to conviction, it is an invaluable exposition both of the principles and the facts of the case. The last is as much required as the first; for the strange partiality of the nation which most abhors negro slavery, to those who are urging an internecine war solely for its propagation, could not have existed for a moment, had there not been, not merely a complete misunderstanding of principles, but an utter ignorance of facts.

We believe that we shall, on the present occasion, do a better service to truth and right by helping to extend the knowledge of the contents of Mr. Cairnes' treatise, than by any comments of our own. Mr. Cairnes opens up the question in so lucid and natural an order, and so exhausts it in all its more important aspects, that a mere condensation of his book would be the most powerful argumentative discourse on the subject, which could well be given in the narrow compass of an article. Not that, as is the case with lax and diffuse writers, his argument gains by ^acondensation. On^a the contrary, it loses greatly. In Mr. Cairnes' book there is nothing verbose, nothing superfluous; the effect is nowhere weakened by expansion, nor the impression of the whole frittered away by undue expatiating on parts; the work is artistic as well as scientific, observing due proportion, dwelling

---

^{a-a}64   condensation: on

long enough, and not too long, on each portion of the subject, and passing to a new point exactly when the mind is prepared for it, by having completely appropriated those preceding. An attempt to convey the substance of such a composition in an abridged form, may give some idea of the skeleton, but none of the nerve and muscle: the greatest merit which it could have would be that of stimulating the reader to have recourse to Mr. Cairnes' own pages.

After sweeping away the idle notion, which never could have been entertained by any one conversant with even the surface of American history, that the quarrel is about tariffs, or anything whatever except slavery, Mr. Cairnes proceeds to the main thesis of his book, viz., that the Slave Power, whose character and aims are the cause of the American contest, is "the most formidable antagonist to civilized progress which has appeared for many centuries, representing a system of society at once retrograde and aggressive, a system which, containing within it no germs from which improvement can spring, gravitates inevitably towards barbarism, while it is impelled by exigencies inherent in its position and circumstances to a constant extension of its territorial domain." [P. 18.] This is what a man of distinguished ability, who has deeply considered the subject, thinks of the new power, which England, by the moral influence of its opinion and sympathies, is helping to raise up. "The vastness," he continues, "of the interests at stake in the American contest, regarded under this aspect, appears to me to be very inadequately conceived in this country, and the purpose of the present work is to bring forward this view of the case more prominently than has yet been done." [*Ibid.*]

Accordingly, in the first place, Mr. Cairnes expounds the economic necessities under which the Slave Power is placed by its fundamental institution.[*] Slavery, as an industrial system, is not capable of being everywhere profitable. It requires peculiar conditions. Originally a common feature of all the Anglo-Saxon settlements in America, it took root and became permanent only in the southern portion of them. What is the explanation of this fact? Several causes have been assigned. One is, diversity of character in the original founders of *b*those*b* communities; New England having been principally colonized by the middle and poorer classes, Virginia and Carolina by the higher. The fact was so, but it goes a very little way towards the explanation of the phenomenon, since "it is certain the New Englanders were not withheld from employing slaves by moral scruples;" and if slave labour had been found suitable for the requirements of the country, they would, without doubt, have adopted it in fact, as they actually did in principle. [P. 36.] Another common explanation of the different fortune of slavery in the Northern and in the Southern States is, that the Southern climate is not adapted to white labourers, and that negroes will not work without slavery. The latter half of

[*Chap. ii, pp. 33-58.]

*b-b*62[2]   these

this statement is opposed to fact. Negroes are willing to work wherever they have the natural inducements to it, inducements equally indispensable to the white race. The climate theory is inapplicable to the Border Slave States, Kentucky, Virginia, and others, whose climate "is remarkably genial, and perfectly suited to the industry of Europeans." [P. 37.] Even in the Gulf States, the alleged fact is only true, as it is in all other parts of the world, of particular localities. The Southern States, it is observed by M. de Tocqueville, "are not hotter than the south of Italy and Spain."[*] In Texas itself there is a flourishing colony of free Germans, who carry on all the occupations of the country, growth of cotton included, by white labour; and "nearly all the heavy out-door work in the city of New Orleans is performed by whites."[Pp. 38-9.]

What the success or failure of slavery as an industrial system depends on, is the adaptation of the productive industry of the country to the qualities and defects of slave labour. There are kinds of cultivation which even in tropical regions cannot advantageously be carried on by slaves; there are others in which, as a mere matter of profit, slave labour has the advantage over the only kind of free labour which, as a matter of fact, comes into competition with it—the labour of peasant proprietors.

The economic advantage of slave labour is, that it admits of complete organization: "it may be combined on an extensive scale, and directed by a controlling mind to a single end." [P. 44.] Its defects are, that it is given reluctantly; it is unskilful; it is wanting in versatility. Being given reluctantly, it can only be depended on as long as the slave is watched; but the cost of watching is too great if the workmen are dispersed over a widely-extended area; their concentration, or, in other words, the employment of many workmen at the same time and place, is a condition *sine quâ non* of slavery as an industrial system; while, to enable it to compete successfully with the intense industry and thrift of workmen who enjoy the entire fruits of their own labour, this concentration and combination of labour must be not merely possible, but also economically preferable. The second disadvantage of slave labour is that it is unskilful: "not only because the slave, having no interest in his work, has no inducement to exert his higher faculties, but because, from the ignorance to which he is of necessity condemned, he is incapable of doing so." [P. 45.] This disqualification restricts the profitableness of slavery to the case of purely unskilled labour. "The slave is unsuited for all branches of industry which require the slightest care, forethought, or dexterity. He cannot be made to co-operate with machinery; he can only be trusted with the commonest implements; he is incapable of all but the rudest labour." [P. 46.] The third defect of slave labour is but a form of the second; its want of versatility. "The difficulty of teaching the slave anything is so great, that the only chance of turning his labour to profit is, when he has once learned a

[*Cairnes, p. 38n, translating Alexis de Tocqueville, *De la démocratie en Amérique*, 4 vols. (Paris: Gosselin, 1835-40), Vol. II, p. 336.]

lesson, to keep him to that lesson for life. Where slaves, therefore, are employed, there can be no variety of production. If tobacco be cultivated, tobacco becomes the sole staple, and tobacco is produced whatever be the state of the market, and whatever be the condition of the soil." [Pp. 46-7.] All this, not as matter of theory merely, but of actual daily experience in the Southern States, is superabundantly proved, as Mr. Cairnes shows, by Southern testimony.[*]

It follows, first, that slave labour is unsuited for manufactures, and can only, in competition with free labour, be profitably carried on in a community exclusively agricultural. Secondly, that even among agricultural employments it is unsuited to those in which the labourers are, or without great economical disadvantage can be, dispersed over a wide surface; among which are nearly all kinds of cereal cultivation, including the two great staples of the Free States, maize and wheat. "A single labourer can cultivate twenty acres of wheat or Indian corn, while he cannot manage more than two of tobacco, or three of cotton." [P. 50.] Tobacco and cotton admit, therefore, the possibility of working large numbers within a limited space: and as they also benefit in a far greater degree than wheat or maize by combination and classification of labour, the characteristic advantage of slave labour is at the highest, while its greatest drawback, the high cost of superintendence, is reduced to the minimum. It is to these kinds of cultivation, together with sugar and rice, that in America slave labour is practically confined. Wherever, even in the Southern States, "the external conditions are especially favourable to cereal crops, as in parts of Virginia, Kentucky, and Missouri, and along the slopes of the Alleghanies, there slavery has always failed to maintain itself." [P. 52.]

But a kind of cultivation suitable to it is not the only condition which the slave system requires in order to be economically profitable. It demands, in addition, an unlimited extent of highly fertile land. This arises from the other two infirmities of slave labour, its unskilfulness and its want of versatility. This point being of the very highest importance, and the foundation of the author's main argument, we give the statement of it in his own words:

When the soils are not of good quality, cultivation needs to be elaborate; a larger capital is expended, and with the increase of capital the processes become more varied, and the agricultural implements of a finer and more delicate construction. With such implements slaves cannot be trusted, and for such processes they are unfit. It is only, therefore, where the natural fertiliy of the soil is so great as to compensate for the inferiority of the cultivation, where nature does so much as to leave little for art, and to supersede the necessity of the more difficult contrivances of industry, that slave labour can be turned to profitable account.

Further, slavery, as a permanent system, has need not merely of a fertile soil, but of a practically unlimited extent of it. This arises from the defect of slave labour in point of versatility. As has been already remarked, the difficulty of teaching the slave anything is so great—the result of the compulsory ignorance in which he is kept, combined with want of intelligent interest in his work—that the only chance of rendering his labour profitable is,

[*Chap. ii, *passim.*]

when he has once learned a lesson, to keep him to that lesson for life. Accordingly, where agricultural operations are carried on by slaves, the business of each gang is always restricted to the raising of a single product. Whatever crop ᶜbeᶜ best suited to the character of the soil and the nature of slave industry, whether cotton, tobacco, sugar, or rice, that crop is cultivated, and that crop only. Rotation of crops is thus precluded by the conditions of the case. The soil is tasked again and again to yield the same product, and the inevitable result follows. After a short series of years its fertility is completely exhausted, the planter abandons the ground which he has rendered worthless, and passes on to seek in new soils for that fertility under which alone the agencies at his disposal can be profitably employed. (Pp. 53-6.)

Accordingly, the ruin, and in many cases the abandonment to nature, of what were once the most productive portions of the older Slave States, are facts palpable to the eye, admitted and loudly proclaimed by slave-holders. And hence that pressing demand for the perpetual extension of the area of slavery, that never-ceasing tendency westward, and unceasing struggle for the opening of fresh regions to slave-owners and their human property, which has grown with the growth of the cotton cultivation, and strengthened with its strength; which produced the seizure of Texas, the war with Mexico, the buccaneering expeditions to Central America, and the sanguinary contest for Kansas; which has been the one determining principle of Southern politics for the last quarter of a century; and because at last, though tardily, resisted by the North, has decided the cotton States to break up the Union.

Such being the economic conditions of a slave community like those of the Southern States, the author proceeds to show how this economic system gives rise to a social and ᵈ political organization tending in the highest degree to aggravate the evils which emanate originally from the economic system itself.

The single merit of slave labour as an industrial instrument consists, as we have seen, in its capacity for organization, its susceptibility of being adjusted with precision to the kind of work to be done, and of being directed on a comprehensive plan towards some distinctly conceived end. Now, to give scope to this quality, the scale on which industry is carried on must be extensive; and to carry on industry on an extensive scale, large capitals are required; (p. 66)

moreover, a capitalist employing slave labour requires funds sufficient not merely to maintain his slaves, but to purchase their fee simple from the first.

Owing to these causes, large capitals are, relatively to small, more profitable, and are at the same time absolutely more required, in countries of slave, than in countries of free labour. It happens, however, that capital is in slave countries a particularly scarce commodity, owing partly to the exclusion from such countries of many modes of creating it—manufactures and commerce, for example—which are open to free communities; and partly to what is also a consequence of the institution, the unthrifty habits of the upper classes. From this state of things result two phenomena, which may be regarded as typical of industry carried on by

ᶜ⁻ᶜ62²   is [Source *agrees with copy-text*]
ᵈ62²   a

slaves—the magnitude of the plantations, and the indebtedness of the planters. Wherever negro slavery has prevailed in modern times, these two phenomena will be found to exist. "Our wealthier planters," says Mr. Clay, "are buying out their poorer neighbours, extending their plantations, and adding to their slave force. The wealthy few, who are able to live on smaller profits, and to give their blasted fields some rest, are thus pushing off the many who are merely independent."[*] At the same time these wealthier planters are, it is well known, very generally in debt, the forthcoming crops being for the most part mortgaged to Northern capitalists, who make the needful advances, and who thus become the instruments by which a considerable proportion of the slave labour of the South is maintained. The tendency of things, therefore, in slave countries, is to a very unequal distribution of wealth. The large capitalists, having a steady advantage over their smaller competitors, engross with the progress of time a larger and larger proportion of the aggregate wealth of the country, and gradually acquire the control of its collective industry. Meantime, amongst the ascendant class a condition of general indebtedness prevails. (Pp. 66-71.)

Side by side with these great land and slave proprietors grows up a white *proletariat* of the worst kind, known in Southern phraseology as "mean whites" or "white trash."[†] The vast districts (becoming, under the deteriorating effects of slave industry, constantly larger,) which are surrendered to nature, and relapse into wilderness,

Become the resort of a numerous horde of people, who, too poor to keep slaves, and too proud to work, prefer a vagrant and precarious life spent in the desert, to engaging in occupations which would associate them with the slaves whom they despise. In the Southern States no less than five millions of human beings are now said to exist in this manner, in a condition little removed from savage life, eking out a wretched subsistence by hunting, by fishing, by hiring themselves out for occasional jobs, by plunder. Combining the restlessness and contempt for regular industry peculiar to the savage, with the vices of the *proletaire* of civilized communities, these people make up a class at once degraded and dangerous; and constantly reinforced as they are by all that is idle, worthless, and lawless among the population of the neighbouring States, form an inexhaustible preserve of ruffianism, ready at hand for all the worst purposes of Southern ambition. The planters complain of these people for their idleness, for corrupting their slaves, for their thievish propensities; but they cannot dispense with them; for in truth they perform an indispensable function in the economy of slave societies, of which they are at once the victims and the principal supporters. It is from their ranks that those filibustering expeditions are recruited, which have been found so effective an instrument in extending the domain of the slave power; they furnish the "Border Ruffians" who in the colonization struggle with the Northern States contend with Freesoilers on the territories, and it is to their antipathy to the negroes that the planters securely trust for repressing every attempt at servile insurrection. (Pp. 75-6.)

Such, then, is the constitution of society in the Slave States; "it resolves itself into three classes—the slaves, on whom devolves all the regular industry; the slaveholders, who reap all its fruits; and an idle and lawless rabble who live dispersed over vast plains in a condition little removed from absolute barbarism."

[*Clement Claiborne Clay, "Address Delivered before the Chunnenuggee Horticultural Society of Alabama," *De Bow's Review*, o.s. XIX (Dec., 1855), 727.]
[†See Cairnes, p. 76.]

[P. 85.] Of a society thus composed, the political structure is determined by an inexorable law.

When the whole wealth of a country is monopolized by a thirtieth part of its population, while the remainder are by physical or moral causes consigned to compulsory poverty and ignorance; when the persons composing the privileged thirtieth part are all engaged in pursuits of the same kind, subject to the influence of the same moral ideas, and identified with the maintenance of the same species of property; political power will of necessity reside with those in whom centre the elements of such power—wealth, knowledge, and intelligence—the small minority for whose exclusive benefit the system exists. The polity of such a society must thus, in essence, be an oligarchy, whatever be the particular mould in which it is cast. Nor is this all. A society so organized tends to develop with a peculiar intensity the distinctive vices of an oligarchy. In a country of free labour, whatever be the form of government to which it is subject, the pursuits of industry are various. Various interests, therefore, take root, and parties grow up which, regarding national questions from various points of view, become centres of opposition, whether against the undue pretensions of any one of their number, or against those of a single ruler. It is not so in the Slave States. That variety of interests which springs from the individual impulses of a free population does not here exist. The elements of a political opposition are wanting. There is but one party, but one set of men who are capable of acting together in political concert. The rest is an undisciplined rabble. From this state of things the only possible result is that which we find—a despotism, in the last degree unscrupulous and impatient of control, wielded by the wealthy few. . . .

To sum up in a few words the general results of the foregoing discussion; the Slave Power—that power which has long held the helm of government in the Union—is, under the forms of a democracy, an uncontrolled despotism, wielded by a compact oligarchy. Supported by the labour of four millions of slaves, it rules a population of five millions of whites—a population ignorant, averse to systematic industry, and prone to irregular adventure. A system of society more formidable for evil, more menacing to the best interests of the human race, it is difficult to conceive. (Pp. 85-7, and 92.)

Are there, in the social and political system which has now been characterized, any elements of improvement, any qualities which leave room for a reasonable hope of the ultimate, however gradual, correction of its inherent evils? Mr. Cairnes has conclusively shown that the very reverse is the case. Instead of raising themselves to the level of free societies, these communities are urged by the most imperious motives to drag down, if possible, free societies to the level of themselves.

It may be thought, perhaps, that American slavery will, from merely natural causes, share the fate of slavery elsewhere. The institution of slavery was once universal, but mankind have nevertheless improved; the most progressive communities in the ancient and modern world—the Greeks, Romans, Hebrews, mediaeval Europeans—have been afflicted with this scourge, but by the natural progress of improvement have got rid of it; and why, it may be said, should not this also happen in the Southern States? and if so, would not an attempt to anticipate this natural progress, and make emancipation move forward more rapidly than the preparation for it, be full of mischief even to the oppressed race itself?

Mr. Cairnes feels all the importance of this question; and no part of his book is more instructive, or more masterly, than the chapter in which he grapples with it.[*] He shows, that "between slavery as it existed in classical and mediaeval times, and the system which now erects itself defiantly in North America," there are such deep-seated distinctions, as render the analogy of the one entirely inapplicable to the other. [P. 98.]

The first distinction is the vital fact of the difference in colour between modern slaves and their masters. In the ancient world, slaves, once freed, became an integral part of free society; their descendants not only were not a class apart, but were the main source from which the members of the free community were recruited; and no obstacle, legal or moral, existed to their attainment of the highest social positions. In America, on the contrary, the freed slave transmits the external brand of his past degradation to all his descendants. However worthy of freedom, they bear an outward mark which prevents them from becoming imperceptibly blended with the mass of the free; and while that odious association lasts, it forms a great additional hindrance to the enfranchisement by their masters, of those whom, even when enfranchised, the masters cannot endure to look upon as their fellow-citizens.

But another difference between ancient and modern slavery, which still more intimately affects the question under discussion, arises from the immense development of international commerce in modern times.

So long as each nation was in the main dependent on the industry of its own members for the supply of its wants, a strong motive would be present for the cultivation of the intelligence, and the improvement of the condition, of the industrial classes. The commodities which minister to comfort and luxury cannot be produced without skilled labour, and skilled labour implies a certain degree of mental cultivation, and a certain progress in social respect. To attain success in the more difficult industrial arts, the workman must respect his vocation, must take an interest in his task; habits of care, deliberation, forethought, must be acquired; in short, there must be such a general awakening of the faculties, intellectual and moral, as by leading men to a knowledge of their rights and of the means of enforcing them, inevitably disqualifies them for the servile condition. Now this was the position in which the slave master found himself in the ancient world. He was, in the main, dependent on the skill of his slaves for obtaining whatever he required. He was therefore naturally led to cultivate the faculties of his slaves, and by consequence to promote generally the improvement of their condition. *His* progress in the enjoyment of the material advantages of civilization depended directly upon *their* progress in knowledge and social consideration. Accordingly the education of slaves was never prohibited in the ancient Roman world, and, in point of fact, no small number of them enjoyed the advantage of a high cultivation. "The youths of promising genius," says Gibbon, "were instructed in the arts and sciences, and almost every profession, liberal and mechanical, might be found in the household of an opulent senator."[†] Modern slaveholders, on the contrary, are independent of the skill, and therefore of the intelligence and social improvement, of their slave population. They have only need to find a

[*Chap. iv, "Tendencies of Slave Societies," pp. 93-118.]

[†Edward Gibbon, *The History of the Decline and Fall of the Roman Empire*, 6 vols. (London: Strahan and Cadell, 1776-88), Vol. I, p. 42.]

commodity which is capable of being produced by crude labour, and at the same time in large demand in the markets of the world; and by applying their slaves to the production of this, they may, through an exchange with other countries, make it the means of procuring for themselves whatever they require. Cotton and sugar, for example, are commodities which fulfil these conditions; they may be raised by crude labour, and they are in large demand throughout the world. Accordingly, Alabama and Louisiana have only to employ their slaves in raising these products, and they are enabled through their means to command the industrial resources of all commercial nations. Without cultivating one of the arts or refinements of civilization, they can possess themselves of all its material comforts. Without employing an artisan, a manufacturer, a skilled labourer of any sort, they can secure the products of the highest manufacturing and mechanical skill. (Pp. 100-3.)

There being thus no inducements *for* cultivating the intelligence of slaves, the mighty motives which always exist *against* suffering it to be cultivated, have had full play; and in all the principal Slave States, teaching a slave to read or write is rigorously prohibited, under most severe penalties both to the teacher and the taught.[*]

There is yet another important distinction between slavery in ancient and in modern times—namely,

the place which the slave trade fills in the organization of modern slavery. Trading in slaves was doubtless practised by the ancients, and with sufficient barbarity. But we look in vain in the records of antiquity for a traffic which, in extent, in systematic character, and above all, in the function discharged by it as the common support of countries breeding and consuming human labour, can with justice be regarded as the analogue of the modern slave trade—of that organized system which has been carried on between Guinea and the coast of America, and of that between Virginia, the Guinea of the New World, and the slave-consuming States of the South and West. [Pp. 107-8.]

The barbarous inhumanity of the slave trade has long been understood; but what has not been so often noticed is the mode in which it operates in giving increased coherence and stability to the system of which it is a part; first, "by bringing the resources of salubrious countries to supplement the waste of human life in torrid regions; and secondly, by providing a new source of profit for slaveholders, which enables them to keep up the institution, when, in the absence of this resource, it would become unprofitable and disappear." [P. 109.] Thus, in Virginia, when slavery, by exhausting the soil, had eaten away its own profits, and the recolonization of the State by free settlers had actually begun, came suddenly the prohibition of the African slave trade, and nearly at the same time the vast enlargement of the field for slave labour by the purchase of Louisiana; and these two events made slavery in Virginia again profitable, as a means of breeding slaves for exportation and sale to the South.

It is through the existence of this abundant breeding ground for slaves, which enables their number to be kept up and increased, in the face of the most frightful mortality in the places to which they are sent, that slavery is enabled, as it exhausts

[*See Cairnes, pp. 104-7.]

old lands, to move on to new ones, preventing that condensation of population which, by depriving the "mean whites" of the means of subsisting without regular work, might render them efficient workmen, instead of, as they now are, "more inefficient, more unreliable, more unmanageable" than even the slaves, and so might gradually effect the substitution of free for slave labour. [P. 126.] The consequence is that population under these institutions increases only by dispersion. Fifteen persons to the square mile are its maximum density in the really slave countries; a state of things under which "popular education becomes impracticable; roads, canals, railways must be losing speculations" [p. 129] (in South Carolina "a train has been known to travel a hundred miles with a single passenger" [p. 131]); all civilizing agencies, all powers capable of making improvement penetrate the mass of the poor white population, are wanting.

There remain, as a source from which the regeneration of slave society is to be looked for, the slave-owners themselves; the chance, whatever it may be, that these may be induced, without external compulsion, to free their slaves, or take some measure, great or small, to prepare the slaves for freedom. An individual here and there may be virtuous enough to do this, if the general sentiment of those by whom he is surrounded will allow him; but no one, we suppose, is simple enough to expect this sacrifice from the entire ruling class of a nation, least of all from the ruling class in the Slave States, with whom the maintenance of slavery has become a matter of social pride and political ambition as much as of pecuniary interest.

It is not simply as a productive instrument that slavery is valued by its supporters. It is far rather for its social and political results, as the means of upholding a form of society in which slaveholders are the sole depositaries of social prestige and political power, as the corner-stone of an edifice of which they are the masters, that the system is prized. Abolish slavery, and you introduce a new order of things, in which the ascendancy of the men who now rule ᵉinᵉ the South would be at an end. An immigration of new men would set in rapidly from various quarters. The planters and their adherents would soon be placed in a hopeless minority in their old dominions. New interests would take root and grow; new social ideas would germinate; new political combinations would be formed; and the power and hopes of the party which has long swayed the politics of the Union, and which now seeks to break loose from that Union in order to secure a free career for the accomplishment of bolder designs, would be gone for ever. [Pp. 138-9.]

Accordingly the South has advanced, from the modest apologies for slavery of a generation ago, to loudly vaunting it as a moral, civilizing, and every way wholesome institution; the fit condition not only for negroes but for the labouring classes of all countries; nay, as an ordinance of God, and a sacred deposit providentially entrusted to the keeping of the Southern Americans, for preservation and extension.[*]

[*See Cairnes, pp. 142-4.]

ᵉ⁻ᵉ–64 [Source *agrees with copy-text*]

The energies of the Southern rulers have long been devoted to protecting themselves against the economical inconveniences of slavery in a manner directly the reverse of either its extinction or its mitigation. To obtain for it an ever wider field is the sole aim of their policy, and, as they are firmly persuaded, the condition of their social existence. "'There is not a slaveholder,' says Judge Warner, of Georgia," and in saying this he only expressed the general sentiment,

"in this house or out of it, but who knows perfectly well that whenever slavery is confined within certain specified limits its future existence is doomed; it is only a question of time as to its final destruction. You may take any single slaveholding county in the Southern States, in which the great staples of cotton and sugar are cultivated to any extent, and confine the present slave population within the limits of that county. Such is the rapid natural increase of the slaves, and the rapid exhaustion of the soil in the cultivation of those crops (which add so much to the commercial wealth of the country), that in a few years it would be impossible to support them within the limits of such county. Both master and slave would be starved out; and what would be the practical effect in any one county, the same result would happen to all the Slaveholding States. Slavery cannot be confined within certain limits without producing the destruction of both master and slave; it requires fresh lands, plenty of wood and water, not only for the comfort and happiness of the slave, but for the benefit of the owner."[*]

And this is the doctrine of the *advocates* of slavery! What, to any mind but that of a slaveholder, would seem at once the *reductio ad absurdum* and the bitterest moral satire on slavery, is by them brought forward—such is the state of their minds—as an unanswerable argument for bringing fresh territory under it as fast as its exhausts the old, until, we suppose, all the remaining soil of our planet is used up and depopulated.

Even were they not prompted to this aggressive ambition by pecuniary interest, they would have a sufficient inducement to it in the passions which are the natural growth of slave society. "That which the necessity for fresh soils is to the political economy of such communities, a lust of power is to their morality. The slaveholder lives from infancy in an atmosphere of *f*despotism; he*f* sees around him none but abject creatures, who, under fearful penalties to be inflicted by himself, are bound to do his slightest, his most unreasonable bidding." [P. 155.] The commerce between master and slave, in the words of Jefferson, himself born and bred a slave-owner, "'is a perpetual exercise of the most boisterous passions—the most unremitting despotism on the one hand, and degrading submission on the other. Our children see this, and learn to imitate it. The parent storms, the child looks on, catches the lineaments of wrath, puts on the same airs in the circle of smaller slaves, gives a loose to the worst passions, and thus nursed, educated, and daily exercised in tyranny, cannot but be stamped with its odious peculiarities.'"[†] The

[*Cairnes, pp. 151-2, quoting Hiram Warner, Speech on Slavery in the Territories (1 Apr., 1856; House of Representatives), *Appendix to the Congressional Globe*, 34th Congress, Sess. I, 1856 (Washington: Rives, 1856), 299-300.]

[†Cairnes, p. 155, quoting Thomas Jefferson, *Notes, on the State of Virginia* (Baltimore: Pechin, 1800), p. 163 ("Query XVIII").]

*f-f*64   despotism. He

arrogance, self-will, and impatience of restraint, which are the natural fruits of the situation, and with which the Southern-American character in all its manifestations is deeply stamped, suffice of themselves to make the slaveholding class throw all their pride and self-importance into the maintenance, extension, and exaltation of their "peculiar institution;"[*] the more, because the institution and its upholders are generally reprobated by mankind, and because they have to defy the opinion of free nations, and may have to resist the exertion of their physical power.

Hence it is that the politicians of the Slave States have devoted themselves, with the ardour of fanaticism, to acquiring, by fair means or foul, ascendancy in the politics of the Union, in order that they might employ that ascendancy in gaining territory for the formation of new Slave States; and again to create more and more Slave States, in order to maintain their ascendancy in the Union. Mr. Cairnes has traced with a vigorous hand the history of these efforts:[†] the struggle between freedom and slavery for the possession of Missouri; the compromise by which that new State was given up to slavery, on condition that no future Slave State should be created north of the parallel 36°30′ of north latitude; the filibustering occupation of Texas in order to detach it from Mexico, its annexation to the Union by means of slavery ascendancy, and the war with Mexico for the acquisition of more slave territory; the Missouri compromise, as soon as all its fruits had been reaped, discovered to be unconstitutional, and repudiated, the principle next set up being "squatter sovereignty"[‡] (the doctrine that Congress could not legislate for the territories, and that the first inhabitants had the right to decide whether they would allow slavery or not); the Northern territories consequently opened to slavery, and the race which followed between Northern and Southern occupants for the possession of Kansas; a slavery constitution for Kansas voted at the rifle's point by bands of "border ruffians"[§] from the South, who did not even intend to settle in the territory; when this nefarious proceeding was frustrated by the crowds of free settlers who flocked in from the North and refused to be bound by the fictitious constitution, the principle of squatter sovereignty also repudiated, since it had failed to effect Southern objects, and the doctrine set up that slavery exists *ipso jure* in all the territories, and that not even the settlers themselves could make it illegal; and finally a decision obtained from the highest tribunal of the United States (which Southern influence had succeeded in filling with Southern lawyers) by which not only this monstrous principle was affirmed, but the right of a slavemaster was recognised to carry his slaves with him to any part of the Free States, and hold them there, any local law to the contrary notwithstanding. This

[*For the term, see Article on emigration to Kansas, *New York Tribune*, 19 Oct., 1854, p. 4.]
[†Cairnes, Chap. vii, pp. 176-226.]
[‡*Ibid.*, p. 195.]
[§*Ibid.*, p. 197.]

was the one step too much in the otherwise well planned progress of the Southern conspiracy. At this point the Northern allies, by whose help alone they could command a majority in the councils of the Federation, fell off from them. The defeat of the Southern candidate for the Presidency[*] followed as a consequence: and this first check to the aggressive and advancing movement of slavery, was the signal for secession and civil war. Well may Mr. Cairnes say that this series of events "is one of the most striking and alarming episodes in modern history, and furnishes a remarkable example of what a small body of men may effect against the most vital interests of human society, when, thoroughly understanding their position and its requirements, they devote themselves, deliberately, resolutely, and unscrupulously, to the accomplishment of their ends." [P. 221.]

Should these conspirators succeed in making good their independence, and possessing themselves of a part of the territories, being those which are in immediate contact with Mexico, nothing is to be expected but the spread of the institution by conquest (unless prevented by some European Power) over that vast country, and ultimately over all Spanish America, and if circumstances permit, the conquest and annexation of the West Indies; while so vast an extension of the field for the employment of slaves would raise up a demand for more, which would in all probability lead to that reopening of the African slave-trade, the legitimacy and necessity of which have long been publicly asserted by many organs of the South. Such are the issues to humanity which are at stake in the present contest between free and slaveholding America; and such is the cause to which a majority of English writers, and of Englishmen who have the ear of the public, have given the support of their sympathies.

What is the meaning of this? Why does the English nation, which has made itself memorable to all time as the destroyer of negro slavery, which has shrunk from no sacrifices to free its own character from that odious stain, and to close all the countries of the world against the slave merchant; why is it that the nation which is at the head of Abolitionism, not only feels no sympathy with those who are fighting against the slaveholding conspiracy, but actually desires its success? Why is the general voice of our press, the general sentiment of our people, bitterly reproachful to the North, while for the South, the aggressors in the war, we have either mild apologies or direct and downright encouragement? and this not only from the Tory and anti-democratic camp, but from Liberals, or *soi-disant* such?

This strange perversion of feeling prevails nowhere else. The public of France, and of the Continent generally, at all events the Liberal part of it, saw at once on which side were justice and moral principle, and gave its sympathies consistently and steadily [8]to[8] the North. Why is England an exception? Several causes may be

[*John Cabell Breckinridge.]

[8-8]64   for

assigned, none of them honourable to this country, though some, more than others, may seem to make the aberration excusable.

In the first place, it must, we fear, be admitted, that the anti-slavery feeling in England, though quite real, is no longer, in point of intensity, what it was. We do not ascribe this to any degeneracy in the public mind. It is because the work, so far as it specially concerns England, is done. Strong feeling on any practical subject is only kept up by constant exercise. A new generation has grown up since the great victory of slavery abolition; composed of persons whose ardour in the cause has never been wrought upon and strung up by contest. The public of the present day think as their fathers did concerning slavery, but their feelings have not been in the same degree roused against its enormities. Their minds have been employed, and their feelings excited, on other topics, on which there still remained, as it might seem, more to be done. Slavery has receded into the background of their mental prospect; it stands, to most of them, as a mere name, the name of one social evil among many others; not as, what in truth it is, the summing-up and concentration of them all; the stronghold in which the principle of tyrannical power, elsewhere only militant, reigns triumphant.

It must be remembered, too, that though the English public are averse to slavery, several of the political and literary organs which have most influence over the public are decidedly not so. For many years the *Times* has taken every opportunity of throwing cold water, as far as decency permitted, on the cause of the negro; had its attempts succeeded, the African squadron would have been withdrawn, and the effort so long and honourably persisted in by England to close the negro coast against the man-stealer would have been ignominiously abandoned. Another of the misleaders of opinion on this subject, more intellectual in its aims, and addressing itself to a more intellectual audience, has been from its first origin, however Liberal on the surface, imbued with a deeply-seated Tory feeling, which makes it prefer even slavery to democratic equality; and it never loses an opportunity of saying a word for slavery, and palliating its evils.[*]

The most operative cause, however, of the wrong direction taken on the American question by English feeling, is the general belief that Americans are hostile to England, and long to insult and humble her if they had but an opportunity; and the accumulated resentment left by a number of small diplomatic collisions, in which America has carried herself with a high hand, has bullied and blustered, or her press has bullied and blustered for her, and in which, through the reluctance of England to push matters to extremities, which do not vitally concern the national honour, bullying and blustering have been allowed to prevail. The facts are too true; but it has not been sufficiently considered, that the most foul-mouthed enemies of England in the American press and in Congress were Southern men, and men in the Southern interest; and that the offensive tone and

[*Apparently a reference to *Fraser's Magazine.*]

encroaching policy of the Federal Government were the tone and policy of a succession of Governments created by the South, and entirely under Southern influence. If some bitterness towards England has shown itself rather widely among the Northern people since the commencement of the war, and has been ministered to in their usual style by the hacks of the newspaper press, it must be said in excuse, that they were smarting under disappointed hopes; that they had found only rebuke where they felt that they deserved, and had counted upon finding, sympathy, and when sympathy would have been of the utmost importance to their cause. "If England had but sympathized with us now," said recently to us one of the first of American writers, "it would have united the two nations almost to the end of time."[*]

But none of these causes would have accounted for the sad aberration of English feeling at this momentous crisis, had they not been combined with an almost total ignorance respecting the antecedents of the struggle. England pays a heavy price for its neglect of general cotemporary history, and inattention to what takes place in foreign countries. The English people did not know the past career or the present policy and purposes of the Slave Power. They did not, nor do they yet, know that the object, the avowed object, of secession was the indefinite extension of slavery; that the sole grievance alleged by the South consisted in being thwarted in this; that the resistance of the North was resistance to the spread of slavery—the aim of the North its confinement within its present bounds, which, in the opinion of the slave-owners themselves, ensures its gradual extinction, and which is the only means whereby the extinction *can* be gradual. The ignorance of the public was shared by the Foreign Minister, whose official attitude in reference to the contest has been everything which it ought to be, but who did unspeakable mischief by the extra-official opinion so often quoted, that the Southern States are in arms for independence, the Northern for dominion.[†]

When this was the view taken of the contest in the quarter supposed to be best informed, what could be expected from the public? Could they fail to bestow their sympathies on the side which, they were told from authority, was fighting for the common right of mankind to a government of their choice, while the other had armed itself for the wicked purpose of exercising power over others against their will? The moral relations of the two parties are misplaced, are almost reversed, in Earl Russell's dictum. Could we consent to overlook the fact that the South are fighting for, and the North against, the most odious form of unjust dominion *h*which*h* ever existed; could we forget the slaves, and view the question as one between two white populations; even then, who, we ask, are fighting for

[*Probably John Lothrop Motley.]

[†John Russell, Speech at Newcastle (14 Oct., 1861), reported in *Spectator*, 19 Oct., 1861, p. 1135.]

*h-h*64   that

dominion, if not those who having always before succeeded in domineering, break off from the Union at the first moment when they find that they can domineer no longer? Did ever any other section of a nation break through the solemn contract which united them with the rest, for no reason but that they were defeated in an election? It is true, indeed, and they are welcome to the admission, that a very serious interest of the slave-owning oligarchy depended on retaining the power to domineer. They had at stake, not dominion only, but the profits of dominion; and those profits were, that the propagation of slavery might be without limit, instead of being circumscribed within the vast unoccupied space already included in the limits of the Slave States, being about half of their entire extent.

But if the South are fighting for slavery, the North, we are told, are, at all events, not fighting against it: their sole object in the struggle is the preservation of the Union.

And if it were so: is there anything so very unjustifiable in resisting, even by arms, the dismemberment of their country? Does public morality require that the United States should abdicate the character of a nation, and be ready at the first summons to allow any discontented section to dissever itself from the rest by a single vote of a local majority, fictitious or real, taken without any established form, or public guarantee for its genuineness and deliberateness? This would be to authorize any State, or part of a State, in a mere fit of ill-temper, or under the temporary influence of intriguing politicians, to detach itself from the Union, and perhaps unite itself to some hostile power; and the end would probably be to break down the Union, from one of the great nations of the world, into as many petty republics as there are States, with lines of custom-houses all round their frontiers, and standing armies always kept up in strength to protect them against their nearest neighbours.

It is so new a thing to consider questions of national morality from the point of view of nations, instead of exclusively from that of rulers, that the conditions have not yet been defined under which it is the duty of an established Government to succumb to a manifestation of hostile feeling by a portion, greater or smaller, of its citizens. Until some rule or maxim shall have grown up to govern this subject, no Government is expected or bound to yield to a rebellion until after a fair trial of strength in the field. Were it not for the certainty of opposition, and the heavy penalties of failure, revolt would be as frequent a fact as it is now an unfrequent; rebellions would be attempted, not as they now are, in cases of almost unanimous discontent, but as often as any object was sought, or offence taken, by the smallest section of the community.

Would the Government or people of the United Kingdom accept for themselves this rule of duty? Would they look on quietly and see the kingdom dismembered? They might renounce transmarine possessions which they hold only as dependencies, which they care little for, and with which they are neither connected by interest nor by neighbourhood; but would England acquiesce, without fighting, in the separation of Ireland or Scotland? and would she be required to do so by any recognised obligation of public morality?

Putting at the very lowest the inducements which can be supposed to have instigated the people of the Northern States to rush into the field with nearly all their available population, and pledge the collective wealth of the country to an unparalleled extent, in order to maintain its integrity; it might still be thought, that a people who *were* supposed to care for nothing in comparison with the "almighty dollar,"[*] ought to have some credit given them for showing, by such decisive proofs, that they are capable of sacrificing that and everything else to a patriotic impulse. It might have been supposed, too, that even had their motives been wholly selfish, all good men would have wished them success when they were fighting for the right; and, considering what it was that they were fighting against, might have been glad that even selfish motives had induced one great nation to shed its blood and expend its substance in doing battle against a monster evil which the other nations, from the height of their disinterested morality, would have allowed to grow up unchecked, until the consequences came home to themselves.

But such a view of the motives of the Northern Americans would be a flagrant injustice to them. True, the feeling which made the heroic impulse pervade the whole country, and descend to the least enlightened classes, was the desire to uphold the Union. But not the Union, simply. Had they consented to give up the Northern interpretation of the pact; had they yielded to the Supreme Court's Southern exposition of it, they would have won back the South to the Federation by an unanimous voice.[†] It was because they valued something else even more highly than the Union, that the Union was ever in a position in which it had to be fought for. The North fights for the Union, but the Union under conditions which deprive the Slave Power of its pernicious ascendancy. People talk as if to support the existing constitution were synonymous with altogether abandoning emancipation, and "giving guarantees to slavery." Nothing of the sort. The Constitution guarantees slavery against nothing but the interference of Congress to legislate for the legally constituted Slave States.[‡] Such legislation, in the opinion equally of North and South, is neither the only, nor the best, nor the most effectual mode of getting rid of slavery. The North may indeed be driven to it; and, in the opinion of near observers, is moving rapidly towards that issue. Mr. Russell, in his letters to

[*Washington Irving, *Chronicles of Wolfert's Roost and Other Papers*, Author's ed. (Edinburgh: Constable; London: Hamilton; Dublin: McGlashan, 1855), p. 30.]

[†See Scott v. Sanford (1856), in *Reports of Cases Argued and Adjudged in the Supreme Court of the United States*, 24 vols. (Washington: Morrison, 1857), Vol. XIX, pp. 393-633.]

[‡*The Constitution or Frame of Government, for the United States of America* (Boston: Fleet, 1787), Art. I, Sect. 9, p. 6.]

*i-i*62² are

the *Times*, was constantly reiterating that the war would before long become an abolition war;[*] and Mr. Dicey, the latest traveller in America who has published his impressions, and whose book should be in every one's hand, says, that this predicted consummation is now rapidly drawing near, through the conviction, becoming general in the North, that slavery and the Union are incompatible.[†] But the Federal Government was bound to keep within the Federal Constitution: and what, that could be done against slavery consistently with the Constitution, has it left undone? The district of Columbia was constitutionally under the authority of Congress; Congress have abolished slavery in that district, granting compensation.[‡] They have offered liberal pecuniary assistance to any Slave State which will take measures for either immediately or gradually emancipating its slaves.[§] They have admitted Western Virginia into the Union as a State, under a provision that all children born after a certain day of 1863 shall be born free.[¶] They have concluded a treaty with England for the better suppression of the slave trade, conceding, what all former American Governments have so obstinately resisted, the right of search.[||] And, what is more important than all, they have, by a legislative act, prohibited slavery in the territories.[**] No human being can henceforth be held in bondage in any possession of the United States which has not yet been erected into a State. A barrier is thus set to all further extension of the legal area of slavery within the dominion of the United States. These things have the United States done, in opposition to the opinion of the Border States which are still true to their allegiance; at the risk of irretrievably offending those States, and deciding them to go over to the enemy. What could the party now dominant in the United States have done more, to prove the sincerity of its aversion to slavery, and its purpose to get rid of it by all lawful means?

And these means would, in all probability, suffice for the object. To prevent the extension of slavery, is, in the general opinion of slaveholders, to ensure its extinction. It is, at any rate, the only means by which that object can be effected through the interest of the slaveholders themselves. If peaceful and gradual is preferable to sudden and violent emancipation (which we grant may in the present case be doubtful), this is the mode in which alone it can be effected. Further

[*See, e.g., William Howard Russell, "The Civil War in America," *The Times*, 13 Sept., 1861, p. 9.]

[†Edward Dicey, *Six Months in the Federal States*, 2 vols. (London and Cambridge: Macmillan, 1863), esp. Vol. I, pp. 315-18.]

[‡37th Congress, Sess. II, c. 54 (1862).]

[§37th Congress, Sess. II, Resolution 26 (1862).]

[¶See "America," *The Times*, 26 July, 1862, p. 14, for a report of the passage through the U.S. Senate of the bill that, after ratification in the House of Representatives in December, was enacted as 37th Congress, Sess. III, c. 6 (1862).]

[||"Treaty between Her Majesty and the United States of America for the Suppression of the African Slave Trade," *PP*, 1862, LXI, 373-85.]

[**37th Congress, Sess. II, c. 111 (1862).]

colonization by slaves and slave-masters being rendered impossible, the process of exhausting the lands fitted for slave cultivation would either continue, or would be arrested. If it continue, the prosperity of the country will progressively decline, until the value of slave property *jwasj* reduced so low, and the need of more efficient labour so keenly felt, that there *kwouldk* be no motive remaining to hold the negroes in bondage. If, on the other hand, the exhaustive process should be arrested, it must be by means implying an entire renovation, economical and social, of Southern society. There would be needed new modes of cultivation, processes more refined and intellectual, and, as an indispensable condition, labourers more intelligent, who must be had either by the introduction of free labour, or by the mental improvement of the slaves. The masters must resign themselves to become efficient men of business, personal and vigilant overseers of their own labourers; and would find that in their new circumstances successful industry was impossible without calling in other motives than the fear of the lash. The immediate mitigation of slavery, and the education of the slaves, would thus be certain consequences, and its gradual destruction by the consent of all concerned, a probable one, of the mere restriction of its area: whether brought about by the subjugation of the Southern States, and their return to the Union under the Constitution according to its Northern interpretation, or by what Mr. Cairnes regards as both more practical and more desirable, the recognition of their independence, with the Mississippi for their western boundary.[*]

Either of these results would be a splendid, and probably a decisive and final, victory over slavery. But the only point on which we hesitate to agree with Mr. Cairnes is in preferring the latter, to the former and more complete issue of the contest. Mr. Cairnes is alarmed by what he thinks the impossibility of governing this group of States after reunion, unless in a manner incompatible with free institutions—as conquered countries, and by military law. We are unable to see the impossibility. If reduced by force, the Slave States must submit at discretion. They could no longer claim to be dealt with according to the Constitution which they had rebelled against. The door which has been left open till now for their voluntary return, would be closed, it is to be presumed, after they had been brought back by force. In that case the whole slave population might, and probably would, be at once emancipated, with compensation to those masters only who had remained loyal to the Federal Government, or who may have voluntarily returned to their allegiance before a time fixed. This having been done, there would be no real danger in restoring the Southern States to their old position in the Union. It would be a diminished position, because the masters would no longer be allowed representatives in Congress in right of three-fifths of their slaves. The slaves once

[*Cairnes, pp. 290-1.]

*j-j*64   is
*k-k*64   will

freed, and enabled to hold property, and the country thrown open to free colonization, in a few years there would be a free population in sympathy with the rest of the Union. The most actively disloyal part of the population, already diminished by the war, would probably in great part emigrate if the North were successful. Even if the negroes were not admitted to the suffrage, or if their former masters were able to control their votes, there is no probability, humbled and prostrated as the Slave Power would be, that in the next few years it would rally sufficiently to render any use which it could make of constitutional freedom again dangerous to the Union. When it is remembered that the thinly-peopled Missouri, Arkansas, Texas, and some parts even of the South-Eastern States, have even now so few slaves that they may be made entirely free at a very trifling expense in the way of redemption; and when the probable great influx of Northern settlers into those provinces is considered; the chance of any dangerous power in the councils of the United States to be exercised by the six or seven Cotton States, if allowed to retain their constitutional freedom, must appear so small, that there could be little temptation to deny them that common right.

It may, however, prove impossible to reduce the seceded States to unconditional submission, without a greater lapse of time, and greater sacrifices, than the North may be willing to endure. If so, the terms of compromise suggested by Mr. Cairnes, which would secure all west of the Mississippi for free labour, would be a great immediate gain to the cause of freedom, and would probably in no long period secure its complete triumph. We agree with Mr. Cairnes[*] that this is the only *kind* of compromise which should be entertained for a moment. That peace should be made by giving up the cause of quarrel, the exclusion of slavery from the territories, would be one of the greatest calamities which could happen to civilization and to mankind. Close the territories, prevent the spread of the disease to countries not now afflicted with it, and much will already have been done to hasten its doom. But that doom would still be distant if the vast uncolonized region of Arkansas, and Texas, which alone is thought sufficient to form five States, were left to be filled up by a population of slaves and their masters; and no treaty of separation can be regarded with any satisfaction but one which should convert the whole country west of the Mississippi into free soil.

[*Pp. 285ff.]

AUSTIN ON JURISPRUDENCE

1863

EDITOR'S NOTE

Dissertations and Discussions, III (1867), 206-74, where the title is footnoted, "*Edinburgh Review*, October 1863.—1. 'Lectures on Jurisprudence; being the Sequel to "The Province of Jurisprudence Determined." To which are added Notes and Fragments, now first published from the Original Manuscripts.' By the late John Austin, Esq., of the Inner Temple, Barrister-at-Law. [Ed. Sarah Austin.] Two vols. 8vo. London: [Murray,] 1863. / 2. 'On the Uses of the Study of Jurisprudence.' By the late John Austin, Esq., of the Inner Temple, Barrister-at-Law. Reprinted from the Third Volume of 'Lectures on Jurisprudence.' [Ed. Sarah Austin.] London: [Murray,] 1863." Reprinted from *Edinburgh Review*, CXVIII (Oct., 1863), 439-82, where it appeared as Art. V, headed by the same information as in the footnote to the title in *D&D*; running titles, "Austin on Jurisprudence." Unsigned. Identified in Mill's bibliography as "A review of Austin's Lectures on Jurisprudence in the Edinburgh Review for October 1863 (omitted in its proper place)" (MacMinn, 96); the entry appears between those for 1865 and for 1866. In the Somerville College copy of an offprint of the *Edinburgh Review* version (repaged 1-44 but otherwise identical) are two corrections in Mill's hand, both of which are adopted in *D&D* (and in the present text): see 167[a-a] and 172[d-d]. In the Somerville College set of *D&D* there is a further correction: at 179.27 "motion" is corrected in pencil to "notion" (as in the *Edinburgh* version and in the 2nd ed. of Vol. III of *D&D* [1875, edited after Mill's death by Helen Taylor]); it too is adopted here. For comment on the essay, see xli-xlviii and lxv-lxvi above.

The text below is that of *D&D*, III (1867), the only edition of that volume in Mill's lifetime. In the footnoted variants, "63[1]" indicates *Edinburgh Review*; "63[2]", the offprint; "67", *D&D*, III.

Austin on Jurisprudence

THESE LECTURES AND FRAGMENTS, with the volume on *The Province of Jurisprudence*,[*] of which they are the continuation, and a very few though very elaborate essays on miscellaneous subjects, published at long intervals, mostly in Reviews, are all that remains of the intellectual life of a most remarkable mind. Mr. Austin's name and writings are little known, except to students of the science which, though only *a*one*a* of those on which his writings prove him to have reflected, was the subject on which he principally wrote. But in that science, even the limited portion of his labours which was before the world had placed him, in the estimation of all competent judges, in the very highest rank; and if such judges are now greatly more numerous than when he began to write, the fact is in no small degree owing to his intellectual influence. He has been in nothing more useful than in forming the minds by which he is, and will hereafter be, judged. No writer whom we know had more of the qualities needed for initiating and disciplining other minds in the difficult art of precise thought. Though the merit and worth of his writings as a contribution to the philosophy of jurisprudence are conspicuous, their educational value, as a training school for the higher class of intellects, will be found, we think, to be still greater. Considered in that aspect, there is not extant any other book which can do for the thinker exactly what this does. Independently of the demands which its subject makes upon the attention, not merely of a particular profession, but of all liberal and cultivated minds, we do not hesitate to say that as a mere organon for certain faculties of the intellect, a practical logic for some of the higher departments of thought, these volumes have a claim to a place in the education of statesmen, publicists, and students of the human mind.

It is not, of course, intended to claim for Mr. Austin a position in the philosophy of law either equal or similar to that which posterity will assign to his great predecessor, Bentham. That illustrious thinker has done, for this important department of human affairs, what can only be done once. But though the work which Mr. Austin did, neither would nor could have been done if Bentham had not given the impulse and pointed out the way, it was of a different character from

---

[*The Province of Jurisprudence Determined* (London: Murray, 1832); 2nd ed., ed. Sarah Austin (London: Murray, 1861), republished (3rd ed.) as Vol. I of the *Lectures*.]

a-a+67 [*corrected by JSM in SC copy of 63²*]

Bentham's work, and not less indispensable. In the confidence of private friendship, Mr. Austin once said of himself, that if he had any special intellectual vocation, it was that of "untying knots." In this judgment he estimated his own qualifications very correctly. The untying of intellectual knots; the clearing up of the puzzles arising from complex combinations of ideas confusedly apprehended, and not analysed into their elements; the building up of definite conceptions where only indefinite ones existed, and where the current phrases disguised and perpetuated the indefiniteness; the disentangling of the classifications and distinctions grounded on differences in things themselves, from those arising out of the mere accidents of their history, and, when disentangled, applying the distinctions (often for the first time) clearly, consistently, and uniformly—these were, of the many admirable characteristics of Mr. Austin's work as a jurist, those which most especially distinguished him. This untying of knots was not particularly characteristic of Bentham. He cut them rather. He preferred to draw his pen through the whole of the past, and begin anew at the beginning. Neither his tastes nor his mental habits were adapted to the other kind of work: but, though his neglect of it led him not unfrequently into errors, yet, all things considered, success has justified his choice. His effect on the world has been greater, and therefore more beneficial, by means of it. The battering ram was of more importance, in Bentham's time, than the builder's trowel. He had to conquer an inveterate superstition. He found an incondite mass of barbarian conceits, obsolete technicalities, and contrivances which had lost their meaning, bound together by sophistical ingenuity into a semblance of legal science, and held up triumphantly to the admiration and applause of mankind. The urgent thing for Bentham was to assault and demolish this castle of unreason, and to try if a foundation could not be laid for a rational science of law by direct consideration of the facts of human life. To rescue from among the ruins such valuable materials as had been built in among rubbish, and give them the new and workmanlike shape which fitted them for a better edifice; to hunt among the irrationalities of law for helps to its rationale, was work for which, even if it had been opportune in his day, Bentham had not time. For Bentham's subject had a wider range than Mr. Austin's. It was the whole, of which the latter is but a part. The one inquiry was ultimate, the other instrumental. Mr. Austin's subject was Jurisprudence, Bentham's was Legislation.

The purpose of Bentham was to investigate principles from which to decide what laws ought to exist—what legal rights, and legal duties or obligations, are fit to be established among mankind. This was also the ultimate end of Mr. Austin's speculations; but the subject of his special labours was theoretically distinct, though subsidiary, and practically indispensable, to the former. It was what may be called the logic of law, as distinguished from its morality or expediency. Its purpose was that of clearing up and defining the notions which the human mind is compelled to form, and the distinctions which it is necessitated to make, by the mere existence of a body of law of any kind, or of a body of law taking cognisance of the concerns of a civilized and complicated state of society. A clear and firm possession of these notions and distinctions is as important to practice as it is to science. For only by means of it can the legislator know how to give effect to his own ideas and his own purposes. Without it, however capable the legislator might be of conceiving good laws in the abstract, he could not possibly so word them, and so combine and arrange them, that they should really do the work intended and expected.

These notions and distinctions form the science of jurisprudence as Mr. Austin conceived it. The readers of what we must now call his first volume, *The Province of Jurisprudence Determined*, have probably often regretted, that though it discussed in a most elaborate and searching manner the "province" (in other words the subject-matter and limits) of jurisprudence, the nature and uses of the study itself were rather taken for granted than expressly set forth. This, which was a real defect in the former volume considered as a separate work, is now supplied by a dissertation on the study of jurisprudence, formed out of the introductory lectures to the two courses which Mr. Austin delivered, at University College and at the Inner Temple. This instructive paper, besides being included in the larger work, has, in order to recommend the study to a more numerous body of readers, been judiciously published separately as a pamphlet.

We have already, in reviewing the second edition of Mr. Austin's *Province of Jurisprudence*,* republished by his widow in 1861, compared and contrasted the method of Mr. Austin with that of another eminent philosophical lawyer, Mr. Maine. The subject-matter of both writers is positive law—the legal institutions which exist, or have existed, among mankind, considered as actual facts. The aim of both is to let in the light of philosophy on these facts; and both do this with great success. Neither writer treats *ex professo* of laws as they ought to be; though, in treating of them as they are and as they have been, it is the declared aim of both to facilitate their improvement. But they pursue this end, for the most part, through different intellectual media. Mr. Maine's operation is essentially historical; not only in the mode of prosecuting his inquiry, but in the nature of the inquiry itself. He investigates, not properly the philosophy of law, but the philosophy of the history of law. In the various legal institutions which obtain, or have formerly obtained, he studies principally the causes that produced them. His book may be called a treatise on the action and reaction between the ideas prevalent among mankind, and their positive institutions. Under each of the principal classes of facts with which law is conversant—family, property, contract, and delict or

*[James Fitzjames Stephen, "English Jurisprudence,"] *Edinburgh Review*, CXIV [(Oct., 1861)], p. 474 *b*(not by the present writer)*b*. [The review (pp. 456-86) is of the 2nd ed. of Austin, and of Henry Maine, *Ancient Law: Its Connection with the Early History of Society, and Its Relation to Modern Ideas* (London: Murray, 1861).]

b-b+67

offence—he historically investigates the primitive ideas of mankind, traces the customs and institutions, which have prevailed ever since, to their origin in those primitive ideas, and shows how institutions which were modelled on the rude notions of an early state of society, have influenced the thoughts of subsequent generations down to the present time. Speculations like these, when directed, as Mr. Maine's are, by a true historical genius, possess in a pre-eminent degree all the uses which can belong to history. The laws and institutions of primitive mankind are the richest indications available for reading their thoughts, entering into their feelings, and understanding their general mode of existence. But the historical value of these studies is the smallest part of their utility. They teach us the highly practical lesson, that institutions which, with more or less of modification, still exist, originated in ideas now universally exploded; and conversely, that ideas and modes of thought which have not lost their hold even on our own time, are often the artificial, and in some sort accidental product of laws and institutions which exist no longer, and of which no one would now approve the revival.

It is not in this manner, except incidentally and occasionally, that Mr. Austin's treatise contributes to the improvement of law; though there is a place allotted to such speculations in his comprehensive conception of the study of jurisprudence. He does not specially contemplate legal systems in reference to their origin, and to the psychological causes of their existence. He considers them in respect of what may be called their organic structure. Every body of law has certain points of agreement with every other; and between those which have prevailed in cultivated and civilized societies, there is a still greater number of features in common. Independently of the resemblances which naturally exist in their substantive provisions (designed as these are for the same world, and for the same human nature), there is also a certain common groundwork of general conceptions or notions, each in itself very wide, and some of them very complex, which can be traced through every body of law, and are the same in all. These conceptions are not pre-existent; they are a result of abstraction, and emerge as soon as the attempt is made to look at any body of laws as a whole, or to compare one part of it with another, or to regard persons, and the facts of life, from a legal point of view. There are certain combinations of facts and of ideas which every system of law must recognise, and certain modes of regarding facts which every such system requires. The proof is, that all legal systems require a variety of names, which are not in use for any other purpose. Whoever has apprehended the full meaning of these names—that is, whoever perfectly understands the facts and the combinations of thoughts which ᶜthe namesᶜ denote—is a master of juristical knowledge; and a well-made lexicon of the legal terms of all systems would be a complete science of jurisprudence: for the objects, whether natural or artificial, with which law has to do, must be the same objects which it also has occasion to name.

ᶜ⁻ᶜ63[1,2]   they

But to conceive distinctly a great mass of objects, partly resembling and partly differing from one another, they must be classed; and to make any set of practical provisions, which cover a large field, definite and intelligible, they must be presented to the mind on some principle of arrangement, grounded on the degree of their connexion and alliance with one another. The details of different legal systems are different, but there is no reason why the main classifications and heads of arrangement should not be in a great measure the same. The facts of which law takes cognisance, though far from being identical in all civilised societies, are sufficiently analogous to enable them to be arranged in the same *cadres*. The more general of the terms employed for legal purposes might stand for the same ideas, and be expounded by the same definitions, in systems otherwise different. The same terminology, nomenclature, and principle of arrangement, which would render one system of law definite, clear, and (in Bentham's language) cognoscible,[*] would serve, with additions and variations in minor details, to render the same office for another.

Such a result, however, has not been attained by the mode in which existing bodies of law have been formed. Laws having in general been made singly, and their mass having grown by mere aggregation, there has usually been no authoritative arrangement but the chronological one, and no uniform or predetermined phraseology, even in the case of statute law; while in many countries, and pre-eminently in England, the greater portion of the law, the part which serves as the basis for all the rest, does not exist at all in the form of general language, but lies imbedded in judicial decisions; of which even the general principle has to be evolved by abstraction, and made the subject of forensic disputation, when the time comes for applying it. Whatever definiteness in detail, and whatever order or consistency as a whole, has been attained by any established system, has in almost all countries been given by private writers on law. All the generalizations of legal ideas, and all explicit statements of the meaning of the principal legal terms, have, speaking generally, been the work of these unauthorized persons—have passed from their writings into professional usage, and have ended by being, either expressly, or oftener by implication, adopted by governments and legislatures. So far as any great body of law has been systematized, this is the mode in which the work has been done; and being done piecemeal, by persons often ill-prepared for the task, and who had seldom any other object in view than the convenience of professional practice, it has been, as a general rule, done very ill. Instead of classing objects together which agree in their main features, or in the points which are of chief importance to the ends of law, the classes formed consist of things which have either no common qualities, or none but such as are common to them with other things. When the bond of connexion is real, it seldom lies in the things

[*Jeremy Bentham, *Papers Relative to Codification and Public Instruction* (1817), in *Works*, ed. John Bowring, 11 vols. (Edinburgh: Tait; London: Simpkin, Marshall; Dublin: Cumming, 1843), Vol. IV, p. 454.]

themselves, but usually in the historical accidents of the particular body of laws. In actual systems of law "most of the leading terms" (it is truly said by Mr. Austin) "are not names of a definite class of objects, but of a heap of heterogeneous objects."*

The only mode of correcting this evil, is to free from confusion and set in a clear light those necessary resemblances and differences, which, if not brought into distinct apprehension by all systems of law, are latent in all, and do not depend on the accidental history of any. These resemblances and differences, while they are the key to all others, are evidently those which, in a scientific point of view, are alone worth understanding in themselves. They are also those which are alone fit to be made use of as the groundwork of a scientific arrangement. The fact that they exist in all legal systems, proves that they go deeper down into the roots of law than any of those which are peculiar to some one system. That the main divisions of the subject should be grounded on these, follows from the first principle of classification, that the general should take precedence of the special: and as they are common to all systems, or to all which are of any scientific importance, the parts of any given system which are peculiar to it will still find, in this arrangement, a proper place in which to lodge themselves; which would not happen if the main arrangement were itself grounded on distinctions purely historical, and belonging only to a particular system.

To clear up these general notions is, therefore, the direct object of the science of jurisprudence, as conceived by Mr. Austin. And the practical result of the science, if carried to the greatest perfection of which it is susceptible, would be to provide, first, such a legal terminology (with a strict and precise meaning attached to every word and phrase) that any system whatever of law might be expressed in it; and next, such a general scheme of arrangement, that any system whatever of law might be distributed according to it; and that when so expressed and distributed, every part of it would be distinctly intelligible, and each part would assist the comprehension of all the rest. Jurisprudence, thus understood, is not so much a science of law, as of the application of logic to law. But by affording a clear and connected view of the whole field of law—illuminating it by large, comprehensive, and exactly discriminated conceptions—and enabling every legal ^{d}fact^d to be classed at once with those with which it has the nearest alliance, it bestows on the student either of the philosophy of law, or of any existing legal system, a command over the subject such as no other course of study would have made attainable.

In the attempt to investigate, and bring out into scientific clearness, the conceptions and distinctions of general jurisprudence, Mr. Austin has built chiefly on the foundation of the Roman law. This has been a cause of disappointment to some earnest students, who expected, and would have preferred, something more

---

*Province of Jurisprudence [Lectures, Vol. I], p. 14.

$^{d\text{-}d}$63   part [corrected by JSM in SC copy of 63²]

decidedly original. The course, however, which Mr. Austin deliberately adopted, admits, we conceive, of full justification. If the conceptions and distinctions which he sought belong to law in general, they must exist in all bodies of law, either explicitly or latently, and might, in strictness, be evolved from any. By stripping off what belongs to the accidental or historical peculiarities of the given system, the elements which are universal will be more surely and completely arrived at, than by any process of construction *à priori*; and with the additional advantage of a knowledge not confined to generals, but including under each generalization a large acquaintance with the concrete particulars contained in it. If this be so, the legal system which has been moulded into the shape it possesses by the greatest number of exact and logical minds, will necessarily be the best adapted for the purpose; for, though the elements sought exist in all systems, this is the one in which the greatest number of them are likely to have been brought out into distinct expression, and the fewest to remain latent. And this superiority is possessed, beyond question, by the Roman law. The eminent systematizing genius of the Roman jurists, and not any over-estimate of the Roman law considered in itself, determined Mr. Austin to make it the basis of his own investigations; as is evident from many passages, and from the following especially:

Much has been talked of the philosophy of the Roman Institutional writers. Of familiarity with Grecian philosophy there are few traces in their writings, and the little that they have borrowed from that source is the veriest foolishness: for example, their account of *Jus Naturale*, in which they confound Law with animal instincts—Law, with all those wants and necessities of mankind which are causes of its institutions.

Nor is the Roman law to be resorted to as a magazine of legislative wisdom. The great Roman Lawyers are, in truth, expositors of a positive or technical system. Not Lord Coke himself is more purely technical.[*] Their real merits lie in their thorough mastery of that system; in their command of its principles; in the readiness with which they recall, and the facility and certainty with which they apply them.

In consequence of this mastery of principles, of their perfect consistency (*elegantia*), and of the clearness of the method in which they are arranged, there is no positive system of law which it is so easy to seize as a whole. The smallness of its volume tends to the same end.

The principles themselves, many of them being derived from barbarous ages, are indeed ill fitted to the ends of law, and the conclusions at which they arrive, being logical consequences of their imperfect principles, necessarily partake of the same defect. (*[On the]* Study of Jurisprudence, pp. 17-19.)*

Mr. Austin, therefore, was justified in seeking for the constituent elements of universal jurisprudence where they were certain to be found, and where (from the superior quality of the minds which had been employed on the system) more of

[*Edward Coke, *The First Part of the Institutes of the Lawes of England* (London: Society of Stationers, 1628).]

*In the outline of his Course of Lectures, prefixed to *The Province of Jurisprudence*, Mr. Austin seems to rest the logical superiority of the Roman over the English legal system mainly on the absence of the darkening distinction between real and personal property—a distinction which has no foundation in the philosophy of law, but solely in its history, and

those elements had been explicitly recognised, and adopted into the scientific arrangement of the law itself, than in any other legal system. There remains, it is true, a question belonging to a later stage of the inquiry: did the Roman jurists select as the foundation of their technology and arrangement those among the conceptions and distinctions of law universal which were best fitted for the purpose? Mr. Austin seems to think that they did; since his own arrangement is merely theirs in an improved form. We shall presently give our reasons for thinking that, with great merits, the arrangement of the Roman jurists has great faults; that, in taking as the ground of their entire system the classification of rights, they adopted a principle suited only to what Bentham called the substantive law,[*] and only to the civil branch of that, and, in so doing, reversed the order of filiation of juristical conceptions, and missed the true aim of scientific classification. But this, though a very important, is still a secondary consideration. To find the absolutely best systematic order for a body of law, would be the ultimate result of a complete science of jurisprudence; but its main problem is to give clearness, precision, and consistency to the juristical conceptions themselves. What Mr. Austin has done towards this object, constitutes the great permanent worth of his speculations, considered as substantive results of thought. No one thoroughly versed in these volumes need ever again miss his way amidst the obscurity and confusion of legal language. He will not only have been made sensible of the absence of meaning in many of the phrases and dogmas of writers on law, but will have been put in the way to detect the true meaning, for which those phrases are the empty substitute. He will have seen this done for him in the *Lectures*, with rare completeness, in regard to a great number of the leading ideas of jurisprudence; and will have served an apprenticeship, enabling him with comparative ease to practise the same operation upon the remainder.

---

which he emphatically characterizes as "a cause of complexness, disorder, and darkness, which nothing but the extirpation of the distinction can thoroughly cure." ([*Lectures*, Vol. I,] p. xciv n.) The following passage shows at once his opinion of the English law, considered as a system, and of the reasons for preferring the Roman law to it, as a guide to general jurisprudence:

"I will venture to affirm that no other body of law, obtaining in a civilized community, has so little of consistency and symmetry as our own. Hence its enormous bulk, and (what is infinitely worse than its mere bulk) the utter impossibility of conceiving it with distinctness and precision. If you would know the English law, you must know all the details which make up the mass. For it has none of those large *coherent* principles which are a sure *index* to details; and, since details are infinite, it is manifest that no man (let his industry be what it may) can compass the whole system.

"Consequently, the knowledge of an English lawyer is nothing but a beggarly account of scraps and fragments. His memory may be stored with numerous particulars, but of the law as a whole, and of the mutual relations of its parts, he has not a conception.

"Compare the best of our English Treatises with the writings of the classical jurists, and of the modern civilians, and you will instantly admit that there is no exaggeration in what I have ventured to state." (Vol. II, pp. 153-4.)

[*See, e.g., *Principles of Judicial Procedure* (1839), in *Works*, Vol. II, p. 6.]

The Course of Lectures, which occupies the greatest part of these volumes, was never completed. The first eleven lectures, condensed (or rather enlarged) into six, form the original volume, lately republished. The remainder have never before appeared in print, but left an indelible impression on the minds of those who heard them delivered, among whom were an unusual number of persons since distinguished as among the foremost minds of the time. Though the Lectures do not conclude the subject, yet, with the loose and unfinished but rich and suggestive memoranda which have been very properly subjoined to them, they fill up the greatest part of the outline given in the first volume; so that, when taken in conjunction with that outline, and with the important and elaborate notes appended to the tables which Mr. Austin prepared of the various known arrangements of the field of law, they give something like an adequate idea of the mode in which he would have treated the entire subject. We may add that, notwithstanding the fragmentary nature of the latter part of these volumes, they will be found, on the whole, easier reading (if that epithet can be applied to anything worth reading on such a subject) than the work already so highly prized by those for whom it was intended.[*] This is an effect of that peculiarity of Mr. Austin's mind, which made his first drafts always more fitted for popularity than his finished performances. For, in deliberate scientific exposition, he was so rigid in his demands on himself, so intolerant of anything short of absolute completeness, so impatient while the slightest shadow rested upon any part of the field he surveyed, that he was apt to overlay his work with excess of matter, and, by the elaboration which he bestowed on minor points, weakened the general effect of his elucidation of those which were greater. But this, while it necessarily diminished the popularity of his writings, added to their intrinsic value. Where most men would have permitted themselves to pass lightly over some detail or difficulty, he developed it at full length; but it was because he well knew that unless the point were cleared up, the matter in hand could not be understood thoroughly. Those who pass on their way leaving dark corners unexplored, and concern themselves only with as much of the subject as lies straight before them, often through that neglect miss the very key of the position. Absence of light and shade, and uniformity of distance, bringing all objects alike into the foreground, are fatal defects in describing things for merely artistic purposes; but Mr. Austin's delineations are like geometrical line-drawing, not intended to exhibit objects in their most impressive aspect, but to show exactly what they are. Whether it would have been possible, by greater artifice of composition, to have somewhat relieved the tension of mind required by the length and intricacy of the fifth and sixth chapters of *The Province of Jurisprudence*;[†] whether somewhat more of rhetoric, in the elevated sense in which the word was understood by Aristotle,[‡] might have conciliated an easier reception for their

[*I.e., *The Province of Jurisprudence Determined*.]

[†*Lectures*, Vol. I, pp. 109-67 and 168-327.]

[‡See *The "Art" of Rhetoric* (Greek and English), trans. J.H. Freese (London: Heinemann; New York: Putnam's Sons, 1926), p. 15 (I, 2).]

severe logic—those who have best learnt from experience the extreme difficulty of such a task will be the most backward to decide. But we feel certain that any competent student of the subject who reads those chapters once, will read them repeatedly, and that each reading will raise higher his estimate of their substance, and reconcile him more, if he ever needed reconciliation, with their manner.

In the very summary view which can alone be taken of the contents of the work, a few words must be premised on the introductory portion, although *published many years earlier*; the rather, as it affords an apt exemplification of what we have said concerning the object and character of the entire treatise. The inquiry into the *Province of Jurisprudence* may be correctly characterized as being from one end to the other an analysis and explanation of a word. It is an examination of what is meant by a law, in the political or juristical sense of the term. And yet it is as far from being a merely verbal discussion, as the inquiry into the meaning of justice, which is the foundation of the greatest and most renowned of the writings of Plato.[*] For the meaning of a name must always be sought in the distinctive qualities of the thing named; and these are only to be detected by an accurate study of the thing itself, and of every other thing from which it requires to be distinguished.

A law is a command. A command is an expression of desire, issuing from a superior, and enforced by a sanction, that is, by something of the nature of a punishment. Law, however, does not mean every command, but only commands which oblige *generally*—which oblige to acts or forbearances of a class, not to *an* act or forbearance individually determined. These several notions having been duly analysed and illustrated, various objects are brought to view, which do not possess all the attributes of a law, but which, bearing a certain analogy to laws, require to be distinguished from them. And even within the limits of the strict meaning of the term, the laws which are the subject of jurisprudence require to be distinguished from laws in the same logical sense but of a different species— namely, divine laws, or the laws of God. The region which these different inquiries travel over is large and important, including the following as its principal parts:

First, the laws of God. Of the six lectures, or chapters, composing the volume, three[†] are occupied in the inquiry, by what means the will of God, concerning the rules of conduct to be observed by his rational creatures, is to be ascertained—ascertained, that is, so far as it has not been revealed, or, if revealed, requires ulterior inquiry respecting the sense intended by the revelation. The

---

[*See *Republic* (Greek and English), trans. Paul Shorey, 2 vols. (London: Heinemann; Cambridge, Mass.: Harvard University Press, 1946), esp. Bk. I (Vol. I, pp. 2-107).]

[†*Lectures*, Vol. I, pp. 1-74.]

*-*63[1,2]   reviewed only two years ago in our own pages

author discusses at considerable length the two rival theories on this subject, that of utility, and that of the moral sense; of the former of which he is an earnest supporter, and has given a most able and instructive defence.[*] His treatment is sometimes such as might suggest the idea that he regarded the binding force of the morals of utility as depending altogether upon the express or implied commands of God. This, however, is a mere appearance, arising from the particular point of view to which he was limited by the nature of his subject. What is called the moral law, was only related to the Law of which Mr. Austin was treating, in so far as it might be considered to possess the distinctive character of laws proper, that of being the command of a superior. If he could have been suspected of encouraging a mere worship of power, by representing the distinction of right and wrong as constituted by the Divine will, instead of merely recognised and sanctioned by it, the supposition would have been conclusively rebutted by a passage at page 116n: "If the laws set by the Deity were not generally useful, or if they did not promote the general happiness of his creatures, or if their great Author were not wise and benevolent, they would not be good, or worthy of praise, but were devilish and worthy of execration."

The laws with which jurisprudence is conversant, having been distinguished from divine laws, have next to be discriminated from what are called laws only by way of analogy—rules prescribed and sanctioned only by opinion: to which Mr. Austin, by a happy extension of the term Positive as applied to law, gives the name of Positive Morality,[†] meaning the moral opinions and sentiments actually prevailing in any given society, as distinguished from Deontology, or morality as it ought to be. Of this character is much that is commonly (to the great confusion of the minds of students) called by the name of Law. What is termed Constitutional Law is, in part, only maxims of morality, considered proper to be observed towards one another by the component members of the sovereign body. But the strongest case is that of International Law, which, as independent nations are not subject to any common political superior, ought not to be termed Law, but Positive International Morality. It is law only in as far as effect is given to its maxims by the tribunals of any particular country; and in that capacity it is not international law, but a part of the particular law of that country.

Lastly, laws properly so called have to be distinguished from laws which are such only in a metaphorical sense—the laws of nature as the expression is understood by physical inquirers, meaning the uniformities of co-existence or succession in the phenomena of the universe. That an ambiguity like this should ever have misled any one—that what are laws only by a metaphor, should be supposed to be laws in the same sense as those which are really the commands of a superior—would hardly *à priori* have appeared probable; yet this confusion is

[*Ibid., pp. 75-108.]
[†Ibid., pp. xxxix, 112n-16n.]

total in the majority of modern writers; among whom Mr. Austin mentions Hooker, Blackstone, and Montesquieu in his celebrated first chapter, which is even now regarded by most French thinkers as profound philosophy.[*] In our own country we are frequently warned by a certain class of writers against disobeying or violating the physical laws of organic life; as if it were not the very meaning of a physical law, that it may be unknown or disregarded, but cannot possibly be violated.

These distinctions, with the many important considerations into which they branch out, bring us to the end of the fifth chapter. The sixth is employed in giving precision to the remainder of the conceptions involved in a law in the positive sense (a law emanating from a sovereign or political superior), by clearing up the meaning of sovereignty, and independent political society: involving incidentally the whole subject of constitutional organization, and the division of the sovereignty among several members; also that of subordinate governments, of federations, and all the various relations in which one political society can stand to another.

In the Lectures newly published, the first subject treated is the most general of all those which come within the scope of jurisprudence—the nature and meaning of Rights (understanding thereby legal rights), and of legal Duties or Obligations. In order to treat of this subject, it was necessary to define certain notions, which are involved in all cases of rights and duties—the notions of person, thing, act, and forbearance. These, accordingly, are the first matters with which the author deals; and he criticizes various cases of confusion of thought or misuse of language on these subjects, in the writings of jurists.

All rights, as he observes, are rights to acts or forbearances, either on the part of persons generally, or of particular persons. When we talk of our right to a thing, we mean, if the thing is in our possession, a right to the forbearance of all persons from taking it, or disturbing us in its enjoyment. If it is in the possession of some other person, we mean a right to an act or forbearance of that person—the act of delivering it to us, or forbearance on his part from detaining it. It is by commanding these acts and forbearances that the law confers the right; and the right, therefore, is essentially and directly a right to them, and only indirectly to the thing itself.

Right is correlative with legal duty or obligation. But though every right supposes a correlative obligation—though the obligation properly constitutes the right—every obligation does not create a right correlative to it. There are duties or

[*Ibid., pp. 163-4, with reference to Richard Hooker, Of the Lawes of Ecclesiastical Polity, 2 vols. (London: Windet, [1593]-97), Vol. I, Bk. I, "Concerning Lawes, and Their Severall Kindes in Generall," esp. pp. 51-5, 91-6; William Blackstone, Commentaries on the Laws of England, 4 vols. (Oxford: Clarendon Press, 1765-69), Vol. I, pp. 38-62; and Charles Louis de Secondat, baron de la Brède et de Montesquieu, De l'esprit des loix, 2 vols. (Geneva: Barrillot, 1748), Vol. I, p. 163.]

obligations which are not relative, but (as the phrase is) absolute. The act commanded is not to be done, or the forbearance observed, towards or in respect to a determinate person; or, if any, not a person distinct from the agent himself. Such absolute duties comprise, first, what are called duties towards oneself. The law may forbid suicide or drunkenness; but it would not be said, by so doing, to give me a right to my life or health as against myself. Secondly, duties towards persons indefinitely, or towards the sovereign or state; such as the political duties of a citizen, which do not correspond to any right vested in determinate individuals. Lastly, duties which do not regard persons—the duty, for instance, of abstaining from cruelty to the lower animals; and religious duties as such, if the law, most improperly, thinks fit to enforce them.

From a comparison between duties which correspond to rights, and duties which have no corresponding rights, and also from a brief review of the different kinds of rights, Mr. Austin endeavours to collect a general definition of a legal right. He rejects the definitions usually given, as not applicable to all cases. He is of opinion that rights have very few properties in common, and that "all that can be affirmed of rights, considered universally, amounts to a brief and barren generality."* The only definition of a right which he finds himself able to give, is, that whenever a legal duty is to be performed *towards* or *in respect of* some determinate person, that person is invested with a right.[*] The idea of a legal right involves, in his opinion, nothing more.

This is one of the points (extremely few, considering the extent and intricacy of the subject) on which we cannot help thinking that Mr. Austin's analysis falls short of perfect exhaustiveness.

Mr. Austin always recognises, as entitled to great consideration, the custom of language—the associations which mankind already have with terms: insomuch that, when a name already stands for a particular notion (provided that, when brought out into distinct consciousness, the notion is not found to be self-contradictory), the definition should rather aim at fixing that notion, and rendering it determinate, than attempt to substitute another notion for it. A definition of right, so wide and general as that of Mr. Austin, does not, as it appears to us, stand this test. It does not satisfy the conception which is in everyone's mind, of the meaning of the word right. Almost every one will feel that there is, somehow, an element left out; an element which is approximately, though perhaps imperfectly, expressed by saying, that the person who has the right, is the person who is meant to be benefited by the imposition of the duty.

In the Lectures as delivered (which included much extemporaneous matter, not preserved in the publication) Mr. Austin anticipated this obvious objection, and combated it. The notion of a right as having necessarily for its purpose the benefit

*Vol. II (first of the new volumes), p. 56.
[*Ibid., pp. 32-4.]

of the person invested with it, is contradicted, he said, by the case of *fiduciary* rights. To these he might have added (and probably did add) the rights of public functionaries—the judge, for instance, or the policeman; which are not created for the benefit of the judge or policeman themselves. These examples are conclusive against the terms of the particular definition contended against; but it will appear, from two considerations, that they do not fully dispose of the subject.

In the first place, Mr. Austin's own definition is amenable to a similar, though contrary, criticism. If the definition which he rejected does not comprise all rights, his own comprises more than rights. It includes cases of obligation to which he himself must have admitted that there were no rights corresponding. For example, the legal duties of jailers. It is a jailer's duty to feed the prisoners in his custody, and to this duty corresponds a correlative right in the prisoners. But it is also his legal duty to keep them in confinement, perhaps in bodily fetters. This case is strictly of the kind contemplated in Mr. Austin's definition of a right; there is a duty to be performed, towards, or in respect to, a determinate person or persons; but would it be said that a corresponding right resided in those persons, or, in other words, that they had a right to be imprisoned, and that their right would be violated by setting them at liberty? Again, it is the duty of the hangman to inflict capital punishment upon all persons lawfully delivered to him for that purpose; but would the culprit himself be spoken of as having a right to be hanged? Certainly not. And the reason is one which Mr. Austin fully recognises. He says, in one place, that "a right in a condition which is purely burthensome is hardly conceivable;"* and, in another, that "a right to a burthen, or to vindicate the enjoyment of a burthen," is "an absurdity."† He also, with writers in general, speaks of many obligations as existing for the sake of the correlative rights.‡ If this is a correct expression, there is more in the idea of a right, than an obligation towards or in respect to a given person; since an obligation cannot exist merely in order that there may be a person towards or in respect to whom it exists.

The truth is, that it is not customary to speak of a person as having a right to anything which is not, in the contemplation of the legislator, a desirable thing; and it is always assumed that the person possessing the right is the person specially interested in enforcing the duty which corresponds to it. Mr. Austin, no less than others, makes this supposition, when, in the common language of jurists, he says, that when a duty is violated, the person who has the right is *wronged* or *injured* by the violation.[*] This desirableness of the right, and this especial vocation on the part of the possessor to defend it, do not necessarily suppose that the right is established for his particular advantage. But it must either be given to him for that reason, or because it is needful for the performance of his own legal duties. It is

Ibid., p. 52.
†*Ibid.*, p. 395.
‡*Ibid.*, p. 423.
[*Ibid.*, p. 231.]

consistent with the meaning of words to call that desirable to us, which is required for the fulfilment of our duties. The alternative covers the case of fiduciary rights, the rights of magistrates, and we think every case in which a person can, consistently with custom and with the ends of language, be said to have a right. And, including all such cases, and no others, it seems to supply what is wanting to Mr. Austin's definition. We submit it therefore to the consideration of his readers.

The analysis of right and duty is not complete without an analysis of wrong or injury—the violation of a duty or of a right. And in order to clear up all that is included in the notion of wrong or injury, it is necessary "to settle the meaning of the following perplexing terms—viz. will, motive, intention, and negligence; including in the term negligence those *modes* of the corresponding complex notion which are styled temerity or rashness, imprudence or heedlessness."* These topics comprise the whole theory of the grounds of imputation; in other words, the *generalia* of criminal or penal law. How much bad law, and bad philosophy of law, have arisen from imperfect comprehension of them, may be seen in the nonsense of English law writers concerning malice. The full elucidation of them by our author occupies a considerable space,[*] and our limits are inconsistent with even the briefest abstract of it. Mr. Austin's special vocation for "untying knots," which would have fitted him as well for the problems of inductive psychology as for those of jurisprudence, is nowhere called into more successful exercise. Without a single metaphysical subtlety, there cannot be a more happy example than he here affords of metaphysical analysis.

With the idea of wrong, that of sanction is inseparably bound up; and after settling the meaning of sanction in its largest sense, Mr. Austin examines the two kinds into which sanctions are divided—namely, civil and criminal;[†] or, as they are sometimes called, private and public. Whoever has even the most superficial acquaintance with the writings of criminalists, knows what a mass of vague and confusing speculation this distinction has given birth to; though, as pointed out by Mr. Austin,[‡] the real difference between civil injuries and crimes consists only in this, that in wrongs of the former class the sanction is enforced at the instance and discretion of the injured party, who has the power of remitting the liability incurred by the wrongdoer; while, when the offence is called a crime (which only means that the procedure is of the kind called criminal), the sanction is enforced at the discretion of the sovereign or state, by whom alone the liability of the wrongdoer can be remitted. This case is an instance of the mode in which a confused apprehension of juristical ideas, in themselves not at all difficult of

*Ibid., p. 79.
[*Ibid., Vol. III, pp. 326-32.]
[†Ibid., Vol. II, p. 189.]
[‡Ibid., pp. 190-1.]

comprehension, reacts mischievously on practical legislation. The unhappy idea of classifying wrongs according to a difference which exists only in the modes appointed for redressing them, has raised up a notion in English lawyers that there is a distinction between civil injuries and crimes considered *per se*, which makes damages the proper remedy for the one, and punishment for the other. And hence that serious defect in English law, by which punishment *eo nomine*, and damages to the injured party, cannot both be awarded in the same cause; while in France, on the contrary, the sufferers by the crime can always be admitted as *parties civiles*, and compensation to them is habitually a part of the sentence. In England, whenever the wrong is of so grave a character as to require punishment over and above the obligation of making amends, the injured party loses the indemnity which he would have been able to exact for a less heinous injury; and the penalty on the criminal is deprived of one of its uses, that of being instrumental to the redress of the particular evil which the crime has inflicted upon an individual.

With the twenty-eighth Lecture[*] Mr. Austin commences a new subject—Law considered with reference to its sources, and to the modes in which it begins and ends; involving the distinction between written and what is called unwritten law; the theory of customary law; the meaning of what is called equity; and the false metaphysical distinction drawn by the Roman lawyers and by nearly all modern jurists, between law natural and positive. These theoretical considerations involve, among other important consequences, the highly practical question of codification, or the reduction of the laws of any country into a compact body, expressed in fixed words, and conforming to a systematic arrangement. Whether we regard the importance of these subjects, or the mass of illogical, unphiloso-phical, and practically misleading speculation in which they have been enveloped, there is no part of the field of jurisprudence on which the value of precise and logical thought is more conspicuous. Mr. Austin was eminently fitted to supply it, both by the general quality of his intellect, and by that accurate special knowledge of the history of institutions and of juristical ideas, which he had in common with Mr. Maine; of whose masterly treatise also a great part of the value has reference to this cluster of subjects.

Even such apparently simple phrases as "written" and "unwritten" law, have their full share of the ambiguity which infects nearly the whole vocabulary of legal science. They are employed to express no less than three different distinctions. "Written law" is used, first, in its literal sense, to denote law which is put into writing at the time of its origin, as distinguished from "law originating in custom, or floating traditionally amongst lawyers."[†] But this last so-called law is not

[*Ibid., pp. 195-212.]
[†Ibid., p. 195.]

really law until re-enacted by the legislature, or enforced judicially by the tribunals.

Secondly, written law, in what is called its juridical sense, means law made directly by the sovereign legislature, as distinguished from that which is made by subordinate legislatures, or by judicial tribunals. In this sense of the term, laws made by provincial or colonial legislatures are unwritten laws, as were also the edicts of the Roman praetors. But the laws made by the Roman emperors, not as legislators by their imperial constitutions, but as supreme judges by their rescripts, would be styled written law, because made directly by the sovereign.

Thirdly (and this is the most important distinction), written law is synonymous with statute law, or law made (whether by supreme or subordinate authorities) in the way of direct legislation. Unwritten law is judiciary law, or law made indirectly, in the way of judicial decision, either by the sovereign in a judicial capacity, or by a subordinate judge. The terms statutory law and judiciary law, being unambiguous, should be exclusively employed where this really fundamental distinction is to be expressed.

Mr. Austin next deals with the strange notion which has prevailed among the Roman and the majority of modern jurists, that customary law exists as law merely by being custom; that it is law not by the will of the legislature, but by the spontaneous act of those who practise it.[*] He exposes the absurdities involved in this notion, and shows that custom in itself belongs not to law, but at most to positive morality, binding only by moral sanctions—by the penalties of opinion. What was originally custom may become law, when either the legislature (supreme or subordinate) enacts a statute in conformity to the custom, or the tribunals recognise it, and enforce it by legal sanctions. In both these ways, custom, in all countries, is continually passing into law. But it has force as law solely by the authority of the sovereign legislator, who either shapes his direct commands in accordance with the custom, or lends his sanctions to the tribunals, which, in the discretion allowed them, annex those sanctions to the particular practice, and render obligatory what before was only voluntary.

The notion of writers on law, "that there are positive laws which exist as positive laws independently of a sovereign authority,"[†] is not limited to customary laws. It extends to the laws which, in the Roman system avowedly, and in all others really, are modelled on the opinions and practices of private lawyers. The *Responsa Prudentum*, and the treatises of institutional writers, gave birth to the whole body of law contained in the Pandects;[‡] and in England "much of the law

[*Ibid., pp. 222-4.]
[†Ibid., p. 221.]
[‡See Johann Gottlieb Heineccius, *Elementa juris civilis, secundum ordinem pandectarum* (1727), 6th ed. (1747), in *Operum ad universam juris prudentiam*, 8 vols. (Geneva: Cramer Heirs and Philibert Bros., 1744-49), Vol. V, pp. 1-812.]

of real property is notoriously taken from opinions and practices which have grown up, and are daily growing up, amongst conveyancers."[*] The English tribunals (by what, when first employed, was an entirely indispensable artifice) keep up what Mr. Austin, with reference to present circumstances, justly calls the "puerile fiction,"[†] that these opinions and practices are mere *evidence* of law already established by custom. But they well know, and every lawyer knows, that the law thus introduced is really new, and, in the case which creates the first precedent, is even *ex post facto*; though not generally liable to the condemnation implied in that term, being commonly shaped for the purpose of fulfilling, not frustrating, the expectations presumed to have been entertained by the parties concerned.

The fact that there is law which the legislature has never expressly announced, but which is, with its tacit consent, made by tribunals which are not regularly authorized to enact law, but only to declare it, has thrown a vagueness over the whole idea of law, which has contributed greatly to obscure the distinction between it and positive morality. The error, that law exists as such independently of legal sanctions, appears in an aggravated shape in the notion that there exists a natural law—a law known by the light of nature, which does not emanate from legislators, but is nevertheless binding on tribunals, and may and ought to be by them enforced by reason of its natural obligation only. This *Jus Naturale* has, as Mr. Austin observes, "thoroughly perplexed and obscured the sciences of jurisprudence and ethics."* As the notion admits only of an historical explanation, Mr. Austin deals with it substantially in the same manner as Mr. Maine.

He expounds the origin of the *Jus Gentium* of the early Roman lawyers;[‡] a different thing not only from international law, to which the term has been perversely transferred by modern jurists, but also from the Natural Law of modern writers on jurisprudence, though of this last it is the real progenitor. The *jus gentium* took its rise from the necessity in which the Romans found themselves, through the growth of their dominion, of administering justice to persons who were not Romans—to whom the laws provided for Roman citizens were not applicable, and who, belonging to different nations and communities, had originally different laws. Provincials of the same province retained, as between themselves, their old laws; but between a provincial and a Roman citizen, or between provincials of one province and those of another, it was neither convenient, nor would in most cases have been just, to decide disputes by a law which was not the law of both parties. The praetors, whose decision in such cases was probably at first arbitrary, were able to find many legal principles and provisions which were not peculiar to either people (as so much of the early Roman law was peculiar to the Romans) but were common to the laws of all or of many

[*Austin, *Lectures*, Vol. II, p. 235.]
[†*Ibid.*, p. 236.]
Ibid., p. 241.
[‡*Ibid.*, pp. 241-3.]

different communities. These principles and provisions there seemed no hardship in applying to cases between persons of what would now be called different nationalities. And where these did not furnish a rule exactly applicable to the case, the praetors were led to supply the deficiency by rules either derived from them by analogy, or suggested by a sense of substantial justice or expediency. In this manner arose the idea of a body of law not peculiar to one, but common to all nations, on which the praetors were supposed, and supposed themselves, to have fashioned the body of positive law which grew up under their hands. This law, being abstracted from the peculiarities both of the *Jus Quiritium* and of all other local and special bodies of law or custom, was, as might naturally be expected, of a more liberal character. It was less charged with technical and circuitous modes of proceeding, invented to evade conflict with local or accidental prejudice. It was less infected by the freaks of fancy which, as Mr. Austin observes, are "omnipotent with barbarians,"[*] but in which one barbarous people is not likely to agree with another. It might be said, by comparison, to represent that portion of all systems, which arose from the wants and feelings of human nature generally. Being, for this reason, as well as from its originating in a more civilized period, far preferable to the old Roman law, it became the model on which the praetors, by their edicts, gradually modified the old law itself; and finally (though not till after many centuries), almost entirely substituted itself for the original Roman law. The provisions of the more liberal *jus gentium*, applied by the praetors as modifying principles to the old law, obtained the name of *Aequitas*, or equity; an appellation which became extended to the somewhat similar process by which the Court of Chancery for ages employed itself in supplying the omissions and mitigating the barbarities of the feudal laws of England. The explanation and elucidation of this one word Equity, in the many senses in which it is used by jurists, forms the subject of several of Mr. Austin's lectures.[†] Both historically and philosophically, they are among the most interesting parts of the Course: though much of the matter they contain, when once stated, appears so obvious, that one is apt to forget how often and by what esteemed authorities it has been misunderstood.*

Now it was this Roman idea of a *jus gentium*, or portion of law common to all nations, which grew insensibly into the modern idea of Natural Law. "The *Jus Naturale*, or law of nature," as Mr. Maine observes, "is simply the *jus gentium*

[*Ibid., Vol. I, p. 58.]

[†In Lectures 31, 34, and 36; Vol. II, pp. 250, 282-9, and 312-15.]

*"I could point," says Mr. Austin, "at books and speeches, by living lawyers of name, wherein the nature of the Equity administered by the Chancellor, or the nature of the jurisdiction (styled extraordinary) which the Chancellor exercises, is thoroughly misunderstood:—wherein the anomalous distinction between Law and Equity is supposed to rest upon principles necessary or universal; or (what is scarcely credible) wherein the functions of the Chancellor, as exercising his extraordinary jurisdiction, are compared to the *arbitrium boni viri*, or to the functions of an *arbiter* released from the observance of rules." (*Ibid.*, pp. 273-4.)

seen in the light of a peculiar theory."* That theory, as both he and Mr. Austin remark, was derived from the precept "Live according to Nature" of the Greek philosophical schools.[*]

After Nature had become a household word in the mouths of the Romans, the belief gradually prevailed among the Roman lawyers that the old *jus gentium* was in fact the lost code of Nature, and that the praetor, in framing an Edictal Jurisprudence on the principles of the *jus gentium*, was gradually restoring a type from which law had only departed to deteriorate.[†]

Being observed or recognised universally, these principles were supposed to have a higher origin than human design, and to be (we quote Mr. Austin) "not so properly rules of human position or establishment, as rules proceeding immediately from the Deity himself, or the intelligent and rational Nature which animates and directs the universe."[‡] This notion, once formed, was, by an obvious process, so enlarged as to include merely moral or merely customary rules which had obtained general acceptance; "every rule, in short, which is common to *all* societies, though the rule may not obtain as positive law in all political communities, or in any political community."[§] In this manner the Natural Law of modern writers was extended to those international usages, and those rules of international morality, which obtained generally among nations. And by a similar process each writer was led to include in his scheme of Natural Law, whatever maxims of justice or utility approved themselves to him as an individual moralist, provided they appeared to be at once self-evident and universal. The writings which profess to treat of the Law of Nature and Nations are a chaos of all these materials. "In studying these writers," says Mr. Maine, "the great difficulty is always to discover whether they are discussing law or morality—whether the state of international relations they describe is actual or ideal—whether they lay down that which is, or that which in their opinion ought to be."[¶] This arose from the confused apprehension of the very meaning of law, engendered by their notion of a Law of Nature according to which what in their opinion ought to be law, was conceived as being, in some strange manner, law already. By this confusion they have spread a thick fog over the distinctions and demarcations which separate the three different notions, positive law, positive morality, and deontology, or morality as it ought to be.

The influence of the imaginary Law of Nature over modern thought has been

---

Ancient Law, p. 52.
[*Austin, *Lectures*, Vol. II, pp. 249, 254; *Ancient Law*, p. 54. For the precept, see Diogenes Laertius, *Lives of Eminent Philosophers* (Greek and English), trans. R.D. Hicks, 2 vols. (London: Heinemann; New York: Putnam's Sons, 1925), Vol. II, p. 194 (VII, 87).]
†*Ancient Law*, p. 56.
‡*Lectures*, Vol. II, p. 261.
§*Ibid.*, p. 260.
¶*Ancient Law*, p. 97.

all-pervading; on the whole, however, still greater on the Continent than in England. Mr. Maine very truly affirms, that "the theory of natural law is the source of almost all the special ideas as to law, politics, and society, which France during the last hundred years has been the instrument of diffusing over the western world. The part" (he continues) "played by jurists in French history, and the sphere of jural conceptions in French thought, have always been remarkably large;"* and in the latter half of the last century, when other old modes of thought were breaking up, the calamitous influence of Rousseau (calamitous at least in this respect) became powerfully operative in strengthening this particular delusion. Coleridge, in the *Friend*, has maintained, with much force of argument, that the thrusting of immutable principles of morality into the province of law, and assuming them as the only legitimate basis of politics, is the essence of Jacobinism.[*] It is the essence not specially of that, but of a general mode of thought which prevails among French thinkers of all political opinions. As a general rule, French speculation knows no distinction or barrier between the province of morals and that of politics or legislation. While, on the one hand, it tends to impose on morals (for this, however, Catholic thought and the influence of the Canonists are partly responsible) all the formality and literalness of juridical rules; on the other, it invests the creations of pure legal institution—the law of property for example— with the sacredness and indefeasibility of the fundamental doctrines of morals; and cannot bear to discuss such a question, for instance, as copyright, on grounds of general expediency, but insists on clenching it by affirming or denying an assumed absolute right in authors to hold the produce of their brain, by themselves or their representatives, as permanent property to the end of time.

The influence, for good and for evil, of the theory of a Law of Nature, is delineated by Mr. Maine more fully than was compatible with Mr. Austin's more extensive design. There is no doubt that for a long period the good side of the influence predominated. It assisted mankind in disencumbering themselves from a superstititous reverence for the institutions which had historically grown up in their several countries. It accustomed them to test particular laws by general principles of some sort, and gave them a type of excellence of which simplicity and symmetry were among the supposed characteristics. Finally, it disregarded all distinctions between man and man, between citizen and foreigner, noble and burgess, burgess and peasant; and Mr. Maine is of opinion "that to the assumption of a Law Natural we owe the doctrine of the fundamental equality of human beings."[†] When almost everything which was artificial was oppressive, the reaction in favour of what was supposed to be natural had a healthy tendency; though we now know that the real natural state (if natural means primitive), instead

*Ibid., p. 80.

[*Samuel Taylor Coleridge, *The Friend*, 3 vols. (London: Rest Fenner, 1818), Vol. I, pp. 308-9.]

[†Ancient Law, p. 92.]

of being the reign of justice and freedom, is a condition of more universal tyranny than any form whatever of civilized life. But whatever power of liberalizing men's minds may once have belonged to the doctrine of Natural Law, that power is now exhausted; the doctrine has done all it can do in that direction, and its remaining influence serves only to make men greater bigots, not indeed to the peculiar vices of any given system, but to whatever vices have existed from the beginning in them all. Meanwhile, the theory of law must be a mass of contradiction as long as the imaginary Natural Law retains any authority in it; for as every actual system of law has been shaped out by conflicting instincts, a theory generalized from what they have in common is necessarily full of conflicting principles, and affords, on both sides of every controverted point, arguments which, if the theory be granted, are all equally unanswerable.

In the thirty-seventh Lecture[*] Mr. Austin commences discussing the differences which distinguish statute from judiciary law; the advantages and disadvantages of judicial legislation, and the possibility and desirableness of excluding it for the future, and converting all judiciary law into statute—in other words, codification. From this excellent discussion we shall permit ourselves, in consideration of its great practical moment, to give a longer quotation than we have ventured to make from any other portion of the Course. It is taken from the place in which, after remarking on some disadvantages erroneously attributed to judiciary law, Mr. Austin points out the evils which are really inherent in it.

First: A judiciary law (or a rule of judiciary law) exists nowhere in fixed or determinate expressions. It lies *in concreto*: or it is implicated with the peculiarities of the particular case or cases, by the decision or decisions whereon, the law or rule was established. Before we can arrive at the rule, we must abstract the *ratio decidendi* (which really constitutes the rule) from all that is peculiar to the case through which the rule was introduced, or to the resolution of which the rule was originally applied. And in trying to arrive at the rule by this process of abstraction and induction, we must not confine our attention to the general positions or expressions which the judicial legislator actually employed. We must look at the whole case which it was his business to decide, and to the whole of the discourse by which he signified his decision. And from the whole of his discourse, combined with the whole of the case, we must extract that *ratio decidendi*, or that general principle or ground, which truly constitutes the law that the particular decision established.

But the process of abstraction and induction to which I now have alluded, is not uncommonly a delicate and difficult process; its difficulty being proportioned to the number and the intricacy of the cases from which the rule that is sought must be abstracted and induced. Consequently, a rule of judiciary law is less accessible and knowable than a statute law. . . . And it must be recollected, that whether it be performed by judges applying the rule to subsequent cases, or by private persons in the course of extra-judicial business, this delicate and difficult process is commonly performed in haste. Insomuch that judges in the exercise of their judicial functions, and private persons in their extra-judicial transactions, must often mistake the import of the rule which they are trying to ascertain and apply.

[*Vol. II, pp. 321-47. The discussion continues through Lectures 38 and 39, from the latter of which Mill takes the long extract below.]

And this naturally conducts me to a *second* objection: namely, that judiciary law (generally speaking) is not only applied in haste, but is also *made* in haste. It is made (generally speaking) in the hurry of judicial business, and not with the mature deliberation which legislation requires, and with which statute law is or might be constructed. . . .

There is more of stability and coherency in judiciary law than might, at the first blush, be imagined. But though it be never so stable and never so coherent, every system of judiciary law has all the evils of a system which is really vague and inconsistent. This arises mainly from two causes: the enormous bulk of the documents in which the law must be sought, and the difficulty of extracting the law (supposing the decisions known) from the particular decided cases in which it lies imbedded.

By consequence, a system of judiciary law (as every candid man will readily admit) is nearly unknown to the bulk of the community, although they are bound to adjust their conduct to the rules or principles of which it consists. Nay, it is known imperfectly to the mass of lawyers, and even to the most experienced of the legal profession. A man of Lord Eldon's legal learning, and of Lord Eldon's acuteness and comprehension, may know where to find the documents in which the law is preserved, and may be able to extract from the documents the rule for which he is seeking. To a man, therefore, of Lord Eldon's learning, and of Lord Eldon's acuteness, the law might really serve as a guide of conduct. But by the great body of the legal profession (when engaged in advising those who resort to them for counsel), the law (generally speaking) is divined rather than ascertained: And whoever has seen opinions even of celebrated lawyers, must know that they are often worded with a discreet and studied ambiguity, which, whilst it saves the credit of the uncertain and perplexed adviser, thickens the doubts of the party who is seeking instruction and guidance. And as to the bulk of the community—the simple-minded laity (to whom, by reason of their simplicity, the law is so benign)—they might as well be subject to the mere *arbitrium* of the tribunals, as to a system of law made by judicial decisions. A few of its rules or principles are extremely simple, and are also exemplified practically in the ordinary course of affairs: Such, for example, are the rules which relate to certain crimes, and to contracts of frequent occurrence. And of these rules or principles, the bulk of the community have some notion. But those portions of the law which are somewhat complex, and are not daily and hourly exemplified in practice, are by the mass of the community utterly unknown, and are by the mass of the community utterly unknowable. Of those, for example, who marry, or of those who purchase land, not one in a hundred (I will venture to affirm) has a distinct notion of the consequences which the law annexes to the transaction.

Consequently, although judiciary law be really certain and coherent, it has all the mischievous effect (in regard to the bulk of the community) of *ex post facto* legislation. Unable to obtain professional advice, or unable to obtain advice which is sound and safe, men enter into transactions of which they know not the consequences, and then (to their surprise and dismay) find themselves saddled with duties which they never contemplated.

The ordinary course is this:—

A man enters into some transaction (say, for example, a contract) either without advice, or with the advice of an incompetent attorney.

By consequence, he gets into a scrape.

Finding himself in a scrape, he submits a case, through his attorney, to counsel.

And, for the fee to attorney and counsel, he has the exquisite satisfaction of learning with certainty that the mischief is irremediable.

[I am far from thinking, that the law ever can be so condensed and simplified, that any considerable portion of the community may know the whole or much of it.

But I think that it may be so condensed and simplified, that *lawyers* may know it: and that at a moderate expense, the rest of the community may learn from lawyers beforehand the legal effect of transactions in which they are about to engage.

Not to mention (as I shall show, when I come to the *rationale* of the distinction between Law of Things and Law of Persons) that the law may be so arranged, that each of the different classes of persons may know something of the part of it with which they are particularly concerned.

Forms, too, for the more usual transactions might be made out by the legislature.]

The evil upon which I am insisting is certainly not *peculiar* to judiciary law. Statute law badly expressed, and made bit by bit, may be just as bulky and just as inaccessible as law of the opposite kind. But there is this essential difference between the kinds of law. The evil is inherent in judiciary law, although it be as well constructed as judiciary law can be. But statute law (though it often is bulky and obscure) *may be* compact and perspicuous, if constructed with care and skill. . . .

Fifthly: I am not aware that there is any *test* by which the validity of a rule made judicially can be ascertained.

Is it the *number* of decisions in which a rule has been followed, that makes it law binding on future judges? Or is it the *elegantia* of the rule (to borrow the language of the Roman lawyers), or its consistency and harmony with the bulk of the legal system? Or is it the *reputation* of the judge or judges by whom the case or cases introducing the rule was decided? . . .

We never can be absolutely certain (so far as I know) that any judiciary rule is good or valid law, and will certainly be followed by future judges in cases resembling the cases by which it has been introduced.

Here, then, is a cause of uncertainty which seems to be of the essence of *judiciary* law. For I am not aware of any contrivance by which the inconvenience could be obviated. . . .

Sixthly: In consequence of the implication of the *ratio decidendi* with the peculiarities of the decided case, the rule established by the decision (or the *ratio*, or the general principle of the decision) is never or rarely comprehensive. It is almost necessarily confined to such future cases as closely resemble the case actually decided: although other cases more remotely resembling may need the care of the legislator. In other words, the rule is necessarily limited to a narrow *species* or sort, although the *genus* or kind, which includes that *species* or sort, ought to be provided for at the same time by one comprehensive law.

This is excellently explained by Sir Samuel Romilly:

"Not only is the judge, who at the very moment when he is making law, is bound to profess that it is his province only to declare it; not only is he thus confined to technical doctrines and to artificial reasoning—he is further compelled to take the narrowest view possible of every subject on which he legislates. *The law he makes is necessarily restricted to the particular case which gives occasion for its promulgation.* Often when he is providing for that particular case, or according to the fiction of our Constitution, is declaring how the ancient and long-forgotten law has provided for it, he represents to himself other cases which probably may arise, though there is no record of their ever having yet occurred, which will as urgently call for a remedy as that which it is his duty to decide. It would be a prudent part to provide, by one comprehensive rule, as well for these possible events, as for the actual case that is in dispute, and, while terminating the existing litigation, to obviate and prevent all future contests. This, however, is, to the judicial legislator, strictly forbidden; and if, in illustrating the grounds of his judgment, he adverts to other and analogous cases, and presumes to anticipate how they should be decided, he is considered as exceeding his province; and the opinions thus delivered are treated by succeeding judges as extra-judicial, and as entitled to no authority."[*]

[*Samuel Romilly, "Bentham on Codification," *Edinburgh Review*, XXIX (Nov., 1817), 231.]

[Hence, exigencies of society provided for bit by bit, and therefore slowly.

Hence, further, immense volume of the documents in which the law is recorded. For in lieu of one comprehensive rule determining a *genus* of cases, we have many several and narrow rules severally determining the species which that *genus* includes.]

And this inconvenience (for a reason which I have noticed above)[*] is probably of the essence of judiciary law. So delicate and difficult is the task of legislation, that any comprehensive rule, made in haste, and under a pressure of business, would probably be ill adapted to meet the contemplated purpose. It is certain that the most experienced, and the most learned and able of our judges, have commonly abstained the most scrupulously from throwing out general propositions which were not as proximate as possible to the case awaiting solution: though the *ratio decidendi* (or ground or *principle* of decision) is necessarily a general position applying to a class of cases, and does not concern exclusively the particular case in question. . . .

Seventhly: Wherever much of the law is judiciary law, the statute law which coexists with it, is imperfect, unsystematic, and bulky.

For the judiciary law is, as it were, the *nucleus* around which the statute law is formed. The judiciary law contains the *legal dictionary*, or the definitions and expositions (in so far as such exist) of the leading technical terms of the entire legal system. The statute law is not a whole of itself, but is formed or fashioned on the judiciary law, and tacitly refers throughout to those leading terms and principles which are expounded by the judiciary. . . .

Wherever, therefore, much of the law consists of judiciary law, the statute law is not of itself complete, but is merely a partial and irregular supplement to that judiciary law which is the mass and bulk of the system. The statute law is not of itself an edifice, but is merely a set of irregular unsystematic patches stuck from time to time upon the edifice reared by judges. . . .

Wherever, therefore, much of the law consists of judiciary law, the entire legal system, or the entire *corpus juris*, is necessarily a monstrous chaos: partly consisting of judiciary law, introduced bit by bit, and imbedded in a measureless heap of particular judicial decisions, and partly of legislative law stuck by patches on the judiciary law, and imbedded in a measureless heap of occasional and supplemental statutes.*

Since such [continues Mr. Austin] are the monstrous evils of judicial legislation, it would seem that the expediency of a Code, or of a complete or exclusive body of statute law, will hardly admit of a doubt. Nor would it, provided that the chaos of judiciary law and of the statute law stuck patchwise on the judiciary could be superseded by a *good* code. For when we contrast the chaos with a positive code, we must not contrast it with the very best of possible or conceivable codes, but with the code which, under the given circumstances of the given community, would probably be the result of an attempt to codify.[†]

The expediency of codification at a particular time and place depends on the question, "Are there men, then and there, competent to the task of successful codification?"[‡] The difficulty of the work no one feels more strongly, or has stated more emphatically, than Mr. Austin. He considers "the technical part of legislation incomparably more difficult than what may be styled the ethical;" holding it "far easier to conceive justly what would be useful law, than so to

[*Lectures, Vol. II, p. 362; quoted at p. 188 above.]
*Lectures, Vol. II, pp. 359-70. [For an explanation of the square-bracketed passages, which were added by Sarah Austin, see her "Preface," *ibid.*, p. ii.]
[†*Ibid.*, p. 370.]
[‡*Ibid.*, p. 373.]

construct that same law that it may accomplish the design of the law-giver:"* an opinion which, in its full breadth of statement, we should hesitate to endorse. But it will readily be admitted that the two qualifications are different, that the one is no guarantee for the other, and that the talent which is merely instrumental is, in any high degree of perfection, nearly if not quite as rare as that to which it is subordinate.

The expediency, therefore, of codification in England and at the present time, Mr. Austin does not discuss; but he shows "the futility of the leading or principal arguments which are advanced against codification, considered generally or in abstract."[*] Unhappily a great part of the matter which he delivered on this subject is missing from the manuscript. But its place is partly supplied by the abundant notes and memoranda relating to the subject, which have been found among his papers, and of which the "Notes on Codification," appended to the third volume, are but a part.[†] We shall quote only one passage, which belongs to the Lectures, and is reproduced in the pamphlet on the *Study of Jurisprudence*. It is a reply to the common objection that statute law cannot include all cases. Mr. Austin shows that it can at least include all those which are covered by judiciary law.

The current objection to codification is the necessary incompleteness of a code. It is said that the individual cases which may arise in fact or practice are infinite, and that, therefore, they cannot be anticipated, and provided for, by a body of general rules. The objection (as applied to statute law generally) is thus put by Lord Mansfield in the case of Omichund and Barker. (He was then Solicitor-General.) "Cases of Law depend upon occasions which give rise to them. All occasions do not arise at once. A statute very seldom can take in all cases. Therefore the common law that works itself pure by rules drawn from the fountains of justice, is superior to an act of parliament."[‡]

My answer to this objection is, that it is equally applicable to all law; and that it implies in the partisans of judiciary law (who are pleased to insist upon it) a profound ignorance, or a complete forgetfulness, of the nature of the law which is established by judicial decisions.

Judiciary law consists of *rules*, or it is merely a heap of particular decisions inapplicable to the solution of future cases. On the last supposition, it is not law at all: and the judges who apply decided cases to the resolution of other cases, are not resolving the latter by any determinate law, but are deciding them arbitrarily.

The truth, however, is, that the general grounds or principles of judicial decisions are as completely law as statute law itself; though they differ considerably from statutes in the manner and form of expression. And being law, it is clear that they are liable to the very imperfection which is objected to statute law. Be the law statute or judiciary, it cannot anticipate all the cases which may possibly arise in practice.

The objection implies, that all judicial decisions which are not applications of statutes are merely arbitrary. It therefore involves a double mistake. It mistakes the nature of judiciary law, and it confounds law with the *arbitrium* of the judge. Deciding arbitrarily, the judge,

---

*Ibid., p. 371.
[*Ibid., p. 373.]
[†Ibid., Vol. III, pp. 275-98.]
[‡William Murray, Speech for the Plaintiff in the Case of Omychund v. Barker, 1744, in 26 *English Reports* 22-3.]

no doubt, may provide for all possible cases. But whether providing for them thus be providing for them by law, I leave it to the judicious to consider.

If law, as reduced into a code, would be incomplete, so is it incomplete as not so reduced. For codification is the re-expression of existing law. It is true that the code might be incomplete, owing to an oversight of redactors. But this is an objection to codification *in particular*. . . .

Repetition and inconsistency are far more likely, where rules are formed one by one (and, perhaps, without concert, by many distinct tribunals), than where all are made at once by a single individual or body, who are trying to embrace the whole field of law, and so to construct every rule as that it may harmonize with the rest.

And here I would make a remark which the objection in question suggests, and which to my understanding is quite conclusive.

Rules of judiciary law are not decided cases, but the *general* grounds or principles (or the *rationes decidendi*) whereon the cases are decided. Now, by the practical admission of those who apply these grounds or principles, they may be codified, or turned into statute laws. For what is that process of induction by which the principle is gathered before it is applied, but this very process of codifying such principles, performed on a particular occasion, and performed on a small scale? If it be possible to extract from a case, or from a few cases, the *ratio decidendi*, or general principle of decision, it is possible to extract from all decided cases their respective grounds of decisions, and to turn them into a body of law, abstract in its form, and therefore compact and accessible. Assuming that judiciary law is really law, it clearly may be codified.

I admit that no code can be complete or perfect. But it may be less incomplete than judge-made law, and (if well constructed) free from the great defects which I have pointed out in the latter. It may be brief, compact, systematic, and therefore knowable as far as it goes. (Vol. II, pp. 374-7.)

The "Notes on Codification" contain, in substance, all that is required to meet any of the objections against codification generally, or in the abstract;* but their form is too completely that of a mere syllabus, to be acceptable to the general reader. We shall quote, however, as a specimen, and for its practical importance, one excellent passage, containing the author's view of the real difficulties of codification, and the conditions necessary for rendering it advisable.

*The most popular, though one of the most superficial, of the objections, is the supposed failure of existing codes, especially the French and the Prussian. To this Mr. Austin answers, substantially, two things: First, that the failure of the French and Prussian codes has been greatly exaggerated, and that, with all their defects, they are still vastly superior to the state of things which preceded them. Secondly, that in so far as those codes do fall short of what is required in a code, it is owing to defects which are obvious and avoidable, and, above all, because *they are not really codes*; for the Code Napoleon is without a single definition, and the Prussian Code has none that are adequate, so that the meaning of all the law terms had either to be fixed by judiciary law, or ascertained by referring back to the old law which was supposed to have been superseded. Far from being any evidence against a code, those compilations are a most satisfactory proof of the great amount of good which can be done even by the merest digest. [See Austin, *Lectures*, Vol. III, pp. 292-4. For the French and Prussian Codes, see *Code civil des Français* (Paris: Imprimerie de la république, 1804; and *Allgemeines Landrecht für die Preussischen Staaten* (5 Feb., 1794).]

The great difficulty is, the impossibility that any one man should perform the whole. But if done by several, it would be incoherent, unless all were imbued with the same principles, and all versed in the power of applying them. The great difficulty, therefore, is to get a sufficient number of competent men, versed in common studies and modes of reasoning. This being given, codification is practicable and expedient.

Peculiarly technical and partial knowledge of English lawyers. No English lawyer is master even of English law, and has, therefore, no notion of that interdependency of parts of a system, on which its successful codification must depend.

A code must be the work of many minds. The project must be the work of one, and revised by a commission. The general outline, the work of one, might be filled up by divers.

All-importance in codification of the first intention. Till minds are trained, it will scarcely succeed. How the difficulty is to be surmounted. Necessity for men versed in theory, and equally versed in practice; or rather, of a combination of theorists and practitioners. Necessity for preliminary digests; or for waiting till successful jurists and jurisprudence are formed through effectual legal education. (Vol. III, pp. 278-9.)

Having concluded the subject of Law in general, regarded under its different aspects, Mr. Austin proceeds to consider the parts of which a *corpus juris* is necessarily composed, and the mutual relations of those parts.[*] As already observed, he adheres in the main, though with some not unimportant improvements, to the classification and arrangement of the Roman law; or rather of its modern expositors, who have carried out the ideas of the classical jurists with a precision still greater than theirs.

Mr. Austin gives excellent reasons for rejecting their primary division, followed by most modern writers, into public and private law, and shows how the various parts which compose the former of these should be disposed of.* This being set aside, the leading division is into what are termed by the Roman lawyers, Law of Persons and Law of Things—*jus personarum* and *jus rerum*, strangely mistranslated by Hale and Blackstone into *rights* of persons and *rights* of things.[†] The original expressions are extremely ill-chosen, and have been an *ignis fatuus* to law writers, both in ancient and modern times. The Law of Persons (agreeably to one of the meanings of the word *persona*) is the law of *Status* or conditions—of the rights and obligations peculiar to certain *classes* of persons, on whom a peculiar legal stamp has been set. And, in contradistinction, the Law of Things is the law common to all persons, together with the peculiar laws relating to other classes of persons not so specially marked out from the rest. But this has seldom been properly understood by law writers. They have imagined that persons (*personae*), in this acceptation, meant persons in the ordinary sense—human beings; and forgetting that in this sense all law, and all rights and obligations, relate to persons, they supposed that the Law of Persons, as distinguished from that of Things, ought

[*Lectures, Vol. II, p. 381.]

*Lecture 44 [*ibid*., pp. 435-9].

[†See *ibid*., pp. 381-449. The references are to Matthew Hale, *An Analysis of the Law* (London: Walthoe, 1713), p. 1; and Blackstone, *Commentaries*, Vol. I, p. 118.]

to contain all law which deals with those interests of persons which have no (or but slight) reference to things. Hence Blackstone places in the Law of Persons what he calls Absolute Rights, being those which belong to all persons without exception, such as the right to life, to personal security, to reputation—rights which, looked at from the point of view of the Roman lawyers, belong even more pre-eminently than any others to the Law of Things.[*]

Those jurists who have understood the meaning of the Roman lawyers more correctly than Blackstone, have exhausted their ingenuity in search of metaphysical reasons why some peculiarities of legal position have been accounted Status, and included in *jus personarum*, while others, equally marked and equally important, have been retained in the Law of Things. Mr. Austin minutely examines and criticizes these subtleties, and, after a full review of them, decides that the division has no logical or metaphysical basis at all.[†] It rests solely on convenience. Executors, heirs, trustees, proprietors, contractors, &c., are as much classes of persons as parents, guardians, infants, magistrates, and the like; yet they are never accounted status, and the laws which concern them are always included in the Law of Things. No reason can be given why the one group should, and the other should not, be detached from the general body of the law and placed apart, except that the laws relating to the one "have no necessary coherency with the bulk of the legal system," and need not, generally speaking, be taken into consideration in order to understand the law as a whole; while the others "have such a coherency with the bulk of the legal system, that if they were detached from it the requisite continuity in the statement or exposition of it would be lost."*

As much of the law, then, as relates to certain peculiar legal positions, is remanded to a separate branch, which naturally should be placed *after* the general law, or *jus rerum*. The Roman institutional writers, by placing the Law of Persons first, gave one among several proofs that even they had not a perfectly clear conception of the distinction which they had themselves drawn.

In proceeding to subdivide the Law of Things, Mr. Austin adopts from the Roman lawyers their principle of grounding the general division of the *corpus juris* upon a classification of rights. But he selects as his primary division of rights (and of the corresponding duties) a distinction not specially recognised by those writers.

The Roman lawyers primarily divided rights into *jura in rem*, or rights availing against all the world, and *jura in personam*, or rights availing against determinate persons only.[†] Of the former, the right of dominion or property is the most

[*Commentaries, Vol. I, pp. 119ff.; Austin, Lectures, Vol. III, pp. 179-80.]
[†Lectures, Vol. II, pp. 400-18.]
*Ibid., p. 413.
†These phrases were devised by the modern civilians. The classical jurists expressed the same distinction by the ambiguous terms *dominium* (in the largest sense in which that word was employed) and *obligatio*, a name which, in the Roman law, is unfortunately given to rights as well as to obligations. [See Austin, *Lectures*, Vol. II, p. 33; Vol. III, p. 190.]

familiar instance. My right of ownership in a thing, is constituted by a duty or obligation imposed on all persons not to deprive me of the thing, or molest me in its enjoyment. Of rights *in personam*, the most prominent example is a right by virtue of a contract. If B has contracted with A to deliver certain goods, A has a right, answering to the legal obligation on B, but the right is against B alone. Until they are delivered, A has acquired no right to the goods as against other persons. If the goods came into the possession of a third party, through (for example) a wrongful resale by B, A would still have his original right as against B, and might have a right to damages besides, but he could not by process of law recover the goods themselves from the new possessor. A's right, therefore, is not *in rem*, but *in personam*, meaning *in personam determinatam*. The distinction between these two classes of rights belongs to universal jurisprudence, for every system of law must establish rights of both kinds; and the difference between them is connected with practical differences in the legal remedies. Among rights *in rem* must be reckoned the right to life, to reputation, to the free disposal of one's person and faculties, to exemption from bodily harm or indignity, and to any external thing of which one is the legal owner. To these must be added the limited right in a thing owned by some one else, which is called *servitus* or easement, such as a right of way over another person's land.

Rights *in personam*, or availing against a determinate person or persons, are divided by Roman jurists into rights (in their unhappy phraseology *obligationes*) *ex contractu*, and rights (or *obligationes*) *ex delicto*, with two miscellaneous appendages, rights *quasi ex contractu* and *quasi ex delicto*. By quasi-contracts are not to be understood *implied* contracts, differing from express ones only in that the engagement is signified by conduct instead of words. Such tacit engagements are real contracts, and are placed in the law of contract. The term quasi-contract applies to cases in which there has not been, and is known not to have been, any engagement, either express or tacit, but in which the ends of legislation require that the same legal obligations shall be imposed as if the party had entered into an engagement. The case commonly used as an illustration is *solutio indebiti*— the obligation of a person to whom a payment has been made under a mistake, to refund the amount. Obligations *quasi ex contractu* are, therefore, simply *miscellaneous* obligations which cannot be reduced to any of the other classes. The third class, obligations (or rights) arising from offences, is, we venture to say, a stumbling-block to all clear-headed persons when they begin the study of the Roman law. Mr. Austin retains it, but suppresses the fourth class, *quasi ex delicto*, it being quite needless to have *two* repositories for merely miscellaneous obligations without any positive feature in common. The term quasi-contracts, rightly understood, includes them all. As Mr. Austin expresses it, "one fiction suffices." "The terms are merely a sink into which such obligatory incidents as are not contracts, or not delicts, but beget an obligation *as if*, &c., are thrown without discrimination. And this is the rational view which Gaius has taken of the subject."*

Though Mr. Austin retains the class of rights *ex delicto*, it is here that his classification most materially deviates from that of the Roman jurists. Instead of making rights *ex delicto* a secondary, he makes them a primary class. Instead of co-ordinating them with rights from contract and from quasi-contract, as species of *jura in personam*, he opposes them to all other rights, *in rem* and *in personam* taken together. His division of rights in general, is into Primary, and what he terms Sanctioning, Rights.[*] The characteristic of these is, that they exist only for the sake of the primary. Primary rights and duties have a legal existence only by virtue of their sanctions. But in order that the sanctions may be applied, legal provisions are necessary, by which other rights are created and duties imposed. These secondary rights and duties are the subject-matter of Penal Law and of the Law of Procedure. They correspond partly (though, as we shall see, not entirely) with the *obligationes ex delicto* of the Romans, and admit of being classed as rights and duties arising out of offences. As such, they are again divided by Mr. Austin into "Rights and Duties arising from Civil Injuries," and "Duties and other Consequences arising from Crimes."[†] The basis which the Roman jurists assumed for their division of rights in general—the distinction between rights *in rem* and *in personam*—is retained by Mr. Austin only for primary rights. The following table,[‡] abridged from one annexed to the author's Outline, will serve as a rough ground-plan of his distribution of the field of law:

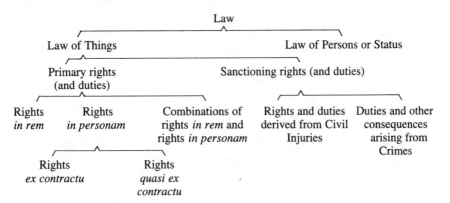

*Ibid., pp. 134-5. [For the reference to Gaius, see Heineccius, *Elementa juris civilis, secundum ordinem pandectarum*, in *Operum*, Vol. V, p. 660 (XLIV, vii, 380).]

[*Austin, *Lectures*, Vol. II, pp. 450-63.]

[†*Ibid.*, pp. 189-91.]

[‡*Ibid.*, Vol. III, Table VIII.]

The remaining Lectures are devoted to the examination and elucidation of the particulars included under these heads. And, with all their incompleteness (which, as with the broken arches in Addison's "Vision," becomes greater as we approach the point where they cease altogether),[*] their value to the student will be found to be very great. We would particularly direct attention to the treatment of *Dominium* or Property, in its various senses, with the contrasted conception of *servitus* or easement.[†] The nature and boundaries of these two kinds of rights are made so transparently clear, that it requires some acquaintance with the speculations of jurists to be able to believe that any one could ever have misunderstood the subject.

But is the division and arrangement of law in general, expressed in the table, wholly unimpeachable? We do not mean in point of mere correctness. It satisfies the fundamental rules of logical division. It covers the whole subject, and no one part overlaps another. It affords an arrangement in which it is at least possible to lay out perspicuously the whole of the matter; and if the proper mode of ordering and setting out a body of law is to ground it upon a classification of rights, no better one for the purpose could probably be made.

But the purely logical requisites are not the only qualities desirable in a scientific classification. There is a further requisite—that the division should turn upon the most important features of the things classified; in order that these, and not points of minor importance, may be the points on which attention is concentrated. A classification which does this, is what men of science mean when they speak of a Natural Classification. To fulfil this condition may require, according to circumstances, different principles of division; since the most important properties may either be those which are most important practically, by their bearing on human interests, or those which are most important scientifically, as rendering it easiest to understand the subject—which will generally be the most *elementary* properties.

In the case now under consideration, both these indications coincide. They both point to the same principle of division. Law is a system of means for the attainment of ends. The different ends for which different portions of the law are designed, are consequently the best foundation for the division of it. They are at once what is most practically important in the laws, and the fundamental element in the conception of them—the one which must be clearly understood to make anything else intelligible. Is, then, this requirement, of distinguishing the parts of the *corpus juris* from one another according to the ends which they subserve, fulfilled by a division which turns entirely upon a classification of rights?

It would be so, if the ends of different portions of the law differed only in respect of the different kinds of Rights which they create. But this is not the fact. The rights

[*Joseph Addison, "The Vision of Mirzah," *Spectator*, No. 160 (1 Sept., 1711), p. 1.]
[†Austin, *Lectures*, Vol. III, pp. 2-3, 13.]

created by a law are sometimes the end or purpose of the law, but are not always so.

In the case of what Mr. Austin terms Primary Rights,[*] the rights created are the very reason and purpose of the law which creates them. That these rights may be enjoyed is the end for which the law is enacted, the duties imposed, and the sanctions established.

In that part of the law, however, which presupposes and grows out of wrongs— the law of civil injuries, of crimes, and of civil and criminal procedure —the case is quite otherwise. There are, it is true, rights (called, by Mr. Austin, Sanctioning Rights)[†] created by this portion of the law, and necessary to its existence. But the laws do not exist for the sake of these rights; the rights, on the contrary, exist for the sake of the laws. They are a portion of the means by which those laws effect their end. The purpose of this part of the law is not the creation of rights, but the application of sanctions, to give effect to the rights created by the law in its other departments. The sanctioning rights are merely instrumental to the sanctions; but the sanctions are themselves instrumental to the primary rights. The filiation of the ideas, proceeding from the simple to the more complex, is as follows:

1. Primary Rights, with the correlative Duties.
2. Sanctions.
3. Laws determining the mode of applying the Sanctions.
4. Rights and Duties established by those laws, for the sake of, and as being necessary to, the application of the Sanctions.

It appears from these considerations, that however suitable a groundwork the classification of rights may be for the arrangement of that portion of the law which treats of Primary Rights (commonly called the Civil Code)—in the Penal Code and Code of Procedure the rights thereby created are but a secondary consideration, on which it is not well to bestow the prominence which is given to them by carrying out into those branches the same principle of classification. We do not mean that rights *ex delicto* can be left out of the classification of rights for the purposes of the Civil Code. They are rights, and being so, cannot be omitted in the catalogue. But they should, we apprehend, be merely mentioned there, and their enumeration and definition reserved for a separate department, of which the subject should be, not Rights, but Sanctions. If this view be correct, the primary division of the body of law should be into two parts. First, the Civil Law, containing the definition and classification of rights and duties: Secondly, the law of Wrongs and Remedies. This last would be subdivided into Penal Law, which treats of offences and punishments, and the law of Procedure. If this were a mere opinion of our own, we should hesitate to assert it against a judge in all respects so much more competent

[*Ibid., Vol. I, pp. lxxv-lxxix, xcviii; Vol. II, pp. 450-63.]
[†Ibid.]

as Mr. Austin; but if his great authority is against us, we have with us that of Bentham, James Mill, and the authors of, we believe, all modern codes.[*]

Not only does this more commonplace distribution and arrangement of the *corpus juris* appear to us more scientific than Mr. Austin's; we apprehend that it is also more convenient. Mr. Austin, in fact, has been driven, by the plan he adopted, to the introduction of a logical anomaly, which he himself acknowledges. There are, as he rightly holds, legal duties which are absolute, that is, which have not only for their ultimate but for their immediate and direct object the *general* good, and not the good of any determinate person or persons, and to which, therefore, there are no correlative rights. Now, in a classification grounded wholly on rights, there is no place for duties which do not correspond to any rights. It being impossible to class these duties with *jura in rem* or *in personam*, Mr. Austin treats of them under the head of Sanctioning Rights. The difficulty, however, is not in knowing under what kind of rights to place them, but in placing them under rights at all. Duties which answer to no rights, have no more natural affinity with Sanctioning than they have with Primary rights. Why then is this, as it undoubtedly is, their proper place in the classification? Because, though the duties have no affinity with rights, the wrongs which are violations of those duties have an affinity with the wrongs which are violations of rights. Violations of absolute duties are Crimes; many violations of rights are also Crimes; and between crimes of these two sorts there is no generic difference which it is necessary that either penal law or criminal procedure should recognise. Now, if the second great division of the law is regarded (which we think it ought to be) as conversant not directly with Rights, but with Wrongs, the wrongs in question, which are violations of absolute duties, take their place among other wrongs as a matter of course. But in a classification grounded on Rights, they are altogether an anomaly and a blot. There is no place marked out for them by the principle of the classification; and to include them in it, recourse must be had to a second principle, which, except for that purpose, the classification does not recognise. It has been seen in the table, that, in the second division of Mr. Austin's Sanctioning Rights, he drops rights altogether, and speaks of "duties and other consequences."

But this is not the only, nor the greatest objection which may be made, both on the ground of scientific symmetry and of practical convenience, against the place assigned by Mr. Austin to the law of Wrongs and Remedies. A still stronger objection is manifest from a mere inspection of the table. It interpolates the entire subjects of Penal Law and Procedure between the general Civil Law of Things and the Law of Status; that is, between two subjects so closely allied, that after a strenuous application of his powerful intellect to the subject, Mr. Austin was unable to draw a definite line, or find any essential or scientific difference between

[*See Jeremy Bentham, *An Introduction to the Principles of Morals and Legislation* (1789), in *Works*, Vol. I, pp. 150-4; James Mill, "Jurisprudence," in *Essays* (London: printed Innis, n.d. [1825]), p. 9.]

them; and was induced to separate them at all, only by the convenience of treating the genus first, and a few of its more complex species afterwards. As he himself says, the law of any and of all Status is "indissolubly connected with that more general matter which is contained in the Law of Things."* These two portions of law are conversant with the same general ideas—namely, rights and their definitions (to a great degree even with the same kinds of rights): and one of them is but a kind of appendix or extension of the other, so that there is often a doubt in which compartment a particular chapter or title of the law may best be placed; yet the one is put at the beginning of the *corpus juris*, the other at the end, and between them lies all that great portion of the law which has to do with the subsequent considerations of Offences, Punishments, Judicature, and Judicial Procedure. We cannot think that this is a mode of arrangement which would have approved itself to Mr. Austin's, on such subjects, almost infallible judgment, had he ever completed his Course.

It may be remarked that, though the arrangement which we have criticized was founded on that of the classical Roman jurists, the criticism is not fairly applicable to those jurists themselves. According to the plan of their treatises, they had no alternative. They could not treat of delicts under any other form than that of "*obligationes quae ex delicto nascuntur.*"[*] For, as Mr. Austin himself observes, their institutional writings were solely on *private* law.[†] Public law was, it is uncertain for what reason, excluded. But crimes, and criminal procedure, belonged to their conception of Public law. Of these, therefore, they had not to treat.† Civil procedure they did treat of; but they placed it in a branch apart, which was neither *jus rerum* nor *personarum*, but a third division co-ordinate with them, called *Jus Actionum*. There remained only the law of civil injuries. Now, the specific character which distinguishes civil injuries from crimes is that, though the sanction is in both cases the leading idea, the mode in which, in the case of civil injuries, the sanction is applied, is by giving to the injured party a right to compensation or redress, which, like his other rights, he may exercise or forego at his pleasure. It is evident that there is not in this case the same impropriety as in the case of crimes or of procedure, in considering the right created as the real purpose of the law. It is true that, even in this case, another purpose of the law is punishment; but the law is willing to forego that object, provided the injured person consents to waive it. The right, therefore, of the injured person, in this

Lectures, Vol. II, pp. 439-40.

[*Heineccius, *Elementa juris civilis, secundum ordinem institutionum* (1726), 6th ed. (1747), in *Operum*, Vol. V, p. 263 (IV, i, title).]

[†*Lectures*, Vol. II, p. 442.]

†The single title appended to Justinian's Institutes, *De Publicis Judiciis*, is supposed to have been an afterthought, and to have had no chapter corresponding to it in the institutional treatises of the classical jurists. [See Heineccius, "De publicis judiciis," *Elementa juris civilis, secundum ordinem institutionum*, Bk. IV, Title xviii, in *Operum*, Vol. V, pp. 333-40.]

particular class of injuries, might without absurdity be treated as the principal object. Being a right availing only against determinate persons—namely, the offender or his representatives—it is a right *in personam*, or, in the language of the classical jurists, an *obligatio*; and its particular nature afforded no reason why it should not, in an arrangement in all other respects dictated by the exigencies of the civil code, take its place where alone, in such an arrangement, a place could be assigned to it—namely, under the general head of *Jura in Personam*, as a sub-species. But this, though it accounts for the place assigned in the Roman law to "*obligationes quae ex delicto nascuntur*," forms no reason for applying the same arrangement to the whole law of wrongs and remedies, and making it the basis of a division including the entire field of the *corpus juris*—crimes, punishments, civil and criminal procedure, among the rest.

After treating of *dominium* in the narrower sense in which it is opposed to *servitus*—a right to use or deal with a thing in a manner which, though not unlimited, is indefinite, as distinguished from a right to use or deal with a thing in a manner not only limited but definite—Mr. Austin proceeds to treat of rights limited or unlimited as to duration; of rights vested and contingent; and of *dominium* or property in the more emphatic sense in which it denotes the largest right which the law recognises over a thing—a right not only indefinite in extent and unlimited in duration, but including the power of aliening the thing from the person who would otherwise take it by succession.[*] The Lectures finally break off, where they were interrupted by ill health, in the middle of the important subject of Title. There is no finer specimen of analytical criticism in these volumes than the comment (in the Notes to the Tables) on the erroneous and confused notions which the Roman jurists connected with their distinction between *Titulus* and *Modus Acquirendi*.[†]

It cannot be too deeply regretted that, through the combined effect of frequently-recurring attacks of depressing illness, and feelings of discouragement which are vividly reproduced in the touching preface of the editor,[‡] Mr. Austin did not complete his Lectures in the form of a systematic treatise. We are fully persuaded that, had he done so, the result would have proved those feelings of discouragement to be ill grounded. The success of the first volume, by no means the most attractive part of the Course, is a proof that even then there was in the more enlightened part of the legal profession a public prepared for such speculations; a public not numerous, but intellectually competent—the only one which Mr. Austin desired. Had he produced a complete work on jurisprudence, such as he, and perhaps only he in his generation, was capable of accomplishing,

[*Austin, *Lectures*, Vol. III, pp. 69-89.]
[†*Ibid.*, pp. 209-13.]
[‡Sarah Austin, his wife.]

he would have attracted to the study every young student of law who had a soul above that of a mere trader in legal learning; and many non-professional students of social and political philosophy (a class now numerous, and eager for an instruction which unhappily, for the most part, does not yet exist) would have been delighted to acquire that insight into the rationale of all legal systems, without which the scientific study of politics can scarcely be pursued with profit, since juristical ideas meet, and, if ill understood, confuse the student at every turning and winding in that intricate subject. Before the end of the period to which Mr. Austin's life was prolonged, he might have stood at the head of a school of scientific jurists, such as England has now little chance of soon possessing. But the remains which he has left, fragmentary though much of them be, are a mine of material for the future. He has shown the way, solved many of the leading problems, and made the path comparatively smooth for those who follow. Among the younger lawyers of the present time, there must surely be several (independently of the brilliant example of Mr. Maine) who possess the capacity, and can acquire the knowledge, required for following up a work so well begun; and whoever does so will find, in the notes and miscellaneous papers which compose the latter part of the third volume, a perfect storehouse of helps and suggestions.

It remains to say a few words on the question of execution. A work left unfinished, and never really composed as a book, however mature and well-digested its thoughts, is not a proper subject for literary criticism. It is from the first volume only that we are able to judge what, in point of composition, Mr. Austin would have made it. But all the merits of expression which were found in that volume reappear in quite an equal degree in the remainder, and even, as far as the case admitted, in the looser memoranda. The language is pure and classical English, though here and there with something of an archaic tinge. In expression as in thought, precision is always his first object. It would probably have been so, whatever had been the subject treated; but on one in which the great and fatal hindrance to rational thought is vague and indefinite phrases, this was especially imperative. Next after precision, clearness is his paramount aim; clearness alike in his phraseology and in the structure of his sentences. His pre-eminent regard to this requisite gives to his style a peculiarity the reverse of agreeable to many readers, since he prefers, on system, the repetition of a noun substantive, or even of an entire clause, in order to dispense with the employment of the little words *it* and *them*, which he is quite right in regarding as one of the most frequent sources of ambiguity and obscurity in composition. If there be some excess here, it is the excess of a good quality, and is a scarcely appreciable evil, while a fault in the contrary direction would have been a serious one. In other respects Mr. Austin's style deserves to be placed very high. His command of apt and vigorous expression is remarkable, and when the subject permits, there is an epigrammatic force in the turn of his sentences which makes them highly effective.

Some readers may be offended at the harsh words which he now and then uses, not towards persons, to whom he is always, at the lowest, respectful, but towards phrases and modes of thought which he considers to have a mischievous tendency. He frequently calls them "absurd," and applies to them such epithets as "jargon," "fustian," and the like.[*] But it would be a great injustice to attribute these vehement expressions to dogmatism, in any bad sense of the word—to undue confidence in himself, or disdain of opponents. They flowed from the very finest part of his character. He was emphatically one who hated the darkness and loved the light. He regarded unmeaning phrases and confused habits of thinking as the greatest hindrance to human intellect, and through it to human virtue and happiness. And, thinking this, he expressed the thought with corresponding warmth: for it was one of his noble qualities that while, whatever he thought, he thought strongly, his feelings always went along with his thoughts. The same *perfervidum ingenium* made him apply the same strong expressions to any mistake which he detected in himself. In a passage of the *Lectures*, he says, referring to a former lecture, "I said so and so. But that remark was absurd; for it would prove," &c.* And in an extemporaneous passage, which some of his hearers may remember, he rated himself soundly for an erroneous opinion which he had expressed, and conjectured, as he might have done respecting a complete stranger to him, what might have been the causes that led him into so gross a misapprehension. That the occasional strength of his denunciations had its source in a naturally enthusiastic character, combined in him with an habitually calm and deliberate judgment, is shown by the corresponding warmth which marks his expressions of eulogium. He was one in whom the feelings of admiration and veneration towards persons and things that deserve it, existed in a strength far too rarely met with among mankind. It is from such feelings that he speaks of "the godlike Turgot;"[†] that, in mentioning Locke, he commemorates "that matchless power of precise and just thinking, with that religious regard for general utility and truth, which marked the incomparable man who emancipated human reason from the yoke of mystery and jargon;"† that he does homage, in many passages of the *Lectures*, to the great intellectual powers of Thibaut and Von Savigny,[‡] and that, in a note at page 248 of his first volume, he devotes to Hobbes perhaps the noblest vindication which that great but unpopular thinker has ever received. That Mr. Austin was capable of similar admiration for the great qualities of those from whose main scheme of thought he dissents, and whose authority he is oftener obliged to thrust aside than enabled to follow, is shown in many passages, and in

[*Austin, *Lectures*, Vol. II, p. 409; Vol. I, pp. 150n, 164.]

Ibid., Vol. III, pp. 24-5.

[†*Ibid.*, Vol. I (i.e., *Province of Jurisprudence*), p. 274.]

†*Ibid.*, p. 150n.

[‡For Thibaut, see *Lectures*, Vol. III, pp. 294-8; for Von Savigny, *ibid.*, Vol. II, pp. 65, 395-7, and Vol. III, pp. 296-8.]

none more than in some remarks on Kant's *Metaphysical Principles of the Science of Law*.* We may add that his praises are not only warm, but (probably without exception) just; that such severity as is shown, is shown towards doctrines, very rarely indeed towards persons, and is never, as with vulgar controversialists, a substitute for refutation, but always and everywhere a consequence of it.

*"A treatise darkened by a philosophy which, I own, is my aversion, but abounding, I must needs admit, with traces of rare sagacity. He has seized a number of notions, complex and difficult in the extreme, with distinctness and precision which are marvellous considering the scantiness of his means. For, of positive systems of law he had scarcely the slightest tincture, and the knowledge of the principles of jurisprudence which he borrowed from other writers, was drawn, for the most part, from the muddiest sources; from books about the fustian which is styled the 'Law of Nature.'" (*Ibid.*, Vol. III, p. 167.) [Immanuel Kant, *Metaphysische Anfangsgründe der Rechtslehre* (1797), in *Sämmtliche Werke*, ed. Karl Rosenkranz and Friedrich Wilhelm Schubert, 14 vols. in 12 (Leipzig: Voss, 1838-42), Vol. IX, pp. 1-214.]

EDUCATIONAL ENDOWMENTS

1866

EDITOR'S NOTE

In "Report of Commissioners on Education in Schools in England, Not Comprised within Her Majesty's Two Recent Commissions on Popular Education and Public Schools," *Parliamentary Papers*, 1867-68, XXVIII, Pt. 2, 67-72. Headed, "John Stuart Mill, Esq., M.P." Signed "J.S. Mill." Not listed in Mill's bibliography. No copy in Somerville College. For comment on the items, see li-lii and lxvi-lxvii above.

Educational Endowments

Blackheath Park, August 9, 1866.

SIR,

I have now the honour of transmitting to the Royal Commissioners for Inquiry into Schools, such answers as it is in my power to give to the queries which the Commissioners did me the honour of addressing to me. Want of time, no less than the understood wishes of the Commissioners, has compelled me to be brief; but, for the further elucidation of the topics to which I have adverted, as well as for many valuable facts and thoughts connected with the subject of their inquiries, I hope I may be permitted to refer the Commissioners to the paper by Mr. Chadwick,[*] mentioned in my answer to the second query, and the evidence appended thereto.

I have, &c.
J.S. Mill

The Secretary of the
Schools Inquiry Commission

* * * * *

1. *The expediency, in the case of endowed schools, of continuing to give gratuitous education to the scholars, and fixed incomes to the teachers.*

I conceive the practice of payment by fixed salaries to be almost fatal to the general usefulness of educational endowments, and quite sufficient in itself to account for the admitted fact of their extensive failure.

If any practical maxim for the conduct of business of any kind by a delegated agent can be called fundamental, it is that of identifying the agent's interest with his duty. But if a schoolmaster's remuneration is neither increased by efficiency, nor diminished by inefficiency, his personal interest is, to have as few pupils as

---

[*Edwin Chadwick, "Copy of Two Papers Submitted to the [Education] Commissioners," *PP*, 1862, XLIII, 1-160. Chadwick's papers were not submitted in time to be included in the *Report* of 1861 (see p. 212 below).]

possible, and to take the least possible trouble with their instruction. I have read of a school where the master's salary was 600*l*. a year, and his object was to drive away the pupils, which he succeeded in effecting by a series of severe floggings.[*] Without vouching for the strict truth of this anecdote, it may be accepted as a warning illustration of what may happen in an extreme case. Every motive that acts upon a teacher thus situated, tends to render his work valueless, except conscience or a disinterested love for his duty; and the insufficiency, in average cases, of these motives, is the principal cause which renders laws and institutions necessary.

The true principle for the remuneration of schoolmasters of all classes and grades, wherever it is possible to apply it, is that of payment for results. The results of their teaching can, in general, only be tested by examinations, conducted by independent public examiners; and if this examination were partly of a competitive character, extending to the pupils of all endowed middle-class schools, somewhat after the model of the Oxford and Cambridge local examinations, it might be made a basis for proportioning, in some degree, the remuneration of schoolmasters to the degree of success which their pupils obtained in the examinations.

It appears to me, generally speaking, undesirable that education should be provided gratuitously for the children of the classes specifically concerned in the present inquiry. Those classes can afford to pay; they are not objects of charity; they have no claim to be relieved from the duty of providing education for their children; and *entire* relief from that obligation on any other ground than inability, appears to me to have a highly demoralizing tendency. The suggestion that exhibitions should be given to pupils of the elementary schools, to be earned by merit, for the purpose of enabling them to prolong their school course, and advance to a higher grade of education, seems to me, on the contrary, to be of a highly moral and improving character, and I would give it my warmest support. I would suggest that these exhibitions be awarded by competitive examination. It is, however, a different question, whether the funds of endowments should be exclusively devoted to this purpose, or to this and to the pensioning of retired teachers. Though endowments are not, I conceive, beneficially employed in educating the children of the middle classes without expense to the parents, I think it a very proper application of them to provide, for those classes, a better quality of education than can be supplied from the contributions of parents as an exclusive resource. They should be called on to pay only what they can, in ordinary cases, well afford, and this having been done, the very best education should be given which can be provided by the addition to those payments, of all other funds legitimately applicable to the purpose.

2. *The best mode of providing for the future management of endowments, and of preventing them from relapsing into inefficiency.*

As the first and most indispensable part of any arrangements for this purpose, I

[*See Chadwick, "Copy of Two Papers," p. 143.]

would urge that the whole of the foundation schools be placed under the regular supervision of the Inspectors of the Privy Council. Nothing but frequent and systematic inspection, by an authority having the power, if not of removing, at least of proposing the removal of the schoolmaster in case of proved unfitness, will ever prevent the majority of such schools from falling back into the state from which it is now desired to rescue them. The inspectors, some of whom are gentlemen of great experience and ability, and the selection of whom will always be the most important of all the duties of the Education Committee of Council, will be the persons most capable of pointing out, in each case, the best arrangements for securing a local superintendence in aid of the general one. The manner in which power and responsibility should be shared between the local and the central authority, and, above all, the question which of the two should exercise, in the last resort, the most important function of all, the appointment and removal of the masters, are matters of deep and serious consideration, with a view to obtain the best security for the efficiency of the work, while avoiding the danger of giving too great a control over the education of the country to a department of the executive. In a country possessing any organized system of local administration, there would be, in every district of a certain size, a school committee, composed of those inhabitants of the locality (whether elected or nominated) who took the greatest practical interest in the subject; and to such a committee, with a representative of the Education Committee of the Privy Council for their regularly appointed adviser, the authority over the local schools might safely and properly be entrusted. But in the chaotic confusion of English local institutions, which throws such obstacles in the way of any systematic improvement in the real government of the country, it would require much more practical experience than I possess, and more meditation than I have been able to bestow on the subject, to enable me to suggest the best constitution for the local superintending body, or to define the powers which ought to be vested in it. It is even possible that both its constitution and its powers ought to be different in different localities, according to the nature of the materials available. For the present, probably, the responsibility of selecting the proper persons from among the leading inhabitants of all denominations, might with advantage be temporarily intrusted to the inspectors; though I would by no means propose this as a permanent arrangement. In whatever manner appointed, I strongly recommend that there should be but one such body for the whole of the endowed schools of a considerable district; comprising, however, persons from various parts of the district, who might severally act as local visitors of the schools nearest to them.

In still further extension of the same principle, I would propose that all the educational endowments of the district, together with all other charitable endowments within the same local limits which are now applied, ostensibly or really, to the relief of the poor in modes which are useless or hurtful, should be brought into a single fund, to be devoted to maintaining one or a few large schools in convenient situations, in preference to a greater number of small ones.

Large schools, with numerous pupils, have a great advantage in point of economy and efficiency over small schools with few pupils. The principal sources of this advantage are—

a. That when the pupils are numerous they can be formed into considerable classes, of about the same degree of proficiency, and capable of profiting by the same teaching; while, if they are few in number, pupils of very unequal degrees of advancement have to be taught together, and either the majority are neglected in favour of the few most proficient, or the teacher's attention is given to them by turns, those to whom the teaching of the moment is unsuited remaining comparatively idle.

b. That by merging many small schools in one large school, it becomes possible to obtain teachers of a far better quality for the same cost, and to economize their labour by confining the superior teachers to the higher departments. A small number of well-paid masters, adapted to the different grades of proficiency, are a vastly superior educational instrument to a large number of ill-paid masters scattered over the country, each of whom has to teach pupils of all grades, and if he is fit for the higher work, is throwing away his labour in teaching mere elements to little boys.

c. And lastly, that large schools economize, in a similar manner, the most important labour of all, and that which requires the highest qualities in the persons intrusted with it, the labour of inspection.

These and other reasons in favour of the consolidation of schools, will be found largely illustrated in a document forming No. 120 of the papers printed by order of the House of Commons in the session of 1862, containing evidence collected by Mr. Chadwick for the former Royal Commission on Education, accompanied by comments of his own on this and other points of the very highest value.[*]

The same Parliamentary paper contains the particulars of a most important practical application of the principles just stated—the case of the Faversham schools.[†] This was a new foundation, growing out of a bequest by a banker of Faversham,[‡] as recently as 1840, of property yielding 2,000*l.* a year, for the general benefit of the poor of that place. The trustees, being thus free to adopt the best ideas of the age, and being evidently men of practical good sense, determined that the purposes of the testator could best be effected by devoting the bequest to an improved scheme of public education for the town and its neighbourhood; and having drawn up a plan for that purpose, obtained the authority of the Court of Chancery for carrying it into execution. The plan comprehends an infant school, a national school, a middle-class or commercial school, and an evening school for

[*Report of the Commissioners Appointed to Inquire into the State of Popular Education in England, PP, 1861, XXI, Pt. I, 1-707; as indicated above, Chadwick's papers are in PP, 1862, XLIII, 1-160.]

[†See Chadwick, "Copy of Two Papers," pp. 52-7, 144.]

[‡Henry Wreight.]

adults under trained masters. The Parliamentary paper already referred to shows the great advantages which have been found to attend the union of all these schools under the same management. Pupils are promoted, as a reward for proficiency, from the national to the commercial school, where they are supplied with books, and their school fees paid, at the expense of the endowment: and there is an annual examination of the commercial school by graduates of one of the Universities, at which exhibitions are awarded, by what is stated to be in effect a competitive examination, to successful pupils, to enable them to continue their studies in an old foundation grammar school which already existed in the town under another trust, and the union of which with the new schools under a common management would complete the scheme. No religious difficulty is experienced; dissenters and churchmen, both lay and clerical, acting together with perfect cordiality, both as trustees and as members of the school committee.

3. *The possibility of securing for purposes of education, endowments that are now wasted.*

There are numerous charitable funds which are now, under the terms of antiquated trusts, distributed in mere doles, to persons supposed to be necessitous, but who have not always even that claim, such as it is. It would be a far more efficacious mode of alleviating the evil of indigence, to employ these funds in making war on its principal cause, the want of education. Full information respecting these wasted endowments could probably be obtained through the Charity Commissioners, within whose special duty it naturally falls to procure such information, when they do not already possess it.[*] The sanction of the Court of Chancery or of Parliament would probably not be refused to the necessary change in the destination of these endowments, due regard being had to the fair claims of living individuals who may have become, in any degree, dependent on them for support.

4. *The best mode of securing, or at least encouraging, a due supply of qualified teachers.*

No part of the subject is more important than this; the wretched incompetency of the great majority of the existing schools for the children of the middle classes being notorious. Mr. Edward Carleton Tufnell, one of the ablest and most experienced of Her Majesty's inspectors of schools, stated in evidence to Mr. Chadwick, "It has frequently occurred to me to cause the dismissal of a master from a pauper school on account of gross ignorance or gross immorality. The useful power of the Poor Law Board[†] prevents such people being again appointed to pauper schools, but I have taken pains to ascertain what has become of those

[*See 16 & 17 Victoria, c. 137 (1853).]
[†See 4 & 5 William IV, c. 76 (1834), Sect. 48.]

masters, and I have generally found that they have got places as ushers in schools for the middle or upper classes."[*]

With a view to correct the extreme deficiency of due qualification in the teachers, all the suggestions referred to in the letter which the Commissioners did me the honour to address to me, appear worthy of adoption, and all of them together are not more than sufficient. It would be highly important that training schools should be established for teachers, where they should learn, not only the things they will have to teach, but how to teach them; for which purpose these training schools must of course be connected with schools of the ordinary kind, where the art of teaching may be practically acquired. It is evidently proper that the restriction, in many foundations, of the office of schoolmaster to persons in holy orders, should be abolished. And it is also right that certificates of fitness for the office of teacher should be granted, after examination, either by the Universities (that of London included) or by examiners appointed by the Committee of Council. I would add a recommendation that on the first appointment of teachers, the principle of competitive examination should be introduced as far as practicable, and that in their subsequent promotion a mode of examination should be resorted to, which might, if possible, test the results of their teaching in the schools where they had already taught. But the greatest security of all, without which no other will permanently avail, is the assured prospect of removal, in case of incompetency proved by experience. The whole chance of success of any reform in the endowed schools rests upon the degree of certainty which can be given to this expectation; and the utmost exertions of the department should, I earnestly urge, be above all directed to this end. With a view to it, the visitorial functions of the Court of Chancery should be transferred to the Privy Council, who might be empowered to avail themselves, if needful, of the aid of the Poor Law Inspectors, as well as of the Charity Commissioners. The arrangements for local visitation I have already touched upon. But all will be ineffective without efficient and vigorous examination of the pupils, by an authority totally independent of the teachers and of those by whom the teachers are appointed; and the value of this examination would be greatly increased if part of it were made competitive among the pupils of all the schools in a given district, or in the whole country.

[*Chadwick, "Copy of Two Papers," p. 143.]

INAUGURAL ADDRESS
DELIVERED TO THE UNIVERSITY OF ST. ANDREWS

1867

EDITOR'S NOTE

2nd ed. London: Longmans, Green, Reader, and Dyer, 1867. Reprinted from 1st ed., *ibid*. Identified in Mill's bibliography as "Inaugural delivered to the University of St. Andrews on February 1st 1867" (MacMinn, 98). The only copy in Somerville College (Boston: Little and Gray, n.d.; double column) has no corrections or emendations. For comment on the work, see lii-lvi and lxvii-lxviii above.

The text below is that of the 2nd ed., the last in Mill's lifetime. There is only one variant between the printed texts (see 245$^{b\text{-}b}$); in the note "67[1]" indicates the 1st ed. A portion of the text exists in early draft form in the Houghton Library, Harvard University; it is printed, with variant notes, in Appendix D.

Inaugural Address
Delivered to the University of St. Andrews

IN COMPLYING WITH THE CUSTOM which prescribes that the person whom you have called by your suffrages to the honorary presidency of your University should embody in an Address a few thoughts on the subjects which most nearly concern a seat of liberal education; let me begin by saying, that this usage appears to me highly commendable. Education, in its larger sense, is one of the most inexhaustible of all topics. Though there is hardly any subject on which so much has been written, by so many of the wisest men, it is as fresh to those who come to it with a fresh mind, a mind not hopelessly filled full with other people's conclusions, as it was to the first explorers of it: and notwithstanding the great mass of excellent things which have been said respecting it, no thoughtful person finds any lack of things both great and small still waiting to be said, or waiting to be developed and followed out to their consequences. Education, moreover, is one of the subjects which most essentially require to be considered by various minds, and from a variety of points of view. For, of all many-sided subjects, it is the one which has the greatest number of sides. Not only does it include whatever we do for ourselves, and whatever is done for us by others, for the express purpose of bringing us somewhat nearer to the perfection of our nature; it does more: in its largest acceptation, it comprehends even the indirect effects produced on character and on the human faculties, by things of which the direct purposes are quite different; by laws, by forms of government, by the industrial arts, by modes of social life; nay even by physical facts not dependent on human will; by climate, soil, and local position. Whatever helps to shape the human being; to make the individual what he is, or hinder him from being what he is not—is part of his education. And a very bad education it often is; requiring all that can be done by cultivated intelligence and will, to counteract its tendencies. To take an obvious instance; the niggardliness of Nature in some places, by engrossing the whole energies of the human being in the mere preservation of life, and her over-bounty in others, affording a sort of brutish subsistence on too easy terms, with hardly any exertion of the human faculties, are both hostile to the spontaneous growth and development of the mind; and it is at those two extremes of the scale that we find human societies in the state of most unmitigated savagery. I shall confine myself, however, to education in the narrower sense; the culture which each generation purposely gives to those who are to be its successors, in order to qualify them for at least keeping up, and if possible for raising, the level of improvement which has been attained. Nearly all here present are daily occupied either in receiving or in giving this sort of education: and the part of it which most concerns you at present is that in which you are yourselves engaged—the stage of education which is the appointed business of a national University.

The proper function of an University in national education is tolerably well understood. At least there is a tolerably general agreement about what an University is not. It is not a place of professional education. Universities are not intended to teach the knowledge required to fit men for some special mode of gaining their livelihood. Their object is not to make skilful lawyers, or physicians, or engineers, but capable and cultivated human beings. It is very right that there should be public facilities for the study of professions. It is well that there should be Schools of Law, and of Medicine, and it would be well if there were schools of engineering, and the industrial arts. The countries which have such institutions are greatly the better for them; and there is something to be said for having them in the same localities, and under the same general superintendence, as the establishments devoted to education properly so called. But these things are no part of what every generation owes to the next, as that on which its civilization and worth will principally depend. They are needed only by a comparatively few, who are under the strongest private inducements to acquire them by their own efforts; and even those few do not require them until after their education, in the ordinary sense, has been completed. Whether those whose speciality they are, will learn them as a branch of intelligence or as a mere trade, and whether, having learnt them, they will make a wise and conscientious use of them or the reverse, depends less on the manner in which they are taught their profession, than upon what sort of minds they bring to it—what kind of intelligence, and of conscience, the general system of education has developed in them. Men are men before they are lawyers, or physicians, or merchants, or manufacturers; and if you make them capable and sensible men, they will make themselves capable and sensible lawyers or physicians. What professional men should carry away with them from an University, is not professional knowledge, but that which should direct the use of their professional knowledge, and bring the light of general culture to illuminate the technicalities of a special pursuit. Men may be competent lawyers without general education, but it depends on general education to make them philosophic lawyers—who demand, and are capable of apprehending, principles, instead of merely cramming their memory with details. And so of all other useful pursuits, mechanical included. Education makes a man a more intelligent shoemaker, if that be his occupation, but not by teaching him how to make shoes; it does so by the mental exercise it gives, and the habits it impresses.

This, then, is what a mathematician would call the higher limit of University education: its province ends where education, ceasing to be general, branches off into departments adapted to the individual's destination in life. The lower limit is more difficult to define. An University is not concerned with elementary instruction: the pupil is supposed to have acquired that before coming here. But where does elementary instruction end, and the higher studies begin? Some have given a very wide extension to the idea of elementary instruction. According to them, it is not the office of an University to give instruction in single branches of knowledge from the commencement. What the pupil should be taught here (they think), is to methodize his knowledge: to look at every separate part of it in its relation to the other parts, and to the whole; combining the partial glimpses which he has obtained of the field of human knowledge at different points, into a general map, if I may so speak, of the entire region; observing how all knowledge is connected, how we ascend to one branch by means of another, how the higher modifies the lower, and the lower helps us to understand the higher; how every existing reality is a compound of many properties, of which each science or distinct mode of study reveals but a small part, but the whole of which must be included to enable us to know it truly as a fact in Nature, and not as a mere abstraction.

This last stage of general education, destined to give the pupil a comprehensive and connected view of the things which he has already learnt separately, includes a philosophic study of the Methods of the sciences; the modes in which the human intellect proceeds from the known to the unknown. We must be taught to generalize our conception of the resources which the human mind possesses for the exploration of nature; to understand how man discovers the real facts of the world, and by what tests he can judge whether he has really found them. And doubtless this is the crown and consummation of a liberal education: but before we restrict an University to this highest department of instruction—before we confine it to teaching, not knowledge, but the philosophy of knowledge—we must be assured that the knowledge itself has been acquired elsewhere. Those who take this view of the function of an University are not wrong in thinking that the schools, as distinguished from the universities, ought to be adequate to teaching every branch of general instruction required by youth, so far as it can be studied apart from the rest. But where are such schools to be found? Since science assumed its modern character, nowhere: and in these islands less even than elsewhere. This ancient kingdom, thanks to its great religious reformers, had the inestimable advantage, denied to its southern sister, of excellent parish schools, which gave, really and not in pretence, a considerable amount of valuable literary instruction to the bulk of the population, two centuries earlier than in any other country. But schools of a still higher description have been, even in Scotland, so few and inadequate, that the Universities have had to perform largely the functions which ought to be performed by schools; receiving students at an early age, and undertaking not only the work for which the schools should have prepared them, but much of the preparation itself. Every Scottish University is not an University only, but a High School, to supply the deficiency of other schools. And if the English Universities do not do the same, it is not because the same need does not exist, but because it is disregarded. Youths come to the Scottish Universities ignorant, and are there taught. The majority of those who come to the English Universities come still more ignorant, and ignorant they go away.

In point of fact, therefore, the office of a Scottish University comprises the whole of a liberal education, from the foundations upwards. And the scheme of your Universities has, almost from the beginning, really aimed at including the whole, both in depth and in breadth. You have not, as the English Universities so long did, confined all the stress of your teaching, all your real effort to teach, within the limits of two subjects, the classical languages and mathematics. You did not wait till the last few years to establish a Natural Science and a Moral Science Tripos. Instruction in both those departments was organized long ago: and your teachers of those subjects have not been nominal professors, who did not lecture: some of the greatest names in physical and in moral science have taught in your Universities, and by their teaching contributed to form some of the most distinguished intellects of the last and present centuries. To comment upon the course of education at the Scottish Universities is to pass in review every essential department of general culture. The best use, then, which I am able to make of the present occasion, is to offer a few remarks on each of those departments, considered in its relation to human cultivation at large: adverting to the nature of the claims which each has to a place in liberal education; in what special manner they each conduce to the improvement of the individual mind and the benefit of the race; and how they all conspire to the common end, the strengthening, exalting, purifying, and beautifying of our common nature, and the fitting out of mankind with the necessary mental implements for the work they have to perform through life.

Let me first say a few words on the great controversy of the present day with regard to the higher education, the difference which most broadly divides educational reformers and conservatives; the vexed question between the ancient languages and the modern sciences and arts; whether general education should be classical—let me use a wider expression, and say literary—or scientific. A dispute as endlessly, and often as fruitlessly agitated as that old controversy which it resembles, made memorable by the names of Swift and Sir William Temple in England and Fontenelle in France—the contest for superiority between the ancients and the moderns.[*] This question, whether we should be taught the

[*Jonathan Swift, *A Full and True Account of the Battle Fought Last Friday, between the Ancient and the Modern Books in St. James's Library* (1704), in *Works*, ed. Walter Scott, 19 vols. (Edinburgh: Constable; London: White, *et al.*; Dublin: Cumming, 1814), Vol. XI, pp. 213-60; William Temple, "An Essay upon the Ancient and Modern Learning" (1690),

classics or the sciences, seems to me, I confess, very like a dispute whether painters should cultivate drawing or colouring, or, to use a more homely illustration, whether a tailor should make coats or trousers. I can only reply by the question, why not both? Can anything deserve the name of a good education which does not include literature and science too? If there were no more to be said than that scientific education teaches us to think, and literary education to express our thoughts, do we not require both? and is not any one a poor, maimed, lopsided fragment of humanity who is deficient in either? We are not obliged to ask ourselves whether it is more important to know the languages or the sciences. Short as life is, and shorter still as we make it by the time we waste on things which are neither business, nor meditation, nor pleasure, we are not so badly off that our scholars need be ignorant of the laws and properties of the world they live in, or our scientific men destitute of poetic feeling and artistic cultivation. I am amazed at the limited conception which many educational reformers have formed to themselves of a human being's power of acquisition. The study of science, they truly say, is indispensable: our present education neglects it: there is truth in this too, though it is not all truth: and they think it impossible to find room for the studies which they desire to encourage, but by turning out, at least from general education, those which are now chiefly cultivated. How absurd, they say, that the whole of boyhood should be taken up in acquiring an imperfect knowledge of two dead languages. Absurd indeed: but is the human mind's capacity to learn, measured by that of Eton and Westminster to teach? I should prefer to see these reformers pointing their attacks against the shameful inefficiency of the schools, public and private, which pretend to teach these two languages and do not. I should like to hear them denounce the wretched methods of teaching, and the criminal idleness and supineness, which waste the entire boyhood of the pupils without really giving to most of them more than a smattering, if even that, of the only kind of knowledge which is even pretended to be cared for. Let us try what conscientious and intelligent teaching can do, before we presume to decide what cannot be done.

Scotland has on the whole, in this respect, been considerably more fortunate than England. Scotch youths have never found it impossible to leave school or the university having learnt somewhat of other things besides Greek and Latin; and why? Because Greek and Latin have been better taught. A beginning of classical instruction has all along been made in the common schools: and the common schools of Scotland, like her Universities, have never been the mere shams that the English Universities were during the last century, and the greater part of the English classical schools still are. The only tolerable Latin grammars for school purposes that I know of, which had been produced in these islands until very lately,

in *Works*, 4 vols. (London: Rivington, *et al.*, 1814), Vol. III, pp. 444-518; and Bernard Le Bovier de Fontenelle, *Digression sur les anciens et les modernes* (1688), in *Oeuvres*, new ed., 10 vols. (Paris: Libraires associés, 1766), Vol. IV, pp. 169-98.]

were written by Scotchmen.[*] Reason, indeed, is beginning to find its way by gradual infiltration even into English schools, and to maintain a contest, though as yet a very unequal one, against routine. A few practical reformers of school tuition, of whom Arnold was the most eminent, have made a beginning of amendment in many things: but reforms, worthy of the name, are always slow, and reform even of governments and churches is not so slow as that of schools, for there is the great preliminary difficulty of fashioning the instruments: of teaching the teachers. If all the improvements in the mode of teaching languages which are already sanctioned by experience, were adopted into our classical schools, we should soon cease to hear of Latin and Greek as studies which must engross the school years, and render impossible any other acquirements. If a boy learnt Greek and Latin on the same principle on which a mere child learns with such ease and rapidity any modern language, namely, by acquiring some familiarity with the vocabulary by practice and repetition, before being troubled with grammatical rules—those rules being "acquired with tenfold greater facility when the cases to which they apply are already familiar to the mind; an average schoolboy, long before the age at which schooling terminates, would be able to read fluently and with intelligent interest any ordinary Latin or Greek author in prose or verse, would have a competent knowledge of the grammatical structure of both languages, and have had time besides for an ample amount of scientific instruction. I might go much further; but I am as unwilling to speak out all that I think practicable in this matter, as George Stephenson was about railways, when he calculated the average speed of a train at ten miles an hour, because if he had estimated it higher, the practical men would have turned a deaf ear to him, as that most unsafe character in their estimation, an enthusiast and a visionary. The results have shewn, in that case, who was the real practical man. What the results would shew in the other case, I will not attempt to anticipate. But I will say confidently, that if the two classical languages were properly taught, there would be no need whatever for ejecting them from the school course, in order to have sufficient time for everything else that need be included therein.

Let me say a few words more on this strangely limited estimate of what it is possible for human beings to learn, resting on a tacit assumption that they are already as efficiently taught as they ever can be. So narrow a conception not only

[*E.g., John Mair, *An Introduction to Latin Syntax* (Edinburgh: Paton, *et al.*, 1750; many subsequent eds.), which was used by Mill in instructing his sisters (see *Autobiography and Literary Essays*, ed. John M. Robson and Jack Stillinger, *CW*, Vol. I [Toronto: University of Toronto Press, 1981], pp. 568-9); Hugh Christie, *A Grammar of the Latin Tongue* (Edinburgh: Donaldson, 1758; many subsequent eds.); and Thomas Ruddiman, *The Rudiments of the Latin Tongue* (Edinburgh: the Author, 1714), often reissued, for example as edited by another Scot, John Hunter (Cupar: Tullis; Edinburgh: Oliver and Boyd; London: Whittaker; Glasgow: Turnbull; Dublin: Johnson and Deas, 1820).]

a-a225[*for a draft of this section, see Appendix D*]

vitiates our idea of education, but actually, if we receive it, darkens our anticipations as to the future progress of mankind. For if the inexorable conditions of human life make it useless for one man to attempt to know more than one thing, what is to become of the human intellect as facts accumulate? In every generation, and now more rapidly than ever, the things which it is necessary that somebody should know are more and more multiplied. Every department of knowledge becomes so loaded with details, that one who endeavours to know it with minute accuracy, must confine himself to a smaller and smaller portion of the whole extent: every science and art must be cut up into subdivisions, until each man's portion, the district which he thoroughly knows, bears about the same ratio to the whole range of useful knowledge that the art of putting on a pin's head does to the field of human industry. Now, if in order to know that little completely, it is necessary to remain wholly ignorant of all the rest, what will soon be the worth of a man, for any human purpose except his own infinitesimal fraction of human wants and requirements? His state will be even worse than that of simple ignorance. Experience proves that there is no one study or pursuit, which, practised to the exclusion of all others, does not narrow and pervert the mind; breeding in it a class of prejudices special to that pursuit, besides a general prejudice, common to all narrow specialities, against large views, from an incapacity to take in and appreciate the grounds of them. We should have to expect that human nature would be more and more dwarfed, and unfitted for great things, by its very proficiency in small ones. But matters are not so bad with us: there is no ground for so dreary an anticipation. It is not the utmost limit of human acquirement to know only one thing, but to combine a minute knowledge of one or a few things with a general knowledge of many things. By a general knowledge I do not mean a few vague impressions. An eminent man, one of whose writings is part of the course of this University, Archbishop Whately, has well discriminated between a general knowledge and a superficial knowledge.[*] To have a general knowledge of a subject is to know only its leading truths, but to know these not superficially but thoroughly, so as to have a true conception of the subject in its great features; leaving the minor details to those who require them for the purposes of their special pursuit. There is no incompatibility between knowing a wide range of subjects up to this point, and some one subject with the completeness required by those who make it their principal occupation. It is this combination which gives an enlightened public: a body of cultivated intellects, each taught by its attainments in its own province what real knowledge is, and knowing enough of other subjects to be able to discern who are those that know them better. The amount of knowledge is not to be lightly estimated, which qualifies us for judging to whom we may have recourse for more. The elements of the more important studies being widely diffused, those who have reached the higher summits find a public capable of

[*See Richard Whately, *Elements of Logic* (London: Mawman, 1826), pp. xii-xiv.]

appreciating their superiority, and prepared to follow their lead. It is thus too that minds are formed capable of guiding and improving public opinion on the greater concerns of practical life. Government and civil society are the most complicated of all subjects accessible to the human mind: and he who would deal competently with them as a thinker, and not as a blind follower of a party, requires not only a general knowledge of the leading facts of life, both moral and material, but an understanding exercised and disciplined in the principles and rules of sound thinking, up to a point which neither the experience of life, nor any one science or branch of knowledge, affords. Let us understand, then, that it should be our aim in learning, not merely to know the one thing which is to be our principal occupation, as well as it can be known, but to do this and also to know something of all the great subjects of human interest: taking care to know that something accurately; marking well the dividing line between what we know accurately and what we do not: and remembering that our object should be to obtain a true view of nature and life in their broad outline, and that it is idle to throw away time upon the details of anything which is to form no part of the occupation of our practical energies.

It by no means follows, however, that every useful branch of general, as distinct from professional, knowledge, should be included in the curriculum of school or university studies. There are things which are better learnt out of school, or when the school years, and even those usually passed in a Scottish university, are over. I do not agree with those reformers who would give a regular and prominent place in the school or university course to modern languages. This is not because I attach small importance to the knowledge of them. No one can in our age be esteemed a well-instructed person who is not familiar with at least the French language, so as to read French books with ease; and there is great use in cultivating a familiarity with German. But living languages are so much more easily acquired by intercourse with those who use them in daily life; a few months in the country itself, if properly employed, go so much farther than as many years of school lessons; that it is really waste of time for those to whom that easier mode is attainable, to labour at them with no help but that of books and masters: and it will in time be made attainable, through international schools and colleges, to many more than at present. Universities do enough to facilitate the study of modern languages, if they give a mastery over that ancient language which is the foundation of most of them, and the possession of which makes it easier to learn four or five of the continental languages than it is to learn one of them without it. Again, it has always seemed to me a great absurdity that history and geography should be taught in schools; except in elementary schools for the children of the labouring classes, whose subsequent access to books is limited. Who ever really learnt history and geography except by private reading? and what an utter failure a system of education must be, if it has not given the pupil a sufficient taste for reading to seek for himself those most attractive and easily intelligible of all kinds of knowledge? Besides, such history and geography as can be taught in schools exercise none of the faculties of the intelligence except the memory. An University is indeed the place where the student should be introduced to the Philosophy of History; where Professors who not merely know the facts but have exercised their minds on them, should initiate him into the causes and explanation, so far as within our reach, of the past life of mankind in its principal features. Historical criticism also—the tests of historical truth—are a subject to which his attention may well be drawn in this stage of his education. But of the mere facts of history, as commonly accepted, what educated youth of any mental activity does not learn as much as is necessary, if he is simply turned loose into an historical library? What he needs on this, and on most other matters of common information, is not that he should be taught it in boyhood, but that abundance of books should be accessible to him.

The only languages, then, and the only literature, to which I would allow a place in the ordinary curriculum, are those of the Greeks and Romans; and to these I would preserve the position in it which they at present occupy. That position is justified, by the great value, in education, of knowing well some other cultivated language and literature than one's own, and by the peculiar value of those particular languages and literatures.

There is one purely intellectual benefit from a knowledge of languages, which I am specially desirous to dwell on. Those who have seriously reflected on the causes of human error, have been deeply impressed with the tendency of mankind to mistake*a* words for things. Without entering into the metaphysics of the subject, we know how common it is to use words glibly and with apparent propriety, and to accept them confidently when used by others, without ever having had any distinct conception of the things denoted by them. To quote again from Archbishop Whately, it is the habit of mankind to mistake familiarity for accurate knowledge.[*] As we seldom think of asking the meaning of what we see every day, so when our ears are used to the sound of a word or a phrase, we do not suspect that it conveys no clear idea to our minds, and that we should have the utmost difficulty in defining it, or expressing, in any other words, what we think we understand by it. Now it is obvious in what manner this bad habit tends to be corrected by the practice of translating with accuracy from one language to another, and hunting out the meanings expressed in a vocabulary with which we have not grown familiar by early and constant use. I hardly know any greater proof of the extraordinary genius of the Greeks, than that they were able to make such brilliant achievements in abstract thought, knowing, as they generally did, no language but their own. But the Greeks did not escape the effects of this deficiency. Their greatest intellects, those who laid the foundation of philosophy and of all our intellectual culture, Plato and Aristotle, are continually led away by words; mistaking the accidents of language for real relations in nature, and supposing that things which have the

[*See *ibid.*, p. 274; and cf. Whately's *Introductory Lectures on Political Economy* (1831), 2nd ed. (London: Fellowes, 1832), p. 224.]

same name in the Greek tongue must be the same in their own essence. There is a well-known saying of Hobbes, the far-reaching significance of which you will more and more appreciate in proportion to the growth of your own intellect: "Words are the counters of wise men, but the money of fools."[*] With the wise man a word stands for the fact which it represents; to the fool it is itself the fact. To carry on Hobbes' metaphor, the counter is far more likely to be taken for merely what it is, by those who are in the habit of using many different kinds of counters. But besides the advantage of possessing another cultivated language, there is a further consideration equally important. Without knowing the language of a people, we never really know their thoughts, their feelings, and their type of character: and unless we do possess this knowledge, of some other people than ourselves, we remain, to the hour of our death, with our intellects only half expanded. Look at a youth who has never been out of his family circle: he never dreams of any other opinions or ways of thinking than those he has been bred up in; or, if he has heard of any such, attributes them to some moral defect, or inferiority of nature or education. If his family are Tory, he cannot conceive the possibility of being a Liberal; if Liberal, of being a Tory. What the notions and habits of a single family are to a boy who has had no intercourse beyond it, the notions and habits of his own country are to him who is ignorant of every other. Those notions and habits are to him human nature itself; whatever varies from them is an unaccountable aberration which he cannot mentally realize: the idea that any other ways can be right, or as near an approach to right as some of his own, is inconceivable to him. This does not merely close his eyes to the many things which every country still has to learn from others: it hinders every country from reaching the improvement which it could otherwise attain by itself. We are not likely to correct any of our opinions or mend any of our ways, unless we begin by conceiving that they are capable of amendment: but merely to know that foreigners think differently from ourselves, without understanding why they do so, or what they really do think, does but confirm us in our self-conceit, and connect our national vanity with the preservation of our own peculiarities. Improvement consists in bringing our opinions into nearer agreement with facts; and we shall not be likely to do this while we look at facts only through glasses coloured by those very opinions. But since we cannot divest ourselves of preconceived notions, there is no known means of eliminating their influence but by frequently using the differently coloured glasses of other people: and those of other nations, as the most different, are the best.

But if it is so useful, on this account, to know the language and literature of any other cultivated and civilized people, the most valuable of all to us in this respect are the languages and literature of the ancients. No nations of modern and civilized

[*Cf. Thomas Hobbes, *Leviathan*, in *English Works*, ed. William Molesworth, 11 vols. (London: Bohn, 1839-45), Vol. III, p. 25 (Pt. I, Chap. iv).]

Europe are so unlike one another, as the Greeks and Romans are unlike all of us; yet without being, as some remote Orientals are, so totally dissimilar, that the labour of a life is required to enable us to understand them. Were this the only gain to be derived from a knowledge of the ancients, it would already place the study of them in a high rank among enlightening and liberalizing pursuits. It is of no use saying that we may know them through modern writings. We may know something of them in that way; which is much better than knowing nothing. But modern books do not teach us ancient thought; they teach us some modern writer's notion of ancient thought. Modern books do not shew us the Greeks and Romans; they tell us some modern writer's opinions about the Greeks and Romans. Translations are scarcely better. When we want really to know what a person thinks or says, we seek it at first hand from himself. We do not trust to another person's impression of his meaning, given in another person's words; we refer to his own. Much more is it necessary to do so when his words are in one language, and those of his reporter in another. Modern phraseology never conveys the exact meaning of a Greek writer; it cannot do so, except by a diffuse explanatory circumlocution which no translator dares use. We must be able, in a certain degree, to think in Greek, if we would represent to ourselves how a Greek thought: and this not only in the abstruse region of metaphysics, but about the political, religious, and even domestic concerns of life. I will mention a further aspect of this question, which, though I have not the merit of originating it, I do not remember to have seen noticed in any book. There is no part of our knowledge which it is more useful to obtain at first hand—to go to the fountain head for—than our knowledge of history. Yet this, in most cases, we hardly ever do. Our conception of the past is not drawn from its own records, but from books written about it, containing not the facts, but a view of the facts which has shaped itself in the mind of somebody of our own or a very recent time. Such books are very instructive and valuable; they help us to understand history, to interpret history, to draw just conclusions from it; at the worst, they set us the example of trying to do all this; but they are not themselves history. The knowledge they give is upon trust, and even when they have done their best, it is not only incomplete but partial, because confined to what a few modern writers have seen in the materials, and have thought worth picking out from among them. How little we learn of our own ancestors from Hume, or Hallam, or Macaulay,[*] compared with what we know if we add to what these tell us, even a little reading of cotemporary authors and documents! The most recent historians are so well aware of this, that they fill their pages with extracts from the original materials, feeling that these extracts are the real history, and their comments and thread of narrative are only helps towards understanding it. Now it is

[*I.e., David Hume, *The History of England* (1754-62), 8 vols. (Oxford: Talboys and Wheeler; London: Pickering, 1826); Henry Hallam, *The Constitutional History of England*, 2 vols. (London: Murray, 1827); and Thomas Babington Macaulay, *The History of England from the Accession of James II*, 5 vols. (London: Longman, *et al.*, 1849-61).]

part of the great worth to us of our Greek and Latin studies, that in them we do read history in the original sources. We are in actual contact with cotemporary minds; we are not dependent on hearsay; we have something by which we can test and check the representations and theories of modern historians. It may be asked, why then not study the original materials of modern history? I answer, it is highly desirable to do so; and let me remark by the way, that even this requires a dead language; nearly all the documents prior to the Reformation, and many subsequent to it, being written in Latin. But the exploration of these documents, though a most useful pursuit, cannot be a branch of education. Not to speak of their vast extent, and the fragmentary nature of each, the strongest reason is, that in learning the spirit of our own past ages, until a comparatively recent period, from cotemporary writers, we learn hardly anything else. Those authors, with a few exceptions, are little worth reading on their own account. While, in studying the great writers of antiquity, we are not only learning to understand the ancient mind, but laying in a stock of wise thought and observation, still valuable to ourselves; and at the same time making ourselves familiar with a number of the most perfect and finished literary compositions which the human mind has produced—compositions which, from the altered conditions of human life, are likely to be seldom paralleled, in their sustained excellence, by the times to come.

Even as mere languages, no modern European language is so valuable a discipline to the intellect as those of Greece and Rome, on account of their regular and complicated structure. Consider for a moment what grammar is. It is the most elementary part of logic. It is the beginning of the analysis of the thinking process. The principles and rules of grammar are the means by which the forms of language are made to correspond with the universal forms of thought. The distinctions between the various parts of speech, between the cases of nouns, the moods and tenses of verbs, the functions of particles, are distinctions in thought, not merely in words. Single nouns and verbs express objects and events, many of which can be cognized by the senses: but the modes of putting nouns and verbs together, express the relations of objects and events, which can be cognized only by the intellect; and each different mode corresponds to a different relation. The structure of every sentence is a lesson in logic. The various rules of syntax oblige us to distinguish between the subject and predicate of a proposition, between the agent, the action, and the thing acted upon; to mark when an idea is intended to modify or qualify, or merely to unite with, some other idea; what assertions are categorical, what only conditional; whether the intention is to express similarity or contrast, to make a plurality of assertions conjunctively or disjunctively; what portions of a sentence, though grammatically complete within themselves, are mere members or sub-ordinate parts of the assertion made by the entire sentence. Such things form the subject-matter of universal grammar; and the languages which teach it best are those which have the most definite rules, and which provide distinct forms for the greatest number of distinctions in thought, so that if we fail to attend precisely and accurately to any of these, we cannot avoid committing a solecism in language. In these qualities the classical languages have an incomparable superiority over every modern language, and over all languages, dead or living, which have a literature worth being generally studied.

But the superiority of the literature itself, for purposes of education, is still more marked and decisive. Even in the substantial value of the matter of which it is the vehicle, it is very far from having been superseded. The discoveries of the ancients in science have been greatly surpassed, and as much of them as is still valuable loses nothing by being incorporated in modern treatises: but what does not so well admit of being transferred bodily, and has been very imperfectly carried off even piecemeal, is the treasure which they accumulated of what may be called the wisdom of life: the rich store of experience of human nature and conduct, which the acute and observing minds of those ages, aided in their observations by the greater simplicity of manners and life, consigned to their writings, and most of which retains all its value. The speeches in Thucydides; the *Rhetoric*, *Ethics*, and *Politics* of Aristotle; the Dialogues of Plato; the Orations of Demosthenes; the *Satires*, and especially the *Epistles* of Horace; all the writings of Tacitus; the great work of Quintilian, a repertory of the best thoughts of the ancient world on all subjects connected with education;[*] and, in a less formal manner, all that is left to us of the ancient historians, orators, philosophers, and even dramatists, are replete with remarks and maxims of singular good sense and penetration, applicable both to political and to private life: and the actual truths we find in them are even surpassed in value by the encouragement and help they give us in the pursuit of truth. Human invention has never produced anything so valuable, in the way both of stimulation and of discipline to the inquiring intellect, as the dialectics of the ancients, of which many of the works of Aristotle illustrate the theory, and those of Plato exhibit the practice. No modern writings come near to these, in teaching, both by precept and example, the way to investigate truth, on those subjects, so vastly important to us, which remain matters of controversy, from the difficulty or impossibility of bringing them to a directly experimental test. To question all things; never to turn away from any difficulty; to accept no doctrine either from

[*For the specific titles referred to, see *Thucydides* (Greek and English), trans. Charles Forster Smith, 4 vols. (London: Heinemann; Cambridge, Mass.: Harvard University Press, 1958); Aristotle, *The "Art" of Rhetoric* (Greek and English), trans. J.H. Freese (London: Heinemann; New York: Putnam's Sons, 1926); Aristotle, *The Nicomachean Ethics* (Greek and English), trans. H. Rackham (London: Heinemann; New York: Putnam's Sons, 1926); Aristotle, *Politics* (Greek and English), trans. H. Rackham (London: Heinemann: New York: Putnam's Sons, 1932); Horace, *Satires*, and *Epistles*, in *Satires, Epistles, and Ars poetica* (Latin and English), trans. H. Rushton Fairclough (London: Heinemann; New York: Putnam's Sons, 1926), pp. 4-244, and 244-440, respectively; and Quintilian, *Institutio oratoria* (Greek and English), trans. H.E. Butler, 4 vols. (London: Heinemann; Cambridge, Mass.: Harvard University Press, 1953). The references to Plato, Demosthenes, and Tacitus are to their writings in general.]

ourselves or from other people without a rigid scrutiny by negative criticism, letting no fallacy, or incoherence, or confusion of thought, slip by unperceived; above all, to insist upon having the meaning of a word clearly understood before using it, and the meaning of a proposition before assenting to it; these are the lessons we learn from the ancient dialecticians. With all this vigorous management of the negative element, they inspire no scepticism about the reality of truth, or indifference to its pursuit. The noblest enthusiasm, both for the search after truth and for applying it to its highest uses, pervades these writers, Aristotle no less than Plato, though Plato has incomparably the greater power of imparting those feelings to others. In cultivating, therefore, the ancient languages as our best literary education, we are all the while laying an admirable foundation for ethical and philosophical culture. In purely literary excellence—in perfection of form—the pre-eminence of the ancients is not disputed. In every department which they attempted, and they attempted almost all, their composition, like their sculpture, has been to the greatest modern artists an example, to be looked up to with hopeless admiration, but of inappreciable value as a light on high, guiding their own endeavours. In prose and in poetry, in epic, lyric, or dramatic, as in historical, philosophical, and oratorical art, the pinnacle on which they stand is equally eminent. I am now speaking of the form, the artistic perfection of treatment: for, as regards substance, I consider modern poetry to be superior to ancient, in the same manner, though in a less degree, as modern science: it enters deeper into nature. The feelings of the modern mind are more various, more complex and manifold, than those of the ancients ever were. The modern mind is, what the ancient mind was not, brooding and self-conscious; and its meditative self-consciousness has discovered depths in the human soul which the Greeks and Romans did not dream of, and would not have understood. But what they had got to express, they expressed in a manner which few even of the greatest moderns have seriously attempted to rival. It must be remembered that they had more time, and that they wrote chiefly for a select class, possessed of leisure. To us who write in a hurry for people who read in a hurry, the attempt to give an equal degree of finish would be loss of time. But to be familiar with perfect models is not the less important to us because the element in which we work precludes even the effort to equal them. They shew us at least what excellence is, and make us desire it, and strive to get as near to it as is within our reach. And this is the value to us of the ancient writers, all the more emphatically, because their excellence does not admit of being copied, or directly imitated. It does not consist in a trick which can be learnt, but in the perfect adaptation of means to ends. The secret of the style of the great Greek and Roman authors, is that it is the perfection of good sense. In the first place, they never use a word without a meaning, or a word which adds nothing to the meaning. They always (to begin with) had a meaning; they knew what they wanted to say; and their whole purpose was to say it with the highest degree of exactness and completeness, and bring it home to the mind with the greatest possible clearness and vividness. It never entered into their thoughts to conceive of a piece of writing as beautiful in itself, abstractedly from what it had to express: its beauty must all be subservient to the most perfect expression of the sense. The *curiosa felicitas* which their critics ascribed in a pre-eminent degree to Horace, expresses the standard at which they all aimed.[*] Their style is exactly described by Swift's definition, "the right words in the right places."[†] Look at an oration of Demosthenes; there is nothing in it which calls attention to itself as style at all: it is only after a close examination we perceive that every word is what it should be, and where it should be, to lead the hearer smoothly and imperceptibly into the state of mind which the orator wishes to produce. The perfection of the workmanship is only visible in the total absence of any blemish or fault, and of anything which checks the flow of thought and feeling, anything which even momentarily distracts the mind from the main purpose. But then (as has been well said) it was not the object of Demosthenes to make the Athenians cry out "What a splendid speaker!" but to make them say "Let us march against Philip!" It was only in the decline of ancient literature that ornament began to be cultivated merely as ornament. In the time of its maturity, not the merest epithet was put in because it was thought beautiful in itself; nor even for a merely descriptive purpose, for epithets purely descriptive were one of the corruptions of style which abound in Lucan, for example: the word had no business there unless it brought out some feature which was wanted, and helped to place the object in the light which the purpose of the composition required. These conditions being complied with, then indeed the intrinsic beauty of the means used was a source of additional effect, of which it behoved them to avail themselves, like rhythm and melody of versification. But these great writers knew that ornament for the sake of ornament, ornament which attracts attention to itself, and shines by its own beauties, only does so by calling off the mind from the main object, and thus not only interferes with the higher purpose of human discourse, which ought, and generally professes, to have some matter to communicate, apart from the mere excitement of the moment, but also spoils the perfection of the composition as a piece of fine art, by destroying the unity of effect. This, then, is the first great lesson in composition to be learnt from the classical authors. The second is, not to be prolix. In a single paragraph, Thucydides can give a clear and vivid representation of a battle, such as a reader who has once taken it into his mind can seldom forget. The most powerful and affecting piece of narrative perhaps in all historical literature, is the account of the Sicilian catastrophe in his seventh book, yet how few pages does it fill![‡] The ancients were concise, because of the extreme pains they took with their

[*Petronius Arbiter, *Satyricon*, in *Petronius; Seneca, "Apocolocyntosis"* (Latin and English), trans. Michael Heseltine and E.H. Warmington (London: Heinemann; Cambridge, Mass.: Harvard University Press, 1969), pp. 1-379.]
[†Cf. Swift, *A Letter to a Young Clergyman* (1720), in *Works*, Vol. VIII, p. 337.]
[‡*Thucydides*, Vol. IV, pp. 159-81 (VII, lxxviii-lxxxvii).]

compositions; almost all moderns are prolix, because they do not. The great ancients could express a thought so perfectly in a few words or sentences, that they did not need to add any more: the moderns, because they cannot bring it out clearly and completely at once, return again and again, heaping sentence upon sentence, each adding a little more elucidation, in hopes that though no single sentence expresses the full meaning, the whole together may give a sufficient notion of it. In this respect I am afraid we are growing worse instead of better, for want of time and patience, and from the necessity we are in of addressing almost all writings to a busy and imperfectly prepared public. The demands of modern life are such—the work to be done, the mass to be worked upon, are so vast, that those who have anything particular to say—who have, as the phrase goes, any message to deliver—cannot afford to devote their time to the production of masterpieces. But they would do far worse than they do, if there had never been masterpieces, or if they had never known them. Early familiarity with the perfect, makes our most imperfect production far less bad than it otherwise would be. To have a high standard of excellence often makes the whole difference of rendering our work good when it would otherwise be mediocre.

For all these reasons I think it important to retain these two languages and literatures in the place they occupy, as a part of liberal education, that is, of the education of all who are not obliged by their circumstances to discontinue their scholastic studies at a very early age. But the same reasons which vindicate the place of classical studies in general education, shew also the proper limitation of them. They should be carried as far as is sufficient to enable the pupil, in after life, to read the great works of ancient literature with ease. Those who have leisure and inclination to make scholarship, or ancient history, or general philology, their pursuit, of course require much more, but there is no room for more in general education. The laborious idleness in which the school-time is wasted away in the English classical schools deserves the severest reprehension. To what purpose should the most precious years of early life be irreparably squandered in learning to write bad Latin and Greek verses? I do not see that we are much the better even for those who end by writing good ones. I am often tempted to ask the favourites of nature and fortune, whether all the serious and important work of the world is done, that their time and energy can be spared for these *nugae difficiles*? I am not blind to the utility of composing in a language, as a means of learning it accurately. I hardly know any other means equally effectual. But why should not prose composition suffice? What need is there of original composition at all? if that can be called original which unfortunate schoolboys, without any thoughts to express, hammer out on compulsion from mere memory, acquiring the pernicious habit which a teacher should consider it one of his first duties to repress, that of merely stringing together borrowed phrases? The exercise in composition, most suitable to the requirements of learners, is that most valuable one, of retranslating from translated passages of a good author: and to this might be added, what still exists in many Continental places of education, occasional practice in talking Latin. There would be something to be said for the time spent in the manufacture of verses, if such practice were necessary for the enjoyment of ancient poetry; though it would be better to lose that enjoyment than to purchase it at so extravagant a price. But the beauties of a great poet would be a far poorer thing than they are, if they only impressed us through a knowledge of the technicalities of his art. The poet needed those technicalities: they are not necessary to us. They are essential for criticizing a poem, but not for enjoying it. All that is wanted is sufficient familiarity with the language, for its meaning to reach us without any sense of effort, and clothed with the associations on which the poet counted for producing his effect. Whoever has this familiarity, and a practised ear, can have as keen a relish of the music of Virgil and Horace, as of Gray, or Burns, or Shelley, though he know not the metrical rules of a common Sapphic or Alcaic. I do not say that these rules ought not to be taught, but I would have a class apart for them, and would make the appropriate exercises an optional, not a compulsory part of the school teaching.

Much more might be said respecting classical instruction, and literary cultivation in general, as a part of liberal education. But it is time to speak of the uses of scientific instruction: or rather its indispensable necessity, for it is recommended by every consideration which pleads for any high order of intellectual education at all.

The most obvious part of the value of scientific instruction, the mere information that it gives, speaks for itself. We are born into a world which we have not made; a world whose phenomena take place according to fixed laws, of which we do not bring any knowledge into the world with us. In such a world we are appointed to live, and in it all our work is to be done. Our whole working power depends on knowing the laws of the world—in other words, the properties of the things which we have to work with, and to work among, and to work upon. We may and do rely, for the greater part of this knowledge, on the few who in each department make its acquisition their main business in life. But unless an elementary knowledge of scientific truths is diffused among the public, they never know what is certain and what is not, or who are entitled to speak with authority and who are not: and they either have no faith at all in the testimony of science, or are the ready dupes of charlatans and impostors. They alternate between ignorant distrust, and blind, often misplaced, confidence. Besides, who is there who would not wish to understand the meaning of the common physical facts that take place under his eye? Who would not wish to know why a pump raises water, why a lever moves heavy weights, why it is hot at the tropics and cold at the poles, why the moon is sometimes dark and sometimes bright, what is the cause of the tides? Do we not feel that he who is totally ignorant of these things, let him be ever so skilled in a special profession, is not an educated man but an ignoramus? It is surely no small part of education to put us in intelligent possession of the most important and most universally interesting facts of the universe, so that the world which surrounds us may not be a sealed book to us, uninteresting because unintelligible. This, however, is but the simplest and most obvious part of the utility of science, and the part which, if neglected in youth, may be the most easily made up for afterwards. It is more important to understand the value of scientific instruction as a training and disciplining process, to fit the intellect for the proper work of a human being. Facts are the materials of our knowledge, but the mind itself is the instrument: and it is easier to acquire facts, than to judge what they prove, and how, through the facts which we know, to get to those which we want to know.

The most incessant occupation of the human intellect throughout life is the ascertainment of truth. We are always needing to know what is actually true about something or other. It is not given to us all to discover great general truths that are a light to all men and to future generations; though with a better general education the number of those who could do so would be far greater than it is. But we all require the ability to judge between the conflicting opinions which are offered to us as vital truths; to choose what doctrines we will receive in the matter of religion, for example; to judge whether we ought to be Tories, Whigs, or Radicals, or to what length it is our duty to go with each; to form a rational conviction on great questions of legislation and internal policy, and on the manner in which our country should behave to dependencies and to foreign nations. And the need we have of knowing how to discriminate truth, is not confined to the larger truths. All through life it is our most pressing interest to find out the truth about all the matters we are concerned with. If we are farmers we want to find what will truly improve our soil; if merchants, what will truly influence the markets of our commodities; if judges, or jurymen, or advocates, who it was that truly did an unlawful act, or to whom a disputed right truly belongs. Every time we have to make a new resolution or alter an old one, in any situation in life, we shall go wrong unless we know the truth about the facts on which our resolution depends. Now, however different these searches for truth may look, and however unlike they really are in their subject-matter, the methods of getting at truth, and the tests of truth, are in all cases much the same. There are but two roads by which truth can be discovered; observation, and reasoning: observation, of course, including experiment. We all observe, and we all reason, and therefore, more or less successfully, we all ascertain truths: but most of us do it very ill, and could not get on at all were we not able to fall back on others who do it better. If we could not do it in any degree, we should be mere instruments in the hands of those who could: they would be able to reduce us to slavery. Then how shall we best learn to do this? By being shewn the way in which it has already been successfully done. The processes by which truth is attained, reasoning and observation, have been carried to their greatest known perfection in the physical sciences. As classical literature furnishes the most perfect types of the art of expression, so do the physical sciences those of the art of thinking. Mathematics, and its application to astronomy and natural philosophy, are the most complete example of the discovery of truths by reasoning;

experimental science, of their discovery by direct observation. In all these cases we know that we can trust the operation, because the conclusions to which it has led have been found true by subsequent trial. It is by the study of these, then, that we may hope to qualify ourselves for distinguishing truth, in cases where there do not exist the same ready means of verification.

In what consists the principal and most characteristic difference between one human intellect and another? In their ability to judge correctly of evidence. Our direct perceptions of truth are so limited; we know so few things by immediate intuition, or, as it used to be called, by simple apprehension—that we depend for almost all our valuable knowledge, on evidence external to itself; and most of us are very unsafe hands at estimating evidence, where an appeal cannot be made to actual eyesight. The intellectual part of our education has nothing more important to do, than to correct or mitigate this almost universal infirmity—this summary and substance of nearly all purely intellectual weakness. To do this with effect needs all the resources which the most perfect system of intellectual training can command. Those resources, as every teacher knows, are but of three kinds: first, models, secondly rules, thirdly, appropriate practice. The models of the art of estimating evidence are furnished by science; the rules are suggested by science; and the study of science is the most fundamental portion of the practice.

Take in the first instance mathematics. It is chiefly from mathematics we realize the fact that there actually is a road to truth by means of reasoning; that anything real, and which will be found true when tried, can be arrived at by a mere operation of the mind. The flagrant abuse of mere reasoning in the days of the schoolmen, when men argued confidently to supposed facts of outward nature without properly establishing their premises, or checking the conclusions by observation, created a prejudice in the modern, and especially in the English mind, against deductive reasoning altogether, as a mode of investigation. The prejudice lasted long, and was upheld by the misunderstood authority of Lord Bacon;[*] until the prodigious applications of mathematics to physical science—to the discovery of the laws of external nature—slowly and tardily restored the reasoning process to the place which belongs to it as a source of real knowledge. Mathematics, pure and applied, are still the great conclusive example of what can be done by reasoning. Mathematics also habituates us to several of the principal precautions for the safety of the process. Our first studies in geometry teach us two invaluable lessons. One is, to lay down at the beginning, in express and clear terms, all the premises from which we intend to reason. The other is, to keep every step in the reasoning distinct and separate from all the other steps, and to make each step safe before proceeding to another; expressly stating to ourselves, at every joint in the reasoning, what new premise we there introduce. It is not necessary that we should do this at all times, in

[*See, e.g., Francis Bacon, *Novum Organum* (1620), in *Works*, ed. James Spedding, *et al.*, 14 vols. (London: Longman, *et al.*, 1857-74), Vol. IV, pp. 80-1 (Bk. I, Aph. 82), and p. 97 (Bk. I, Aph. 104).]

all our reasonings. But we must be always able and ready to do it. If the validity of our argument is denied, or if we doubt it ourselves, that is the way to check it. In this way we are often enabled to detect at once the exact place where paralogism or confusion get in: and after sufficient practice we may be able to keep them out from the beginning. It is to mathematics, again, that we owe our first notion of a connected body of truth; truths which grow out of one another, and hang together so that each implies all the rest; that no one of them can be questioned without contradicting another or others, until in the end it appears that no part of the system can be false unless the whole is so. Pure mathematics first gave us this conception; applied mathematics extends it to the realm of physical nature. Applied mathematics shews us that not only the truths of abstract number and extension, but the external facts of the universe, which we apprehend by our senses, form, at least in a large part of all nature, a web similarly held together. We are able, by reasoning from a few fundamental truths, to explain and predict the phenomena of material objects: and what is still more remarkable, the fundamental truths were themselves found out by reasoning; for they are not such as are obvious to the senses, but had to be inferred by a mathematical process from a mass of minute details, which alone came within the direct reach of human observation. When Newton, in this manner, discovered the laws of the solar system, he created, for all posterity, the true idea of science. He gave the most perfect example we are ever likely to have, of that union of reasoning and observation, which by means of facts that can be directly observed, ascends to laws which govern multitudes of other facts—laws which not only explain and account for what we see, but give us assurance beforehand of much that we do not see, much that we never could have found out by observation, though, having been found out, it is always verified by the result.

While mathematics, and the mathematical sciences, supply us with a typical example of the ascertainment of truth by reasoning; those physical sciences which are not mathematical, such as chemistry, and purely experimental physics, shew us in equal perfection the other mode of arriving at certain truth, by observation, in its most accurate form, that of experiment. The value of mathematics in a logical point of view is an old topic with mathematicians, and has even been insisted on so exclusively as to provoke a counter-exaggeration, of which a well-known essay by Sir William Hamilton is an example:[*] but the logical value of experimental science is comparatively a new subject, yet there is no intellectual discipline more important than that which the experimental sciences afford. Their whole occupation consists in doing well, what all of us, during the whole of life, are engaged in doing, for the most part badly. All men do not affect to be reasoners, but all profess, and really attempt, to draw inferences from experience: yet hardly

[*"Study of Mathematics—University of Cambridge," *Edinburgh Review*, LXII (Jan., 1836), 409-55.]

any one, who has not been a student of the physical sciences, sets out with any just idea of what the process of interpreting experience really is. If a fact has occurred once or oftener, and another fact has followed it, people think they have got an experiment, and are well on the road towards shewing that the one fact is the cause of the other. If they did but know the immense amount of precaution necessary to a scientific experiment; with what sedulous care the accompanying circumstances are contrived and varied, so as to exclude every agency but that which is the subject of the experiment—or, when disturbing agencies cannot be excluded, the minute accuracy with which their influence is calculated and allowed for, in order that the residue may contain nothing but what is due to the one agency under examination; if these things were attended to, people would be much less easily satisfied that their opinions have the evidence of experience; many popular notions and generalizations which are in all mouths, would be thought a great deal less certain than they are supposed to be; but we should begin to lay the foundation of really experimental knowledge, on things which are now the subjects of mere vague discussion, where one side finds as much to say and says it as confidently as another, and each person's opinion is less determined by evidence than by his accidental interest or prepossession. In politics, for instance, it is evident to whoever comes to the study from that of the experimental sciences, that no political conclusions of any value for practice can be arrived at by direct experience. Such specific experience as we can have, serves only to verify, and even that insufficiently, the conclusions of reasoning. Take any active force you please in politics, take the liberties of England, or free trade: how should we know that either of these things conduced to prosperity, if we could discern no tendency in the things themselves to produce it? If we had only the evidence of what is called our experience, such prosperity as we enjoy might be owing to a hundred other causes, and might have been obstructed, not promoted, by these. All true political science is, in one sense of the phrase, à priori, being deduced from the tendencies of things, tendencies known either through our general experience of human nature, or as the result of an analysis of the course of history, considered as a progressive evolution. It requires, therefore, the union of induction and deduction, and the mind that is equal to it must have been well disciplined in both. But familiarity with scientific experiment at least does the useful service of inspiring a wholesome scepticism about the conclusions which the mere surface of experience suggests.

The study, on the one hand, of mathematics and its applications, on the other, of experimental science, prepares us for the principal business of the intellect, by the practice of it in the most characteristic cases, and by familiarity with the most perfect and successful models of it. But in great things as in small, examples and models are not sufficient: we want rules as well. Familiarity with the correct use of a language in conversation and writing does not make rules of grammar un-necessary; nor does the amplest knowledge of sciences of reasoning and experiment dispense with rules of logic. We may have heard correct reasonings and seen skilful experiments all our lives—we shall not learn by mere imitation to do the like, unless we pay careful attention to how it is done. It is much easier in these abstract matters, than in purely mechanical ones, to mistake bad work for good. To mark out the difference between them is the province of logic. Logic lays down the general principles and laws of the search after truth; the conditions which, whether recognised or not, must actually have been observed if the mind has done its work rightly. Logic is the intellectual complement of mathematics and physics. Those sciences give the practice, of which Logic is the theory. It declares the principles, rules, and precepts, of which they exemplify the observance.

The science of Logic has two parts; ratiocinative and inductive logic. The one helps to keep us right in reasoning from premises, the other in concluding from observation. Ratiocinative logic is much older than inductive, because reasoning in the narrower sense of the word is an easier process than induction, and the science which works by mere reasoning, pure mathematics, had been carried to a considerable height while the sciences of observation were still in the purely empirical period. The principles of ratiocination, therefore, were the earliest understood and systematized, and the logic of ratiocination is even now suitable to an earlier stage in education than that of induction. The principles of induction cannot be properly understood without some previous study of the inductive sciences: but the logic of reasoning, which was already carried to a high degree of perfection by Aristotle, does not absolutely require even a knowledge of mathematics, but can be sufficiently exemplified and illustrated from the practice of daily life.

Of Logic I venture to say, even if limited to that of mere ratiocination, the theory of names, propositions, and the syllogism, that there is no part of intellectual education which is of greater value, or whose place can so ill be supplied by anything else. Its uses, it is true, are chiefly negative; its function is, not so much to teach us to go right, as to keep us from going wrong. But in the operations of the intellect it is so much easier to go wrong than right; it is so utterly impossible for even the most vigorous mind to keep itself in the path but by maintaining a vigilant watch against all deviations, and noting all the byways by which it is possible to go astray—that the chief difference between one reasoner and another consists in their less or greater liability to be misled. Logic points out all the possible ways in which, starting from true premises, we may draw false conclusions. By its analysis of the reasoning process, and the forms it supplies for stating and setting forth our reasonings, it enables us to guard the points at which a fallacy is in danger of slipping in, or to lay our fingers upon the place where it has slipped in. When I consider how very simple the theory of reasoning is, and how short a time is sufficient for acquiring a thorough knowledge of its principles and rules, and even considerable expertness in applying them, I can find no excuse for omission to study it on the part of any one who aspires to succeed in any intellectual pursuit.

Logic is the great disperser of hazy and confused thinking: it clears up the fogs which hide from us our own ignorance, and make us believe that we understand a subject when we do not. We must not be led away by talk about inarticulate giants who do great deeds without knowing how, and see into the most recondite truths without any of the ordinary helps, and without being able to explain to other people how they reach their conclusions, nor consequently to convince any other people of the truth of them. There may be such men, as there are deaf and dumb persons who do clever things, but for all that, speech and hearing are faculties by no means to be dispensed with. If you want to know whether you are thinking rightly, put your thoughts into words. In the very attempt to do this you will find yourselves, consciously or unconsciously, using logical forms. Logic compels us to throw our meaning into distinct propositions, and our reasonings into distinct steps. It makes us conscious of all the implied assumptions on which we are proceeding, and which, if not true, vitiate the entire process. It makes us aware what extent of doctrine we commit ourselves to by any course of reasoning, and obliges us to look the implied premises in the face, and make up our minds whether we can stand to them. It makes our opinions consistent with themselves and with one another, and forces us to think clearly, even when it cannot make us think correctly. It is true that error may be consistent and systematic as well as truth; but this is not the common case. It is no small advantage to see clearly the principles and con-sequences involved in our opinions, and which we must either accept, or else abandon those opinions. We are much nearer to finding truth when we search for it in broad daylight. Error, pursued rigorously to all that is implied in it, seldom fails to get detected by coming into collision with some known and admitted fact.

You will find abundance of people to tell you that logic is no help to thought, and that people cannot be taught to think by rules. Undoubtedly rules by themselves, without practice, go but a little way in teaching anything. But if the practice of thinking is not improved by rules, I venture to say it is the only difficult thing done by human beings that is not so. A man learns to saw wood principally by practice, but there are rules for doing it, grounded on the nature of the operation, and if he is not taught the rules, he will not saw well until he has discovered them for himself. Wherever there is a right way and a wrong, there must be a difference between them, and it must be possible to find out what the difference is; and when found out and expressed in words, it is a rule for the operation. If any one is inclined to disparage rules, I say to him, try to learn anything which there are rules for, without knowing the rules, and see how you succeed. To those who think lightly of the school logic, I say, take the trouble to learn it. You will easily do so in a few weeks, and you will see whether it is of no use to you in making your mind clear, and keeping you from stumbling in the dark over the most outrageous fallacies. Nobody, I believe, who has really learnt it, and who goes on using his mind, is insensible to its benefits, unless he started with a prejudice, or, like some eminent English and Scottish thinkers of the past century, is under the influence of a reaction against the exaggerated pretensions made by the schoolmen, not so much in behalf of logic as of the reasoning process itself. Still more highly must the use of logic be estimated, if we include in it, as we ought to do, the principles and rules of Induction as well as of Ratiocination. As the one logic guards us against bad deduction, so does the other against bad generalization, which is a still more universal error. If men easily err in arguing from one general proposition to another, still more easily do they go wrong in interpreting the observations made by themselves and others. There is nothing in which an untrained mind shows itself more hopelessly incapable, than in drawing the proper general conclusions from its own experience. And even trained minds, when all their training is on a special subject, and does not extend to the general principles of induction, are only kept right when there are ready opportunities of verifying their inferences by facts. Able scientific men, when they venture upon subjects in which they have no facts to check them, are often found drawing conclusions or making generalizations from their experimental knowledge, such as any sound theory of induction would shew to be utterly unwarranted. So true is it that practice alone, even of a good kind, is not sufficient without principles and rules. Lord Bacon had the great merit of seeing that rules were necessary, and conceiving, to a very considerable extent, their true character.[*] The defects of his conception were such as were inevitable while the inductive sciences were only in the earliest stage of their progress, and the highest efforts of the human mind in that direction had not yet been made. Inadequate as the Baconian view of induction was, and rapidly as the practice outgrew it, it is only within a generation or two that any considerable improvement has been made in the theory; very much through the impulse given by two of the many distinguished men who have adorned the Scottish universities, Dugald Stewart and Brown.

I have given a very incomplete and summary view of the educational benefits derived from instruction in the more perfect sciences, and in the rules for the proper use of the intellectual faculties which the practice of those sciences has suggested. There are other sciences, which are in a more backward state, and tax the whole powers of the mind in its mature years, yet a beginning of which may be beneficially made in university studies, while a tincture of them is valuable even to those who are never likely to proceed further. The first is physiology; the science of the laws of organic and animal life, and especially of the structure and functions of the human body. It would be absurd to pretend that a profound knowledge of this difficult subject can be acquired in youth, or as a part of general education. Yet an acquaintance with its leading truths is one of those acquirements which ought not to be the exclusive property of a particular profession. The value of such knowledge for daily uses has been made familiar to us all by the sanitary dis-

[*See *Novum Organum*, Vol. IV, pp. 80-1 (Bk. I, Aph. 82), and pp. 97-8 (Bk. I, Aphs. 104-6).]

cussions of late years. There is hardly one among us who may not, in some position of authority, be required to form an opinion and take part in public action on sanitary subjects. And the importance of understanding the true conditions of health and disease—of knowing how to acquire and preserve that healthy habit of body which the most tedious and costly medical treatment so often fails to restore when once lost, should secure a place in general education for the principal maxims of hygiene, and some of those even of practical medicine. For those who aim at high intellectual cultivation, the study of physiology has still greater recommendations, and is, in the present state of advancement of the higher studies, a real necessity. The practice which it gives in the study of nature is such as no other physical science affords in the same kind, and is the best introduction to the difficult questions of politics and social life. Scientific education, apart from professional objects, is but a preparation for judging rightly of Man, and of his requirements and interests. But to this final pursuit, which has been called *par excellence* the proper study of mankind,[*] physiology is the most serviceable of the sciences, because it is the nearest. Its subject is already Man: the same complex and manifold being, whose properties are not independent of circumstance, and immovable from age to age, like those of the ellipse and hyperbola, or of sulphur and phosphorus, but are infinitely various, indefinitely modifiable by art or accident, graduating by the nicest shades into one another, and reacting upon one another in a thousand ways, so that they are seldom capable of being isolated and observed separately. With the difficulties of the study of a being so constituted, the physiologist, and he alone among scientific enquirers, is already familiar. Take what view we will of man as a spiritual being, one part of his nature is far more like another than either of them is like anything else. In the organic world we study nature under disadvantages very similar to those which affect the study of moral and political phenomena: our means of making experiments are almost as limited, while the extreme complexity of the facts makes the conclusions of general reasoning unusually precarious, on account of the vast number of circumstances that conspire to determine every result. Yet in spite of these obstacles, it is found possible in physiology to arrive at a considerable number of well-ascertained and important truths. This therefore is an excellent school in which to study the means of overcoming similar difficulties elsewhere. It is in physiology too that we are first introduced to some of the conceptions which play the greatest part in the moral and social sciences, but which do not occur at all in those of inorganic nature. As, for instance, the idea of predisposition, and of predisposing causes, as distinguished from exciting causes. The operation of all moral forces is immensely influenced by predisposition: without that element, it is impossible to explain the commonest facts of history and social life. Physiology is also the first science in

[*Alexander Pope, *An Essay on Man* (1733-34), in *Works*, ed. J. Warton, *et al.*, 10 vols. (London: Priestley, and Hearne, 1822-25), Vol. III, p. 53 (Epist. II, l. 2).]

which we recognise the influence of habit—the tendency of something to happen again merely because it has happened before. From physiology, too, we get our clearest notion of what is meant by development or evolution. The growth of a plant or animal from the first germ is the typical specimen of a phenomenon which rules through the whole course of the history of man and society—increase of function, through expansion and differentiation of structure by internal forces. I cannot enter into the subject at greater length; it is enough if I throw out hints which may be germs of further thought in yourselves. Those who aim at high intellectual achievements may be assured that no part of their time will be less wasted, than that which they employ in becoming familiar with the methods and with the main conceptions of the science of organization and life.

Physiology, at its upper extremity, touches on Psychology, or the Philosophy of Mind: and without raising any disputed questions about the limits between Matter and Spirit, the nerves and brain are admitted to have so intimate a connexion with the mental operations, that the student of the last cannot dispense with a considerable knowledge of the first. The value of psychology itself need hardly be expatiated upon in a Scottish university; for it has always been there studied with brilliant success. Almost everything which has been contributed from these islands towards its advancement since Locke and Berkeley, has until very lately, and much of it even in the present generation, proceeded from Scottish authors and Scottish professors. Psychology, in truth, is simply the knowledge of the laws of human nature. If there is anything that deserves to be studied by man, it is his own nature and that of his fellow-men: and if it is worth studying at all, it is worth studying scientifically, so as to reach the fundamental laws which underlie and govern all the rest. With regard to the suitableness of this subject for general education, a distinction must be made. There are certain observed laws of our thoughts and of our feelings which rest upon experimental evidence, and, once seized, are a clue to the interpretation of much that we are conscious of in ourselves, and observe in one another. Such, for example, are the laws of association. Psychology, so far as it consists of such laws—I speak of the laws themselves, not of their disputed applications—is as positive and certain a science as chemistry, and fit to be taught as such. When, however, we pass beyond the bounds of these admitted truths, to questions which are still in controversy among the different philosophical schools—how far the higher operations of the mind can be explained by association, how far we must admit other primary principles —what faculties of the mind are simple, what complex, and what is the composition of the latter—above all, when we embark upon the sea of metaphysics properly so called, and enquire, for instance, whether time and space are real existences, as is our spontaneous impression, or forms of our sensitive faculty, as is maintained by Kant,[*] or complex ideas generated by association; whether

[*See Immanuel Kant, *Kritik der reinen Vernunft*, in *Sämmtliche Werke*, ed. Karl Rosenkrantz and Friedrich Schubert, 14 vols. in 12 (Leipzig: Voss, 1838-40), Vol. II, pp. 34-54.]

matter and spirit are conceptions merely relative to our faculties, or facts existing *per se*, and in the latter case, what is the nature and limit of our knowledge of them; whether the will of man is free or determined by causes, and what is the real difference between the two doctrines; matters on which the most thinking men, and those who have given most study to the subjects, are still divided; it is neither to be expected nor desired that those who do not specially devote themselves to the higher departments of speculation should employ much of their time in attempting to get to the bottom of these questions. But it is a part of liberal education to know that such controversies exist, and, in a general way, what has been said on both sides of them. It is instructive to know the failures of the human intellect as well as its successes, its imperfect as well as its perfect attainments; to be aware of the open questions, as well as of those which have been definitively resolved. A very summary view of these disputed matters may suffice for the many; but a system of education is not intended solely for the many: it has to kindle the aspirations and aid the efforts of those who are destined to stand forth as thinkers above the multitude: and for these there is hardly to be found any discipline comparable to that which these metaphysical controversies afford. For they are essentially questions about the estimation of evidence; about the ultimate grounds of belief; the conditions required to justify our most familiar and intimate convictions; and the real meaning and import of words and phrases which we have used from infancy as if we understood all about them, which are even at the foundation of human language, yet of which no one except a metaphysician has rendered to himself a complete account. Whatever philosophical opinions the study of these questions may lead us to adopt, no one ever came out of the discussion of them without increased vigour of understanding, an increased demand for precision of thought and language, and a more careful and exact appreciation of the nature of proof. There never was any sharpener of the intellectual faculties superior to the Berkeleian controversy. There is even now no reading more profitable to students—confining myself to writers in our own language, and notwithstanding that so many of their speculations are already obsolete—than Hobbes and Locke, Reid and Stewart, Hume, Hartley, and Brown: on condition that these great thinkers are not read passively, as masters to be followed, but actively, as supplying materials and incentives to thought. To come to our own cotemporaries, he who has mastered Sir William Hamilton and your own lamented Ferrier as distinguished representatives of one of the two great schools of philosophy, and an eminent Professor in a neighbouring University, Professor Bain, probably the greatest living authority in the other, has gained a practice in the most searching methods of philosophic investigation applied to the most arduous subjects, which is no inadequate preparation for any intellectual difficulties that he is ever likely to be called on to resolve.

In this brief outline of a complete scientific education, I have said nothing about direct instruction in that which it is the chief of all the ends of intellectual education to qualify us for—the exercise of thought on the great interests of mankind as moral and social beings—ethics and politics, in the largest sense. These things are not, in the existing state of human knowledge, the subject of a science, generally admitted and accepted. Politics cannot be learnt once for all, from a text-book, or the instructions of a master. What we require to be taught on that subject, is to be our own teachers. It is a subject on which we have no masters to follow; each must explore for himself, and exercise an independent judgment. Scientific politics do not consist in having a set of conclusions ready made, to be applied everywhere indiscriminately, but in setting the mind to work in a scientific spirit to discover in each instance the truths applicable to the given case. And this, at present, scarcely any two persons do in the same way. Education is not entitled, on this subject, to recommend any set of opinions as resting on the authority of established science. But it can supply the student with materials for his own mind, and helps to use them. It can make him acquainted with the best speculations on the subject, taken from different points of view: none of which will be found complete, while each embodies some considerations really relevant, really requiring to be taken into the account. Education may also introduce us to the principal facts which have a direct bearing on the subject, namely the different modes or stages of civilization that have been found among mankind, and the characteristic properties of each. This is the true purpose of historical studies, as prosecuted in an University. The leading facts of ancient and modern history should be known by the student from his private reading: if that knowledge be wanting, it cannot possibly be supplied here. What a Professor of History has to teach, is the meaning of those facts. His office is to help the student in collecting from history what are the main differences between human beings, and between the institutions of society, at one time or place and at another: in picturing to himself human life and the human conception of life, as they were at the different stages of human development: in distinguishing between what is the same in all ages and what is progressive, and forming some incipient conception of the causes and laws of progress. All these things are as yet very imperfectly understood even by the most philosophic enquirers, and are quite unfit to be taught dogmatically. The object is to lead the student to attend to them; to make him take interest in history not as a mere narrative, but as a chain of causes and effects still unwinding itself before his eyes, and full of momentous consequences to himself and his descendants; the unfolding of a great epic or dramatic action, to terminate in the happiness or misery, the elevation or degradation, of the human race; an unremitting conflict between good and evil powers, of which every act done by any of us, insignificant as we are, forms one of the incidents; a conflict in which even the smallest of us cannot escape from taking part, in which whoever does not help the right side is helping the wrong, and for our share in which, whether it be greater or smaller, and let its actual consequences be visible or in the main invisible, no one of us can escape the responsibility. Though education cannot arm and equip its pupils for this fight with any complete philosophy either of politics or of history, there is much positive instruction that it can give them, having a direct bearing on the duties of citizenship. They should be taught the outlines of the civil and political institutions of their own country, and in a more general way, of the more advanced of the other civilized nations. Those branches of politics, or of the laws of social life, in which there exists a collection of facts or thoughts sufficiently sifted and methodized to form the beginning of a science, should be taught *ex professo*. Among the chief of these is Political Economy; the sources and conditions of wealth and material prosperity for aggregate bodies of human beings. This study approaches nearer to the rank of a science, in the sense in which we apply that name to the physical sciences, than anything else connected with politics yet does. I need not enlarge on the important lessons which it affords for the guidance of life, and for the estimation of laws and institutions, or on the necessity of knowing all that it can teach in order to have true views of the course of human affairs, or form plans for their improvement which will stand actual trial. The same persons who cry down Logic will generally warn you against Political Economy. It is unfeeling, they will tell you. It recognises unpleasant facts. For my part, the most unfeeling thing I know of is the law of gravitation: it breaks the neck of the best and most amiable person without scruple, if he forgets for a single moment to give heed to it. The winds and waves too are very unfeeling. Would you advise those who go to sea to deny the winds and waves—or to make use of them, and find the means of guarding against their dangers? My advice to you is to study the great writers on Political Economy, and hold firmly by whatever in them you find true; and depend upon it that if you are not selfish or hard-hearted already, Political Economy will not make you so. Of no less importance than Political Economy is the study of what is called Jurisprudence; the general principles of law; the social necessities which laws are required to meet; the features common to all systems of law, and the differences between them; the requisites of good legislation, the proper mode of constructing a legal system, and the best constitution of courts of justice and modes of legal procedure. These things are not only the chief part of the business of government, but the vital concern of every citizen; and their improvement affords a wide scope for the energies of any duly prepared mind, ambitious of contributing towards the better condition of the human race. For this, too, admirable helps have been provided by writers of our own or of a very recent time. At the head of them stands Bentham; undoubtedly the greatest master who ever devoted the labour of a life to let in light on the subject of law; and who is the more intelligible to non-professional persons, because, as his way is, he builds up the subject from its foundation in the facts of human life, and shows by careful consideration of ends and means, what law might and ought to be, in deplorable contrast with what it is. Other enlightened jurists have followed with contributions of two kinds, as the type of which I may take two works, equally admirable in their respective *b*lines*b*. Mr. Austin, in his *Lectures on Jurisprud-*

---

*b-b*67[1]   times [*printer's error?*]

ence,[*] takes for his basis the Roman law, the most elaborately consistent legal system which history has shewn us in actual operation, and that which the greatest number of accomplished minds have employed themselves in harmonizing. From this he singles out the principles and distinctions which are of general applicability, and employs the powers and resources of a most precise and analytic mind to give to those principles and distinctions a philosophic basis, grounded in the universal reason of mankind, and not in mere technical convenience. Mr. Maine, in his treatise on *Ancient Law in its relations to Modern Thought*,[†] shews from the history of law, and from what is known of the primitive institutions of mankind, the origin of much that has lasted till now, and has a firm footing both in the laws and in the ideas of modern times; shewing that many of these things never originated in reason, but are relics of the institutions of barbarous society, modified more or less by civilization, but kept standing by the persistency of ideas which were the offspring of those barbarous institutions, and have survived their parent. The path opened by Mr. Maine has been followed up by others, with additional illustrations of the influence of obsolete ideas on modern institutions, and of obsolete institutions on modern ideas; an action and reaction which perpetuate, in many of the greatest concerns, a mitigated barbarism: things being continually accepted as dictates of nature and necessities of life, which, if we knew all, we should see to have originated in artificial arrangements of society, long since abandoned and condemned.

To these studies I would add International Law; which I decidedly think should be taught in all universities, and should form part of all liberal education. The need of it is far from being limited to diplomatists and lawyers; it extends to every citizen. What is called the Law of Nations is not properly law, but a part of ethics: a set of moral rules, accepted as authoritative by civilized states. It is true that these rules neither are nor ought to be of eternal obligation, but do and must vary more or less from age to age, as the consciences of nations become more enlightened and the exigencies of political society undergo change. But the rules mostly were at their origin, and still are, an application of the maxims of honesty and humanity to the intercourse of states. They were introduced by the moral sentiments of mankind, or by their sense of the general interest, to mitigate the crimes and sufferings of a state of war, and to restrain governments and nations from unjust or dishonest conduct towards one another in time of peace. Since every country stands in numerous and various relations with the other countries of the world, and many, our own among the number, exercise actual authority over some of these, a knowledge of the established rules of international morality is essential to the duty of every nation, and therefore of every person in it who helps to make up the

[*John Austin, *Lectures on Jurisprudence*, ed. Sarah Austin, 3 vols. (London: Murray, 1863).]

[†Henry Maine, *Ancient Law: Its Connection with the Early History of Society, and Its Relation to Modern Ideas* (London: Murray, 1861).]

nation, and whose voice and feeling form a part of what is called public opinion. Let not any one pacify his conscience by the delusion that he can do no harm if he takes no part, and forms no opinion. Bad men need nothing more to compass their ends, than that good men should look on and do nothing. He is not a good man who, without a protest, allows wrong to be committed in his name, and with the means which he helps to supply, because he will not trouble himself to use his mind on the subject. It depends on the habit of attending to and looking into public transactions, and on the degree of information and solid judgment respecting them that exists in the community, whether the conduct of the nation as a nation, both within itself and towards others, shall be selfish, corrupt, and tyrannical, or rational and enlightened, just and noble.

Of these more advanced studies, only a small commencement can be made at schools and universities; but even this is of the highest value, by awakening an interest in the subjects, by conquering the first difficulties, and inuring the mind to the kind of exertion which the studies require, by implanting a desire to make further progress, and directing the student to the best tracks and the best helps. So far as these branches of knowledge have been acquired, we have learnt, or been put into the way of learning, our duty, and our work in life. Knowing it, however, is but half the work of education; it still remains, that what we know, we shall be willing and determined to put in practice. Nevertheless, to know the truth is already a great way towards disposing us to act upon it. What we see clearly and apprehend keenly, we have a natural desire to act out. "To see the best, and yet the worst pursue,"[*] is a possible but not a common state of mind; those who follow the wrong have generally first taken care to be voluntarily ignorant of the right. They have silenced their conscience, but they are not knowingly disobeying it. If you take an average human mind while still young, before the objects it has chosen in life have given it a turn in any bad direction, you will generally find it desiring what is good, right, and for the benefit of all; and if that season is properly used to implant the knowledge and give the training which shall render rectitude of judgment more habitual than sophistry, a serious barrier will have been erected against the inroads of selfishness and falsehood. Still, it is a very imperfect education which trains the intelligence only, but not the will. No one can dispense with an education directed expressly to the moral as well as the intellectual part of his being. Such education, so far as it is direct, is either moral or religious; and these may either be treated as distinct, or as different aspects of the same thing. The subject we are now considering is not education as a whole, but scholastic education, and we must keep in view the inevitable limitations of what schools and universities can do. It is beyond their power to educate morally or religiously. Moral and religious education consist in training the feelings and the daily habits;

[*Cf. Ovid, *Metamorphoses* (Latin and English), trans. Frank Justus Miller, 2 vols. (London: Heinemann; New York: Putnam's Sons, 1916), Vol. I, p. 342 (VII, 20-1).]

and these are, in the main, beyond the sphere and inaccessible to the control of public education. It is the home, the family, which gives us the moral or religious education we really receive: and this is completed, and modified, sometimes for the better, often for the worse, by society, and the opinions and feelings with which we are there surrounded. The moral or religious influence which an university can exercise, consists less in any express teaching, than in the pervading tone of the place. Whatever it teaches, it should teach as penetrated by a sense of duty; it should present all knowledge as chiefly a means to worthiness of life, given for the double purpose of making each of us practically useful to his fellow-creatures, and of elevating the character of the species itself; exalting and dignifying our nature. There is nothing which spreads more contagiously from teacher to pupil than elevation of sentiment: often and often have students caught from the living influence of a professor, a contempt for mean and selfish objects, and a noble ambition to leave the world better than they found it, which they have carried with them throughout life. In these respects, teachers of every kind have natural and peculiar means of doing with effect, what every one who mixes with his fellow-beings, or addresses himself to them in any character, should feel bound to do to the extent of his capacity and opportunities. What is special to an university on these subjects belongs chiefly, like the rest of its work, to the intellectual department. An university exists for the purpose of laying open to each succeeding generation, as far as the conditions of the case admit, the accumulated treasure of the thoughts of mankind. As an indispensable part of this, it has to make known to them what mankind at large, their own country, and the best and wisest individual men, have thought on the great subjects of morals and religion. There should be, and there is in most universities, professorial instruction in moral philosophy; but I could wish that this instruction were of a somewhat different type from what is ordinarily met with. I could wish that it were more expository, less polemical, and above all less dogmatic. The learner should be made acquainted with the principal systems of moral philosophy which have existed and been practically operative among mankind, and should hear what there is to be said for each: the Aristotelian, the Epicurean, the Stoic, the Judaic, the Christian in the various modes of its interpretation, which differ almost as much from one another as the teachings of those earlier schools. He should be made familiar with the different standards of right and wrong which have been taken as the basis of ethics: general utility, natural justice, natural rights, a moral sense, principles of practical reason, and the rest. Among all these, it is not so much the teacher's business to take a side, and fight stoutly for some one against the rest, as it is to direct them all towards the establishment and preservation of the rules of conduct most advantageous to mankind. There is not one of these systems which has not its good side; not one from which there is not something to be learnt by the votaries of the others; not one which is not suggested by a keen, though it may not always be a clear, perception of some important truths, which are the prop of the system, and the neglect or undervaluing of which in other systems is their characteristic infirmity. A system which may be as a whole erroneous, is still valuable, until it has forced upon mankind a sufficient attention to the portion of truth which suggested it. The ethical teacher does his part best, when he points out how each system may be strengthened even on its own basis, by taking into more complete account the truths which other systems have realized more fully and made more prominent. I do not mean that he should encourage an essentially sceptical eclecticism. While placing every system in the best aspect it admits of, and endeavouring to draw from all of them the most salutary consequences compatible with their nature, I would by no means debar him from enforcing by his best arguments his own preference for some one of the number. They cannot be all true; though those which are false as theories may contain particular truths, indispensable to the completeness of the true theory. But on this subject, even more than on any of those I have previously mentioned, it is not the teacher's business to impose his own judgment, but to inform and discipline that of his pupil.

And this same clue, if we keep hold of it, will guide us through the labyrinth of conflicting thought into which we enter when we touch the great question of the relation of education to religion. As I have already said, the only really effective religious education is the parental—that of home and childhood. All that social and public education has in its power to do, further than by a general pervading tone of reverence and duty, amounts to little more than the information which it can give; but this is extremely valuable. I shall not enter into the question which has been debated with so much vehemence in the last and present generation, whether religion ought to be taught at all in universities and public schools, seeing that religion is the subject of all others on which men's opinions are most widely at variance. On neither side of this controversy do the disputants seem to me to have sufficiently freed their minds from the old notion of education, that it consists in the dogmatic inculcation from authority, of what the teacher deems true. Why should it be impossible, that information of the greatest value, on subjects connected with religion, should be brought before the student's mind; that he should be made acquainted with so important a part of the national thought, and of the intellectual labours of past generations, as those relating to religion, without being taught dogmatically the doctrines of any church or sect? Christianity being a historical religion, the sort of religious instruction which seems to me most appropriate to an University is the study of ecclesiastical history. If teaching, even on matters of scientific certainty, should aim quite as much at showing how the results are arrived at, as at teaching the results themselves, far more, then, should this be the case on subjects where there is the widest diversity of opinion among men of equal ability, and who have taken equal pains to arrive at the truth. This diversity should of itself be a warning to a conscientious teacher that he has no right to impose his opinion authoritatively upon a youthful mind. His teaching should not be in the spirit of dogmatism, but in that of enquiry. The pupil should not be addressed as if his religion had been chosen for him, but as one who will have to choose it for himself. The various Churches, established and unestablished, are quite competent to the task which is peculiarly theirs, that of teaching each its own doctrines, as far as necessary, to its own rising generation. The proper business of an University is different: not to tell us from authority what we ought to believe, and make us accept the belief as a duty, but to give us information and training, and help us to form our own belief in a manner worthy of intelligent beings, who seek for truth at all hazards, and demand to know all the difficulties, in order that they may be better qualified to find, or recognise, the most satisfactory mode of resolving them. The vast importance of these questions—the great results as regards the conduct of our lives, which depend upon our choosing one belief or another—are the strongest reasons why we should not trust our judgment when it has been formed in ignorance of the evidence, and why we should not consent to be restricted to a one-sided teaching, which informs us of what a particular teacher or association of teachers receive as true doctrine and sound argument, but of nothing more.

I do not affirm that an University, if it represses free thought and enquiry, must be altogether a failure, for the freest thinkers have often been trained in the most slavish seminaries of learning. The great Christian reformers were taught in Roman Catholic Universities; the sceptical philosophers of France were mostly educated by the Jesuits. The human mind is sometimes impelled all the more violently in one direction, by an over zealous and demonstrative attempt to drag it in the opposite. But this is not what Universities are appointed for—to drive men from them, even into good, by excess of evil. An University ought to be a place of free speculation. The more diligently it does its duty in all other respects, the more certain it is to be that. The old English Universities, in the present generation, are doing better work than they have done within human memory in teaching the ordinary studies of their curriculum; and one of the consequences has been, that whereas they formerly seemed to exist mainly for the repression of independent thought, and the chaining up of the individual intellect and conscience, they are now the great foci of free and manly enquiry, to the higher and professional classes, south of the Tweed. The ruling minds of those ancient seminaries have at last remembered that to place themselves in hostility to the free use of the understanding, is to abdicate their own best privilege, that of guiding it. A modest deference, at least provisional, to the united authority of the specially instructed, is becoming in a youthful and imperfectly formed mind; but when there is no united authority—when the specially instructed are so divided and scattered that almost any opinion can boast of some high authority, and no opinion whatever can claim all; when, therefore, it can never be deemed extremely improbable that one who uses his mind freely may see reason to change his first opinion; then, whatever you do, keep, at all risks, your minds open: do not barter away your freedom of thought. Those of you who are destined for the clerical profession are, no doubt, so far held to a certain number of doctrines, that if they ceased to believe them they would not be justified in remaining in a position in which they would be required to teach insincerely. But use your influence to make those doctrines as few as possible. It is not right that men should be bribed to hold out against conviction—to shut their ears against objections, or, if the objections penetrate, to continue professing full and unfaltering belief when their confidence is already shaken. Neither is it right that if men honestly profess to have changed some of their religious opinions, their honesty should as a matter of course exclude them from taking a part for which they may be admirably qualified, in the spiritual instruction of the nation. The tendency of the age, on both sides of the ancient Border, is towards the relaxation of formularies, and a less rigid construction of articles. This very circumstance, by making the limits of orthodoxy less definite, and obliging every one to draw the line for himself, is an embarrassment to consciences. But I hold entirely with those clergymen who elect to remain in the national church, so long as they are able to accept its articles and confessions in any sense or with any interpretation consistent with common honesty, whether it be the generally received interpretation or not. If all were to desert the church who put a large and liberal construction on its terms of communion, or who would wish to see those terms widened, the national provision for religious teaching and worship would be left utterly to those who take the narrowest, the most literal, and purely textual view of the formularies; who, though by no means necessarily bigots, are under the great disadvantage of having the bigots for their allies, and who, however great their merits may be, and they are often very great, yet if the church is improvable, are not the most likely persons to improve it. Therefore, if it were not an impertinence in me to tender advice in such a matter, I should say, let all who conscientiously can, remain in the church. A church is far more easily improved from within than from without. Almost all the illustrious reformers of religion began by being clergymen: but they did not think that their profession as clergymen was inconsistent with being reformers. They mostly indeed ended their days outside the churches in which they were born; but it was because the churches, in an evil hour for themselves, cast them out. They did not think it any business of theirs to withdraw. They thought they had a better right to remain in the fold, than those had who expelled them.

I have now said what I had to say on the two kinds of education which the system of schools and universities is intended to promote—intellectual education, and moral education: knowledge and the training of the knowing faculty, conscience and that of the moral faculty. These are the two main ingredients of human culture; but they do not exhaust the whole of it. There is a third division, which, if subordinate, and owing allegiance to the two others, is barely inferior to them, and not less needful to the completeness of the human being; I mean the aesthetic branch; the culture which comes through poetry and art, and may be described as the education of the feelings, and the cultivation of the beautiful. This department of things deserves to be regarded in a far more serious light than is the custom of these countries. It is only of late, and chiefly by a superficial imitation of foreigners, that we have begun to use the word Art by itself, and to speak of Art as we speak of Science, or Government, or Religion: we used to talk of the Arts, and more specifically of the Fine Arts: and even by them were vulgarly meant only two forms of art, Painting and Sculpture, the two which as a people we cared least about—which were regarded even by the more cultivated among us as little more than branches of domestic ornamentation, a kind of elegant upholstery. The very words "Fine Arts" called up a notion of frivolity, of great pains expended on a rather trifling object—on something which differed from the cheaper and commoner arts of producing pretty things, mainly by being more difficult, and by giving fops an opportunity of pluming themselves on caring for it and on being able to talk about it. This estimate extended in no small degree, though not altogether, even to poetry; the queen of arts, but, in Great Britain, hardly included under the name. It cannot exactly be said that poetry was little thought of; we were proud of our Shakespeare and Milton, and in one period at least of our history, that of Queen Anne, it was a high literary distinction to be a poet; but poetry was hardly looked upon in any serious light, or as having much value except as an amusement or excitement, the superiority of which over others principally consisted in being that of a more refined order of minds. Yet the celebrated saying of Fletcher of Saltoun, "Let who will make the laws of a people if I write their songs,"[*] might have taught us how great an instrument for acting on the human mind we were undervaluing. It would be difficult for anybody to imagine that "Rule Britannia," for example, or "Scots wha hae,"[†] had no permanent influence on the higher region of human character; some of Moore's songs have done more for Ireland than all Grattan's speeches: and songs are far from being the highest or most impressive form of poetry. On these subjects, the mode of thinking and feeling of other countries was not only not intelligible, but not credible, to an average Englishman. To find Art ranking on a complete equality, in theory at least, with Philosophy, Learning, and Science—as holding an equally important place among the agents of civilization and among the elements of the worth of humanity; to find even painting and sculpture treated as great social powers, and the art of a country as a feature in its character and condition, little inferior in importance to either its religion or its government; all this only did not amaze and puzzle Englishmen, because it was too strange for them to be able to realize it, or, in truth, to believe it possible: and the radical difference of feeling on this matter between the British

[*Cf. Andrew Fletcher, *An Account of a Conversation Concerning a Right Regulation of Governments for the Common Good of Mankind* (Edinburgh: n.p., 1704), p. 10.]

[†James Thomson and David Mallet, "An Ode" ["Rule, Britannia"], in *Alfred: A Masque* (London: Millar, 1740), and Robert Burns, "Scots wha hae wi Wallace bled" (1794), in *Works*, new ed., 2 pts. (London: Tegg, *et al.*; Dublin: Milliken, *et al.*; Glasgow: Griffin, 1824), Pt. II, p. 254.]

people and those of France, Germany, and the Continent generally, is one among the causes of that extraordinary inability to understand one another, which exists between England and the rest of Europe, while it does not exist to anything like the same degree between one nation of Continental Europe and another. It may be traced to the two influences which have chiefly shaped the British character since the days of the Stuarts: commercial money-getting business, and religious Puritanism. Business, demanding the whole of the faculties, and whether pursued from duty or the love of gain, regarding as a loss of time whatever does not conduce directly to the end; Puritanism, which looking upon every feeling of human nature, except fear and reverence for God, as a snare, if not as partaking of sin, looked coldly, if not disapprovingly, on the cultivation of the sentiments. Different causes have produced different effects in the Continental nations; among whom it is even now observable that virtue and goodness are generally for the most part an affair of the sentiments, while with us they are almost exclusively an affair of duty. Accordingly, the kind of advantage which we have had over many other countries in point of morals—I am not sure that we are not losing it—has consisted in greater tenderness of conscience. In this we have had on the whole a real superiority, though one principally negative; for conscience is with most men a power chiefly in the way of restraint—a power which acts rather in staying our hands from any great wickedness, than by the direction it gives to the general course of our desires and sentiments. One of the commonest types of character among us is that of a man all whose ambition is self-regarding; who has no higher purpose in life than to enrich or raise in the world himself and his family; who never dreams of making the good of his fellow-creatures or of his country an habitual object, further than giving away, annually or from time to time, certain sums in charity; but who has a conscience sincerely alive to whatever is generally considered wrong, and would scruple to use any very illegitimate means for attaining his self-interested objects. While it will often happen in other countries that men whose feelings and whose active energies point strongly in an unselfish direction, who have the love of their country, of human improvement, of human freedom, even of virtue, in great strength, and of whose thoughts and activity a large share is devoted to disinterested objects, will yet, in the pursuit of these or of any other objects that they strongly desire, permit themselves to do wrong things which the other man, though intrinsically, and taking the whole of his character, farther removed from what a human being ought to be, could not bring himself to commit. It is of no use to debate which of these two states of mind is the best, or rather the least bad. It is quite possible to cultivate the conscience and the sentiments too. Nothing hinders us from so training a man that he will not, even for a disinterested purpose, violate the moral law, and also feeding and encouraging those high feelings, on which we mainly rely for lifting men above low and sordid objects, and giving them a higher conception of what constitutes success in life. If we wish men to practise virtue, it is worth while trying to make them love virtue, and feel it an object in itself, and not a tax paid for leave to pursue other objects. It is worth training them to feel, not only actual wrong or actual meanness, but the absence of noble aims and endeavours, as not merely blameable but also degrading: to have a feeling of the miserable smallness of mere self in the face of this great universe, of the collective mass of our fellow creatures, in the face of past history and of the indefinite future—the poorness and insignificance of human life if it is to be all spent in making things comfortable for ourselves and our kin, and raising ourselves and them a step or two on the social ladder. Thus feeling, we learn to respect ourselves only so far as we feel capable of nobler objects: and if unfortunately those by whom we are surrounded do not share our aspirations, perhaps disapprove the conduct to which we are prompted by them—to sustain ourselves by the ideal sympathy of the great characters in history, or even in fiction, and by the contemplation of an idealized posterity: shall I add, of ideal perfection embodied in a Divine Being? Now, of this elevated tone of mind the great source of inspiration is poetry, and all literature so far as it is poetical and artistic. We may imbibe exalted feelings from Plato, or Demosthenes, or Tacitus, but it is in so far as those great men are not solely philosophers or orators or historians, but poets and artists. Nor is it only loftiness, only the heroic feelings, that are bred by poetic cultivation. Its power is as great in calming the soul as in elevating it—in fostering the milder emotions, as the more exalted. It brings home to us all those aspects of life which take hold of our nature on its unselfish side, and lead us to identify our joy and grief with the good or ill of the system of which we form a part; and all those solemn or pensive feelings, which, without having any direct application to conduct, incline us to take life seriously, and predispose us to the reception of anything which comes before us in the shape of duty. Who does not feel a better man after a course of Dante, or of Wordsworth, or, I will add, of Lucretius or the *Georgics*, or after brooding over Gray's *Elegy*, or Shelley's "Hymn to Intellectual Beauty"?[*] I have spoken of poetry, but all the other modes of art produce similar effects in their degree. The races and nations whose senses are naturally finer and their sensuous perceptions more exercised than ours, receive the same kind of impressions from painting and sculpture: and many of the more delicately organized among ourselves do the same. All the arts of expression tend to keep alive and in activity the feelings they express. Do you think that the great Italian painters would have filled the place they did in the European mind, would

[*For the specific titles referred to, see Lucretius, *De rerum natura* (Latin and English), trans. W.H.D. Rouse (London: Heinemann; New York: Putnam's Sons, 1924); Virgil, *Georgics*, in *Virgil* (Latin and English), trans. H. Rushton Fairclough, 2 vols. (London: Heinemann; New York: Putnam's Sons, 1922), Vol. I, pp. 80-236; Thomas Grey, *An Elegy Wrote in a Country Church Yard*, in *Works*, ed. Thomas James Mathias, 2 vols. (London: Porter, 1814), Vol. I, pp. 57-63; and Percy Bysshe Shelley, "Hymn to Intellectual Beauty," in *Rosalind and Helen, a Modern Eclogue; with Other Poems* (London: Ollier, 1819), pp. 87-91. The references to Dante and Wordsworth are to their writings in general.]

have been universally ranked among the greatest men of their time, if their productions had done nothing for it but to serve as the decoration of a public hall or a private *salon*? Their Nativities and Crucifixions, their glorious Madonnas and Saints, were to their susceptible Southern countrymen the great school not only of devotional, but of all the elevated and all the imaginative feelings. We colder Northerns may approach to a conception of this function of art when we listen to an oratorio of Handel, or give ourselves up to the emotions excited by a Gothic cathedral. Even apart from any specific emotional expression, the mere contemplation of beauty of a high order produces in no small degree this elevating effect on the character. The power of natural scenery addresses itself to the same region of human nature which corresponds to Art. There are few capable of feeling the sublimer order of natural beauty, such as your own Highlands and other mountain regions afford, who are not, at least temporarily, raised by it above the littlenesses of humanity, and made to feel the puerility of the petty objects which set men's interests at variance, contrasted with the nobler pleasures which all might share. To whatever avocations we may be called in life, let us never quash these susceptibilities within us, but carefully seek the opportunities of maintaining them in exercise. The more prosaic our ordinary duties, the more necessary it is to keep up the tone of our minds by frequent visits to that higher region of thought and feeling, in which every work seems dignified in proportion to the ends for which, and the spirit in which, it is done; where we learn, while eagerly seizing every opportunity of exercising higher faculties and performing higher duties, to regard all useful and honest work as a public function, which may be ennobled by the mode of performing it—which has not properly any other nobility than what that gives—and which, if ever so humble, is never mean but when it is meanly done, and when the motives from which it is done are mean motives. There is, besides, a natural affinity between goodness and the cultivation of the Beautiful, when it is real cultivation, and not a mere unguided instinct. He who has learnt what beauty is, if he be of a virtuous character, will desire to realize it in his own life—will keep before himself a type of perfect beauty in human character, to light his attempts at self-culture. There is a true meaning in the saying of Goethe, though liable to be misunderstood and perverted, that the Beautiful is greater than the Good;[*] for it includes the Good, and adds something to it: it is the Good made perfect, and fitted with all the collateral perfections which make it a finished and completed thing. Now, this sense of perfection, which would make us demand from every creation of man the very utmost that it ought to give, and render us intolerant of the smallest fault in ourselves or in anything we do, is one of the results of Art cultivation. No other human productions come so near to perfection as works of pure Art. In all other things, we are, and may reasonably be, satisfied if the degree of excellence

[*This saying has not been found in Johann Wolfgang von Goethe; Mill very likely took it from Thomas Carlyle, *On Heroes, Hero-Worship, and the Heroic in History* (London: Fraser, 1841), p. 132.]

is as great as the object immediately in view seems to us to be worth: but in Art, the perfection is itself the object. If I were to define Art, I should be inclined to call it, the endeavour after perfection in execution. If we meet with even a piece of mechanical work which bears the marks of being done in this spirit—which is done as if the workman loved it, and tried to make it as good as possible, though something less good would have answered the purpose for which it was ostensibly made—we say that he has worked like an artist. Art, when really cultivated, and not merely practised empirically, maintains, what it first gave the conception of, an ideal Beauty, to be eternally aimed at, though surpassing what can be actually attained; and by this idea it trains us never to be completely satisfied with imperfection in what we ourselves do and are: to idealize, as much as possible, every work we do, and most of all, our own characters and lives.

And now, having travelled with you over the whole range of the materials and training which an University supplies as a preparation for the higher uses of life, it is almost needless to add any exhortation to you to profit by the gift. Now is your opportunity for gaining a degree of insight into subjects larger and far more ennobling than the minutiae of a business or a profession, and for acquiring a facility of using your minds on all that concerns the higher interests of man, which you will carry with you into the occupations of active life, and which will prevent even the short intervals of time which that may leave you, from being altogether lost for noble purposes. Having once conquered the first difficulties, the only ones of which the irksomeness surpasses the interest; having turned the point beyond which what was once a task becomes a pleasure; in even the busiest after-life, the higher powers of your mind will make progress imperceptibly, by the spontaneous exercise of your thoughts, and by the lessons you will know how to learn from daily experience. So, at least, it will be if in your early studies you have fixed your eyes upon the ultimate end from which those studies take their chief value—that of making you more effective combatants in the great fight which never ceases to rage between Good and Evil, and more equal to coping with the ever new problems which the changing course of human nature and human society present to be resolved. Aims like these commonly retain the footing which they have once established in the mind; and their presence in our thoughts keeps our higher faculties in exercise, and makes us consider the acquirements and powers which we store up at any time of our lives, as a mental capital, to be freely expended in helping forward any mode which presents itself of making mankind in any respect wiser or better, or placing any portion of human affairs on a more sensible and rational footing than its existing one. There is not one of us who may not qualify himself so to improve the average amount of opportunities, as to leave his fellow creatures some little the better for the use he has known how to make of his intellect. To make this little greater, let us strive to keep ourselves acquainted with the best thoughts that are brought forth by the original minds of the age; that we may know what movements stand most in need of our aid, and that, as far as depends on us, the good seed may not fall on a rock, and perish without reaching the soil in which it might have germinated and flourished.[*] You are to be a part of the public who are to welcome, encourage, and help forward the future intellectual benefactors of humanity; and you are, if possible, to furnish your contingent to the number of those benefactors. Nor let any one be discouraged by what may seem, in moments of despondency, the lack of time and of opportunity. Those who know how to employ opportunities will often find that they can create them: and what we achieve depends less on the amount of time we possess, than on the use we make of our time. You and your like are the hope and resource of your country in the coming generation. All great things which that generation is destined to do, have to be done by some like you; several will assuredly be done by persons for whom society has done much less, to whom it has given far less preparation, than those whom I am now addressing. I do not attempt to instigate you by the prospect of direct rewards, either earthly or heavenly; the less we think about being rewarded in either way, the better for us. But there is one reward which will not fail you, and which may be called disinterested, because it is not a consequence, but is inherent in the very fact of deserving it; the deeper and more varied interest you will feel in life: which will give it tenfold its value, and a value which will last to the end. All merely personal objects grow less valuable as we advance in life: this not only endures but increases.

[*Cf. Luke, 8:6.]

THE SUBJECTION OF WOMEN

1869

EDITOR'S NOTE

3rd ed. London: Longmans, Green, Reader, and Dyer, 1870. Reprinted without variants from 1st and 2nd eds., *ibid.*, both 1869. Not listed in Mill's bibliography. There are no corrections in the Somerville College copy of the 2nd ed. For comment on the work, see xxix-xxxvii and lxviii-lxxi above.

Chapter I

THE OBJECT OF THIS ESSAY is to explain as clearly as I am able, the grounds of an opinion which I have held from the very earliest period when I had formed any opinions at all on social or political matters, and which, instead of being weakened or modified, has been constantly growing stronger by the progress of reflection and the experience of life: That the principle which regulates the existing social relations between the two sexes—the legal subordination of one sex to the other—is wrong in itself, and now one of the chief hindrances to human improvement; and that it ought to be replaced by a principle of perfect equality, admitting no power or privilege on the one side, nor disability on the other.

The very words necessary to express the task I have undertaken, show how arduous it is. But it would be a mistake to suppose that the difficulty of the case must lie in the insufficiency or obscurity of the grounds of reason on which my conviction rests. The difficulty is that which exists in all cases in which there is a mass of feeling to be contended against. So long as an opinion is strongly rooted in the feelings, it gains rather than loses in stability by having a preponderating weight of argument against it. For if it were accepted as a result of argument, the refutation of the argument might shake the solidity of the conviction; but when it rests solely on feeling, the worse it fares in argumentative contest, the more persuaded its adherents are that their feeling must have some deeper ground, which the arguments do not reach; and while the feeling remains, it is always throwing up fresh intrenchments of argument to repair any breach made in the old. And there are so many causes tending to make the feelings connected with this subject the most intense and most deeply-rooted of all those which gather round and protect old institutions and customs, that we need not wonder to find them as yet less undermined and loosened than any of the rest by the progress of the great modern spiritual and social transition; nor suppose that the barbarisms to which men cling longest must be less barbarisms than those which they earlier shake off.

In every respect the burthen is hard on those who attack an almost universal opinion. They must be very fortunate as well as unusually capable if they obtain a hearing at all. They have more difficulty in obtaining a trial, than any other litigants have in getting a verdict. If they do extort a hearing, they are subjected to a set of logical requirements totally different from those exacted from other people. In all other cases, the burthen of proof is supposed to lie with the affirmative. If a person is charged with a murder, it rests with those who accuse him to give proof of his guilt, not with himself to prove his innocence. If there is a difference of opinion about the reality of any alleged historical event, in which the feelings of men in general are not much interested, as the Siege of Troy for example, those who maintain that the event took place are expected to produce their proofs, before those who take the other side can be required to say anything; and at no time are these required to do more than show that the evidence produced by the others is of no value. Again, in practical matters, the burthen of proof is supposed to be with those who are against liberty; who contend for any restriction or prohibition; either any limitation of the general freedom of human action, or any disqualification or disparity of privilege affecting one person or kind of persons, as compared with others. The *à priori* presumption is in favour of freedom and impartiality. It is held that there should be no restraint not required by the general good, and that the law should be no respecter of persons, but should treat all alike, save where dissimilarity of treatment is required by positive reasons, either of justice or of policy. But of none of these rules of evidence will the benefit be allowed to those who maintain the opinion I profess. It is useless for me to say that those who maintain the doctrine that men have a right to command and women are under an obligation to obey, or that men are fit for government and women unfit, are on the affirmative side of the question, and that they are bound to show positive evidence for the assertions, or submit to their rejection. It is equally unavailing for me to say that those who deny to women any freedom or privilege rightly allowed to men, having the double presumption against them that they are opposing freedom and recommending partiality, must be held to the strictest proof of their case, and unless their success be such as to exclude all doubt, the judgment ought to go against them. These would be thought good pleas in any common case; but they will not be thought so in this instance. Before I could hope to make any impression, I should be expected not only to answer all that has ever been said by those who take the other side of the question, but to imagine all that could be said by them—to find them in reasons, as well as answer all I find: and besides refuting all arguments for the affirmative, I shall be called upon for invincible positive arguments to prove a negative. And even if I could do all this, and leave the opposite party with a host of unanswered arguments against them, and not a single unrefuted one on their side, I should be thought to have done little; for a cause supported on the one hand by universal usage, and on the other by so great a preponderance of popular sentiment, is supposed to have a presumption in its favour, superior to any conviction which an appeal to reason has power to produce in any intellects but those of a high class.

I do not mention these difficulties to complain of them; first, because it would be useless; they are inseparable from having to contend through people's understandings against the hostility of their feelings and practical tendencies: and truly the understandings of the majority of mankind would need to be much better cultivated than has ever yet been the case, before they can be asked to place such reliance in their own power of estimating arguments, as to give up practical principles in which they have been born and bred and which are the basis of much of the existing order of the world, at the first argumentative attack which they are not capable of logically resisting. I do not therefore quarrel with them for having too little faith in argument, but for having too much faith in custom and the general feeling. It is one of the characteristic prejudices of the reaction of the nineteenth century against the eighteenth, to accord to the unreasoning elements in human nature the infallibility which the eighteenth century is supposed to have ascribed to the reasoning elements. For the apotheosis of Reason we have substituted that of Instinct; and we call everything instinct which we find in ourselves and for which we cannot trace any rational foundation. This idolatry, infinitely more degrading than the other, and the most pernicious of the false worships of the present day, of all of which it is now the main support, will probably hold its ground until it gives way before a sound psychology, laying bare the real root of much that is bowed down to as the intention of Nature and the ordinance of God. As regards the present question, I am willing to accept the unfavourable conditions which the prejudice assigns to me. I consent that established custom, and the general feeling, should be deemed conclusive against me, unless that custom and feeling from age to age can be shown to have owed their existence to other causes than their soundness, and to have derived their power from the worse rather than the better parts of human nature. I am willing that judgment should go against me, unless I can show that my judge has been tampered with. The concession is not so great as it might appear; for to prove this, is by far the easiest portion of my task.

The generality of a practice is in some cases a strong presumption that it is, or at all events once was, conducive to laudable ends. This is the case, when the practice was first adopted, or afterwards kept up, as a means to such ends, and was grounded on experience of the mode in which they could be most effectually attained. If the authority of men over women, when first established, had been the result of a conscientious comparison between different modes of constituting the government of society; if, after trying various other modes of social organization —the government of women over men, equality between the two, and such mixed and divided modes of government as might be invented—it had been decided, on the testimony of experience, that the mode in which women are wholly under the rule of men, having no share at all in public concerns, and each in private being under the legal obligation of obedience to the man with whom she has associated her destiny, was the arrangement most conducive to the happiness and well being of both; its general adoption might then be fairly thought to be some evidence that, at the time when it was adopted, it was the best: though even then the considerations which recommended it may, like so many other primeval social facts of the greatest importance, have subsequently, in the course of ages, ceased to exist. But the state of the case is in every respect the reverse of this. In the first place, the opinion in favour of the present system, which entirely subordinates the weaker sex to the stronger, rests upon theory only; for there never has been trial made of any other: so that experience, in the sense in which it is vulgarly opposed to theory, cannot be pretended to have pronounced any verdict. And in the second place, the adoption of this system of inequality never was the result of deliberation, or forethought, or any social ideas, or any notion whatever of what conduced to the benefit of humanity or the good order of society. It arose simply from the fact that from the very earliest twilight of human society, every woman (owing to the value attached to her by men, combined with her inferiority in muscular strength) was found in a state of bondage to some man. Laws and systems of polity always begin by recognising the relations they find already existing between individuals. They convert what was a mere physical fact into a legal right, give it the sanction of society, and principally aim at the substitution of public and organized means of asserting and protecting these rights, instead of the irregular and lawless conflict of physical strength. Those who had already been compelled to obedience became in this manner legally bound to it. Slavery, from being a mere affair of force between the master and the slave, became regularized and a matter of compact among the masters, who, binding themselves to one another for common protection, guaranteed by their collective strength the private possessions of each, including his slaves. In early times, the great majority of the male sex were slaves, as well as the whole of the female. And many ages elapsed, some of them ages of high cultivation, before any thinker was bold enough to question the rightfulness, and the absolute social necessity, either of the one slavery or of the other. By degrees such thinkers did arise: and (the general progress of society assisting) the slavery of the male sex has, in all the countries of Christian Europe at least (though, in one of them, only within the last few years) been at length abolished, and that of the female sex has been gradually changed into a milder form of dependence. But this dependence, as it exists at present, is not an original institution, taking a fresh start from considerations of justice and social expediency—it is the primitive state of slavery lasting on, through successive mitigations and modifications occasioned by the same causes which have softened the general manners, and brought all human relations more under the control of justice and the influence of humanity. It has not lost the taint of its brutal origin. No presumption in its favour, therefore, can be drawn from the fact of its existence. The only such presumption which it could be supposed to have, must be grounded on its having lasted till now, when so many other things which came down from the same odious source have been done away with. And this, indeed, is what makes it strange to ordinary ears, to hear it asserted that the inequality of rights between men and women has no other source than the law of the strongest.

That this statement should have the effect of a paradox, is in some respects creditable to the progress of civilization, and the improvement of the moral sentiments of mankind. We now live—that is to say, one or two of the most advanced nations of the world now live—in a state in which the law of the strongest seems to be entirely abandoned as the regulating principle of the world's affairs: nobody professes it, and, as regards most of the relations between human beings, nobody is permitted to practise it. When any one succeeds in doing so, it is under cover of some pretext which gives him the semblance of having some general social interest on his side. This being the ostensible state of things, people flatter themselves that the rule of mere force is ended; that the law of the strongest cannot be the reason of existence of anything which has remained in full operation down to the present time. However any of our present institutions may have begun, it can only, they think, have been preserved to this period of advanced civilization by a well-grounded feeling of its adaptation to human nature, and conduciveness to the general good. They do not understand the great vitality and durability of institutions which place right on the side of might; how intensely they are clung to; how the good as well as the bad propensities and sentiments of those who have power in their hands, become identified with retaining it; how slowly these bad institutions give way, one at a time, the weakest first, beginning with those which are least interwoven with the daily habits of life; and how very rarely those who have obtained legal power because they first had physical, have ever lost their hold of it until the physical power had passed over to the other side. Such shifting of the physical force not having taken place in the case of women; this fact, combined with all the peculiar and characteristic features of the particular case, made it certain from the first that this branch of the system of right founded on might, though softened in its most atrocious features at an earlier period than several of the others, would be the very last to disappear. It was inevitable that this one case of a social relation grounded on force, would survive through generations of institutions grounded on equal justice, an almost solitary exception to the general character of their laws and customs; but which, so long as it does not proclaim its own origin, and as discussion has not brought out its true character, is not felt to jar with modern civilization, any more than domestic slavery among the Greeks jarred with their notion of themselves as a free people.

The truth is, that people of the present and the last two or three generations have lost all practical sense of the primitive condition of humanity; and only the few who have studied history accurately, or have much frequented the parts of the world occupied by the living representatives of ages long past, are able to form any mental picture of what society then was. People are not aware how entirely, in former ages, the law of superior strength was the rule of life; how publicly and openly it was avowed, I do not say cynically or shamelessly—for these words imply a feeling that there was something in it to be ashamed of, and no such notion could find a place in the faculties of any person in those ages, except a philosopher or a saint. History gives a cruel experience of human nature, in shewing how exactly the regard due to the life, possessions, and entire earthly happiness of any class of persons, was measured by what they had the power of enforcing; how all who made any resistance to authorities that had arms in their hands, however dreadful might be the provocation, had not only the law of force but all other laws, and all the notions of social obligation against them; and in the eyes of those whom they resisted, were not only guilty of crime, but of the worst of all crimes, deserving the most cruel chastisement which human beings could inflict. The first small vestige of a feeling of obligation in a superior to acknowledge any right in inferiors, began when he had been induced, for convenience, to make some promise to them. Though these promises, even when sanctioned by the most solemn oaths, were for many ages revoked or violated on the most trifling provocation or temptation, it is probable that this, except by persons of still worse than the average morality, was seldom done without some twinges of conscience. The ancient republics, being mostly grounded from the first upon some kind of mutual compact, or at any rate formed by an union of persons not very unequal in strength, afforded, in consequence, the first instance of a portion of human relations fenced round, and placed under the dominion of another law than that of force. And though the original law of force remained in full operation between them and their slaves, and also (except so far as limited by express compact) between a commonwealth and its subjects, or other independent commonwealths; the banishment of that primitive law even from so narrow a field, commenced the regeneration of human nature, by giving birth to sentiments of which experience soon demonstrated the immense value even for material interests, and which thenceforward only required to be enlarged, not created. Though slaves were no part of the commonwealth, it was in the free states that slaves were first felt to have rights as human beings. The Stoics were, I believe, the first (except so far as the Jewish law constitutes an exception) who taught as a part of morality that men were bound by moral obligations to their slaves. No one, after Christianity became ascendant, could ever again have been a stranger to this belief, in theory; nor, after the rise of the Catholic Church, was it ever without persons to stand up for it. Yet to enforce it was the most arduous task which Christianity ever had to perform. For more than a thousand years the Church kept up the contest, with hardly any perceptible success. It was not for want of power over men's minds. Its power was prodigious. It could make kings and nobles resign their most valued possessions to enrich the Church. It could make thousands, in the prime of life and the height of worldly advantages, shut themselves up in convents to work out their salvation by poverty, fasting, and prayer. It could send hundreds of thousands across land and sea, Europe and Asia, to give their lives for the deliverance of the Holy Sepulchre. It could make kings relinquish wives who were the object of their passionate attachment, because the Church declared that they were within the seventh (by our calculation the fourteenth) degree of relationship. All this it did; but it could not make men fight less with one another, nor tyrannize less cruelly over the serfs, and when they were able, over burgesses. It could not make them renounce either of the applications of force; force militant, or force triumphant. This they could never be induced to do until they were themselves in their turn compelled by superior force. Only by the growing power of kings was an end put to fighting except between kings, or competitors for kingship; only by the growth of a wealthy and warlike bourgeoisie in the fortified towns, and of a plebeian infantry which proved more powerful in the field than the undisciplined chivalry, was the insolent tyranny of the nobles over the bourgeoisie and peasantry brought within some bounds. It was persisted in not only until, but long after, the oppressed had obtained a power enabling them often to take conspicuous vengeance; and on the Continent much of it continued to the time of the French Revolution, though in England the earlier and better organization of the democratic classes put an end to it sooner, by establishing equal laws and free national institutions.

If people are mostly so little aware how completely, during the greater part of the duration of our species, the law of force was the avowed rule of general conduct, any other being only a special and exceptional consequence of peculiar ties—and from how very recent a date it is that the affairs of society in general have been even pretended to be regulated according to any moral law; as little do people remember or consider, how institutions and customs which never had any ground but the law of force, last on into ages and states of general opinion which never would have permitted their first establishment. Less than forty years ago, Englishmen might still by law hold human beings in bondage as saleable property: within the present century they might kidnap them and carry them off, and work them literally to death. This absolutely extreme case of the law of force, condemned by those who can tolerate almost every other form of arbitrary power, and which, of all others, presents features the most revolting to the feelings of all who look at it from an impartial position, was the law of civilized and Christian England within the memory of persons now living: and in one half of Anglo-Saxon America three or four years ago, not only did slavery exist, but the slave trade, and the breeding of slaves expressly for it, was a general practice between slave states. Yet not only was there a greater strength of sentiment against it, but, in England at least, a less amount either of feeling or of interest in favour of it, than of any other of the customary abuses of force: for its motive was the love of gain, unmixed and undisguised; and those who profited by it were a very small numerical fraction of the country, while the natural feeling of all who were not personally interested in it, was unmitigated abhorrence. So extreme an instance makes it almost superfluous to refer to any other: but consider the long duration of absolute monarchy. In England at present it is the almost universal conviction that military despotism is a case of the law of force, having no other origin or justification. Yet in all the great nations of Europe except England it either still exists, or has only just ceased to exist, and has even now a strong party favourable to it in all ranks of the people, especially among persons of station and consequence. Such is the power of an established system, even when far from universal; when not only in almost every period of history there have been great and well-known examples of the contrary system, but these have almost invariably been afforded by the most illustrious and most prosperous communities. In this case, too, the possessor of the undue power, the person directly interested in it, is only one person, while those who are subject to it and suffer from it are literally all the rest. The yoke is naturally and necessarily humiliating to all persons, except the one who is on the throne, together with, at most, the one who expects to succeed to it. How different are these cases from that of the power of men over women! I am not now prejudging the question of its justifiableness. I am showing how vastly more permanent it could not but be, even if not justifiable, than these other dominations which have nevertheless lasted down to our own time. Whatever gratification of pride there is in the possession of power, and whatever personal interest in its exercise, is in this case not confined to a limited class, but common to the whole male sex. Instead of being, to most of its supporters, a thing desirable chiefly in the abstract, or, like the political ends usually contended for by factions, of little private importance to any but the leaders; it comes home to the person and hearth of every male head of a family, and of every one who looks forward to being so. The clodhopper exercises, or is to exercise, his share of the power equally with the highest nobleman. And the case is that in which the desire of power is the strongest: for every one who desires power, desires it most over those who are nearest to him, with whom his life is passed, with whom he has most concerns in common, and in whom any independence of his authority is oftenest likely to interfere with his individual preferences. If, in the other cases specified, powers manifestly grounded only on force, and having so much less to support them, are so slowly and with so much difficulty got rid of, much more must it be so with this, even if it rests on no better foundation than those. We must consider, too, that the possessors of the power have facilities in this case, greater than in any other, to prevent any uprising against it. Every one of the subjects lives under the very eye, and almost, it may be said, in the hands, of one of the masters—in closer intimacy with him than with any of her fellow-subjects; with no means of combining against him, no power of even locally overmastering him, and, on the other hand, with the strongest motives for seeking his favour and avoiding to give him offence. In struggles for political emancipation, everybody knows how often its champions are bought off by bribes, or daunted by terrors. In the case of women, each individual of the subject-class is in a chronic state of bribery and intimidation combined. In setting up the standard of resistance, a large number of the leaders, and still more of the followers, must make an almost complete sacrifice of the pleasures or the alleviations of their own individual lot. If ever any system of privilege and enforced subjection had its yoke tightly riveted on the necks of those who are kept down by it, this has. I have not yet shown that it is a wrong system: but every one who is capable of thinking on the subject must see that even if it is, it was certain to outlast all other forms of unjust authority. And when some of the grossest of the other forms still exist in many civilized countries, and have only recently been got rid of in others, it would be strange if that which is so much the deepest-rooted had yet been perceptibly shaken anywhere. There is more reason to wonder that the protests and testimonies against it should have been so numerous and so weighty as they are.

Some will object, that a comparison cannot fairly be made between the government of the male sex and the forms of unjust power which I have adduced in illustration of it, since these are arbitrary, and the effect of mere usurpation, while it on the contrary is natural. But was there ever any domination which did not appear natural to those who possessed it? There was a time when the division of mankind into two classes, a small one of masters and a numerous one of slaves, appeared, even to the most cultivated minds, to be a natural, and the only natural, condition of the human race. No less an intellect, and one which contributed no less to the progress of human thought, than Aristotle, held this opinion without doubt or misgiving; and rested it on the same premises on which the same assertion in regard to the dominion of men over women is usually based, namely that there are different natures among mankind, free natures, and slave natures; that the Greeks were of a free nature, the barbarian races of Thracians and Asiatics of a slave nature.[*] But why need I go back to Aristotle? Did not the slaveowners of the Southern United States maintain the same doctrine, with all the fanaticism with which men cling to the theories that justify their passions and legitimate their personal interests? Did they not call heaven and earth to witness that the dominion of the white man over the black is natural, that the black race is by nature incapable of freedom, and marked out for slavery? some even going so far as to say that the freedom of manual labourers is an unnatural order of things anywhere. Again, the theorists of absolute monarchy have always affirmed it to be the only natural form of government; issuing from the patriarchal, which was the primitive and spontaneous form of society, framed on the model of the paternal, which is anterior to society itself, and, as they contend, the most natural authority of all. Nay, for that matter, the law of force itself, to those who could not plead any other, has always seemed the most natural of all grounds for the exercise of authority. Conquering races hold it to be Nature's own dictate that the conquered should obey the conquerors, or, as they euphoniously paraphrase it, that the feebler and more unwarlike races should submit to the braver and manlier. The smallest acquaintance with human life in the middle ages, shows how supremely natural the dominion of the feudal nobility over men of low condition appeared to the nobility themselves, and how unnatural the conception seemed, of a person of the inferior class claiming equality with them, or exercising authority over them. It hardly seemed less so to the class held in subjection. The emancipated serfs and burgesses, even in their most vigorous struggles, never made any pretension to a share of authority; they only demanded more or less of limitation to the power

[*See *Politics* (Greek and English), trans. H. Rackham (London: Heinemann; New York: Putnam's Sons, 1932), pp. 565-6 (VII, vii, 1; 1327^b).]

of tyrannizing over them. So true is it that unnatural generally means only uncustomary, and that everything which is usual appears natural. The subjection of women to men being a universal custom, any departure from it quite naturally appears unnatural. But how entirely, even in this case, the feeling is dependent on custom, appears by ample experience. Nothing so much astonishes the people of distant parts of the world, when they first learn anything about England, as to be told that it is under a queen: the thing seems to them so unnatural as to be almost incredible. To Englishmen this does not seem in the least degree unnatural, because they are used to it; but they do feel it unnatural that women should be soldiers or members of Parliament. In the feudal ages, on the contrary, war and politics were not thought unnatural to women, because not unusual; it seemed natural that women of the privileged classes should be of manly character, inferior in nothing but bodily strength to their husbands and fathers. The independence of women seemed rather less unnatural to the Greeks than to other ancients, on account of the fabulous Amazons (whom they believed to be historical), and the partial example afforded by the Spartan women; who, though no less subordinate by law than in other Greek states, were more free in fact, and being trained to bodily exercises in the same manner with men, gave ample proof that they were not naturally disqualified for them. There can be little doubt that Spartan experience suggested to Plato, among many other of his doctrines, that of the social and political equality of the two sexes.[*]

But, it will be said, the rule of men over women differs from all these others in not being a rule of force: it is accepted voluntarily; women make no complaint, and are consenting parties to it. In the first place, a great number of women do not accept it. Ever since there have been women able to make their sentiments known by their writings (the only mode of publicity which society permits to them), an increasing number of them have recorded protests against their present social condition: and recently many thousands of them, headed by the most eminent women known to the public, have petitioned Parliament for their admission to the Parliamentary Suffrage.[†] The claim of women to be educated as solidly, and in the same branches of knowledge, as men, is urged with growing intensity, and with a great prospect of success; while the demand for their admission into professions and occupations hitherto closed against them, becomes every year more urgent. Though there are not in this country, as there are in the United States, periodical Conventions and an organized party to agitate for the Rights of Women, there is a numerous and active Society organized and managed by women, for the

[*See *Republic* (Greek and English), trans. Paul Shorey, 2 vols. (London: Heinemann; Cambridge, Mass.: Harvard University Press, 1946), Vol. I, pp. 444-52 (V).]

[†Petition for Extension (of the Elective Franchise) to All Householders without Distinction of Sex (Public Petition no. 8501, Presented 7 June, 1866), *Reports of Select Committee on Public Petitions*, 1866, p. 697, and Appendix, p. 305. Presented by Mill to the House of Commons.]

more limited object of obtaining the political franchise. Nor is it only in our own country and in America that women are beginning to protest, more or less collectively, against the disabilities under which they labour. France, and Italy, and Switzerland, and Russia now afford examples of the same thing. How many more women there are who silently cherish similar aspirations, no one can possibly know; but there are abundant tokens how many *would* cherish them, were they not so strenuously taught to repress them as contrary to the proprieties of their sex. It must be remembered, also, that no enslaved class ever asked for complete liberty at once. When Simon de Montfort called the deputies of the commons to sit for the first time in Parliament, did any of them dream of demanding that an assembly, elected by their constituents, should make and destroy ministries, and dictate to the king in affairs of state? No such thought entered into the imagination of the most ambitious of them. The nobility had already these pretensions; the commons pretended to nothing but to be exempt from arbitrary taxation, and from the gross individual oppression of the king's officers. It is a political law of nature that those who are under any power of ancient origin, never begin by complaining of the power itself, but only of its oppressive exercise. There is never any want of women who complain of ill usage by their husbands. There would be infinitely more, if complaint were not the greatest of all provocatives to a repetition and increase of the ill usage. It is this which frustrates all attempts to maintain the power but protect the woman against its abuses. In no other case (except that of a child) is the person who has been proved judicially to have suffered an injury, replaced under the physical power of the culprit who inflicted it. Accordingly wives, even in the most extreme and protracted cases of bodily ill usage, hardly ever dare avail themselves of the laws made for their protection: and if, in a moment of irrepressible indignation, or by the interference of neighbours, they are induced to do so, their whole effort afterwards is to disclose as little as they can, and to beg off their tyrant from his merited chastisement.

All causes, social and natural, combine to make it unlikely that women should be collectively rebellious to the power of men. They are so far in a position different from all other subject classes, that their masters require something more from them than actual service. Men do not want solely the obedience of women, they want their sentiments. All men, except the most brutish, desire to have, in the woman most nearly connected with them, not a forced slave but a willing one, not a slave merely, but a favourite. They have therefore put everything in practice to enslave their minds. The masters of all other slaves rely, for maintaining obedience, on fear; either fear of themselves, or religious fears. The masters of women wanted more than simple obedience, and they turned the whole force of education to effect their purpose. All women are brought up from the very earliest years in the belief that their ideal of character is the very opposite to that of men; not self-will, and government by self-control, but submission, and yielding to the control of others. All the moralities tell them that it is the duty of women, and all the current sentimentalities that it is their nature, to live for others; to make complete abnegation of themselves, and to have no life but in their affections. And by their affections are meant the only ones they are allowed to have—those to the men with whom they are connected, or to the children who constitute an additional and indefeasible tie between them and a man. When we put together three things—first, the natural attraction between opposite sexes; secondly, the wife's entire dependence on the husband, every privilege or pleasure she has being either his gift, or depending entirely on his will; and lastly, that the principal object of human pursuit, consideration, and all objects of social ambition, can in general be sought or obtained by her only through him, it would be a miracle if the object of being attractive to men had not become the polar star of feminine education and formation of character. And, this great means of influence over the minds of women having been acquired, an instinct of selfishness made men avail themselves of it to the utmost as a means of holding women in subjection, by representing to them meekness, submissiveness, and resignation of all individual will into the hands of a man, as an essential part of sexual attractiveness. Can it be doubted that any of the other yokes which mankind have succeeded in breaking, would have subsisted till now if the same means had existed, and had been as sedulously used, to bow down their minds to it? If it had been made the object of the life of every young plebeian to find personal favour in the eyes of some patrician, of every young serf with some seigneur; if domestication with him, and a share of his personal affections, had been held out as the prize which they all should look out for, the most gifted and aspiring being able to reckon on the most desirable prizes; and if, when this prize had been obtained, they had been shut out by a wall of brass from all interests not centering in him, all feelings and desires but those which he shared or inculcated; would not serfs and seigneurs, plebeians and patricians, have been as broadly distinguished at this day as men and women are? and would not all but a thinker here and there, have believed the distinction to be a fundamental and unalterable fact in human nature?

The preceding considerations are amply sufficient to show that custom, however universal it may be, affords in this case no presumption, and ought not to create any prejudice, in favour of the arrangements which place women in social and political subjection to men. But I may go farther, and maintain that the course of history, and the tendencies of progressive human society, afford not only no presumption in favour of this system of inequality of rights, but a strong one against it; and that, so far as the whole course of human improvement up to this time, the whole stream of modern tendencies, warrants any inference on the subject, it is, that this relic of the past is discordant with the future, and must necessarily disappear.

For, what is the peculiar character of the modern world—the difference which chiefly distinguishes modern institutions, modern social ideas, modern life itself, from those of times long past? It is, that human beings are no longer born to their place in life, and chained down by an inexorable bond to the place they are born to, but are free to employ their faculties, and such favourable chances as offer, to achieve the lot which may appear to them most desirable. Human society of old was constituted on a very different principle. All were born to a fixed social position, and were mostly kept in it by law, or interdicted from any means by which they could emerge from it. As some men are born white and others black, so some were born slaves and others freemen and citizens; some were born patricians, others plebeians; some were born feudal nobles, others commoners and *roturiers*. A slave or serf could never make himself free, nor, except by the will of his master, become so. In most European countries it was not till towards the close of the middle ages, and as a consequence of the growth of regal power, that commoners could be ennobled. Even among nobles, the eldest son was born the exclusive heir to the paternal possessions, and a long time elapsed before it was fully established that the father could disinherit him. Among the industrious classes, only those who were born members of a guild, or were admitted into it by its members, could lawfully practise their calling within its local limits; and nobody could practise any calling deemed important, in any but the legal manner—by processes authoritatively prescribed. Manufacturers have stood in the pillory for presuming to carry on their business by new and improved methods. In modern Europe, and most in those parts of it which have participated most largely in all other modern improvements, diametrically opposite doctrines now prevail. Law and government do not undertake to prescribe by whom any social or industrial operation shall or shall not be conducted, or what modes of conducting them shall be lawful. These things are left to the unfettered choice of individuals. Even the laws which required that workmen should serve an apprenticeship, have in this country been repealed: there being ample assurance that in all cases in which an apprenticeship is necessary, its necessity will suffice to enforce it. The old theory was, that the least possible should be left to the choice of the individual agent; that all he had to do should, as far as practicable, be laid down for him by superior wisdom. Left to himself he was sure to go wrong. The modern conviction, the fruit of a thousand years of experience, is, that things in which the individual is the person directly interested, never go right but as they are left to his own discretion; and that any regulation of them by authority, except to protect the rights of others, is sure to be mischievous. This conclusion, slowly arrived at, and not adopted until almost every possible application of the contrary theory had been made with disastrous result, now (in the industrial department) prevails universally in the most advanced countries, almost universally in all that have pretensions to any sort of advancement. It is not that all processes are supposed to be equally good, or all persons to be equally qualified for everything; but that freedom of individual choice is now known to be the only thing which procures the adoption of the best processes, and throws each operation into the hands of those who are best qualified for it. Nobody thinks it necessary to make a law that only a strong-armed man shall be a blacksmith. Freedom and competition suffice to make blacksmiths strong-armed men, because the weak-armed can earn more by engaging in occupations for which they are more fit. In consonance with this doctrine, it is felt to be an overstepping of the proper bounds of authority to fix beforehand, on some general presumption, that certain persons are not fit to do certain things. It is now thoroughly known and admitted that if some such presumptions exist, no such presumption is infallible. Even if it be well grounded in a majority of cases, which it is very likely not to be, there will be a minority of exceptional cases in which it does not hold: and in those it is both an injustice to the individuals, and a detriment to society, to place barriers in the way of their using their faculties for their own benefit and for that of others. In the cases, on the other hand, in which the unfitness is real, the ordinary motives of human conduct will on the whole suffice to prevent the incompetent person from making, or from persisting in, the attempt.

If this general principle of social and economical science is not true; if individuals, with such help as they can derive from the opinion of those who know them, are not better judges than the law and the government, of their own capacities and vocation; the world cannot too soon abandon this principle, and return to the old system of regulations and disabilities. But if the principle is true, we ought to act as if we believed it, and not to ordain that to be born a girl instead of a boy, any more than to be born black instead of white, or a commoner instead of a nobleman, shall decide the person's position through all life—shall interdict people from all the more elevated social positions, and from all, except a few, respectable occupations. Even were we to admit the utmost that is ever pretended as to the superior fitness of men for all the functions now reserved to them, the same argument applies which forbids a legal qualification for members of Parliament. If only once in a dozen years the conditions of eligibility exclude a fit person, there is a real loss, while the exclusion of thousands of unfit persons is no gain; for if the constitution of the electoral body disposes them to choose unfit persons, there are always plenty of such persons to choose from. In all things of any difficulty and importance, those who can do them well are fewer than the need, even with the most unrestricted latitude of choice: and any limitation of the field of selection deprives society of some chances of being served by the competent, without ever saving it from the incompetent.

At present, in the more improved countries, the disabilities of women are the only case, save one, in which laws and institutions take persons at their birth, and ordain that they shall never in all their lives be allowed to compete for certain things. The one exception is that of royalty. Persons still are born to the throne; no one, not of the reigning family, can ever occupy it, and no one even of that family can, by any means but the course of hereditary succession, attain it. All other dignities and social advantages are open to the whole male sex: many indeed are only attainable by wealth, but wealth may be striven for by any one, and is actually obtained by many men of the very humblest origin. The difficulties, to the majority, are indeed insuperable without the aid of fortunate accidents; but no male human being is under any legal ban: neither law nor opinion superadd artificial obstacles to the natural ones. Royalty, as I have said, is excepted: but in this case every one feels it to be an exception—an anomaly in the modern world, in marked opposition to its customs and principles, and to be justified only by extraordinary special expediencies, which, though individuals and nations differ in estimating their weight, unquestionably do in fact exist. But in this exceptional case, in which a high social function is, for important reasons, bestowed on birth instead of being put up to competition, all free nations contrive to adhere in substance to the principle from which they nominally derogate; for they circumscribe this high function by conditions avowedly intended to prevent the person to whom it ostensibly belongs from really performing it; while the person by whom it is performed, the responsible minister, does obtain the post by a competition from which no full-grown citizen of the male sex is legally excluded. The disabilities, therefore, to which women are subject from the mere fact of their birth, are the solitary examples of the kind in modern legislation. In no instance except this, which comprehends half the human race, are the higher social functions closed against any one by a fatality of birth which no exertions, and no change of circumstances, can overcome; for even religious disabilities (besides that in England and in Europe they have practically almost ceased to exist) do not close any career to the disqualified person in case of conversion.

The social subordination of women thus stands out an isolated fact in modern social institutions; a solitary breach of what has become their fundamental law; a single relic of an old world of thought and practice exploded in everything else, but retained in the one thing of most universal interest; as if a gigantic dolmen, or a vast temple of Jupiter Olympius, occupied the site of St. Paul's and received daily worship, while the surrounding Christian churches were only resorted to on fasts and festivals. This entire discrepancy between one social fact and all those which accompany it, and the radical opposition between its nature and the progressive movement which is the boast of the modern world, and which has successively swept away everything else of an analogous character, surely affords, to a con-scientious observer of human tendencies, serious matter for reflection. It raises a *primâ facie* presumption on the unfavourable side, far outweighing any which custom and usage could in such circumstances create on the favourable; and should at least suffice to make this, like the choice between republicanism and royalty, a balanced question.

The least that can be demanded is, that the question should not be considered as prejudged by existing fact and existing opinion, but open to discussion on its merits, as a question of justice and expediency: the decision on this, as on any of the other social arrangements of mankind, depending on what an enlightened estimate of tendencies and consequences may show to be most advantageous to humanity in general, without distinction of sex. And the discussion must be a real discussion, descending to foundations, and not resting satisfied with vague and general assertions. It will not do, for instance, to assert in general terms, that the experience of mankind has pronounced in favour of the existing system. Experience cannot possibly have decided between two courses, so long as there has only been experience of one. If it be said that the doctrine of the equality of the sexes rests only on theory, it must be remembered that the contrary doctrine also has only theory to rest upon. All that is proved in its favour by direct experience, is that mankind have been able to exist under it, and to attain the degree of improvement and prosperity which we now see; but whether that prosperity has been attained sooner, or is now greater, than it would have been under the other system, experience does not say. On the other hand, experience does say, that every step in improvement has been so invariably accompanied by a step made in raising the social position of women, that historians and philosophers have been led to adopt their elevation or debasement as on the whole the surest test and most correct measure of the civilization of a people or an age. Through all the progressive period of human history, the condition of women has been approaching nearer to equality with men. This does not of itself prove that the assimilation must go on to complete equality; but it assuredly affords some presumption that such is the case.

Neither does it avail anything to say that the *nature* of the two sexes adapts them to their present functions and position, and renders these appropriate to them. Standing on the ground of common sense and the constitution of the human mind, I deny that any one knows, or can know, the nature of the two sexes, as long as they have only been seen in their present relation to one another. If men had ever been found in society without women, or women without men, or if there had been a society of men and women in which the women were not under the control of the men, something might have been positively known about the mental and moral differences which may be inherent in the nature of each. What is now called the nature of women is an eminently artificial thing—the result of forced repression in some directions, unnatural stimulation in others. It may be asserted without scruple, that no other class of dependents have had their character so entirely distorted from its natural proportions by their relation with their masters; for, if conquered and slave races have been, in some respects, more forcibly repressed, whatever in them has not been crushed down by an iron heel has generally been let alone, and if left with any liberty of development, it has developed itself according to its own laws; but in the case of women, a hot-house and stove cultivation has always been carried on of some of the capabilities of their nature, for the benefit and pleasure of their masters. Then, because certain products of the general vital force sprout luxuriantly and reach a great development in this heated atmosphere and under this active nurture and watering, while other shoots from the same root, which are left outside in the wintry air, with ice purposely heaped all round them, have a stunted growth, and some are burnt off with fire and disappear; men, with that inability to recognise their own work which distinguishes the unanalytic mind, indolently believe that the tree grows of itself in the way they have made it grow, and that it would die if one half of it were not kept in a vapour bath and the other half in the snow.

Of all difficulties which impede the progress of thought, and the formation of well-grounded opinions on life and social arrangements, the greatest is now the unspeakable ignorance and inattention of mankind in respect to the influences which form human character. Whatever any portion of the human species now are, or seem to be, such, it is supposed, they have a natural tendency to be: even when the most elementary knowledge of the circumstances in which they have been placed, clearly points out the causes that made them what they are. Because a cottier deeply in arrears to his landlord is not industrious, there are people who think that the Irish are naturally idle. Because constitutions can be overthrown when the authorities appointed to execute them turn their arms against them, there are people who think the French incapable of free government. Because the Greeks cheated the Turks, and the Turks only plundered the Greeks, there are persons who think that the Turks are naturally more sincere: and because women, as is often said, care nothing about politics except their personalities, it is supposed that the general good is naturally less interesting to women than to men. History, which is now so much better understood than formerly, teaches another lesson: if only by showing the extraordinary susceptibility of human nature to external influences, and the extreme variableness of those of its manifestations which are supposed to be most universal and uniform. But in history, as in travelling, men usually see only what they already had in their own minds; and few learn much from history, who do not bring much with them to its study.

Hence, in regard to that most difficult question, what are the natural differences between the two sexes—a subject on which it is impossible in the present state of society to obtain complete and correct knowledge—while almost everybody dogmatizes upon it, almost all neglect and make light of the only means by which any partial insight can be obtained into it. This is, an analytic study of the most important department of psychology, the laws of the influence of circumstances on character. For, however great and apparently ineradicable the moral and intellectual differences between men and women might be, the evidence of their being natural differences could only be negative. Those only could be inferred to be natural which could not possibly be artificial—the residuum, after deducting every characteristic of either sex which can admit of being explained from education or external circumstances. The profoundest knowledge of the laws of the formation of character is indispensable to entitle any one to affirm even that there is any difference, much more what the difference is, between the two sexes considered as moral and rational beings; and since no one, as yet, has that knowledge, (for there is hardly any subject which, in proportion to its importance, has been so little studied), no one is thus far entitled to any positive opinion on the subject. Conjectures are all that can at present be made; conjectures more or less probable, according as more or less authorized by such knowledge as we yet have of the laws of psychology, as applied to the formation of character.

Even the preliminary knowledge, what the differences between the sexes now are, apart from all question as to how they are made what they are, is still in the crudest and most incomplete state. Medical practitioners and physiologists have ascertained, to some extent, the differences in bodily constitution; and this is an important element to the psychologist: but hardly any medical practitioner is a psychologist. Respecting the mental characteristics of women; their observations are of no more worth than those of common men. It is a subject on which nothing final can be known, so long as those who alone can really know it, women themselves, have given but little testimony, and that little, mostly suborned. It is easy to know stupid women. Stupidity is much the same all the world over. A stupid person's notions and feelings may confidently be inferred from those which prevail in the circle by which the person is surrounded. Not so with those whose opinions and feelings are an emanation from their own nature and faculties. It is only a man here and there who has any tolerable knowledge of the character even of the women of his own family. I do not mean, of their capabilities; these nobody knows, not even themselves, because most of them have never been called out. I mean their actually existing thoughts and feelings. Many a man thinks he perfectly understands women, because he has had amatory relations with several, perhaps with many of them. If he is a good observer, and his experience extends to quality as well as quantity, he may have learnt something of one narrow department of their nature—an important department, no doubt. But of all the rest of it, few persons are generally more ignorant, because there are few from whom it is so carefully hidden. The most favourable case which a man can generally have for studying the character of a woman, is that of his own wife: for the opportunities are greater, and the cases of complete sympathy not so unspeakably rare. And in fact, this is the source from which any knowledge worth having on the subject has, I believe, generally come. But most men have not had the opportunity of studying in this way more than a single case: accordingly one can, to an almost laughable degree, infer what a man's wife is like, from his opinions about women in general. To make even this one case yield any result, the woman must be worth knowing, and the man not only a competent judge, but of a character so sympathetic in itself, and so well adapted to hers, that he can either read her mind by sympathetic intuition, or has nothing in himself which makes her shy of disclosing it. Hardly anything, I believe, can be more rare than this conjunction. It often happens that there is the most complete unity of feeling and community of interests as to all external things, yet the one has as little admission into the internal life of the other as if they were common acquaintance. Even with true affection, authority on the one side and subordination on the other prevent perfect confidence. Though nothing may be intentionally withheld, much is not shown. In the analogous relation of parent and child, the corresponding phenomenon must have been in the observation of every one. As between father and son, how many are the cases in which the father, in spite of real affection on both sides, obviously to all the world does not know, nor suspect, parts of the son's character familiar to his companions and equals. The truth is, that the position of looking up to another is extremely unpropitious to complete sincerity and openness with him. The fear of losing ground in his opinion or in his feelings is so strong, that even in an upright character, there is an unconscious tendency to show only the best side, or the side which, though not the best, is that which he most likes to see: and it may be confidently said that thorough knowledge of one another hardly ever exists, but between persons who, besides being intimates, are equals. How much more true, then, must all this be, when the one is not only under the authority of the other, but has it inculcated on her as a duty to reckon everything else subordinate to his comfort and pleasure, and to let him neither see nor feel anything coming from her, except what is agreeable to him. All these difficulties stand in the way of a man's obtaining any thorough knowledge even of the one woman whom alone, in general, he has sufficient opportunity of studying. When we further consider that to understand one woman is not necessarily to understand any other woman; that even if he could study many women of one rank, or of one country, he would not thereby understand women of other ranks or countries; and even if he did, they are still only the women of a single period of history; we may safely assert that the knowledge which men can acquire of women, even as they have been and are, without reference to what they might be, is wretchedly imperfect and superficial, and always will be so, until women themselves have told all that they have to tell.

And this time has not come; nor will it come otherwise than gradually. It is but of yesterday that women have either been qualified by literary accomplishments, or permitted by society, to tell anything to the general public. As yet very few of them dare tell anything, which men, on whom their literary success depends, are unwilling to hear. Let us remember in what manner, up to a very recent time, the expression, even by a male author, of uncustomary opinions, or what are deemed eccentric feelings, usually was, and in some degree still is, received; and we may form some faint conception under what impediments a woman, who is brought up to think custom and opinion her sovereign rule, attempts to express in books anything drawn from the depths of her own nature. The greatest woman who has left writings behind her sufficient to give her an eminent rank in the literature of her country, thought it necessary to prefix as a motto to her boldest work, "Un homme peut braver l'opinion; une femme doit s'y soumettre."* The greater part of what women write about women is mere sycophancy to men. In the case of unmarried women, much of it seems only intended to increase their chance of a husband. Many, both married and unmarried, overstep the mark, and inculcate a servility

*Title-page of Mme. de Staël's *Delphine*. [4 vols. (Geneva: Paschoud, 1802).]

beyond what is desired or relished by any man, except the very vulgarest. But this is not so often the case as, even at a quite late period, it still was. Literary women are becoming more freespoken, and more willing to express their real sentiments. Unfortunately, in this country especially, they are themselves such artificial products, that their sentiments are compounded of a small element of individual observation and consciousness, and a very large one of acquired associations. This will be less and less the case, but it will remain true to a great extent, as long as social institutions do not admit the same free development of originality in women which is possible to men. When that time comes, and not before, we shall see, and not merely hear, as much as it is necessary to know of the nature of women, and the adaptation of other things to it.

I have dwelt so much on the difficulties which at present obstruct any real knowledge by men of the true nature of women, because in this as in so many other things "opinio copiae inter maximas causas inopiae est;"[*] and there is little chance of reasonable thinking on the matter, while people flatter themselves that they perfectly understand a subject of which most men know absolutely nothing, and of which it is at present impossible that any man, or all men taken together, should have knowledge which can qualify them to lay down the law to women as to what is, or is not, their vocation. Happily, no such knowledge is necessary for any practical purpose connected with the position of women in relation to society and life. For, according to all the principles involved in modern society, the question rests with women themselves—to be decided by their own experience, and by the use of their own faculties. There are no means of finding what either one person or many can do, but by trying—and no means by which any one else can discover for them what it is for their happiness to do or leave undone.

One thing we may be certain of—that what is contrary to women's nature to do, they never will be made to do by simply giving their nature free play. The anxiety of mankind to interfere in behalf of nature, for fear lest nature should not succeed in effecting its purpose, is an altogether unnecessary solicitude. What women by nature cannot do, it is quite superfluous to forbid them from doing. What they can do, but not so well as the men who are their competitors, competition suffices to exclude them from; since nobody asks for protective duties and bounties in favour of women; it is only asked that the present bounties and protective duties in favour of men should be recalled. If women have a greater natural inclination for some things than for others, there is no need of laws or social inculcation to make the majority of them do the former in preference to the latter. Whatever women's services are most wanted for, the free play of competition will hold out the strongest inducements to them to undertake. And, as the words imply, they are most wanted for the things for which they are most fit; by the apportionment of

[*Francis Bacon, *Novum Organum* (1620), in *Works*, ed. James Spedding, *et al.*, 14 vols. (London: Longman, *et al.*, 1857-74), Vol. I, p. 125.]

which to them, the collective faculties of the two sexes can be applied on the whole with the greatest sum of valuable result.

The general opinion of men is supposed to be, that the natural vocation of a woman is that of a wife and mother. I say, is supposed to be, because, judging from acts—from the whole of the present constitution of society—one might infer that their opinion was the direct contrary. They might be supposed to think that the alleged natural vocation of women was of all things the most repugnant to their nature; insomuch that if they are free to do anything else—if any other means of living, or occupation of their time and faculties, is open, which has any chance of appearing desirable to them—there will not be enough of them who will be willing to accept the condition said to be natural to them. If this is the real opinion of men in general, it would be well that it should be spoken out. I should like to hear somebody openly enunciating the doctrine (it is already implied in much that is written on the subject)—"It is necessary to society that women should marry and produce children. They will not do so unless they are compelled. Therefore it is necessary to compel them." The merits of the case would then be clearly defined. It would be exactly that of the slaveholders of South Carolina and Louisiana. "It is necessary that cotton and sugar should be grown. White men cannot produce them. Negroes will not, for any wages which we choose to give. *Ergo* they must be compelled." An illustration still closer to the point is that of impressment. Sailors must absolutely be had to defend the country. It often happens that they will not voluntarily enlist. Therefore there must be the power of forcing them. How often has this logic been used! and, but for one flaw in it, without doubt it would have been successful up to this day. But it is open to the retort—First pay the sailors the honest value of their labour. When you have made it as well worth their while to serve you, as to work for other employers, you will have no more difficulty than others have in obtaining their services. To this there is no logical answer except "I will not:" and as people are now not only ashamed, but are not desirous, to rob the labourer of his hire,[*] impressment is no longer advocated. Those who attempt to force women into marriage by closing all other doors against them, lay themselves open to a similar retort. If they mean what they say, their opinion must evidently be, that men do not render the married condition so desirable to women, as to induce them to accept it for its own recommendations. It is not a sign of one's thinking the boon one offers very attractive, when one allows only Hobson's choice, "that or none." And here, I believe, is the clue to the feelings of those men, who have a real antipathy to the equal freedom of women. I believe they are afraid, not lest women should be unwilling to marry, for I do not think that any one in reality has that apprehension; but lest they should insist that marriage should be on equal conditions; lest all women of spirit and capacity should prefer doing almost anything else, not in their own eyes degrading, rather than marry, when marrying

[*Luke, 10:7.]

is giving themselves a master, and a master too of all their earthly possessions. And truly, if this consequence were necessarily incident to marriage, I think that the apprehension would be very well founded. I agree in thinking it probable that few women, capable of anything else, would, unless under an irresistible *entrainement*, rendering them for the time insensible to anything but itself, choose such a lot, when any other means were open to them of filling a conventionally honourable place in life: and if men are determined that the law of marriage shall be a law of despotism, they are quite right, in point of mere policy, in leaving to women only Hobson's choice. But, in that case, all that has been done in the modern world to relax the chain on the minds of women, has been a mistake. They never should have been allowed to receive a literary education. Women who read, much more women who write, are, in the existing constitution of things, a contradiction and a disturbing element: and it was wrong to bring women up with any acquirements but those of an odalisque, or of a domestic servant.

Chapter II

IT WILL BE WELL TO COMMENCE the detailed discussion of the subject by the particular branch of it to which the course of our observations has led us: the conditions which the laws of this and all other countries annex to the marriage contract. Marriage being the destination appointed by society for women, the prospect they are brought up to, and the object which it is intended should be sought by all of them, except those who are too little attractive to be chosen by any man as his companion; one might have supposed that everything would have been done to make this condition as eligible to them as possible, that they might have no cause to regret being denied the option of any other. Society, however, both in this, and, at first, in all other cases, has preferred to attain its object by foul rather than fair means: but this is the only case in which it has substantially persisted in them even to the present day. Originally women were taken by force, or regularly sold by their father to the husband. Until a late period in European history, the father had the power to dispose of his daughter in marriage at his own will and pleasure, without any regard to hers. The Church, indeed, was so far faithful to a better morality as to require a formal "yes" from the woman at the marriage ceremony; but there was nothing to shew that the consent was other than compulsory; and it was practically impossible for the girl to refuse compliance if the father persevered, except perhaps when she might obtain the protection of religion by a determined resolution to take monastic vows. After marriage, the man had anciently (but this was anterior to Christianity) the power of life and death over his wife. She could invoke no law against him; he was her sole tribunal and law. For a long time he could repudiate her, but she had no corresponding power in regard to him. By the old laws of England, the husband was called the *lord* of the wife; he was literally regarded as her sovereign, inasmuch that the murder of a man by his wife was called treason (*petty* as distinguished from *high* treason), and was more cruelly avenged than was usually the case with high treason, for the penalty was burning to death. Because these various enormities have fallen into disuse (for most of them were never formally abolished, or not until they had long ceased to be practised)[*] men suppose that all is now as it should be in regard to the marriage

[*See 26 George II, c. 33 (1753); 20 & 21 Victoria, c. 85 (1857); and 24 & 25 Victoria, c. 100 (1861).]

contract; and we are continually told that civilization and Christianity have restored to the woman her just rights. Meanwhile the wife is the actual bondservant of her husband: no less so, as far as legal obligation goes, than slaves commonly so called. She vows a lifelong obedience to him at the altar, and is held to it all through her life by law. Casuists may say that the obligation of obedience stops short of participation in crime, but it certainly extends to everything else. She can do no act whatever but by his permission, at least tacit. She can acquire no property but for him; the instant it becomes hers, even if by inheritance, it becomes *ipso facto* his. In this respect the wife's position under the common law of England is worse than that of slaves in the laws of many countries: by the Roman law, for example, a slave might have his peculium, which to a certain extent the law guaranteed to him for his exclusive use. The higher classes in this country have given an analogous advantage to their women, through special contracts setting aside the law, by conditions of pin-money, &c.: since parental feeling being stronger with fathers than the class feeling of their own sex, a father generally prefers his own daughter to a son-in-law who is a stranger to him. By means of settlements, the rich usually contrive to withdraw the whole or part of the inherited property of the wife from the absolute control of the husband: but they do not succeed in keeping it under her own control; the utmost they can do only prevents the husband from squandering it, at the same time debarring the rightful owner from its use. The property itself is out of the reach of both; and as to the income derived from it, the form of settlement most favourable to the wife (that called "to her separate use") only precludes the husband from receiving it instead of her: it must pass through her hands, but if he takes it from her by personal violence as soon as she receives it, he can neither be punished, nor compelled to restitution. This is the amount of the protection which, under the laws of this country, the most powerful nobleman can give to his own daughter as respects her husband. In the immense majority of cases there is no settlement: and the absorption of all rights, all property, as well as all freedom of action, is complete. The two are called "one person in law," for the purpose of inferring that whatever is hers is his, but the parallel inference is never drawn that whatever is his is hers; the maxim is not applied against the man, except to make him responsible to third parties for her acts, as a master is for the acts of his slaves or of his cattle. I am far from pretending that wives are in general no better treated than slaves; but no slave is a slave to the same lengths, and in so full a sense of the word, as a wife is. Hardly any slave, except one immediately attached to the master's person, is a slave at all hours and all minutes; in general he has, like a soldier, his fixed task, and when it is done, or when he is off duty, he disposes, within certain limits, of his own time, and has a family life into which the master rarely intrudes. "Uncle Tom" under his first master had his own life in his "cabin,"[*] almost as much as any man whose work

[*In Harriet Beecher Stowe, *Uncle Tom's Cabin*, 2 vols. (Boston: Jewett, 1852).]

takes him away from home, is able to have in his own family. But it cannot be so with the wife. Above all, a female slave has (in Christian countries) an admitted right, and is considered under a moral obligation, to refuse to her master the last familiarity. Not so the wife: however brutal a tyrant she may unfortunately be chained to—though she may know that he hates her, though it may be his daily pleasure to torture her, and though she may feel it impossible not to loathe him—he can claim from her and enforce the lowest degradation of a human being, that of being made the instrument of an animal function contrary to her inclinations. While she is held in this worst description of slavery as to her own person, what is her position in regard to the children in whom she and her master have a joint interest? They are by law *his* children. He alone has any legal rights over them. Not one act can she do towards or in relation to them, except by delegation from him. Even after he is dead she is not their legal guardian, unless he by will has made her so. He could even send them away from her, and deprive her of the means of seeing or corresponding with them, until this power was in some degree restricted by Serjeant Talfourd's Act.[*] This is her legal state. And from this state she has no means of withdrawing herself. If she leaves her husband, she can take nothing with her, neither her children nor anything which is rightfully her own. If he chooses, he can compel her to return, by law, or by physical force; or he may content himself with seizing for his own use anything which she may earn, or which may be given to her by her relations. It is only legal separation by a decree of a court of justice, which entitles her to live apart, without being forced back into the custody of an exasperated jailer—or which empowers her to apply any earnings to her own use, without fear that a man whom perhaps she has not seen for twenty years will pounce upon her some day and carry all off. This legal separation, until lately,[†] the courts of justice would only give at an expense which made it inaccessible to any one out of the higher ranks. Even now it is only given in cases of desertion, or of the extreme of cruelty; and yet complaints are made every day that it is granted too easily. Surely, if a woman is denied any lot in life but that of being the personal body-servant of a despot, and is dependent for everything upon the chance of finding one who may be disposed to make a favourite of her instead of merely a drudge, it is a very cruel aggravation of her fate that she should be allowed to try this chance only once. The natural sequel and corollary from this state of things would be, that since her all in life depends upon obtaining a good master, she should be allowed to change again and again until she finds one. I am not saying that she ought to be allowed this privilege. That is a totally different consideration. The question of divorce, in the sense involving liberty of remarriage, is one into which it is foreign to my purpose to enter. All I now say is, that to those to whom nothing but servitude is allowed, the free choice of servitude is the only, though a

[*2 & 3 Victoria, c. 54 (1839), Sect. 1.]
[†20 & 21 Victoria, c. 85 (1857).]

most insufficient, alleviation. Its refusal completes the assimilation of the wife to the slave—and the slave under not the mildest form of slavery: for in some slave codes the slave could, under certain circumstances of ill usage, legally compel the master to sell him. But no amount of ill usage, without adultery superadded, will in England free a wife from her tormentor.

I have no desire to exaggerate, nor does the case stand in any need of exaggeration. I have described the wife's legal position, not her actual treatment. The laws of most countries are far worse than the people who execute them, and many of them are only able to remain laws by being seldom or never carried into effect. If married life were all that it might be expected to be, looking to the laws alone, society would be a hell upon earth. Happily there are both feelings and interests which in many men exclude, and in most, greatly temper, the impulses and propensities which lead to tyranny: and of those feelings, the tie which connects a man with his wife affords, in a normal state of things, incomparably the strongest example. The only tie which at all approaches to it, that between him and his children, tends, in all save exceptional cases, to strengthen, instead of conflicting with, the first. Because this is true; because men in general do not inflict, nor women suffer, all the misery which could be inflicted and suffered if the full power of tyranny with which the man is legally invested were acted on; the defenders of the existing form of the institution think that all its iniquity is justified, and that any complaint is merely quarrelling with the evil which is the price paid for every great good. But the mitigations in practice, which are compatible with maintaining in full legal force this or any other kind of tyranny, instead of being any apology for despotism, only serve to prove what power human nature possesses of reacting against the vilest institutions, and with what vitality the seeds of good as well as those of evil in human character diffuse and propagate themselves. Not a word can be said for despotism in the family which cannot be said for political despotism. Every absolute king does not sit at his window to enjoy the groans of his tortured subjects, nor strips them of their last rag and turns them out to shiver in the road. The despotism of Louis XVI was not the despotism of Philippe le Bel, or of Nadir Shah, or of Caligula; but it was bad enough to justify the French Revolution, and to palliate even its horrors. If an appeal be made to the intense attachments which exist between wives and their husbands, exactly as much may be said of domestic slavery. It was quite an ordinary fact in Greece and Rome for slaves to submit to death by torture rather than betray their masters. In the proscriptions of the Roman civil wars it was remarked that wives and slaves were heroically faithful, sons very commonly treacherous. Yet we know how cruelly many Romans treated their slaves. But in truth these intense individual feelings nowhere rise to such a luxuriant height as under the most atrocious institutions. It is part of the irony of life, that the strongest feelings of devoted gratitude of which human nature seems to be susceptible, are called forth in human beings towards those who, having the power entirely to crush their earthly existence, voluntarily refrain from using that power. How great a place in most men this sentiment fills, even in religious devotion, it would be cruel to inquire. We daily see how much their gratitude to Heaven appears to be stimulated by the contemplation of fellow-creatures to whom God has not been so merciful as he has to themselves.

Whether the institution to be defended is slavery, political absolutism, or the absolutism of the head of a family, we are always expected to judge of it from its best instances; and we are presented with pictures of loving exercise of authority on one side, loving submission to it on the other—superior wisdom ordering all things for the greatest good of the dependents, and surrounded by their smiles and benedictions. All this would be very much to the purpose if any one pretended that there are no such things as good men. Who doubts that there may be great goodness, and great happiness, and great affection, under the absolute government of a good man? Meanwhile, laws and institutions require to be adapted, not to good men, but to bad. Marriage is not an institution designed for a select few. Men are not required, as a preliminary to the marriage ceremony, to prove by testimonials that they are fit to be trusted with the exercise of absolute power. The tie of affection and obligation to a wife and children is very strong with those whose general social feelings are strong, and with many who are little sensible to any other social ties; but there are all degrees of sensibility and insensibility to it, as there are all grades of goodness and wickedness in men, down to those whom no ties will bind, and on whom society has no action but through its *ultima ratio*, the penalties of the law. In every grade of this descending scale are men to whom are committed all the legal powers of a husband. The vilest malefactor has some wretched woman tied to him, against whom he can commit any atrocity except killing her, and, if tolerably cautious, can do that without much danger of the legal penalty. And how many thousands are there among the lowest classes in every country, who, without being in a legal sense malefactors in any other respect, because in every other quarter their aggressions meet with resistance, indulge the utmost habitual excesses of bodily violence towards the unhappy wife, who alone, at least of grown persons, can neither repel nor escape from their brutality; and towards whom the excess of dependence inspires their mean and savage natures, not with a generous forbearance, and a point of honour to behave well to one whose lot in life is trusted entirely to their kindness, but on the contrary with a notion that the law has delivered her to them as their thing, to be used at their pleasure, and that they are not expected to practise the consideration towards her which is required from them towards everybody else. The law, which till lately left even these atrocious extremes of domestic oppression practically unpunished, has within these few years made some feeble attempts to repress them. But its attempts have done little, and cannot be expected to do much, because it is contrary to reason and experience to suppose that there can be any real check to brutality, consistent with leaving the victim still in the power of the executioner. Until a conviction for personal violence, or at all events a repetition of it after a first conviction, entitles the woman *ipso facto* to a divorce, or at least to a judicial separation, the attempt to repress these "aggravated assaults"[*] by legal penalties will break down for want of a prosecutor, or for want of a witness.

When we consider how vast is the number of men, in any great country, who are little higher than brutes, and that this never prevents them from being able, through the law of marriage, to obtain a victim, the breadth and depth of human misery caused in this shape alone by the abuse of the institution swells to something appalling. Yet these are only the extreme cases. They are the lowest abysses, but there is a sad succession of depth after depth before reaching them. In domestic as in political tyranny, the case of absolute monsters chiefly illustrates the institution by showing that there is scarcely any horror which may not occur under it if the despot pleases, and thus setting in a strong light what must be the terrible frequency of things only a little less atrocious. Absolute fiends are as rare as angels, perhaps rarer: ferocious savages, with occasional touches of humanity, are however very frequent: and in the wide interval which separates these from any worthy representatives of the human species, how many are the forms and gradations of animalism and selfishness, often under an outward varnish of civilization and even cultivation, living at peace with the law, maintaining a creditable appearance to all who are not under their power, yet sufficient often to make the lives of all who are so, a torment and a burthen to them! It would be tiresome to repeat the commonplaces about the unfitness of men in general for power, which, after the political discussions of centuries, every one knows by heart, were it not that hardly any one thinks of applying these maxims to the case in which above all others they are applicable, that of power, not placed in the hands of a man here and there, but offered to every adult male, down to the basest and most ferocious. It is not because a man is not known to have broken any of the Ten Commandments,[†] or because he maintains a respectable character in his dealings with those whom he cannot compel to have intercourse with him, or because he does not fly out into violent bursts of ill-temper against those who are not obliged to bear with him, that it is possible to surmise of what sort his conduct will be in the unrestraint of home. Even the commonest men reserve the violent, the sulky, the undisguisedly selfish side of their character for those who have no power to withstand it. The relation of superiors to dependents is the nursery of these vices of character, which, wherever else they exist, are an overflowing from that source. A man who is morose or violent to his equals, is sure to be one who has lived among inferiors, whom he could frighten or worry into submission. If the family in its best forms is, as it is often said to be, a school of sympathy, tenderness, and loving forgetfulness of self, it is still oftener, as respects its chief, a

[*See 24 & 25 Victoria, c. 100 (1861), Sect. 43.]
[†Exodus, 20:3-17.]

school of wilfulness, overbearingness, unbounded self-indulgence, and a double-dyed and idealized selfishness, of which sacrifice itself is only a particular form: the care for the wife and children being only care for them as parts of the man's own interests and belongings, and their individual happiness being immolated in every shape to his smallest preferences. What better is to be looked for under the existing form of the institution? We know that the bad propensities of human nature are only kept within bounds when they are allowed no scope for their indulgence. We know that from impulse and habit, when not from deliberate purpose, almost every one to whom others yield, goes on encroaching upon them, until a point is reached at which they are compelled to resist. Such being the common tendency of human nature; the almost unlimited power which present social institutions give to the man over at least one human being—the one with whom he resides, and whom he has always present—this power seeks out and evokes the latent germs of selfishness in the remotest corners of his nature—fans its faintest sparks and smouldering embers—offers to him a license for the indulgence of those points of his original character which in all other relations he would have found it necessary to repress and conceal, and the repression of which would in time have become a second nature. I know that there is another side to the question. I grant that the wife, if she cannot effectually resist, can at least retaliate; she, too, can make the man's life extremely uncomfortable, and by that power is able to carry many points which she ought, and many which she ought not, to prevail in. But this instrument of self-protection—which may be called the power of the scold, or the shrewish sanction—has the fatal defect, that it avails most against the least tyrannical superiors, and in favour of the least deserving dependents. It is the weapon of irritable and self-willed women; of those who would make the worst use of power if they themselves had it, and who generally turn this power to a bad use. The amiable cannot use such an instrument, the highminded disdain it. And on the other hand, the husbands against whom it is used most effectively are the gentler and more inoffensive; those who cannot be induced, even by provocation, to resort to any very harsh exercise of authority. The wife's power of being disagreeable generally only establishes a counter-tyranny, and makes victims in their turn chiefly of those husbands who are least inclined to be tyrants.

What is it, then, which really tempers the corrupting effects of the power, and makes it compatible with such amount of good as we actually see? Mere feminine blandishments, though of great effect in individual instances, have very little effect in modifying the general tendencies of the situation; for their power only lasts while the woman is young and attractive, often only while her charm is new, and not dimmed by familiarity; and on many men they have not much influence at any time. The real mitigating causes are, the personal affection which is the growth of time, in so far as the man's nature is susceptible of it, and the woman's character sufficiently congenial with his to excite it; their common interests as regards the children, and their general community of interest as concerns third persons (to which however there are very great limitations); the real importance of the wife to his daily comforts and enjoyments, and the value he consequently attaches to her on his personal account, which, in a man capable of feeling for others, lays the foundation of caring for her on her own; and lastly, the influence naturally acquired over almost all human beings by those near to their persons (if not actually disagreeable to them): who, both by their direct entreaties, and by the insensible contagion of their feelings and dispositions, are often able, unless counteracted by some equally strong personal influence, to obtain a degree of command over the conduct of the superior, altogether excessive and unreasonable. Through these various means, the wife frequently exercises even too much power over the man; she is able to affect his conduct in things in which she may not be qualified to influence it for good—in which her influence may be not only unenlightened, but employed on the morally wrong side; and in which he would act better if left to his own prompting. But neither in the affairs of families nor in those of states is power a compensation for the loss of freedom. Her power often gives her what she has no right to, but does not enable her to assert her own rights. A Sultan's favourite slave has slaves under her, over whom she tyrannizes; but the desirable thing would be that she should neither have slaves nor be a slave. By entirely sinking her own existence in her husband; by having no will (or persuading him that she has no will) but his, in anything which regards their joint relation, and by making it the business of her life to work upon his sentiments, a wife may gratify herself by influencing, and very probably perverting, his conduct, in those of his external relations which she has never qualified herself to judge of, or in which she is herself wholly influenced by some personal or other partiality or prejudice. Accordingly, as things now are, those who act most kindly to their wives, are quite as often made worse, as better, by the wife's influence, in respect to all interests extending beyond the family. She is taught that she has no business with things out of that sphere; and accordingly she seldom has any honest and conscientious opinion on them; and therefore hardly ever meddles with them for any legitimate purpose, but generally for an interested one. She neither knows nor cares which is the right side in politics, but she knows what will bring in money or invitations, give her husband a title, her son a place, or her daughter a good marriage.

But how, it will be asked, can any society exist without government? In a family, as in a state, some one person must be the ultimate ruler. Who shall decide when married people differ in opinion? Both cannot have their way, yet a decision one way or the other must be come to.

It is not true that in all voluntary association between two people, one of them must be absolute master: still less that the law must determine which of them it shall be. The most frequent case of voluntary association, next to marriage, is partnership in business: and it is not found or thought necessary to enact that in every partnership, one partner shall have entire control over the concern, and the others shall be bound to obey his orders. No one would enter into partnership on terms which would subject him to the responsibilities of a principal, with only the powers and privileges of a clerk or agent. If the law dealt with other contracts as it does with marriage, it would ordain that one partner should administer the common business as if it was his private concern; that the others should have only delegated powers; and that this one should be designated by some general presumption of law, for example as being the eldest. The law never does this: nor does experience show it to be necessary that any theoretical inequality of power should exist between the partners, or that the partnership should have any other conditions than what they may themselves appoint by their articles of agreement. Yet it might seem that the exclusive power might be conceded with less danger to the rights and interests of the inferior, in the case of partnership than in that of marriage, since he is free to cancel the power by withdrawing from the connexion. The wife has no such power, and even if she had, it is almost always desirable that she should try all measures before resorting to it.

It is quite true that things which have to be decided every day, and cannot adjust themselves gradually, or wait for a compromise, ought to depend on one will: one person must have their sole control. But it does not follow that this should always be the same person. The natural arrangement is a division of powers between the two; each being absolute in the executive branch of their own department, and any change of system and principle requiring the consent of both. The division neither can nor should be pre-established by the law, since it must depend on individual capacities and suitabilities. If the two persons chose, they might pre-appoint it by the marriage contract, as pecuniary arrangements are now often pre-appointed. There would seldom be any difficulty in deciding such things by mutual consent, unless the marriage was one of those unhappy ones in which all other things, as well as this, become subjects of bickering and dispute. The division of rights would naturally follow the division of duties and functions; and that is already made by consent, or at all events not by law, but by general custom, modified and modifiable at the pleasure of the persons concerned.

The real practical decision of affairs, to whichever may be given the legal authority, will greatly depend, as it even now does, upon comparative qualifications. The mere fact that he is usually the eldest, will in most cases give the preponderance to the man; at least until they both attain a time of life at which the difference in their years is of no importance. There will naturally also be a more potential voice on the side, whichever it is, that brings the means of support. Inequality from this source does not depend on the law of marriage, but on the general conditions of human society, as now constituted. The influence of mental superiority, either general or special, and of superior decision of character, will necessarily tell for much. It always does so at present. And this fact shows how little foundation there is for the apprehension that the powers and responsibilities of partners in life (as of partners in business), cannot be satisfactorily apportioned by agreement between themselves. They always are so apportioned, except in cases in which the marriage institution is a failure. Things never come to an issue of downright power on one side, and obedience on the other, except where the connexion altogether has been a mistake, and it would be a blessing to both parties to be relieved from it. Some may say that the very thing by which an amicable settlement of differences becomes possible, is the power of legal compulsion known to be in reserve; as people submit to an arbitration because there is a court of law in the background, which they know that they can be forced to obey. But to make the cases parallel, we must suppose that the rule of the court of law was, not to try the cause, but to give judgment always for the same side, suppose the defendant. If so, the amenability to it would be a motive with the plaintiff to agree to almost any arbitration, but it would be just the reverse with the defendant. The despotic power which the law gives to the husband may be a reason to make the wife assent to any compromise by which power is practically shared between the two, but it cannot be the reason why the husband does. That there is always among decently conducted people a practical compromise, though one of them at least is under no physical or moral necessity of making it, shows that the natural motives which lead to a voluntary adjustment of the united life of two persons in a manner acceptable to both, do on the whole, except in unfavourable cases, prevail. The matter is certainly not improved by laying down as an ordinance of law, that the superstructure of free government shall be raised upon a legal basis of despotism on one side and subjection on the other, and that every concession which the despot makes may, at his mere pleasure, and without any warning, be recalled. Besides that no freedom is worth much when held on so precarious a tenure, its conditions are not likely to be the most equitable when the law throws so prodigious a weight into one scale; when the adjustment rests between two persons one of whom is declared to be entitled to everything, the other not only entitled to nothing except during the good pleasure of the first, but under the strongest moral and religious obligation not to rebel under any excess of oppression.

A pertinacious adversary, pushed to extremities, may say, that husbands indeed are willing to be reasonable, and to make fair concessions to their partners without being compelled to it, but that wives are not: that if allowed any rights of their own, they will acknowledge no rights at all in any one else, and never will yield in anything, unless they can be compelled, by the man's mere authority, to yield in everything. This would have been said by many persons some generations ago, when satires on women were in vogue, and men thought it a clever thing to insult women for being what men made them. But it will be said by no one now who is worth replying to. It is not the doctrine of the present day that women are less susceptible of good feeling, and consideration for those with whom they are united by the strongest ties, than men are. On the contrary, we are perpetually told that women are better than men, by those who are totally opposed to treating them as if they were as good; so that the saying has passed into a piece of tiresome cant, intended to put a complimentary face upon an injury, and resembling those celebrations of royal clemency which, according to Gulliver, the king of Lilliput always prefixed to his most sanguinary decrees.[*] If women are better than men in anything, it surely is in individual self-sacrifice for those of their own family. But I lay little stress on this, so long as they are universally taught that they are born and created for self-sacrifice. I believe that equality of rights would abate the exaggerated self-abnegation which is the present artificial ideal of feminine character, and that a good woman would not be more self-sacrificing than the best man: but on the other hand, men would be much more unselfish and self-sacrificing than at present, because they would no longer be taught to worship their own will as such a grand thing that it is actually the law for another rational being. There is nothing which men so easily learn as this self-worship: all privileged persons, and all privileged classes, have had it. The more we descend in the scale of humanity, the intenser it is; and most of all in those who are not, and can never expect to be, raised above any one except an unfortunate wife and children. The honourable exceptions are proportionally fewer than in the case of almost any other human infirmity. Philosophy and religion, instead of keeping it in check, are generally suborned to defend it; and nothing controls it but that practical feeling of the equality of human beings, which is the theory of Christianity, but which Christianity will never practically teach, while it sanctions institutions grounded on an arbitrary preference of one human being over another.

There are, no doubt, women, as there are men, whom equality of consideration will not satisfy; with whom there is no peace while any will or wish is regarded but their own. Such persons are a proper subject for the law of divorce. They are only fit to live alone, and no human beings ought to be compelled to associate their lives with them. But the legal subordination tends to make such characters among women more, rather than less, frequent. If the man exerts his whole power, the woman is of course crushed: but if she is treated with indulgence, and permitted to assume power, there is no rule to set limits to her encroachments. The law, not determining her rights, but theoretically allowing her none at all, practically declares that the measure of what she has a right to, is what she can contrive to get.

The equality of married persons before the law, is not only the sole mode in which that particular relation can be made consistent with justice to both sides, and conducive to the happiness of both, but it is the only means of rendering the daily life of mankind, in any high sense, a school of moral cultivation. Though the truth may not be felt or generally acknowledged for generations to come, the only school of genuine moral sentiment is society between equals. The moral education

[*See Jonathan Swift, *Travels into Several Remote Nations of the World. By Lemuel Gulliver* (1726), in *Works*, ed. Walter Scott, 19 vols. (Edinburgh: Constable; London: White, Cochrane, *et al.*; Dublin: Cumming, 1814), Vol. XII, pp. 95-6 (Voyage I, Chap. vii).]

of mankind has hitherto emanated chiefly from the law of force, and is adapted almost solely to the relations which force creates. In the less advanced states of society, people hardly recognise any relation with their equals. To be an equal is to be an enemy. Society, from its highest place to its lowest, is one long chain, or rather ladder, where every individual is either above or below his nearest neighbour, and wherever he does not command he must obey. Existing moralities, accordingly, are mainly fitted to a relation of command and obedience. Yet command and obedience are but unfortunate necessities of human life: society in equality is its normal state. Already in modern life, and more and more as it progressively improves, command and obedience become exceptional facts in life, equal association its general rule. The morality of the first ages rested on the obligation to submit to power; that of the ages next following, on the right of the weak to the forbearance and protection of the strong. How much longer is one form of society and life to content itself with the morality made for another? We have had the morality of submission, and the morality of chivalry and generosity; the time is now come for the morality of justice. Whenever, in former ages, any approach has been made to society in equality, Justice has asserted its claims as the foundation of virtue. It was thus in the free republics of antiquity. But even in the best of these, the equals were limited to the free male citizens; slaves, women, and the unenfranchised residents were under the law of force. The joint influence of Roman civilization and of Christianity obliterated these distinctions, and in theory (if only partially in practice) declared the claims of the human being, as such, to be paramount to those of sex, class, or social position. The barriers which had begun to be levelled were raised again by the northern conquests; and the whole of modern history consists of the slow process by which they have since been wearing away. We are entering into an order of things in which justice will again be the primary virtue; grounded as before on equal, but now also on sympathetic association; having its root no longer in the instinct of equals for self-protection, but in a cultivated sympathy between them; and no one being now left out, but an equal measure being extended to all. It is no novelty that mankind do not distinctly foresee their own changes, and that their sentiments are adapted to past, not to coming ages. To see the futurity of the species has always been the privilege of the intellectual élite, or of those who have learnt from them; to have the feelings of that futurity has been the distinction, and usually the martyrdom, of a still rarer élite. Institutions, books, education, society, all go on training human beings for the old, long after the new has come; much more when it is only coming. But the true virtue of human beings is fitness to live together as equals; claiming nothing for themselves but what they as freely concede to every one else; regarding command of any kind as an exceptional necessity, and in all cases a temporary one; and preferring, whenever possible, the society of those with whom leading and following can be alternate and reciprocal. To these virtues, nothing in life as at present constituted gives cultivation by exercise. The family is a school of despotism, in which the virtues of despotism, but also its vices, are largely nourished. Citizenship, in free countries, is partly a school of society in equality; but citizenship fills only a small place in modern life, and does not come near the daily habits or inmost sentiments. The family, justly constituted, would be the real school of the virtues of freedom. It is sure to be a sufficient one of everything else. It will always be a school of obedience for the children, of command for the parents. What is needed is, that it should be a school of sympathy in equality, of living together in love, without power on one side or obedience on the other. This it ought to be between the parents. It would then be an exercise of those virtues which each requires to fit them for all other association, and a model to the children of the feelings and conduct which their temporary training by means of obedience is designed to render habitual, and therefore natural, to them. The moral training of mankind will never be adapted to the conditions of the life for which all other human progress is a preparation, until they practise in the family the same moral rule which is adapted to the normal constitution of human society. Any senti-ment of freedom which can exist in a man whose nearest and dearest intimacies are with those of whom he is absolute master, is not the genuine or Christian love of freedom, but, what the love of freedom generally was in the ancients and in the middle ages—an intense feeling of the dignity and importance of his own personality; making him disdain a yoke for himself, of which he has no abhorrence whatever in the abstract, but which he is abundantly ready to impose on others for his own interest or glorification.

I readily admit (and it is the very foundation of my hopes) that numbers of married people even under the present law, (in the higher classes of England probably a great majority,) live in the spirit of a just law of equality. Laws never would be improved, if there were not numerous persons whose moral sentiments are better than the existing laws. Such persons ought to support the principles here advocated; of which the only object is to make all other married couples similar to what these are now. But persons even of considerable moral worth, unless they are also thinkers, are very ready to believe that laws or practices, the evils of which they have not personally experienced, do not produce any evils, but (if seeming to be generally approved of) probably do good, and that it is wrong to object to them. It would, however, be a great mistake in such married people to suppose, because the legal conditions of the tie which unites them do not occur to their thoughts once in a twelvemonth, and because they live and feel in all respects as if they were legally equals, that the same is the case with all other married couples, wherever the husband is not a notorious ruffian. To suppose this, would be to show equal ignorance of human nature and of fact. The less fit a man is for the possession of power—the less likely to be allowed to exercise it over any person with that person's voluntary consent—the more does he hug himself in the consciousness of the power the law gives him, exact its legal rights to the utmost point which custom (the custom of men like himself) will tolerate, and take pleasure in using the power, merely to enliven the agreeable sense of possessing it. What is more; in the most naturally brutal and morally uneducated part of the lower classes, the legal slavery of the woman, and something in the merely physical subjection to their will as an instrument, causes them to feel a sort of disrespect and contempt towards their own wife which they do not feel towards any other woman, or any other human being, with whom they come in contact; and which makes her seem to them an appropriate subject for any kind of indignity. Let an acute observer of the signs of feeling, who has the requisite opportunities, judge for himself whether this is not the case: and if he finds that it is, let him not wonder at any amount of disgust and indignation that can be felt against institutions which lead naturally to this depraved state of the human mind.

We shall be told, perhaps, that religion imposes the duty of obedience; as every established fact which is too bad to admit of any other defence, is always presented to us as an injunction of religion. The Church, it is very true, enjoins it in her formularies,[*] but it would be difficult to derive any such injunction from Christianity. We are told that St. Paul said, "Wives, obey your husbands:" but he also said, "Slaves, obey your masters."[†] It was not St. Paul's business, nor was it consistent with his object, the propagation of Christianity, to incite any one to rebellion against existing laws. The apostle's acceptance of all social institutions as he found them, is no more to be construed as a disapproval of attempts to improve them at the proper time, than his declaration, "The powers that be are ordained of God,"[‡] gives his sanction to military despotism, and to that alone, as the Christian form of political government, or commands passive obedience to it. To pretend that Christianity was intended to stereotype existing forms of government and society, and protect them against change, is to reduce it to the level of Islamism or of Brahminism. It is precisely because Christianity has not done this, that it has been the religion of the progressive portion of mankind, and Islamism, Brahminism, &c., have been those of the stationary portions; or rather (for there is no such thing as a really stationary society) of the declining portions. There have been abundance of people, in all ages of Christianity, who tried to make it something of the same kind; to convert us into a sort of Christian Mussulmans, with the Bible for a Koran, prohibiting all improvement: and great has been their power, and many have had to sacrifice their lives in resisting them. But they have been resisted, and the resistance has made us what we are, and will yet make us what we are to be.

After what has been said respecting the obligation of obedience, it is almost superfluous to say anything concerning the more special point included in the

[*See "The Form of Solemnization of Matrimony," in *The Annotated Book of Common Prayer*, ed. John Henry Blunt, 7th ed. (London, Oxford, and Cambridge: Rivingtons, 1876), pp. 261-74.]
[†Colossians, 3:18, 22.]
[‡Romans, 13:1.]

general one—a woman's right to her own property; for I need not hope that this treatise can make any impression upon those who need anything to convince them that a woman's inheritance or gains ought to be as much her own after marriage as before. The rule is simple: whatever would be the husband's or wife's if they were not married, should be under their exclusive control during marriage; which need not interfere with the power to tie up property by settlement, in order to preserve it for children. Some people are sentimentally shocked at the idea of a separate interest in money matters, as inconsistent with the ideal fusion of two lives into one. For my own part, I am one of the strongest supporters of community of goods, when resulting from an entire unity of feeling in the owners, which makes all things common between them. But I have no relish for a community of goods resting on the doctrine, that what is mine is yours but what is yours is not mine; and I should prefer to decline entering into such a compact with any one, though I were myself the person to profit by it.

This particular injustice and oppression to women, which is, to common apprehensions, more obvious than all the rest, admits of remedy without interfering with any other mischiefs: and there can be little doubt that it will be one of the earliest remedied. Already, in many of the new and several of the old States of the American Confederation, provisions have been inserted even in the written Constitutions, securing to women equality of rights in this respect:[*] and thereby improving materially the position, in the marriage relation, of those women at least who have property, by leaving them one instrument of power which they have not signed away; and preventing also the scandalous abuse of the marriage institution, which is perpetrated when a man entraps a girl into marrying him without a settlement, for the sole purpose of getting possession of her money. When the support of the family depends, not on property, but on earnings, the common arrangement, by which the man earns the income and the wife superintends the domestic expenditure, seems to me in general the most suitable division of labour between the two persons. If, in addition to the physical suffering of bearing children, and the whole responsibility of their care and education in early years, the wife undertakes the careful and economical application of the husband's earnings to the general comfort of the family; she takes not only her fair share, but usually the larger share, of the bodily and mental exertion required by their joint existence. If she undertakes any additional portion, it seldom relieves her from this, but only prevents her from performing it properly. The care which she is

[*See, e.g., *Constitution of Texas 1845*, Art. VII, Sect. 19, in *The Constitutions of the State of Texas*, annotated by John Sayles, 4th ed. (St. Louis, Mo.: Gilbert, 1893), p. 209; *Constitution of the State of California 1849* (San Francisco: printed at the office of the *Alta California*, 1849), Art. XI, Sect. 14, p. 13; *Constitution of the State of Nevada 1864*, Art. IV, Sect. 31, in *Statutes of the State of Nevada Passed at the First Session of the Legislature, 1864-65* (Carson City, Nev.: Church, 1865), p. 48; and *Constitution of the State of Georgia 1868*, Art. VII, Sect. 2 (Augusta, Ga.: Pughe, 1868), p. 11.]

herself disabled from taking of the children and the household, nobody else takes; those of the children who do not die, grow up as they best can, and the management of the household is likely to be so bad, as even in point of economy to be a great drawback from the value of the wife's earnings. In an otherwise just state of things, it is not, therefore, I think, a desirable custom, that the wife should contribute by her labour to the income of the family. In an unjust state of things, her doing so may be useful to her, by making her of more value in the eyes of the man who is legally her master; but, on the other hand, it enables him still farther to abuse his power, by forcing her to work, and leaving the support of the family to her exertions, while he spends most of his time in drinking and idleness. The *power* of earning is essential to the dignity of a woman, if she has not independent property. But if marriage were an equal contract, not implying the obligation of obedience; if the connexion were no longer enforced to the oppression of those to whom it is purely a mischief, but a separation, on just terms (I do not now speak of a divorce), could be obtained by any woman who was morally entitled to it; and if she would then find all honourable employments as freely open to her as to men; it would not be necessary for her protection, that during marriage she should make this particular use of her faculties. Like a man when he chooses a profession, so, when a woman marries, it may in general be understood that she makes choice of the management of a household, and the bringing up of a family, as the first call upon her exertions, during as many years of her life as may be required for the purpose; and that she renounces, not all other objects and occupations, but all which are not consistent with the requirements of this. The actual exercise, in a habitual or systematic manner, of outdoor occupations, or such as cannot be carried on at home, would by this principle be practically interdicted to the greater number of married women. But the utmost latitude ought to exist for the adaptation of general rules to individual suitabilities; and there ought to be nothing to prevent faculties exceptionally adapted to any other pursuit, from obeying their vocation notwith-standing marriage: due provision being made for supplying otherwise any falling-short which might become inevitable, in her full performance of the ordinary functions of mistress of a family. These things, if once opinion were rightly directed on the subject, might with perfect safety be left to be regulated by opinion, without any interference of law.

Chapter III

ON THE OTHER POINT which is involved in the just equality of women, their admissibility to all the functions and occupations hitherto retained as the monopoly of the stronger sex, I should anticipate no difficulty in convincing any one who has gone with me on the subject of the equality of women in the family. I believe that their disabilities elsewhere are only clung to in order to maintain their subordination in domestic life; because the generality of the male sex cannot yet tolerate the idea of living with an equal. Were it not for that, I think that almost every one, in the existing state of opinion in politics and political economy, would admit the injustice of excluding half the human race from the greater number of lucrative occupations, and from almost all high social functions; ordaining from their birth either that they are not, and cannot by any possibility become, fit for employments which are legally open to the stupidest and basest of the other sex, or else that however fit they may be, those employments shall be interdicted to them, in order to be preserved for the exclusive benefit of males. In the last two centuries, when (which was seldom the case) any reason beyond the mere existence of the fact was thought to be required to justify the disabilities of women, people seldom assigned as a reason their inferior mental capacity; which, in times when there was a real trial of personal faculties (from which all women were not excluded) in the struggles of public life, no one really believed in. The reason given in those days was not women's unfitness, but the interest of society, by which was meant the interest of men: just as the *raison d'état*, meaning the convenience of the government, and the support of existing authority, was deemed a sufficient explanation and excuse for the most flagitious crimes. In the present day, power holds a smoother language, and whomsoever it oppresses, always pretends to do so for their own good: accordingly, when anything is forbidden to women, it is thought necessary to say, and desirable to believe, that they are incapable of doing it, and that they depart from their real path of success and happiness when they aspire to it. But to make this reason plausible (I do not say valid), those by whom it is urged must be prepared to carry it to a much greater length than any one ventures to do in the face of present experience. It is not sufficient to maintain that women on the average are less gifted than men on the average, with certain of the higher mental faculties, or that a smaller number of women than of men are fit for occupations and functions of the highest intellectual character. It is necessary to maintain that no women at all are fit for them, and that the most eminent women are inferior in mental faculties to the most mediocre of the men on whom those functions at present devolve. For if the performance of the function is decided either by competition, or by any mode of choice which secures regard to the public interest, there needs be no apprehension that any important employments will fall into the hands of women inferior to average men, or to the average of their male competitors. The only result would be that there would be fewer women than men in such employments; a result certain to happen in any case, if only from the preference always likely to be felt by the majority of women for the one vocation in which there is nobody to compete with them. Now, the most determined depreciator of women will not venture to deny, that when we add the experience of recent times to that of ages past, women, and not a few merely, but many women, have proved themselves capable of everything, perhaps without a single exception, which is done by men, and of doing it successfully and creditably. The utmost that can be said is, that there are many things which none of them have succeeded in doing as well as they have been done by some men—many in which they have not reached the very highest rank. But there are extremely few, dependent only on mental faculties, in which they have not attained the rank next to the highest. Is not this enough, and much more than enough, to make it a tyranny to them, and a detriment to society, that they should not be allowed to compete with men for the exercise of these functions? Is it not a mere truism to say, that such functions are often filled by men far less fit for them than numbers of women, and who would be beaten by women in any fair field of competition? What difference does it make that there may be men somewhere, fully employed about other things, who may be still better qualified for the things in question than these women? Does not this take place in all competitions? Is there so great a superfluity of men fit for high duties, that society can afford to reject the service of any competent person? Are we so certain of always finding a man made to our hands for any duty or function of social importance which falls vacant, that we lose nothing by putting a ban upon one-half of mankind, and refusing beforehand to make their faculties available, however distinguished they may be? And even if we could do without them, would it be consistent with justice to refuse to them their fair share of honour and distinction, or to deny to them the equal moral right of all human beings to choose their occupation (short of injury to others) according to their own preferences, at their own risk? Nor is the injustice confined to them: it is shared by those who are in a position to benefit by their services. To ordain that any kind of persons shall not be physicians, or shall not be advocates, or shall not be members of parliament, is to injure not them only, but all who employ physicians or advocates, or elect members of parliament, and who are deprived of the stimulating effect of greater competition on the exertions of the competitors, as well as restricted to a narrower range of individual choice.

It will perhaps be sufficient if I confine myself, in the details of my argument, to functions of a public nature: since, if I am successful as to those, it probably will be readily granted that women should be admissible to all other occupations to which it is at all material whether they are admitted or not. And here let me begin by marking out one function, broadly distinguished from all others, their right to which is entirely independent of any question which can be raised concerning their faculties. I mean the suffrage, both parliamentary and municipal. The right to share in the choice of those who are to exercise a public trust, is altogether a distinct thing from that of competing for the trust itself. If no one could vote for a member of parliament who was not fit to be a candidate, the government would be a narrow oligarchy indeed. To have a voice in choosing those by whom one is to be governed, is a means of self-protection due to every one, though he were to remain for ever excluded from the function of governing: and that women are considered fit to have such a choice, may be presumed from the fact, that the law already gives it to women in the most important of all cases to themselves: for the choice of the man who is to govern a woman to the end of life, is always supposed to be voluntarily made by herself. In the case of election to public trusts, it is the business of constitutional law to surround the right of suffrage with all needful securities and limitations; but whatever securities are sufficient in the case of the male sex, no others need be required in the case of women. Under whatever conditions, and within whatever limits, men are admitted to the suffrage, there is not a shadow of justification for not admitting women under the same. The majority of the women of any class are not likely to differ in political opinion from the majority of the men of the same class, unless the question be one in which the interests of women, as such, are in some way involved; and if they are so, women require the suffrage, as their guarantee of just and equal consideration. This ought to be obvious even to those who coincide in no other of the doctrines for which I contend. Even if every woman were a wife, and if every wife ought to be a slave, all the more would these slaves stand in need of legal protection: and we know what legal protection the slaves have, where the laws are made by their masters.

With regard to the fitness of women, not only to participate in elections, but themselves to hold offices or practise professions involving important public responsibilities; I have already observed that this consideration is not essential to the practical question in dispute: since any woman, who succeeds in an open profession, proves by that very fact that she is qualified for it. And in the case of public offices, if the political system of the country is such as to exclude unfit men, it will equally exclude unfit women: while if it is not, there is no additional evil in the fact that the unfit persons whom it admits may be either women or men. As long therefore as it is acknowledged that even a few women may be fit for these duties, the laws which shut the door on those exceptions cannot be justified by any opinion which can be held respecting the capacities of women in general. But, though this last consideration is not essential, it is far from being irrelevant. An unprejudiced view of it gives additional strength to the arguments against the disabilities of women, and reinforces them by high considerations of practical utility.

Let us at first make entire abstraction of all psychological considerations tending to show, that any of the mental differences supposed to exist between women and men are but the natural effect of the differences in their education and circumstances, and indicate no radical difference, far less radical inferiority, of nature. Let us consider women only as they already are, or as they are known to have been; and the capacities which they have already practically shown. What they have done, that at least, if nothing else, it is proved that they can do. When we consider how sedulously they are all trained away from, instead of being trained towards, any of the occupations or objects reserved for men, it is evident that I am taking a very humble ground for them, when I rest their case on what they have actually achieved. For, in this case, negative evidence is worth little, while any positive evidence is conclusive. It cannot be inferred to be impossible that a woman should be a Homer, or an Aristotle, or a Michael Angelo, or a Beethoven, because no woman has yet actually produced works comparable to theirs in any of those lines of excellence. This negative fact at most leaves the question uncertain, and open to psychological discussion. But it is quite certain that a woman can be a Queen Elizabeth, or a Deborah,[*] or a Joan of Arc, since this is not inference, but fact. Now it is a curious consideration, that the only things which the existing law excludes women from doing, are the things which they have proved that they are able to do. There is no law to prevent a woman from having written all the plays of Shakspeare, or composed all the operas of Mozart. But Queen Elizabeth or Queen Victoria, had they not inherited the throne, could not have been intrusted with the smallest of the political duties, of which the former showed herself equal to the greatest.

If anything conclusive could be inferred from experience, without psychological analysis, it would be that the things which women are not allowed to do are the very ones for which they are peculiarly qualified; since their vocation for government has made its way, and become conspicuous, through the very few opportunities which have been given; while in the lines of distinction which apparently were freely open to them, they have by no means so eminently distinguished themselves. We know how small a number of reigning queens history presents, in comparison with that of kings. Of this smaller number a far larger proportion have shown talents for rule; though many of them have occupied the throne in difficult periods. It is remarkable, too, that they have, in a great number of instances, been distinguished by merits the most opposite to the imaginary and conventional character of women: they have been as much remarked for the firmness and vigour of their rule, as for its intelligence. When, to queens and empresses, we add regents, and viceroys of provinces, the list of

[*See Judges, 4-5.]

women who have been eminent rulers of mankind swells to a great length.* This fact is so undeniable, that some one, long ago, tried to retort the argument, and turned the admitted truth into an additional insult, by saying that queens are better than kings, because under kings women govern, but under queens, men.

It may seem a waste of reasoning to argue against a bad joke; but such things do affect people's minds; and I have heard men quote this saying, with an air as if they thought that there was something in it. At any rate, it will serve as well as anything else for a starting point in discussion. I say, then, that it is not true that under kings, women govern. Such cases are entirely exceptional: and weak kings have quite as often governed ill through the influence of male favourites, as of female. When a king is governed by a woman merely through his amatory propensities, good government is not probable, though even then there are exceptions. But French history counts two kings who have voluntarily given the direction of affairs during many years, the one to his mother, the other to his sister:[*] one of them, Charles VIII, was a mere boy, but in doing so he followed the intentions of his father Louis XI, the ablest monarch of his age. The other, Saint Louis, was the best, and one of the most vigorous rulers, since the time of Charlemagne. Both these princesses ruled in a manner hardly equalled by any prince among their cotemporaries. The emperor Charles V, the most politic prince of his time, who had as great a number of able men in his service as a ruler ever had, and was one of the least likely of all sovereigns to sacrifice his interest to personal feelings, made two princesses of his family successively Governors of the Netherlands, and kept one or other of them in that post during his whole life, (they were afterwards succeeded by a third).[†] Both ruled very successfully, and one of them, Margaret of Austria, was one of the ablest politicians of the age. So much for one side of the question. Now

*Especially is this true if we take into consideration Asia as well as Europe. If a Hindoo principality is strongly, vigilantly, and economically governed; if order is preserved without oppression; if cultivation is extending, and the people prosperous, in three cases out of four that principality is under a woman's rule. This fact, to me an entirely unexpected one, I have collected from a long official knowledge of Hindoo governments. There are many such instances: for though, by Hindoo institutions, a woman cannot reign, she is the legal regent of a kingdom during the minority of the heir; and minorities are frequent, the lives of the male rulers being so often prematurely terminated through the effect of inactivity and sensual excesses. When we consider that these princesses have never been seen in public, have never conversed with any man not of their own family except from behind a curtain, that they do not read, and if they did, there is no book in their languages which can give them the smallest instruction on political affairs; the example they afford of the natural capacity of women for government is very striking.

[*Blanche of Castile, mother of Louis IX, was regent for several periods during his reign; Anne, duchesse de Beaujeu, sister of Charles VIII, was regent during part of his reign, as designated by Louis XI.]

[†Margaret of Austria, aunt of Charles V, was regent 1507-30; Mary of Hungary, sister of Charles V (and widow of Louis II of Hungary), was regent 1531-52; Margaret, Duchess of Parma, natural daughter of Charles V, was regent 1559-67.]

as to the other. When it is said that under queens men govern, is the same meaning to be understood as when kings are said to be governed by women? Is it meant that queens choose as their instruments of government, the associates of their personal pleasures? The case is rare even with those who are as unscrupulous on the latter point as Catherine II: and it is not in these cases that the good government, alleged to arise from male influence, is to be found. If it be true, then, that the administration is in the hands of better men under a queen than under an average king, it must be that queens have a superior capacity for choosing them; and women must be better qualified than men both for the position of sovereign, and for that of chief minister; for the principal business of a prime minister is not to govern in person, but to find the fittest persons to conduct every department of public affairs. The more rapid insight into character, which is one of the admitted points of superiority in women over men, must certainly make them, with anything like parity of qualifications in other respects, more apt than men in that choice of instruments, which is nearly the most important business of every one who has to do with governing mankind. Even the unprincipled Catherine de' Medici could feel the value of a Chancellor de l'Hôpital. But it is also true that most great queens have been great by their own talents for government, and have been well served precisely for that reason. They retained the supreme direction of affairs in their own hands: and if they listened to good advisers, they gave by that fact the strongest proof that their judgment fitted them for dealing with the great questions of government.

Is it reasonable to think that those who are fit for the greater functions of politics, are incapable of qualifying themselves for the less? Is there any reason in the nature of things, that the wives and sisters of princes should, whenever called on, be found as competent as the princes themselves to *their* business, but that the wives and sisters of statesmen, and administrators, and directors of companies, and managers of public institutions, should be unable to do what is done by their brothers and husbands? The real reason is plain enough; it is that princesses, being more raised above the generality of men by their rank than placed below them by their sex, have never been taught that it was improper for them to concern themselves with politics; but have been allowed to feel the liberal interest natural to any cultivated human being, in the great transactions which took place around them, and in which they might be called on to take a part. The ladies of reigning families are the only women who are allowed the same range of interests and freedom of development as men; and it is precisely in their case that there is not found to be any inferiority. Exactly where and in proportion as women's capacities for government have been tried, in that proportion have they been found adequate.

This fact is in accordance with the best general conclusions which the world's imperfect experience seems as yet to suggest, concerning the peculiar tendencies and aptitudes characteristic of women, as women have hitherto been. I do not say, as they will continue to be; for, as I have already said more than once, I consider it presumption in any one to pretend to decide what women are or are not, can or cannot be, by natural constitution. They have always hitherto been kept, as far as regards spontaneous development, in so unnatural a state, that their nature cannot but have been greatly distorted and disguised; and no one can safely pronounce that if women's nature were left to choose its direction as freely as men's, and if no artificial bent were attempted to be given to it except that required by the conditions of human society, and given to both sexes alike, there would be any material difference, or perhaps any difference at all, in the character and capacities which would unfold themselves. I shall presently show, that even the least contestable of the differences which now exist, are such as may very well have been produced merely by circumstances, without any difference of natural capacity. But, looking at women as they are known in experience, it may be said of them, with more truth than belongs to most other generalizations on the subject, that the general bent of their talents is towards the practical. This statement is conformable to all the public history of women, in the present and the past. It is no less borne out by common and daily experience. Let us consider the special nature of the mental capacities most characteristic of a woman of talent. They are all of a kind which fits them for practice, and makes them tend towards it. What is meant by a woman's capacity of intuitive perception? It means, a rapid and correct insight into present fact. It has nothing to do with general principles. Nobody ever perceived a scientific law of nature by intuition, nor arrived at a general rule of duty or prudence by it. These are results of slow and careful collection and comparison of experience; and neither the men nor the women of intuition usually shine in this department, unless, indeed, the experience necessary is such as they can acquire by themselves. For what is called their intuitive sagacity makes them peculiarly apt in gathering such general truths as can be collected from their individual means of observation. When, consequently, they chance to be as well provided as men are with the results of other people's experience, by reading and education, (I use the word chance advisedly, for, in respect to the knowledge that tends to fit them for the greater concerns of life, the only educated women are the self-educated) they are better furnished than men in general with the essential requisites of skilful and successful practice. Men who have been much taught, are apt to be deficient in the sense of present fact; they do not see, in the facts which they are called upon to deal with, what is really there, but what they have been taught to expect. This is seldom the case with women of any ability. Their capacity of "intuition" preserves them from it. With equality of experience and of general faculties, a woman usually sees much more than a man of what is immediately before her. Now this sensibility to the present, is the main quality on which the capacity for practice, as distinguished from theory, depends. To discover general principles, belongs to the speculative faculty: to discern and discriminate the particular cases in which they are and are not applicable, constitutes practical talent: and for this, women as they now are have a peculiar aptitude. I admit that there can be no good practice without principles, and that the predominant place which quickness of observation holds among a woman's faculties, makes her particularly apt to build over-hasty generalizations upon her own observation; though at the same time no less ready in rectifying those generalizations, as her observation takes a wider range. But the corrective to this defect, is access to the experience of the human race; general knowledge—exactly the thing which education can best supply. A woman's mistakes are specifically those of a clever self-educated man, who often sees what men trained in routine do not see, but falls into errors for want of knowing things which have long been known. Of course he has acquired much of the pre-existing knowledge, or he could not have got on at all; but what he knows of it he has picked up in fragments and at random, as women do.

But this gravitation of women's minds to the present, to the real, to actual fact, while in its exclusiveness it is a source of errors, is also a most useful counteractive of the contrary error. The principal and most characteristic aberration of speculative minds as such, consists precisely in the deficiency of this lively perception and ever-present sense of objective fact. For want of this, they often not only overlook the contradiction which outward facts oppose to their theories, but lose sight of the legitimate purpose of speculation altogether, and let their speculative faculties go astray into regions not peopled with real beings, animate or inanimate, even idealized, but with personified shadows created by the illusions of metaphysics or by the mere entanglement of words, and think these shadows the proper objects of the highest, the most transcendant, philosophy. Hardly anything can be of greater value to a man of theory and speculation who employs himself not in collecting materials of knowledge by observation, but in working them up by processes of thought into comprehensive truths of science and laws of conduct, than to carry on his speculations in the companionship, and under the criticism, of a really superior woman. There is nothing comparable to it for keeping his thoughts within the limits of real things, and the actual facts of nature. A woman seldom runs wild after an abstraction. The habitual direction of her mind to dealing with things as individuals rather than in groups, and (what is closely connected with it) her more lively interest in the present feelings of persons, which makes her consider first of all, in anything which claims to be applied to practice, in what manner persons will be affected by it—these two things make her extremely unlikely to put faith in any speculation which loses sight of individuals, and deals with things as if they existed for the benefit of some imaginary entity, some mere creation of the mind, not resolvable into the feelings of living beings. Women's thoughts are thus as useful in giving reality to those of thinking men, as men's thoughts in giving width and largeness to those of women. In depth, as distinguished from breadth, I greatly doubt if even now, women, compared with men, are at any disadvantage.

If the existing mental characteristics of women are thus valuable even in aid of speculation, they are still more important, when speculation has done its work, for carrying out the results of speculation into practice. For the reasons already given, women are comparatively unlikely to fall into the common error of men, that of sticking to their rules in a case whose specialities either take it out of the class to which the rules are applicable, or require a special adaptation of them. Let us now consider another of the admitted superiorities of clever women, greater quickness of apprehension. Is not this pre-eminently a quality which fits a person for practice? In action, everything continually depends upon deciding promptly. In speculation, nothing does. A mere thinker can wait, can take time to consider, can collect additional evidence; he is not obliged to complete his philosophy at once, lest the opportunity should go by. The power of drawing the best conclusion possible from insufficient data is not indeed useless in philosophy; the construction of a provisional hypothesis consistent with all known facts is often the needful basis for further inquiry. But this faculty is rather serviceable in philosophy, than the main qualification for it: and, for the auxiliary as well as for the main operation, the philosopher can allow himself any time he pleases. He is in no need of the capacity of doing rapidly what he does; what he rather needs is patience, to work on slowly until imperfect lights have become perfect, and a conjecture has ripened into a theorem. For those, on the contrary, whose business is with the fugitive and perishable—with individual facts, not kinds of facts—rapidity of thought is a qualification next only in importance to the power of thought itself. He who has not his faculties under immediate command, in the contingencies of action, might as well not have them at all. He may be fit to criticize, but he is not fit to act. Now it is in this that women, and the men who are most like women, confessedly excel. The other sort of man, however pre-eminent may be his faculties, arrives slowly at complete command of them: rapidity of judgment and promptitude of judicious action, even in the things he knows best, are the gradual and late result of strenuous effort grown into habit.

It will be said, perhaps, that the greater nervous susceptibility of women is a disqualification for practice, in anything but domestic life, by rendering them mobile, changeable, too vehemently under the influence of the moment, incapable of dogged perseverance, unequal and uncertain in the power of using their faculties. I think that these phrases sum up the greater part of the objections commonly made to the fitness of women for the higher class of serious business. Much of all this is the mere overflow of nervous energy run to waste, and would cease when the energy was directed to a definite end. Much is also the result of conscious or unconscious cultivation; as we see by the almost total disappearance of "hysterics" and fainting fits, since they have gone out of fashion. Moreover, when people are brought up, like many women of the higher classes (though less so in our own country than in any other) a kind of hot-house plants, shielded from the wholesome vicissitudes of air and temperature, and untrained in any of the occupations and exercises which give stimulus and development to the circulatory and muscular system, while their nervous system, especially in its emotional department, is kept in unnaturally active play; it is no wonder if those of them who do not die of consumption, grow up with constitutions liable to derangement from slight causes, both internal and external, and without stamina to support any task, physical or mental, requiring continuity of effort. But women brought up to work for their livelihood show none of these morbid characteristics, unless indeed they are chained to an excess of sedentary work in confined and unhealthy rooms. Women who in their early years have shared in the healthful physical education and bodily freedom of their brothers, and who obtain a sufficiency of pure air and exercise in after-life, very rarely have any excessive susceptibility of nerves which can disqualify them for active pursuits. There is indeed a certain proportion of persons, in both sexes, in whom an unusual degree of nervous sensibility is constitutional, and of so marked a character as to be the feature of their organization which exercises the greatest influence over the whole character of the vital phenomena. This constitution, like other physical conformations, is hereditary, and is transmitted to sons as well as daughters; but it is possible, and probable, that the nervous temperament (as it is called) is inherited by a greater number of women than of men. We will assume this as a fact: and let me then ask, are men of nervous temperament found to be unfit for the duties and pursuits usually followed by men? If not, why should women of the same temperament be unfit for them? The peculiarities of the temperament are, no doubt, within certain limits, an obstacle to success in some employments, though an aid to it in others. But when the occupation is suitable to the temperament, and sometimes even when it is unsuitable, the most brilliant examples of success are continually given by the men of high nervous sensibility. They are distinguished in their practical manifestations chiefly by this, that being susceptible of a higher degree of excitement than those of another physical constitution, their powers when excited differ more than in the case of other people, from those shown in their ordinary state: they are raised, as it were, above themselves, and do things with ease which they are wholly incapable of at other times. But this lofty excitement is not, except in weak bodily constitutions, a mere flash, which passes away immediately, leaving no permanent traces, and incompatible with persistent and steady pursuit of an object. It is the character of the nervous temperament to be capable of *sustained* excitement, holding out through long continued efforts. It is what is meant by *spirit*. It is what makes the high-bred racehorse run without slackening speed till he drops down dead. It is what has enabled so many delicate women to maintain the most sublime constancy not only at the stake, but through a long preliminary succession of mental and bodily tortures. It is evident that people of this temperament are particularly apt for what may be called the executive department of the leadership of mankind. They are the material of great orators, great preachers, impressive diffusers of moral influences. Their constitution might be deemed less favourable to the qualities required from a statesman in the cabinet, or from a judge. It would be so, if the consequence necessarily followed that because people are excitable they must always be in a state of excitement. But this is wholly a question of training. Strong feeling is the instrument and element of strong self-control: but it requires to be cultivated in that direction. When it is, it forms not the heroes of impulse only, but those also of self-conquest. History and experience prove that the most passionate characters are the most fanatically rigid in their feelings of duty, when their passion has been trained to act in that direction. The judge who gives a just decision in a case where his feelings are intensely interested on the other side, derives from that same strength of feeling the determined sense of the obligation of justice, which enables him to achieve this victory over himself. The capability of that lofty enthusiasm which takes the human being out of his every-day character, reacts upon the daily character itself. His aspirations and powers when he is in this exceptional state, become the type with which he compares, and by which he estimates, his sentiments and proceedings at other times: and his habitual purposes assume a character moulded by and assimilated to the moments of lofty excitement, although those, from the physical nature of a human being, can only be transient. Experience of races, as well as of individuals, does not show those of excitable temperament to be less fit, on the average, either for speculation or practice, than the more unexcitable. The French, and the Italians, are undoubtedly by nature more nervously excitable than the Teutonic races, and, compared at least with the English, they have a much greater habitual and daily emotional life: but have they been less great in science, in public business, in legal and judicial eminence, or in war? There is abundant evidence that the Greeks were of old, as their descendants and successors still are, one of the most excitable of the races of mankind. It is superfluous to ask, what among the achievements of men they did not excel in. The Romans, probably, as an equally southern people, had the same original temperament: but the stern character of their national discipline, like that of the Spartans, made them an example of the opposite type of national character; the greater strength of their natural feelings being chiefly apparent in the intensity which the same original temperament made it possible to give to the artificial. If these cases exemplify what a naturally excitable people may be made, the Irish Celts afford one of the aptest examples of what they are when left to themselves (if those can be said to be left to themselves who have been for centuries under the indirect influence of bad government, and the direct training of a Catholic hierarchy and of a sincere belief in the Catholic religion). The Irish character must be considered, therefore, as an unfavourable case: yet, whenever the circumstances of the individual have been at all favourable, what people have shown greater capacity for the most varied and multifarious individual eminence? Like the French compared with the English, the Irish with the Swiss, the Greeks or Italians compared with the German races, so women compared with men may be found, on the average, to do the same things with some variety in the particular kind of excellence. But, that they would do them fully as well on the whole, if their education and cultivation were adapted to correcting instead of aggravating the infirmities incident to their temperament, I see not the smallest reason to doubt.

Supposing it, however, to be true that women's minds are by nature more mobile than those of men, less capable of persisting long in the same continuous effort, more fitted for dividing their faculties among many things than for travelling in any one path to the highest point which can be reached by it: this may be true of women as they now are (though not without great and numerous exceptions), and may account for their having remained behind the highest order of men in precisely the things in which this absorption of the whole mind in one set of ideas and occupations may seem to be most requisite. Still, this difference is one which can only affect the kind of excellence, not the excellence itself, or its practical worth: and it remains to be shown whether this exclusive working of a part of the mind, this absorption of the whole thinking faculty in a single subject, and concentration of it on a single work, is the normal and healthful condition of the human faculties, even for speculative uses. I believe that what is gained in special development by this concentration, is lost in the capacity of the mind for the other purposes of life; and even in abstract thought, it is my decided opinion that the mind does more by frequently returning to a difficult problem, than by sticking to it without interruption. For the purposes, at all events, of practice, from its highest to its humblest departments, the capacity of passing promptly from one subject of consideration to another, without letting the active spring of the intellect run down between the two, is a power far more valuable; and this power women pre-eminently possess, by virtue of the very mobility of which they are accused. They perhaps have it from nature, but they certainly have it by training and education; for nearly the whole of the occupations of women consist in the management of small but multitudinous details, on each of which the mind cannot dwell even for a minute, but must pass on to other things, and if anything requires longer thought, must steal time at odd moments for thinking of it. The capacity indeed which women show for doing their thinking in circumstances and at times which almost any man would make an excuse to himself for not attempting it, has often been noticed: and a woman's mind, though it may be occupied only with small things, can hardly ever permit itself to be vacant, as a man's so often is when not engaged in what he chooses to consider the business of his life. The business of a woman's ordinary life is things in general, and can as little cease to go on as the world to go round.

But (it is said) there is anatomical evidence of the superior mental capacity of men compared with women: they have a larger brain. I reply, that in the first place the fact itself is doubtful. It is by no means established that the brain of a woman is smaller than that of a man. If it is inferred merely because a woman's bodily frame generally is of less dimensions than a man's, this criterion would lead to strange consequences. A tall and large-boned man must on this showing be wonderfully superior in intelligence to a small man, and an elephant or a whale must prodigiously excel mankind. The size of the brain in human beings, anatomists say, varies much less than the size of the body, or even of the head, and the one cannot be at all inferred from the other. It is certain that some women have as large a brain as any man. It is within my knowledge that a man who had weighed many human brains, said that the heaviest he knew of, heavier even than Cuvier's (the heaviest previously recorded,) was that of a woman.[*] Next, I must observe that the precise relation which exists between the brain and the intellectual powers is not yet well understood, but is a subject of great dispute. That there is a very close relation we cannot doubt. The brain is certainly the material organ of thought and feeling: and (making abstraction of the great unsettled controversy respecting the appropriation of different parts of the brain to different mental faculties) I admit that it would be an anomaly, and an exception to all we know of the general laws of life and organization, if the size of the organ were wholly indifferent to the function; if no accession of power were derived from the greater magnitude of the instrument. But the exception and the anomaly would be fully as great if the organ exercised influence by its magnitude *only*. In all the more delicate operations of nature—of which those of the animated creation are the most delicate, and those of the nervous system by far the most delicate of these—differences in the effect depend as much on differences of quality in the physical agents, as on their quantity: and if the quality of an instrument is to be tested by the nicety and delicacy of the work it can do, the indications point to a greater average fineness of quality in the brain and nervous system of women than of men. Dismissing abstract difference of quality, a thing difficult to verify, the efficiency of an organ is known to depend not solely on its size but on its activity: and of this we have an approximate measure in the energy with which the blood circulates through it, both the stimulus and the reparative force being mainly dependent on the circulation. It would not be surprising—it is indeed an hypothesis which accords well with the differences actually observed between the mental operations of the two sexes—if men on the average should have the advantage in the size of the brain, and women in activity of cerebral circulation. The results which conjecture, founded on analogy, would lead us to expect from this difference of organization, would correspond to some of those which we most commonly see. In the first place, the mental operations of men might be expected to be slower. They would neither be so prompt as women in thinking, nor so quick to feel. Large bodies take more time to get into full action. On the other hand, when once got thoroughly into play, men's brain would bear more work. It would be more persistent in the line first taken; it would have more difficulty in changing from one mode of action to another, but, in the one thing it was doing, it could go on longer without loss of

[*See Rudolph Virchow, *Untersuchungen über die Entwickelung des Schädelgrundes* (Berlin: Reimer, 1857), p. 101.]

power or sense of fatigue. And do we not find that the things in which men most excel women are those which require most plodding and long hammering at a single thought, while women do best what must be done rapidly? A woman's brain is sooner fatigued, sooner exhausted; but given the degree of exhaustion, we should expect to find that it would recover itself sooner. I repeat that this speculation is entirely hypothetical; it pretends to no more than to suggest a line of enquiry. I have before repudiated the notion of its being yet certainly known that there is any natural difference at all in the average strength or direction of the mental capacities of the two sexes, much less what that difference is. Nor is it possible that this should be known, so long as the psychological laws of the formation of character have been so little studied, even in a general way, and in the particular case never scientifically applied at all; so long as the most obvious external causes of difference of character are habitually disregarded—left unnoticed by the observer, and looked down upon with a kind of supericilious contempt by the prevalent schools both of natural history and of mental philosophy: who, whether they look for the source of what mainly distinguishes human beings from one another, in the world of matter or in that of spirit, agree in running down those who prefer to explain these differences by the different relations of human beings to society and life.

To so ridiculous an extent are the notions formed of the nature of women, mere empirical generalizations, framed, without philosophy or analysis, upon the first instances which present themselves, that the popular idea of it is different in different countries, according as the opinions and social circumstances of the country have given to the women living in it any speciality of development or non-development. An Oriental thinks that women are by nature peculiarly voluptuous; see the violent abuse of them on this ground in Hindoo writings. An Englishman usually thinks that they are by nature cold. The sayings about women's fickleness are mostly of French origin; from the famous distich of Francis I,[*] upward and downward. In England it is a common remark, how much more constant women are than men. Inconstancy has been longer reckoned discreditable to a woman, in England than in France; and Englishwomen are besides, in their inmost nature, much more subdued to opinion. It may be remarked by the way, that Englishmen are in peculiarly unfavourable circumstances for attempting to judge what is or is not natural, not merely to women, but to men, or to human beings altogether, at least if they have only English experience

---

[*"Toute femme varie," the comment of Francis I, carved in stone in his room at Chambord, is recorded in Pierre de Bourdeille, seigneur de Brantôme, *Les vies des dames galantes* (1666), in *Mémoires de Messire Pierre de Bourdeille, seigneur de Brantôme*, 10 vols. (Leyden: Sambix le jeune, 1665-1722), Vol. III, p. 233. However, Mill in referring to a "distich" is probably thinking of the version given to Francis I in Victor Hugo's *Le roi s'amuse* (Paris: Renduel, 1832), p. 129 (IV, ii): "Souvent femme varie, / Bien fol est qui s'y fie!"]

to go upon: because there is no place where human nature shows so little of its original lineaments. Both in a good and a bad sense, the English are farther from a state of nature than any other modern people. They are, more than any other people, a product of civilization and discipline. England is the country in which social discipline has most succeeded, not so much in conquering, as in suppressing, whatever is liable to conflict with it. The English, more than any other people, not only act but feel according to rule. In other countries, the taught opinion, or the requirement of society, may be the stronger power, but the promptings of the individual nature are always visible under it, and often resisting it: rule may be stronger than nature, but nature is still there. In England, rule has to a great degree substituted itself for nature. The greater part of life is carried on, not by following inclination under the control of rule, but by having no inclination but that of following a rule. Now this has its good side doubtless, though it has also a wretchedly bad one; but it must render an Englishman peculiarly ill-qualified to pass a judgment on the original tendencies of human nature from his own experience. The errors to which observers elsewhere are liable on the subject, are of a different character. An Englishman is ignorant respecting human nature, a Frenchman is prejudiced. An Englishman's errors are negative, a Frenchman's positive. An Englishman fancies that things do not exist, because he never sees them; a Frenchman thinks they must always and necessarily exist, because he does see them. An Englishman does not know nature, because he has had no opportunity of observing it; a Frenchman generally knows a great deal of it, but often mistakes it, because he has only seen it sophisticated and distorted. For the artificial state superinduced by society disguises the natural tendencies of the thing which is the subject of observation, in two different ways: by extinguishing the nature, or by transforming it. In the one case there is but a starved residuum of nature remaining to be studied; in the other case there is much, but it may have expanded in any direction rather than that in which it would spontaneously grow.

I have said that it cannot now be known how much of the existing mental differences between men and women is natural, and how much artificial; whether there are any natural differences at all; or, supposing all artificial causes of difference to be withdrawn, what natural character would be revealed. I am not about to attempt what I have pronounced impossible: but doubt does not forbid conjecture, and where certainty is unattainable, there may yet be the means of arriving at some degree of probability. The first point, the origin of the differences actually observed, is the one most accessible to speculation; and I shall attempt to approach it, by the only path by which it can be reached; by tracing the mental consequences of external influences. We cannot isolate a human being from the circumstances of his condition, so as to ascertain experimentally what he would have been by nature; but we can consider what he is, and what his circumstances have been, and whether the one would have been capable of producing the other.

Let us take, then, the only marked case which observation affords, of apparent inferiority of women to men, if we except the merely physical one of bodily strength. No production in philosophy, science, or art, entitled to the first rank, has been the work of a woman. Is there any mode of accounting for this, without supposing that women are naturally incapable of producing them?

In the first place, we may fairly question whether experience has afforded sufficient grounds for an induction. It is scarcely three generations since women, saving very rare exceptions, have begun to try their capacity in philosophy, science, or art. It is only in the present generation that their attempts have been at all numerous; and they are even now extremely few, everywhere but in England and France. It is a relevant question, whether a mind possessing the requisites of first-rate eminence in speculation or creative art could have been expected, on the mere calculation of chances, to turn up during that lapse of time, among the women whose tastes and personal position admitted of their devoting themselves to these pursuits. In all things which there has yet been time for—in all but the very highest grades in the scale of excellence, especially in the department in which they have been longest engaged, literature (both prose and poetry)—women have done quite as much, have obtained fully as high prizes and as many of them, as could be expected from the length of time and the number of competitors. If we go back to the earlier period when very few women made the attempt, yet some of those few made it with distinguished success. The Greeks always accounted Sappho among their great poets; and we may well suppose that Myrtis, said to have been the teacher of Pindar, and Corinna, who five times bore away from him the prize of poetry, must at least have had sufficient merit to admit of being compared with that great name. Aspasia did not leave any philosophical writings; but it is an admitted fact that Socrates resorted to her for instruction, and avowed himself to have obtained it.

If we consider the works of women in modern times, and contrast them with those of men, either in the literary or the artistic department, such inferiority as may be observed resolves itself essentially into one thing: but that is a most material one; deficiency of originality. Not total deficiency; for every production of mind which is of any substantive value, has an originality of its own—is a conception of the mind itself, not a copy of something else. Thoughts original, in the sense of being unborrowed—of being derived from the thinker's own observations or intellectual processes—are abundant in the writings of women. But they have not yet produced any of those great and luminous new ideas which form an era in thought, nor those fundamentally new conceptions in art, which open a vista of possible effects not before thought of, and found a new school. Their compositions are mostly grounded on the existing fund of thought, and their creations do not deviate widely from existing types. This is the sort of inferiority which their works manifest: for in point of execution, in the detailed application of thought, and the perfection of style, there is no inferiority. Our best novelists in point of composition, and of the management of detail, have mostly been women;

and there is not in all modern literature a more eloquent vehicle of thought than the style of Madame de Staël, nor, as a specimen of purely artistic excellence, anything superior to the prose of Madame Sand, whose style acts upon the nervous system like a symphony of Haydn or Mozart. High originality of conception is, as I have said, what is chiefly wanting. And now to examine if there is any manner in which this deficiency can be accounted for.

Let us remember, then, so far as regards mere thought, that during all that period in the world's existence, and in the progress of cultivation, in which great and fruitful new truths could be arrived at by mere force of genius, with little previous study and accumulation of knowledge—during all that time women did not concern themselves with speculation at all. From the days of Hypatia to those of the Reformation, the illustrious Heloisa is almost the only woman to whom any such achievement might have been possible; and we know not how great a capacity of speculation in her may have been lost to mankind by the misfortunes of her life. Never since any considerable number of women have began to cultivate serious thought, has originality been possible on easy terms. Nearly all the thoughts which can be reached by mere strength of original faculties, have long since been arrived at; and originality, in any high sense of the word, is now scarcely ever attained but by minds which have undergone elaborate discipline, and are deeply versed in the results of previous thinking. It is Mr. Maurice, I think, who has remarked on the present age, that its most original thinkers are those who have known most thoroughly what had been thought by their predecessors:[*] and this will always henceforth be the case. Every fresh stone in the edifice has now to be placed on the top of so many others, that a long process of climbing, and of carrying up materials, has to be gone through by whoever aspires to take a share in the present stage of the work. How many women are there who have gone through any such process? Mrs. Somerville, alone perhaps of women, knows as much of mathematics as is now needful for making any considerable mathematical discovery: is it any proof of inferiority in women, that she has not happened to be one of the two or three persons who in her lifetime have associated their names with some striking advancement of the science? Two women, since political economy has been made a science, have known enough of it to write usefully on the subject:[†] of how many of the innumerable men who have written on it during the same time, is it possible with truth to say more? If no woman has hitherto been a great historian, what woman has had the necessary erudition? If no woman is a great philologist, what woman has studied Sanscrit and Slavonic, the Gothic of Ulphila and the Persic of the Zendavesta? Even in practical matters we all know

[*See Frederick Denison Maurice, Review of James Montgomery's *Pelican Island*, *Westminster Review*, VIII (Oct., 1827), 309-15.]

[†Probably Mill intends Jane Marcet, *Conversations on Political Economy* (London: Longman, *et al.*, 1816); and Harriet Martineau, *Illustrations of Political Economy*, 9 vols. (London: Fox, 1832-34).]

what is the value of the originality of untaught geniuses. It means, inventing over again in its rudimentary form something already invented and improved upon by many successive inventors. When women have had the preparation which all men now require to be eminently original, it will be time enough to begin judging by experience of their capacity for originality.

It no doubt often happens that a person, who has not widely and accurately studied the thoughts of others on a subject, has by natural sagacity a happy intuition, which he can suggest, but cannot prove, which yet when matured may be an important addition to knowledge: but even then, no justice can be done to it until some other person, who does possess the previous acquirements, takes it in hand, tests it, gives it a scientific or practical form, and fits it into its place among the existing truths of philosophy or science. Is it supposed that such felicitous thoughts do not occur to women? They occur by hundreds to every woman of intellect. But they are mostly lost, for want of a husband or friend who has the other knowledge which can enable him to estimate them properly and bring them before the world: and even when they are brought before it, they generally appear as his ideas, not their real author's. Who can tell how many of the most original thoughts put forth by male writers, belong to a woman by suggestion, to themselves only by verifying and working out? If I may judge by my own case, a very large proportion indeed.

If we turn from pure speculation to literature in the narrow sense of the term, and the fine arts, there is a very obvious reason why women's literature is, in its general conception and in its main features, an imitation of men's. Why is the Roman literature, as critics proclaim to satiety, not original, but an imitation of the Greek? Simply because the Greeks came first. If women lived in a different country from men, and had never read any of their writings, they would have had a literature of their own. As it is, they have not created one, because they found a highly advanced literature already created. If there had been no suspension of the knowledge of antiquity, or if the Renaissance had occurred before the Gothic cathedrals were built, they never would have been built. We see that, in France and Italy, imitation of the ancient literature stopped the original development even after it had commenced. All women who write are pupils of the great male writers. A painter's early pictures, even if he be a Raffaelle, are undistinguishable in style from those of his master. Even a Mozart does not display his powerful originality in his earliest pieces. What years are to a gifted individual, generations are to a mass. If women's literature is destined to have a different collective character from that of men, depending on any difference of natural tendencies, much longer time is necessary than has yet elapsed, before it can emancipate itself from the influence of accepted models, and guide itself by its own impulses. But if, as I believe, there will not prove to be any natural tendencies common to women, and distinguishing their genius from that of men, yet every individual writer among them has her individual tendencies, which at present are still subdued by the influence of precedent and example: and it will require generations more, before their individuality is sufficiently developed to make head against that influence.

It is in the fine arts, properly so called, that the *primâ facie* evidence of inferior original powers in women at first sight appears the strongest: since opinion (it may be said) does not exclude them from these, but rather encourages them, and their education, instead of passing over this department, is in the affluent classes mainly composed of it. Yet in this line of exertion they have fallen still more short than in many others, of the highest eminence attained by men. This shortcoming, however, needs no other explanation than the familiar fact, more universally true in the fine arts than in anything else; the vast superiority of professional persons over amateurs. Women in the educated classes are almost universally taught more or less of some branch or other of the fine arts, but not that they may gain their living or their social consequence by it. Women artists are all amateurs. The exceptions are only of the kind which confirm the general truth. Women are taught music, but not for the purpose of composing, only of executing it: and accordingly it is only as composers, that men, in music, are superior to women. The only one of the fine arts which women do follow, to any extent, as a profession, and an occupation for life, is the histrionic; and in that they are confessedly equal, if not superior, to men. To make the comparison fair, it should be made between the productions of women in any branch of art, and those of men not following it as a profession. In musical composition, for example, women surely have produced fully as good things as have ever been produced by male amateurs. There are now a few women, a very few, who practise painting as a profession, and these are already begining to show quite as much talent as could be expected. Even male painters (*pace* Mr. Ruskin) have not made any very remarkable figure these last centuries, and it will be long before they do so. The reason why the old painters were so greatly superior to the modern, is that a greatly superior class of men applied themselves to the art. In the fourteenth and fifteenth centuries the Italian painters were the most accomplished men of their age. The greatest of them were men of encyclopaedical acquirements and powers, like the great men of Greece. But in their times fine art was, to men's feelings and conceptions, among the grandest things in which a human being could excel; and by it men were made, what only political or military distinction now makes them, the companions of sovereigns, and the equals of the highest nobility. In the present age, men of anything like similar calibre find something more important to do, for their own fame and the uses of the modern world, than painting: and it is only now and then that a Reynolds or a Turner (of whose relative rank among eminent men I do not pretend to an opinion) applies himself to that art. Music belongs to a different order of things; it does not require the same general powers of mind, but seems more dependant on a natural gift: and it may be thought surprising that no one of the great musical composers has been a woman. But even this natural gift, to be made available for great creations, requires study, and professional devotion to the pursuit. The only countries which have produced first-rate composers, even of the male sex, are Germany and Italy—countries in which, both in point of special and of general cultivation, women have remained far behind France and England, being generally (it may be said without exaggeration) very little educated, and having scarcely cultivated at all any of the higher faculties of mind. And in those countries the men who are acquainted with the principles of musical composition must be counted by hundreds, or more probably by thousands, the women barely by scores: so that here again, on the doctrine of averages, we cannot reasonably expect to see more than one eminent woman to fifty eminent men; and the last three centuries have not produced fifty eminent male composers either in Germany or in Italy.

There are other reasons, besides those which we have now given, that help to explain why women remain behind men, even in the pursuits which are open to both. For one thing, very few women have time for them. This may seem a paradox; it is an undoubted social fact. The time and thoughts of every woman have to satisfy great previous demands on them for things practical. There is, first, the superintendence of the family and the domestic expenditure, which occupies at least one woman in every family, generally the one of mature years and acquired experience; unless the family is so rich as to admit of delegating that task to hired agency, and submitting to all the waste and malversation inseparable from that mode of conducting it. The superintendence of a household, even when not in other respects laborious, is extremely onerous to the thoughts; it requires incessant vigilance, an eye which no detail escapes, and presents questions for consideration and solution, foreseen and unforeseen, at every hour of the day, from which the person responsible for them can hardly ever shake herself free. If a woman is of a rank and circumstances which relieve her in a measure from these cares, she has still devolving on her the management for the whole family of its intercourse with others—of what is called society, and the less the call made on her by the former duty, the greater is always the development of the latter: the dinner parties, concerts, evening parties, morning visits, letter writing, and all that goes with them. All this is over and above the engrossing duty which society imposes exclusively on women, of making themselves charming. A clever woman of the higher ranks finds nearly a sufficient employment of her talents in cultivating the graces of manner and the arts of conversation. To look only at the outward side of the subject: the great and continual exercise of thought which all women who attach any value to dressing well (I do not mean expensively, but with taste, and perception of natural and of artificial *convenance*) must bestow upon their own dress, perhaps also upon that of their daughters, would alone go a great way towards achieving respectable results in art, or science, or literature, and does actually exhaust much of the time and mental power they might have to spare for either.* If it were possible that all this number of little practical interests (which are made great to them) should leave them either much leisure, or much energy and freedom of mind, to be devoted to art or speculation, they must have a much greater original supply of active faculty than the vast majority of men. But this is not all. Independently of the regular offices of life which devolve upon a woman, she is expected to have her time and faculties always at the disposal of everybody. If a man has not a profession to exempt him from such demands, still, if he has a pursuit, he offends nobody by devoting his time to it; occupation is received as a valid excuse for his not answering to every casual demand which may be made on him. Are a woman's occupations, especially her chosen and voluntary ones, ever regarded as excusing her from any of what are termed the calls of society? Scarcely are her most necessary and recognised duties allowed as an exemption. It requires an illness in the family, or something else out of the common way, to entitle her to give her own business the precedence over other people's amusement. She must always be at the beck and call of somebody, generally of everybody. If she has a study or a pursuit, she must snatch any short interval which accidentally occurs to be employed in it. A celebrated woman, in a work which I hope will some day be published, remarks truly that everything a woman does is done at odd times.[*] Is it wonderful, then, if she does not attain the highest eminence in things which require consecutive attention, and the concentration on them of the chief interest of life? Such is philosophy, and such, above all, is art, in which, besides the devotion of the thoughts and feelings, the hand also must be kept in constant exercise to attain high skill.

There is another consideration to be added to all these. In the various arts and intellectual occupations, there is a degree of proficiency sufficient for living by it, and there is a higher degree on which depend the great productions which immortalize a name. To the attainment of the former, there are adequate motives in the case of all who follow the pursuit professionally: the other is hardly ever

*"It appears to be the same right turn of mind which enables a man to acquire the *truth*, or the just idea of what is right, in the ornaments, as in the more stable principles of art. It has still the same centre of perfection, though it is the centre of a smaller circle.—To illustrate this by the fashion of dress, in which there is allowed to be a good or bad taste. The component parts of dress are continually changing from great to little, from short to long; but the general form still remains: it is still the same general dress which is comparatively fixed, though on a very slender foundation; but it is on this which fashion must rest. He who invents with the most success, or dresses in the best taste, would probably, from the same sagacity employed to greater purposes, have discovered equal skill, or have formed the same correct taste, in the highest labours of art." (Sir Joshua Reynolds' *Discourses* [1776], Discourse VII [in *Works*, ed. Edmond Malone, 4th ed., 3 vols. (London: Cadell and Davies, 1809), Vol. I, pp. 230-1].)

[*Florence Nightingale, *Suggestions for Thought to the Searchers after Truth among the Artizans of England*, 3 vols. (London: printed Eyre and Spottiswoode [not published], 1860), Vol. II, p. 392.]

attained where there is not, or where there has not been at some period of life, an ardent desire of celebrity. Nothing less is commonly a sufficient stimulus to undergo the long and patient drudgery, which, in the case even of the greatest natural gifts, is absolutely required for great eminence in pursuits in which we already possess so many splendid memorials of the highest genius. Now, whether the cause be natural or artificial, women seldom have this eagerness for fame. Their ambition is generally confined within narrower bounds. The influence they seek is over those who immediately surround them. Their desire is to be liked, loved, or admired, by those whom they see with their eyes: and the proficiency in knowledge, arts, and accomplishments, which is sufficient for that, almost always contents them. This is a trait of character which cannot be left out of the account in judging of women as they are. I do not at all believe that it is inherent in women. It is only the natural result of their circumstances. The love of fame in men is encouraged by education and opinion: to "scorn delights and live laborious days" for its sake, is accounted the part of "noble minds," even if spoken of as their "last infirmity,"[*] and is stimulated by the access which fame gives to all objects of ambition, including even the favour of women; while to women themselves all these objects are closed, and the desire of fame itself considered daring and unfeminine. Besides, how could it be that a woman's interests should not be all concentrated upon the impressions made on those who come into her daily life, when society has ordained that all her duties should be to them, and has contrived that all her comforts should depend on them? The natural desire of consideration from our fellow creatures is as strong in a woman as in a man; but society has so ordered things that public consideration is, in all ordinary cases, only attainable by her through the consideration of her husband or of her male relations, while her private consideration is forfeited by making herself individually prominent, or appearing in any other character than that of an appendage to men. Whoever is in the least capable of estimating the influence on the mind of the entire domestic and social position and the whole habit of a life, must easily recognise in that influence a complete explanation of nearly all the apparent differences between women and men, including the whole of those which imply any inferiority.

As for moral differences, considered as distinguished from intellectual, the distinction commonly drawn is to the advantage of women. They are declared to be better than men; an empty compliment, which must provoke a bitter smile from every woman of spirit, since there is no other situation in life in which it is the established order, and considered quite natural and suitable, that the better should obey the worse. If this piece of idle talk is good for anything, it is only as an admission by men, of the corrupting influence of power; for that is certainly the only truth which the fact, if it be a fact, either proves or illustrates. And it *is* true

[*John Milton, *Lycidas* (1638), in *Poems upon Several Occasions*, included in *The Poetical Works* (London: Tonson, 1695), p. 2 (ll. 70-2).]

that servitude, except when it actually brutalizes, though corrupting to both, is less so to the slaves than to the slave-masters. It is wholesomer for the moral nature to be restrained, even by arbitrary power, than to be allowed to exercise arbitrary power without restraint. Women, it is said, seldomer fall under the penal law—contribute a much smaller number of offenders to the criminal calendar, than men. I doubt not that the same thing may be said, with the same truth, of negro slaves. Those who are under the control of others cannot often commit crimes, unless at the command and for the purposes of their masters. I do not know a more signal instance of the blindness with which the world, including the herd of studious men, ignore and pass over all the influences of social circumstances, than their silly depreciation of the intellectual, and silly panegyrics on the moral, nature of women.

The complimentary dictum about women's superior moral goodness may be allowed to pair off with the disparaging one respecting their greater liability to moral bias. Women, we are told, are not capable of resisting their personal partialities: their judgment in grave affairs is warped by their sympathies and antipathies. Assuming it to be so, it is still to be proved that women are oftener misled by their personal feelings than men by their personal interests. The chief difference would seem in that case to be, that men are led from the course of duty and the public interest by their regard for themselves, women (not being allowed to have private interests of their own) by their regard for somebody else. It is also to be considered, that all the education which women receive from society inculcates on them the feeling that the individuals connected with them are the only ones to whom they owe any duty—the only ones whose interest they are called upon to care for; while, as far as education is concerned, they are left strangers even to the elementary ideas which are presupposed in any intelligent regard for larger interests or higher moral objects. The complaint against them resolves itself merely into this, that they fulfil only too faithfully the sole duty which they are taught, and almost the only one which they are permitted to practise.

The concessions of the privileged to the unprivileged are so seldom brought about by any better motive than the power of the unprivileged to extort them, that any arguments against the prerogative of sex are likely to be little attended to by the generality, as long as they are able to say to themselves that women do not complain of it. That fact certainly enables men to retain the unjust privilege some time longer; but does not render it less unjust. Exactly the same thing may be said of the women in the harem of an Oriental: they do not complain of not being allowed the freedom of European women. They think our women insufferably bold and unfeminine. How rarely it is that even men complain of the general order of society; and how much rarer still would such complaint be, if they did not know of any different order existing anywhere else. Women do not complain of the general lot of women; or rather they do, for plaintive elegies on it are very common in the writings of women, and were still more so as long as the lamentations could not be suspected of having any practical object. Their complaints are like the complaints which men make of the general unsatisfactoriness of human life; they are not meant to imply blame, or to plead for any change. But though women do not complain of the power of husbands, each complains of her own husband, or of the husbands of her friends. It is the same in all other cases of servitude, at least in the commencement of the emancipatory movement. The serfs did not at first complain of the power of their lords, but only of their tyranny. The Commons began by claiming a few municipal privileges; they next asked an exemption for themselves from being taxed without their own consent; but they would at that time have thought it a great presumption to claim any share in the king's sovereign authority. The case of women is now the only case in which to rebel against established rules is still looked upon with the same eyes as was formerly a subject's claim to the right of rebelling against his king. A woman who joins in any movement which her husband disapproves, makes herself a martyr, without even being able to be an apostle, for the husband can legally put a stop to her apostleship. Women cannot be expected to devote themselves to the emancipation of women, until men in considerable number are prepared to join with them in the undertaking.

Chapter IV

THERE REMAINS A QUESTION, not of less importance than those already discussed, and which will be asked the most importunately by those opponents whose conviction is somewhat shaken on the main point. What good are we to expect from the changes proposed in our customs and institutions? Would mankind be at all better off if women were free? If not, why disturb their minds, and attempt to make a social revolution in the name of an abstract right?

It is hardly to be expected that this question will be asked in respect to the change proposed in the condition of women in marriage. The sufferings, immoralities, evils of all sorts, produced in innumerable cases by the subjection of individual women to individual men, are far too terrible to be overlooked. Unthinking or uncandid persons, counting those cases alone which are extreme, or which attain publicity, may say that the evils are exceptional; but no one can be blind to their existence, nor, in many cases, to their intensity. And it is perfectly obvious that the abuse of the power cannot be very much checked while the power remains. It is a power given, or offered, not to good men, or to decently respectable men, but to all men; the most brutal, and the most criminal. There is no check but that of opinion, and such men are in general within the reach of no opinion but that of men like themselves. If such men did not brutally tyrannize over the one human being whom the law compels to bear everything from them, society must already have reached a paradisiacal state. There could be no need any longer of laws to curb men's vicious propensities. Astraea must not only have returned to earth, but the heart of the worst man must have become her temple. The law of servitude in marriage is a monstrous contradiction to all the principles of the modern world, and to all the experience through which those principles have been slowly and painfully worked out. It is the sole case, now that negro slavery has been abolished, in which a human being in the plenitude of every faculty is delivered up to the tender mercies of another human being, in the hope forsooth that this other will use the power solely for the good of the person subjected to it. Marriage is the only actual bondage known to our law. There remain no legal slaves, except the mistress of every house.

It is not, therefore, on this part of the subject, that the question is likely to be asked, *Cui bono?* We may be told that the evil would outweigh the good, but the reality of the good admits of no dispute. In regard, however, to the larger question, the removal of women's disabilities—their recognition as the equals of men in all that belongs to citizenship—the opening to them of all honourable employments, and of the training and education which qualifies for those employments—there are many persons for whom it is not enough that the inequality has no just or legitimate defence; they require to be told what express advantage would be obtained by abolishing it.

To which let me first answer, the advantage of having the most universal and pervading of all human relations regulated by justice instead of injustice. The vast amount of this gain to human nature, it is hardly possible, by any explanation or illustration, to place in a stronger light than it is placed by the bare statement, to any one who attaches a moral meaning to words. All the selfish propensities, the self-worship, the unjust self-preference, which exist among mankind, have their source and root in, and derive their principal nourishment from, the present constitution of the relation between men and women. Think what it is to a boy, to grow up to manhood in the belief that without any merit or any exertion of his own, though he may be the most frivolous and empty or the most ignorant and stolid of mankind, by the mere fact of being born a male he is by right the superior of all and every one of an entire half of the human race: including probably some whose real superiority to himself he has daily or hourly occasion to feel; but even if in his whole conduct he habitually follows a woman's guidance, still, if he is a fool, he thinks that of course she is not, and cannot be, equal in ability and judgment to himself; and if he is not a fool, he does worse—he sees that she is superior to him, and believes that, notwithstanding her superiority, he is entitled to command and she is bound to obey. What must be the effect on his character, of this lesson? And men of the cultivated classes are often not aware how deeply it sinks into the immense majority of male minds. For, among right-feeling and well-bred people, the inequality is kept as much as possible out of sight; above all, out of sight of the children. As much obedience is required from boys to their mother as to their father: they are not permitted to domineer over their sisters, nor are they accustomed to see these postponed to them, but the contrary; the compensations of the chivalrous feeling being made prominent, while the servitude which requires them is kept in the background. Well brought-up youths in the higher classes thus often escape the bad influences of the situation in their early years, and only experience them when, arrived at manhood, they fall under the dominion of facts as they really exist. Such people are little aware, when a boy is differently brought up, how early the notion of his inherent superiority to a girl arises in his mind; how it grows with his growth and strengthens with his strength; how it is inoculated by one schoolboy upon another; how early the youth thinks himself superior to his mother, owing her perhaps forbearance, but no real respect; and how sublime and sultan-like a sense of superiority he feels, above all, over the woman whom he honours by admitting her to a partnership of his life. Is it imagined that all this does not pervert the whole manner of existence of the man, both as an individual and as a social being? It is an exact parallel to the feeling of a hereditary king that he is excellent above others by being born a king, or a noble by being born a noble. The relation between husband and wife is very like that between lord and vassal, except that the wife is held to more unlimited obedience than the vassal was. However the vassal's character may have been affected, for better and for worse, by his subordination, who can help seeing that the lord's was affected greatly for the worse? whether he was led to believe that his vassals were really superior to himself, or to feel that he was placed in command over people as good as himself, for no merits or labours of his own, but merely for having, as Figaro says, taken the trouble to be born.[*] The self-worship of the monarch, or of the feudal superior, is matched by the self-worship of the male. Human beings do not grow up from childhood in the possession of unearned distinctions, without pluming themselves upon them. Those whom privileges not acquired by their merit, and which they feel to be disproportioned to it, inspire with additional humility, are always the few, and the best few. The rest are only inspired with pride, and the worst sort of pride, that which values itself upon accidental advantages, not of its own achieving. Above all, when the feeling of being raised above the whole of the other sex is combined with personal authority over one individual among them; the situation, if a school of conscientious and affectionate forbearance to those whose strongest points of character are conscience and affection, is to men of another quality a regularly constituted Academy or Gymnasium for training them in arrogance and overbearingness; which vices, if curbed by the certainty of resistance in their intercourse with other men, their equals, break out towards all who are in a position to be obliged to tolerate them, and often revenge themselves upon the unfortunate wife for the involuntary restraint which they are obliged to submit to elsewhere.

The example afforded, and the education given to the sentiments, by laying the foundation of domestic existence upon a relation contradictory to the first principles of social justice, must, from the very nature of man, have a perverting influence of such magnitude, that it is hardly possible with our present experience to raise our imaginations to the conception of so great a change for the better as would be made by its removal. All that education and civilization are doing to efface the influences on character of the law of force, and replace them by those of justice, remains merely on the surface, as long as the citadel of the enemy is not attacked. The principle of the modern movement in morals and politics, is that conduct, and conduct alone, entitles to respect: that not what men are, but what they do, constitutes their claim to deference; that, above all, merit, and not birth, is the only rightful claim to power and authority. If no authority, not in its nature temporary, were allowed to one human being over another, society would not be

[*See Pierre Augustin Caron de Beaumarchais, *La folle journée, ou Le mariage de Figaro* (1785), in *Oeuvres complètes*, 7 vols. (Paris: Collin, 1809), Vol. II, p. 274 (V, iii, 13-15).]

employed in building up propensities with one hand which it has to curb with the other. The child would really, for the first time in man's existence on earth, be trained in the way he should go, and when he was old there would be a chance that he would not depart from it. But so long as the right of the strong to power over the weak rules in the very heart of society, the attempt to make the equal right of the weak the principle of its outward actions will always be an uphill struggle; for the law of justice, which is also that of Christianity, will never get possession of men's inmost sentiments; they will be working against it, even when bending to it.

The second benefit to be expected from giving to women the free use of their faculties, by leaving them the free choice of their employments, and opening to them the same field of occupation and the same prizes and encouragements as to other human beings, would be that of doubling the mass of mental faculties available for the higher service of humanity. Where there is now one person qualified to benefit mankind and promote the general improvement, as a public teacher, or an administrator of some branch of public or social affairs, there would then be a chance of two. Mental superiority of any kind is at present everywhere so much below the demand; there is such a deficiency of persons competent to do excellently anything which it requires any considerable amount of ability to do; that the loss to the world, by refusing to make use of one-half of the whole quantity of talent it possesses, is extremely serious. It is true that this amount of mental power is not totally lost. Much of it is employed, and would in any case be employed, in domestic management, and in the few other occupations open to women; and from the remainder indirect benefit is in many individual cases obtained, through the personal influence of individual women over individual men. But these benefits are partial; their range is extremely circumscribed; and if they must be admitted, on the one hand, as a deduction from the amount of fresh social power that would be acquired by giving freedom to one-half of the whole sum of human intellect, there must be added, on the other, the benefit of the stimulus that would be given to the intellect of men by the competition; or (to use a more true expression) by the necessity that would be imposed on them of deserving precedency before they could expect to obtain it.

This great accession to the intellectual power of the species, and to the amount of intellect available for the good management of its affairs, would be obtained, partly, through the better and more complete intellectual education of women, which would then improve *pari passu* with that of men. Women in general would be brought up equally capable of understanding business, public affairs, and the higher matters of speculation, with men in the same class of society; and the select few of the one as well as of the other sex, who were qualified not only to comprehend what is done or thought by others, but to think or do something considerable themselves, would meet with the same facilities for improving and training their capacities in the one sex as in the other. In this way, the widening of the sphere of action for women would operate for good, by raising their education to the level of that of men, and making the one participate in all improvements made in the other. But independently of this, the mere breaking down of the barrier would of itself have an educational virtue of the highest worth. The mere getting rid of the idea that all the wider subjects of thought and action, all the things which are of general and not solely of private interest, are men's business, from which women are to be warned off—positively interdicted from most of it, coldly tolerated in the little which is allowed them—the mere consciousness a woman would then have of being a human being like any other, entitled to choose her pursuits, urged or invited by the same inducements as any one else to interest herself in whatever is interesting to human beings, entitled to exert the share of influence on all human concerns which belongs to an individual opinion, whether she attempted actual participation in them or not—this alone would effect an immense expansion of the faculties of women, as well as enlargement of the range of their moral sentiments.

Besides the addition to the amount of individual talent available for the conduct of human affairs, which certainly are not at present so abundantly provided in that respect that they can afford to dispense with one-half of what nature proffers; the opinion of women would then possess a more beneficial, rather than a greater, influence upon the general mass of human belief and sentiment. I say a more beneficial, rather than a greater influence; for the influence of women over the general tone of opinion has always, or at least from the earliest known period, been very considerable. The influence of mothers on the early character of their sons, and the desire of young men to recommend themselves to young women, have in all recorded times been important agencies in the formation of character, and have determined some of the chief steps in the progress of civilization. Even in the Homeric age, αἰδώς towards the Τρωάδας ἑλκεσιπέπλους is an acknow-ledged and powerful motive of action in the great Hector.[*] The moral influence of women has had two modes of operation. First, it has been a softening influence. Those who were most liable to be the victims of violence, have naturally tended as much as they could towards limiting its sphere and mitigating its excesses. Those who were not taught to fight, have naturally inclined in favour of any other mode of settling differences rather than that of fighting. In general, those who have been the greatest sufferers by the indulgence of selfish passion, have been the most earnest supporters of any moral law which offered a means of bridling passion. Women were powerfully instrumental in inducing the northern conquerors to adopt the creed of Christianity, a creed so much more favourable to women than any that preceded it. The conversion of the Anglo-Saxons and of the Franks may be said to have been begun by the wives of Ethelbert and Clovis.[†] The other mode in which

[*Homer, The Iliad (Greek and English), trans. A.T. Murray, 2 vols. (London: Heinemann; Cambridge, Mass.: Harvard University Press, 1946), Vol. I, p. 294 (VI, 441-2).]

[†Bertha of Kent and Clotilda of the Franks.]

the effect of women's opinion has been conspicuous, is by giving a powerful stimulus to those qualities in men, which, not being themselves trained in, it was necessary for them that they should find in their protectors. Courage, and the military virtues generally, have at all times been greatly indebted to the desire which men felt of being admired by women: and the stimulus reaches far beyond this one class of eminent qualities, since, by a very natural effect of their position, the best passport to the admiration and favour of women has always been to be thought highly of by men. From the combination of the two kinds of moral influence thus exercised by women, arose the spirit of chivalry: the peculiarity of which is, to aim at combining the highest standard of the warlike qualities with the cultivation of a totally different class of virtues—those of gentleness, generosity, and self-abnegation, towards the non-military and defenceless classes generally, and a special submission and worship directed towards women; who were distinguished from the other defenceless classes by the high rewards which they had it in their power voluntarily to bestow on those who endeavoured to earn their favour, instead of extorting their subjection. Though the practice of chivalry fell even more sadly short of its theoretic standard than practice generally falls below theory, it remains one of the most precious monuments of the moral history of our race; as a remarkable instance of a concerted and organized attempt by a most disorganized and distracted society, to raise up and carry into practice a moral ideal greatly in advance of its social conditions and institutions; so much so as to have been completely frustrated in the main object, yet never entirely inefficacious, and which has left a most sensible, and for the most part a highly valuable impress on the ideas and feelings of all subsequent times.

The chivalrous ideal is the acme of the influence of women's sentiments on the moral cultivation of mankind: and if women are to remain in their subordinate situation, it were greatly to be lamented that the chivalrous standard should have passed away, for it is the only one at all capable of mitigating the demoralizing influences of that position. But the changes in the general state of the species rendered inevitable the substitution of a totally different ideal of morality for the chivalrous one. Chivalry was the attempt to infuse moral elements into a state of society in which everything depended for good or evil on individual prowess, under the softening influences of individual delicacy and generosity. In modern societies, all things, even in the military department of affairs, are decided, not by individual effort, but by the combined operations of numbers; while the main occupation of society has changed from fighting to business, from military to industrial life. The exigencies of the new life are no more exclusive of the virtues of generosity than those of the old, but it no longer entirely depends on them. The main foundations of the moral life of modern times must be justice and prudence; the respect of each for the rights of every other, and the ability of each to take care of himself. Chivalry left without legal check all forms of wrong which reigned unpunished throughout society; it only encouraged a few to do right in preference to wrong, by the direction it gave to the instruments of praise and admiration. But the real dependence of morality must always be upon its penal sanctions—its power to deter from evil. The security of society cannot rest on merely rendering honour to right, a motive so comparatively weak in all but a few, and which on very many does not operate at all. Modern society is able to repress wrong through all departments of life, by a fit exertion of the superior strength which civilization has given it, and thus to render the existence of the weaker members of society (no longer defenceless but protected by law) tolerable to them, without reliance on the chivalrous feelings of those who are in a position to tyrannize. The beauties and graces of the chivalrous character are still what they were, but the rights of the weak, and the general comfort of human life, now rest on a far surer and steadier support; or rather, they do so in every relation of life except the conjugal.

At present the moral influence of women is no less real, but it is no longer of so marked and definite a character: it has more nearly merged in the general influence of public opinion. Both through the contagion of sympathy, and through the desire of men to shine in the eyes of women, their feelings have great effect in keeping alive what remains of the chivalrous ideal—in fostering the sentiments and continuing the traditions of spirit and generosity. In these points of character, their standard is higher than that of men; in the quality of justice, somewhat lower. As regards the relations of private life it may be said generally, that their influence is, on the whole, encouraging to the softer virtues, discouraging to the sterner: though the statement must be taken with all the modifications dependent on individual character. In the chief of the greater trials to which virtue is subject in the concerns of life—the conflict between interest and principle—the tendency of women's influence is of a very mixed character. When the principle involved happens to be one of the very few which the course of their religious or moral education has strongly impressed upon themselves, they are potent auxiliaries to virtue: and their husbands and sons are often prompted by them to acts of abnegation which they never would have been capable of without that stimulus. But, with the present education and position of women, the moral principles which have been impressed on them cover but a comparatively small part of the field of virtue, and are, moreover, principally negative; forbidding particular acts, but having little to do with the general direction of the thoughts and purposes. I am afraid it must be said, that disinterestedness in the general conduct of life—the devotion of the energies to purposes which hold out no promise of private advantages to the family—is very seldom encouraged or supported by women's influence. It is small blame to them that they discourage objects of which they have not learnt to see the advantage, and which withdraw their men from them, and from the interests of the family. But the consequence is that women's influence is often anything but favourable to public virtue.

Women have, however, some share of influence in giving the tone to public moralities since their sphere of action has been a little widened, and since a considerable number of them have occupied themselves practically in the promotion of objects reaching beyond their own family and household. The influence of women counts for a great deal in two of the most marked features of modern European life—its aversion to war, and its addiction to philanthropy. Excellent characteristics both; but unhappily, if the influence of women is valuable in the encouragement it gives to these feelings in general, in the particular applications the direction it gives to them is at least as often mischievous as useful. In the philanthropic department more particularly, the two provinces chiefly cultivated by women are religious proselytism and charity. Religious proselytism at home, is but another word for embittering of religious animosities: abroad, it is usually a blind running at an object, without either knowing or heeding the fatal mischiefs—fatal to the religious object itself as well as to all other desirable objects—which may be produced by the means employed. As for charity, it is a matter in which the immediate effect on the persons directly concerned, and the ultimate consequence to the general good, are apt to be at complete war with one another: while the education given to women—an education of the sentiments rather than of the understanding—and the habit inculcated by their whole life, of looking to immediate effects on persons, and not to remote effects on classes of persons—make them both unable to see, and unwilling to admit, the ultimate evil tendency of any form of charity or philanthropy which commends itself to their sympathetic feelings. The great and continually increasing mass of unenlightened and shortsighted benevolence, which, taking the care of people's lives out of their own hands, and relieving them from the disagreeable consequences of their own acts, saps the very foundations of the self-respect, self-help, and self-control which are the essential conditions both of individual prosperity and of social virtue—this waste of resources and of benevolent feelings in doing harm instead of good, is immensely swelled by women's contributions, and stimulated by their influence. Not that this is a mistake likely to be made by women, where they have actually the practical management of schemes of beneficence. It sometimes happens that women who administer public charities—with that insight into present fact, and especially into the minds and feelings of those with whom they are in immediate contact, in which women generally excel men—recognise in the clearest manner the demoralizing influence of the alms given or the help afforded, and could give lessons on the subject to many a male political economist. But women who only give their money, and are not brought face to face with the effects it produces, how can they be expected to foresee them? A woman born to the present lot of women, and content with it, how should she appreciate the value of self-dependence? She is not self-dependent; she is not taught self-dependence; her destiny is to receive everything from others, and why should what is good enough for her be bad for the poor? Her familiar notions of good are of blessings descending from a superior. She forgets that she is not free, and that the poor are; that if what they need is given to them unearned, they cannot be compelled to earn it: that everybody cannot be taken care of by everybody, but there must be some motive to induce people to take care of themselves; and that to be helped to help themselves, if they are physically capable of it, is the only charity which proves to be charity in the end.

These considerations shew how usefully the part which women take in the formation of general opinion, would be modified for the better by that more enlarged instruction, and practical conversancy with the things which their opinions influence, that would necessarily arise from their social and political emancipation. But the improvement it would work through the influence they exercise, each in her own family, would be still more remarkable.

It is often said that in the classes most exposed to temptation, a man's wife and children tend to keep him honest and respectable, both by the wife's direct influence, and by the concern he feels for their future welfare. This may be so, and no doubt often is so, with those who are more weak than wicked; and this beneficial influence would be preserved and strengthened under equal laws; it does not depend on the woman's servitude, but is, on the contrary, diminished by the disrespect which the inferior class of men always at heart feel towards those who are subject to their power. But when we ascend higher in the scale, we come among a totally different set of moving forces. The wife's influence tends, as far as it goes, to prevent the husband from falling below the common standard of approbation of the country. It tends quite as strongly to hinder him from rising above it. The wife is the auxiliary of the common public opinion. A man who is married to a woman his inferior in intelligence, finds her a perpetual dead weight, or, worse than a dead weight, a drag, upon every aspiration of his to be better than public opinion requires him to be. It is hardly possible for one who is in these bonds, to attain exalted virtue. If he differs in his opinion from the mass—if he sees truths which have not yet dawned upon them, or if, feeling in his heart truths which they nominally recognise, he would like to act up to those truths more conscientiously than the generality of mankind—to all such thoughts and desires, marriage is the heaviest of drawbacks, unless he be so fortunate as to have a wife as much above the common level as he himself is.

For, in the first place, there is always some sacrifice of personal interest required; either of social consequence, or of pecuniary means; perhaps the risk of even the means of subsistence. These sacrifices and risks he may be willing to encounter for himself; but he will pause before he imposes them on his family. And his family in this case means his wife and daughters; for he always hopes that his sons will feel as he feels himself, and that what he can do without, they will do without, willingly, in the same cause. But his daughters—their marriage may depend upon it: and his wife, who is unable to enter into or understand the objects for which these sacrifices are made—who, if she thought them worth any sacrifice, would think so on trust, and solely for his sake—who can participate in none of the enthusiasm or the self-approbation he himself may feel, while the things which he is disposed to sacrifice are all in all to her; will not the best and most unselfish man hesitate the longest before bringing on her this consequence? If it be not the comforts of life, but only social consideration, that is at stake, the burthen upon his conscience and feelings is still very severe. Whoever has a wife and children has given hostages to Mrs. Grundy.[*] The approbation of that potentate may be a matter of indifference to him, but it is of great importance to his wife. The man himself may be above opinion, or may find sufficient compensation in the opinion of those of his own way of thinking. But to the women connected with him, he can offer no compensation. The almost invariable tendency of the wife to place her influence in the same scale with social consideration, is sometimes made a reproach to women, and represented as a peculiar trait of feebleness and childishness of character in them: surely with great injustice. Society makes the whole life of a woman, in the easy classes, a continued self-sacrifice; it exacts from her an unremitting restraint of the whole of her natural inclinations, and the sole return it makes to her for what often deserves the name of a martyrdom, is consideration. Her consideration is inseparably connected with that of her husband, and after paying the full price for it, she finds that she is to lose it, for no reason of which she can feel the cogency. She has sacrificed her whole life to it, and her husband will not sacrifice to it a whim, a freak, an eccentricity; something not recognised or allowed for by the world, and which the world will agree with her in thinking a folly, if it thinks no worse! The dilemma is hardest upon that very meritorious class of men, who, without possessing talents which qualify them to make a figure among those with whom they agree in opinion, hold their opinion from conviction, and feel bound in honour and conscience to serve it, by making profession of their belief, and giving their time, labour, and means, to anything undertaken in its behalf. The worst case of all is when such men happen to be of a rank and position which of itself neither gives them, nor excludes them from, what is considered the best society; when their admission to it depends mainly on what is thought of them personally—and however unexceptionable their breeding and habits, their being identified with opinions and public conduct unacceptable to those who give the tone to society would operate as an effectual exclusion. Many a woman flatters herself (nine times out of ten quite erroneously) that nothing prevents her and her husband from moving in the highest society of her neighbourhood—society in which others well known to her, and in the same class of life, mix freely—except that her husband is unfortunately a Dissenter, or has the reputation of mingling in low radical politics. That it is, she thinks, which hinders George from getting a commission or a place, Caroline from making an advantageous match, and prevents her and her husband from obtaining invitations,

[*Mill is combining a maxim from Francis Bacon's "Of Marriage and Single Life" (1612), in *Works*, Vol. VI, p. 391, with the name, become proverbial, of a character in Thomas Morton's play, *Speed the Plough* (London: Longman and Rees, 1800).]

perhaps honours, which, for aught she sees, they are as well entitled to as some folks. With such an influence in every house, either exerted actively, or operating all the more powerfully for not being asserted, is it any wonder that people in general are kept down in that mediocrity of respectability which is becoming a marked characteristic of modern times?

There is another very injurious aspect in which the effect, not of women's disabilities directly, but of the broad line of difference which those disabilities create between the education and character of a woman and that of a man, requires to be considered. Nothing can be more unfavourable to that union of thoughts and inclinations which is the ideal of married life. Intimate society between people radically dissimilar to one another, is an idle dream. Unlikeness may attract, but it is likeness which retains; and in proportion to the likeness is the suitability of the individuals to give each other a happy life. While women are so unlike men, it is not wonderful that selfish men should feel the need of arbitrary power in their own hands, to arrest *in limine* the life-long conflict of inclinations, by deciding every question on the side of their own preference. When people are extremely unlike, there can be no real identity of interest. Very often there is conscientious difference of opinion between married people, on the highest points of duty. Is there any reality in the marriage union where this takes place? Yet it is not uncommon anywhere, when the woman has any earnestness of character; and it is a very general case indeed in Catholic countries, when she is supported in her dissent by the only other authority to which she is taught to bow, the priest. With the usual barefacedness of power not accustomed to find itself disputed, the influence of priests over women is attacked by Protestant and Liberal writers, less for being bad in itself, than because it is a rival authority to the husband, and raises up a revolt against his infallibility. In England, similar differences occasionally exist when an Evangelical wife has allied herself with a husband of a different quality; but in general this source at least of dissension is got rid of, by reducing the minds of women to such a nullity, that they have no opinions but those of Mrs. Grundy or those which the husband tells them to have. When there is no difference of opinion, differences merely of taste may be sufficient to detract greatly from the happiness of married life. And though it may stimulate the amatory propensities of men, it does not conduce to married happiness, to exaggerate by differences of education whatever may be the native differences of the sexes. If the married pair are well-bred and well-behaved people, they tolerate each other's tastes; but is mutual toleration what people look forward to, when they enter into marriage? These differences of inclination will naturally make their wishes different, if not restrained by affection or duty, as to almost all domestic questions which arise. What a difference there must be in the society which the two persons will wish to frequent, or be frequented by! Each will desire associates who share their own tastes: the persons agreeable to one, will be indifferent or positively disagreeable to the other; yet there can be none who are not common to both, for married people do not now live in different parts of the house and have totally different visiting lists, as in the reign of Louis XV. They cannot help having different wishes as to the bringing up of the children: each will wish to see reproduced in them their own tastes and sentiments: and there is either a compromise, and only a half-satisfaction to either, or the wife has to yield—often with bitter suffering; and, with or without intention, her occult influence continues to counterwork the husband's purposes.

It would of course be extreme folly to suppose that these differences of feeling and inclination only exist because women are brought up differently from men, and that there would not be differences of taste under any imaginable circumstances. But there is nothing beyond the mark in saying that the distinction in bringing-up immensely aggravates those differences, and renders them wholly inevitable. While women are brought up as they are, a man and a woman will but rarely find in one another real agreement of tastes and wishes as to daily life. They will generally have to give it up as hopeless, and renounce the attempt to have, in the intimate associate of their daily life, that *idem velle, idem nolle*, which is the recognised bond of any society that is really such: or if the man succeeds in obtaining it, he does so by choosing a woman who is so complete a nullity that she has no *velle* or *nolle* at all, and is as ready to comply with one thing as another if anybody tells her to do so. Even this calculation is apt to fail; dulness and want of spirit are not always a guarantee of the submission which is so confidently expected from them. But if they were, is this the ideal of marriage? What, in this case, does the man obtain by it, except an upper servant, a nurse, or a mistress? On the contrary, when each of two persons, instead of being a nothing, is a something; when they are attached to one another, and are not too much unlike to begin with; the constant partaking in the same things, assisted by their sympathy, draws out the latent capacities of each for being interested in the things which were at first interesting only to the other; and works a gradual assimilation of the tastes and characters to one another, partly by the insensible modification of each, but more by a real enriching of the two natures, each acquiring the tastes and capacities of the other in addition to its own. This often happens between two friends of the same sex, who are much associated in their daily life: and it would be a common, if not the commonest, case in marriage, did not the totally different bringing-up of the two sexes make it next to an impossibility to form a really well-assorted union. Were this remedied, whatever differences there might still be in individual tastes, there would at least be, as a general rule, complete unity and unanimity as to the great objects of life. When the two persons both care for great objects, and are a help and encouragement to each other in whatever regards these, the minor matters on which their tastes may differ are not all-important to them; and there is a foundation for solid friendship, of an enduring character, more likely than anything else to make it, through the whole of life, a greater pleasure to each to give pleasure to the other, than to receive it.

I have considered, thus far, the effects on the pleasures and benefits of the marriage union which depend on the mere unlikeness between the wife and the husband: but the evil tendency is prodigiously aggravated when the unlikeness is inferiority. Mere unlikeness, when it only means difference of good qualities, may be more a benefit in the way of mutual improvement, than a drawback from comfort. When each emulates, and desires and endeavours to acquire, the other's peculiar qualities, the difference does not produce diversity of interest, but increased identity of it, and makes each still more valuable to the other. But when one is much the inferior of the two in mental ability and cultivation, and is not actively attempting by the other's aid to rise to the other's level, the whole influence of the connexion upon the development of the superior of the two is deteriorating: and still more so in a tolerably happy marriage than in an unhappy one. It is not with impunity that the superior in intellect shuts himself up with an inferior, and elects that inferior for his chosen, and sole completely intimate, associate. Any society which is not improving, is deteriorating: and the more so, the closer and more familiar it is. Even a really superior man almost always begins to deteriorate when he is habitually (as the phrase is) king of his company: and in his most habitual company the husband who has a wife inferior to him is always so. While his self-satisfaction is incessantly ministered to on the one hand, on the other he insensibly imbibes the modes of feeling, and of looking at things, which belong to a more vulgar or a more limited mind than his own. This evil differs from many of those which have hitherto been dwelt on, by being an increasing one. The association of men with women in daily life is much closer and more complete than it ever was before. Men's life is more domestic. Formerly, their pleasures and chosen occupations were among men, and in men's company: their wives had but a fragment of their lives. At the present time, the progress of civilization, and the turn of opinion against the rough amusements and convivial excesses which formerly occupied most men in their hours of relaxation—together with (it must be said) the improved tone of modern feeling as to the reciprocity of duty which binds the husband towards the wife—have thrown the man very much more upon home and its inmates, for his personal and social pleasures: while the kind and degree of improvement which has been made in women's education, has made them in some degree capable of being his companions in ideas and mental tastes, while leaving them, in most cases, still hopelessly inferior to him. His desire of mental communion is thus in general satisfied by a communion from which he learns nothing. An unimproving and unstimulating companionship is substituted for (what he might otherwise have been obliged to seek) the society of his equals in powers and his fellows in the higher pursuits. We see, accordingly, that young men of the greatest promise generally cease to improve as soon as they marry, and, not improving, inevitably degenerate. If the wife does not push the husband forward, she always holds him back. He ceases to care for what she does not care for; he no longer desires, and ends by disliking and shunning, society congenial to his former aspirations, and which would now shame his falling-off from them; his higher faculties both of mind and heart cease to be called into activity. And this change coinciding with the new and selfish interests which are created by the family, after a few years he differs in no material respect from those who have never had wishes for anything but the common vanities and the common pecuniary objects.

What marriage may be in the case of two persons of cultivated faculties, identical in opinions and purposes, between whom there exists that best kind of equality, similiarity of powers and capacities with reciprocal superiority in them—so that each can enjoy the luxury of looking up to the other, and can have alternately the pleasure of leading and of being led in the path of development—I will not attempt to describe. To those who can conceive it, there is no need; to those who cannot, it would appear the dream of an enthusiast. But I maintain, with the profoundest conviction, that this, and this only, is the ideal of marriage; and that all opinions, customs, and institutions which favour any other notion of it, or turn the conceptions and aspirations connected with it into any other direction, by whatever pretences they may be coloured, are relics of primitive barbarism. The moral regeneration of mankind will only really commence, when the most fundamental of the social relations is placed under the rule of equal justice, and when human beings learn to cultivate their strongest sympathy with an equal in rights and in cultivation.

Thus far, the benefits which it has appeared that the world would gain by ceasing to make sex a disqualification for privileges and a badge of subjection, are social rather than individual; consisting in an increase of the general fund of thinking and acting power, and an improvement in the general conditions of the association of men with women. But it would be a grievous understatement of the case to omit the most direct benefit of all, the unspeakable gain in private happiness to the liberated half of the species; the difference to them between a life of subjection to the will of others, and a life of rational freedom. After the primary necessities of food and raiment, freedom is the first and strongest want of human nature. While mankind are lawless, their desire is for lawless freedom. When they have learnt to understand the meaning of duty and the value of reason, they incline more and more to be guided and restrained by these in the exercise of their freedom; but they do not therefore desire freedom less; they do not become disposed to accept the will of other people as the representative and interpreter of those guiding principles. On the contrary, the communities in which the reason has been most cultivated, and in which the idea of social duty has been most powerful, are those which have most strongly asserted the freedom of action of the individual—the liberty of each to govern his conduct by his own feelings of duty, and by such laws and social restraints as his own conscience can subscribe to.

He who would rightly appreciate the worth of personal independence as an element of happiness, should consider the value he himself puts upon it as an ingredient of his own. There is no subject on which there is a greater habitual difference of judgment between a man judging for himself, and the same man judging for other people. When he hears others complaining that they are not allowed freedom of action—that their own will has not sufficient influence in the regulation of their affairs—his inclination is, to ask, what are their grievances? what positive damage they sustain? and in what respect they consider their affairs to be mismanaged? and if they fail to make out, in answer to these questions, what appears to him a sufficient case, he turns a deaf ear, and regards their complaint as the fanciful querulousness of people whom nothing reasonable will satisfy. But he has a quite different standard of judgment when he is deciding for himself. Then, the most unexceptionable administration of his interests by a tutor set over him, does not satisfy his feelings: his personal exclusion from the deciding authority appears itself the greatest grievance of all, rendering it superfluous even to enter into the question of mismanagement. It is the same with nations. What citizen of a free country would listen to any offers of good and skilful administration, in return for the abdication of freedom? Even if he could believe that good and skilful administration can exist among a people ruled by a will not their own, would not the consciousness of working out their own destiny under their own moral responsibility be a compensation to his feelings for great rudeness and imperfection in the details of public affairs? Let him rest assured that whatever he feels on this point, women feel in a fully equal degree. Whatever has been said or written, from the time of Herodotus to the present, of the ennobling influence of free government[*]—the nerve and spring which it gives to all the faculties, the larger and higher objects which it presents to the intellect and feelings, the more unselfish public spirit, and calmer and broader views of duty, that it engenders, and the generally loftier platform on which it elevates the individual as a moral, spiritual, and social being—is every particle as true of women as of men. Are these things no important part of individual happiness? Let any man call to mind what he himself felt on emerging from boyhood—from the tutelage and control of even loved and affectionate elders—and entering upon the responsibilities of manhood. Was it not like the physical effect of taking off a heavy weight, or releasing him from obstructive, even if not otherwise painful, bonds? Did he not feel twice as much alive, twice as much a human being, as before? And does he imagine that women have none of these feelings? But it is a striking fact, that the satisfactions and mortifications of personal pride, though all in all to most men when the case is their own, have less allowance made for them in the case of other people, and are less listened to as a ground or a justification of conduct, than any other natural human feelings; perhaps because men compliment them in their own case with the names of so many other qualities, that they are seldom conscious how mighty an influence

[*See *Herodotus* (Greek and English), trans. A.D. Godley, 4 vols. (London: Heinemann; New York: Putnam's Sons, 1926-30), Vol. II, pp. 105-7 (III, 80).]

these feelings exercise in their own lives. No less large and powerful is their part, we may assure ourselves, in the lives and feelings of women. Women are schooled into suppressing them in their most natural and most healthy direction, but the internal principle remains, in a different outward form. An active and energetic mind, if denied liberty, will seek for power: refused the command of itself, it will assert its personality by attempting to control others. To allow to any human beings no existence of their own but what depends on others, is giving far too high a premium on bending others to their purposes. Where liberty cannot be hoped for, and power can, power becomes the grand object of human desire; those to whom others will not leave the undisturbed management of their own affairs, will compensate themselves, if they can, by meddling for their own purposes with the affairs of others. Hence also women's passion for personal beauty, and dress and display; and all the evils that flow from it, in the way of mischievous luxury and social immorality. The love of power and the love of liberty are in eternal antagonism. Where there is least liberty, the passion for power is the most ardent and unscrupulous. The desire of power over others can only cease to be a depraving agency among mankind, when each of them individually is able to do without it: which can only be where respect for liberty in the personal concerns of each is an established principle.

But it is not only through the sentiment of personal dignity, that the free direction and disposal of their own faculties is a source of individual happiness, and to be fettered and restricted in it, a source of unhappiness, to human beings, and not least to women. There is nothing, after disease, indigence, and guilt, so fatal to the pleasurable enjoyment of life as the want of a worthy outlet for the active faculties. Women who have the cares of a family, and while they have the cares of a family, have this outlet, and it generally suffices for them: but what of the greatly increasing number of women, who have had no opportunity of exercising the vocation which they are mocked by telling them is their proper one? What of the women whose children have been lost to them by death or distance, or have grown up, married, and formed homes of their own? There are abundant examples of men who, after a life engrossed by business, retire with a competency to the enjoyment, as they hope, of rest, but to whom, as they are unable to acquire new interests and excitements that can replace the old, the change to a life of inactivity brings ennui, melancholy, and premature death. Yet no one thinks of the parallel case of so many worthy and devoted women, who, having paid what they are told is their debt to society—having brought up a family blamelessly to manhood and womanhood—having kept a house as long as they had a house needing to be kept—are deserted by the sole occupation for which they have fitted themselves; and remain with undiminished activity but with no employment for it, unless perhaps a daughter or daughter-in-law is willing to abdicate in their favour the discharge of the same functions in her younger household. Surely a hard lot for the old age of those who have worthily discharged, as long as it was given to them to discharge, what the world accounts their only social duty. Of such women, and of those others to whom this duty has not been committed at all—many of whom pine through life with the consciousness of thwarted vocations, and activities which are not suffered to expand—the only resources, speaking generally, are religion and charity. But their religion, though it may be one of feeling, and of ceremonial observance, cannot be a religion of action, unless in the form of charity. For charity many of them are by nature admirably fitted; but to practise it usefully, or even without doing mischief, requires the education, the manifold preparation, the knowledge and the thinking powers, of a skilful administrator. There are few of the administrative functions of government for which a person would not be fit, who is fit to bestow charity usefully. In this as in other cases (pre-eminently in that of the education of children), the duties permitted to women cannot be performed properly, without their being trained for duties which, to the great loss of society, are not permitted to them. And here let me notice the singular way in which the question of women's disabilities is frequently presented to view, by those who find it easier to draw a ludicrous picture of what they do not like, than to answer the arguments for it. When it is suggested that women's executive capacities and prudent counsels might sometimes be found valuable in affairs of state, these lovers of fun hold up to the ridicule of the world, as sitting in parliament or in the cabinet, girls in their teens, or young wives of two or three and twenty, transported bodily, exactly as they are, from the drawing-room to the House of Commons. They forget that males are not usually selected at this early age for a seat in Parliament, or for responsible political functions. Common sense would tell them that if such trusts were confided to women, it would be to such as having no special vocation for married life, or preferring another employment of their faculties (as many women even now prefer to marriage some of the few honourable occupations within their reach), have spent the best years of their youth in attempting to qualify themselves for the pursuits in which they desire to engage; or still more frequently perhaps, widows or wives of forty or fifty, by whom the knowledge of life and faculty of government which they have acquired in their families, could by the aid of appropriate studies be made available on a less contracted scale. There is no country of Europe in which the ablest men have not frequently experienced, and keenly appreciated, the value of the advice and help of clever and experienced women of the world, in the attainment both of private and of public objects; and there are important matters of public administration to which few men are equally competent with such women; among others, the detailed control of expenditure. But what we are now discussing is not the need which society has of the services of women in public business, but the dull and hopeless life to which it so often condemns them, by forbidding them to exercise the practical abilities which many of them are conscious of, in any wider field than one which to some of them never was, and to others is no longer, open. If there is anything vitally important to the happiness of human beings, it is that they should relish their habitual pursuit. This requisite of an enjoyable life is very imperfectly granted, or altogether denied, to a large part of mankind; and by its absence many a life is a failure, which is provided, in appearance, with every requisite of success. But if circumstances which society is not yet skilful enough to overcome, render such failures often for the present inevitable, society need not itself inflict them. The injudiciousness of parents, a youth's own inexperience, or the absence of external opportunities for the congenial vocation, and their presence for an uncongenial, condemn numbers of men to pass their lives in doing one thing reluctantly and ill, when there are other things which they could have done well and happily. But on women this sentence is imposed by actual law, and by customs equivalent to law. What, in unenlightened societies, colour, race, religion, or in the case of a conquered country, nationality, are to some men, sex is to all women; a peremptory exclusion from almost all honourable occupations, but either such as cannot be fulfilled by others, or such as those others do not think worthy of their acceptance. Sufferings arising from causes of this nature usually meet with so little sympathy, that few persons are aware of the great amount of unhappiness even now produced by the feeling of a wasted life. The case will be even more frequent, as increased cultivation creates a greater and greater disproportion between the ideas and faculties of women, and the scope which society allows to their activity.

When we consider the positive evil caused to the disqualified half of the human race by their disqualification—first in the loss of the most inspiriting and elevating kind of personal enjoyment, and next in the weariness, disappointment, and profound dissatisfaction with life, which are so often the substitute for it; one feels that among all the lessons which men require for carrying on the struggle against the inevitable imperfections of their lot on earth, there is no lesson which they more need, than not to add to the evils which nature inflicts, by their jealous and prejudiced restrictions on one another. Their vain fears only substitute other and worse evils for those which they are idly apprehensive of: while every restraint on the freedom of conduct of any of their human fellow creatures, (otherwise than by making them responsible for any evil actually caused by it), dries up *pro tanto* the principal fountain of human happiness, and leaves the species less rich, to an inappreciable degree, in all that makes life valuable to the individual human being.

TREATY OBLIGATIONS

1870

EDITOR'S NOTE

Fortnightly Review, XIV (Dec., 1870), 715-20. Signed "J.S. Mill." Running titles as title. Reprinted posthumously in *Dissertations and Discussions*, IV (1875), 119-29. Identified in Mill's bibliography as "An article on 'Treaty obligations' in the Fortnightly Review of Dec. 1st 1870" (MacMinn, 100). For comment on the essay, see xxix and lxxi above.

Treaty Obligations

WHILE IT IS UNDOUBTEDLY TRUE that, in the practical application even of the best established and most universally received rules of morality, in ninety-nine cases out of a hundred an honest man seldom doubts by which he is to guide his conduct; yet no one, I presume, will deny that there will be found a hundredth case in which different moral obligations conflict. But, though this is not likely to be denied, there exists very generally a cowardly reluctance to look the fact in the face, and make provision for it, as one of the unavoidable inconveniences of an imperfect condition. People are afraid lest the force of recognised duties should be weakened, by admitting the liability of one duty to be overruled by another; and, though well knowing that this does happen, and not prepared to deny that it sometimes ought to happen, they prefer to be excused from giving their appro- bation beforehand to so unpleasant-looking a fact. The consequence is, that those who, having the responsibility of action, are forced to make for themselves some path through these moral entanglements, finding no rules or principles laid down for them but such as ignore instead of meeting the difficulties of the case, decide according to the dictate either of their selfish interests, or of some pre- vailing sentiment, which, if more disinterested, is not necessarily a truer guide. And since national concerns, by reason of their superior complication, afford by far the greatest number of these disputable questions of obligation, this is one (and not the smallest) among the causes of that laxity of principle which has almost always prevailed in public matters, even when the moralities of private life have met with a tolerable amount of observance.

There is no case which more flagrantly exemplifies these general observations than the case of international treaties. Through the greater part of the present century, the conscience of Europe has been habituated to the demoralising spectacle of treaties made only to be broken. In 1814 and 1815, a set of treaties were made by a general Congress of the States of Europe, which affected to regulate the external, and some of the internal, concerns of the European nations, for a time altogether unlimited. These treaties, having been concluded at the termination of a long war, which had ended in the signal discomfiture of one side, were imposed by some of the contracting parties, and reluctantly submitted to by others. Their terms were regulated by the interests, and relative strength at the time, of the victors and vanquished; and were observed as long as those interests and that relative strength remained the same. But as fast as any alteration took place in these elements, the powers, one after another, without asking leave, threw off, and were allowed with impunity to throw off, such of the obligations of the treaties as were distasteful to them, and not sufficiently important to the others to be worth a fight. The general opinion sustained some of those violations as being perfectly right; and even those which were disapproved, were not regarded as justifying a resort to war. Europe did not interpose when Russia annihilated Poland; when Prussia, Austria, and Russia extinguished the Republic of Cracow; or when a second Bonaparte mounted the throne of France. England alone, among the great contracting powers, never actively violated this set of treaties; though England, too, was a party after the fact to one of the most justifiable of the violations—the separation of Belgium from Holland. Such is the spectacle which Europe has had before her for half a century; and it is well calculated, one would think, to moderate her surprise, when another treaty, made forty years later, in the same wild hope of fixing a certain condition of the affairs of Europe in perpetuity, has in a similar manner broken down.[*] If we ask ourselves why this case has aroused more anger in this country than any of the others had done, the reply, if given with a full remembrance of the previous cases, can scarcely be, that it is more shocking to the conscience than any of them; for the annihilation of the Republic of Cracow was not merely the infringement of a treaty, it was also, had there existed no treaty to forbid it, in itself a gross violation of public rights and morality. But it did not touch so nearly what we had been taught to fancy our own interests, and was not so liable to be imagined a defiance to us in particular. Not to a greater tenderness of the public conscience, but to the different aspect affronts and injuries wear to the unreflecting when addressed to ourselves and when addressed to others, must, I fear, be attributed our special perception of the moral value of treaties on this occasion. We may fairly be complimented with being so far in advance of some of the other great States of Europe, that it is a disputable point whether we have of late years infringed any of our treaty obligations: although we must remember that the announcement, by one of our leading states-men, that almost the last treaty we entered into was only to be considered binding by ourselves if adhered to by the others who entered into the same obligation, met with very general approval.[†] Yet the public, if actuated purely by moral feeling, ought to have been more startled by the suggestion of a possible breach of morality

[*General Treaty between Great Britain, Austria, France, Prussia, Russia, Sardinia and Turkey, for the Re-establishment of Peace, with Three Conventions Annexed Thereto; Signed at Paris, March 30, 1856, PP, 1856, Vol. LXI, pp. 1-34; for Russia's intention to repudiate it, see "The Treaty of 1856: Prince Gortschakoff's Note," The Times, 18 Nov., 1870, p. 3.]

[†Edward George Stanley, Speech (4 July, 1867; Lords), PD, 3rd ser., Vol. 188, cols. 968-74, with reference to the "Treaty Relative to the Grand Duchy of Luxemburg" (11 May, 1867), PP, 1867, LXXIV, 415-22.]

on our own part, than by the certainty of an actual breach of it on the part of somebody else. The fact is, we have not yet advanced so far as to regard these questions purely from the moral point of view. Our indignation is hot or cold according to circumstances quite foreign to the morality of the case; and is likely to continue so until the morality of such cases has been placed on a firmer and more clearly defined basis than it has yet received.

I am ready to join with any one in averring that this is an evil state of things, most injurious to public morality. No honest man can see with indifference a condition in which treaties do not bind; in which it rests with the party who deems himself aggrieved by them, to say whether they shall be observed or not; in which nations cannot trust each other's pledged word. It does not follow, however, that this evil is likely to be remedied by ignoring the fact, that there are treaties which never will, and even which never ought to be permanently observed by those who have been obliged to submit to them; far less, therefore, to be permanently enforced. It is not necessary to go far back for one of the most signal examples which the entire history of mankind affords. Did any impartial person blame Prussia or Austria, because, in 1813, they violated the treaties which bound them to the first Napoleon, and not only did not fight in his ranks, as their engagements required, but brought their whole military force into the field against him, and pursued him to his destruction? Ought they, instead of cancelling the treaties, to have opened a negotiation with Napoleon, and entreated him to grant them a voluntary release from their obligations; and if he did not comply with their request to be allowed to desert him, ought they to have faithfully fought in his defence? Yet it was as true of those treaties, as it is of the treaty of 1856, that disadvantageous and dishonourable as they might be, they had been submitted to as the purchase-money of peace, when the prolongation of war would have been most disastrous; for, had the terms been refused, Napoleon could with ease have conquered the whole of Prussia, and at least the German dominions of Austria; which is considerably more, I presume, than England and France could have done to Russia, after the fall of Sebastopol. I already seem to hear some uncandid reader crying out, "Do you pretend that Russia has as complete a justification, and even positive obligation, to break her treaties, as Prussia and Austria then had?" Certainly not. The case of Austria and Prussia was about as extreme a case as, in the nature of national affairs, could possibly occur: Russia herself could not pretend that her own approaches within a great distance of theirs. But the principle may be the same; and principles are best tested by extreme cases. If a principle will not stand good in every case which it covers, it is a proof that some other principle requires to be considered along with it.

What means, then, are there of reconciling, in the greatest practicable degree, the inviolability of treaties and the sanctity of national faith, with the undoubted fact that treaties are not always fit to be kept, while yet those who have imposed them upon others weaker than themselves are not likely, if they retain confidence in their own strength, to grant a release from them? To effect this reconcilement, so far as it is capable of being effected, nations should be willing to abide by two rules. They should abstain from imposing conditions which, on any just and reasonable view of human affairs, cannot be expected to be kept. And they should conclude their treaties, as commercial treaties are usually concluded, only for terms of years.

To the first of these rules it is essential that the obligations should be defined, which nations are not warranted in imposing on one another. I do not pretend to enter exhaustively into so large a subject. But one great principle one can clearly see, and it is the only one which need concern us at present. The community of nations is essentially a republic of equals. Its purposes require that it should know no distinction of grades, no rights or privileges enjoyed by some and refused to others. The basis of international law—without which the weak, for whose protection chiefly international law exists, would never be secure—is, that the smallest and least powerful nation, in its capacity of a nation, is the equal of the strongest. Whatever rights belong to one belong to all, and can only be temporarily forfeited, even by misconduct, unless the erring nation is to be treated as a savage, and thrust out of the communion of civilised nations altogether. Now, all treaties which bind a nation, within itself and in its own affairs, by restrictions not common to all the rest, violate this principle. Of this nature is a stipulation that a country shall maintain one form of goverment, or abjure another; that she shall abstain from fortifying places situated within her own territory; that she shall limit to a prescribed amount her army or her fleet, or the portion of each stationed in a particular part of her dominions, no equivalent limitation of armaments being consented to by the other parties to the treaty, or by nations in general. I do not say that some of these restrictions cannot ever be admissible as a temporary penalty for crimes committed against other states; though in general some penalty would be preferable which could be completed by a single act. The period, however, for which such exceptional disabilities can justly be imposed, ought not, I conceive, to exceed the length of a generation; or, more properly, the period at the end of which a majority of the adult population will have grown up from childhood subsequently to the offence, so that the people suffering the penalty are no longer, as a body, the same with those who shared in the fault.

But the end in view would be in a still greater degree attained, were nations to decline concluding any treaties except for limited periods. Nations cannot rightfully bind themselves or others beyond the period to which human foresight can be presumed to extend; thus aggravating the danger which, to some extent, always exists, that the fulfilment of the obligation may, by change of circumstances, become either wrong or unwise. I am not aware of any good reason why engagements reciprocally entered into by nations for their joint advantage, should not be subject to periodical renewal. There are few, if any, contracts between nations, the terms of which might not be so framed as to protect either party from sustaining undue loss or injury in case of the non-renewal of the contract. And with respect to the other kind of treaties, those which nations inflict upon one another, there is a very much greater chance of their being faithfully observed, if a legitimate and peaceful emancipation from them is looked forward to at the end of a moderate length of time. The treaty of 1856, vainly affecting to be perpetual, has been repudiated in fourteen years. Had it been concluded for twenty, or even for twenty-five years, it would probably have lasted out the term. It is, perhaps, necessary to say, that the expiration of a treaty does not imply that a money indemnity exacted by it should be repaid, or a ceded territory restored. Possession, once transferred, is an accomplished fact; and to disturb it, after an interval of peace, would imply a fresh aggression, which requires no stipulation of treaties to constitute it a *casus belli*. The lapse of the treaty would merely reinstate the nation that had been punished, in those common rights of all nations, the enjoyment of which is the normal condition of an independent State; rights which no nation ought to be, and no high-spirited nation will ever consent to be, permanently dispossessed of.

If these principles are sound, it remains to be considered how they are to be applied to past treaties, which, though containing stipulations which, to be legitimate, must be temporary, have been concluded without such limitation, and are afterwards violated, or, as by Russia at present, repudiated, on the assumption of a right superior to the faith of engagements.

It is the misfortune of such stipulations, even if as temporary arrangements they might have been justifiable, that if concluded for permanency, they are seldom to be got rid of without some lawless act on the part of the nation bound by them. If a lawless act, then, has been committed in the present instance, it does not entitle those who imposed the conditions to consider the lawlessness only, and to dismiss the more important consideration, whether, even if it was wrong to throw off the obligation, it would not be still more wrong to persist in enforcing it. If, though not fit to be perpetual, it has been imposed in perpetuity, the question when it becomes right to throw it off is but a question of time. No time having been fixed, Russia fixed her own time, and naturally chose the most convenient. She had no reason to believe that the release she sought would be voluntarily granted, on any conditions which she would accept; and she chose an opportunity which, if not seized, might have been long before it occurred again, when the other contracting parties were in a more than usually disadvantageous position for going to war.

Had this been all, there would have been little in the conduct of Russia but what most other powers in her position would have done, and what there are, at all events, but too many precedents for doing. Her special offence is, that in asserting what she might, without being entirely unreasonable or unscrupulous, believe to be her right, she showed no desire whatever that the wound inflicted upon the confidence, so necessary to mankind, in the faith of treaties, should be the smallest possible. She showed herself perfectly indifferent to any such consequence. She made her claim in the manner most calculated to startle mankind, and to destroy their faith in the observance of all treaties which any one of the contracting parties thinks it has an interest in shaking off. Not but that it is in itself a less immoral act, if a promise is to be broken, to give notice beforehand of the intention, than to keep it hidden, and break the engagement without notice, while the other party is relying on its being kept. This is too obvious not to be seen in private life, and it is as true of public treaties as of private promises. Had Russia, however, thought the trust of nations in each other's engagements a thing of the highest importance, she would, even if determined to assert finally at all costs what she claims as her right, have first exhausted all endeavours, and consented to some sacrifices, to attain the freedom she claimed by the general consent of Europe. If Russia had acted in this honourable manner, she would have set, perhaps for the first time in history, an example which neither we ourselves who blame her, nor any other state, would find it easy to show in their own annals. She has chosen a less honourable course. But this misconduct of Russia (misconduct not so much before the bar of history and the past practice of nations, as before that of true morality, and of what we may hope will become the future customs) does not entitle us to bring upon millions of innocent persons the unspeakable evils of war, in order to enforce an obligation which it was wrong to impose, and which we ought therefore plainly to declare that we do not desire to reimpose. The notice which the high-handed proceeding of the Russian Government demanded at our hands, was to protest (as Lord Granville immediately did)[*] against the claim of a contracting party to set aside a treaty by a mere announcement of its will; and, for the rest, to follow the precedent set by the French Government, when three of the powers who were parties to the treaties of Vienna, destroyed the Republic of Cracow and confiscated its territory. M. Guizot, then Foreign Minister of France, made a public declaration, that France took notice of this violation of treaties; that she did not intend to oppose herself, by arms or otherwise, to the proceeding; but that she reserved to herself the full exercise of whatever rights the infringement of a treaty, to which she was a contracting party, restored to her.[†] If we are unable to arrange any joint peaceable action with the other powers concerned, an intimation somewhat like this would be the only dignified notice we could take of the mode of a demand, the substance of which the intrinsic merits of the case forbid us to resent. We may, however, hope that if our Government stands firm against the unreasonable clamour of the war party, some arrangement may be come to by which the obnoxious stipulations may be abrogated with the consent of all concerned.

[*See "Lord Granville's Answer to the Russian Circular," *The Times*, 17 Nov., 1870, p. 9.]

[†François Pierre Guillaume Guizot, Despatch to Metternich on the Incorporation of Cracow (3 Dec., 1846), in *La Presse*, 4 Dec., 1846, p. 1; the relevant passages are cited from *La Presse* in *The Times*, 7 Dec., 1846, p. 4.]

THE CONTAGIOUS DISEASES ACTS

1871

EDITOR'S NOTE

The Evidence of John Stuart Mill, Taken before the Royal Commission of 1870, on the Administration and Operation of the Contagious Diseases Acts of 1866 and 1869. Reprinted Verbatim from the Blue Book (London: Association for the Repeal of the Contagious Diseases Acts, [1871]). Reprinted from "Minutes of Evidence Taken before the Commission upon the Administration and Operation of the Contagious Diseases Acts," *Parliamentary Papers*, 1871, XIX, 1818-25. The Acts are 29 Victoria, c. 35 (1866), and 32 & 33 Victoria, c. 96 (1869). Not listed in Mill's bibliography. No copy in the Somerville College Library. Mill's evidence was taken on 13 May, 1871 (in the House of Lords), with William Nathaniel Massey in the Chair, and the following members of the Committee present: Robert Applegarth, John Henry Bridges, Richard Collinson, Holmes Coote, Robert Gregory, John Hannah, Timothy Holmes, Walter Charles James, Frederick Denison Maurice (whose name is omitted from the list in the pamphlet and in *PP*), Anthony John Mundella, John Somerset Pakington, and Peter Rylands. The text is headed: "Mr. John Stuart Mill gave evidence as follows:". Mill's examination included questions 19,990 to 20,101 of the evidence before the Committee. For comment on the evidence, see xxxvii-xxxviii and lxxi-lxxii above.

The text below is taken from the pamphlet reprint of the evidence. It has been collated with the version in *PP*, which is signified in the variant notes by "71[1]".

The Contagious Diseases Acts

WILLIAM NATHANIEL MASSEY: *Are you acquainted with the Acts of Parliament which are the subject of inquiry by this Commission?* I have a general acquaintance with them.

Have you any practical knowledge of the working of them? No practical knowledge.

Then any opinion you express with regard to these Acts, refers to the principles on which they are founded? Yes; the general principles of legislation. I have not studied the details.

The principal Act now in force is entitled "An Act for the better prevention of contagious diseases at certain naval and military stations." [*] *And are you aware that the policy which dictated this legislation in the first instance, was a desire to maintain the health of soldiers and sailors, whose physical efficiency was reported to be very seriously affected by the disease which they contracted at garrison and seaport towns, those towns and garrisons being the resort, in a peculiar manner, of common prostitutes?* Yes; I am aware of that.

Do you consider that such legislation as that is justifiable on principle? I do not consider it justifiable on principle, because it appears to me to be opposed to one of the greatest principles of legislation, the security of personal liberty. It appears to me that legislation of this sort takes away that security, almost entirely from a particular class of women intentionally, but incidentally and unintentionally, one may say, from all women whatever, inasmuch as it enables a woman to be apprehended by the police on suspicion and taken before a magistrate, and then by that magistrate she is liable to be confined for a term of imprisonment which may amount, I believe, to six months, for refusing to sign a declaration consenting to be examined.

The Act of Parliament in express terms applies only to common prostitutes, plying their trade as prostitutes within the protected districts. The police have express instructions to confine their action to the women specified in the Act. We have it in evidence before us that those orders have been most carefully obeyed by a select body of police detached upon this particular duty [a]. *In point of fact,* [a] I do

[*29 Victoria, c. 35 (1866).]

[a-a]71[1]   , in point of fact. [*transcriber's error?*]

not know whether that would make any difference in your opinion. The Commission, I may say, are satisfied that no practical abuse of the Act has taken place by the police; that in fact, women who are not intended by the Legislature to be subjected to these provisions have not been molested by it. We so far qualify that by saying it is possible that in some particular instances the suspicion of the police may have rested upon women who are not within the description of common prostitutes, but practically the Act has been carried out with great care. Is your objection confined to the possibility of a modest woman being brought up under these Acts? That is a very great part of my objection. Although I am quite aware that the Act only authorises the apprehension of prostitutes, still a discretion must necessarily be left in the police to prevent the entire evasion of the Act: and I have understood that it is held by its supporters, medical men and others, that the powers must be very considerable if the Acts are not to be very seriously evaded. What number of cases there have been in which modest women, or women at any rate not prostitutes, have been apprehended by the police on suspicion, I do not know, but it appears to me that the police have that power, and that they must have the power; it is impossible to enforce the Acts unless they have the power; the Acts cannot be made really effectual unless those powers are strengthened. But in any case it seems to me that we ought not to assume, even supposing *b*that*b* no case of abuse has been found out as yet, that abuses will not occur. When power is given which may be easily abused, we ought always to presume that it will be abused, and although it is possible that great precautions will be taken at first, those precautions are likely to be relaxed in time. We ought not to give powers liable to very great abuse, and easily abused, and then presume that those powers will not be abused.

What power do you refer to? The power of apprehending women on suspicion, and then requiring them to enter into engagements subjecting themselves to examination.

Then setting aside the tendency to which these Acts are liable in their execution of invading the liberty of modest women, do you consider it objectionable in itself that the Legislature should make provision for the periodical examination of common prostitutes who let out their bodies for hire? I think that it is objectionable. If any penalty is to be imposed, and this must be considered a penalty, for being a common prostitute, she ought to have power to defend herself in the same manner as before any ordinary tribunal, and of being heard by counsel, in order to prove that she is not a prostitute if she can. There are great numbers of prostitutes, I believe in this country, certainly in foreign countries, who are not registered, and the effect of the examination which the Act requires, and similar examinations which are required in foreign countries, is said to be, and I believe with a great deal of truth, to lead to a great amount of clandestine prostitution, and the Acts therefore are not effectual unless clandestine prostitution is touched also.

b-b+71[2]

The provision of the Act is this, that a woman shall be permitted, if she ᶜthinksᶜ fit, to acknowledge herself to be a common prostitute upon paper; that is called in the Act a voluntary submission, and she may deposit that in the hands of the police or the authorities of the hospital, and in pursuance of that submission she is examined and subjected to the same examination with regard to periodical attendance as if ordered to attend before the magistrate; the alternative being that if she declines to sign a voluntary submission, she may be taken before a magistrate, and the question whether she is a common prostitute, will be a question for the magistrate to try. She may be heard by counsel, and the only difference between that mode of trial and the ordinary mode of trial is the absence of a jury. She is tried, in fact, by a tribunal analogous to that which has been created by recent legislation in an Act called the "Criminal Justice Act,"[*] which in fact merely extends summary jurisdiction which already obtained in this country. Do I understand you to say that you think the protection of a jury is necessary in such a case? I have not considered that subject, but I think all the protection, which is necessary in other cases of judicial investigation would be necessary in this. There can be hardly any more serious case to the person concerned than that of being charged with being a prostitute, if she is not really so. With regard to the first part of your question, supposing that her declaration of her being a prostitute is voluntary, and that her submission to examination is strictly spontaneous on her part, I have nothing to say against it then; but I do not think it is the business of Government to provide the means of such examinations.

To follow up that, supposing a woman had voluntarily submitted her person to examination, and her person was found to be diseased, would you consider it an unjustifiable violation of her ᵈlibertyᵈ if she was sent to hospital, and detained in the hospital against her will until she was cured? I should think the objection less strong than in the other case, but I still think it objectionable because I do not think it is part of the business of the Government to provide securities beforehand against the consequences of immoralities of any kind. That is a totally different thing from remedying the consequences after they occur. That I see no objection to at all. I see no objection to having hospitals for the cure of patients, but I see considerable objection to consigning them to hospitals against their will.

The condition which I took the liberty of putting to you was the voluntary submission of the women? Yes.

Upon that voluntary submission the woman is found diseased. Now the woman being found diseased and being a common prostitute, upon her voluntary submission the law assumes the right of sending her to a hospital, and detaining her in that hospital, until she is no longer in a condition to communicate contagion.

[*27 & 28 Victoria, c. 80 (1864), which extended 18 & 19 Victoria, c. 126 (1855).]

ᶜ⁻ᶜ71¹   *think*
ᵈ⁻ᵈ71¹   *liability [transcriber's error?]*

Do you think that a warrantable violation of the woman's liberty, which is the first question? Do you consider that a proper course for legislation to take? I do not consider it a violation of the woman's liberty in that case, because she would know beforehand to what she would subject herself. If she voluntarily underwent this examination, she might well be made to undertake that if she was examined and found diseased, she should consent beforehand to go to the hospital, and be there detained until cured; therefore, on the score of personal liberty, I have no objection to it. But I have a still remaining objection to the Government undertaking, even on the solicitation of the parties concerned, to provide beforehand the means of practising certain indulgences with safety. Of course the objection on the ground of personal liberty does not occur in that case, but the other objection does. It applies to this case as much as the other. I think if a woman comes and asks to be examined and asks it to be ascertained that she is in a healthy condition, and to be submitted to treatment until she is healthy in order that she may be fitter to follow a certain profession, the State is in fact going out of its way to provide facilities for the practice of that profession, which I do not think the State is called upon, or can without considerable disadvantage undertake, to do.

Would your objection be modified by this consideration. It is in evidence before this Commission, and we will assume for the purpose of your answer that it is proved to your satisfaction that the contagious disease extends far beyond the guilty persons, and may be communicated to innocent wives, and be transmitted to innocent children? That opens another point on which I should like to express an opinion. Of course I understand it is not the object of the Act of Parliament to afford facilities for indulgence. The object of the Act is not to protect those who voluntarily seek indulgence, but to protect the innocent from having these diseases communicated to them; that I understand to be the object. Now a woman cannot communicate the disease but to a person who seeks it, and who knowingly places himself in the way of it. A woman can only communicate it through a man; it must be the man who communicates it to innocent women and children afterwards. It seems to me, therefore, if the object is to protect those who are not unchaste, the way to do that is to bring motives to bear on the man and not on the woman, who cannot have anything to do directly with the communication of it to persons entirely innocent, whereas the man can and does. If you ask whether I think it possible to bring motives to bear on the man, I think there are various ways in which it may be done. In the first place, the same degree of *espionage* which is necessary to detect women would detect also the men who go with them, because very often they are detected only by the circumstance of being seen to go into certain houses with men. In that case, if the women can be laid hold of, the men can also, and be obliged to give an account why they are there. But without the exercise of *espionage* on either men or women, there are other means which can be had recourse to; very severe damages in case a man is proved to have communicated this disease to a modest woman, and in the case of his wife, divorce as a matter of right; I think that a stronger case in which to apply the remedy of divorce can hardly be conceived.

Supposing for a moment that the enactment in law making it penal to communicate the disease to another person was objectionable on the ground that it would lead to extortion, and that a wife so affected would not be able to overcome all those influences which her own affections have over her to induce her not to take the extreme step of seeking divorce, what remedy would you provide for the innocent children? The evil could only reach the children through the wife. The unborn children could only be infected by the mother being first infected. If it was proved that a man had been the means of communicating to his wife, she being a modest woman, or to his children, any of these diseases, the law should grant the woman a divorce, and compel the man in proportion to his means to pay very heavy damages to them for their support apart from himself. That, in my opinion, is what the law ought to do in the case. I quite see there would be often great difficulty in enforcing it; probably it would only be enforced in a certain proportion of cases, and very likely not in the majority of cases, but still the knowledge that it could be enforced would operate as a considerable check on the evil; and even the fact that the law declared this a very great crime, not only rendering the person who committed it subject to heavy penalties, but deemed so serious as to warrant the dissolving of the marriage tie, the mere effect of placing its mark on the conduct in this way would have very great influence, and would make this crime be considered, as in truth it is, one of the gravest a man could possibly commit.

REV. JOHN HANNAH: *Would you think it worth while to make an effort to stop it, viewed simply as a plague?* That is, of course, a question to be considered, but I have heard and read that many medical men, and other strong supporters of the Act, think it cannot be made effectual enough to stamp out these diseases unless it is made much more strict than it is, consequently much more oppressive to women, and still more liable to abuse; besides which I have understood that several medical men who were warm supporters of the Acts nevertheless think it impossible for the Acts to be made to that degree effectual, or any degree approaching that, unless men are subject to it as well as women, and the reason they do not propose this is because they do not think that men would consent to it.

Confining you to the one point of detention, I think I gather your objections to it arise from collateral considerations which admit of removal: I mean the consideration that the detention is simply to facilitate an immoral purpose; an objection which you dwelt upon, did you not? It seems to me always liable to that objection, even if it is not liable to others.

Still, is not the policy of detention separable from what is clearly a bad reason; viz., to make sin safe? I do not see how it can be separated. I do not see how that which makes illicit indulgence of that sort safe, or is supposed to do so, can be prevented from giving some degree of encouragement to it, though far, I know, from the intention of the Act.

The point, I apprehend, is really this: in case it is really a plague, differing only from other plagues by the intermixture of the moral element, then is not the Legislature justified in the interests of the innocent in endeavouring, so far as it can, to stamp it out, even if there is no hope of complete success? I should say this question is very much affected by the degree of hope there is of complete success. It seems to me there ought to be a very good prospect of complete extirpation to justify anything of that kind, and I do not understand that such hope is entertained by those who are now most in favour of the Acts.

SIR WALTER JAMES: *You mentioned that personal examination of men and women was a degrading thing, and in itself illegal?* I did. I think it is exceedingly degrading to the women subjected to it, not in the same degree to men; therefore there is more reason that if it is applied at all it should be applied to men as well as *ᵉ* women, or if not to both, rather to men than to women. Men are not lowered in their own eyes as much by exposure of their persons, besides which it is not a painful operation in the case of a man, which I believe in the case of a woman it often is, and they very much detest it.

With regard to the cost of these Acts, I understand on the continent these Acts are self-supporting, are you aware of that? are you aware that such is the case? I am not aware whether it is so.

Is it your opinion that it would be right and just that those persons for whose safety these Acts were passed should pay for them? It depends on who those are who are affected by the Acts.

Should you consider it more just that they should pay for it by licenses as on the continent, or that the British taxpayer, the poor man should pay for it? It seems to me that all the objections which exist against the Acts, exist in an extreme degree against licenses, because they have still more the character of toleration of that kind of vicious indulgence, than exists under the Acts at present, or can exist in any other way.

I think on this point you will agree with me that licenses should be paid for by ᶠ prostitutes themselves, and the brothel-keepers, rather than as in the present case by the English people? If the thing was really justifiable on the ground on which it is defended, namely, as a great sanitary measure for the protection of all classes, I think it would be very fair that the English people should pay: but it is not professed, and could not be with truth asserted to be the object of these Acts, to protect persons in vicious indulgence or to protect the class of prostitutes. The strongest argument for the Acts has been the protection of those who are liable to take the disease without any voluntary exposure to it on their own part.

But supposing the opposite to be the case, would not the hardship of the case be greater, that is, that the innocent should pay the cost of these Acts rather than the guilty? I should think such considerations of such extremely small importance

ᵉ71¹   to
ᶠ71¹   *the*

compared with the general bearing of the Acts, that I should think them hardly worth regarding. The very expense in any case would not be great.

But the expense would be very considerable if extended to other classes? If applied to the whole population the expense no doubt would be very much greater.

Would you consider, if applied to the whole population, it would be a justifiable subject to tax the people for? I think it would; I do not think it belongs to the class of measures which, if justifiable at all, it would be unjust to make a charge on the whole community. The health of the community is a subject now considered, I think with reason, to be within the province of Government. But I do not think this consideration material in comparison with the inconvenience that I see in the fact, that the expense could not be charged on the prostitutes themselves without in a manner licensing their profession. Moreover it is not the prostitutes themselves mainly who are protected, but their customers, and I do not see how you can get at them especially to make them pay. You can make prostitutes pay, but you cannot make those who frequent them pay.

Undoubtedly you can according to the principles of political economy, by making a prostitute recoup by charging a larger sum to customers, because we have heard in evidence that these registered women charge a higher price than the others. A gentleman said the officers gave a higher price to those licensed women than the others, so that you see in that case the cost would not fall upon the woman but upon her customers? In that case this particular objection fails, but the objection is still unanswered that it involves special licensing of persons to practise that profession.

Do you think that evil is at all avoided by the present Acts? By no means. I think one of the objections to the present Acts is that they do not avoid that evil, but still they are not attended with so much of it as the licensing system would be.

You are aware that a woman has an order to attend the next examination? I am.

And that it is their custom to show their tickets? Yes; that comes very near to the licensing.

Can you draw a distinction between it and licensing? There is hardly any distinction. It makes some difference that it is not called a license. That makes a considerable difference in the feeling about it, not by the public, but by the women themselves.

We have strong evidence that they are considered equivalent to it? That may very possibly be the case.

Do you see a substantial difference between medical ⁸examinations⁸ under these Acts, and the continental system? I do not see any substantial difference. It seems to me that the same objections apply to both.

Except that it is applied to a smaller population here, and that on the continent it is applied to all? More extensively.

---

⁸⁻⁸71[1]   *examination*

REV. FREDERICK DENISON MAURICE: *Supposing the whole of these Acts were repealed so far as regards the military and naval population, so that the whole purpose to supply prostitutes for them was taken away, would you then think that there might be hospitals for this purpose established by Government; would you see any objection to such hospitals being under Government control?* I do not see any reason. I by no means wish that there should not be hospital accommodation for those cases to the utmost extent for which it may be required. But I think the objection that applies to the Acts would apply in some degree to having hospitals for this express purpose. The great defect now is that these patients are not admitted into most hospitals. It would be desirable that the restrictive regulations which exclude them from all except a few hospitals should be removed in some way or other, and hospital accommodation provided for this disease in the same way as for others, but not by Government taking that charge on itself, which would be liable to the same objection as licensing prostitutes.

Do you not think the Government ought to exert itself for the purpose of putting down this disease? I think the Government ought, so far as it can, to exert itself in putting down all diseases—this among the rest, but I certainly do see some degree of objection to anything special being done by the Government distinguishing between this and other diseases in that respect.

Then if the Act really fulfilled its purpose, and was for all contagious diseases, by there being one department in each hospital, you would not think that objectionable? No. Supposing the opinion of Parliament was that contagious diseases generally, all sorts of infectious and contagious diseases, were proper subjects for the Government to take in hand administratively, and to provide proper means for curing, I should say there was no objection in including this among the others.

You would not think it bad legislation? No, because it would not single out diseases of this kind to meet with particular favour.

DR. JOHN HENRY BRIDGES: *I understood one of your objections to the Act was that the State thereby gave security for the consequences of committing an immoral act?* It facilitates the act beforehand; which is a totally different thing and always recognized in legislation as a different thing from correcting the evils which are the consequences of vices and faults. If we were never to interfere with the evil consequences which persons have brought upon themselves, or are likely to have brought upon themselves, we should help one another very little. Undoubtedly it is quite true that interfering to remedy evils which we have brought on ourselves has in some degree the same bad consequences, since it does in the same degree diminish the motive we have to guard against bringing evils on ourselves. Still a line must be drawn somewhere, and a marked line can be drawn there. You may draw a line between attacking evils when they occur, in order to remedy them as far as we are able, and making arrangements beforehand which will enable the objectionable practices to be carried on without incurring the danger of the evil.

*[h]*These*[h]* two things I take to be distinct, and capable of being kept distinct in practice. As long as hospitals are not peculiarly for that class of diseases, and do not give that class of disease any favour as compared with others, they are not liable to objection, because their operation consists in remedying the effects of past evils; they do not hold out a special facility beforehand to practising illicit indulgence with a security which it would not otherwise enjoy. The interference is not preventive but remedial.

By attacking the evil after it has occurred, you would, I presume, prefer dealing with a woman after she is diseased? Yes; I mean having hospitals, and taking means of curing people of diseases either of this kind or other kinds, which they have brought upon themselves by their own fault.

You are probably aware speaking of the country generally that there are not a very large number of hospitals, for the treatment of these diseases? I believe there are not.

And that it is excluded to a very large extent from our provincial hospitals? Yes.

Now would not the effect of having wards for the admission of venereal disease in all our hospitals scattered about the country have the effect which you deprecate, that is, of making fornication more secure from the chance of disease than it is at present? No doubt it would. No doubt everything you do to relieve people from what may be the *[i]*consequence*[i]* of their own fault, does in some degree diminish the motives to refrain from that fault. Still if we are to help one another at all, we must not stretch this argument to its full extent. Relieving people who are in danger of starvation is liable to the same objection. All poor laws, all relief whatever to the indigences or distresses of our fellow creatures are liable to it, since the people themselves are often very much to blame for bringing themselves into a position in which they require relief, and no doubt the relief does in some not inconsiderable degree diminish the prudential motives for abstaining. But still all our experience, and the consideration given to the question by thinkers and legislators, have ended in the recognition of this, that we ought not to abstain from helping one another through the evils of life, provided we do it in such a way as that it shall not provide facilities beforehand, but only deal with the evil when it has been incurred.

Apart from the existence of venereal disease, will you be prepared to lay down as a principle that the State should not take cognizance of the existence of prostitution? Of course a good deal will depend on the sort of cognizance, but I do not think that prostitution should be classed and recognised as such by the State. It seems to me there are inconveniences of many kinds in that.

You do not see your way to any improved legislation, for instance, with reference to brothels? That is a different question and a very difficult one. The

*[h-h]*71[1] Those
*[i-i]*71[1] consequences

question of the regulation of brothels, whether they should be systematically put down, or let alone to a certain degree, enters into very wide reaching considerations as to the degree in which the law should interfere in questions of simple morality, and also how far it should attack one portion of the persons who conspire to do a particular act, while it tolerates the others. I have always felt it very difficult to lay down a general rule on the subject, and I am not prepared to do so now, but I do not think it material to the consideration of these Acts.

SIR JOHN SOMERSET PAKINGTON: *Am I right in inferring from the evidence you have been so good as to give us, that you would not consider the fact of a very large proportion of the crews of our men-of-war and the soldiers of our army, being incapacitated for rendering service to the State by this terrible disease, an adequate reason for legislation of this kind?* Not for legislation of this kind; but it might be for legislation of other kinds. I cannot say that I have considered the subject much, but I do not see why the State should not subject its own soldiers and sailors to medical examination, and impose penalties on them in case they are found diseased. I would not undertake to say that it might not, by measures directly acting on soldiers and sailors, in a very considerable degree discourage that kind of indulgence. It is certain, at least I have understood so, that the impression on the minds of soldiers and sailors, is that it is not discouraged, that it is considered by Parliament a necessity which may be regulated, but which must be accepted, and that Parliament does not entertain any serious disapprobation of immoral conduct of that kind. Now the State might exercise an influence opposite to that, by making the being found diseased a ground for military penalties in the case of soldiers and sailors. I do not pretend to have made up my mind on the subject, or to have anything definite to propose. I only throw that out as a possibility.

Are you aware that in the case of soldiers, the very thing you recommend has been now in practice for many years, and is still in practice? I have understood that soldiers are examined.

Under those circumstances the remedy you suggest can hardly be regarded as a fresh security? Not an entirely fresh security, certainly. I have mentioned that I have not considered or studied that part of the subject.

I infer from your answer that the fact to which I have adverted of the known suffering in the way I have described must be regarded as a great public evil? No doubt it is a great public evil.

Do you think it is an evil which the State would not be justified in endeavouring to avert? If the State endeavours to avert it by any means which are not objectionable in a greater degree than the evil itself.

Do you think that the State had better rather continue to suffer from the evil than to pass such Acts as these for its prevention? I think the State had better continue to suffer as much of that evil as it cannot prevent in other ways, by the application of military discipline and the correction of these practices among the soldiers.

Can you suggest any way other than that already adverted to, and which I have told you is already in exercise? You mentioned that the soldiers are liable to examination, but you have not mentioned, and I am not aware, to what degree, if the result of that examination proves them to be diseased, they are liable to penalties.

I cannot describe the exact penalty, but the principle has been in action. I do not say with regard to the whole army, but can you suggest any other description? I have not considered that part of the subject, but certainly I am not prepared to suggest any other.

And I understand you to be of opinion that in no case should the State resort to such a remedy as is found in these Acts? Exactly. I do not think that the State should resort to any remedy which operates by taking means beforehand to make the indulgence safe.

I think you told us that you have only a general knowledge of ʲtheseʲ Acts, and no practical experience of their working? That is so.

You spoke of the violation of personal liberty, and I think you also, if I took down your words correctly, objected to the power of apprehending women on suspicion.[*] *Do you think, as far as you know the Act, that the expression "apprehend the woman on suspicion" is an expression taken in its ordinary sense, which is applicable to the powers which these Acts give?* It seems to me that it is applicable as far as I understand the subject; inasmuch as when women have not voluntarily declared themselves to be prostitutes, they may be, as I understand, watched by policemen, and if the policeman thinks a woman is practising prostitution, although not registered, he has it in his power, on any grounds of suspicion which appear to him to be adequate, to require the woman to enter into an undertaking to submit herself to examination, or to take her before a magistrate, who will make her do so.

I am glad I asked you the question, because it is very clear you are under a mis-apprehension. There is no such power calling on a woman to make a declaration compelling her to be examined. The only power of the police in this case is where they have good reason to suppose a woman to be practising common prostitution, if she does not voluntarily sign a paper stating she is willing to be examined, to lay an information before a magistrate, and proceed in the ordinary course before that magistrate. You would hardly call that apprehension on suspicion, would you? Certainly, I should call that apprehending a woman on suspicion. It is apprehending a woman on grounds which, in the opinion of the policeman, place her under suspicion of practising prostitution without acknowledgment. I am aware that policemen have no power of using any compulsion for making a woman enter into an engagement subjecting herself to examination. I am aware that that can only be done before a magistrate, and after such inquiries as he

[*See pp. 351 and 352 above.]

ʲ⁻ʲ71¹ *those*

might hold; but the policeman has it in his power, whether he uses the power or not, to use threats to induce the woman to enter into this engagement.

I have no wish to raise any question on the narrow meaning of the word "apprehend," but as you have said it is a violation of personal liberty, I will ask you whether you are aware that the liberty of such women, as of all other persons, is protected by law, until interrupted under the authority of law? Yes, I did not make that distinction as I ought to have done. I admit its relevancy.

When you said that a prostitute ought to have the power of defending herself before the ordinary tribunals, I think you would admit that she has that power, because she is brought before the magistrate, and that magistrate is not only free but bound in duty to hear everything that a woman has got to say, and judge of the evidence before deciding her case as he would in any other? That depends on whether it is explained to her that she may be defended by counsel.

The attack on personal liberty is subject to those usual grounds of protection which the law gives to all parties? It may be so.

In the case, which is not only a possible case but I fear from the evidence we have had the not very uncommon one of disease being communicated to innocent wives and innocent children, would you really trust to the power of divorce as the only remedy in such a ᵏcase? shouldᵏ you not endeavour at least to resort to prevention as being better than trusting to so uncertain a cure? I think that if prevention is to be applied at all, it should be applied to the man, who alone has the power of committing this offence in a direct way. When a woman infects anyone the man must always be a consenting party to running the risk: it is only a man who having been infected himself can communicate infection to an innocent person, and therefore if there is any argument for prevention, it should be for preventive measures applied to men who infect these women, and not to the women themselves.

Do you know or have you ever thought of any process by which prevention could be applied to men? I think that it could. No doubt it would fail very often; but inasmuch as it certainly does happen frequently that women are brought under the operation of these Acts through being watched by the police, and its being ascertained that they frequent certain houses along with men, the police can equally ascertain who the men are who go ˡ with them; and when they find that men have been seen to frequent along with prostitutes houses of this description, those men might be compelled to undergo examination for a certain period afterwards.

Am I to understand you seriously to propose that in this country we should adopt a system of espionage over every man seen going into a brothel, and that men seen to go into a brothel should be subject all alike to personal examination? I am not suggesting espionage; but if it is already in practice on women who go to brothels,

ᵏ⁻ᵏ71¹   *case, should*
ˡ71¹   *there*

with a view of ascertaining whether a woman is a prostitute by her being seen there, I think the woman should not be singled out to be subject to examination, but the men should be subjected to it also, or even if the women were not subjected the men might be, but if the one is, certainly I should say both.

Therefore you do, as I understand, recommend such a system of espionage as I have described? I do not recommend it, because I do not recommend the Acts at all; I do not recommend that there be any espionage practised upon women, and therefore not on men either.

Do ^m^you not^m^ recommend it to this extent, if any remedy is attempted for the evils complained of, it should be done in that shape? If any preventive measures are to be taken I should say it should be in that shape. But penal measures, or remedial measures by means of hospitals, could be adopted independently of that: increasing the hospitals, and increasing the facilities for admission of those who are diseased, and laying severe penalties on the man who communicates this disease to an innocent woman.

If the Legislature did enact with a view to preventing such cases as this, that the woman affected should have the remedy of divorce, would your knowledge of human nature lead you to the conclusion that that remedy would be resorted to in one case in a hundred, or one case in a thousand? A good many more than that, though probably not the majority.

WILLIAM NATHANIEL MASSEY: *Are you aware that for a man to give his wife a disease of that description would be adjudged cruelty by the Court of Divorce, and would be a ground for a divorce, at all events a mensa?* Yes, but not complete dissolution of the matrimonial tie.

SIR JOHN PAKINGTON: *Would you make it so?* Yes.

WILLIAM NATHANIEL MASSEY: *You would make it a vinculo?* Yes, *a vinculo*, accompanied with heavy pecuniary damages for the benefit of the sufferers, the wife or children.

SIR JOHN PAKINGTON: *We have received very strong evidence before this Commission, that at one, at least, I think more, but at one of the most populous places to which these Acts apply, one result has been that whereas there were previously hundreds of children—when I say children, girls under 13, 14, and 15 years of age—practising habitual prostitution, that since these Acts have passed that class has almost, if not quite, disappeared; now, assuming that evidence to be correct, would it reconcile your mind to the operation of the Acts producing so blessed an effect as that?* It would not remove the objections by any means. I have not examined into the statistics of the question, which I have no doubt are very contradictory, because very opposite results are stated at different places, with the effect of creating very great distrust in statistics altogether on that subject. In the experience of those countries where Acts similar to these have been very much

^m-m^71[1] *not you*

longer in operation, it is certainly found that a vast quantity of prostitutes escape the operation of them altogether; that the process to which women are subjected by it is so extremely offensive and odious, that there is a great quantity of clandestine prostitution; and therefore it may well happen—I do not pretend knowledge on the subject—that the introduction of these Acts in places where they have not prevailed before, may be attended with a considerable diminution of avowed prostitution, without any diminution of real prostitution. I may now say, as I did not say it before, that another reason which appears to me very strong against the system of these Acts is, that they have a decided tendency to increase the class of prostitutes. Even if it is only by the fact that a considerable number of them are withdrawn from their profession periodically, the vacancy or gap that is thus made, as the demand calls forth a supply, has a natural tendency to be filled up by additional prostitutes being brought into the profession. That is independent of another argument, which may also be urged, that in so far as the Acts are supposed to afford increased security to the men who frequent these women, it is liable to produce an increased demand for prostitutes, and therefore bring forth in that way an increased supply. But independently of that, which is an argument I have no doubt the Commission are perfectly familiar with—the mere taking away forcibly from the competition of a certain per-centage of the prostitutes for a certain time, naturally tends to have that vacancy filled up by healthy persons from other quarters.

I think I may ask you whether that is not rather a fear than any fact established by proof? As I have already mentioned, I have not studied the details, and cannot say that I know as a matter of fact that it is so, though accounts I have read, and which appear to me reliable, as to what takes place on the Continent, appear to me very strong evidence that that is actually the case there. Whether it is the case here may be matter of dispute. It may perhaps not be the case yet—it may be the case hereafter, though not the case already, or it may be the case without being detected. I know nothing practically about the matter, but it appears to me that there is the tendency, and that the law which produces it is as strong as any law in political economy.

Excuse me saying that I think your answer to my question about children did not quite meet the question. I asked you whether, assuming such to be the case, having first told you the strong evidence we had, whether that fact would reconcile you in any degree to the operation of the Acts, and your answer was that you distrusted such statistics. I did not ask you that, but assuming those to be accurate, whether such an important fact would reconcile you in any degree to the operation of the Acts? If we are to enter into one part of the question only, the degree of efficacy of the Acts for their professed purpose, of course any increased efficacy furnishes an additional argument for the Acts. But no argument that can be produced of that kind, or I believe ever has been produced, would seem to me to overbear the very strong arguments of other kinds against the operation of such Acts; therefore my opinion would not be favourable to the Acts, supposing the circumstances you mention to be finally confirmed.

If the existence of such a fact would not reconcile you to the "principles" of the Acts, would it not at least make you thankful that such a result had ensued? Of course anybody must be thankful for such a result, from whatever cause.

In following up the same part of the subject, may I ask you whether you think it would be inconsistent with due regard to the liberty of the subject, if such young creatures as I have referred to, and you must be aware that such must be the case in all our crowded populations, if the law authorised the detention of such young creatures as I have described, when once convicted of prostitution, in homes or refuges for their subsequent reclamation? I am not prepared to say that might not be a good measure. I perhaps would go further for the protection of extremely young persons than most people would. I should not be adverse to strengthening and extending the laws which at present exist against intercourse of any kind with girls below a certain age. I should not be at all adverse to raising considerably the age below which it should be prohibited.

We have had strong evidence with regard to the moral effects of these Acts, and a number of cases in which through the agency of these Acts, by first being taken into a hospital, where moral effects are produced as well as physical, and then being sent to a refuge, numbers of young women have been reclaimed from vice and restored to a virtuous life, and in many instances married. Would such a fact as that reconcile you to the operation of these Acts? I think *°these°* effects might just as well be produced by the mere existence of hospitals; by receiving them into hospitals, having proper hospital accommodation for them, and when there having them attended by those benevolent and excellent people who undertake their reclamation.

Are you now contemplating voluntary hospitals or hospitals supported by the State? Either. I have already stated I should object to hospitals supported by the State for this particular disease exclusively, but if contagious diseases generally were considered a proper subject for the State to take under its charge, I should not object to those being included.

Supposing these abandoned women did not go into them, what would you do then? Suppose they did not go in, I do not see how anything could be done.

Then your remedy would fail? Yes; but the women who would not go in would be those on whom the remedy would be the least likely to be effectual.

Supposing they did go in and would not stay when they were there, what would you do? I should not be prepared to give any compulsory power to detain them.

You would let them come out and spread disease right and left, rather than do good? I do not think it is the business of legislation of this kind to take special care

*n-n*71¹   principle
*o-o*71¹   those

either of the women who practise this profession, or of the men who frequent them. I apprehend that the real object for which these Acts are most defensible, if defensible at all, is the protection of the innocent, and as long as people are not liable to be infected without exposing themselves to it, I should say you do enough for them if you offer them the means of cure provided they accept it.

We have very strong evidence before us to this effect, that the Acts in certain localities have greatly diminished the number of common prostitutes, and have had the effect of raising the lowest and most demoralised portion of that class to a comparatively more decent and more respectable state of life—would not you acknowledge that to be a good effect? Stated as you have stated it, any such effect, however produced, is good *pro tanto*.

I am only putting to you that which we have before us in evidence. Precisely so: but I should consider, if any effect of that sort is produced, it is produced by a process, not applicable specially to prostitution, but to the criminal and vicious classes, the dangerous classes altogether, all of whom may have some amount of good done them if attention is paid to them by benevolent persons, or, it may be by persons employed by the Government. It would not be beyond the proper function of the State to take means of making these persons understand that they are not considered as totally unworthy of any kind of regard or consideration by the rest of their fellow-creatures, but that it is the object to reclaim them, and do them as much good as their condition makes them susceptible of. Such measures, at all events, might be applied to the dangerous classes generally, much more than ever has been done yet. I should not see the least objection to applying such measures to prostitutes also, but that would not require Acts of this description.

We have before us evidence of such a nature as I think hardly you or anybody else whose attention has not been called to it can imagine, with regard to the state not only of degradation but of physical disease, amounting to absolute rottenness, that the women have been found in in the neighbourhood of our camps, I think if I remember right such a state as almost to lead to the idea of falling to pieces; now looking at the fact of a human being in such a horrible state as this, would you leave those women to rot and die under the hedges, rather than pass such Acts as these to save them? I do not think it is quite fair to put the question exactly in that manner, because I am inclined to think that I should approve very much more decided measures of that sort with regard to the destitute classes generally than are now in practice. I should say, if you found a person in this last stage of consumption, or any other very wretched disease, it might be advisable and right to lay hold of that person and give him or her relief or proper medical treatment, and under proper medical regulation, and whatever relief of that sort I gave to others I would give to these women. What I object to is having special legislation for those women, which would have the effect of singling them out for a special cure, to which persons with other equally bad diseases are not subject.

I apprehend that I may take your answer as being in effect in the affirmative. You would rather leave these women to die and rot under hedges than pass these Acts and save them? I do not think that a fair way of putting the question, because I think they could be just as well saved without these Acts. I would do a great deal for the purpose of affording relief to persons who were found in an extremely bad state of disease, and in a state of destitution. I would not do more for those than others; and certainly the fact that there are such persons would not reconcile me to these Acts, because I think these Acts do a great deal of mischief in other ways, which is not at all necessary to be done for the sake of affording relief to those people, without giving it in common to all others who have an equal claim to it.

I apprehend that I can take that as an affirmative answer. My inference is that you would trust in such a case to the ordinary operation of the poor law?[*] I have not such a very high opinion of the administration of the poor laws as not to think it admits of great improvement in that respect as in others, and such improvement I should be glad to see, though I am not prepared to say exactly what it should be.

But the poor law has long been in operation and has not had the effect of res- cuing these poor creatures from suffering, therefore is it not a fair inference that they are insufficient to meet that case? That is a defect in the poor law, but some other means should be in practice for the relief of disease. Disease is a proper subject for a special branch of administration.

You would suggest that some remedy should be afforded for so horrible an evil, but you would rather it should not be the remedy we are now trusting to? Precisely.

Though that remedy has been proved signally successful? Yes, but if it has been signally successful, I think it has been by means and in a manner which ought equally to be applied to other diseases, if applied at all, and it would be equally effectual without the Acts.

We have before us evidence to the effect that from the fear of coming under the cognizance of the police, these Acts have had the effect of deterring young women from practising that clandestine prostitution which they previously did. Now assuming this evidence to be consistent with the facts, I would ask you whether you do not consider, that whatever your objections to the ᴾprinciplesᴾ of these Acts are, they have produced good results? Undoubtedly that result taken by itself, must be considered a good result by every one. It is, however, to be weighed against the probability that in other cases an opposite result might be produced, for which also strong presumption can be shown.

You stated an opinion, and it is an opinion which other witnesses also strongly stated, that the examination of the persons which is authorised by the Acts is very degrading to those women, that is your opinion? I dare say there are some of them to whom nothing is degrading, they are so degraded already; but there is reason to

[*4 & 5 William IV, c. 76 (1834).]

ᴾ⁻ᴾ71[1] *principle*

believe that there are many of them who have a considerable quantity of modesty left, and to whom therefore it is degrading.

Your answer rather anticipates the next question I was going to put to you, which is whether taking the case of a woman who submits herself daily to prostitution in three or four instances, and lives that miserable life, which do you think is the real degradation to that woman; is it the life that she leads, or the fact that she subsequently undergoes examination in order to cure the evils which have arisen from that disgraceful life? I think both are degrading, but degradation for degradation, that which is compulsory seems to me always more degrading in its effects on the character than what is done voluntarily.

Am I to understand from that answer that you think the fact of such an examination is more degrading to such a woman than the debauched life she leads? I think it adds considerably to the degradation already caused by the debauched life.

SIR WALTER JAMES: *It is an additional degradation?* An additional degradation.

ANTHONY JOHN MUNDELLA: *If we have evidence before us that many young people have been removed from prostitution in the streets by the operation of the Acts, are you not of opinion that we might also remove those young persons from the streets without subjecting them to this examination and making them healthy for prostitution?* Certainly I think so. I think that what removes them from the streets is the moral effect which is produced in their minds, and the chance of producing this effect is likely to be lessened by subjecting them to an offensive and what must be considered a tyrannical operation by the force of law. I should think that must tend in some degree to counteract the good effect which no doubt was produced by the moral influences that were brought to bear on them during their detention, which are no doubt the real cause of reclaiming them so far as they are reclaimed, and therefore they might be applied more effectually without the machinery of the Acts.

You are familiar with the compulsory education which exists on the continent and elsewhere, and have written a good deal on the duties of the State towards young children. Should you think it any interference with personal liberty, if girls under a certain age found practising prostitution were taken up and put into some industrial home? I certainly do not think there would be any objection to that. I think the objection to the interference with personal liberty begins when the age of education, properly so called, ceases. Where a person is under age, and in a position which must counteract very much all the good influences of education, and substitute bad ones, it is always open to the consideration of the State whether they cannot withdraw young persons from those bad influences. I have already mentioned that I would go still further, and be inclined to extend very much the operation of the penal laws which now exist against intercourse with girls under age. I would raise the age below which that is an offence by law, very considerably, though I have not considered up to what point.

I was going to ask you up to what age you would think the State would be justified in interfering to prevent prostitution? I should think certainly up to 17 or 18, up to the age when what is commonly called education ordinarily finishes. Possibly it might be extended with propriety until the girl was legally of age, but on that I would not undertake to give an opinion.

Do you think it any interference with the liberty of the subject to prevent solicitation in the streets? No; I think that is the duty of the police, in order to preserve the order of the streets.

Sir John Pakington has referred to the wretched women who haunt the camps.[*] *Do you see any means of clearing the camps from those wretched women, without subjecting them to these examinations and healing them for the purpose of prostitution with soldiers?* That is a matter of police and the military discipline of camps, which I am not conversant with. I should think much stronger things than that are justified by military discipline.

As I have understood your evidence, from what I heard in cross-examination, I gather that you would attack this evil of prostitution rather in its cause than deal with its consequences? I would deal with the consequences by means of hospitals, and combat the disease after it has been contracted, only taking care not to do this in such a way as would seem to take the persons who have that disease under the special protection of the State in a degree in which others persons equally diseased were not taken.

If we have evidence before us that brothel-keepers are constantly communicated with by the police, and that beer-houses and public-houses are used as brothels in large numbers, and are well known to the local authorities, do not you think the State would be justified in interfering with that class of persons? Clearly it ought to be a forfeiture of the license of a public-house or beer-house to use it as a brothel.

But suppose it is not a beer-house, would you prosecute brothel-keepers? That is an extremely difficult question, and I would rather not give a positive opinion about it, because so many *pros* and *cons* have occurred to me when I have thought about it that I have found it very difficult to make up my mind.

ROBERT APPLEGARTH: *You conceive it to be the duty of the State to deal with girls and boys up to the age of 16; may I ask you whether you consider it to be the duty of the State to insist that children should be sent to school up to that age?* I cannot pretend to say exactly up to what age. I do think the State has a right, and is bound whenever circumstances admit, to insist on all children who are born into the community receiving education up to a certain point, and also to give facilities for educating them still higher.

And I suppose you consider that if the State did its duty in that respect, we should have in addition to better educated people, a higher standard of morality amongst the people? That is one of the greatest reasons for desiring it.

[*See p. 366 above.]

And therefore we should probably have less prostitution? I should think so.

Is it your opinion that sending children to work at a young age instead of to school leads to immoral practices, and ultimately prostitution? I should think it extremely probable from what I have heard and read. I have no knowledge on the subject.

In your opinion, if the laws in existence against seduction and bastardy and in other respects were strengthened and made of real practical use, would it have a tendency to diminish prostitution? I do not know whether it would have a tendency to reduce prostitution, but that is not the only thing to be considered, because it might have a tendency to increase other kinds of illicit intercourse. When the laws relating to bastardy made a greater attempt to enforce the obligation upon the seducer than is the case now, they did produce very demoralizing effects upon many women.[*] I do not mean to give an express opinion as to how far the law might properly go on that subject. At present my feeling is against any attempt, however much it may be agreeable to one's moral feelings, to restrain illicit intercourse in that way.

Whilst you are opposed to the Acts, I understand you are not opposed to an attempt being made by the State to diminish the amount of disease by providing hospitals? Yes, providing always it is not done with special favour to this class of diseases, but forms part of a general system, such a system as it may be thought advisable by the State to adopt, with a view of getting rid of serious and especially contagious diseases, as far as possible, throughout the community.

And would you advise that there should be provided special Lock Hospitals, or that people suffering from this disease should be treated in lock wards in general hospitals? I should prefer lock wards; because lock hospitals are a special provision for this particular class of disease, and that appears to me to be undesirable.

Do you think providing Lock Hospitals for the treatment of this disease would have a tendency to induce inquiries on the part of young children which parents would be ashamed to answer, and thus produce a bad moral effect? That might be one objection; but the grand objection I have to it is to any measure taken specially with reference to this class of disease. The general impression it would make, however contrary to the intention of those who support it, would be that the State patronises the class of practices by which these diseases are engendered, since it considers those who contract *q*these*q* diseases as worthy of more attention, and takes more pains to remedy the consequences, than those who have other diseases equally serious.

[*The former laws include 18 Elizabeth, c. 3 (1576), 6 George II, c. 31 (1733), and 49 George III, c. 68 (1809); laws in effect include 4 & 5 William IV, c. 76 (1834), Sects. 69-72, and 7 & 8 Victoria, c. 101 (1844).]

*q-q*71[1]   those [*transcriber's error?*]

Is it your opinion that these Acts have done any physical good at all? I have really no means of judging. I am not acquainted with the details. No doubt the evidence taken before this Commission will be expected to throw light on this subject.

Is it your opinion that morally they have done harm? I cannot tell whether they have actually done harm, but it seems to me their natural effect is to do harm.

You think that the tendency of them is to do moral injury? I do think so, because I hardly think it possible for thoughtless people not to infer, when special precautions are taken to make a course which is generally considered worthy of disapprobation safer than it would naturally be, that it cannot be considered very bad by the law, and possibly may be considered as either not bad at all, or at any rate a necessary evil.

APPENDICES

[79]

... be subservience to the will for a time, for the express purpose of raising the condition of women, I should come to you to know the means — The purpose would be to remove all interference with affection, or with any thing which is, or which even ought be supposed to be, demonstration of affection. In the present state of women's ... perfectly unstudied, and with whatever of timidity & dependance is natural to them increased a thousand fold by their habits of utter dependance it would probably be mischievous to remove at once all restraints, they would bring themselves prostitutes at a dearer cost than even at present — but without raising their natures at all, it seems to me, that only give women the desire to raise their social condition, and they have a power which in the present state of civilization of mind characters, might be made of ...

Folio 1r of "On Marriage" by Harriet Taylor

Appendix A

ON MARRIAGE (1832-33?)

by Harriet Taylor

Holograph MS, Mill-Taylor Collection, British Library of Political and Economic Science, London School of Economics. Untitled and unsigned, but in Taylor's hand. Dated on physical evidence. Not published. For a description of the MS, and comment on it, see xxx-xxxi and lviii-lix above.

IF I COULD BE PROVIDENCE to the world for a time, for the express purpose of raising the condition of women, I should come to you to know the *means*—the *purpose* would be to remove all interference with affection, or with any thing which is, or which even might be supposed to be, demonstrative of affection—In the present state of womens minds, perfectly uneducated, and with whatever of timidity and dependance is natural to them increased a thousand fold by their habits of utter dependance, it would probably be mischievous to remove at once all restraints, they would buy themselves protectors at a dearer cost than even at present—but without raising their natures at all, it seems to me, that once give women the desire to raise their social condition, and they have a power which in the present state of civilization and of mens characters, might be made of tremendous effect. Whether nature made a difference in the nature of men and women or not, it seems now that all men, with the exception of a few lofty minded, are sensualists more or less—Women on the contrary are quite exempt from this trait, however it may appear otherwise in the cases of some—It seems strange that it should be so, unless it was meant to be a source of power in demi-civilized states such as the present—or it may not be so—it may be only that the habits of freedom and low indulgence in which boys grow up and the contrary notion of what is called purity in girls may have produced the appearance of different natures in the two sexes—As certain it is that there is equality in nothing, now—all the pleasures such as there are being mens, and all the disagreables and pains being womens, as that every pleasure would be infinitely heightened both in kind and degree by the perfect equality of the sexes. Women are educated for one single object, to gain their living by marrying—(some poor souls get it without the churchgoing in the same way—they do not seem to me a bit worse than their honoured sisters)—To be married is the object of their existence and that object being gained they do really cease to exist as to anything worth calling life or any useful purpose. One observes very few marriages where there is any real sympathy or enjoyment of companionship between the parties—The woman knows what her power is, and gains by it what she has been taught to consider "proper" to her state—The woman who would gain power by such means is unfit for power, still they *do* use this power for paltry advantages and I am astonished it has never occurred to them to gain some large purpose: but their minds are degenerated by habits of dependance—I should think that 500 years hence none of the follies of their ancestors will so excite wonder and contempt as the fact of legislative restraint as to matters of feeling—or rather in the expressions of feeling. When once the law undertakes to say which demonstration of feeling shall be given to which, it seems quite inconsistent not to legislate for *all*, and say how many shall be seen, how many heard, and what kind and degree of feeling allows of shaking hands—The Turks is the only consistent mode—

I have no doubt that when the whole community is really educated, tho' the present laws of marriage were to continue they would be perfectly disregarded, because no one would marry—The widest and perhaps the quickest means to do away with its evils is to be found in promoting education—as it is the means of all good—but meanwhile it is hard that those who suffer most from its evils and who are always the best people, should be left without remedy. Would not the best plan be divorce which could be attained by *any, without any reason assigned*, and at small expence, but which could only be finally pronounced after a long period? not *less* time than two years should elapse between suing for divorce and permission to contract again—but what the decision will be *must* be certain at the moment of asking for it—*unless* during that time the suit should be withdrawn—

(I feel like a lawyer in talking of it only! O how absurd and little it all is!) In the present system of habits and opinions, girls enter into what is called a contract perfectly ignorant of the conditions of it, and that they should be so is considered absolutely essential to their fitness for it!—But after all the one argument of the matter which I think might be said so as to strike both high and low natures is—Who would wish to have the person without the inclination? Whoever would take the benefit of a law of divorce must be those whose inclination is to separate and who on earth would wish another to remain with them against their inclination? I should think no one—people sophisticate about the matter now and will not believe that one "*really would wish to go.*" Suppose instead of calling it a "law of divorce" it were to be called "Proof of affection"—They would like it better then—

At this present time, in this state of civilization, what evil would be caused by, first placing women on the most entire equality with men, as to all rights and privileges, civil and political, and then doing away with all laws whatever relating to marriage? Then if a woman had children she must take the charge of them, women would not then have children without considering how to maintain them. Women would have no more reason to barter person for bread, or for any thing else, than men have—public offices being open to them alike, all occupations would be divided between the sexes in their natural arrangement. Fathers would provide for their daughters in the same manner as for their sons—

All the difficulties about divorce seem to be in the consideration for the children—but on this plan it would be the women's *interest* not to have children—*now* it is thought to be the womans interest to have children as so many *ties* to the man who feeds her.

Sex in its true and finest meaning, seems to be the way in which is manifested all that is highest best and beautiful in the nature of human beings—none but poets have approached to the perception of the beauty of the material world—still less of the spiritual—and there never yet existed a poet, except by the inspiration of that feeling which is the perception of beauty in all forms and by all the means which are given us, as well as by *sight*. Are we not born with the *five* senses, merely as a foundation for others which we may make by them—and who extends and refines those material senses to the highest—into infinity—best fulfils the end of creation—That is only saying—*Who enjoys most, is most virtuous*—It is for *you*—the most worthy to be the apostle of all loftiest virtue—to teach, such as may be taught, that the higher the *kind* of enjoyment, the *greater* the *degree*—perhaps there is but one class to whom this *can* be *taught*—the poetic nature struggling with superstition: *you* are fitted to be the saviour of such—

Appendix B

PAPERS ON WOMEN'S RIGHTS (1847-50?)

by Harriet Taylor and J.S. Mill

Holograph MSS, Mill-Taylor Collection, British Library of Political and Economic Science, London School of Economics. The title of the first fragment is in Harriet Taylor's hand at the end; those of the second, third, and fourth fragments are in Mill's hand; that of the fifth has been supplied. The MSS are in Mill's hand (except for a few corrections in pencil by Taylor in the first and fourth, indicated in variant notes, and in repeated parts of the second); however, her title for the first, our knowledge of their working habits, and the apparent status of these fragments as preparatory for her "Enfranchisement of Women" suggest that they should be attributed jointly, if not solely to her. For descriptions of the MSS, and comment on them, see lxxii-lxxiv above.

1. Rights of Women—and Especially with Regard to the Elective Franchise—By a Woman— Dedicated to Queen Victoria

A GREAT NUMBER of progressive changes are constantly going forward in human affairs and ideas, which escape the notice of unreflecting people, because of their slowness. As each successive step requires a whole generation or several generations to effect it, and is then only one step, things in reality very changeable remain a sufficient length of time without perceptible progress, to be, by the majority of cotemporaries, mistaken for things permanent and immovable—and it is only by looking at a long series of generations that they are seen to be, in reality, always moving, and always in the same direction.

This is remarkably the case with respect to Privileges and Exclusions. In every generation, the bulk of mankind imagine that all privileges and all exclusions, then existing by law or usage, are natural, fit and proper, even necessary: *except* such as happen to be, just at that time, in the very crisis of the struggle which puts an end to them—which rarely happens to more than one set or class of them at a time. But

---

*a-a*unless indeed [*first cancelled by HTM*]

when we take all history into view we find that its whole course is a getting rid of privileges and exclusions. Anciently all was privilege and exclusion. There was not a person or class of persons who had not a line marked round them which they were in no case permitted to overstep. There was not a function or operation in society, sufficiently desirable to be thought worth guarding, which was not rigidly confined to a circumscribed class or body of persons. Some functions were confined to particular families—some to particular guilds, corporations, or societies. Whoever has any knowledge of ancient times knows that privilege and exclusion was not only the general rule in point of fact, but *b*that nothing else was in*b* accordance with the ideas of mankind. Whenever any action or occupation, private or public, was thought of, it seemed natural to everybody that there should be some persons who were allowed to do the action or follow the occupation, and others who were not. People never thought of inquiring why it should be so, or what there was in the nature of the particular case to require it. People seldom ask reasons for what is in accordance with the whole spirit of what they see round them, but only for what jars with that spirit. Even bodily freedom, the right to use one's own labour for one's own benefit, was once a privilege, and the great majority of mankind were excluded from it. This seems to the people of our day something monstrously unnatural: to people of former days it seemed the most natural of all things. It was very gradually that this was got rid of; through many intermediate stages, of serfage, villenage &c. Where this did not exist, the system of castes did: and that appears profoundly unnatural to us, but so profoundly natural to Hindoos that they have not yet given it up. Among the early Romans fathers had the power of putting their sons to death, or selling them into slavery: this seemed perfectly natural to them, most unnatural to us. To hold land, in property, was throughout feudal Europe the privilege of a noble. This was only gradually relaxed and in Germany there is still much land which can only be so held. Up to the Reformation to teach religion was the exclusive privilege of a male separate class, even to read the Bible was a privilege: Those who lived at the time of the Reformation and who adopted it, ceased to recognize this case of privilege and exclusion, but did not therefore call in question any others. Throughout the Continent political office and military rank were exclusive privileges of a hereditary noblesse, till the French revolution destroyed these privileges. Trades and occupations have almost everywhere ceased to be privileges. Thus exclusion after exclusion has disappeared, until privilege has ceased to be the general rule, and tends more and more to become the exception: it now no longer seems a matter of course that there should be an exclusion, but it is conceded that freedom and admissibility ought to prevail, wherever there is not some special reason for limiting them. Whoever considers how immense a change this is from primitive

---

b-b[*first read*] was in entire [*altered by JSM to*] was alone in [*which was cancelled, first by HTM, and replaced, first by HTM, by interlined final version*]

opinions and feelings, will think it nothing less than the very most important advance which has hitherto been made in human society. It is nothing less than the beginning of the reign of justice, or the first dawn of it at least. It is the introduction of the principle that distinctions, and inequalities of rights, are not good things in themselves, and that none ought to exist for which there is not a special justification, grounded on the greatest good of the whole community, privileged and excluded taken together.

Considering how slowly this change has taken place and how very recent is its date, it would be surprising if many exclusions did not still exist, by no means fitted to stand the test which until lately no one ever thought of applying to them. The fact that any particular exclusion exists, and has existed hitherto, is in such a case no presumption whatever that it ought to exist. We may rather surmise that it is probably a remaining relic of that past state of things, in which privilege and exclusion were the general rule. That the opinions of mankind have not yet put an end to it is not even a presumption that they ought not, or that they will not hereafter do so.

We propose to examine how far this may be the case with one of the principal remaining cases of privilege, the privilege of sex: and to consider whether the civil and political disabilities of women have any better foundation in justice or the interest of society than any of the other exclusions which have successively disappeared.[*]

In the first place it must be observed that the disabilities of women are exactly of the class which modern times most pride themselves on getting rid of—disabilities by birth. It is the boast of England that if some persons are privileged by birth, at least none are disqualified by it—that anybody may rise to be a peer, or a member of parliament, or a minister—that the path to distinction is not closed to the humblest. But it *is* closed irrevocably to women. A woman is born disqualified, and cannot by any exertion get rid of her disabilities. This makes her case an entirely peculiar one in modern Europe. It is like that of the negro in America, and worse than that of the roturier formerly in Europe, for *he* might receive or perhaps buy a patent of nobility. Women's disqualifications are the only indelible ones.

It is also a peculiarity in the case, that the persons disqualified are of the same race, the same blood, the same parents, as the privileged, and have even been brought up and educated along with them. There are none of the excuses grounded on their belonging to a different class in society. The excluded, have the same advantages of breeding and social culture, as the admitted, and have or might have the same educational advantages of all sorts.

[*The last paragraph, especially the last line, which concludes f. 2v, is crowded in (the final word is interlined below), as though to conclude, or else to avoid disturbing what was already written on 3r.]

It is necessary to protest first of all against a mode of thought on the subject of political exclusions which though less common than it once was is still very common, viz. that a prohibition, an exclusion, a disability, is not an evil or a grievance in itself. This is the opinion of many grave, dignified people, who think that by uttering it they are shewing themselves to be sound, sage, and rational, superior to nonsense and sentimentality. Where is the grievance, they say, of not being allowed to be an elector? What good would it do you to be an elector? Why should you wish to be one? They always require you to point out some distinct loss or suffering, some positive inconvenience which befals you from anything you complain of. This class of persons are enemies of all sorts of liberty. They say to those who complain, Have you not liberty enough? What do you want to do more than you do at present? And what is strange is, that they think this is shewing peculiar good sense and sobriety. It is a doctrine however which they are not fond of applying to their own liberties. Suppose that a law were made forbidding them ever to go beyond the British isles, and that when they complained they were answered thus: Is not Great Britain large enough for you? Are not England, Scotland and Ireland fine countries? Is there not variety enough in them for any reasonable taste? Why do you want to go to foreign countries? Your proper place is at home. Your duties are there. You have no duties to perform abroad: you are not a sailor, or a merchant, or an ambassador. Stay at home.—Would they not say—"My good friend, it is possible that I may never wish to go abroad at all; or that if I do wish, it may not be convenient: but that does not give you any right to say I *shall* not go abroad. It is an injustice and a hardship to be told that even if I do wish to go I shall not be permitted. I shall probably live all my life in this house, but that is a very different thing from being imprisoned in it."—What these people (who deem their notions wise because they are limited) think there is no harm in cutting off from the life of anybody, except themselves, is precisely what makes the chief value of life. They think you lose nothing as long as you are not prevented from having what you have and doing what you do: now the value of life does not consist in what you have or do, but in what you may have and may do. Freedom, power, and hope, are the charms of existence. If you are outwardly comfortable they think it nothing to cut off hope, to close the region of possibilities, to say that you shall have no carrière, no excitement, that neither chance nor your own exertions shall ever make you anything more or other than you now are. This is essentially the doctrine of people legislating for others. Nobody legislates in this way for himself. When it comes home to them personally all feel that it is precisely the *inconnu*, the indefinite, to be cut off from which would be unbearable. They know that it is not the thing they please to do, but the power of doing *as* they please, that makes to them the difference between contentment and dissatisfaction. Everybody, for himself, values his position just in proportion to the freedom of it: yet the same people think that freedom is the very thing which you may subtract from in the case of others, without doing them any wrong. The grievance they think is merely ideal: but they find in their own case that these ideal grievances are among the most real of any.[*]

"The proper sphere of women is domestic life." Putting aside the word "proper" which begs the question, what does this assertion mean? That no woman is qualified for any other social functions than those of domestic life? This will hardly be asserted, in opposition to the fact not only of the numerous women who have distinguished themselves as writers, but of the great number of eminent sovereigns who have been women—not only in Europe but in the East where they are shut up in zenanas. The assertion therefore can only be supposed to mean that a large proportion of mankind must devote themselves mainly to domestic management, the bringing up of children &c. and that this kind of employment is one particularly suitable for women. Now, taking this for what it is worth, is it in other cases thought necessary to dedicate a multitude of people from their birth to one exclusive employment lest there should not be people enough, or people qualified enough, to fill it? It is necessary that there should be coalheavers, paviours, ploughmen, sailors, shoemakers, clerks and so forth, but is it therefore necessary that people should be *born* all these things, and not permitted to quit those particular occupations? Still more, is it necessary that because people are clerks or shoemakers they should have no thoughts or opinions beyond clerking or shoemaking? for that is the implication involved in denying them votes.

The occupations of men, however engrossing they may be considered, are not supposed to make them either less interested in the good management of public affairs, or less entitled to exercise their share of influence in those affairs by their votes. It is not supposed that nobody ought to have a vote except idle people. A shoemaker, a carpenter, a farmer have votes. Those who say that a scavenger or a coalheaver should *not* have a vote, do not say so on account of his occupation but on account of his poverty or want of education. Let this ground of exclusion be admitted for one sex just as far as for the other. Whatever class of men are allowed the franchise, let the same class of women have it.

If a woman's habitual employment, whether chosen *for* or *by* her, is the management of a family, she will be no more withdrawn from that occupation by voting in an election than her neighbour will be withdrawn by it from his shop or his office.[†]

The feeling, however, which expresses itself in such phrases as "The proper sphere of women is private life," "Women have nothing to do with politics" and the like, is, I believe, not so much any feeling regarding women as women, as a feeling against any new and unexpected claimants of political rights. In England especially there is always a grudging feeling towards all persons who unexpectedly

[*The text here stops about nine lines above the bottom of f. 4v.]
[†The text here stops about two lines above the bottom of f. 5v.]

profess an opinion in politics, or indeed in any matter not concerning their own speciality. There is always a disposition to say, What business is that of yours? When people hear that their tradespeople, or their workpeople, concern themselves about politics, there is almost always a feeling of dislike accompanying the remark. It seems as if people were vexed at finding more persons than they expected in a condition to give them trouble on that subject. Men have the same feeling about their sons unless the sons are mere echoes of their own opinions: and if their wives and daughters claimed the same privilege, their feeling would be that of having an additional disagreeable from a quarter they did not expect.

The truth is, everybody feels that whether in classes or individuals, having an opinion of their own makes them more troublesome and difficult to manage: and everybody is aware, in all cases but his own, that the intrinsic value of the opinion is very seldom much of an equivalent. But this is no more than the ministers of despotic monarchs feel with regard to popular opinion altogether. It is an exact picture of the state of mind of Metternich. It is much more consistent in *him*. He says, or would say, Leave politics to those whose business it is. But these other people say, No: some whose business it is not peculiarly may and ought to have opinions on it, but others, workpeople for instance, and women, ought not. Constitutionalists and Liberals are right against Metternich only on grounds which prove them to be wrong against those whom they would exclude. Metternich is wrong because if none but those who make politics their business, had opinions and could give votes, all the rest would be delivered blindfold into the hands of those professional politicians. This argument is good against excluding anybody, especially any class or kind of persons. It is a very great evil that any portion of the community should be left politically defenceless. To justify it in any case it must be shewn that still greater evils would arise from arming the class with opinions and votes. It may possibly admit of being maintained that this *would* be the result of giving votes to very ignorant or even in some cases to very poor people. But it is impossible to shew that any evils would arise from admitting women of the same social rank as the men who have votes.

Objection. "You would have perpetual domestic discussion." If people cannot differ in opinion on any important matter and remain capable of living together without quarrelling, there cannot be a more complete condemnation of marriage: for if so, two people cannot live together at all unless one of them is a mere cipher, abdicating all will and opinion into the hands of the other, and marriage can only be fit for tyrants and nobodies.

But the proposition is false. Do not married people live together in perfect harmony although they differ in opinions and even feelings on things which come much nearer home than politics do to most people? Does it not often happen for instance that they hold different opinions in religion? And have they not continually different opinions or wishes on innumerable private matters without quarrelling? People with whose comfort it is incompatible that the person they live with should think differently from them in politics or religion will if they marry at all generally marry a person who has either no opinions or the same sort of opinions with themselves. Besides, by discouraging political opinions in women, you only prevent independent disinterested opinions. In a woman, to have no political opinions, practically means to have the political opinions which conduce to the pecuniary interest or social vanity of the family. If honest opinions on both sides would make dissension between married people, will there not be dissension between a man who has an opinion and a conscience in politics and a woman who sees what she thinks the interests of the family sacrificed to what seems to her a matter of indifference? except indeed that the man's public spirit is seldom strong enough to hold out long against the woman's opposition, especially if he really cares for her. Now when women and men really live together, and are each other's most intimate associates, (which in the ancient republics they were not) men never can or will be patriotic or public spirited unless women are so too. People cannot long maintain a higher tone of feeling than that of their favourite society. The wife is the incarnate spirit of family selfishness unless she has accustomed herself to cultivate feelings of a larger and more generous kind: while, when she has, her (in general) greater susceptibility of emotion and more delicate conscience makes her the great inspirer of those nobler feelings in the men with whom she habitually associates.

A part of the feeling which makes many men *dislike* the idea of political women, is, I think, the idea that politics altogether are a necessary evil, a source of quarrelsome and unamiable feelings, and that their sphere of action should be restricted as much as possible, and especially that home, and social intercourse, should be kept free from them, and be retained as much as possible under influences counteractive of those of politics. One would imagine from this manner of looking at the subject, that the danger in modern times was that of too much political earnestness: that people generally felt so strongly about politics as to require a strong curb to prevent them from quarrelling about it when they meet. The fact however we know to be that people in general are quite lukewarm about politics, except where their personal interests or the social position of their class are at stake, and when that is the case women have already as strong political feelings as men have. And this wish to keep the greater interests of mankind from being thought of and dwelt on when people are brought together in private, does not really prevent ill feeling and ill blood in society, but only causes it to exist about things not worth it. Where is the benefit of hindering people from disliking each other on matters involving the liberty or the progress of mankind, only to make them hate each other from petty personal jealousies and piques? Active minds and susceptible feelings will and must interest themselves about something, and if you deny them all subjects of interest except personal ones, you reduce the personal interests to a petty scale, and make personal or social vanities the primum mobile of life: now personal rivalities are a much more fruitful source of hatred and malice than differences of political opinion.

How vain the idea that the way to make mankind amiable is to make them care for nothing except themselves and the individuals immediately surrounding them. Does not all experience shew that when people care only for themselves and their families, then unless they are held down by despotism, every one's hand is against every one, and that only so far as they care about the public or about some abstract principle is there a basis for real social feeling of any sort? One reason why there is scarcely any social feeling in England, but every man, entrenched within his family, feels a kind of dislike and repugnance to every other, is because there is hardly any concern in England for great ideas and the larger interests of humanity. The moment you kindle any such concern, if it be only about negroes or prisoners in gaols, you not only elevate but soften individual character; because each begins to move in an element of sympathy, having a common ground, even if a narrow one, to sympathize on. And yet you would prevent the sympathetic influence of women from exercising itself on the great interests. Observe, by the way, that almost all the popular movements towards any object of social improvement which have been successful in this country, have been those in which women have taken an active part, and have fraternized thoroughly with the men who were engaged about them: Slavery abolition, establishment of schools, improvement of prisons. In the last we know that a woman[*] was one of the principal leaders, and in all three the victory was chiefly due to the Quakers among whom women are in all points of public exertion as active as men. Probably none of these things would have been effected if women had not taken so strong an interest in them—if the men engaged had not found a constant stimulus in the feelings of the women connected with them, and a necessity for excusing themselves in the eyes of the women in every case of failure or shortcoming. And will any one say that the harmony of domestic life or of social intercourse was rendered less because women took interest in these subjects? It will be said, they were questions peculiarly concerning the sympathies and therefore suitable to women. But they were also subjects which concerned people's self interest and were therefore sources of antipathy as well as sympathy: and there have been few subjects on which there has been more party spirit and more vehement opposition of political feeling, than on West India slavery and on the Bell and Lancaster schools.[†]

"What is the use of giving women votes?" Before answering this question it may be well to put another: What is the use of votes at all? Whatever use there is in any case, there is in the case of women. Are votes given to protect the particular interests of the voters? Then women need votes, for the state of the law as to their

[*Elizabeth Fry.]

[†Similar, but competing, systems, founded by Andrew Bell and Joseph Lancaster. The text here stops about seven lines above the bottom of f. 9v.]

property, their rights with regard to children, their right to their own person, together with the extreme maladministration of the courts of justice in cases of even the most atrocious violence when practised by men to their wives, contributes a mass of grievances greater than exists in the case of any other class or body of persons. Are votes given as a means of fostering the intelligence of the voters, and enlarging their feelings by directing them to a wider class of interests? This would be as beneficial to women as to men. Are votes given as a means of exalting the voters in social position and estimation? and to avoid making an offensive distinction to their disadvantage? This reason is strong in the case of women. And this reason would suffice in the absence of any other. Women should have votes because otherwise they are not the equals but the inferiors of men.

So clear is this, that any one who maintains that it is right in itself to exclude women from votes, can only do it for the express purpose of stamping on them the character of inferiors.

* * * * *

2. Women—(Rights of)

THE RIGHTS OF WOMEN are no other than the rights of human beings. The phrase has come into use, and become necessary, only because law and opinion, having been made chiefly by men, have refused to recognize in women the universal claims of humanity. When opinion on this subject shall be further advanced towards rectification, neither "rights of women" nor even "equality of women" will be terms in use, because neither of them fully expresses the real object to be aimed at, viz. the negation of all distinctions among persons, grounded on the accidental circumstance of sex.

The present legal and moral subjection of women is the principal, and likely to be the latest remaining relic of the primitive condition of society, the tyranny of physical force. Society sets out from the state of lawlessness in which every one's hand is against every one, and each robs and slays a weaker than himself when he has any object to gain by it: the next stage is that in which the races and tribes which are vanquished in war are made slaves, the absolute property of their conquerors: this by degrees changes into serfdom, or some other limited form of dependence, and in the course of ages mankind pass through various decreasing stages of subjection on one side and privilege on the other, up to complete democracy which the advanced guard of the human species are now just reaching: so that the only arbitrary distinction among human beings, which the one or two most advanced nations do not now, at least in principle, repudiate, is that between women and men. And even this distinction, although still essentially founded on despotism, has assumed a more mitigated form with each step in the general improvement of mankind, whether we compare age with age, people with people or class with class: which was also the case with all the other social tyrannies, in their progress towards extinction.

It deserves particular remark, that at every period in this gradual progress, the prevailing morality of the time (with or without the exception of a few individuals superior to their age) invariably consecrated all existing facts. It assumed every existing unjust power or privilege as right and proper, contenting itself with inculcating a mild and forbearing exercise of them: by which inculcation no doubt it did considerable good, but which it never failed to balance by enjoining on the sufferers an unresisting and uncomplaining submission to the power itself. Morality recommended kind treatment of slaves by their masters, and just rule by despots over their subjects, but it never justified or tolerated either slaves or subjects in throwing off the yoke, and wherever they have done so it has been by a plain violation of the then established morality. It is needless to point out how exactly the parallel holds in the case of women and men.

In the position of women as society has now made it, there are two distinct peculiarities. The first is, the domestic subjection of the larger portion of them. From this, unmarried women who are either in independent or in self-dependent pecuniary circumstances are exempt; so that by the admission of society itself, there is no inherent necessity for it; and the time cannot be far off when to hold any human being, who has past the age which requires to be taken care of and educated by others, in a state of compulsory obedience to any other human being (except as the mere organ and minister of the law) will be acknowledged to be as monstrous an infraction of the rights and dignity of humanity, as slavery is at last, though tardily, among a small, comparatively advanced part of the human race, felt to be. Practically the evil varies, in the case of women, (as it did in the case of slaves) from being slowly murdered by continued bodily torture, to being only subdued in spirit and thwarted of all those higher and finer developements of individual character of which personal liberty has in all ages been felt to be the indispensable condition.

The other point of the question relates to the numberless disabilities imposed on women by law or by custom equivalent to law; their exclusion from most public and from a great number of private occupations, and the direction of all the forces of society towards educating them for, and confining them to, a small number of functions, on the plea that these are the most conformable to their nature and powers. It is impossible here to enter, with any detail, into this part of the subject. Three propositions however may be laid down as certain. First; that the alleged superior adaptation of women to certain occupations, and of men to certain others, does not, even now, exist, to anything like the extent that is pretended. Secondly; that so far as it does exist, a rational analysis of human character and circumstances tends more and more to shew, that the difference is principally if not wholly the effect of differences in education and in social circumstances, or of physical characteristics by no means peculiar to one or the other sex. Lastly; even if the alleged differences of aptitude did exist, it would be a reason why women and men would generally occupy themselves differently but no reason why they should be forced to do so. It is one of the aberrations of early and rude legislation to attempt to convert every supposed natural fitness into an imperative obligation. There was an apparent natural reason why the children should follow the occupation of their parents; they were often familiar with it from childhood, and had always peculiar facilities for being instructed in it: but this natural fitness, converted into a law, became the oppressive and enslaving system of Castes. Good laws, laws which pay any due regard to human liberty, will not class human beings according to mere general presumptions, nor require them to do one thing and to abstain from another on account of any supposed suitableness to their natural or acquired gifts, but will leave them to class *themselves* under the natural influence of those and of all the other peculiarities of their situation, which if left free they will not fail to do quite as well, not to say much better, than any inflexible laws made for them by pedantic legislators or conceited soi-disant philosophers are ever likely to do.

* * * * *

3. The Rights of Women to the Elective Franchise and Its Advantages

STATEMENT OF THE PRINCIPLE—perfect equality.

Although this requires no proof, necessary to consider the subject as usually treated and reply categorically to objections either to it as a principle or as a matter of practice.

Prevailing opinion is that some change is needed but not fundamental, only of degree—above all that the change shall not alter the principle of inequality, foundation of present condition.

Present state of opinion *divided into* the following:

Largest class, both men and women, composed of those who take things for granted because they are so and have always been so—have a natural fear of making any alteration in the relations on which they are accustomed to think the best things in life depend. We would prove to them that tho' the best things in life *did* depend on those relations as they are, the relation under its present conditions is worn out and no longer affords to either party a life either well or sufficiently filled for the spirit of the present time which requires more developement of the spiritual and less of the physical instead of the contrary. True, education is the great want of the time, but people have scarce begun to perceive in what *sense* of education—

that which modern developement requires should be the desire, power and habit of using the person's own mind, instead of (as almost all educationists seem to think) *filling* the mind with an undigested mass from the minds of others, in consequence of which process the most educated people now are among the most ignorant— witness not only the (absurdly) called educated *classes* but preeminently the collegiate, legal, clerical, professional men. Placeman, clergyman, barrister, doctor, has each something to say on one subject—in the majority of cases this something is what he has heard from others and therefore comes from him deadborn—if an active minded person, he is found to talk interestingly on his one subject, but let conversation be anything worthy the name of general, and the profound ignorance and inactivity of intellect presented by the educated classes in England is the only thing capable of exciting the mind in intercourse with them.

After all the objections that are made both by men and women have been considered, one may perhaps put it down as a fact that they are all based on the supposition that conceding equal political rights to women would be contrary to the interests of men. Some think it would be contrary to their *real* interests, some to their *selfish* interests. We think they would be not only in accordance with, but greatly advantageous to, the interests of men with perhaps the exception of interests if such they can be called, as no man in the present day would venture to &c. It would probably put a stop to the sort of license of indulgence which everybody is now agreed in discountenancing.—

A great part of the feeling which resists the political equality of women is a feeling of the contrast it would make with their domestic servitude.

The evils of women's present condition all lie in the necessity of dependence: the just cause of complaint lies here and not elsewhere.

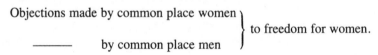

Objections made by common place women ⎫
⎬ to freedom for women.
———— by common place men ⎭

Historical parallel between men and women sovereigns.

The expression "Rights of Women," it is the fashion among women and among a certain vulgar class of men to affect to receive with a sneer and to endeavour to drown with ridicule. In neither case does this appear to be because they really regard it as meaningless, for if the same people are asked why they receive it so, they invariably grow angry and this mode of reception perpetuates itself because the intense constitutional shyness of Englishmen makes them of all things fear ridicule and this phrase as well as the idea it includes has always hitherto been put down by ridicule. Commonplace women's aversion to it has more meaning—it contains the everlasting dread of the givers of the loaves and fishes[*]—their lively

[*See Luke, 9:11-15.]

imagination exaggerates the disagreeables of having to work instead of being worked for, which their education having precluded all notions of public spirit or personal dignity, far from being revolted at the idea of dependence, elevates submission into a virtue *per se*. They enormously exaggerate both the talent and the labour required for the external details of life, unaware that they give as much labour and fritter away as much talent in executing badly those domestic details which they enlarge upon as arguments against women's emancipation, as would be sufficient to conduct both the public and private affairs of either an individual or a family. Is it not true that half the time of half the women in existence is passed in worthless and trashy work, of no benefit to any human being?

Objection. Well bred people never exercise the power which the law gives them. But all their conduct takes the bent which has been given to the two characters by the relation which the law establishes. The woman's whole talent goes into the inducing, persuading, coaxing, caressing, in reality the seducing, capacity. In whatever class in life, the woman gains her object by seducing the man. This makes her character quite unconsciously to herself, petty and paltry.

* * * * *

4. Why Women Are Entitled to the Suffrage

1st. Because it is just.

2nd. Because women have many serious practical grievances from the state of the law as it regards them.

3rd. Because the general condition of women, being one of dependence, is in itself a grievance, which their exclusion from the suffrage stamps and perpetuates.

4th. Reply to objections.

The exclusion of women from the suffrage becomes a greater offence and degradation in proportion as the suffrage is opened widely to all men. When the only privileged class is the aristocracy of sex the slavery of the excluded sex is more marked and complete.

Notion that giving the suffrage does no good; a shallow fallacy. The greatest good that can be done for women and the preparation of all others is to recognize them as citizens—as substantive members of the community instead of mere *things* belonging to members of the community. One of the narrownesses of modern times, in England, is that the indirect effects produced by the *spirit* of institutions are not recognized and therefore the immense influence on the whole life of a person produced by the fact of *citizenship* is not at all felt.

Even according to the most moderate reformers the suffrage should include clerks and other educated persons who are dependent on employers. These are not turned out of their employments for voting against their employers, only because there is a point of honour on the subject. There ought to be the same between married people.—

To suppose that one person's freedom of opinion must merge in that of the other and that they could not vote differently at an election without quarrelling is a satire on marriage and a reductio ad absurdum of it. All persons, men and women, in the present age, are entitled to mental independence and marriage like other institutions must reconcile itself to this necessity.

The queen professes to live and act perfectly conscientiously: does she ask her husband's opinion and submit to it in all her acts as queen? is not this a case of married persons exercising their separate freedom of opinion and conduct?

The principle that all who are taxed should be represented, would give votes not only to single women but to married women whose property is settled.

Women should either not be allowed to have property or should have all which follows from the possession of property.

The man acquires the points of character that belong to one who is always having homage paid to the power vested in him; self-important, domineering, with more or less politeness of form according to his breeding; and more or less suavity according to his temper—the difference in the case of a well bred man being mainly this, that as he does not need to assert what never is disputed, so he does not do so, but contents himself with accepting the position which the law assigns and which the woman yields to him: it being a main point in the ways of well bred people that all occasions of bringing wills into active collision, are avoided, sometimes by a tacit compromise in which however the chief part always remains with the strongest, sometimes because that which knows itself to be the weakest makes a graceful retreat in time. In this as in other relations, good breeding does not so much affect the substance of conduct as the manner *of it*. When the man is ill bred the manner is coarse, tyrannical, brutal, either in a greater or in a less degree; there is superfluous self assertion, and of an offensive kind: well bred people's self assertion is only tacit, until their claims are in some way resisted, but they are not therefore less tenacious of all that *the law* gives them, and are often not less really inflated by self-worship caused by the *worship* they receive from dependents of every description.

* * * * *

a-a[*marked for deletion in pencil by HTM*]
b-b[*altered in pencil by HTM to*] law or custom
c-c[*altered in pencil by HTM to*] deference

5. [Reform: Ends and Means]

Political

No hereditary privileges whatever.

No exclusion from the suffrage, but an educational qualification (qu. what?).

Complete freedom of speech, printing, public meetings and associations, locomotion, and industry in all its branches.

No church establishment or paid clergy; but national schools and colleges without religion.

Social

All occupations to be alike open to men and women; and all kinds and departments of instruction.

Marriage to be like any other partnership, dissoluble at pleasure, and not merging any of the individual rights of either of the parties to the contract. All the interests arising out of marriage to be provided for by special agreement.

The property of intestates to belong to the state, which then undertakes the education, and setting out in life, of all descendants not otherwise provided for.

No one to acquire by gift or bequest more than a limited amount.

Appendix C

ENFRANCHISEMENT OF WOMEN (1851)

by Harriet Taylor Mill

Westminster and Foreign Quarterly Review, LV (July, 1851), 289-311. Headed, "Art. I.—*The New York Tribune for Europe*. October 29th, 1850"; running titles, "Enfranchisement of Women"; unsigned. Offprinted with title, repaged 1-23, and identified as "Reprinted from the 'Westminster and Foreign Quarterly Review,' for July, 1851," with the printer's identification ("London: Waterlow and Sons, Printers, 65 to 66, London Wall, London") added at the end, but otherwise identical. Reprinted in *Dissertations and Discussions*, II, 411-49, where the title is footnoted, "*Westminster Review*, July 1851." Issued as a pamphlet, London: Trübner, 1868, where the title page reads, "*Enfranchisement of Women* by Mrs. Stuart Mill / Reprinted from the 'Westminster Review' for July, 1851. / London / Trübner and Co., 60, Paternoster Row. / 1868. / Price One Penny"; paged 1-22; title repeated on 1; no running heads. Not listed in Mill's bibliography of his writings, where various items are identified as "joint productions" with Harriet Taylor Mill. There are no corrections or emendations in the copies of the offprint and pamphlet in the Somerville College Library. For comment on the essay, see xxxi-xxxii and lxxiv-lxxvii above.

The text below is that of the *Westminster*, the last in Harriet Taylor Mill's lifetime (she died in 1858, before the 1st ed. of *D&D*), which has been collated with the offprint, the 1st and 2nd eds. of *D&D*, and the pamphlet. In the footnoted variants, "59" indicates *D&D*, 1st ed.; "67", *D&D*, 2nd ed.; and "68", the pamphlet.

Though the copy-text is that of 1851, the text below is headed by the introductory note written by Mill for the version in *D&D*; it is separated from the main text by a row of asterisks.

ALL THE MORE RECENT of these papers[*] were joint productions of myself and of one[†] whose loss, even in a merely intellectual point of view, can never be repaired or alleviated. But the following Essay is hers in a peculiar sense, my share in it being little more than that of an editor and amanuensis. Its authorship having been known at the time, and publicly attributed to her, it is proper to state, that she never regarded it as a complete discussion of the subject which it treats of: and, highly as

[*I.e., of those in *Dissertations and Discussions*, 2 vols. (London: Parker, 1859).]
[†Harriet Taylor Mill, his wife, who died in 1858.]

I estimate it, I would rather it remained unacknowledged, than that it should be read with the idea that even the faintest image can be found in it of a mind and heart which in their union of the rarest, and what are deemed the most conflicting *excellences*, were unparalleled in any human being that I have known or read of. While she was the light, life, and grace of every society in which she took part, the foundation of her character was a deep seriousness, resulting from the combination of the strongest and most sensitive feelings with the highest principles. All that excites admiration when found separately in others, seemed brought together in her: a conscience at once healthy and tender; a generosity, bounded only by a sense of justice which often forgot its own claims, but never those of others; a heart so large and loving, that whoever was capable of making the smallest return of sympathy, always received tenfold; and in the intellectual department, a vigour and truth of imagination, a delicacy of perception, an accuracy and nicety of observation, only equalled by her profundity of speculative thought, and by a practical judgment and discernment next to infallible. So elevated was the general level of her faculties, that the highest poetry, philosophy, oratory, or art, seemed trivial by the side of her, and equal only to expressing some small part of her mind. And there is no one of those modes of manifestation in which she could not easily have taken the highest rank, had not her inclination led her for the most part to content herself with being the inspirer, prompter, and unavowed coadjutor of others.

The present paper was written to promote a cause which she had deeply at heart, and though appealing only to the severest reason, was meant for the general reader. The question, in her opinion, was in a stage in which no treatment but the most calmly argumentative could be useful, while many of the strongest arguments were necessarily omitted, as being unsuited for popular effect. Had she lived to write out all her thoughts on this great question, she would have produced something as far transcending in profundity the present Essay, as, had she not placed a rigid restraint on her feelings, she would have excelled it in fervid eloquence. Yet nothing which even she could have written on any single subject, would have given an adequate idea of the depth and compass of her mind. As during life she continually detected, before any one else had seemed to perceive them, those changes of times and circumstances which ten or twelve years later became subjects of general remark, so I venture to prophecy that if mankind continue to improve, their spiritual history for ages to come will be the progressive working out of her thoughts, and realization of her conceptions.

* * * * *

MOST OF OUR READERS will probably learn from these pages for the first time, that there has arisen in the United States, and in the most civilized and enlightened

---

*a-a*59   excellencies

portion of them, an organised agitation on a new question—new, not to thinkers, nor to any one by whom the principles of free and popular government are felt as well as acknowledged, but new, and even unheard of, as a subject for public meetings and practical political action. This question is, the enfranchisement of women; their admission, in law and in fact, to equality in all rights, political, civil, and social, with the male citizens of the community.

It will add to the surprise with which many will receive this intelligence, that the agitation which has commenced is not a pleading by male writers and orators *for* women, those who are professedly to be benefitted remaining either indifferent or ostensibly *b*hostile: it*b* is a political movement, practical in its objects, carried on in a form which denotes an intention to persevere. And it is a movement not merely *for* women, but *by* them. Its first public manifestation appears to have been a Convention of Women, held in the State of Ohio, in the spring of 1850. Of this meeting we have seen no report. On the 23rd and 24th of October last, a succession of public meetings was held at Worcester, in Massachusetts, under the name of a "Women's Rights Convention," of which the president was a woman,[*] and nearly all the chief speakers women; numerously reinforced, however, by men, among whom were some of the most distinguished leaders in the kindred cause of negro emancipation. A general and four special committees were nominated, for the purpose of carrying on the undertaking until the next annual meeting.

According to the report in the New York *Tribune*, above a thousand persons were present throughout, and "if a larger place could have been had, many thousands more would have attended." The place was described as "crowded from the beginning with attentive and interested listeners."[†] In regard to the quality of the speaking, the proceedings bear an advantageous comparison with those of any popular movement with which we are acquainted, either in this country or in America. Very rarely in the oratory of public meetings is the part of verbiage and declamation so small, that of calm good sense and reason so considerable. The result of the Convention was in every respect encouraging to those by whom it was summoned: and it is probably destined to inaugurate one of the most important of the movements towards political and social reform, which are the best characteristic of the present age.

That the promoters of this new agitation take their stand on principles, and do not fear to declare these in their widest extent, without time-serving or compromise, will be seen from the resolutions adopted by the Convention, part of which we transcribe:

Resolved—That every human being, of full age, and resident for a proper length of time on the soil of the nation, who is required to obey the law, is entitled to a voice in its

[*Paulina Kellogg Wright Davis.]
[†Jacob Gilbert Forman, "Women's Rights Convention at Worcester, Mass.," *New York Daily Tribune*, 26 Oct., 1850, p. 6.]

*b-b*59,67 hostile. It

enactment; that every such person, whose property or labour is taxed for the support of the government, is entitled to a direct share in such government; therefore,

Resolved—That women are entitled to the right of suffrage, and to be considered eligible to office, . . . and that every party which claims to represent the humanity, the civilization, and the progress of the age, is bound to inscribe on its banners, equality before the law, without distinction of sex or colour.

Resolved—That civil and political rights acknowledge no sex, and therefore the word "male" should be struck from every State Constitution.[*]

Resolved—That, since the prospect of honourable and useful employment in after life is the best stimulus to the use of educational advantages, and since the best education is that we give ourselves, in the struggles, employments, and discipline of life; therefore it is impossible that women should make full use of the instruction already accorded to them, or that their career should do justice to their faculties, until the avenues to the various civil and professional employments are thrown open to them.

Resolved—That every effort to educate women, without according to them their rights, and arousing their conscience by the weight of their responsibilities, is futile, and a waste of labour.

Resolved—That the laws of property, as affecting married persons, demand a thorough revisal, so that all rights be equal between them; that the wife have, during life, an equal control over the property gained by their mutual toil and sacrifices, and be heir to her husband precisely to that extent that he is heir to her, and entitled at her death to dispose by will of the same share of the joint property as he is.[†]

The following is a brief summary of the principal demands:

1. *Education* in primary and high schools, universities, medical, legal, and theological institutions.
2. *Partnership* in the labours and gains, risks and remunerations, of productive industry.
3. *A coequal share* in the formation and administration of laws—municipal, state, and national—through legislative assemblies, courts, and executive offices.[‡]

It would be difficult to put so much true, just, and reasonable meaning into a style so little calculated to recommend it as ᶜthatᶜ of some of the resolutions. But whatever objection may be made to some of the expressions, none, in our opinion, can be made to the demands themselves. As a question of justice, the case seems to us too clear for dispute. As one of expediency, the more thoroughly it is examined the stronger it will appear.

That women have as good a claim as men have, in point of personal right, to the suffrage, or to a place in the jury-box, it would be difficult for anyone to deny. It cannot certainly be denied by the United States of America, as a people or as a community. Their democratic institutions rest avowedly on the inherent right of everyone to a voice in the government. Their Declaration of Independence, framed by the men who are still their great constitutional authorities—that document

---

[*Ibid., 25 Oct., 1850, p. 6.]
[†Ibid., 26 Oct., 1850, p. 6.]
[‡Ibid.]

ᶜ⁻ᶜ68   the style

which has been from the first, and is now, the acknowledged basis of their polity, commences with this express statement:

We hold these truths to be self-evident: that all men are created equal; that they are endowed by their Creator with certain inalienable rights; that among these are life, liberty, and the pursuit of happiness; that to secure these rights, governments are instituted among men, deriving their just powers from the consent of the governed.[*]

We do not imagine that any American democrat will evade the force of these expressions by the dishonest or ignorant subterfuge, that "men," in this memorable document, does not stand for human beings, but for one sex only; that "life, liberty, and the pursuit of happiness" are "inalienable rights" of only one moiety of the human species; and that "the governed," whose consent is affirmed to be the only source of just power, are meant for that half of mankind only, who, in relation to the other, have hitherto assumed the character of *dgovernorsd*. The contradiction between principle and practice cannot be explained away. A like dereliction of the fundamental maxims of their political creed has been committed by the Americans in the flagrant instance of the negroes; of this they are learning to recognise the turpitude. After a struggle which, by many of its incidents, deserves the name of heroic, the abolitionists are now so strong in numbers and in influence that they hold the balance of parties in the United States. It was fitting that the men whose names will remain associated with the extirpation, from the democratic soil of America, of the aristocracy of colour, should be among the originators, for America and for the rest of the world, of the first collective protest against the aristocracy of sex; a distinction as accidental as that of colour, and fully as irrelevant to all questions of government.

Not only to the democracy of America, the claim of women to civil and political equality makes an irresistible appeal, but also to those radicals and chartists in the British islands, and democrats on the Continent, who claim what is called universal suffrage as an inherent right, unjustly and oppressively withheld from them. For with what truth or rationality could the suffrage be termed universal, while half the human species *eremaine* excluded from it? To declare that a voice in the government is the right of all, and demand it only for a part—the part, namely, to which the claimant himself belongs—is to renounce even the appearance of principle. The chartist who denies the suffrage to women, is a chartist only because he is not a lord;[†] he is one of those levellers who would level only down to themselves.

[*A *Declaration by the Representatives of the United States of America, in General Congress Assembled* (Philadelphia: Dunlap, 1776).]

[†For another version of this charge, see Edward Barrington de Fonblanque, *The Life and Labours of Albany Fonblanque* (London: Bentley, 1874), p. 6, and Mill, *Essays on England, Ireland, and the Empire, CW*, Vol. VI (Toronto: University of Toronto Press, 1982), p. 353n.]

d-d67   governors
e-e67   remained

Even those who do not look upon a voice in the government as a matter of personal right, nor profess principles which require that it should be extended to all, have usually traditional maxims of political justice with which it is impossible to reconcile the exclusion of all women from the common rights of citizenship. It is an axiom of English freedom that taxation and representation should be co-extensive. Even under the laws which give the wife's property to the husband, there are many unmarried women who pay taxes. It is one of the fundamental doctrines of the British constitution, that all persons should be tried by their peers: yet women, whenever tried, are tried by male judges and a male jury. To foreigners the law accords the privilege of claiming that half the jury should be composed of themselves; not so to women. Apart from maxims of detail, which represent local and national rather than universal ideas; it is an acknowledged dictate of justice to make no degrading distinctions without necessity. In all things the presumption ought to be on the side of equality. A reason must be given why anything should be permitted to one person and interdicted to another. But when that which is interdicted includes nearly everything which those to whom it is permitted most prize, and to be deprived of which they feel to be most insulting; when not only political liberty but personal freedom of action is the prerogative of a caste; when even in the exercise of industry, almost all employments which task the higher faculties in an important field, which lead to distinction, riches, or even pecuniary independence, are fenced round as the exclusive domain of the predominant section, scarcely any doors being left open to the dependent class, except such as all who can enter elsewhere disdainfully pass by; the miserable expediencies which are advanced as excuses for so grossly partial a dispensation, would not be sufficient, even if they were real, to render it other than a flagrant injustice. While, far from being expedient, we are firmly convinced that the division of mankind into two castes, one born to rule over the other, is in this case, as in all cases, an unqualified mischief; a source of perversion and demoralization, both to the favoured class and to those at whose expense they are favoured; producing none of the good which it is the custom to ascribe to it, and forming a bar, almost insuperable while it lasts, to any really vital improvement, either in the character or in the social condition of the human race.

These propositions it is now our purpose to maintain. But before entering on them, we would endeavour to dispel the preliminary objections which, in the minds of persons to whom the subject is new, are apt to prevent a real and conscientious examination of it. The chief of these obstacles is that most formidable one, custom. Women never have had equal rights with men. The claim in their behalf, of the common rights of mankind, is looked upon as barred by universal practice. This strongest of prejudices, the prejudice against what is new and unknown, has, indeed, in an age of changes like the present, lost much of its force; if it had not, there would be little hope of prevailing against it. Over three-fourths of the habitable world, even at this day, the answer, "it has always been so," closes all discussion. But it is the boast of modern Europeans, and of their American kindred, that they know and do many things which their forefathers neither knew nor did; and it is perhaps the most unquestionable point of superiority in the present above former ages, that habit is not now the tyrant it formerly was over opinions and modes of action, and that the worship of custom is a declining idolatry. An uncustomary thought, on a subject which touches the greater interests of life, still startles when first presented; but if it can be kept before the mind until the impression of strangeness wears off, it obtains a hearing, and as rational a consideration as the intellect of the hearer is accustomed to bestow on any other subject.

In the present case, the prejudice of custom is doubtless on the unjust side. Great thinkers, indeed, at different times, from Plato to Condorcet,[*] besides some of the most eminent names of the present age, have made emphatic protests in favour of the equality of women. And there have been voluntary societies, religious or secular, of which the Society of Friends is the most known, by whom that principle was recognised. But there has been no political community or nation in which, by law, and usage, women have not been in a state of political and civil inferiority. In the ancient world the same fact was alleged, with equal truth, in behalf of slavery. It might have been alleged in favour of the mitigated form of slavery, serfdom, all through the middle ages. It was urged against freedom of industry, freedom of conscience, freedom of the press; none of these liberties were thought compatible with a well-ordered state, until they had proved their possibility by actually existing as facts. That an institution or a practice is customary is no presumption of its goodness, when any other sufficient cause can be assigned for its existence. There is no difficulty in understanding why the subjection of women has been a custom. No other explanation is needed than physical force.

That those who were physically weaker should have been made legally inferior, is quite conformable to the mode in which the world has been governed. Until very lately, the rule of physical strength was the general law of human affairs. Throughout history, the nations, races, classes, which found themselves the strongest, either in muscles, in riches, or in military discipline, have conquered and held in subjection the rest. If, even in the most improved nations, the law of the sword is at last discountenanced as unworthy, it is only since the calumniated eighteenth century. Wars of conquest have only ceased since democratic revolutions began. The world is very young, and has but just begun to cast off injustice. It is only now getting rid of negro slavery. It is only now getting rid of monarchical despotism. It is only now getting rid of hereditary feudal nobility. It is

[*Plato, *Republic* (Greek and English), trans. Paul Shorey, 2 vols. (London: Heinemann; Cambridge, Mass.: Harvard University Press, 1946), Vol. I, pp. 444-52 (Bk. V); and Marie Jean Antoine Nicolas Caritat, marquis de Condorcet, *Esquisse d'un tableau historique des progrès de l'esprit humain* (Paris: Agasse, 1795), p. 367.]

only now getting rid of disabilities on the ground of religion. It is only beginning to treat *ᶠany menᶠ* as citizens, except the rich and a favoured portion of the middle class. Can we wonder that it has not yet done as much for women? As society was constituted until the last few generations, inequality was its very basis; association grounded on equal rights scarcely existed; to be equals was to be enemies; two persons could hardly co-operate in anything, or meet in any amicable relation, without the law's appointing that one of them should be the superior of the other. Mankind have outgrown this state, and all things now tend to substitute, as the general principle of human relations, a just equality, instead of the dominion of the strongest. But of all relations, that between men and women being the nearest and most intimate, and connected with the greatest number of strong emotions, was sure to be the last to throw off the old rule and receive the new: for in proportion to the strength of a feeling, is the tenacity with which it clings to the forms and circumstances with which it has even accidentally become associated.

When a prejudice, which has any hold on the feelings, finds itself reduced to the unpleasant necessity of assigning reasons, it thinks it has done enough when it has re-asserted the very point in dispute, in phrases which appeal to the pre-existing feeling. Thus, many persons think they have sufficiently justified the restrictions on women's field of action, when they have said that the pursuits from which women are excluded are *unfeminine*, and that the *proper sphere* of women is not politics or publicity, but private and domestic life.

We deny the right of any portion of the species to decide for another portion, or any individual for another individual, what is and what is not their "proper sphere." The proper sphere for all human beings is the largest and highest which they are able to attain to. What this is, cannot be ascertained, without complete liberty of choice. The speakers at the Convention in America have therefore done wisely and right, in refusing to entertain the question of the peculiar aptitudes either of women or of men, or the limits within which this or that occupation may be supposed to be more adapted to the one or to the other.[*] They justly maintain, that these questions can only be satisfactorily answered by perfect freedom. Let every occupation be open to all, without favour or discouragement to any, and employments will fall into the hands of those men or women who are found by experience to be most capable of worthily exercising them. There need be no fear that women will take out of the hands of men any occupation which men perform better than they. Each individual will prove his or her capacities, in the only way in which capacities can be proved—by trial; and the world will have the benefit of the best faculties of all its inhabitants. But to interfere beforehand by an arbitrary limit, and declare that whatever be the genius, talent, energy, or force of mind of an individual of a certain sex or class, those faculties shall not be exerted, or shall be

[*See Forman, "Women's Rights Convention," 25 Oct., 1850, p. 6.]

ᶠ⁻ᶠ68   men

exerted only in some few of the many modes in which others are permitted to use theirs, is not only an injustice to the individual, and a detriment to society, which loses what it can ill spare, but is also the most effectual mode of providing that, in the sex or class so fettered, the qualities which are not permitted to be exercised shall not exist.

We shall follow the very proper example of the Convention, in not entering into the question of the alleged differences in physical or mental qualities between the sexes; not because we have nothing to say, but because we have too much; to discuss this one point tolerably would need all the space we have to bestow on the entire subject.* But if those who assert that the "proper sphere" for women is the domestic, mean by this that they have not shown themselves qualified for any other, the assertion evinces great ignorance of life and of history. Women have shown fitness for the highest social functions, exactly in proportion as they have been admitted to them. By a curious anomaly, though ineligible to even the lowest offices of state, they are in some countries admitted to the highest of all, the regal; and if there is any one function for which they have shown a decided vocation, it is that of reigning. Not to go back to ancient history, we look in vain for abler or firmer rulers than Elizabeth; than Isabella of Castile; than Maria Teresa; than Catherine of Russia; than Blanche, mother of Louis IX of France; than Jeanne d'Albret, mother of Henri Quatre. There are few kings on record who contended with more difficult circumstances, or overcame them more triumphantly, than *h* these. Even in semi-barbarous Asia, princesses who have never been seen by men, other than those of their own family, or ever spoken with them unless from behind a curtain, have as regents, during the minority of their sons, exhibited many of the most brilliant examples of just and vigorous administration. In the middle ages,

---

*An excellent passage on this part of the subject, from one of Sydney Smith's contributions to the *Edinburgh Review*, we ^{g}will^g not refrain from quoting: "A great deal has been said of the original difference of capacity between men and women, as if women were more quick and men more judicious—as if women were more remarkable for delicacy of association, and men for stronger powers of attention. All this, we confess, appears to us very fanciful. That there is a difference in the understandings of the men and the women we every day meet with, everybody, we suppose, must perceive; but there is none surely which may not be accounted for by the difference of circumstances in which they have been placed, without referring to any conjectural difference of original conformation of mind. As long as boys and girls run about in the dirt, and trundle hoops together, they are both precisely alike. If you catch up one-half of these creatures, and train them to a particular set of actions and opinions, and the other half to a perfectly opposite set, of course their understandings will differ, as one or the other sort of occupations has called this or that talent into action. There is surely no occasion to go into any deeper or more abstruse reasoning, in order to explain so very simple a phenomenon." (["Female Education" (1810), in] Sydney Smith's *Works*, [2nd ed., 3 vols. (London: Longman, *et al.*, 1840),] Vol. I, p. 200.)

$^{g-g}$68   must
^{h}68   most of

when the distance between the upper and lower ranks was greater than even between women and men, and the women of the privileged class, however subject to tyranny from the men of the same class, were at a less distance below them than any one else *was*, and often in their absence represented them in their functions and authority—numbers of heroic chatelaines, like Jeanne de Montfort, or the great Countess of Derby[*] as late even as the time of Charles I, distinguished themselves not only by their political but their military capacity. In the centuries immediately before and after the Reformation, ladies of royal houses, as diplomatists, as governors of provinces, or as the confidential advisers of kings, equalled the first statesmen of their time: and the treaty of Cambray, which gave peace to Europe, was negociated in conferences where no other person was present, by the aunt of the Emperor Charles V, and the mother of Francis I.[†]

Concerning the fitness, then, of women for politics, there can be no question: but the dispute is more likely to turn upon the fitness of politics for women. When the reasons alleged for excluding women from active life in all its higher departments, are stripped of their garb of declamatory phrases, and reduced to the simple expression of a meaning, they seem to be mainly three: [j] the incompatibility of active life with maternity, and with the cares of a household; secondly, its alleged hardening effect on the character; and thirdly, the inexpediency of making an addition to the already excessive pressure of competition in every kind of professional or lucrative employment.

The first, the maternity argument, is usually laid most stress upon: although (it needs hardly be said) this reason, if it be one, can apply only to mothers. It is neither necessary nor just to make imperative on women that they *shall* be either mothers or nothing; or that if they *have* been mothers once, they shall be nothing else during the whole remainder of their lives. Neither women nor men need any law to exclude them from an occupation, if they have undertaken another which is incompatible with it. No one proposes to exclude the male sex from Parliament because a man may be a soldier or sailor in active service, or a merchant whose business requires all his time and energies. Nine-tenths of the occupations of men exclude them *de facto* from public life, as effectually as if they were excluded by law; but that is no reason for making laws to exclude even the nine-tenths, much less the remaining tenth. The reason of the case is the same for women as for men. There is no need to make provision by law that a woman shall not carry on the

---

[*Charlotte de la Tremoille Stanley.]
[†Margaret of Austria and Louise of Savoy, respectively.]

[i-i]−68
[j]59,67 first,
[k-k]68 should
[l-l]68 had

active details of a household, or of the education of children, and at the same time practise a profession or be elected to Parliament. Where incompatibility is real, it will take care of itself: but there is gross injustice in making the incompatibility a pretence for the exclusion of those in whose case it does not exist. And these, if they were free to choose, would be a very large proportion. The maternity argument deserts its supporters in the case of single women, a large and increasing class of the population; a fact which, it is not irrelevant to remark, by tending to diminish the excessive competition of numbers, is calculated to assist greatly the prosperity of all. There is no inherent reason or necessity that all women should voluntarily choose to devote their lives to one animal function and its consequences. Numbers of women are wives and mothers only because there is no other career open to them, no other occupation for their feelings or their activities. Every improvement in their education, and enlargement of their faculties—everything which renders them more qualified for any other mode of life, increases the number of those to whom it is an injury and an oppression to be denied the choice. To say that women must be excluded from active life because maternity disqualifies them for it, is in fact to say, that every other career should be forbidden them in order that maternity may be their only resource.

But secondly, it is urged, that to give the same freedom of occupation to women as to men, would be an injurious addition to the crowd of competitors, by whom the avenues to almost all kinds of employment are choked up, and its remuneration depressed. This argument, it is to be observed, does not reach the political question. It gives no excuse for withholding from women the rights of citizenship. The suffrage, the jury-box, admission to the legislature and to office, it does not touch. It bears only on the industrial branch of the subject. Allowing it, then, in an economical point of view, its full force; assuming that to lay open to women the employments now monopolized by men, would tend, like the breaking down of other monopolies, to lower the rate of remuneration in those employments; let us consider what is the amount of this evil consequence, and what the compensation for it. The worst ever asserted, much worse than is at all likely to be realized, is that if women competed with men, a man and a woman could not together earn more than is now earned by the man alone. Let us make this supposition, the most unfavourable supposition possible: the joint income of the two would be the same as before, while the woman would be raised from the position of a servant to that of a partner. Even if every woman, as matters now stand, had a claim on some man for support, how infinitely preferable is it that part of the income should be of the woman's earning, even if the aggregate sum were but little increased by it, rather than that she should be compelled to stand aside in order that men may be the sole earners, and the sole dispensers of what is *m*earned.*m* Even under the present laws

*m-m*68   earned!

respecting the property of women,* a woman who contributes materially to the support of the family, cannot be treated in the same contemptuously tyrannical manner as one who, however she may toil as a domestic drudge, is a dependent on the man for subsistence. As for the depression of wages by increase of competition, remedies will be found for it in time. Palliatives might be applied immediately; for instance, a more rigid exclusion of children from industrial employment, during the years in which they ought to be working only to strengthen their bodies and minds for after life. Children are "necessarily" dependent, and under the power of others; and their labour, being not for themselves but for the gain of their parents, is a proper subject for legislative regulation. With respect to the future, we neither believe that improvident multiplication, and the consequent excessive difficulty of gaining a subsistence, will *always* continue, nor that the division of mankind into capitalists and hired labourers, and the regulation of the reward of labourers mainly by demand and supply, will be for ever, or even much longer, the rule of the world. But so long as competition is the general law of human life, it is tyranny to shut out one half of the competitors. All who have attained the age of self-government, have an equal claim to be permitted to sell whatever kind of useful labour they are capable of, for the price which it will bring.

The third objection to the admission of women to political or professional life, its alleged hardening tendency, belongs to an age now past, and is scarcely to be comprehended by people of the present time. There are still, however, persons who say that the world and its avocations render men selfish and unfeeling; that the struggles, rivalries and collisions of business and of politics make them harsh and unamiable; that if half the species must unavoidably be given up to these things, it is the more necessary that the other half should be kept free from them; that to preserve women from the bad influences of the world, is the only chance of preventing men from being wholly given up to them.

There would have been plausibility in this argument when the world was still in the age of violence, when life was full of physical conflict, and every man had to redress his injuries or those of others, by the sword or by the strength of his arm. Women, like priests, by being exempted from such responsibilities, and from some part of the accompanying dangers, may have been enabled to exercise a

---

*The truly horrible effects of the present state of the law among the lowest of the working population, is exhibited in those cases of hideous maltreatment of their wives by working men, with which every newspaper, every police report, teems. Wretches unfit to have the smallest authority over any living thing, have a helpless woman for their household slave. These excesses could not exist, if women both earned, and had the right to possess, a part of the income of the family. [This note is appended to the end of the sentence in 59, 67, 75.]

*n-n*68   *necessarily*
*o-o*68   eternally

beneficial influence. But in the present condition of human life, we do not know where those hardening influences are to be found, to which men are subject and from which women are at present exempt. Individuals now-a-days are seldom called upon to fight hand to hand, even with peaceful weapons; personal enmities and rivalities count for little in worldly transactions; the general pressure of circumstances, not the adverse will of individuals, is the obstacle men now have to make head against. That pressure, when excessive, breaks the spirit, and cramps and sours the feelings, but not less of women than of men, since they suffer certainly not less from its evils. There are still quarrels and dislikes, but the sources of them are changed. The feudal chief once found his bitterest enemy in his powerful neighbour, the minister or courtier in his rival for place: but opposition of interest in active life, as a cause of personal animosity, is out of date; the enmities of the present day arise not from great things but small, from what people say of one another, more than from what they do; and if there are hatred, malice, and all uncharitableness, they are to be found among women fully as much as among men. In the present state of civilization, the notion of guarding women from the hardening influences of the world, could only be realized by secluding them from society altogether. The common duties of common life, as at present constituted, are incompatible with any other softness in women than weakness. Surely weak minds in weak bodies must ere long cease to be even supposed to be either attractive or amiable.

But, in truth, none of these arguments and considerations touch the foundations of the subject. The real question is, whether it is right and expedient that one-half of the human race should pass through life in a state of forced subordination to the other half. If the best state of human society is that of being divided into two parts, one consisting of persons with a will and a substantive existence, the other of humble companions to these persons, attached, each of them to one, for the purpose of bringing up *his* children, and making *his* home pleasant to him; if this is the place assigned to women, it is but kindness to educate them for this; to make them believe that the greatest good fortune which can befal them, is to be chosen by some man for this purpose; and that every other career which the world deems happy or honourable, is closed to them by the law, not of social institutions, but of nature and destiny.

When, however, we ask why the existence of one-half the species should be merely ancillary to that of the other—why each woman should be a mere appendage to a man, allowed to have no interests of her own, that there may be nothing to compete in her mind with his interests and his pleasure; the only reason which can be given is, that men like it. It is agreeable to them that men should live for their own sake, women for the sake of men: and the qualities and conduct in subjects which are agreeable to rulers, they succeed for a long time in making the subjects themselves consider as their appropriate virtues. Helvetius has met with much obloquy for asserting, that persons usually mean by virtues the qualities which are useful or convenient to themselves.[*] How truly this is said of mankind in general, and how wonderfully the ideas of virtue set afloat by the powerful, are caught and imbibed by those under their dominion, is exemplified by the manner in which the world were once persuaded that the supreme virtue of subjects was loyalty to kings, and are still persuaded that the paramount virtue of womanhood is loyalty to *p*men*p*. Under a nominal recognition of a moral code common to both, in practice self-will, and self-assertion form the type of what are designated as manly virtues, while abnegation of self, patience, resignation, and submission to power, unless when resistance is commanded by other interests than their own, have been stamped by general consent as pre-eminently the duties and graces required of *q*women. The*q* meaning being merely, that power makes itself the centre of moral obligation, and that a man likes to have his own will, but does not like that his domestic companion should have a will different from his.

We are far from pretending that in modern and civilized times, no reciprocity of obligation is ackowleged on the part of the stronger. Such an assertion would be very wide of the truth. But even *r*this*r* reciprocity, which has disarmed tyranny, at least in the higher and middle classes, of its most revolting features, yet when combined with the original evil of the dependent condition of women, has introduced in its turn serious evils.

In the beginning, and *s*among*s* tribes which are still in a primitive condition, women were and are the slaves of men for *t*the*t* purposes of toil. All the hard bodily labour devolves on them. The Australian savage is idle, while women painfully dig up the roots on which he lives. An American Indian, when he has killed a deer, leaves it, and sends a woman to carry it home. In a state somewhat more advanced, as in Asia, women were and are the slaves of men for *u*the*u* purposes of sensuality. In Europe there early succeeded a third and milder dominion, secured not by blows, nor by locks and bars, but by sedulous inculcation on the mind; feelings also of kindness, and ideas of duty, such as a superior owes to inferiors under his protection, became more and more involved in the relation. But it did not for many ages become a relation of companionship, even between *v*unequals; the*v* lives of the two persons were apart. The wife was part of the furniture of home, of the resting-place to which the man returned from business or pleasure. His occupations were, as they still are, among men; his pleasures and excitements also

[*See, e.g., Claude Adrien Helvétius, *De l'esprit* (Paris: Durand, 1758), pp. 53-5.]

*p-p*68   man
*q-q*68   women,—the
*r-r*68   the
*s-s*68   amongst
t-t−59,67,68
u-u−59,67
*v-v*59,67   unequals. The

were, for the most part, among men—among his equals. He was a patriarch and a despot within four walls, and irresponsible power had its effect, greater or less according to his disposition, in rendering him domineering, exacting, self-worshipping, when not capriciously or brutally tyrannical. But if the moral part of his nature suffered, it was not necessarily so, in the same degree, with the intellectual or the active portion. He might have as much vigour of mind and energy of character as his nature enabled him, and as the circumstances of his times allowed. He might write the *Paradise Lost*,[*] or win the battle of Marengo.[†] This was the condition of the Greeks and Romans, and of the moderns until a recent date. Their relations with their domestic subordinates occupied a mere corner, though a cherished one, of their lives. Their education as men, the formation of their character and faculties, depended mainly on a different class of influences.

It is otherwise now. The progress of improvement has imposed on all possessors of power, and of domestic power among the rest, an increased and increasing sense of correlative obligation. No man now thinks that his wife has no claim upon his actions but such as he may accord to her. All men of any conscience believe that their duty to their wives is one of the most binding of their obligations. Nor is it supposed to consist solely in protection, which, in the present state of civilization, women have almost ceased to need: it involves care for their happiness and consideration of their wishes, with a not unfrequent sacrifice of their own to them. The power of husbands has reached the stage which the power of kings had arrived at, when opinion did not yet question the rightfulness of arbitrary power, but in theory, and to a certain extent in practice, condemned the selfish use of it. This improvement in the moral sentiments of mankind, and increased sense of the consideration due by every man to those who "have" no one but himself to look to, has tended to make home more and more the centre of interest, and domestic circumstances and society a larger and larger part of life, and of its pursuits and pleasures. The tendency has been strengthened by the changes of tastes and manners which have so remarkably distinguished the last two or three generations. In days not far distant, men found their excitement and filled up their time in violent bodily exercises, noisy merriment, and intemperance. They have now, in all but the very poorest classes, lost their inclination for these things, and for the coarser pleasures generally; they have now scarcely any tastes but those which they have in common with women, and, for the first time in the world, men and women are really companions. A most beneficial change, if the companionship were between equals; but being between unequals, it produces, what good

[*John Milton, *Paradise Lost* (1667), in *The Poetical Works* (London: Tonson, 1695), pp. 1-343.]

[†As did Napoleon I.]

w-w68 had

observers have noticed, though without perceiving its cause, a progressive deterioration among men in what had hitherto been considered the masculine excellences. Those who are so careful that women should not become men, do not see that men are becoming, what they have decided that women should be—are falling into the feebleness which they have so long cultivated in their companions. Those who are associated in their lives, tend to become assimilated in character. In the present closeness of association between the sexes, men cannot retain manliness unless women acquire it.

There is hardly any situation more unfavourable to the maintenance of elevation of character or force of intellect, than to live in the society, and seek by preference the sympathy, of inferiors in mental endowments. Why is it that we constantly see in life so much of intellectual and moral promise followed by such inadequate performance, but because the aspirant has compared himself only with those below himself, and has not sought improvement or stimulus from measuring himself with his equals or *superiors.* In the present state of social life, this is becoming the general condition of men. They care less and less for any sympathies, and are less and less under any personal influences, but those of the domestic roof. Not to be misunderstood, it is necessary that we should distinctly disclaim the belief, that women are even now inferior in intellect to men. There are women who are the equals in intellect of any men who ever lived: and comparing ordinary women with ordinary men, the varied though petty details which compose the occupation of most women, call forth probably as much of mental ability, as the uniform routine of the pursuits which are the habitual occupation of a large majority of men. It is from nothing in the faculties themselves, but from the petty subjects and interests on which alone they are exercised, that the companionship of women, such as their present circumstances make them, so often exercises a dissolvent influence on high faculties and aspirations in men. If one of the two has no knowledge and no care about the great ideas and purposes which dignify life, or about any of its practical concerns save personal interests and personal vanities, her conscious, and still more her unconscious influence, will, except in rare cases, reduce to a secondary place in his mind, if not entirely extinguish, those interests which she cannot or does not share.

Our argument here brings us into collision with what may be termed the moderate reformers of the education of women; a sort of persons who cross the path of improvement on all great questions; those who would maintain the old bad principles, mitigating their consequences. These say, that women should be, not slaves, nor servants, but companions; and educated for that office: (they do not say that men should be educated to be the companions of women). But since uncultivated women are not suitable companions for cultivated men, and a man who feels interest in things above and beyond the family circle wishes that his

---

*-*68   superiors?

companion should sympathize with him in that interest; they therefore say, let women improve their understanding and taste, acquire general knowledge, cultivate poetry, art, even coquet with science, and some stretch their liberality so far as to say, inform themselves on politics; not as pursuits, but sufficiently to feel an interest in the subjects, and to be capable of holding a conversation on them with the husband, or at least of understanding and imbibing his wisdom. Very agreeable to him, no doubt, but unfortunately the reverse of improving. It is from having intellectual communion only with those to whom they can lay down the law, that so few men continue to advance in wisdom beyond the first stages. The most eminent men cease to improve, if they associate only with disciples. When they have overtopped those who immediately surround them, if they wish for further growth, they must seek for others of their own stature to consort with. The mental companionship which is improving, is communion between active minds, not mere contact between an active mind and a passive. This inestimable advantage is even now enjoyed, when a strong-minded man and a strong-minded woman are, by a rare chance, united: and would be had far oftener, if education took the same pains to form strong-minded women which it takes to prevent them from being formed. ʸThe modern, and what are regarded as the improved and enlightened modes of education of women, abjure, as far as words go, an education of mere show, and profess to aim at solid instruction, but mean by that expression, superficial information on solid subjects. Except accomplishments, which are now generally regarded as to be taught well if taught at all, nothing is taught to women thoroughly. Small portions only of what it is attempted to teach thoroughly to boys, are the whole of what it is intended or desired to teach to women.ʸ What makes intelligent beings is the power of thought: the stimuli which call forth that power are the interest and dignity of thought itself, and a field for its practical application. Both motives are cut off from those who are told from infancy that thought, and all its greater applications, are other people's business, while theirs is to make themselves agreeable to other people. High mental powers in women will be but an exceptional accident, until every career is open to them, and until they, as well as men, are educated for themselves and for the world—not one sex for the other.

In what we have said on the effect of the inferior position of women, combined with the present constitution of married life, we have thus far had in view only the most favourable cases, those in which there is some real approach to that union and blending of characters and of lives, which the theory of the relation contemplates as its ideal standard. But if we look to the great majority of cases, the effect of women's legal inferiority on the character both of women and of men must be

---

ʸ⁻ʸ68   But this supposes other than mere *dilettante* instruction, given as an elegant amusement or agreeable accomplishment, not as a power to be used. Mental cultivation adapted for show and not for use, which makes pigmies of men, is the only kind given or proposed to be given to women by the present reformers of their education.

painted in far darker colours. We do not speak here of the grosser brutalities, nor of the man's power to seize on the woman's earnings, or compel her to live with him against her will. We do not address ourselves to any one who requires to have it proved that these things should be remedied. We suppose average cases, in which there is neither complete union nor complete disunion of feelings and ^{z}of^z character; and we affirm that in such cases the influence of the dependence on the woman's side, is demoralizing to the character of both.

The common opinion is, that whatever may be the case with the intellectual, the moral influence of women over men is almost always salutary. It is, we are often told, the great counteractive of selfishness. However the case may be as to personal influence, the influence of the position tends eminently to promote selfishness. The most insignificant of men, the man who can obtain influence or consideration nowhere else, finds one place where he is chief and head. There is one person, often greatly his superior in understanding, who is obliged to consult him, and whom he is not obliged to consult. He is judge, magistrate, ruler, over their joint concerns; arbiter of all differences between them. The justice or conscience to which her appeal must be made, is his justice and conscience: it is his to hold the balance and adjust the scales between his own claims or wishes and those of another. His is now the only tribunal, in civilized life, in which the same person is judge and party. A generous mind, in such a situation, makes the balance incline against its own side, and gives the other not less, but more, than a fair equality; and thus the weaker side may be enabled to turn the very fact of dependence into an instrument of power, and in default of justice, take an ungenerous advantage of generosity; rendering the unjust power, to those who make an unselfish use of it, a torment and a burthen. But how is it when average men are invested with this power, without reciprocity and without responsibility? Give such a man the idea that he is first in law and in opinion—that to will is his part, and hers to submit; it is absurd to suppose that this idea merely glides over his mind, without sinking into it, or having any effect on his feelings and practice. The propensity to make himself the first object of consideration, and others at most the second, is not so rare as to be wanting where everything seems purposely arranged for ^{a}permitting^a its indulgence. If there is any self-will in the man, he becomes either the conscious or unconscious despot of his household. The wife, indeed, often succeeds in gaining her objects, but it is by some of the many various forms of indirectness and management.

Thus the position is corrupting equally to both; in the one it produces the vices of power, in the other those of artifice. Women, in their present physical and moral state, having stronger impulses, would naturally be franker and more direct than men; yet all the old saws and traditions represent them as artful and dissembling. Why? Because their only way to their objects is by indirect paths. In all countries where women have strong wishes and active minds, this consequence is inevitable: and if it is less conspicuous in England than in some other places, it is because Englishwomen, saving occasional exceptions, have ceased to have either strong wishes or active minds.

We are not now speaking of cases in which there is anything deserving the name of strong affection on both sides. That, where it exists, is too powerful a principle not to modify greatly the bad influences of the situation; it seldom, however, destroys them entirely. Much oftener the bad influences are too strong for the affection, and destroy it. The highest order of durable and happy attachments would be a hundred times more frequent than they are, if the affection which the two sexes sought from one another were that genuine friendship, which only exists between equals in privileges as in faculties. But with regard to what is commonly called affection in married life—the habitual and almost mechanical feeling of kindliness, and pleasure in each other's society, which generally grows up between persons who constantly live together, unless there is actual dislike—there is nothing in this to contradict or qualify the mischievous influence of the unequal relation. Such feelings often exist between a sultan and his favourites, between a master and his servants; they are merely examples of the pliability of human nature, which accommodates itself in some degree even to the worst circumstances, and the commonest natures always the most easily.

With respect to the influence personally exercised by women over men, it, no doubt, renders them less harsh and brutal; in ruder times, it was often the only softening influence to which they were accessible. But the assertion, that the wife's influence renders the man less selfish, contains, as things now are, fully as much error as truth. Selfishness towards the wife herself, and towards those in whom she is interested, the children, though favoured by [b]their[b] dependence, the wife's influence, no doubt, tends to counteract. But the general effect on him of her character, so long as her interests are concentrated in the family, tends but to substitute for individual selfishness a family selfishness, wearing an amiable guise, and putting on the mask of duty. How rarely is the wife's influence on the side of public virtue: how rarely does it do otherwise than discourage any effort of principle by which the private interests or worldly vanities of the family can be expected to [c]suffer.[c] Public spirit, sense of duty towards the public good, is of all virtues, as women are now educated and situated, the most rarely to be found among them; they have seldom even, what in men is often a partial substitute for public spirit, a sense of personal honour connected with any public duty. Many a man, whom no money or personal flattery would have bought, has bartered his political opinions against [d]a title[d] or invitations [e]for[e] his wife; and a still greater number are made mere hunters after the puerile vanities of society, because their

[b-b]59,67   her
[c-c]68   suffer!
[d-d]68   titles
[e-e]68   to

wives value them. As for opinions; in Catholic countries, the wife's influence is another name for that of the priest: he gives her, in the hopes and emotions connected with a future life, a consolation for the sufferings and disappointments which are her ordinary lot in this. Elsewhere, her weight is thrown into the scale either of the most common-place, or of the most outwardly prosperous opinions: either those by which censure will be escaped, or by which worldly advancement is likeliest to be procured. In England, the wife's influence is usually on the illiberal and anti-popular side: this is generally the gaining side for personal interest and vanity; and what to her is the democracy or liberalism in which she has no part—which leaves her the Pariah it found her? The man himself, when he marries, usually declines into Conservatism; begins to sympathize with the holders of power, more than with its victims, and thinks it his part to be on the side of authority. As to mental progress, except those *vulgarer* attainments by which vanity or ambition are promoted, there is generally an end to it in a man who marries a woman mentally his inferior; unless, indeed, he is unhappy in marriage, or becomes indifferent. From a man of twenty-five or thirty, after he is married, an experienced observer seldom expects any further progress in mind or feelings. It is rare that the progress already made is maintained. Any spark of the *mens divinior*[*] which might otherwise have spread and become a flame, seldom survives for any length of time unextinguished. For a mind which learns to be satisfied with what it already is—which does not incessantly look forward to a degree of improvement not yet reached—becomes relaxed, self-indulgent, and loses the spring and the tension which maintain it even at the point already attained. And there is no fact in human nature to which experience bears more invariable testimony than to this—that all social or sympathetic influences which do not raise up, pull down; if they do not tend to stimulate and exalt the mind, they tend to vulgarize it.

For the interest, therefore, not only of women but of men, and of human improvement in the widest sense, the emancipation of women, which the modern world often boasts of having effected, and for which credit is sometimes given to civilization, and sometimes to Christianity, cannot stop where it is. If it were either necessary or just that one portion of mankind should remain mentally and spiritually only half developed, the development of the other portion ought to have been made, as far as possible, independent of their influence. Instead of this, they have become the most intimate, and it may now be said, the only intimate associates of those to whom yet they are sedulously kept inferior; and have been raised just high enough to drag the others down to themselves.

[*Horace, *Satires*, in *Satires, Epistles and Ars poetica*, trans. H. Rushton Fairclough (London: Heinemann; Cambridge, Mass.: Harvard University Press, 1939), p. 52 (I, iv, 43-4).]

*f-f*67 vulgar

We have left behind a host of vulgar objections, either as not worthy of an answer, or as answered by the general course of our remarks. A few words, however, must be said on one plea, which in England is made much use of for giving an unselfish air to the upholding of selfish privileges, and which, with unobserving, unreflecting people, passes for much more than it is worth. Women, it is said, do not desire—do not seek, what is called their emancipation. On the contrary, they generally disown such claims when made in their behalf, and fall with *acharnement* upon any one of themselves who identifies herself with their common cause.

Supposing the fact to be true in the fullest extent ever asserted, if it proves that European women ought to remain as they are, it proves exactly the same with respect to Asiatic women; for they too, instead of murmuring at their seclusion, and at the restraint imposed upon them, pride themselves on it, and are astonished at the effrontery of women who receive visits from male acquaintances, and are seen in the streets unveiled. Habits of submission make men as well as women servile-minded. The vast population of Asia do not desire or value, probably would not accept, political liberty, nor the savages of the forest, civilization; which does not prove that either of those things is undesirable for them, or that they will not, at some future time, enjoy it. Custom hardens human beings to any kind of degradation, by deadening the part of their nature which would resist it. And the case of women is, in this respect, even a peculiar one, for no other inferior caste that we have heard of, have been taught to regard their degradation as their honour. The argument, however, implies a secret consciousness that the alleged preference of women for their dependent state is merely apparent, and arises from their being allowed no choice; for if the preference be natural, there can be no necessity for enforcing it by law. To make laws compelling people to follow their inclination, has not hitherto been thought necessary by any legislator. The plea that women do not desire any change, is the same that has been urged, times out of mind, against the proposal of abolishing any social evil—"there is no complaint;" which is generally not true, and when true, only so because there is not that hope of success, without which complaint seldom makes itself audible to unwilling ears. How does the objector know that women do not desire equality and freedom? He never knew a woman who did not, or would not, desire it for herself individually. It would be very simple to suppose, that if they do desire it they will say so. Their position is like that of the tenants or labourers who vote against their own political interests to please their landlords or employers; with the unique addition, that submission is inculcated on them from childhood, as the peculiar attraction and grace of their character. They are taught to think, that to repel actively even an admitted injustice done to themselves, is somewhat unfeminine, and had better be left to some male friend or protector. To be accused of rebelling against anything which admits of being called an ordinance of society, they are taught to regard as an imputation of a serious offence, to say the least, against the proprieties of their sex. It requires unusual moral courage as well as disinterestedness in a woman, to express opinions favourable to women's enfranchisement, until, at least, there is some prospect of obtaining it. The comfort of her individual life, and her social consideration, usually depend on the goodwill of those who hold the undue power; and to possessors of power any complaint, however bitter, of the misuse of it, is a less flagrant act of insubordination than to protest against the power itself. The professions of women in this matter remind us of the state offenders of old, who, on the point of execution, used to protest their love and devotion to the sovereign by whose unjust mandate they suffered. Griselda herself might be matched from the speeches put by Shakspeare into the mouths of male victims of kingly caprice and tryanny: the Duke of Buckingham, for example, in *Henry the Eighth*, and even Wolsey.[*] The literary class of women, especially in England, are ostentatious in disclaiming the desire for equality or citizenship, and proclaiming their complete satisfaction with the place which society assigns to them; exercising in this, as in many other respects, a most noxious influence over the feelings and opinions of men, who unsuspectingly accept the servilities of toadyism as concessions to the force of truth, not considering that it is the personal interest of these women to profess whatever opinions they expect will be agreeable to men. It is not among men of talent, sprung from the people, and patronized and flattered by the aristocracy, that we look for the leaders of a democratic movement. Successful literary women are just as unlikely to prefer the cause of women to their own social consideration. They depend on men's opinion for their literary as well as for their feminine successes; and such is their bad opinion of men, that they believe there is not more than one in ten thousand who does not dislike and fear strength, sincerity, or high spirit in a woman. They are therefore anxious to earn pardon and toleration for whatever of these qualities their writings may exhibit on other subjects, by a studied display of submission on this: that they may give no occasion for vulgar men to say (what nothing will prevent vulgar men from saying), that learning makes women unfeminine, and that literary ladies are likely to be bad wives.

But enough of this; especially as the fact which affords the occasion for this gnoticeg, makes it impossible any longer to assert the universal acquiescence of women (saving individual exceptions) in their dependent condition. In the United States at least, there are women, seemingly numerous, and now organised for action on the public mind, who demand equality in the fullest acceptation of the

[*Griselda is the heroine of Story 10, Day 10, of Giovanni Boccaccio, *Decameron* (1353), whose loyal patience became proverbial; for the speeches, see William Shakespeare, *Henry the Eighth*, II, i, 55-78 and 100-36 (Buckingham), and III, ii, 407-21 and 428-57 (Wolsey), in *The Riverside Shakespeare*, ed. G. Blakemore Evans (Boston: Houghton Mifflin, 1974), pp. 990-1 and 1005, respectively.]

g-g68   paper

word, and demand it by a straightforward appeal to men's sense of justice, not plead for it with a timid deprecation of their displeasure.

Like other popular movements, however, this may be seriously retarded by the blunders of its adherents. Tried by the ordinary standard of public meetings, the speeches at the Convention are remarkable for the preponderance of the rational over the declamatory element; but there are some exceptions; and things to which it is impossible to attach any rational meaning, have found their way into the resolutions. Thus, the resolution which sets forth the claims made in behalf of women, after claiming equality in education, in industrial pursuits, and in political rights, enumerates as a fourth head of demand something under the name of "social and spiritual union," and "a medium of expressing the highest moral and spiritual views of justice,"[*] with other similar verbiage, serving only to mar the simplicity and rationality of the other demands [h]: resembling those who would weakly attempt to combine nominal equality between men and women, with enforced distinctions in their privileges and functions[h]. What is wanted for women is equal rights, equal admission to all social privileges; not a position apart, a sort of sentimental priesthood. To this, the only just and rational principle, both the resolutions and the speeches, for the most part, adhere. They contain so little which is akin to the nonsensical paragraph in question, that we suspect it not to be the work of the same hands as most of the other resolutions. The strength of the cause lies in the support of those who are influenced by reason and principle; and to attempt to recommend it by sentimentalities, absurd in reason, and inconsistent with the principle on which the movement is founded, is to place a good cause on a level with a bad one.

There are indications that the example of America will be followed on this side of the Atlantic; and the first step has been taken in that part of England where every serious movement in the direction of political progress has its commencement —the manufacturing districts of the North. On the 13th of February 1851, a petition of women, agreed to by a public meeting at Sheffield, and claiming the elective franchise, was presented to the House of Lords by the Earl of Carlisle.[†]

[*Forman, "Women's Rights Convention," 26 Oct., 1850, p. 6.]
[†"A Petition of the Female Inhabitants of the Borough of Sheffield in the County of York, in Public Meeting Assembled, Praying Their Lordships 'to Take into Their Serious Consideration the Propriety of Enacting an Electoral Law Which Will Include Adult Females within Its Provisions'" (13 Feb., 1851), *Journals of the House of Lords*, 1851, LXXXIII, 23.]

[h-h]-68

Appendix D

DRAFT OF A PORTION OF THE *INAUGURAL ADDRESS* (1866)

MS (evidently first draft), Houghton Library, Harvard University, part of the miscellaneous papers bought by George Herbert Palmer from the Avignon bookseller, J. Roumanille.

The variant notes to the text below give the differences between the draft and the printed versions, the latter indicated by "67". The comparable passage in the printed versions appears at 222-5 above.

acquired with tenfold greater facility when the *a*examples of their application*a* are already *b*present in*b* the *c*mind—if this were but done,*c* an average schoolboy long before the age at which schooling *d*generally*d* terminates, *e*might easily*e* be able to read *f*with ease, fluency, and*f* intelligent interest any ordinary Latin or Greek author, in prose or verse, *g*might*g* have a competent knowledge of the grammatical structure of both languages, and have had time besides for an ample amount of scientific instruction. *h* I am as unwilling to *i*mention*i* all that I think practicable in this matter, as George Stephenson was *j*in the matter of locomotion*j*, when he calculated the average speed of a *k*railway*k* train at ten miles an hour because if he had estimated it *l*at more*l* the practical men *m*whose cooperation he needed*m* would have *n*distrusted*n* him as that most unsafe character in their estimation an

*a-a*67   cases to which they apply
*b-b*67   familiar to
*c-c*67   mind;
*d-d*_67
*e-e*67   would
*f-f*67   fluently and with
*g-g*67   would
*h*67   I might go much further; but
*i-i*67   speak out
*j-j*67   about railways
*k-k*_67
*l-l*67   higher,
*m-m*_67
*n-n*67   turned a deaf ear to

enthusiast and a visionary. The results have shewn, in ^{o}this^o case, who was the real practical man. What the results would shew in the other case I will not ^{p} anticipate. ^{q}It is enough to be able to say with confidence^q, that if the two classical languages were properly taught, there would be no need whatever for ^{r}turning them out of^r the school course in order to have sufficient ^{s}room^s for everything else that ^{t}needs^t be included therein.

^{u}This wonderfully^u limited estimate of what it is possible for human beings to learn, resting upon a tacit assumption that they are already as efficiently taught as they ever can ^{v}be,^{v} not only vitiates ^{w}the general conception^w of education, but actually, if we receive it, darkens our anticipations as to the future progress of mankind. For if the inexorable conditions of human life make it useless for one man to attempt to know more than one thing, what is to become of the human intellect as facts accumulate? In every generation, and ^{x}more rapidly now^x than ever ^{y}before, the number of things increases,^{y} which it is necessary that somebody should ^{z}learn^z. Every department of ^{a}our knowledge of the universe^a becomes so loaded with details that ^{b}if a person^b endeavours to know ^{c}all that is known of it, he^c must confine himself to a smaller and smaller portion of the whole ^{d}field,^{d} every science and art must be ^{e}divided and subdivided^e, until each man's ^{f}speciality, the region^f which he thoroughly knows, bears about the same ^{g}proportion^g to the whole ^{h}field^h of useful knowledge that the art of putting on a pin's head does to the field of human industry. Now, ^{i}when we take this along with the fact certified by experience,^{i} that there is no one study or pursuit which,

$^{o\text{-}o}$67   that
^{p}67   attempt to
$^{q\text{-}q}$67   But I will say confidently
$^{r\text{-}r}$67   ejecting them from
$^{s\text{-}s}$67   time
$^{t\text{-}t}$67   need
$^{u\text{-}u}$67   Let me say a few words more on this strangely
$^{v\text{-}v}$67   be. So narrow a conception
$^{w\text{-}w}$67   our idea
$^{x\text{-}x}$67   now more rapidly
$^{y\text{-}y}$67   , the things
$^{z\text{-}z}$67   know are more and more multiplied
$^{a\text{-}a}$67   knowledge
$^{b\text{-}b}$67   one who
$^{c\text{-}c}$67   it with minute accuracy,
$^{d\text{-}d}$67   extent:
$^{e\text{-}e}$67   cut up into subdivisions
$^{f\text{-}f}$67   portion, the district
$^{g\text{-}g}$67 ratio
$^{h\text{-}h}$67   range
$^{i\text{-}i}$67   if in order to know that little completely, it is necessary to remain wholly ignorant of all the rest, what will soon be the worth of a man, for any human purpose except his own infinitesimal fraction of human wants and requirements? His state will be even worse than that of simple ignorance. Experience proves

practised to the exclusion of all others, does not narrow and pervert the mind [j], breed[j] in it a class of prejudices special to that [k]particular pursuit, and[k] a general prejudice common to all narrow specialities against [l]general ideas of all sorts, grounded on[l] an incapacity to take [m]them in or to judge[m] of them. [n]What prospect have we before us but that of a human intellect[n] more and more dwarfed and unfitted for [o]all[o] great things, [p]actually by its progress[p] in small ones [q]? But things[q] are not so bad with us: [r]this is not the fate we need look forward to[r]. It is not the utmost limit of human acquirement to know only one thing, but to combine a minute knowledge of one or a few things with a general knowledge of many things. By a general knowledge I do not mean a [s]mere vague impression[s]. An eminent man one of whose writings is part of the course of this University, Abp. Whately, has well [t]pointed out, that[t] a general knowledge [u]is a totally different thing from[u] a superficial knowledge. To have a general knowledge of a subject is to know [v] its leading truths, but to [w]learn them with understanding,[w] not superficially but thoroughly, so as to have a true conception of the subject [x]as a whole,[x] leaving the minor details to those who require [y]the knowledge of[y] them [z]because it is their business to follow them out and to apply them. This kind of knowledge does not tend to narrow but to enlarge the mind; it forms[z] a body of cultivated intellects, [a]capable of illuminating each his own special studies by the lights derived from the other branches of human knowledge, and constituting a public able to understand and appreciate the processes of thought in other people's special departments and intelligently follow the lead of those specialists who by their general powers and

[j-j]67   ; breeding
[k-k]67   pursuit, besides
[l-l]67   large views, from
[m-m]67   in and appreciate the grounds
[n-n]67   We should have to expect that human nature would be
[o-o]–67
[p-p]67   by its very proficiency
[q-q]67   . But matters
[r-r]67   there is no ground for so dreary an anticipation
[s-s]67   few vague impressions
[t-t]67   discriminated between
[u-u]67   and
[v]67   only
[w-w]67   know these
[x-x]67   in its great features
[y-y]–67
[z-z]67   for the purposes of their special pursuit. There is no incompatibility between knowing a wide range of subjects up to this point, and some one subject with the completeness required by those who make it their principal occupation. It is this combination which gives an enlightened public:
[a-a]67   each taught by its attainments in its own province what real knowledge is, and knowing enough of other subjects to be able to discern who are those that know them better. The amount of knowledge is not to be lightly estimated, which qualifies us for judging to whom we may have recourse for more. The elements of the more important studies being widely diffused, those who have reached the higher summits find a public capable of appreciating their superiority, and prepared to follow their lead. It is thus too that minds are formed

cultivation of their minds are most capable of leading rightly. Above all, it is this alone which can form minds^a capable of ^bdirecting^b and improving public opinion in the greater concerns of ^chuman^c life. Government and civil society are the most complicated of all subjects accessible to the human mind, and ^dto be competent to deal with them there is great need not only of^d a general knowledge of the leading facts of ^ethe universe in almost all its departments, but of^e an understanding exercised and disciplined in the principles and rules of sound thinking up to a point which ^fno^f one science or branch of knowledge affords ^g, and to obtain which it is necessary to be more or less conversant with many^g. Let us understand then, that it ^hought to be our object^h in learning, not merely to know ⁱsome one thing, the thingⁱ which is to be our principal occupation, as well as it can be known but to do this and also to know something of all the great ^jdepartments^j of human ^kknowledge;^k taking care to know that something ^laccurately, or at all events^l marking well the dividing line between what we know accurately and what we do not; and remembering that our object should be to obtain a true view of nature and ^mthe world in its^m broad outline, ⁿbutⁿ that it is ^ouseless^o to throw away time upon the ^pminute^p details of anything which is ^qnot to be^q part of the occupation of our practical energies.

It by no means follows, however, that ^reverything which deserves to be known, and which is capable of being known by everybody who has received a liberal education^r, should be included in the ^scourse^s of school or university studies. ^tSome things, very desirable to be learnt, are learnt better^t out of school or ^uafter^u school years ^v are over. ^wFor this reason^w I do not agree with those reformers who

---

^{b-b}67   guiding

^{c-c}67   practical

^{d-d}67   he who would deal competently with them as a thinker, and not as a blind follower of a party, requires not only

^{e-e}67   life, both moral and material, but

^{f-f}67   neither the experience of life, nor any

^{g-g}–67

^{h-h}67   should be our aim

ⁱ⁻ⁱ67   the one thing

^{j-j}67   subjects

^{k-k}67   interest:

^{l-l}67   accurately;

^{m-m}67   life in their

ⁿ⁻ⁿ67   and

^{o-o}67   idle

^{p-p}–67

^{q-q}67   to form no

^{r-r}67   every useful branch of general, as distinct from professional, knowledge

^{s-s}67   curriculum

^{t-t}67   There are things which are better learnt

^{u-u}67   when the

^v67   , and even those usually passed in a Scottish university,

^{w-w}–67

would [x]assign a place, and an important place,[x] in the school [y] course, to modern languages. This is not because I attach small importance to [z]them*; no[z] one can [a] be [b]considered well-instructed or cultivated[b] who is not familiar with at least the French language [c]and able[c] to read French books with ease; and there is great [d]advantage[d] in cultivating a familiarity with German. But living languages are so much more easily acquired [e]later in life,[e] by intercourse with those who use them in daily[f] life,[f] that it is really waste of time [g] to labour at [h]their acquisition without any[h] help but that of books and masters [i] . Again, it has always seemed to me a great absurdity that [j]such things as[j] history and geography should be taught in schools, except [k]a few of the leading facts of both[k] in elementary schools for the [l]mass of the people[l]. Who ever really learnt history and geography except by private reading? and what an utter failure [m]your[m] education must be if it has not given [n]your[n] pupil a sufficient taste for reading to [o]make him seek by that easy process the most interesting[o] of all kinds of knowledge? Besides such history and geography as can be taught in schools exercise none of the faculties of the [p]intellect except that of mere[p] memory. [q]At an University indeed it is very important that the pupil[q] should be introduced to the Philosophy of History [r]—that a Professor[r] who

*[−67]Acquaintance with the literature and forms of thought of other nations is the most effectual of all preservatives against a narrow nationality, against mistaking one local type of human nature for the universal laws of it, and against the habit of accepting custom both in opinion and practice, as a test of right, for want of knowing that perfectly opposite customs prevail elsewhere.

[x-x]67   give a regular and prominent place
[y]67   or university
[z-z]67   the knowledge of them. No
[a]67   in our age
[b-b]67   esteemed a well-instructed person
[c-c]67   , so as
[d-d]67   use
[e-e]−67
[f-f]67   life; a few months in the country itself, if properly employed, go so much farther than as many years of school lessons;
[g]67   for those to whom that easier mode is attainable,
[h-h]67   them with no
[i]67   : and it will in time be made attainable, through international schools and colleges, to many more than at present. Universities do enough to facilitate the study of modern languages, if they give a mastery over that ancient language which is the foundation of most of them, and the possession of which makes it easier to learn four or five of the continental languages than it is to learn one of them without it
[j-j]−67
[k-k]−67
[l-l]67   children of the labouring classes, whose subsequent access to books is limited
[m-m]67   a system of
[n-n]67   the
[o-o]67   seek for himself those most attractive and easily intelligible
[p-p]67   intelligence except the
[q-q]67   An University is indeed the place where the student
[r-r]67   ; where Professors

not merely *knows*[s] the facts but [t]has[t] exercised [u]his mind[u] on them, should initiate [v]the pupils[v] into the causes and explanation, [w]as[w] far as [x]an explanation is possible[x] of the past life of mankind in its [y]more important features and vicissitudes[y]. But of the mere facts of history as commonly [z]believed and understood[z], what educated [a]person[a] of any mental activity does not learn [b]all that is of primary importance[b] if he is [c]only[c] turned loose in an historical library? What [d]is wanted on this subject[d] is not that he should be taught it in boyhood, but that [e] books should be accessible to him.

The only languages [f]therefore[f] and the only [g]literatures[g] to which I would allow a place in the ordinary [h]course of a liberal education[h] are those of the Greeks and Romans; to these I would preserve the position [i] they at present occupy [j]in it. The importance of these languages in education is twofold: first, the value of languages in general, of studying and knowing[j] some other cultivated language and [k]some other[k] literature than one's own [l]: secondly,[l] the peculiar value of those particular languages [m] .

[n]The value, to the human mind, of knowing, and knowing well, more than one language; or I should rather say, the extreme disadvantage of knowing no language but one's own, is scarcely, I think, generally felt and recognized in all its force. Every thinker or writer who has[n] reflected on the causes of human error [o]has[o] been deeply impressed with the [p]natural[p] tendency of mankind to mistake

[s-s]67 know
[t-t]67 have
[u-u]67 their minds
[v-v]67 him
[w-w]67 so
[x-x]67 within our reach,
[y-y]67 principal features. Historical criticism also—the tests of historical truth—are a subject to which his attention may well be drawn in this stage of his education
[z-z]67 accepted
[a-a]67 youth
[b-b]67 as much as is necessary,
[c-c]67 simply
[d-d]67 he needs on this, and on most other matters of common information,
[e]67 abundance of
[f-f]67 , then,
[g-g]67 literature,
[h-h]67 curriculum,
[i]67 in it which
[j-j]67 That position is justified, by the great value, in education, of knowing well
[k-k]_67
[l-l]67 , and by
[m]67 and literatures
[n-n]67 There is one purely intellectual benefit from a knowledge of languages, which I am specially desirous to dwell on. Those who have seriously
[o-o]67 have
[p-p]_67

Appendix E

JAMAICA COMMITTEE: PUBLIC DOCUMENTS (1866, 1868)

1. Statement of the Jamaica Committee (1866)

Jamaica Papers, No. III, *Statement of the Committee and Other Documents* (London: Jamaica Committee, [1866]), 3-7. Concludes: "Signed, on behalf of the Committee, / J.S. Mill, Chairman. / P.A. Taylor, Treasurer. / F.W. Chesson, Hon. Sec. / 65, Fleet Street, / 27*th July*, 1866." Not listed in Mill's bibliography. Printed, with a few substantive differences, in the *Daily News*, 30 July, 1866, 3, and, without substantive differences, in the *Diplomatic Review*, 5 Sept., 1866, 118-19; the variants between the version in the *Daily News* and the copy-text are given in notes, in which "DN" indicates *Daily News*.

For comment on this and the other Jamaica documents, see xxvi-xxviii and lxxviii above.

THE JAMAICA COMMITTEE[*] wish to explain to the public the motives by which they are actuated, and the objects which they have in view.

When there is reason to believe that a British subject has been illegally put to death, or otherwise illegally punished by a person in authority, it is the duty of the Government to inquire into the case; and if it appears that the offence has been committed, to vindicate the law by bringing the offender to public justice.

From the facts recorded in the Report of the Royal Commissioners of Inquiry,[†] and in other documents relating to the late disturbances in Jamaica, coupled with the legal opinion of Mr. Edward James and Mr. Fitzjames Stephen, published by

[*The Committee had been formed in December, 1865, to attempt the prosecution for murder of the former Governor of Jamaica, Edward John Eyre, for his responsibility for the deaths of Jamaicans following the Morant Bay rebellion in October, 1865. See *LL*, *CW*, Vol. XVI, pp. 1117-18, 1191-2. Mill had become Chairman of the Committee on 9 July, 1866. The Jamaica Committee included those whose names appear in the headnote to the second paper, at p. 427 below, and others such as Charles Darwin and Thomas Henry Huxley.]

[†A Royal Commission of Inquiry appointed to investigate the case reported on 9 April, 1866; the *Report of the Jamaica Royal Commission*, released to the public on 18 June, 1866, appeared in *PP*, 1866, XXX, 489-531, and XXXI, 1-1172. Other documents include *Papers Laid before the Royal Commission of Inquiry by Governor Eyre*, *PP*, 1866, XXX, 1-488, and *Papers Relating to the Disturbances in Jamaica*, *ibid.*, LI, 145-506.]

the Committee,[*] there appeared strong reason to believe that George William Gordon, Samuel Clarke, Edward Fleming, Charles Mitchell, William Grant, Henry Lawrence, and many other subjects of Her Majesty, both male and female, had been illegally put to death, or flogged, and in some cases flogged and afterwards put to death, and *a* the houses of many others *b* illegally burnt, by Ex-Governor Eyre, Brigadier Nelson,[†] and their subordinates and coadjutors. The attention of the Government was therefore called to these cases in Parliament by Mr. Mill, the Chairman of the Committee.[‡]

The Government not only declined to take any steps for the vindication of the law, but declined on grounds and in a tone which appear to the Committee to aggravate the dangerous aspect of the proceedings in question as infractions of the constitutional liberty of the subject.[§]

The duty now devolves upon private citizens of taking such measures as the constitution may point out for the defence of those legal and chartered rights which protect the lives and liberties of all.

In undertaking to discharge this duty, so far as circumstances and the means placed at their disposal may permit, the Committee are not, any more than the ordinary ministers of public justice, actuated by vindictive feelings towards those whom they believe to have violated the law. Their aim, besides upholding the obligation of justice and humanity towards all races beneath the Queen's sway, is to vindicate, by an appeal to judicial authority, the great legal and constitutional principles which have been violated in the late proceedings, and deserted by the Government.

They desire in the first instance to establish, by a judicial sentence, the principle that the illegal execution of a British subject by a person in authority is not merely an error which superiors in office may at their discretion visit with displeasure or condone, but a crime which will certainly be punished by the law. The condition of a British subject will be altered if, for the offence of taking his life without law, a public functionary is to be responsible only to a Minister of the Crown who, in the case most dangerous to public liberty, would obviously be not the censor of his subordinate but his abettor. Our lives and liberties have not been, nor can they be safely allowed to be, under the guardianship of the Executive Government alone; they have been, and it is essential that they should remain, under the guardian-

[*See "The Jamaica Committee," *The Times*, 16 Jan., 1866, p. 3.]

[†Alexander Abercromby Nelson.]

[‡Speech on the Outbreak in Jamaica (19 July, 1866; Commons), *PD*, 3rd ser., Vol. 184, cols. 1064-6. Mill also spoke on this matter on 31 July and 10 Aug., 1866, and 1 Aug., 1867; see *ibid.*, cols. 1797-1806, 2160, and Vol. 189, cols. 598-9.]

[§Benjamin Disraeli, Speech on the Outbreak in Jamaica (19 July, 1866; Commons), *ibid.*, Vol. 184, col. 1069.]

*a*DN that
*b*DN had been

ship of the law. ^{c}A Royal Commission of Inquiry, the report of which it is proposed to substitute for the regular inquest of a court of justice in a case affecting the life of the subject, is a tribunal unknown to the constitution, not independent of the Executive, incapable even of entertaining a criminal charge, much more of passing any sentence upon the guilty, and therefore, though useful in instructing the Government, not competent to protect the lives of British citizens, or to fulfil the ends of public justice. ^{c}

In the second place, the Committee desire to challenge in a Court of Justice the jurisdiction of courts of martial law, which, as the late events show, may be made engines of indiscriminate butchery and torture; to obtain a judicial answer to the question whether military and naval officers, untrained to judicial investigation, and inflamed, probably, by the passions of the crisis, can legally try and torture or put to death the subjects of Her Majesty for high treason and other civil offences without a jury or any adequate security for justice, and without necessarily keeping even a record of the proceedings; and to have it determined by authority whether the law which these courts assume to administer is really law at all, or sanguinary licence which the law will repress and punish.

The mere refusal of Mr. Eyre's superiors in office to reinstate him in his government affords little satisfaction to the community as regards the first of these objects, and none at all as regards the second. In the Dispatch conveying that decision some parts of his conduct are disapproved; but he is not pronounced to have violated the law; and the resolution not to retain him in office is put at last mainly on the ground that a new form of government is about to be inaugurated in the Island, and that it is better to intrust this "arduous task" to some person "who may approach it free from all the difficulties inseparable from a participation in the questions raised by the recent troubles."[*] The execution of Mr. Gordon is condemned in more positive terms; but it is condemned as a stretch of severity uncalled for in the particular case, not as an infraction of public rights and principles of justice sacred in all cases alike. The practice of trying British subjects for high treason and other civil offences by court-martial is not repudiated in this Dispatch; while the language of Mr. Disraeli, in his reply to Mr. Mill's questions, admits that the proclamation of martial law is the suspension of all law,[†] and exposes the lives of British subjects to irresponsible butchery.

The form of the legal proceedings prescribed by the law in such a case, and the issue in the event of those proceedings proving successful, the Committee must leave to be determined by the law itself, of which they take ^{d}the regulation of the penalty by the exercise of^d the prerogative of mercy to be a part. It is not their fault

[*Despatch from the Right Hon. Edward Cardwell, M.P., to Lieut.-Gen. Sir H.K. Storks, *PP*, 1866, LI, 137-43.]

[†Disraeli, speech of 19 July, 1866, col. 1067.]

$^{c\text{-}c}$–DN
$^{d\text{-}d}$–DN

if the law of England, instead of assigning a specific remedy against a public functionary guilty of contriving the death of an English citizen, includes the offence among those the common remedy for which is an indictment for murder;[*] nor can the Committee admit that public justice ought on that account to be allowed to fail.

In deciding on their legal course, however, the Committee have hitherto consulted,[†] and will continue to consult, professional advisers of the highest eminence and the most unbiassed judgment.

When indeed the Committee consider the circumstances of such a case as that of Mr. Gordon—the political antagonism which previously subsisted between him and Governor Eyre—the apparent absence of any ground of military necessity for taking the life of a man who was a helpless captive in the hands of the authorities—the eagerness with which the Governor personally interposed to arrest him and carry him *e* from the place where he was living under the protection of the common law to one where it was supposed that his life might with impunity be taken without a regular trial—*f*the voice of warning raised in vain by a member of the Council,[‡] who, seeing the Governor's intention, suggested that Mr. Gordon should be tried before a civil court—*f* the composition of the court, which, by its combined incompetence and ruthlessness, cut off all hope alike of justice and of mercy—the pitiless manner in which the accused was deprived of all legal advice and assistance, and of the benefit of evidence which might have been given in his favour—the interception and destruction of the letter of advice sent open to the Brigadier-General for the guidance of the prisoner in pleading,[§] and the refusal of the brief delay necessary to call a most important witness[¶] who resided almost on the spot—the evidence on which the conviction was founded, and the total insufficiency of which to support the charge must have been palpable to any man of common understanding—the warm approval of the sentence upon that evidence by the Governor[||] after the date at which, by his own account, the insurrection had been got under,[**] and when, consequently, the plea of military necessity could no longer have any force—they must confess that this is not a case

[*42 George III, c. 85 (1802).]

[†James Fitzjames Stephen as barrister, and William Shaen as solicitor.]

[‡Henry Westmorland; see *Minutes of Evidence Taken before the Jamaica Royal Commission, PP*, 1866, XXXI, 890.]

[§William Wemyss Anderson, Letter to George W. Gordon (Oct., 1865), *ibid.*, p. 805.]

[¶Edward Major.]

[||Edward Eyre, Letter to Brigadier-General Nelson (22 Oct., 1865), in *Minutes of Evidence*, p. 636.]

[**Eyre, Despatch to Mr. [Edward] Cardwell (20 Oct., 1865), *The Times*, 20 Nov., 1865, p. 9.]

*e*DN   in a war ship
f-f–DN

which they would particularly shrink from submitting to the investigation of a court of justice.

If the execution of Mr. Gordon was illegal, and, in the eye of the law, a murder, it was a murder of which Mr. Eyre was not only constructively but personally guilty; which was committed not only under his authority, but, to all intents and purposes, with his own hand.

To lay it down that proof of private malice is indispensable in order to make an illegal execution a murder, would be to hold out impunity to the crime which is the most dangerous of all to the community—the crime of a public functionary who abuses the power entrusted to him to compass, under the forms of justice, the death of a citizen obnoxious to the Government. *To lay it down that the plea of good intentions is sufficient to divest an act of criminality would be, in like manner, to hold out impunity to all political homicide: since all who commit political homicide, whether the agents of a Government or its opponents, believe that the political object which they have in view is good.*

The Government of Jamaica institutes a prosecution for murder against Mr. Ramsay,[*] the Provost-Marshal, though it is not suggested that his cruelties were committed from any feelings of private malice against the victims. Mr. Cardwell advises Sir Henry Storks, as Governor of Jamaica, to cause careful investigation to be made in those cases which appear to require it, with a view to such further proceedings as may be requisite and just. "Great offences," he says, "must be punished."[†] It is to be presumed that he would not except the great offences of great offenders.

In attempting to vindicate the law against the violence of persons in authority, the Committee will take care to give no pretence for the charge that they are showing sympathy with disorder. The gentlemen who represented them in Jamaica[‡] went out with strict instructions to lend no assistance or countenance to any persons who had suffered for real complicity in the late disturbances. The Committee will themselves act in the spirit of these instructions; and they will further abstain from founding proceedings on any case which appears to be fairly covered by the plea of *h* necessity. They have no desire to abet resistance to lawful authority or to weaken the arm of the magistrate in preserving public order. But, on the other hand, they would remind their fellow-citizens that hopeless wrong is the sure parent of rebellion, and that its best antidote is the hope of constitutional redress.

The Committee, then, submit that they are endeavouring to defend public

[*Gordon Duberry Ramsay.]
[†Cardwell, Despatch, p. 143.]
[‡John Gorrie and J. Horne Payne.]

8-8–DN
*h*DN   military

liberty against aggression from public motives, and by the means pointed out by law; and that they may justly claim the sympathy and support of all to whom public liberty is dear.

* * * * *

2. Address to Friends of the Jamaica Committee (1866)

Examiner, 13 Oct., 1866 (2nd ed.), 647. Headed: "The Jamaica Committee. / The Jamaica Committee have issued the following address to their friends throughout the country: / 65, Fleet-street, London, October, 1866." Not listed in Mill's bibliography. Printed also, without substantive variants, and with the same heading, in the *Daily News*, 12 Oct., 1866, 3. Signed: John Stuart Mill, M.P., Chairman. / P.A. Taylor, M.P., Treasurer. / F.W. Chesson, Hon. Secretary. / Thomas Barnes, M.P., John Bright, M.P., Joseph Cowen, M.P., J.E. Cairnes, Henry Fawcett, M.P., Thomas Hughes, M.P., Wilfrid Lawson, Bart., J.M. Ludlow, Duncan M'Laren, M.P., S. Morley, F.W. Newman, R.N. Philips, M.P., T.B. Potter, M.P., Humphrey Sandwith, C.B., Goldwin Smith, Herbert Spencer, James White, M.P.

SIR,—For the reasons set forth in the accompanying "Statement"[*]—to which particular attention is requested—the Jamaica Committee resolved to undertake the duty which the Government had declined, of submitting to judicial investigation the conduct of Governor Eyre and his subordinates in putting to death Mr. Gordon and other British subjects for treason, sedition, and other alleged offences without a lawful trial.

The subscriptions and guarantees already received have justified the committee in taking the first steps; and they hope, by the time the courts resume their sittings, to be in possession of the opinion of eminent counsel as to the form of indictment and method of procedure.

The process, owing to the distance of Jamaica and other circumstances, will be very expensive; and it is evident that the committee will have to encounter a powerful resistance backed by all the resources of wealth. They deem it necessary, therefore, to appeal to the public to raise the fund to 10,000*l*. Your personal aid is earnestly requested, both in the form of subscription or guarantee, and in that of endeavouring to secure the co-operation of your friends.

In making this appeal, the committee desire once more to state that their sole object is to vindicate the law.

That the law has not yet been vindicated, that the principles of public liberty and justice impugned by the acts of Governor Eyre and his subordinates have not yet been effectively asserted, that no adequate security has been obtained against a

[*I.e., the preceding paper.]

repetition of such acts by men in power for the future, the Southampton banquet, the sentiments expressed at that banquet,[*] the doctrines propounded by the chairman and other members of the Eyre Defence and Aid Committee,[†] and the bearing of Mr. Eyre himself, are sufficient proofs. The conduct of the ex-governor, so far from being repented of or repudiated, is held up as a model for imitation; and the committee submit that, as the matter at present stands, the public cannot feel assured that British subjects, who may have given offence to a party in power, will not again be put to death without lawful trial; or that those who have been concerned in such proceedings will not again be applauded, caressed, and marked out for future reward and honour by peers, members of parliament, chaplains of her Majesty, magistrates, and other persons in high station.

The only adequate, as well as the only constitutional safeguard, is the decision of a court of justice, which, as the committee submit, those supporters of the ex-governor who believe that Mr. Gordon, Mr. Clarke, and Mr. Lawrence came lawfully and fairly to their ends ought to be the last to decline.

The committee also desire once more, in reply to persistent misrepresentation, to repeat that the acts for which they are about to prosecute were not done in the suppression of the so-called rebellion. Mr. Gordon, Mr. Clarke, and Mr. Lawrence all suffered after the period at which, as Mr. Eyre himself expressly stated, the insurrection had been completely crushed.[‡] They suffered, there is reason to suspect, for offence given to the party in power, quite independently of the disturbances, with which no one of the three was proved to have been connected in any way whatever.

While the interests of public liberty form the most obvious ground for an effectual protest against the lawless violence of persons in authority, it must not be forgotten that justice is also due to the memory, and to the families of those who have been put to a felon's death, and buried as felons beneath the gallows, for crimes of which there is reason to believe they were not lawfully or justly convicted.

The committee commend to your support an undertaking which they believe to be essential to the interests of public liberty and justice. They have come forward as private individuals to put the law in motion only on the positive and almost contumacious refusal of the Government to do its duty, by inquiring into the cases in which there was reason to believe the lives of subjects of her Majesty had been

[*See "Ex-Governor Eyre at Southampton," *The Times*, 23 Aug., 1866, p. 7.]

[†This Committee, formed in August, 1866, was chaired by Henry John Chetwynd Talbot, Earl of Shrewsbury, and included Thomas Carlyle and Roderick Impey Murchison (Vice-Presidents), Hamilton Hume (Secretary), and other notables such as John Ruskin and Henry Kingsley. Carlyle expressed their views in a letter to Hamilton Hume (23 Aug., 1866), *The Times*, 12 Sept., 1866, p. 6.]

[‡See Paper 1 above, p. 425.]

illegally taken. But having come forward, they will not fail the public, if the public will not fail them.

P.S.—Subcriptions should be forwarded to the treasurer, Mr. P.A. Taylor, M.P., Aubrey-house, Notting-hill; or to Mr. F. W. Chesson, the hon. secretary, 65 Fleet-street, London.

* * * * *

3. Statement of the Jamaica Committee (1868)

London: The Jamaica Committee, 1868. Headed: "To the Members of the Jamaica Committee"; signed: "John Stuart Mill, *Chairman*. / P.A. Taylor, *Treasurer*. / F.W. Chesson, *Hon. Sec*.", and dated London, 15 July, 1868. Not listed in Mill's bibliography. Accompanied by the following letter from Chesson, dated as the statement, from 65 Fleet St.: "Dear Sir, / I beg to send you, as a Member of the (General) Jamaica Committee, the enclosed statement, explanatory of the course which your Executive Committee has followed, and of the conclusion at which they have arrived. / The Executive Committee propose to call together the whole body of Subscribers in the course of the Autumn, of which you will of course receive due notice. / In the meantime I need hardly say we shall be happy to receive any suggestions or opinions with which you may please to favour us." The only copies of the statement located are in the Mill-Taylor Collection, British Library of Political and Economic Science.

THE ATTEMPT to call Mr. Eyre to account for his conduct as Governor of Jamaica, under the Colonial Governors' Act,[*] being at an end, the Grand Jury of Middlesex having thrown out the Bill,[†] the Executive Committee are of opinion that the duty which they undertook of exhausting all the methods afforded by the criminal law of bringing the case under the cognizance of justice has now been performed.

So much misconception has prevailed, and has been fostered by the language of those who were opposed to an inquiry, that it may be desirable to recall to mind the leading facts.

A district in the Island of Jamaica had been the scene of a disturbance, caused as it appears, in part at least, by a system of misrule under which (according to the testimony of the present Governor, Sir J.P. Grant) in minor criminal cases, those mainly affecting the people, the system of legal procedure was extremely bad, and in civil matters for the poorer classes there was no justice at all, while there was

[*42 George III, c. 85 (1802).]
[†See "Ex-Governor Eyre," *The Times*, 3 June, 1868, pp. 9-10.]

nothing worthy to be called a police.* The disturbance, though sanguinary in its first outbreak, was suppressed without difficulty, no stand being ever made by the peasantry against the troops engaged in its suppression. The outbreak having occurred on October 11th, on the 20th the Governor reported, in a letter to the Colonial Secretary, that "the rebellion had been crushed."[*] Nevertheless, for more than three weeks after this date, and even for many days after he had, on the 30th October, issued a proclamation of amnesty, declaring that the rebellion had been subdued—when all excuse of military necessity for summary proceedings was at end, and every person suspected of complicity in the disturbance might have been brought before the regular courts of justice—he continued to license the shooting, hanging and flogging of the peasantry, without distinction of sex, and the destruction of their houses and property, under the name and colour of martial law. According to the Report of the Royal Commissioners of Inquiry, 439 persons in all were put to death, not less than 600 were flogged, and 1000 houses were burned.[†] For a whole month there was a reign of terror. At one place, on a single day, 30 men and 20 women were flogged; the men with cats twisted with piano-wire, of which the Royal Commissioners of Inquiry, before whom portions of some of the cats were produced, say that it is painful to think that any man should have used such an instrument for the torturing of his fellow-creatures.[‡] Persons were tried and put to death under martial law for acts done, and even for words spoken, before the proclamation of martial law. A peasant, named Samuel Clarke, was hanged some days after the proclamation of amnesty, for words spoken two months before the proclamation of martial law, his only specified offence being that he had, at that time, declared with an oath that a letter signed by the Secretary of State for the Colonies was a lie.[§] The case of the Hon. G.W. Gordon was in its constitutional aspect still more grave.[¶] A member of the Legislature of Jamaica, and a leading opponent of the government of Mr. Eyre, he was taken by the Governor himself out of the protection of the common law, carried into the proclaimed district, handed over to a so-called court-martial presided over by Lieutenant Brand, of whose fitness to sit as judge in a case of life or death the public has since had sufficient means of forming an opinion, and put to death, with the express sanction of Mr. Eyre;[‖] to whom the sentence had been specially submitted, with an intimation from the commanding officer, General

---

*Speech of Sir J.P. Grant to the Legislative Council, Oct. 16, 1866. [In *The Times*, 13 Nov., 1866, p. 7.]

[*See Paper 1 above, p. 425.]

[†*Report of the Jamaica Royal Commission; with Minutes of Evidence and Appendix*, *PP*, 1866, XXX, 515.]

[‡*Ibid.*, pp. 515-16.]

[§*Ibid.*, XXXI, 1159; the Colonial Secretary was Edward Cardwell.]

[¶*Ibid.*, XXX, 518-28.]

[‖See p. 425 above.]

Nelson, that there was no military necessity for a summary execution: and this on evidence which the Royal Commissioners pronounce to have been wholly insufficient to support the charge,[*] and which is characterized by the Lord Chief Justice of the Queen's Bench, not only as legally "inadmissible before any properly-constituted tribunal," but as "morally worthless."[†] "No one, I think," says the same authority, "who has the faintest idea of what the administration of justice involves, could deem the proceedings on this trial consistent with justice, or, to use a homely phrase, with that fair play which is the right of the commonest criminal." "All I can say," proceeds the Lord Chief Justice, "is that if, on martial law being proclaimed, a man can lawfully be thus tried, condemned and sacrificed, such a state of things is a scandal and a reproach to the institutions of this great and free country; and, as a minister of justice, profoundly imbued with a sense of what is due to the first and greatest of earthly obligations, I enter my solemn and emphatic protest against the lives of men being thus dealt with in the time to come."[‡]

The gravity of these events, in a constitutional point of view, and the necessity of bringing the case before a legal tribunal in the interest of public liberty and justice, were enhanced by the language of certain classes and of certain journalists in this country, who applauded the arbitrary violence of Mr. Eyre; by the publications of legal writers, the advocates of prerogative, who took occasion to uphold martial law as exemplified in the acts of the Governor and his subordinates in Jamaica (and notably in the trial and execution of Mr. Gordon) putting forth doctrines which the Lord Chief Justice denounces as "dangerous and pernicious," and of which he says that he "almost shuddered when he read them;"[§] and, above all, by the attitude of the ministers of the Crown, one of whom, when questioned on the subject in Parliament, maintained, in effect, that martial law, when proclaimed, exempted those assuming to act under it from responsibility for their actions, however criminal and oppressive, to the laws and legal tribunals of the land,* while his colleague defended the execution of Mr. Gordon, without reference to legality, as "practically just."[†]

Acting, as they have acted throughout, under the legal guidance of counsel at once eminent and dispassionate,[¶] the Executive Committee proceeded to try the question whether an officer of the Crown, who had illegally taken the life of a

[*Report of the Jamaica Royal Commission, p. 528.]

[†Alexander James Edmund Cockburn, Charge of the Lord Chief Justice of England to the Grand Jury at the Central Criminal Court, in the Case of the Queen against Nelson and Brand, ed. Frederick Cockburn (London: Ridgway, 1867), pp. 153, 115.]

[‡Ibid., p. 165.]

[§Ibid., pp. 155, 153.]

*Speech of Mr. Disraeli (Chancellor of the Exchequer), July 19, 1866. [PD, 3rd ser., Vol. 184, col. 1067.]

†Speech of Mr. [Charles Bowyer] Adderley, July 31, 1866 [ibid., col. 1794].

[¶See p. 425 above. Robert Porrett Collier succeeded Stephen as counsel.]

British subject, was or was not responsible to the law. This was done by proceeding at common law against Mr. Eyre and his subordinates, General Nelson and Lieut. Brand, for the illegal execution of Mr. Gordon. The subordinates were committed for trial by Sir Thomas Henry, the chief magistrate of the metropolitan district, but the Grand Jury of London threw out the Bill.[*] Mr. Eyre himself, acting, as was stated, under the advice of his Committee, had retired into Shropshire, where he was under the jurisdiction of the county magistrates, who, upon application being made to them, refused to commit him for trial.[†] The case against Mr. Eyre was now laid in its completeness before the Attorney-General, that the investigation, which the Shropshire Justices of the Peace refused, might, under his authority and on his motion, be obtained; but the Attorney-General declined to act.[‡] Much time was next spent in endeavouring to bring Mr. Eyre, who had left Shropshire, but whose movements the Solicitor of the Committee found great difficulty in tracing, before a magistrate legally educated, and upon whose impartiality reliance could be placed. When, at length, this was effected, the magistrate[§] refused to commit, on the technical ground that General Nelson and Lieutenant Brand were the principals in the execution of Mr. Gordon, while Mr. Eyre was only an accessory, and that the Bill against the principals having been thrown out by the Grand Jury, the accessory ought not to be committed on that charge. Thus baffled by the forms of law, the Executive Committee made a final attempt, under the advice of their counsel, to bring the case before a jury under the Colonial Governors' Act. Under that Act the magistrate,[¶] after first seeking the direction of the Court of Queen's Bench as to his jurisdiction in the matter, committed Mr. Eyre for trial; but the Grand Jury of Middlesex threw out the Bill.

In accordance with their pledge, and in consistency with the instructions given by them to their legal representatives in Jamaica, the Executive Committee have abstained from calling in question any act done by an officer of the Crown in the suppression of insurrection. They have confined the proceedings to acts done after the insurrection had, in the recorded opinion of the Governor himself, been put down, and when, in the judgment of his chief military subordinate, the military necessity was at an end.

Nor would the Executive Committee have assumed to themselves and their constituents in any case the invidious function of setting the law in motion, if the

[*See "The Jamaica Prosecutions," *The Times*, 12 Apr., 1867, p. 11.]

[†See *ibid.*, 30 Mar., 1867, p. 12.]

[‡See "The Jamaica Committee and Mr. Eyre," *ibid.*, 29 July, 1867, p. 12, in which appear Shaen's request of 10 July to John Rolt, the Attorney-General, and Rolt's reply of 13 July refusing to prosecute.]

[§Again Thomas Henry. See "Prosecution of Ex-Governor Eyre," *The Times*, 28 Feb., 1868, p. 10.]

[¶James Vaughan.]

Government had shewn any disposition to perform that duty. Once, as has already been stated, they attempted, and they would at any time have been ready, to transfer the matter to the hands of the Law Officers of the Crown. But the Government, though it instituted proceedings against some of the subordinate agents in Jamaica, wholly refused to take any steps for submitting the conduct of the principal agents to a judicial investigation here.[*] The duty of vindicating the law, when thus abandoned by the Government, is cast, by the principles of the English constitution, on private citizens; if private citizens declined it, there would be no check on the illegal conduct of officers of the Crown.

For the inappropriateness, uncertainty and awkwardness of the remedies provided by the law against a Colonial Governor guilty of oppression, and the protraction of the legal proceedings thereby occasioned, the Executive Committee are not responsible. Nor are they responsible for the unavoidable delay incurred in bringing witnesses from Jamaica, or for that caused by the difficulty of finding Mr. Eyre within the jurisdiction of a professional minister of the law. Due allowance being made for these impediments, the proceedings have been carried on with all possible despatch.

The difficulty of bringing evidence from Jamaica not only occasioned loss of time and expenditure of money, but prevented the case from being presented before the public in the Courts of Law, with its full moral force, the Executive Committee being compelled to content themselves with no more testimony than what was technically sufficient to support the charge.

The proceedings of the Committee may be said to have had three objects—to obtain a judicial inquiry into the conduct of Mr. Eyre and his subordinates; to settle the law in the interest of justice, liberty and humanity; and to arouse public morality against oppression generally, and particularly against the oppression of subject and dependent races.

The first object has not been attained. The Grand Jury in Jamaica threw out the Bill in the case of Provost-Marshal Ramsay (who had hanged a man for a gesture made, or an exclamation uttered under the torture of the lash) notwithstanding the declaration of the presiding judge that a trial was essential to the interests of public justice.[†] The county Magistrates of Shropshire, and the Grand Juries of London and Middlesex, have interposed their authority to prevent a judicial inquiry into the case of a British citizen put to death "unlawfully and unjustifiably," in the words of the Lord Chief Justice,[‡] by an officer of the Crown. In each case the public must be left to judge whether the result was due to the want of ground for an inquiry, or to the determination of those who interposed that no inquiry should take place. On

[* See The Times, 29 Oct., 1866, p. 10; 13 Nov., 1866, p. 7; 1 Jan., 1867, p. 9; and 2 Mar., 1867, p. 12.]

[†Gordon Duberry Ramsay hanged George Marshall; the judge was Alan Ker. See The Times, 13 Nov., 1866, p. 7.]

[‡Cockburn, Charge, p. 114.]

the other hand, it is needless to say that Mr. Eyre is in error when he speaks of himself as having been twice acquitted.[*] As there has been no trial, there can have been no acquittal; and in that respect the question remains exactly where it was before these proceedings were commenced.

The second object has been attained. The memorable charge of the Lord Chief Justice in the case of Nelson and Brand will remain, as the Executive Committee believe, a lasting barrier against the encroachment of martial law and its upholders on the rights and liberties of British subjects. If the subsequent charge of Mr. Justice Blackburn[†] in some respects differed from that of the Lord Chief Justice, the opinion of the Lord Chief Justice is known to be shared by every other member of the Court. But even Mr. Justice Blackburn did not maintain, as some lawyers had maintained, that the power of proclaiming martial law formed a part of the prerogative of the Crown in England. His doctrine was limited to Jamaica, and was founded on Acts of the Colonial Legislature, which, with all Colonial Acts of a similar character, have now, and in consequence of the manifestation of public opinion respecting the events in Jamaica, been repealed.[‡] British jurisprudence, therefore, has been finally purged of martial law. The committal of Mr. Eyre, General Nelson and Lieutenant Brand, for trial, by London Magistrates, has moreover confirmed the principle that the officers of the Crown are responsible in the ordinary course of justice to the Courts of Law for acts done by them in the suppression, or alleged suppression, of insurrection.

With regard to the third object, also, the Executive Committee feel that the efforts of the Jamaica Committee have been well repaid. A great amount of sound public opinion has been called forth; and it is not unreasonable to think that this has contributed to the escape of the nation from any thing which could leave a stain on its humanity or honour in the suppression of the recent disturbances in Ireland, where there were not wanting cruel and panic-stricken advocates of a proclamation of martial law. That sympathy with Mr. Eyre and with his policy should at the same time be exhibited in the quarters where it prevailed, was inevitable. It was inevitable also, that this sympathy should take the form of charges of vindictiveness, malignity and persecution against those who, without the slightest personal feeling, were endeavouring to discharge the unwelcome but indispensable duty of guarding public liberty and vindicating the law; nor was it unnatural that such charges should find acceptance among the unthinking, when, from the lapse of time, the agony of so many hundreds of sufferers had been forgotten, and the annoyance inflicted by legal proceedings on the author of the suffering alone remained present to the mind. In answer to the charge of persecution, so far as it is

[*Eyre, Letter to the Editor (2 June, 1868), *The Times*, 4 June, 1868, p. 7.]

[†Colin Blackburn, Charge to the Middlesex Grand Jury (2 June, 1868), in "Ex-Governor Eyre," *The Times*, 3 June, 1868, pp. 9-10.]

[‡See Henry Howard Molyneux Herbert, "Circular Despatch to Colonial Governors, Dated 30th January, 1867, on the Subject of Martial Law," *PP*, 1867, XLIX, 395.]

founded on the protraction of the proceedings, the Executive Committee repeat, that for this protraction they are not responsible. Had Mr. Eyre been advised to meet justice like his subordinates, his case would have been brought to as prompt a hearing as those of General Nelson and Lieutenant Brand.

Appendix F

TEXTUAL EMENDATIONS

IN THIS LIST, following the page and line numbers, the reading of the copy-text is given first, and then the emended reading in square brackets, with explanations if required. "SC" indicates Mill's own copies of the texts in Somerville College, Oxford. Typographical errors in versions other than the copy-text are ignored. When the copy-text is a manuscript, end-of-line punctuation, frequently omitted by Mill, is supplied when necessary for the sense.

5.10   end.† [end."†] [*restyled in this ed.*]
5n.7   parceque [parce que] [*as in* Source]
6.3   libel. [libel?] [*for sense*]
7.11   reason, [reason] [*as elsewhere in paragraph*]
18.24   reign—. [reign?] [*as in* Source]
24n.3   Wils. [*Wils. K.B.*] [*as in* Source]
27.38   defence." [defence.'] [*restyled in this ed.*]
29.20   Yorke, ...) [Yorke . . .).] [*to conform to usual practice*]
29n.1   Holt's Rep. [*Holt K.B.*] [*for consistency*]
31.20   begins [begin] [*as in* Source]
31.21   formed' [formed.'] [*restyled in this ed.*]
32.14   party" [party.'] [*restyled in this ed.*]
33.41   witness' [witness.'] [*restyled in this ed.*]
53.1   early a brilliant [early or brilliant] [*corrected by JSM in SC copy*]
54.19   people. Our [people; our] [*altered to* people; Our *by JSM in SC copy; treated as incomplete revision*]
56.10   an author [our author] [*corrected by JSM in SC copy*]
67.32   three [3] [*for consistency*]
67n.1   .) [).]
68.39   No." ["No."]
72.15   avoirdupoise [avoirdupois] [*as in* Source]
78.6   another? [another.] [*corrected by JSM in SC copy*]
79.17   merely [surely] [*corrected by JSM in SC copy*]
79.25   self defence [self-defence] [*as elsewhere in paragraph*]
93.39   highest [briefest] [*corrected by JSM in SC copy*]
113.41   *refrein* [*refrain*] [*as in* 59[1,2]]
150.42   lawless, [lawless] [*as in* Source *and* 64]
152.29   as [as,] [*as in* Source *and* 64]

152.34   His [*His*] [*as in* Source]

155.5-6   "There . . . slaveholder," . . . Georgia, . . . "in ['"There . . . slaveholder,' . . . Georgia," . . . '"in] [*restyled in this ed.*]

155.18   owner." [owner.'"] [*restyled in this ed.*]

155.33-8   "is . . . peculiarities." ['"is . . . peculiarities.'"]

164.24   made [made by] [*as in* 62[1,2],64, *and for sense*]

173.24   as as a [as a]

179.28   motion [notion] [*as in* 63,75]

179.33   every one [everyone] [*as in previous sentence, and* 63[1,2]]

270.10   parliament [Parliament] [*as elsewhere in work*]

309.33   themselves; (if [themselves (if] [*to conform to usual practice*]

309.36   .) [).] [*to conform to usual practice*]

315.2   Stael [Staël]

324.20   she [he] [*for sense*]

347.1   nations, [nations] [*as in* 75, *and for sense*]

351.23   imprisonmənt [imprisonment]

353.11   analagous [analogous] [*incorrect also in* 71[1]]

355.1   , that, [that] [*as in* 71[1]]

355.1   divorce, [divorce] [*as in* 71[1]]

356.18   self supporting [self-supporting] [*as in* 71[1]]

356.23   licences [licenses] [*as in answer,* 71[1], *and elsewhere*]

356.30   brothel keepers [brothel-keepers] [*as elsewhere in passage*]

357.23   practice [practise] [*as in* 71[1]]

358.5   Goverment [Government]

358.35   themselves we [themselves, we] [*as in* 71[1]]

359.5   before-hand [beforehand] [*as elsewhere in passage; end-of-line hyphen in* 71[1]]

359.5   practicing [practising] [*as in* 71[1]]

359.21   fault; [fault.]

359.25   from [for] [*for sense*]

360.2   alone, [alone] [*as in* 71[1]]

360.3   into [in] [*as in* 71[1]]

361.14   working. [working?] [*as in* 71[1]]

362.13   council [counsel] [*as in* 71[1] *and elsewhere in passage*]

364.8   anotherreason [another reason]

365.7   inconsistent, [inconsistent] [*for sense*]

366.12   evidence? [evidence.]

366.34-5   more / generally than are now in practice. I should say, if you found a / decided measures of that sort with regard to the destitute classes / person [*lines restored to their proper order as in* 71[1]]

367.22   remdy [remedy]

368.23   cousidered [considered]

368.39   still go [go still] [*as in* 71[1] *and for sense*]

369.26   licence [license] [*as in* 71[1], *and elsewhere in passage*]

371.3   commission [Commission] [*as in* 71[1], *and elsewhere in passage*]

378.4   changable [changeable] [*slip of the pen?*]

379.26   this [This] [*slip of the pen?*]

381.7   elector, [elector?] [*as elsewhere in passage*]

381.11   what [What] [*as elsewhere in passage*]

381.15   they were [they] [*slip of the pen*]

381.19   there, [there.] [*for consistency*]

381.32   They [they] [*incomplete revision*]
382.19   occupations; [occupations?] [*end of page*]
382.36   life" [life,"]
383.35   other. [other,] [*incomplete revision*]
388.22   it is [it as] [*slip of the pen*]
389.7   majority [the majority] [*slip of the pen*]
389.30   Women" It [Women," it] [*incomplete revision*]
395.37   [*½-line space added*]
403.2   parliament [Parliament] [*as elsewhere in passage*]
417.13   accumulate. [accumulate?] [*as in printed version*]
417.18   man' [man's] [*slip of the pen*]
430.22   Clark [Clarke] [*as in* Source]
431.24   "he almost [he "almost]
431.29   land,"* [land,*] [*the passage is not a quotation, and the opening quotation marks are not in the text*]
434.23   Committe [Committee]

Appendix G

Bibliographical Index of Persons and Works Cited, with Variants and Notes

LIKE MOST NINETEENTH-CENTURY AUTHORS, Mill is cavalier in his approach to sources, sometimes identifying them with insufficient care, and occasionally quoting them inaccurately. This Appendix is intended to help correct these deficiencies, and to serve as an index of names and titles (which are consequently omitted in the Index proper). Included here also are (at the end of the appendix) references to parliamentary documents, entered in order of date under the heading "Parliamentary Papers," and references to statute law, entered by country in order of date under the heading "Statutes." The material otherwise is arranged in alphabetical order, with an entry for each person or work quoted or referred to. Anonymous articles in newspapers are entered in order of date under the title of the particular newspaper. References to mythical and fictional characters are excluded. The following abbreviations are used: *PD* for Hansard's *Parliamentary Debates*, and *PP* for *Parliamentary Papers*.

The entries take the following form:

1. Identification: author, title, etc. in the usual bibliographic form. When only a surname is given, no other identification has been found.

2. Notes (if required) giving information about JSM's use of the source, indication if the work is in his library, Somerville College, Oxford (referred to as SC), and any other relevant information.

3. Lists of the pages where works are reviewed, quoted, and referred to.

4. In the case of quotations, a list of substantive variants between Mill's text and his source, in this form: Page and line reference to the present text. Reading in the present text] Reading in the source (page reference in the source).

The list of substantive variants also attempts to place quoted passages in their contexts by giving the beginnings and endings of sentences. The original wording is supplied where Mill has omitted two sentences or less; only the length of other omissions is given. There being uncertainty about the actual Classical texts used by Mill, the Loeb editions are cited when possible.

ABBOTT, CHARLES.
  NOTE: the quotation and the reference are from Thomas Jonathan Wooler, *A Verbatim Report* (*q.v.* for the collation).
  QUOTED: 31
  REFERRED TO: 30

ABERDEEN, LORD. See George Gordon.

ADDERLEY, CHARLES BOWYER. Speech on the Disturbances in Jamaica (31 July, 1866; Commons), *PD*, 3rd ser., Vol. 184, cols. 1785-97.
QUOTED: 431
431.30   "practically just"] At all events, I do not wish to press that point, but I may say that, although there is some question about the illegality of the arrest, and the sufficiency of evidence, there is less question about the practical justice of the result. (col. 1794)

ADDISON, JOSEPH. *The Spectator*, No. 160 (1 Sept., 1711).
NOTE: reprinted in collections under the title "The Vision of Mirzah."
REFERRED TO: 198

AESOP. *Aesop's Fables*. Trans. Vernon Stanley Vernon Jones. London: Heinemann; New York: Doubleday, Page, 1912.
NOTE: this ed. used for ease of reference. *Aesopi Phrygis fabulae graece et latine, cum aliis opusculis* (Pladunes Collection) (Basel: Heruagius, 1544) is in SC. The reference at 53 is to the fable of "The Lioness and the Vixen"; that at 112 is to "The Fox without a Tail."
REFERRED TO: 53, 112

ALBRET, JEANNE D'.
NOTE: mother of Henri IV of France.
REFERRED TO: 401

ANDERSON, WILLIAM WEMYSS. Letter to George W. Gordon (Oct., 1865). In *Minutes of Evidence Taken before the Jamaica Royal Commission*, *PP*, 1866, XXXI, 805.
REFERRED TO: 425

ANNE (of England). Referred to: 252

ANON. "Mr. Carlyle on the Negroes," *The Inquirer*, VIII (8 Dec., 1849), 769-70.
QUOTED: 95
95.28 "a . . . devil"] It is a . . . Devil, the fostering of a tyrannical prejudice. (770)

ANON. Review of *Report on the State of Public Instruction in Prussia*, by M. Victor Cousin. Translated by Sarah Austin. *Monthly Repository*, n.s. VIII (May, 1834), 383.
NOTE: in the list of "New Publications."
REFERRED TO: 63

APPLEGARTH, ROBERT. "Minutes of Evidence Taken before the Royal Commission on the Administration and Operation of the Contagious Diseases Acts of 1866 and 1869," *PP*, 1871, XIX, 818-25.
NOTE: the "quotations" are questions asked by Applegarth, a member of the Commission.
QUOTED: 369-71
REFERRED TO: 350

ARISTOTLE. Referred to: 225, 229, 230, 238, 302

———— *The "Art" of Rhetoric* (Greek and English). Trans. J.H. Freese. London: Heinemann; New York: Putnam's Sons, 1926.
NOTE: this ed. used for ease of reference. *De rhetorica seu arte dicendi libri* (Greek and Latin), ed. Theodor Goulston (London: Griffin, 1619), is in SC.
REFERRED TO: 175, 229

———— *The Nicomachean Ethics* (Greek and English). Trans. H. Rackham. London: Heinemann; New York: Putnam's Sons, 1926.
NOTE: this ed. used for ease of reference. Another ed. (Oxford: Sheldonian Theatre, 1716) in SC.
REFERRED TO: 229

———— *Politics* (Greek and English). Trans. H. Rackham. London: Heinemann; New York: Putnam's Sons, 1932.

172.2-4 In . . . law "most . . . terms" . . . "are not names of . . . objects."] Though that, indeed, is a name which will hardly denote them distinctly: for, like most . . . terms in . . . law, it is not the name of . . . objects.* [*footnote omitted*] (I, 14)

174n.1-2 "a cause . . . nothing . . . cure."] To the absence of this distinction (a cause . . . naught . . . cure), the greater compactness of the Roman system, with its greater symmetry and clearness, are mainly imputable. (I, xciv n)

174n.10 mass] mess (II, 154)

177.14 "If] But to say this is to talk absurdly: for every object which is measured, or every object which is brought to a test, is compared with a given object other than itself.—If (I, 116n)

179.16 "all] [*paragraph*] Now (as I shall endeavour to demonstrate in this evening's discourse) all (II, 56)

179.17 considered universally] *considered universally* (II, 56)

179.17 generality."] generality, and may be compressed into a single proposition, or into a few short propositions. (II, 56)

180.21 "a] Now a (II, 52)

180.23-4 "a right . . . burthen," . . . "an absurdity."] [*paragraph*] For, 1st, in purely onerous conditions, the mark is *not* to be found: a right . . . burthen, being an absurdity. (II, 395)

181.9 "to] [*paragraph*] But before we can determine the import "Injury" and "Sanction" (or can distinguish the compulsion or restraint, which is implied in Duty or Obligation, from that compulsion or restraint which is merely physical), we must try to (II, 79)

182.36-7 "law . . . lawyers."] For law . . . lawyers, is not committed to writing *ab initio*, although it may afterwards be recorded in legal treatises, or may be adopted by the supreme legislature and promulged in a written form. (II, 195)

183.31-2 "that . . . authority,"] [*paragraph*] But though every positive law exists *as positive law* through the position or institution given to it by a sovereign government, it is supposed by a multitude of writers on general and particular jurisprudence, that . . . authority. (II, 221)

183.36 "much] [*paragraph*] Again: Much (II, 235)

184.4-5 "puerile fiction,"] But the opinions of both, as determining the decisions of the tribunals, may be considered as *causes* of that law, which (in spite of the puerile fiction about immemorial usage) is notoriously introduced by judges acting in their judicial capacity. (II, 236)

184.20 "thoroughly] Since it is peculiar to Ulpian, and since no attempt to apply it occurs in the Pandects or Institutes, it can scarcely be considered the *natural Law of the Romans,** [*footnote omitted*] nor can it be fairly imputed to the body of the Classical Jurists: who (heaven knows) have enough to answer for, in that they adopted from the Greeks the other *jus naturale*, and were thus the remote authors of that modern Law of Nature which has so thoroughly (II, 240-1)

185.14 "omnipotent with barbarians"] They arose in early ages, and in the infancy of the human mind, partly from caprices of the fancy (which are nearly omnipotent with barbarians), and partly from the imperfect apprehension of general utility which is the consequence of narrow experience. (I, 58)

185n.3 "I could point," . . . "at] If I liked, I could point at (II, 273)

185n.5-6 misunderstood] misapprehended (II, 273)

186.10-11 "not . . . human] [*paragraph*] But since their human authors copied them from divine originals, which were known to those human authors through a perfectly infallible index, they are not . . . *human* (II, 261)

186.15-17 "every . . . any] It comprises *every . . . any* (II, 260)

188.22 First: A] First: As I showed in my last lecture, a (II, 359)

188.38 "law. . . . And] law: provided (that is to say) that the statute law with which the rule is compared, be not only expressed in *abstract* and *brief* expressions, but also in such expressions as are *apt* and *unambiguous* as may be. For (as I shall show immediately) the very indeterminateness of its form (or the very indeterminateness of the signs by which it is signified or indicated) renders a judiciary law less uncertain in effect than a statute law unaptly and dubiously worded. But, assuming that a statute law is aptly and unambiguously worded, (or as aptly and unambiguously worded as the subject and language will permit,) it is more accessible and knowable than a rule of judiciary law which must be obtained through the process to which I have adverted above. [*paragraph*] And (II, 360)

189.5-6 constructed. . . . [*paragraph*] There] constructed. [*ellipsis indicates 8-paragraph omission*] [*paragraph*] Fourthly: For the reasons which I assigned in my last lecture, and for others which I passed in silence, there (II, 361-2)

189.48 [I] [*v.v.* I (II, 364)

190.3 Not] *v.v.* Not (II, 364)

190.7 Forms, . . . legislature.] [*paragraph*] The] *v.v.* Forms, . . . legislature.] [*2-paragraph omission*] [*paragraph*] The (II, 364)

190.13-14 skill. . . . [*paragraph*] Fifthly] skill. [*ellipsis indicates 4-paragraph omission*] [*paragraph*] Fifthly (II, 365)

190.19-20 rule was decided? . . . [*paragraph*] We] rule were decided? [*ellipsis indicates 1-paragraph omission*] [*paragraph*] In fine, we (II, 365-6)

190.25-6 obviated. . . . [*paragraph*] Sixthly] obviated. [*ellipsis indicates 4-paragraph and 2-note omission*] [*paragraph*] Sixthly (II, 366-7)

190.32-3 Romilly: [*paragraph*] "Not] Romilly, in that admirable article on Codification which I ventured to criticize in my last evening's discourse. [*paragraph*] The passage is as follows: [*paragraph*] "Not (II, 367)

190.48 authority." [*paragraph*] [Hence] authority."* [*footnote and 1 paragraph omitted*] [*paragraph*] *v.v.* Hence (II, 368)

191.2 Hence] *v.v.* Hence (II, 368)

191.11 though the] though (for the reasons which I stated in my last lecture, and to which I shall revert immediately) the (II, 368)

191.13-14 question. . . . [*paragraph*] Seventhly] question. I have heard Lord Eldon declare (more than once) that nothing should provoke him to decide more than the decision of the case in question absolutely required. [*ellipsis indicates 1-paragraph omission*] [*paragraph*] Seventhly (II, 368-9)

191.20-1 judiciary. . . . [*paragraph*] Wherever] judiciary. [*ellipsis indicates 3-sentence omission*] [*paragraph*] Wherever (II, 369)

191.25-6 irregular unsystematic . . . judges. . . . [*paragraph*] Wherever . . . judiciary] irregular or unsystematic . . . judges. [*ellipsis indicates 5-paragraph omission*] [*paragraph*] Wherever . . . *judiciary* (II, 369-70)

191.32 a Code, or . . . law, will] *a Code* (or . . . law) will (II, 370)

——— *On the Uses of the Study of Jurisprudence.* London: Murray, 1863.
NOTE: reprinted from Vol. III of *Lectures on Jurisprudence, q.v.*
REVIEWED: 165-205
QUOTED: 173

173.29 (*elegentia*)] "elegentia"† [*footnote omitted*] (19)

———— *The Province of Jurisprudence Determined*. London: Murray, 1832.
REVIEWED: 51-60
QUOTED: 58-9, 59-60
REFERRED TO: 167, 169, 175
58.37 vigour] rigour (83) [*printer's error?*]
59.9 indifferency] "indifferency" (84)
59.12 *are*] are (84)
59.18 charge] change (84) [*printer's error?*]
59.20 *In*] In (84)
60.21 Hoadleys] Hoadlys (81)

———— 2nd ed. Ed. Sarah Austin. London: Murray, 1861.
NOTE: see also 1st ed. (1832), and *Lectures on Jurisprudence*, 3 vols. (1863), Vol. I of which is
identified as the 3rd ed. of *The Province*. The collations and references are given under the
Lectures (because it is the work under review).
REFERRED TO: 167, 169

AUSTIN, SARAH.
NOTE: the references at 167 and 169 are to her as editor of John Austin's *Province*, 2nd ed. (*q.v.*);
that at 202 is to her as editor of his *Lectures* (*q.v.*). See also Cousin.
REFERRED TO: 167, 169, 202

BACON, FRANCIS. *Novum Organum* (1620). In *Works*. Ed. James Spedding, *et al.* 14
vols. London: Longman, *et al.*, 1857-74, I, 119-365 (Latin); IV, 38-248 (English).
NOTE: in SC.
QUOTED: 280
REFERRED TO: 235, 240
280.14 "opinio . . . inopiae est;"] Atque cum opinio . . . inopiae sit; quumque ex fiducia
praesentium vera auxilia negligantur in posterum; ex usa est, et plane ex necessitate, ut ab illis
quae adhuc inventa sunt in ipso operis nostri limine (idque relictis ambagibus et non
dissimulanter) honoris et admirationis excessus tollatur; utili monito, ne homines eorum aut
copiam aut utilitatem in majus accipiant aut celebrent. (125)

———— "Of Marriage and Single Life" (1612). In *Works*, VI, 391-2.
REFERRED TO: 332

BAIN, ALEXANDER.
NOTE: a professor at Aberdeen University.
REFERRED TO: 243

BAKER, ELIZABETH.
NOTE: a nurse whose cruelty led to the death of a child (Albert Monks).
REFERRED TO: 103

BARKER.
NOTE: not otherwise identified. The reference, in a quotation from Austin, is to the case of
Omychund *v.* Barker in 1744.
REFERRED TO: 192

BARNES, THOMAS. Referred to: 427

BEAUJEU, ANNE, DUCHESSE DE.
NOTE: sister of Charles VIII of France, regent 1483-91 as designated by their father, Louis XI.
REFERRED TO: 303

BEAUMARCHAIS, PIERRE AUGUSTIN CARON DE. *La folle journée, ou Le mariage de
Figaro* (1785). In *Oeuvres complètes*. 7 vols. Paris: Collin, 1809, II, 57-320.
NOTE: a 2-vol. *Oeuvres complètes* was formerly in SC.
REFERRED TO: 325

69.34   not] *not* (168)
69.37   calculating spirit] [*in italics*] (168)
69.38   reward tickets] [*in italics*] (168)
69.41   Mammon of unrighteousness] [*in italics*] (168)
70.2-3   pay . . . dismissed] [*in italics*] (168)
70.3-4   those . . . them] [*in italics*] (169)
70.5-6   in . . . them] [*in italics*] (169)
70.31   round the school-room] [*in italics*] (170)
70.32   proclaim] *proclaim* (170)
70.32-3   they . . . learning] [*in italics*] (170)
70.33   two . . . school] [*in italics*] (170)
71.7   The] [*no paragraph*] However that may be, it is certain that the (172)
71.7   and, as] and that, as (172)
71.21   grafted upon] grafted in upon (173)
72.25   beef] *beef* (175)
72.35   connecting] *connecting* (175)
73.18   at] for (176)

BIBLE. Referred to: 296

———— Colossians.

QUOTED: 296

296.16   "Wives, obey your husbands:"] Wives, submit yourselves unto your own husbands, as it
is fit in the Lord. (3:18)

296.17   "Slaves, obey your masters."] Servants, obey in all things your masters according to the
flesh; not with eyeservice, as menpleasers; but in singleness of heart, fearing God. (3:22)

———— I Corinthians.

NOTE: the reference is in a quotation from Biber.

REFERRED TO: 69

———— Deuteronomy.

REFERRED TO: 58

———— Exodus.

NOTE: the reference is to the Ten Commandments.

REFERRED TO: 288

———— Genesis.

QUOTED: 37

37.7   "it . . . good for man to be alone"] It . . . good that man should be alone. (2:18)

———— Hosea.

NOTE: the quotations are in a quotation from Biber.

QUOTED: 69

69.28   "love a reward upon every cornfloor"] Rejoice not, O Israel, for joy, as other people: for
thou hast gone a whoring from thy God, thou hast loved a reward upon every cornfloor. (9:1)

————Isaiah.

NOTE: the quotation is in a quotation from Biber.

QUOTED: 69

69.30   "love gifts, and follow after rewards"] Thy princes are rebellious, and companions of
thieves: every one loveth gifts, and followeth after rewards: they judge not the fatherless,
neither doth the cause of the widow come unto them. (1:23)

———— Judges.

NOTE: the reference is to Deborah.

REFERRED TO: 302

———— Luke.

NOTE: the quotation is in a quotation from Biber; the reference at 68 is in a quotation from Biber;
that at 257 is to the parable of the sower.

QUOTED: 69

REFERRED TO: 68, 257, 281, 389

69.41 "Mammon of unrighteousness."] And I say unto you, Make to yourselves friends of the mammon of unrighteousness; that, when ye fail, they may receive you into everlasting habitations. (16:9)

———— Matthew.

QUOTED: 87

87.7 "as one having authority"] For he taught them as one having authority, and not as the scribes. (7:29)

———— Proverbs.

NOTE: the quotation is in a quotation from Biber.

QUOTED: 71

71.15-16 him,"] him. (27:22)

———— Romans.

QUOTED: 296

296.21-2 "The powers . . . God,"] For there is no power but of God: the powers . . . God. (13:1)

———— Titus.

QUOTED: 39

39.19 "to the pure all things are pure"] Unto the pure all things are pure: but unto them that are defiled and unbelieving is nothing pure; but even their mind and conscience is defiled. (1:15)

BLACKBURN, COLIN. Charge to Middlesex Grand Jury in the Case of Governor Eyre (2 June, 1868). In "Ex-Governor Eyre," *The Times*, 3 June, 1868, 9-10.

REFERRED TO: 434

BLACKSTONE, WILLIAM. *Commentaries on the Laws of England.* 4 vols. Oxford: Clarendon Press, 1765-69.

NOTE: the reference at 21 is to Blackstone's *Commentaries* (IV, 150) as one of the six legal authorities cited by Holt, *q.v.* The references at 178, 194 and 195 are cited by Austin, who used the 1st ed. The 5th ed. (1773) is in SC.

REFERRED TO: 21, 178, 194, 195

BLANCHE (of Castile).

NOTE: mother of Louis IX of France, regent for several periods during his reign.

REFERRED TO: 303, 401

BLUNT, JOHN HENRY, ed. *The Annotated Book of Common Prayer, Being an Historical, Ritual, and Theological Commentary on the Devotional System of the Church of England.* 7th ed. London, Oxford, and Cambridge: Rivingtons, 1876.

NOTE: this version used for ease of reference. The reference is to "The Form of Solemnization of Matrimony," 261-74.

REFERRED TO: 296

BOCCACCIO, GIOVANNI. *Decameron* (1353).

NOTE: as the reference is simply to Griselda, the heroine of one of the stories, no ed. is cited.

REFERRED TO: 414

The Book of Common Prayer. See John Henry Blunt.

BOURDEILLE, PIERRE DE, SEIGNEUR DE BRANTÔME. *Les vies des dames galantes* (1666). Vols. II and III of *Mémoires de Messire Pierre de Bourdeille, seigneur de Brantôme.* 10 vols. Leyden: Sambix le jeune, 1665-1722.

NOTE: see also Francis I, and Victor Hugo, *Le roi s'amuse.*

REFERRED TO: 312

BOURGUIGNON, LOUIS DOMINIQUE ("Cartouche").

NOTE: his name became proverbial for highway robbers.

REFERRED TO: 137

BRAND, HERBERT CHARLES ALEXANDER. Referred to: 430, 432, 434, 435

BRAYNE, WILLIAM.
NOTE: the reference is in a quotation from Carlyle.
REFERRED TO: 92

BRECKINRIDGE, JOHN CABELL. Referred to: 157

BRIDGES, JOHN HENRY. "Minutes of Evidence Taken before the Royal Commission on
the Administration and Operation of the Contagious Diseases Acts of 1866 and
1869," *PP*, 1871, XIX, 818-25.
NOTE: the "quotations" are questions asked by Bridges as member of the Commission.
QUOTED: 358-9
REFERRED TO: 350

BRIGHT, JOHN. Referred to: 427

BROUGHAM, HENRY PETER (Lord Brougham). Speech on the Address on the King's
Speech (29 Jan., 1828; Commons), *PD*, n.s., Vol. 18, cols. 49-58.
NOTE: the quotation, in a quotation from *The Cornish Guardian*, is indirect.
QUOTED: 66-7

——— Speech on National Education (14 Mar., 1833; Lords), *PD*, 3rd ser., Vol. 16,
cols. 632-8.
REFERRED TO: 64, 65, 71

BROWN, JOHN.
NOTE: the reference is in a quotation from Phillips.
REFERRED TO: 133n

——— Last Speech (2 Nov., 1859). Reported in "Brown's Trial," *New-York Daily
Tribune*, 3 Nov., 1859, 5.
NOTE: the reference is in a quotation from Phillips.
REFERRED TO: 133n

BROWN, THOMAS. Referred to: 240, 243

BULLER, FRANCIS. Judgment in the Case of R. *v.* Archer (25 Jan., 1788). 100 *English
Reports* 113.
NOTE: the quotation is taken from Holt (*q.v.* for the collation). The "writing like the present"
refers to the books of the corporation of Yarmouth, which recorded the payment to Watson of
£2300 as just compensation for his fine of £1500 for a libel against a man called Hurry, wherein
Watson had claimed that the recently acquitted Hurry would soon be indicted again. Originally
appeared in 2 *Term Reports* 205.
QUOTED: 32
32.25 *law . . . remedy*] [*not in italics*] (113)
32.27 by writing] by a writing (113)

BUONARROTI, MICHELANGELO. See Michelangelo.

BURNET, GILBERT.
NOTE: the reference is in a quotation from Austin.
REFERRED TO: 60

BURNS, ROBERT.
NOTE: the reference is to his poetry in general.
REFERRED TO: 233

——— "Scots wha hae wi Wallace bled" (1794). In *Works*. New ed. 2 pts. London:
Tegg, *et al.*; Dublin: Milliken, *et al.*; Glasgow: Griffin, 1824, Pt. II, 254.
NOTE: this ed. in SC, as was formerly *The Poetical Works*, 2 vols. (London: Pickering, 1830).
REFERRED TO: 252

BUTLER, JOSEPH.
NOTE: the reference is in a quotation from Austin.
REFERRED TO: 60

CAIRNES, JOHN ELLIOT. Referred to: 145-6, 427

—— *The Slave Power: Its Character, Career, and Probable Designs: Being an Attempt to Explain the Real Issues Involved in the American Contest.* London: Parker, *et al.*, 1862.

NOTE: dedicated to JSM; 2nd ed. (1863) is in SC, inscribed "With the author's regards."

REVIEWED: 143-64

QUOTED: 146, 147, 147-8, 148, 148-9, 149, 149-50, 150, 151, 152, 152-3, 154, 155, 156, 157

146.11 "the most] In the following pages an attempt will be made to resolve this system into its component elements, to trace the connexion of the several parts with each other, and of the whole with the foundation on which it rests, and to estimate generally the prospects which it holds out to the people who compose it, as well as the influence it is likely to exercise on the interests of other nations; and, if I do not greatly mistake the purport of the considerations which shall be adduced, their effect will be to show that this Slave Power constitutes the most (18)

146.19 "The vastness," . . . "of] The vastness of (18)

146.33-4 "it is . . . scruples;"] It is . . . scruples, and, if the system had been found suitable to the requirements of the country, it is to be presumed that they would have gradually extended its basis, and that, like their neighbours, especially since the treaty of Utrecht had secured for English enterprise the African slave-trade, they would have availed themselves of this means of recruiting their labour market. (36)

147.4-5 "is . . . Europeans."] The climate of the oldest of the Slave States—Virginia, Maryland, Delaware, North and South Carolina—is . . . Europeans;* [*footnote:*] *Olmsted's *Slave States*, pp. 131, 462-3. [*text:*] and, though the same is not true in the same degree of the Gulf States, yet it is a fact that these regions also afford examples of free European communities increasing in numbers under a semi-tropical climate, and rising to opulence through the labour of their own hands. (37)

147.7-8 "are . . . and Spain."] "The Southern parts of the Union," says De Tocqueville, "are . . . and of Spain; and it may be asked why the European cannot work as well there as in the two latter countries." (38n)

147.10 "nearly] Nearly (38) [Cairnes is quoting Weston, *Progress of Slavery*, pp. 160-1]

147.19-20 "it . . . end."] Slave labour, therefore, admits of the most complete organization, that is to say, it . . . end, and its cost can never rise above that which is necessary to maintain the slave in health and strength. (44)

147.29 "not] [*paragraph*] Secondly, slave labour is unskilful, and this, not (45)

147.33 "The slave is unsuited] He is therefore unsuited (46)

147.36 commonest] coarsest (46)

147.37 labour."] forms of labour.* [*footnote quoting Olmsted omitted*] (46)

148.4 soil."] soil.* [*footnote:*] *Olmsted's *Seaboard Slave States*, pp. 337 to 339. (46-7)

148.13 labourer can] labourer, Mr. Russell tells us,* [*footnote:*] *Russell's *North America*, pp. 141, 164. [*text:*] can (50)

148.21 "the] And, in confirmation of this view it may be added that wherever in the Southern States the (52)

148.33 unfit.] unfit.* [*footnote quoting Olmsted omitted*] (53)

148.35 cultivation,] cultivation,* [*footnote quoting Russell omitted*] (53)

148.37 account.] account.† [*footnote omitted*] (53)

149.3 product.] product.* [*footnote quoting Olmsted omitted*] (54)

149.27 The] [*no paragraph*] The (66)

149.28 susceptibility of] susceptibility, that is to say, of (66)

149.32 required;] required. (66)

149.40 classes. From] classes. We arrive therefore at this singular conclusion, that, while large capitals in countries of slave labour enjoy peculiar advantages, and while the aggregate capital needed in them for the conduct of a given amount of industry is greater than in countries where labour is free, capital nevertheless in such countries is extremely scarce. From (75)

150.2-3 exist. "Our] exist. They form the burthen of most of what has been written on our West Indian Islands while under the *régime* of slavery; and they are not less prominently the characteristic features of the industrial system of the Southern States. "Our (75-6)

150.16-17   "mean whites" or "white trash."] Such are the "Mean whites" or "white trash" of the Southern States. (76)

150.20   Become the] [*no paragraph*] For the tracts thus left, or made, desolate become in time the (75)

150.34   supporters] supports (75)

150.40   "it] [*paragraph*] The constitution of a slave society, it has been seen, is sufficiently simple: it (85)

150.41   classes—] classes, broadly distinguished from each other, and connected by no common interest— (85)

151.3   "When] [*no paragraph*] When (85)

151.7   property; political] property—in a society so constituted, political (86)

151.19   party,] party,* [*footnote omitted*] (86)

151.22   few. . . . [*paragraph*] To] [*ellipsis indicates 5-page omission*] (87-92)

152.2   "between] The truth is, between (98)

152.3   America,"] America, there exist the most deep reaching distinctions. (98)

152.22   wants, a] wants, it is obvious that a (101)

152.34   His] *His* (101) [*treated as typographical error in this ed.*]

152.40   senator." Modern slaveholders, on the contrary, are rendered independent] senator." The industrial necessities of Roman society (and the same was true of society in the middle ages) in this way provided for the education of at least a large proportion of the slave population; and education, accompanied as it was by a general elevation of their condition, led, by a natural and almost inevitable tendency, to emancipation.* [*footnote quoting Congreve's* Politics of Aristotle *omitted*] [*text:*] [*paragraph*] But in the position of slavery in North America there is nothing which corresponds to this. Owing to the vast development in modern times of international trade, modern slaveholders are independent (102-3)

153.19   "the] [*paragraph*] But there is yet another distinction between the slavery of modern times and slavery as it was known among the progressive communities of former ages, which deserves to be noticed—I mean the (107)

153.23   labour, can] labour, which can [*sic*] (108)

153.25   and] or (108)

153.26   West."] West.* [*footnote omitted*] (108)

153.29   "by] Now, it does this in two ways, by (109)

154.2-4   "mean whites" . . . "more . . . unmanageable"] It is universally agreed that the labour of the mean whites* [*footnote:*] *And it may be added, of such free labourers as will consent to the degradation of living in a slave community. [*text:*] is more . . . unmanageable than even the crude efforts of the slaves. (126)

154.8-9   "popular . . . speculations"] Under such conditions social intercourse cannot exist; popular . . . speculations; in short, all the civilizing agencies of highest value are, by the very nature of the case, excluded. (129)

154.10-11   "a . . . passenger"] In South Carolina a . . . passenger.* [*footnote:*] *See Stirling's *Letters from the Slave States*, p. 265. (131)

154.26   corner-stone] "corner stone" (139)

155.5-6   "'There . . . Georgia," . . . "in] "There . . . Georgia, "in (151) [*Cairnes's quotation marks adopted in this ed.*]

155.16   certain limits] certain specified limits (152)

155.18   owner."] owner."* [*footnote:*] *Progress of Slavery*, p. 227. (152) [*Cairnes's quotation marks adopted in this ed.*]

155.29   despotism; he] despotism. He (155)

155.33   "'is] "The commerce between master and slave," says a slaveowner, "is (155) [*Cairnes's quotation marks adopted in this ed.*]

155.35   it. The] it. . . . The (155)

155.38   peculiarities.'"] peculiarities."* [*footnote:*] Jefferson's *Notes on Virginia*, p. 39. (155) [*Cairnes's quotation marks adopted in this ed.*]

156.22   "squatter sovereignty"] By this bill [the Kansas and Nebraska Bill] the Missouri Compromise was abrogated, and in its place a principle was established, popularly known as that of "squatter sovereignty," by which it was resolved that the future settlement of the Territories should be determined. (195)

156.27   "border ruffians"] Bands of border ruffians were mustered on the Missouri frontier, and held in leash to be let slip at the decisive moment. (197)

157.7   "is one] It forms, as it seems to me, one (221)

CALIGULA (Gaius Caesar). Referred to: 286

CAMDEN, LORD. See Charles Pratt.

CARAFA, ANTONIO.
NOTE: for the collation see De Thou.
QUOTED: 66

CARDWELL, EDWARD (Viscount).
NOTE: the reference is to him as the Secretary of State for the Colonies.
REFERRED TO: 430

———— Despatch from the Right Hon. Edward Cardwell, M.P., to Lieut.-Gen. Sir H.K. Storks, *PP*, 1866, LI, 137-43.
QUOTED: 424, 426

424.24-6   "arduous task" to some person "who . . . troubles."] It remains, therefore, to decide whether the inauguration of the new Government shall be accomplished by Mr. Eyre, or whether Her Majesty shall be advised to intrust that arduous task to some other person who . . . troubles. (143)

426.21-2   "Great offences," . . . "must be punished."] But great offences ought to be punished. (143)

CAREY, HENRY CHARLES. *The French and American Tariffs Compared; in a Series of Letters Addressed to Mons. Michel Chevalier.* Philadelphia: printed Collins, 1861.
REFERRED TO: 132, 138

CARLISLE, EARL OF. See George William Frederick Howard.

CARLYLE, THOMAS. "Biography," *Fraser's Magazine*, V (Apr., 1832), 253-60.
QUOTED: 39

39.14-15   "an open loving heart."] One grand, invaluable secret there is, however, which includes all the rest, and, what is comfortable, lies clearly in every man's power: *To have an open loving heart, and what follows from the possession of such!* (259)

———— Letter to Hamilton Hume (23 Aug., 1866), *The Times*, 12 Sept. 1866, 6.
REFERRED TO: 428n

———— "Occasional Discourse on the Negro Question," *Fraser's Magazine*, XL (Dec., 1849), 670-9.
NOTE: when Carlyle republished the essay, after Mill's attack, he retitled it "The Nigger Question." JSM's "The Negro Question" (85-95), is a reply to Carlyle's essay, not strictly a review.
QUOTED: 87, 88, 89, 89-90, 90, 91, 92, 94
REFERRED TO: 87-95

87.1   "rights of Negroes"] My Philanthropic Friends,—It is my painful duty to address some words to you, this evening, on the Rights of Negroes. (670)

87.4   "immortal gods"] Both these things, we may be assured, the immortal gods have decided upon, passed their eternal act of parliament for: and both of them, though all terrestrial Parliaments and entities oppose it to the death, shall be done. (675)

87.4   "The Powers"] If Quashee will not honestly aid in bringing out those sugars, cinnamons, and nobler products of the West Indian Islands, for the benefit of all mankind, then I say neither will the Powers permit Quashee to continue growing pumpkins there for his own lazy benefit; but will sheer him out, by and by, like a lazy gourd overshadowing rich ground; him and all that partake with him,—perhaps in a very terrible manner. (675)

87.4 "the Destinies"] For, under favour of Exeter Hall, the 'terrible manner' is not yet quite extinct with the Destinies in this Universe; nor will it quite cease, I apprehend, for soft sawder or philanthropic stump-oratory now or henceforth. (675)

87.5-6 "have . . . for."] [see collation for 87.4 above]

87.9 "eternal . . . Parliament"] [see collation for 87.4 above]

87.12-13 "born lord" . . . "servant"] You are not 'slaves' now; nor do I wish, if it can be avoided, to see you slaves again: but decidedly you will have to be servants to those that are born wiser than you, that are born lords of you,—servants to the whites, if they are (as what mortal can doubt they are?) born wiser than you. (676-7)

87.13-14 "compelled to work" . . . "beneficent whip" . . . "other . . . not."] Quashee, if he will not help in bringing out the spices, will get himself made a slave again (which state will be a little less ugly than his present one), and with beneficent whip, since other methods avail not, will be compelled to work. (675)

87.15 "the gods"] The gods are long-suffering; but the law from the beginning was, He that will not work shall perish from the earth, and the patience of the gods has limits! (675)

88.4 jargon," . . . "hearts] jargon,—sad product of a sceptical Eighteenth Century, and of poor human hearts (671)

88.4 destitute] destitute (671)

88.5-6 heathen," . . . "human species" . . . "reduced . . . alone."] Heathen, and reduced . . . alone, and to cultivate the same under its Christian, Antichristian, Broad-brimmed, Brutus-headed and other forms,—has not the human species gone strange roads, during that period? (671)

89.16-18 "wish to see" . . . "if . . . avoided;" . . . "decidedly" . . . "will . . . servants," "servants . . . whites,"] [see collation for 87.12-13 above]

89.18 "compelled to labour" . . . "not . . . minute."] And I incessantly pray Heaven, all men, the whitest alike and the blackest, the richest and the poorest, in other regions of the world, had attained precisely the same right, the divine right of being compelled (if 'permitted' will not answer) to do what work they are appointed for, and not to go idle another minute, in a life so short! (674)

89.19 "Black Quashee"] And now observe, my friends, it was not Black Quashee or those he represents that made those West India Islands what they are, or can by any hypothesis be considered to have the right of growing pumpkins there. (674)

89.19 "up . . . pumpkins"] Sitting yonder with their beautiful muzzles up . . . pumpkins, imbibing sweet pulps and juices; the grinder and incisor teeth ready for every new work, and the pumpkins cheap as grass in those rich climates: while the sugar-crops rot round them uncut, because labour cannot be hired,so cheap are the pumpkins;—and at home we are but required to rasp from the breakfast loaves of our own English labourers some slight 'differential sugar-duties,' and lend a poor half-million or a few poor millions now and then, to keep that beautiful state of matters going. (671)

89.20 "working . . . day"] The West Indies, it appears, are short of labour; as indeed is very conceivable in those circumstances: where a Black man by working . . . a-day (such is the calculation) can supply himself, by aid of sun and soil, with as much pumpkin as will suffice, he is likely to be a little stiff to raise into hard work! (672)

89.32 "an eye-sorrow" . . . "blister . . . state"] Any poor idle Black man, any idle White man, rich or poor, is a mere eye-sorrow to the State; a perpetual blister . . . State. (676)

89.35 world."] world; and woe is to every man who, by friend or by foe, is prevented from fulfilling this the end of his being. (673)

89.36-7 "sacred . . . earth" . . . "his . . . enemy."] Whatsoever prohibits or prevents a man from this his sacred . . . earth,—that, I say, is the man's deadliest enemy; and all men are called upon to do what is in their power or opportunity towards delivering him from it. (673)

89.37-90.2 "his own indolence" . . . "the first right he has" . . . "by some wise means compel . . . for."] If it be his own indolence that prevents and prohibits him, then his own indolence is the enemy he must be delivered from: and the first "right" he has,—poor indolent blockhead, black or white, is, that every unprohibited man, whatsoever wiser, more industrious person may be passing that way, shall endeavour to "emancipate" him from his indolence and by some wise means, as I said, compel . . . for. (673)

90.6-7 "divine . . . for"] [*see collation for* 89.18 *above*]

90.9-10 "the eternal . . . will"] The one perfect eternal proprietor is the Maker who created them: the temporary better or worse proprietor is he whom the Maker has sent on that mission; he who the best hitherto can educe from said lands the beneficent gifts the Maker endowed them with; or, which is but another definition of the same person, he who leads hitherto the manfullest life on that bit of soil, doing, better than another yet found can do, the Eternal Purpose and Supreme Will there. (674)

90.10-11 "injustice" . . . "for . . . accursed"] For injustice is *for ever* accursed: and precisely our unfairness toward the enslaved black man has,—by inevitable revulsion and fated turn of the wheel,—brought about these present Confusions. (676)

91.3-5 "spices." "The gods . . . Indies"] No; the gods . . . Indies; thus much they have declared in so making the West Indies:—infinitely more they wish, that manful industrious men occupy their West Indies, not indolent two-legged cattle, however 'happy' over their abundant pumpkins! (675)

91.5 "noble . . . grey"] For countless ages, since they first mounted oozy, on the back of earthquakes, from their dark bed in the Ocean deeps, and reeking saluted the tropical Sun, and ever onwards till the European white man first saw them some three short centuries ago, those Islands had produced mere jungle, savagery, poison-reptiles and swamp-malaria: till the white European first saw them, they were as if not yet created,—their noble . . . grey, lying all asleep, waiting the white Enchanter who should say to them, Awake! (674-5)

91.6 "things . . . pumpkins."] The Islands are good withal for pepper, for sugar, for sago, arrowroot, for coffee, perhaps for cinnamon and precious spices; things . . . pumpkins; and leading towards commerces, arts, polities, and social developements, which alone are the noble product, where men (and not pigs with pumpkins) are the parties concerned! (674)

91.8 "immortal gods"] [*see collation for* 87.4 *above*]

91.9-10 "towards . . . developements"] [*see collation for* 91.6 *above*]

92.3 "divine right"] [*see collation for* 89.18 *above*]

92.9-11 "It was . . . are"] And now observe, my friends, it was . . . are, or can by any hypothesis be considered to have the right of growing pumpkins there. (674)

92.12-14 "Under . . . men" . . . "had . . . laid"] But under the soil of Jamaica, before it could even produce spices or any pumpkin, the bones of many thousand British men had to be laid. (676)

92.13-14 "brave . . . Brayne"] Brave . . . Brayne,—the dust of many thousand strong old English hearts lies there; worn down swiftly in frightful travail, chaining the Devils, which were manifold. (676)

92.18 "compel;"] And his own happiness, and that of others round him, will alone be possible by his and their getting into such a relation that this can be permitted him, and in case of need that this can be compelled him. (673-4)

92.20-1 "Never . . . his" . . . "could . . . throat."] Never . . . his could . . .throat; nothing but savagery and reeking putrefaction could have grown there. (675)

92.23-5 "Little . . . jungle."] Let him, by his ugliness, idleness, rebellion, banish all White men from the West Indies, and make it all one Haiti,—with little . . . jungle,—does he think that will for ever continue pleasant to gods and men? (675)

92.31-4 "You . . . you."] [*see collation for* 87.12-13 *above*]

94.5-6 "the new . . . little" . . . "take . . . others"] If the new . . . little, take . . . others, what remedy is there? (672)

94.8 "a black Ireland."] To have 'emancipated' the West Indies into a *Black Ireland*; 'free' indeed, but an Ireland, and black! (672)

94.30 "Universal . . . Association"] Taking, as we hope we do, an extensive survey of social affairs, which we find all in a state of the frightfullest embroilment, and as it were, of inextricable final bankruptcy, just at present; and being desirous to adjust ourselves in that huge upbreak, and unutterable welter of tumbling ruins, and to see well that our grand proposed Association of Associations, the UNIVERSAL ABOLITION-OF-PAIN ASSOCIATION, which is meant to be the consummate golden flower and summary of modern Philanthropisms all in one, do not issue as a universal 'Sluggard-and-Scoundrel Protection Society,'—we have judged that, before constituting ourselves, it would be very proper to commune earnestly with one

another, and discourse together on the leading elements of our great Problem, which surely is
one of the greatest. (670)

94.34-6 "the Destinies" . . . "terrible manner" . . . "for soft . . . stump-oratory;"] [*see collation
for 87.4 above*]

―――― *On Heroes, Hero-Worship, and the Heroic in History*. London: Fraser, 1841.
NOTE: in SC. JSM is citing Goethe (in whose work the passage has not been found), but there is
little doubt that he took the reference from Carlyle, who says: "In this point of view, too, a
saying of Goethe's, which has staggered several, may have meaning: 'The Beautiful,' he
intimates, 'is higher than the Good; the Beautiful includes in it the Good.'" (132)
REFERRED TO: 255

―――― *Past and Present*. London: Chapman and Hall, 1843.
NOTE: in SC.
REFERRED TO: 90

―――― *Sartor Resartus* (1833-34). 2nd ed. Boston: Munroe, 1837.
NOTE: in SC.
REFERRED TO: 90

―――― "Signs of the Times," *Edinburgh Review*, XLIX (June, 1829), 439-59.
REFERRED TO: 90

CARNARVON, 4TH EARL OF. See Henry Howard Molyneux Herbert.

CARRINGTON, NATHAN.
NOTE: the reference is to the case of Entick *v*. Carrington in 1765 over which Lord Camden (*q.v.*)
presided.
REFERRED TO: 24

CARTOUCHE. See Louis Dominique Bourguignon.

CATHERINE II (of Russia).
NOTE: known as Catherine the Great.
REFERRED TO: 304, 401

CATHERINE DE' MEDICI. Referred to: 304

CHADWICK, EDWIN. "Copy of Two Papers Submitted to the [Education] Commission by
Mr. Chadwick, as to Half-Time Teaching and Military and Naval Drill, and on Time
and Cost of Popular Education on a Large and Small Scale; with a Further Return,
Being a Letter to Mr. Senior, Explanatory of the Former Paper," *PP*, 1862, XLIII,
1-160.
NOTE: the quotation is of evidence by Tufnell, *q.v.*
QUOTED: 213-14
REFERRED TO: 209, 210, 212
213.34 It] As a proof of this, I may mention that it (143)

CHARLEMAGNE. Referred to: 303

CHARLES I (of England). Referred to: 402

CHARLES V (Holy Roman Emperor). Referred to: 303, 402

CHARLES VIII (of France). Referred to: 303

CHESSON, FREDERICK WILLIAM.
NOTE: the references are to him as Honorary Secretary of the Jamaica Committee, co-signer of the
accounts published here as App. E.
REFERRED TO: 422, 427, 429

CHRISTIE, HUGH. *A Grammar of the Latin Tongue. After a New and Easy Method,
Adapted to the Capacities of Children*. Edinburgh: Donaldson, 1758.
REFERRED TO: 221-2

Code Napoléon. See Statutes, France.

COKE, EDWARD. *The First Part of the Institutes of the Lawes of England; or, A Commentarie upon Littleton, Not the Name of a Lawyer Onely, but of the Law It Selfe.* London: Society of Stationers, 1628.
NOTE: the reference at 173 is in a quotation from Austin.
REFERRED TO: 22, 173

——— Judgment in the Case de Libellis Famosis, 1606. 77 *English Reports* 250.
NOTE: one of the six legal authorities cited by Holt, *q.v.* Originally appeared in 5 *Coke* 125.
REFERRED TO: 21

COLERIDGE, SAMUEL TAYLOR. *The Friend: A Series of Essays, in Three Volumes, to Aid in the Formation of Fixed Principles in Politics, Morals, and Religion, with Literary Amusements Interspersed.* 3 vols. London: Rest Fenner, 1818.
NOTE: in SC.
REFERRED TO: 187

COLLIER, ROBERT PORRETT (Lord Monkswell).
NOTE: counsel to the Jamaica Committee.
REFERRED TO: 431, 432

COLLINSON, RICHARD. Referred to: 350

A Complete Collection of State Trials. See Howell.

CONDORCET, MARIE JEAN ANTOINE NICOLAS CARITAT, MARQUIS DE. *Esquisse d'un tableau historique des progrès de l'esprit humain.* Paris: Agasse, 1795.
REFERRED TO: 399

COOTE, HOLMES. Referred to: 350

CORINNA. Referred to: 314

The Cornish Guardian and Western Chronicle. Leading article, 13 June, 1834, 4.
QUOTED: 66-7
66.32-67.1 "The schoolmaster," . . . "the schoolmaster may be abroad, but] "The school-master" *may* "be abroad," but (4)
67.2 ungratefully,"] ungratefully. (4)

COUSIN, VICTOR. *Report on the State of Public Instruction in Prussia.* Trans. Sarah Austin. London: Wilson, 1834.
REVIEWED: 61-74
QUOTED: 64
64.6 "Constituted," says she, "as] Constituted as (viii)

COWEN, JOSEPH. Referred to: 427

COWPER, WILLIAM. "Tirocinium." In *The Task, a Poem, in Six Books, to Which Are Added by the Same Author, An Epistle to Joseph Hill, Esq., Tirocinium, or a Review of Schools, and The History of John Gilpin.* London: Johnson, 1785, 289-341.
NOTE: the quotation is in a quotation from William Smith.
QUOTED: 83-4
84.1 he who runs may read] [*paragraph*] Truths that the learn'd pursue with eager thought, / Are not important always as dear-bought, / Proving at last, though told in pompous strains, / A childish waste of philosophic pains; / But truths on which depends our main concern, / That 'tis our shame and mis'ry not to learn, / Shine by the side of ev'ry path we tread / With such a lustre, he that runs may read. (297; 73-80)

CUVIER, GEORGES LÉOPOLD CHRÉTIEN FRÉDÉRIC DAGOBERT, BARON. Referred to: 311

DANTE ALIGHIERI. Referred to: 254

DAVIS, JEFFERSON. Referred to: 141, 141n

DAVIS, PAULINA KELLOGG WRIGHT. Referred to: 395

FITZROY, HENRY.
  NOTE: the references derive from the introduction by Fitzroy (Under-Secretary of State for the
  Home Department) of "A Bill for the Better Prevention and Punishment of Aggravated Assaults
  upon Women and Children," *q.v.*
  REFERRED TO: 101-8 *passim*

────── Speech in Introducing "A Bill for the Better Prevention and Punishment of
  Aggravated Assaults upon Women and Children" (10 Mar., 1853; Commons), *PD*,
  3rd ser., Vol. 124, cols. 1414-19.
  REFERRED TO: 103, 105

FLEMING, EDWARD. Referred to: 423

FLETCHER, ANDREW. *An Account of a Conversation Concerning a Right Regulation of
  Governments for the Common Good of Mankind. In a Letter to the Marquiss of
  Montrose, the Earls of Rothes, Roxburg, and Hadington, from London the 1st of
  December, 1703.* Edinburgh: n.p., 1704.
  NOTE: known as Fletcher of Saltoun.
  QUOTED: 252
  252.21 "Let . . . songs"] *I said, I knew a very wise man so much of* Sir Chr──'s
  [Christopher's] sentiment, that he believed if a man were permitted to make all the Ballads, he
  need not care who should make the Laws of a Nation. (10)

FONBLANQUE, EDWARD BARRINGTON DE. *The Life and Labours of Albany Fonblanque.*
  London: Bentley, 1874.
  NOTE: the reference arises from a phrase JSM attributes to "somebody," and Fonblanque
  attributes to JSM. It is a variation on the phrase, "a Radical because he is not a lord." See *CW*,
  VI, 353.
  REFERRED TO: 397

FONTENELLE, BERNARD LE BOVIER DE. *Digression sur les anciens et les modernes*
  (1688). In *Oeuvres.* New ed. 10 vols. Paris: Libraires associés, 1766, IV, 169-98.
  NOTE: in SC.
  REFERRED TO: 220

FORMAN, JACOB GILBERT. "Women's Rights Convention at Worcester, Mass.,"
  New York Daily Tribune, 25 Oct., 1850, 5-6.
  QUOTED: 395-6
  REFERRED TO: 400, 415
  396.3 are entitled] are clearly entitled (6)
  396.4 office . . . and] office, the omission to demand which on their part is a palpable
  recreancy to duty; and the denial of which is a gross usurpation on the part of man—no longer
  to be endured—and (6)
  396.8 struck] stricken (6)

────── "Women's Rights Convention at Worcester, Mass.," *New York Daily Tribune*,
  26 Oct., 1850, 5-6.
  QUOTED: 395, 396, 415
  REFERRED TO: 415
  395.22 "if] If (6)
  395.23-4 "crowded from the beginning with] This hall had been crowded from the beginning
  thus far with (6)
  396.9 in after-life . . . and] in after life, for the faculties we are laboring to discipline, is the
  honest stimulus to fidelity, in the use of Educational advantages; and (6)
  396.12 women] Woman (6)
  396.12 them] her (6)
  396.13 their . . . their] her . . . her (6)
  396.14 open to them.] open, to arouse her ambition, and call forth all her nature. (6)

NOTE: the quotation is in a quotation from Cairnes.
QUOTED: 152
152.38-9 "The youths of promising genius," . . . "were] The youths of a promising genius were (I, 42)
152.39 and almost every] and their price was ascertained by the degree of their skill and talents.[56] [*footnote omitted*] Almost every (I, 42)
152.39-40 liberal and mechanical] either liberal[57] [*footnote omitted*] or mechanical (I, 42)

GIFFORD, ROBERT.
NOTE: Master of the Rolls in 1825, but Solicitor-General in 1817, when the Attorney-General was Samuel Shepherd, *q.v.*
REFERRED TO: 30

GODWIN, WILLIAM. *Things As They Are; or, The Adventures of Caleb Williams*. 3 vols. London: Crosby, 1794.
NOTE: the phrase (indirectly quoted) was popular in an ironic sense, occurring, for example, as a heading in James Mill's Commonplace Book (London Library), Vol. III, f. 145r.
QUOTED: 12

GOETHE, JOHANN WOLFGANG VON.
NOTE: see also Thomas Carlyle, *On Heroes*.
REFERRED TO: 255

GORDON, GEORGE WILLIAM. Referred to: 422-35

GORRIE, JOHN. Referred to: 426, 432

GRANT, JOHN PETER. Referred to: 429

—— Speech to the Legislative Council of Jamaica (16 Oct., 1866), *The Times*, 13 Nov., 1866, 7.
REFERRED TO: 429-30

GRANT, WILLIAM. Referred to: 423

GRANVILLE, LORD. See Granville George Leveson-Gower.

GRATTAN, HENRY.
NOTE: the reference is to his speeches.
REFERRED TO: 252

GRAY, THOMAS.
NOTE: the reference is to his poetry in general.
REFERRED TO: 233

—— *An Elegy Wrote in a Country Church Yard* (1751). In *The Works of Thomas Gray, with Memoirs of His Life and Writings by William Mason*. Ed. Thomas James Mathias. 2 vols. London: Porter, 1814, I, 57-63.
NOTE: in SC.
REFERRED TO: 254

GREGORY, ROBERT. Referred to: 350

GUIZOT, FRANÇOIS PIERRE GUILLAUME. Despatch to Metternich on the Incorporation of Cracow (3 Dec., 1846), *La Presse*, 4 Dec., 1846, 1.
NOTE: the relevant passages were quoted from *La Presse* in *The Times*, 7 Dec., 1846, 4.
REFERRED TO: 348

HABEAS CORPUS ACT. See 31 Charles II, c. 2.

HALE, MATTHEW. *An Analysis of the Law: Being a Scheme, or Abstract, of the Several Titles and Partitions of the Law of England, Digested into Method*. London: Walthoe, 1713.
REFERRED TO: 194

HERBERT, HENRY HOWARD MOLYNEUX (4th Earl of Carnarvon). "Circular Despatch to
Colonial Governors, Dated 30th January, 1867, on the Subject of Martial Law," *PP*,
1867, XLIX, 395.
REFERRED TO: 434

HERODOTUS. *Herodotus* (Greek and English). Trans. A.D. Godley. 4 vols. London:
Heinemann; New York: Putnam's Sons, 1926-30.
NOTE: this ed. used for ease of reference. Two Greek and Latin eds. (Glasgow: Foulis, 1761; and
Edinburgh: Laing, 1806) were formerly in SC.
REFERRED TO: 337

HOADLEY, BENJAMIN (Bishop of Winchester).
NOTE: the reference is in a quotation from Austin.
REFERRED TO: 60

HOBBES, THOMAS.
NOTE: the second reference at 58 is in a quotation from Austin; that at 204 derives from Austin.
REFERRED TO: 58, 204, 243

——— *Leviathan; or, The Matter, Form, and Power of a Commonwealth Ecclesiastical
and Civil* (1651). In *The English Works*. Ed. William Molesworth. 11 vols. London:
Bohn, 1839-45, III.
NOTE: in SC, as is ed. of 1855.
QUOTED: 226
226.4   "Words are the counters of wise men, but the money of fools."] For words are wise
men's counters, they do but reckon by them; but they are the money of fools, that value
them by the authority of an Aristotle, a Cicero, or a Thomas, or any other doctor whatsoever,
if but a man. (III, 25; Pt. I, Chap. iv)

HOBSON, TOBIAS.
NOTE: the quotation is traditionally ascribed to Hobson, a Cambridge hosteler, who gave his
customers the choice of one horse or none.
QUOTED: 281
REFERRED TO: 282

HOLMES, TIMOTHY. Referred to: 350

HOLT, FRANCIS LUDLOW. *The Law of Libel: In Which Is Contained, a General History
of This Law in the Ancient Codes, and of Its Introduction, and Successive
Alterations, in the Law of England, Comprehending a Digest of All the Leading
Cases upon Libels, from the Earliest to the Present Time*. London: Reed; Dublin:
Phelan, 1812.
QUOTED: 18, 21, 23, 24, 25, 25-6, 26, 27, 28, 29, 30, 32
REFERRED TO: 15, 20, 29, 32
18.13   Our] [*no paragraph*] Our (39)
18.24   reign—.] reign? (40)
18.31   *every society*] every society (45)
18.32   to maintain the] to the above ends; which are necessary to maintain the (45)
18.33   exercise.] exercise, and, without which, governments would be successively adopted and
rejected like opposite paradoxes in the schools,—and, without which, no magistrate, no
corporation, could execute their duties. (46)
21.1   A] [*paragraph*] A (50)
21.1-2 A . . . writing] [*in italics*] (50)
21.2   signs, pictures, &c.] [*in italics*] (50)
21.4   contempt and] contempt, or (50)
23.29   to subvert] to attempt to subvert (74)
23.35   *wantonly to defame . . . indecorously to calumniate*] [*not in italics*] (74)
24.34   governments must] governments," says Lord Camden[+], [*footnote:*] [+]Entick *v.* Carrington, 2 Wils. 275. [*text:*] "must (75)
25.40   truth] fruit (76)
27.3-7 [*see quotation at* 27.28-38]

28.12   "The law," . . . "in] [*paragraph*] The law, in (103)
28.13   duty. Invective] Duty. [*paragraph*] Invective (103)
28.40   reflecting on the government] [*in italics*] (108)
29.7   LORD CHIEF JUSTICE RAYMOND. Even a] [*no paragraph*] His lordship added, "even a (110-11)
29.20   SIR PHILIP YORKE (afterwards Lord Chancellor Hardwicke). He (the printer) is] [*no paragraph*] He may lawfully print and publish what belongs to his own trade; but he is (112)
29.22   *administration*] administration (112)
29.22   ministers.] ministers; nor yet to stain the character or reputation of any of his subjects. (112)
29.27   "that the] [*paragraph*] The second of these points [urged by defence council] the court said they would not suffer to be argued; "for the (55)
30.1   LORD ELLENBOROUGH. It] [*no paragraph*] It (119)
30.2   *bringing . . . disesteem*] [*not in italics*] (119)
30.4   crime, it] crime. It (119)
32.11   peaceable] decent (144)
32.14   party.] party*. [*footnote omitted*] (144)
32.15   reflection," . . . "on] reflection on (144)
32.21   Justice BULLER. Nothing can] In this case Buller, justice, observed, "nothing can (145)
32.25   *law . . . remedy*] [*not in italics*] (145)

HOLT, JOHN. Referred to: 31

———— Charge to the Jury in the Trial of John Tutchin, 1704. In Howell, *A Complete Collection* (*q.v.*), Vol. XIV, cols. 1125-9.
NOTE: the quotation is taken from Francis Holt, *q.v.* This speech is also located in 90 *English Reports* 1133 and originally appeared in *Holt K.B.* 424.
QUOTED: 28-9
28.39   They] They say they are innocent papers, and no libels, and they (1128)
28.40   on] upon (1128)
28.42   such stations] Such or such stations (1128)
28.42   army. To] Army. [*paragraph*] To (1128)
29.2   men] people (1128)
29.3   subsist.] subsist; for it is very necessary for every Government, that the people should have a good opinion of it. (1128)

———— Judgment in the Trial of Beare, 1698. 91 *English Reports* 363.
NOTE: one of the six legal authorities cited by Holt, *q.v.* Originally appeared in 1 *Salkeld* 417.
REFERRED TO: 21

HOMER. Referred to: 302

———— *Iliad* (Greek and English). Trans. A.T. Murray. 2 vols. London: Heinemann; Cambridge, Mass.: Harvard University Press, 1946.
NOTE: this ed. used for ease of reference. *Iliad and Odyssey* (Greek), 2 vols. (Oxford, 1800), was formerly in SC.
QUOTED: 327

HOOKER, RICHARD. *Of the Lawes of Ecclesiasticall Politie.* 2 vols. London: Windet, [1593]-97.
NOTE: the reference derives from Austin.
REFERRED TO: 178

HORACE (Quintus Horatius Flaccus). Referred to: 231, 233

———— *Epistles.* In *Satires, Epistles and Ars poetica* (Latin and English). Trans. H. Rushton Fairclough. London: Heinemann; New York: Putnam's Sons, 1926, 248-440.
NOTE: this ed. used for ease of reference. *Opera,* ed. William Baxter (Glasgow: Mundell, 1796), is in SC.
REFERRED TO: 229

—— *Satires. Ibid.*, 4-244.

QUOTED: 412

REFERRED TO: 229

412.18-19 *mens divinior*] ingenium cui sit, cui mens divinior atque os magna sonaturum, des nominis huius honorem. (52; I, iv, 43-4)

HORSLEY, SAMUEL. *The Speeches in Parliament of Samuel Horsley*. Ed. H. Horsley. Dundee: Chalmers, 1813.

NOTE: the quotation is indirect. The comment was made by Bishop Horsley in Committee of the House of Lords on the Treason Bill introduced by Lord Grenville on 6 November, 1795. On the third reading, 13 November, the remark was attacked by Lord Lauderdale, and defended by Horsley.

QUOTED: 17

17.22-3 They [the people] have nothing to do with their rulers except to obey them] All that the people had to do with the laws of the country was to obey them (167-8)

HORTH, SAMUEL. Referred to: 107n

HOWARD, BENJAMIN C. *Reports of Cases Argued and Adjudged in the Supreme Court of the United States*. 24 vols. Washington, D.C.: Morrison, 1857.

NOTE: the reference is to Dred Scott *v*. John F.A. Sanford (December term, 1856).

REFERRED TO: 161

HOWARD, GEORGE WILLIAM FREDERICK (7th Earl of Carlisle). Referred to: 415

HOWARD, JOHN. Referred to: 94

HOWELL, THOMAS BAYLY, ed. *A Complete Collection of State Trials and Proceedings for High Treason and Other Crimes and Misdemeanors from the Earliest Period to the Year 1783, with Notes and Illustrations: Compiled by T.B. Howell, Esq. F.R.S., F.S.A., and Continued from the Year 1783 to the Present Time by Thomas Jones Howell, Esq.* 34 vols. London: Longman, *et al.*, 1809-28.

NOTE: the reference at 22 is to Lord Ellenborough's definition of libel as "*any thing which hurts the feelings of any body*." Ellenborough's statement formed part of his summing up in the case of the King against Cobbett, 24 May, 1804. On that occasion, Ellenborough stated: "Upon the subject of libel, it may be as well for me to observe, before I enter upon the question, that, by the law of England, there is no impunity to any person publishing any thing injurious to the feelings and happiness of an individual, or prejudicial to the general interests of the state" (Vol. XXIX, col. 49). The quotation at 22-3 is to the Indictment in the Trial of John Lambert and James Perry, for a libel upon His Majesty George III, which is cited as representative, there being no standard form of indictment. For example, the indictment of William Cobbett for libel in 1804 uses the term "dislike" rather than "contempt." The 1819 Libel Act (60 George III & 1 George IV, c. 8) also uses the phrase "tending to bring into Hatred and Contempt the Person of His Majesty, His Heirs or Successors, or the Regent, or the Government and Constitution of the United Kingdom as by Law established, or either House of Parliament. . . ." The quotations at 28-9 and 29 are taken from Francis Holt (*q.v.* for the collations), from speeches by Edward Law, Robert Raymond, and Philip Yorke, *q.v.*

QUOTED: 22, 22-3, 28-9, 29

HUGHES, THOMAS. Referred to: 427

HUGO, VICTOR. *Le roi s'amuse*. Paris: Renduel, 1832.

NOTE: JSM's reference is to the "famous distich" of Francis I, but tradition has it that his comment on women's fickleness, carved in stone in his room at Chambord, was merely "Toute femme varie." See Pierre de Bourdeille, *Les vies des dames galantes*. It seems certain that JSM is taking the distich "Souvent femme varie, " Bien fol est qui s'y fie!" from the King's (Francis I's) song in *Le roi s'amuse*, IV, ii.

REFERRED TO: 312

HUME, DAVID. Referred to: 243

—— *The History of England* (1754-62). 8 vols. in 4. Oxford: Talboys and Wheeler; London: Pickering, 1826.

NOTE: formerly in SC.
REFERRED TO: 227

HUME, HAMILTON.
NOTE: the reference is to him as one of the members of the Eyre Defence Committee.
REFERRED TO: 428

HUNT, JOHN.
NOTE: the reference is to his trial for libelling the deceased king, George III, in 1824.
REFERRED TO: 31

HUNTER, JOHN. See Thomas Ruddiman, *The Rudiments of the Latin Tongue*.

HYPATIA. Referred to: 315

Institutes. See Heineccius.

IRVING, WASHINGTON. *Chronicles of Wolfert's Roost and Other Papers*. Author's ed. Edinburgh: Constable; London: Hamilton; Dublin: McGlashan, 1855.
QUOTED: 161
161.8 "almighty dollar,"] In a word, the almighty dollar, that great object of universal devotion throughout our land, seems to have no genuine devotees in these peculiar villages; and unless some of its missionaries penetrate there, and erect banking-houses and other pious shrines, there is no knowing how long the inhabitants may remain in their present state of contented poverty. (30)

ISABELLA I (of Spain).
NOTE: known as Isabella of Castile.
REFERRED TO: 401

JACKSON, ANDREW. Referred to: 132

JAMES, EDWARD.
NOTE: see also *The Times*, 16 Jan., 1866.
REFERRED TO: 422

JAMES, WALTER CHARLES. "Minutes of Evidence Taken before the Royal Commission on the Administration and Operation of the Contagious Diseases Acts of 1866 and 1869," *PP*, 1871, XIX, 818-25.
NOTE: the "quotations" are questions asked by James, a member of the Commission.
QUOTED: 356-7, 368
REFERRED TO: 350

JARVIS, WILLIAM. Referred to: 107n

JEFFERSON, THOMAS. *Notes, on the State of Virginia*. Baltimore: Pechin, 1800.
NOTE: the quotation is taken from Cairnes, who gives a reference to p. 39; the ed. Cairnes used has not been located, but the passage appears in all eds. in "Query XVIII."
QUOTED: 155

JEHANGIR (Mogul Emperor).
NOTE: see also William Finch.
REFERRED TO: 26

JEVONS, THOMAS. *Remarks on Criminal Law; with a Plan for an Improved System, and Observations on the Prevention of Crime*. London: Hamilton, Adams; Edinburgh: Waugh and Innes; Dublin: Curry; Liverpool: Marples, 1834.
REVIEWED: 77-9
QUOTED: 78, 79
78.14 man," . . . "in] man, in (72)
78.18 certainty."] certainty: how much less then can this punishment be justified, if its effects are uniformly bad, as concerns both the individual object of it and the public at large, which there is too much reason to believe is the actual result at the present time, as well as in all past ages. (72)

78.19 "for example's sake,"] [*see next collation*]

78.20 "earnest] [*paragraph*] When we consider the history of the punishments that have from time to time been inflicted for *example's sake*, it is enough to make us shudder at the degraded state to which our species has in some countries been reduced by this debasing practice, and to express our earnest (72-3)

79.3 "the fundamental] [*paragraph*] The fundamental (23)

79.3 should govern] should alone govern (23)

79.4 state, viz. protection] state appears, from what has been said, to be simply *protection—* protection (23)

79.4 and property,"] and of property; and all beyond this is superfluous, and belongs not to the province of the state. (23)

JOAN OF ARC. Referred to: 302

KANT, IMMANUEL. *Kritik der reinen Vernunft*. In *Sämmtliche Werke*. Ed. Karl Rosenkrantz and Friedrich Schubert. 14 vols. in 12. Leipzig: Voss, 1838-40, II.
REFERRED TO: 242

——— *Metaphysische Anfangsgründe der Rechtslehre* (1797). *Ibid.*, IX, 1-214.
NOTE: the reference at 205 derives from, that at 205n is in a quotation from, John Austin.
REFERRED TO: 205, 205n

KENYON, LLOYD. Judgment in the Trial of Topham, 1791. 100 *English Reports* 931.
NOTE: one of the six legal authorities cited by Holt, *q.v.* The original report appeared in 4 *Term Reports* 126.
REFERRED TO: 21

KER, ALAN. Referred to: 433

KINGSLEY, HENRY.
NOTE: the reference is to him as a member of the Eyre Defence Committee.
REFERRED TO: 428

KORAN. Referred to: 296

LAMBERT, JOHN. See Thomas Bayly Howell, *State Trials*.

LANCASTER, JOSEPH. Referred to: 385

LAW, EDWARD (Lord Ellenborough).
NOTE: the remark attributed to Law, referred to in both places, has not been located.
REFERRED TO: 18, 20

——— Charge to the Jury in the Trial of William Cobbett, 1804. In Howell, *State Trials* (*q.v.*), Vol. XXIX, cols. 49-54.
NOTE: the quotation at 30 is from Holt (*q.v.* for the collation).
QUOTED: 22, 30

LAWRENCE, HENRY. Referred to: 423, 428

LAWSON, WILFRID (2nd Baronet). Referred to: 427

LEVESON-GOWER, GRANVILLE GEORGE (2nd Earl Granville).
NOTE: see also *The Times*, 17 Nov., 1870.
REFERRED TO: 348

LINCOLN, ABRAHAM.
NOTE: the references at 130, 131, and 131n are to Lincoln's government; that at 140 is erroneously to a Presidential "Message."
REFERRED TO: 130, 131, 131n, 132, 135, 140

——— *Emancipation Proclamation*. Washington: n.p., 1863.
NOTE: in effect 1 Jan., 1863.
REFERRED TO: 139

———— *Ancient Law: Its Connection with the Early History of Society, and Its Relation to Modern Ideas*. London: Murray, 1861.
QUOTED: 185-6, 186, 187
REFERRED TO: 169-70, 182, 184, 246
185.32-186.1 "The *Jus Naturale*, or law of nature," . . . "is simply the *jus gentium* seen] [*paragraph*] The Jus Naturale, or Law of Nature, is simply the Jus Gentium or Law of Nations seen (52)
186.5 *jus gentium*] Jus Gentium (56)
186.7 *jus gentium*] Jus Gentium (56)
186.24 writers," . . . "the] writers, the (97)
187.2 "the] The doctrines and institutions which may be attributed to it are the material of some of the most violent controversies debated in our time, as will be seen when it is stated that the (80)
187.5 the part" . . . "played] the part played (80)
187.34 "that] There cannot, I conceive, be any question that (92)

MAIR, JOHN. *An Introduction to Latin Syntax; or, An Exemplification of the Rules of Construction, as Delivered in Mr. Ruddiman's Rudiments, without Anticipating Posterior Rules*. Edinburgh: Paton, *et al.*, 1750.
REFERRED TO: 221-2

MAJOR, EDWARD WILLIAM.
NOTE: the reference is to a witness in the Gordon case.
REFERRED TO: 425

MANSFIELD, LORD. See William Murray.

Manual of the System of Teaching Reading, Writing, and Arithmetic, in the Elementary Schools of the British and Foreign School Society. See Biber.

MARCET, JANE. *Conversations on Political Economy, in Which the Elements of That Science Are Familiarly Explained*. London: Longman, *et al.*, 1816.
REFERRED TO: 315

MARGARET (of Austria).
NOTE: aunt of Emperor Charles V, regent of the Netherlands 1507-30.
REFERRED TO: 303, 402

MARGARET (Duchess of Parma).
NOTE: natural daughter of Emperor Charles V, regent of the Netherlands 1559-67.
REFERRED TO: 303

MARIA THERESA (of Austria). Referred to: 401

MARSHALL, GEORGE. Referred to: 433

MARTINEAU, HARRIET. *Illustrations of Political Economy*. 9 vols. London: Fox, 1832-34.
REFERRED TO: 315

———— "The United States under the Presidentship of Mr. Buchanan," *Edinburgh Review*, CXII (Oct., 1860), 545-82.
REFERRED TO: 136

MARY (of Hungary).
NOTE: widow of Louis II of Hungary, sister of Emperor Charles V, regent of the Netherlands 1531-52.
REFERRED TO: 303

MASON, JAMES MURRAY. Referred to: 130

4.37 deposition] definition (3)
5.2-3 means. [*paragraph*] As] means. [*1-paragraph omission*] [*paragraph*] As (3-4)
5.9 or theft] or a theft (4)
13.30 Religion] *Religion* (34)

——— *Schools for All, in Preference to Schools for Churchmen Only: (or the State of the Controversy between the Advocates for the Lancasterian System of Universal Education, and Those Who Have Set Up an Exclusive and Partial System under the Name of the Church and Dr. Bell)*. London: Longman, *et al.*, 1812.
NOTE: reprinted from *Philanthropist*, II (1812), 57-108. The quotation, of the title, is indirect.
QUOTED: 63

MILL, JOHN STUART. "Corporation and Church Property," *Jurist*, IV (Feb., 1833), 1-26. In *CW*, IV, 193-222.
NOTE: the reference is to the pamphlet reprint, which has the same pagination. The passage has been collated with *CW*, and the substantive differences recorded as variants.
QUOTED: 65-6

——— Jamaica—Question (10 Aug., 1866; Commons), *PD*, 3rd ser., Vol. 184, col. 2160.
REFERRED TO: 423n

——— Speech on the Outbreak in Jamaica (19 July, 1866; Commons), *PD*, 3rd ser., Vol. 184, cols. 1064-6.
REFERRED TO: 423

——— Speech on the Disturbances in Jamaica (31 July, 1866; Commons), *PD*, 3rd ser., Vol. 184, cols. 1797-1806.
REFERRED TO: 423n

——— Speech on the Recent Court Martial in Jamaica (1 Aug., 1867; Commons), *PD*, 3rd ser., Vol. 189, cols. 598-9.
REFERRED TO: 423n

MILTON, JOHN. Referred to: 252

——— *Lycidas* (1638). In *The Poetical Works of Mr. John Milton*. London: Tonson, 1695, 1-3.
NOTE: the volume includes, separately paged, *Poems upon Several Occasions*, 3rd ed. (London: Tonson, 1695), of which *Lycidas* is the first.
QUOTED: 320
320.14-16 "scorn delights and live laborious days" . . . "noble minds," . . . "last infirmity."] *Fame* is the spur that the clear spirit doth raise / (That last infirmity of Noble mind) / To scorn delights, and live laborious days; / But the fair Guerdon when we hope to find, / And think to burst out into sudden blaze, / Comes the blind *Fury* with th'abhorred shears, / And slits the thin spun life. (2; 70-6)

——— *Paradise Lost* (1667). *Ibid.*, 1-343.
REFERRED TO: 407

MITCHELL, CHARLES. Referred to: 423

MOLESWORTH, WILLIAM. Speech on National Education, *The Cornish Guardian and Western Chronicle* (Truro), 13 June, 1834, 2-3.
QUOTED; 64, 66, 67
64.21 "In] [*no paragraph*] He will then see how it is, that in (2)
66.27 "The so-called] [*no paragraph*] For my own part, sir, I am prepared to maintain, that the so called (2)
66.28 quality; as] quality; that, as (2)
66.30 null. All] null. [*9-sentence omission*] A system such as that now exists in England, in which all (2)

NADIR QULI BEG.
NOTE: known as Nadir Shah.
REFERRED TO: 286

NAPOLEON I (of France). Referred to: 345, 407

NAPOLEON III (of France).
NOTE: the reference at 132 is to his free-trade tariff *vis-à-vis* Britain.
REFERRED TO: 132, 344

NELSON, ALEXANDER ABERCROMBY. Referred to: 423, 425, 430-1, 432, 434, 435

NERO, CLAUDIUS CAESAR.
NOTE: the reference is in a quotation from Holt.
REFERRED TO: 18

New York Tribune. Article on emigration to Kansas, 19 Oct., 1854, 4.
QUOTED: 139, 156
139.14-15 "peculiar institution"] We do not know how much the number of emigrants has been increased by their exertions, but the fact that before the season is concluded not far from two thousand will have been forwarded from this vicinity alone, while those from New-England have been much more numerous, sufficiently indicates the utility of this peculiar institution. (4)
156.5 [*see collation for* 139.14-15 *above*]

NEWMAN, FRANCIS WILLIAM. Referred to: 427

NEWTON, ISAAC. Referred to: 236

NIGHTINGALE, FLORENCE. *Suggestions for Thought to the Searchers after Truth among the Artizans of England.* 3 vols. London: printed Eyre and Spottiswoode (not published), 1860.
REFERRED TO: 319

OLDHAM, MARY ANN.
NOTE: a nurse whose cruelty led to the death of a child (John Gaywood).
REFERRED TO: 103-4

OLMSTED, FREDERICK LAW. *The Cotton Kingdom: A Traveller's Observations on Cotton and Slavery in the American Slave States.* 2 vols. New York: Mason; London: Low, 1861.
NOTE: dedicated to JSM.
REFERRED TO: 134, 136

OMYCHUND.
NOTE: not otherwise identified. The reference, in a quotation from Austin, is to the case of Omychund *v.* Barker in 1744. Austin (JSM following) uses the spelling Omichund.
REFERRED TO: 192

OVID (Publius Ovidius Naso). *Metamorphoses* (Latin and English). Trans. Frank Justus Miller. 2 vols. London: Heinemann; New York: Putnam's Sons, 1916.
NOTE: this ed. used for ease of reference. *Opera omnia* (Amsterdam: Blaviana, 1683) is in SC.
QUOTED: 247

OWEN, ROBERT. Referred to: 77

——— "The Address of Robert Owen, at the Great Public Meeting, Held at the National Labour Exchange, Charlotte-street, Fitzroy-square, on the 1st of May, 1833, Denouncing the Old System of the World, and Announcing the Commencement of the New," *The Crisis,* II (11 May, 1833), 140-3.
NOTE: see also Robert Owen and Alexander Campbell, *Debate.* The passage referred to reads (in "The Address"): "All will then be fully conscious, and will openly acknowledge, that pure chastity consists in forming this connexion only when affection exists between the parties, and that it is a vile, abominable, and injurious prostitution to form or continue this connexion when

there is no affection between the parties, even when they are what is called legally bound to each other." (141)
REFERRED TO: 48-9

———— *A New View of Society*. London: Cadell and Davies, 1813.
NOTE: the reference is in a quotation from Biber.
REFERRED TO: 71

———— and Alexander Campbell. *Debate on the Evidences of Christianity; Containing an Examination of the "Social System," and of All the Systems of Scepticism of Ancient and Modern Times. Held in the City of Cincinnati, Ohio, from the 13th to the 21st of April, 1829*. 2 vols. Bethany, Va.: Campbell, 1829.
NOTE: Owen's definitions of chastity and prostitution appear in several formulations in various of his works, and there is no clue as to which of them JSM had in mind. Unfortunately, the only hard evidence as to the dating of JSM's manuscript is the watermark date, 1832. The closest approximation to JSM's wording is found in the *Debate* of 1829: "For real chastity consists, in connexion with affection, and prostitution, in connexion without affection." (I, 120; Wed. forenoon, 15 Apr.) It may be, however, that JSM was writing later than 1832, in which case he might have been alluding to the version in Robert Owen, "The Address" (1833), *q.v.*
REFERRED TO: 48-9

PAKINGTON, JOHN SOMERSET. "Minutes of Evidence Taken before the Royal Commission on the Administration and Operation of the Contagious Diseases Acts of 1866 and 1869," *PP*, 1871, XIX, 818-25.
NOTE: the "quotations" are questions asked by Pakington, a member of the Commission.
QUOTED: 360-3, 363, 363-8
REFERRED TO: 350, 369

PALEY, WILLIAM.
NOTE: the reference is in a quotation from Austin.
REFERRED TO: 59

———— *The Principles of Moral and Political Philosophy* (1785). 15th ed. 2 vols. London: Faulder, 1804.
NOTE: the reference is from a quotation from John Austin. This ed. is in SC.
REFERRED TO: 59

PALMERSTON, LORD. See Henry John Temple.

Pandects. See Heineccius.

PARKER, JOHN WILLIAM, JR.
NOTE: contributed a headnote to JSM's "The Negro Question," which is here quoted as a footnote; JSM's article appeared as a letter to the editor.
QUOTED: 87n

PAYNE, J. HORNE. Referred to: 426, 432

PERRY, JAMES. See Thomas Bayly Howell, *State Trials*.

PESTALOZZI, JOHANN HEINRICH.
NOTE: the reference is in a self-quotation from "Corporation and Church Property."
REFERRED TO: 65

PETRONIUS ARBITER. *Satyricon*. In *Petronius; Seneca, "Apocolocyntos"* (Latin and English). Trans. Michael Heseltine, rev. E.H. Warmington. London: Heinemann; Cambridge, Mass.: Harvard University Press, 1969, 1-379.
NOTE: this ed. used for ease of reference. SC contains the *Satyricon*, ed. Gabbema (Utrecht, 1654).
QUOTED: 231
231.3 *curiosa felicitas*] Homerus testis et lyrici Romanusque Vergilius et Horatii curiosa felicitas. (294; 118, 17-18)

PHILIP IV (of France).
NOTE: called Philippe le Bel.
REFERRED TO: 286

PHILIP (of Macedon). Referred to: 231

PHILIPS, ROBERT NEEDHAM. Referred to: 427

PHILLIPS, WENDELL. Letter to John Stuart Mill.
NOTE: no copy of the letter has been located.
QUOTED: 133n

PHINN, THOMAS. Speech in Amendment to Mr. Fitzroy's Bill (10 Mar., 1853;
    Commons), PD, 3rd ser., Vol. 124, cols. 1419-21.
REFERRED TO: 105, 106

PINDAR. Referred to: 314

PITT, WILLIAM.
NOTE: see also under Parliamentary Papers, "The King's Proclamation," 21 May, 1792.
REFERRED TO: 26

PLACE, FRANCIS. Referred to: 3

——— On the Law of Libel; with Strictures on the Self-Styled "Constitutional
    Association." London: Hunt, 1823.
NOTE: all the essays, except the last, first appeared in weekly front-page instalments in the British
    Luminary and Weekly Intelligencer, from 3 Nov. to 22 Dec., 1822.
REVIEWED: 1-34
QUOTED: 33
33.26-7   boasting . . . We . . . boasting of] boasting of (5)

PLATO.
NOTE: the reference at 229 is to the Dialogues in general.
REFERRED TO: 225, 229, 230, 254

——— Republic (Greek and English). Trans. Paul Shorey. 2 vols. London: Heinemann;
    Cambridge, Mass.: Harvard University Press, 1946.
NOTE: this ed. used for ease of reference. Opera omnia, ed. Immanuel Bekker, 11 vols. (London:
    Priestley, 1826), is in SC.
REFERRED TO: 176, 270, 399

POLLOCK, JONATHAN FREDERICK. Referred to: 107

POPE, ALEXANDER. An Essay on Man (1733-34). In The Works of Alexander Pope: with
    Notes and Illustrations by Joseph Warton and Others. Ed. Joseph Warton, et al. 9
    vols. and Supplementary Vol. London: Priestley, 1822 (Suppl. Vol., London:
    Hearne, 1825), III, 1-160.
NOTE: the quotation is indirect. This ed. is in SC.
QUOTED: 241
241.15   the proper study of mankind,] Know then thyself, presume not God to scan, / The
    proper study of Mankind is Man. (53; II, 2)

POTTER, THOMAS BAYLEY. Referred to: 427

PRATT, CHARLES (Lord Camden). Referred to: 25

——— Charge to the Jury in the Case of Entick v. Carrington, 1704. 95 English
    Reports 814.
NOTE: the quotation derives from Francis Holt, q.v. Originally appeared in 2 Wils. K.B. 286.
QUOTED: 24
24.34   "All] One word more for ourselves; we are no advocates for libels, all (818)
24.34   libels] them (818)
24.35   a court] us (818)

24.35   they will] we shall (818)
24.35   their] our (818)

PROUDFOOT, ANN. Referred to: 107

PRUSSIAN CODE. See under Statutes, Prussia.

QUINTILIAN (Marcus Fabius Quintilianus). *The Institutio Oratoria of Quintilian* (Latin and English). Trans. H.E. Butler. 4 vols. London: Heinemann; Cambridge, Mass.: Harvard University Press, 1953.
REFERRED TO: 229

RACINE, JEAN BAPTISTE. *Les plaideurs* (1668). In *Oeuvres, avec des commentaires par I.L. Geoffroy*. 7 vols. Paris: Le Normant, 1808, II, 259-423.
NOTE: in SC. The quotation is in a quotation from Biber.
QUOTED: 69
69.34   *"Point d'argent, point de Suisse."*] Point d'argent, point de suisse; ma porte étoit close. (II, 277; I, i, 15)

RAMSAY, GORDON DUBERRY. Referred to: 426, 433

RAMSAY, JAMES ANDREW BROUN (Earl of Dalhousie). "Minute by the Governor-General of India, Concurred in by the Commander-in-Chief" (13 Feb., 1856), *PP*, XLV, 643-53.
REFERRED TO: 120

RAPHAEL (Raphael Sanzio).
NOTE: JSM uses the spelling Raffaelle.
REFERRED TO: 316

RAYMOND, ROBERT. Speech in the Trial of Richard Francklin, 1731. In *A Complete Collection of State Trials*. Ed. Thomas Bayly Howell. 34 vols. London: Longman, *et al.*, 1809-28, Vol. XVII, cols. 658-9.
NOTE: the quotation is from Francis Holt (*q.v.* for the collation).
QUOTED: 29

———— Speech in the Trial of Thomas Woolston, 1729. 94 *English Reports* 113.
NOTE: originally appeared in 1 *Barn. K.B.* 163.
QUOTED: 29
29.27   "that the] But the second of these points the Court said, they would not suffer to be argued; for the (113)
29.29   written] writ (113)

REID, THOMAS. Referred to: 463

REYNOLDS, JOSHUA. Referred to: 317

———— *Discourse VII* (1776). In *Works*. Ed. Edmond Malone. 4th ed. 3 vols. London: Cadell and Davies, 1809, I, 187-242.
NOTE: in SC.
QUOTED: 319n
319n.1   "It] [*paragraph*] It (I, 230)
319n.3   Circle.—To] circle. [*paragraph*] To (I, 230)

ROEBUCK, JOHN ARTHUR. Speech in Introducing a Motion on National Education (3 June, 1834; Commons), *PD*, 3rd ser., Vol. 24, cols. 127-30.
REFERRED TO: 63

ROLT, JOHN.
NOTE: the reference is to the Attorney-General. See also "The Jamaica Committee and Mr. Eyre," *The Times*, 29 July, 1867.
REFERRED TO: 423

ROMILLY, SAMUEL. "Bentham on Codification," *Edinburgh Review*, XXIX (Nov., 1817), 217-37.
NOTE: the quotation is in a quotation from Austin.
QUOTED: 190
190.37-8 *The . . . promulgation.*] [*not in italics*] (231)

ROUSSEAU, JEAN JACQUES. Referred to: 187

RUDDIMAN, THOMAS. *The Rudiments of the Latin Tongue; or, A Plain and Easy Introduction to Latin Grammar.* Edinburgh: the Author, 1714.
NOTE: a popular nineteenth-century edition of this work is that edited by another Scotsman: John Hunter, *Ruddiman's Rudiments of the Latin Tongue; with an Appendix on the Moods and Tenses of the Greek and Latin Verb* (Cupar: Tullis; Edinburgh: Oliver and Boyd; London: Whittaker; Glasgow: Turnbull; Dublin: Johnston and Deas, 1820).
REFERRED TO: 221

RUSKIN, JOHN.
NOTE: the reference at 428 is to him as one of the members of the Eyre Defence and Aid Committee.
REFERRED TO: 317, 428

RUSSELL, JOHN (Lord). Speech on Public Business (10 Feb., 1853; Commons), *PD*, 3rd ser., Vol. 124, cols. 17-23.
REFERRED TO: 106

—— Speech at Newcastle (14 Oct., 1861), *Spectator*, 19 Oct., 1861, 1135.
REFERRED TO: 159

RUSSELL, WILLIAM HOWARD. "The Civil War in America," *The Times*, 13 Sept., 1861, 9.
NOTE: one of a series of articles which ran from 16 Apr., 1861, to 23 Apr., 1862.
REFERRED TO: 135, 161-2

RYLANDS, PETER. Referred to: 350

SÁ DE BANDEIRA, BERNARDO.
NOTE: one of the chiefs of the Portuguese rebellion of 1847, who later became Prime Minister.
REFERRED TO: 122

SAND, GEORGE. See Dupin.

SANDWITH, HUMPHREY. Referred to: 427

SAPPHO. Referred to: 314

SAVIGNY, FRIEDRICH KARL VON.
NOTE: the reference derives from Austin.
REFERRED TO: 204

SCOTT, JOHN (Lord Eldon).
NOTE: the reference is in a quotation from Austin.
REFERRED TO: 189

SCOTT, WALTER. *Rob Roy.* 3 vols. Edinburgh: Constable, 1818.
NOTE: the quotation is indirect.
QUOTED: 92

SEDGWICK, ROBERT.
NOTE: the reference is in a quotation from Carlyle.
REFERRED TO: 92

SEWARD, WILLIAM HENRY. Letter to Lord Lyons, 26 Dec., 1861. In "The Trent Affair," *The Times*, 13 Jan., 1862, 9.
QUOTED: 131n
REFERRED TO: 130

—— *The Theory of Moral Sentiments; or, An Essay towards an Analysis of the Principles by Which Men Naturally Judge Concerning the Conduct and Character, First of Their Neighbours, and Afterwards of Themselves. To Which Is Added, A Dissertation on the Origin of Languages* (1759). 6th ed. 2 vols. London: Strahan and Cadell; Edinburgh: Creech and Bell, 1790.

NOTE: this ed., in which the passage referred to first appeared, is in SC.
REFERRED TO: 13

SMITH, GOLDWIN. Referred to: 427

SMITH, SYDNEY. "Female Education." In *The Works of the Rev. Sydney Smith* (1839-40). 2nd ed. 3 vols. London: Longman, *et al.*, 1840, I, 200-20.

NOTE: reprinted from *Edinburgh Review*, XV (Jan., 1810), 299-315. Harriet Mill's page reference conforms to the 2nd ed.
QUOTED: 401n
401n.2 "A] [*paragraph*] A (I, 200)

SMITH, WILLIAM HENRY. *Remarks on Law Reform: Addressed More Particularly to the General Reader*. London: Maxwell, 1840.

REVIEWED: 81-4
QUOTED: 83-4
84.8   rules] rule (8)
84.16   its origin] *its origin* (9)
84.21   English] *English* (9)
84.22   history.] history! (9)
84.24   with it] with *it* (9)
84.28   monks. Must] monks; must (9)

SOCRATES. Referred to: 314

SOMERVILLE, MARY. Referred to: 315

SPENCER, HERBERT. Referred to: 427

STAËL-HOLSTEIN, ANNE LOUISE GERMAINE NECKER, BARONNE DE. Referred to: 315

—— *Delphine*. 4 vols. Geneva: Paschoud, 1802.

NOTE: in SC. The title page (from which JSM quotes) identifies the passage as coming from her *Mélanges*.
QUOTED: 279
279.37   peut] doit (title page)
279.37   femme doit s'y] femme s'y (title page)

STANLEY, CHARLOTTE (Countess of Derby). Referred to: 402

STANLEY, EDWARD GEORGE GEOFFREY SMITH (Earl of Derby). Speech on the Treaty Relative to the Grand Duchy of Luxemburg (4 July, 1867; Lords), *PD*, 3rd ser., Vol. 188, cols. 968-74.

NOTE: the reference is to "one of our leading statesmen."
REFERRED TO: 344

STEPHEN, JAMES FITZJAMES.
NOTE: counsel to the Jamaica Committee.
REFERRED TO: 425, 427, 431

—— "English Jurisprudence," *Edinburgh Review*, CXIV (Oct., 1861), 456-86.
REFERRED TO: 169, 176n

STEPHENSON, GEORGE. Referred to: 222

STEWART, DUGALD. Referred to: 240, 463

STORKS, HENRY KNIGHT. Referred to: 424n, 426

THIBAUT, ANTON FRIEDRICH JUSTUS.
NOTE: the reference derives from John Austin.
REFERRED TO: 204

THOMSON, JAMES, and David Mallet. "An Ode" ["Rule, Britannia"]. In *Alfred: A Masque*. London: Millar, 1740.
NOTE: the reference is simply to the commonly applied title.
REFERRED TO: 252

THOU, JACQUES AUGUSTE DE. *Historia sui temporis*. 5 vols. Paris: Drouart, 1604-08.
NOTE: the quotation is in a quotation from Biber; for the rest of the maxim, see Franck, *Paradoxa*.
QUOTED: 66
66.14-15 *Mundus vult decipi, ergo decipiatur*;] inde Carafa Lutetiam regni metropolim, tanquam Pontificis legatus solita pompa ingreditur; ubi cum signum crucis, ut fit, ederet, verborum, quae proferri mos est, loco, ferunt, eum, ut erat securo de numine animo et summus relligionis derisor, occursante passim populo et in genua ad ipsius conspectum procumbente, saepius secreta murmuratione haec verba ingeminasse, Quandoquidem populus iste vult decipi, decipiatur. (II, 298-9; XII)

THUCYDIDES. *Thucydides* (Greek and English). Trans. Charles Forster Smith. 4 vols. London: Heinemann; Cambridge, Mass.: Harvard University Press, 1958.
NOTE: the reference at 229 is to the "speeches in Thucydides." Two other Greek eds., *Opera*, ed. Baverus and Beckius, 2 vols. (Leipzig, 1790-1804), and *Polemos Peloponnesiakos*, 8 vols. (Glasgow: Foulis, 1759), were formerly in SC.
REFERRED TO: 229, 231

TIBERIUS CLAUDIUS NERO.
NOTE: the reference is in a quotation from Holt.
REFERRED TO: 18

TILLOTSON, JOHN (Archbishop of Canterbury).
NOTE: the reference is in a quotation from John Austin.
REFERRED TO: 60

The Times.
NOTE: anonymous articles follow chronologically.
REFERRED TO: 158

———— Article on the Norfolk Circuit, 21 Mar., 1853, 7.
REFERRED TO: 107

———— Article on the Police Courts, 25 Mar., 1853, 7.
NOTE: Hammill is not otherwise identified than as a London police magistrate.
QUOTED: 105n
105n.8 Mr. Hammill. "Though he] Mr. HAMMILL said that this was one of the worst cases of the kind that had ever come under his notice, and, although he (7)

———— "America," 26 July, 1862, 14.
NOTE: this column reports the passage in the Senate of a bill to admit West Virginia as a state. On 30 July, *The Times* reported (11) that the vote in the House was deferred until December. The bill passed into law on 31 Dec., 1862, as 37th Congress, Sess. III, c. 6, An Act for the Admission of the State of West Virginia into the Union and for Other Purposes (*q.v*).
REFERRED TO: 162

———— "The Jamaica Committee," 16 Jan., 1866, 3.
REFERRED TO: 422-3

———— "Ex-Governor Eyre at Southampton," 23 Aug., 1866, 7.
REFERRED TO: 428

———— "The Jamaica Prosecutions," 30 Mar., 1867, 12.
REFERRED TO: 432

———— "The Jamaica Prosecutions," 12 Apr., 1867, 11.
REFERRED TO: 432

———— "The Jamaica Committee and Mr. Eyre," 29 July, 1867, 12.
NOTE: containing William Shaen's request of 10 July, 1867, to the Attorney-General, John Rolt, and the latter's refusal of 13 July.
REFERRED TO: 432

———— "Prosecution of Ex-Governor Eyre," 28 Feb., 1868, 10.
REFERRED TO: 432

———— "Ex-Governor Eyre," 3 June, 1868, 9-10.
REFERRED TO: 429

———— "Lord Granville's Answer to the Russian Circular," 17 Nov., 1870, 9.
REFERRED TO: 348

———— "The Treaty of 1856: Prince Gortschakoff's Note," 18 Nov., 1870, 3.
NOTE: Gortschakoff's Note was dated 19 (i.e., 31 new style) Oct., 1870.
REFERRED TO: 344, 347-8

TOCQUEVILLE, ALEXIS CHARLES HENRI MAURICE CLÉREL DE. *De la démocratie en Amérique*. 4 vols. Paris: Gosselin, 1835-40.
NOTE: in SC.
QUOTED: 147
147.7-8 "are . . . Spain."] [*translated from:*] Il ne fait pas plus chaud dans le sud de l'Union que dans le sud de l'Espagne et de l'Italie (2). [*footnote omitted*] (II, 336)

TUFNELL, EDWARD CARLETON.
NOTE: the quotation is in Chadwick's "Copy' of Two Papers" (*q.v.* for the collation).
QUOTED: 213-14

TURGOT, ANNE ROBERT JACQUES, BARON DE L'AULNE.
NOTE: the reference is in a quotation from John Austin.
REFERRED TO: 204

TURNER, JOSEPH MALLORD WILLIAM. Referred to: 317

TURPIN, RICHARD ("DICK").
NOTE: his name became proverbial for highway robbers.
REFERRED TO: 137

ULFILAS.
NOTE: JSM uses the spelling Ulphila.
REFERRED TO: 315

VAUGHAN, JAMES. Referred to: 432

VICTORIA (of England). Referred to: 270, 302, 378, 423, 424

VIRCHOW, RUDOLPH. *Untersuchungen über die Entwickelung des Schädelgrundes*. Berlin: Reimer, 1857.
REFERRED TO: 311

VIRGIL (Publius Virgilius Maro).
NOTE: the reference is to his poetry in general.
REFERRED TO: 233

———— *Georgics*. In *Virgil* (Latin and English). Trans. H. Rushton Fairclough. 2 vols. London: Heinemann; New York: Putnam's Sons, 1922, I, 80-236.
NOTE: this ed. used for ease of reference. Two editions of *Opera*, 2 vols. (London, 1800) and (London: Priestley, 1821) are in SC.
REFERRED TO: 254

WALKER, ROBERT JAMES. *Jefferson Davis and Repudiation. Letter of Hon. Robert J. Walker.* London: Ridgway, 1863.

NOTE: Walker was the financial agent of the United States in Britain and Europe, working to secure war loans. This work (dated 1 July, 1863), which went through three editions in the year, is in answer to a letter in *The Times* of 25 March that denied Jefferson Davis's involvement and indicated that there was confusion between Jefferson Davis and Reuben Davis. Walker vehemently argues that Jefferson Davis was involved in the repudiation of the Mississippi Union Bank bonds. His assertions are not founded on fact. In 1840 the Legislature of the State of Mississippi repudiated the Union Bank bonds on the ground that their issue was contrary to the state constitution. However, until 1843, when he ran unsuccessfully for a seat in the Legislature, Jefferson Davis played no political role in Mississippi. This Civil War propaganda may have found its source in Reuben Davis's sneers at the protests of the bondholders, and was carried to Britain by a former U.S. senator from Mississippi to rally support for the North among those British investors who had lost heavily in the repudiation of the bank bonds. Although Jefferson Davis denied the story for his whole life, and there was plenty of evidence to support his claims, as late as 1887 Theodore Roosevelt, in his *Life of Thomas H. Benton* (Boston and New York: Houghton Mifflin), reiterated the propaganda. The uncertainty behind the story may have prompted Mill to delete this passage.

REFERRED TO: 141n

WARNER, HIRAM. Speech on Slavery in the Territories (1 Apr., 1856; House of Representatives), *Appendix to the Congressional Globe*, 34th Congress, Sess. I, 1856. Washington: Rives, 1856, 297-300.

QUOTED: 155

155.5-7   slaveholder,' . . . "in] slaveholder in (299)
155.14   starved out] *starved out* (300)
155.16   certain limits] certain specified limits (300)

WELLES, GIDEON. Referred to: 130

WESTMORLAND, HENRY.

NOTE: see his evidence in *Minutes of Evidence Taken before the Jamaica Royal Commission, PP*, 1866, XXXI, 866-92.

REFERRED TO: 425

WHATELY, RICHARD. Referred to: 145

———— *Elements of Logic.* London: Mawman, 1826.

NOTE: this ed. and the 9th ed. (London: Parker, 1848) in SC. The indirect quotation is of phrasing that also appears in Whately's *Introductory Lectures on Political Economy*, *q.v.*

QUOTED: 225

REFERRED TO: 223

225.25-6   to mistake familiarity for accurate knowledge.] *Familiar acquaintance* is perpetually mistaken for *accurate knowledge.* (274)

———— *Introductory Lectures on Political Economy* (1831). 2nd ed. London: Fellowes, 1832.

NOTE: Lecture IX, from which the indirect quotation is taken, is not in the 1st ed. Similar phrasing appears in Whately's *Elements of Logic*, *q.v.*

QUOTED: 225

225.25-6   to mistake familiarity for accurate knowledge.] Whereas this circumstance adds to the difficulty, on account of our liability, in any subject, to mistake *familiar acquaintance* for accurate *knowledge*;—from our having, in addition to all that is to be learnt, much also to unlearn, of prejudices insensibly imbibed,—and from the influence of personal interests and feelings in biassing the judgment, on almost every question that can arise. (224)

WHITE, JAMES. Referred to: 427

WILDERSPIN, SAMUEL. *The Infant System, for Developing the Intellectual and Moral Powers of All Children from One to Seven Years of Age* (1823). 6th ed. London: Simpkin and Marshall, 1834.

NOTE: the quotation is in a quotation from Biber. The 1st ed. had as its title *On the Importance of*

PARLIAMENTARY PAPERS

"Treaty with the Nawaub Vizier, Saadit Ali" (10 Nov., 1801). In *Hertslet's Commercial Treaties*. Ed. Lewis Hertslet, *et al.* 31 vols. in 24. London: Butterworth, 1820-1925, VIII, 663.
REFERRED TO: 120

"Report from the Select Committee on the State of Education; with the Minutes of Evidence, and Index," *PP*, 1834, IX, 1-261.
REFERRED TO: 63, 67

"Report from His Majesty's Commissioners for Inquiry into the Administration and Practical Operation of the Poor Laws," *PP*, 1834, XXVII-XXXIX.
REFERRED TO: 105

"First Report of the Commissioners Appointed to Inquire into the Municipal Corporations in England and Wales," *PP*, 1835, XXIII, 1-49.
REFERRED TO: 67

"An Account Showing the Imports into the United Kingdom of Sugar, Molasses, Rum, Coffee, and Cocoa, from the West Indies and British Guiana, for the Years 1831 to 1847 Both Inclusive," *PP*, 1847-48, LVIII, 547-9.
REFERRED TO: 89

"First Report from the Select Committee on Ceylon and British Guiana; Together with the Minutes of Evidence, and an Appendix," *PP*, 1849, XI, 1-466.
REFERRED TO: 89

"A Petition of the Female Inhabitants of the Borough of Sheffield in the County of York, in Public Meeting Assembled, Praying Their Lordships 'to Take into Their Serious Consideration the Propriety of Enacting an Electoral Law Which Will Include Adult Females within Its Provisions'" (13 Feb., 1851), *Journals of the House of Lords*, 1851, LXXXIII, 23.
REFERRED TO: 415

"A Bill for the Better Prevention and Punishment of Assaults on Women and Children," 16 Victoria (10 Mar., 1853), *PP*, 1852-53, I, 9-12.
NOTE: referred to by JSM as "Mr. Fitzroy's Bill." Enacted as 16 & 17 Victoria, c. 30, An Act for the Better Prevention and Punishment of Aggravated Assaults upon Women and Children, and for Preventing Delay and Expense in the Administration of Certain Parts of the Criminal Law (14 June, 1853). The quotation at 104 is indirect.
REVIEWED: 101-8
QUOTED: 104

104.14-15 *with or without hard labour*] When any Person shall be charged before Two Justices of the Peace, or any Magistrate of the Police Courts of the Metropolis sitting at any such Police Court, with an Assault upon a Female or upon a Male Child under the Age of *Twelve* Years, either upon the Complaint of the Party aggrieved or otherwise, it shall be lawful for the said Justices or Police Magistrate, if the Assault is of such an aggravated Nature that it cannot in their opinion be sufficiently punished by them under the Provisions of the Statute Ninth George the Fourth, Chapter Thirty-one, and if it shall appear to them that a Prosecution of it by Indictment is not likely to be effectual (owing to the Sex or Age of the Party injured), to proceed to hear and determine the same in a summary Way, and if they shall find the Charge to be proved, to convict the Person accused; and every Offender so convicted shall be liable to be imprisoned in the Common Gaol or House of Correction, with or without Hard Labour, for a Period not exceeding *Six* Calendar Months, or to pay a Fine not exceeding (together with Costs) the Sum of *Twenty Pounds*; and in default of Payment to be imprisoned as aforesaid, with or without Hard Labour, for *Six* Calendar Months unless such Fine and Costs be sooner paid; and such Conviction shall be a Bar to all future Proceedings, civil or criminal, for or in respect of the same Assault. (9-10)

"General Treaty between Great Britain, Austria, France, Prussia, Russia, Sardinia and Turkey, for the Re-establishment of Peace, with Three Conventions Annexed Thereto; Signed at Paris, March 30, 1856," *PP*, 1856, LXI, 1-34.
REFERRED TO: 344, 345, 347

"Draft of Treaty between the East India Company and the King of Oude," *PP*, 1856, XLV, 597-9.
REFERRED TO: 120

"Treaty of Commerce between Her Majesty and the Emperor of the French" (23 Jan., 1860), *PP*, 1860, LXVIII, 467-77.
NOTE: the reference is to "Cobden's Treaty."
REFERRED TO: 132

"Report of the Commissioners Appointed to Inquire into the State of Popular Education in England," *PP*, 1861, XXI, Pt. I, 1-707.
REFERRED TO: 209n, 212

"Treaty between Her Majesty and the United States of America for the Suppression of the African Slave Trade," *PP*, 1862, LXI, 373-85.
NOTE: signed 7 Apr., 1862.
REFERRED TO: 162

"Petition for Extension [of the Elective Franchise] to All Householders without Distinction of Sex" (Public Petition no. 8501, presented 7 June, 1866), *Reports of Select Committee on Public Petitions*, 1866, 697, and Appendix, 305.
NOTE: presented by JSM to the House of Commons.
REFERRED TO: 270

"Papers Laid before the Royal Commission of Inquiry by Governor Eyre," *PP*, 1866, XXX, 1-488.
NOTE: the reference is to other documents relating to the Jamaica disturbances.
REFERRED TO: 422

"Report of the Jamaica Royal Commission; with Minutes of Evidence and Appendix," *PP*, 1866, XXX, 489-531; XXXI, 1-1172.
REFERRED TO: 422, 424, 430, 431

"Papers Relating to the Disturbances in Jamaica," *PP*, 1866, LI, 145-506.
NOTE: the reference is to other documents relating to the Jamaica disturbances.
REFERRED TO: 422

"Treaty Relative to the Grand Duchy of Luxemburg" (11 May, 1867), *PP*, 1867, LXXIV, 415-22.
NOTE: the reference is to "almost the last treaty we entered into."
REFERRED TO: 344

"Report of Commissioners on Education in Schools in England, Not Comprised within Her Majesty's Two Recent Commissions on Popular Education and Public Schools; with Appendices, Miscellaneous Papers, Answers to the Commissioners' Questions, and Minutes of Evidence" (21 vols.), *PP*, 1867-68, XXVIII, Pts. I-XVII.
NOTE: JSM's evidence is in "Miscellaneous Papers," *PP*, XXVIII, Pt. II, 67-72.
REFERRED TO: 209-14

STATUTES

Following the British statutes, those of France, Prussia, and the United States are listed; each list is chronological. In the British section information is taken from the *Statutes at Large*.

18 Elizabeth, c. 3. An Act for Setting of the Poor on Work, and for Avoiding of Idleness (1576).
REFERRED TO: 370

43 Elizabeth, c. 2. An Act for the Reliefe of the Poore (1601).
REFERRED TO: 105

31 Charles II, c. 2. An Act for the Better Securing the Liberty of the Subject, and for the Prevention of Imprisonments beyond the Seas (27 May, 1679).
NOTE: known as the Habeas Corpus Act.
REFERRED TO: 7, 26, 131n

6 George II, c. 31. An Act for the Relief of Parishes and Other Places from Such Charges as May Arise from Bastard Children Born within the Same (1733).
REFERRED TO: 370

26 George II, c. 33. An Act for the Better Preventing of Clandestine Marriages (1753).
NOTE: one of the statutes which abolished what JSM calls the "enormities" in marriage law, in this case the binding nature of marriage contracts.
REFERRED TO: 283

34 George III, c. 54. An Act to Empower His Majesty to Secure and Detain Such Persons as His Majesty Shall Suspect Are Conspiring against His Person and Government (23 May, 1794).
REFERRED TO: 26

42 George III, c. 85. An Act for the Trying and Punishing in Great Britain Persons Holding Publick Employments for Offences Committed Abroad; and for Extending the Provisions of an Act, Passed in the Twenty-first Year of the Reign of King James, Made for the Ease of Justices and Others in Pleading in Suits Brought against Them, to All Persons, Either in or out of This Kingdom, Authorized to Commit to Safe Custody (22 June, 1802).
NOTE: the Colonial Governors' Act under which the indictment of Governor Eyre was attempted (not the earlier 11 & 12 William III, c. 12).
REFERRED TO: 425, 429, 433

49 George III, c. 68. An Act to Explain and Amend the Law of Bastardy, So Far as Relates to Indemnifying Parishes in Respect Thereof (3 June, 1809).
REFERRED TO: 370

60 George III and 1 George IV, c. 8. An Act for the More Effectual Prevention and Punishment of Blasphemous and Seditious Libels (30 Dec., 1819). See Thomas Bayly Howell, *State Trials*.

9 George IV, c. 31. An Act for Consolidating and Amending the Statutes in England Relative to Offences against the Person (27 June, 1828).
REFERRED TO: 104

3 & 4 William IV, c. 73. An Act for the Abolition of Slavery Throughout the British Colonies; for Promoting the Industry of the Manumitted Slaves; and for Compensating the Persons Hitherto Entitled to the Services of Such Slaves (28 Aug., 1833).
NOTE: the reference at 112 is to the Compensating Clause.
REFERRED TO: 106, 112

4 & 5 William IV, c. 76. An Act for the Amendment and Better Administration of the Laws Relating to the Poor in England and Wales (14 Aug., 1834).
NOTE: the reference at 213, to sect. 48, is in a quotation from Tufnell; that at 214 is to the Poor Law Inspectors.
REFERRED TO: 105, 213, 214, 367, 370

2 & 3 Victoria, c. 54. An Act to Amend the Law Relating to the Custody of Infants (17 Aug., 1839).

NOTE: known as Serjeant Talfourd's Act.
REFERRED TO: 285

7 & 8 Victoria, c. 101. An Act for the Further Amendment of the Laws Relating to the Poor in England (9 Aug., 1844).
NOTE: primarily deals with the support of bastards.
REFERRED TO: 370

11 Victoria, c. 20. An Act to Authorize for One Year, and to the End of the Then Next Session of Parliament, the Removal of Aliens from the Realm (9 June, 1848).
REFERRED TO: 131n

11 & 12 Victoria, c. 35. An Act to Empower the Lord Lieutenant or Other Chief Governor or Governors of Ireland to Apprehend, and Detain until the First Day of March 1849, Such Persons as He or They Shall Suspect of Conspiring against Her Majesty's Person and Government (25 July, 1848).
NOTE: suspended the Habeas Corpus Act.
REFERRED TO: 131n

12 Victoria, c. 2. An Act to Continue until the First Day of September 1849 an Act of the Last Session, for Empowering the Lord Lieutenant or Other Chief Governor or Governors of Ireland to Apprehend and Detain Such Persons as He or They Shall Suspect of Conspiring against Her Majesty's Person and Government (27 Feb., 1849).
REFERRED TO: 131n

16 & 17 Victoria, c. 30 (14 June, 1853). See, under Parliamentary Papers, "A Bill for the Better Prevention and Punishment of Assaults on Women and Children" (10 Mar., 1853).

16 & 17 Victoria, c. 137. An Act for the Better Administration of Charitable Trusts (20 Aug., 1853).
REFERRED TO: 213, 214

18 & 19 Victoria, c. 126. An Act for Diminishing Expense and Delay in the Administration of Criminal Justice in Certain Cases (14 Aug., 1855).
NOTE: see 27 & 28 Victoria, c. 80.
REFERRED TO: 353

20 & 21 Victoria, c. 85. An Act to Amend the Law Relating to Divorce and Matrimonial Clauses in England (28 Aug., 1857).
NOTE: the reference at 283 is to this statute as one of those which abolished what JSM calls the "enormities" in marriage law; that at 285 is to its provision for legal separation.
REFERRED TO: 283, 285

24 & 25 Victoria, c. 100. An Act to Consolidate and Amend the Statute Law of England and Ireland Relating to Offences Against the Person (6 Aug., 1861).
NOTE: see sect. 43 for assaults against women. The reference at 283 is to this as one of the statutes which abolished what JSM calls the "enormities" in marriage law.
QUOTED: 288
REFERRED TO: 283, 288
288.3 "aggravated assaults"] Persons convicted of aggravated Assaults on Females and Boys under Fourteen Years of Age may be imprisoned or fined. (margin note, 573)

27 & 28 Victoria, c. 80. An Act to Extend the Provisions of "The Criminal Justice Act, 1855" to the Liberties of the Cinque Ports and to the District of Romney Marsh in the County of Kent (29 July, 1864).
NOTE: this Act extended, as its title indicates, the provisions of 18 & 19 Victoria, c. 126 (q.v.). The Cinque Ports and Romney Marsh had been excluded by 19 & 20 Victoria, c. 118.
REFERRED TO: 353

29 Victoria, c. 35. An Act for the Better Prevention of Contagious Diseases at Certain Naval and Military Stations (11 June, 1866).
NOTE: superseded the first Contagious Diseases Act, 27 & 28 Victoria, c. 85, An Act for the Prevention of Contagious Diseases at Certain Naval and Military Stations (29 July, 1864).
REFERRED TO: 351-71

32 & 33 Victoria, c. 96. An Act to Amend the Contagious Diseases Act, 1866 (11 Aug., 1869).
REFERRED TO: 351-71

FRANCE

Code civil des Français. Paris: Imprimerie de la république, 1804.
NOTE: known after 1807 as the *Code Napoléon*. The reference derives from Austin.
REFERRED TO: 193n

PRUSSIA

Allgemeines Landrecht für die Preussischen Staaten (5 Feb., 1794).
NOTE: the reference derives from Austin.
REFERRED TO: 193n

UNITED STATES OF AMERICA

A Declaration by the Representatives of the United States of America, in General Congress Assembled. In Congress, July 4, 1776. Philadelphia: Dunlap, 1776.
NOTE: known as the Declaration of Independence.
QUOTED: 397
397.6 governed.] governed, that Whenever any Form of Government becomes destructive of these Ends, it is the Right of the People to alter or abolish it, and to institute new Government, laying its Foundation on such Principles, and organizing its Powers in such Form, as to them shall seem most likely to effect their Safety and Happiness.

The Constitution or Frame of Government, for the United States of America. Boston: Fleet, 1787.
NOTE: the references at 133n are in a quotation from Phillips.
REFERRED TO: 132, 133n, 140, 161, 162, 163

2nd Congress, Sess. II, c. 7. An Act Respecting Fugitives from Justice, and Persons Escaping from the Service of Their Masters (12 Feb., 1793).
NOTE: one of the fugitive slave laws. They were abolished in 1864 (38th Congress, Sess. I, c. 166).
REFERRED TO: 133n

Constitution of Texas 1845. In *The Constitutions of the State of Texas, with the Reconstruction Acts of Congress, the Constitution of the Confederate States, and of the United States.* Annotated by John Sayles. 4th ed. St. Louis, Mo.: Gilbert, 1893, 185-222.
REFERRED TO: 297

Constitution of the State of California 1849. San Francisco: printed at the office of the *Alta California*, 1849.
REFERRED TO: 297

31st Congress, Sess. I, c. 60. An Act to Amend, and Supplementary to, the Act Entitled "An Act Respecting Fugitives from Justice, and Persons Escaping from the Service of Their Masters," Approved February Twelfth, One Thousand Seven Hundred and Ninety-three (18 Sept., 1850).
NOTE: one of the fugitive slave laws. They were abolished in 1864 (38th Congress, Sess. I, c. 166).
REFERRED TO: 133n

36th Congress, Sess. II, c. 68. An Act to Provide for the Payment of Outstanding Treasury Notes, to Authorize a Loan, to Regulate and Fix the Duties on Imports, and for Other Purposes (2 Mar., 1861).
REFERRED TO: 132

Constitution, Adopted Unanimously by the Congress of the Confederate States of America, March 11, 1861. In The Federal and the Confederate Constitutions, for the Use of Government Officers and for the People. Cincinnati: Watkin, 1862.
REFERRED TO: 127, 132, 135, 140

37th Congress, Sess. II, Resolution 26. Joint Resolution Declaring that the United States Ought to Coöperate with, Affording Pecuniary Aid to Any State Which May Adopt the Gradual Abolishment of Slavery (10 Apr., 1862).
REFERRED TO: 162

37 Congress, Sess. II, c. 54. An Act for the Release of Certain Persons Held to Service or Labor in the District of Columbia (16 Apr., 1862).
REFERRED TO: 132, 162

37th Congress, Sess. II, c. 111. An Act to Secure Freedom to All Persons within the Territories of the United States (19 June, 1862).
REFERRED TO: 162

37th Congress, Sess. II, c. 195. An Act to Suppress Insurrection, to Punish Treason and Rebellion, to Seize and Confiscate the Property of Rebels, and for Other Purposes (17 July, 1862).
NOTE: see sects. 9, 10.
REFERRED TO: 139

37th Congress, Sess. III, c. 6. An Act for the Admission of the State of West Virginia into the Union, and for Other Purposes (31 Dec., 1862).
NOTE: this Act was reported as having been passed by the Senate in "America," The Times, 26 July, 1862 (q.v.). The vote by the House was deferred until Dec., 1862, at which time the bill was passed.
REFERRED TO: 162

Constitution of the State of Nevada 1864. In Statutes of the State of Nevada Passed at the First Session of the Legislature, 1864-65. Carson City, Nev.: Church, 1865, 39-71.
REFERRED TO: 297

Constitution of the State of Georgia as Passed by the Constitutional Convention Assembled at Atlanta, Ga., March 11th, 1868. Augusta, Ga.: Pughe, 1868.
REFERRED TO: 297

Index

References in italic type are to the Appendices; when, in Appendix D, they simply reproduce references in the main text, they are also in parentheses. "HTM" refers to writings (both before and after her marriage to JSM) by Harriet Taylor Mill (Apps. A and C).